GLOBAL LAWMAKERS

International Organizations in the Crafting of World Markets

Global lawmaking by international organizations holds the potential for enormous influence over world trade and national economies. Representatives from states, industries, and professions produce laws for worldwide adoption in an effort to alter state lawmaking and commercial behaviors, whether of giant multi-national corporations or micro, small and medium-sized businesses. Who makes that law and who benefits affects all states and all market players. *Global Lawmakers* offers the first extensive empirical study of commercial lawmaking within the United Nations. It shows who makes law for the world, how they make it, and who comes out ahead. Using extensive and unique data, the book investigates three episodes of lawmaking between the late 1990s and 2012. Through its original socio-legal orientation, it reveals dynamics of competition, cooperation and competitive cooperation within and between international organizations, including the UN, World Bank, IMF and UNIDROIT, as these IOs craft international laws. *Global Lawmakers* proposes an original theory of international organizations that seek to construct transnational legal orders within social ecologies of lawmaking. The book concludes with an appraisal of creative global governance by the UN in international commerce over the past fifty years and examines prospective challenges for the twenty-first century.

SUSAN BLOCK-LIEB is the Cooper Family Professor in Urban Legal Issues at Fordham University's School of Law.

TERENCE C. HALLIDAY is Co-Director, Center on Law and Globalization, and Research Professor, American Bar Foundation. He is Honorary Professor, School of Regulation and Global Governance, The Australian National University, and Adjunct Professor of Sociology, Northwestern University.

CAMBRIDGE STUDIES IN LAW AND SOCIETY

Cambridge Studies in Law and Society aims to publish the best scholarly work on legal discourse and practice in its social and institutional contexts, combining theoretical insights and empirical research.

The fields that it covers are: studies of law in action; the sociology of law; the anthropology of law; cultural studies of law, including the role of legal discourses in social formations; law and economics; law and politics; and studies of governance. The books consider all forms of legal discourse across societies, rather than being limited to lawyers' discourses alone.

The series editors come from a range of disciplines: academic law; socio-legal studies; sociology; and anthropology. All have been actively involved in teaching and writing about law in context.

A list of books in the series can be found at the back of this book.

Global Lawmakers

INTERNATIONAL ORGANIZATIONS IN THE CRAFTING OF WORLD MARKETS

SUSAN BLOCK-LIEB
Fordham University

TERENCE C. HALLIDAY
American Bar Foundation

CAMBRIDGE
UNIVERSITY PRESS

CAMBRIDGE
UNIVERSITY PRESS

University Printing House, Cambridge CB2 8BS, United Kingdom

One Liberty Plaza, 20th Floor, New York, NY 10006, USA

477 Williamstown Road, Port Melbourne, VIC 3207, Australia

314-321, 3rd Floor, Plot 3, Splendor Forum, Jasola District Centre, New Delhi - 110025, India

79 Anson Road, #06-04/06, Singapore 079906

Cambridge University Press is part of the University of Cambridge.

It furthers the University's mission by disseminating knowledge in the pursuit of education, learning and research at the highest international levels of excellence.

www.cambridge.org
Information on this title: www.cambridge.org/9781107187580
DOI: 10.1017/9781316941508

First published 2017

A catalogue record for this publication is available from the British Library

Library of Congress Cataloging in Publication data
NAMES: Block-Lieb, Susan, 1958– author. | Halliday, Terence C. (Terence Charles), author.
TITLE: Global lawmakers : International organizations in the crafting of world markets / Susan Block-Lieb, fordham University, New York; Terence C. Halliday, American Bar Foundation.
DESCRIPTION: Cambridge [UK] ; New York : Cambridge University Press, 2017. | Series: Cambridge studies in law and society | Includes bibliographical references and index.
IDENTIFIERS: LCCN 2017014835| ISBN 9781107187580 (hardback : alk. paper) | ISBN 9781316638163 (pbk. : alk. paper)
SUBJECTS: LCSH: Legislation. | Legislative bodies. | Foreign trade regulation. | International organization.
CLASSIFICATION: LCC K3316 .B59 2017 | DDC 343.08/7–DC23
LC record available at https://lccn.loc.gov/2017014835

ISBN 978-1-107-18758-0 Hardback
ISBN 978-1-316-63816-3 Paperback

To Peter
S.B.L.

To Holly
T.C.H.

Contents

Figures

Tables

Acknowledgments

Writing a book on a global institution over many years can feel like an endless reshuffling of odd-fitting pieces of a puzzle into some sort of recognizable landscape. A delegate from Australia and a delegation from Cameroon; a shipping line veteran and a UN diplomat; UN meeting chambers and elegant city dining venues; a week in one decade and a week in another; a banker from India and a judge from France; a nineteenth century happening and a twenty-first century repercussion; reports from one IO and retorts from its rival; snippets of conversations in coffee lines and breakfast on the East River; attendance spreadsheets and UN documents – together, these and many other bits of research activity yield a mountain of intelligence spread over fragments of time, and we authors are required to make sense of it.

And thus our sense-making stands atop a very large accumulation of indebtedness. Most of our appreciation is owed to the officials of the United Nations Commission on International Trade Law (UNCITRAL), who endured endless conversations and queries over many years and took the admirable risk of opening their practices and minds to academic observers. We are especially indebted to Jenny Clift, Secretary of the Insolvency Working Group, for introducing us to UNCITRAL and for her continuing insights, as we are to Spiros Bazinas, Kate Lannan, and Renaud Sorieul who also were the UNCITRAL Working Group Secretaries responsible for production of the treaty and legislative guides we study. We are most grateful for all their support. Needless to say, we hold none of them responsible for our interpretations. We owe a great deal to Jernej Sekolec, the Secretary who led UNCITRAL during the most intense period of our fieldwork, and to his successor, Renaud Sorieul, not only for enabling our research but also for insight into the institutional challenges and opportunities faced by the Secretariat. We also appreciate the extensive efforts of Claudia Gross to compile many years of attendance data for delegates and delegations over the three UNCITRAL Working Groups.

We conducted hundreds of hours of formal and informal interviews with UNCITRAL delegates from states and international organizations. Our ethics of research do not permit us to list them by name but readers will recognize that there would be no research and no book worthy of UNCITRAL's enterprise without delegates' willingness to talk, to invite us to informal events, to share documents, and to offer and test ideas about the processes and products of their participation in lawmaking. We extend similar appreciation to officials of the very many non-state organizations of professions, industry, clubs of nations, and international financial institutions, among others, who shared their time, insights, and materials.

A great deal of valuable work and intellectual exchange occurred in conjunction with research assistants and associates. We were most fortunate to be joined at different points by the highly talented Scott Parrott and Josh Pacewicz, with whom we worked closely and with immense benefit. Administrators Amy Schlueter and research assistant Lauren Buxbaum constantly, effectively, and amiably kept apace with project logistics and coordination.

This longstanding project, following international lawmaking in real time, was expensive. The American Bar Foundation (ABF) offered extensive and sustained research funding supplemented by a generous grant from the US National Science Foundation (SES-0214301) to Bruce Carruthers and Terence Halliday for an earlier project. Fordham Law School provided important funding throughout.

Our project extends several strands of theory introduced in *Bankrupt: Global Lawmaking and Systemic Financial Crisis*, and we express our gratitude to Bruce Carruthers for his contributions to the generativity of that book. Readers of *Global Lawmakers* will observe how much we have benefitted from intense intellectual engagement with Sida Liu on social ecology theory and Gregory Shaffer on the theory of transnational legal orders.

Several institutions hosted our research program, most notably the ABF, which housed the research team, and Fordham Law School and its Corporate Law Center, which sponsored our manuscript conference. We thank ABF Directors Robert Nelson and Ajay Mehrotra, and Fordham Law School Deans Matthew Diller, Mike Martin, William Treanor and John Feerick, for their sustaining support, both financial as well as intellectual. The School of Regulation and Global Governance, Australian National University, hosted and supported Terry Halliday for part of each year over the length of the project, as did Sciences Po, Paris, for a visit in 2013.

Many scholars have contributed to the critique and development of ideas in the articles and chapters that led to this volume whom we have thanked previously. In addition, we express our thanks to John Braithwaite, Peter Drahos, Ian Hurd, Gregoire Mallard, Steve Nelson, Sigrid Quack, Britta Rehder, Jerome Sgard, and to the insightful readers at our Fordham book manuscript conference – Julian Arato, Nitsan Chorev, Edward Cohen, Sarah Dadush, Martin Flaherty, Ted Janger, Tom Lee, Sida Liu, Josh Pacewicz, and Mark Suchman.

We learned a great deal from constructive comments in many seminars and presentations over the life of the project, including the Max Planck Institute for Study of Societies, American Bar Foundation, University of New South Wales, Australian National University, University of Queensland, Fordham University, University of Minnesota, Northwestern University, China University of Politics and Law, *CSO: Sciences Po*, Brooklyn Law School, Temple Law School, Dedman School of Law at Southern Methodist University, and IIT Kent Law School. Many colleagues offered valuable insights at academic conferences including the American Sociological Association, International Studies Association, Law and Society Association, American Association of Law Schools, American Society of Comparative Law, International Academy of Commercial and Consumer Law, Midwest Colloquium on International Organizations/International Law, the Conference on Governance of Transnational Economic Relations, Villa Vigoni, Italy, and World Bank Conference on Secured Transactions at University of Newcastle.

Earlier versions of several chapters and segments of the book have been previously published in the *Brooklyn Journal of International Law, European Socio-Economic Review, Regulation & Governance, Texas International Law Journal*, and in several edited volumes published by Cambridge University, Oxford University Press, and Routledge.

Two anonymous reviewers for Cambridge University Press provided insightful guidance for revision. We are indebted to Kristine Tobin for her excellent index. As ever, Cambridge University Press Senior Editor John Berger and Series Editor Sally Engle Merry have been a pleasure to work with.

Not least, we thank our spouses, who have been terribly long-suffering, invariably encouraging, and mostly restrained from asking year after year when this book would finally be on the newsstands. At last we can all be happy.

Abbreviations

AAR: Association of American Railroads
ABA: American Bar Association
ABCNY: Association of the Bar of the City of New York
ABF: American Bar Foundation
ADB: Asian Development Bank
ASIL: American Society of International Law
BIMCO: Baltic and International Maritime Council
BRICS: Brazil, Russia, India, China, and South Africa
CEELI: Central and East European Law Institute
CFA: Commercial Finance Association
CILS: Center for International Legal Studies
CISG: Convention on the International Sale of Goods
CMI: *Comité Maritime International*
COGSA: Carriage of Goods by Sea Act, US Code, Title 46, Chapter 28
EBRD: European Bank for Reconstruction and Development
EC: European Community
ECOSOC: United Nations Economic and Social Council
ELSA: European Law Students Association
ECSA: European Community Ship Owners' Association
EU: European Union
FinCoNet: International Financial Consumer Protection Organization
FIATA: International Federation of Freight Forwarders Association
FSB: Financial Stability Board
G-7: Group of Seven, Club of Nations
G-20: Group of Twenty, Club of Nations
G-22: Group of Twenty Two, Club of Nations

G-77: Group of Seventy Seven, Club of Nations
GA: UN General Assembly
GATT: General Agreement on Tariffs and Trade
GRIP 21: *Groupe de Réflexion sur L'Insolvabilité et sa Prévention*
HCCH: Hague Conference on Private International Law
IBA: International Bar Association
ICC: International Chamber of Commerce
ICS: International Chamber of Shipping
IFI: international financial institutions
IGO: international governmental organization
III: International Insolvency Institute
IL: international law
ILA: International Law Association
ILC: International Law Commission
ILO: International Labor Organization
IMA: International Maritime Association
IMF: International Monetary Fund
IMMTA: International Multimodal Transport Association
IMO: International Maritime Organization
INGO: international nongovernmental organization
INSOL: International Association of Restructuring, Insolvency and Bankruptcy Professionals
IO: international organization
IOSCO: International Organization of Securities Commissions
IR: international relations
NIEO: New International Economic Order
NGO: nongovernmental organizations
OAS: Organization of American States
OECD: Organization for Economic Cooperation and Development
OHADA: *Organisation pour l'Harmonistion en Afrique du Droit des Affaires*
OTIF: Intergovernmental Organization for International Carriage by Rail
P&I Clubs: clubs of mutual maritime insurance providers, including especially protection and indemnity insurance
ROSC: Reports on the Observance of Standards and Codes, promulgated by World Bank and International Monetary Fund
ROT: retention of title
TLO: transnational legal order
UCC: Uniform Commercial Code, US uniform state law
UNCITRAL: United Nations Commission on International Trade Law
UNCTAD: United Nations Conference on Trade and Development

UNIDROIT:	International Institute for the Unification of Private Law
UNECE:	United Nations Economic Commission for Europe
WB:	World Bank
WG:	working group
WHO:	World Health Organization
WIPO:	World Intellectual Property Organization
WTO:	World Trade Organization

Introduction

This book had a serendipitous beginning. In June 1999, we found ourselves seated next to each other in an enormous chamber at the United Nations headquarters in New York. Our seats were made available to us at the invitation of the UN's Commission on International Trade Law (UNCITRAL).[1] We had been invited as observer delegates to UNCITRAL's Working Group on Insolvency and, between 1999 and 2004, stayed to participate and observe in the making of what would become UNCITRAL's Legislative Guide on Insolvency Law.[2] This participation became not Act 3 but Act 1 of a much larger research enterprise on lawmaking by UNCITRAL and other global lawmakers.[3]

1 What UNCITRAL calls "trade law," and why insolvency law belongs as a part of the "trade laws" over which UNCITRAL asserts competence, is itself a long and complex conversation, which we explore more fully in Chapter 2. Many practitioners view "trade law" as the laws and customs governing trade between countries, prohibitions on "unfair trade" practices, and more recently the pronouncements of the WTO on such norms on trade. But the UN General Assembly created its Commission on International Trade Law in 1966, well before the World Trade Organization was formed. The General Assembly Resolution constituting UNCITRAL provides that the Commission "shall have for its object the promotion of the progressive harmonization and unification of the law of international trade." UN General Assembly Resolution 2205 (XXI), Establishment of Commission on International Trade Law, Art. I (17 Dec. 1966). In 1966, then, the UN's General Assembly was defining any laws creating obstacles to global trade as "trade laws" that UNCITRAL should strive to reform. But creation of the World Trade Organization in 1995 altered this parlance considerably. In current terminological usages, UNCITRAL produces commercial law to govern transactions, mostly among private parties.

2 Our observations of UNCITRAL's Insolvency Working Group extended well beyond its completion of the Legislative Guide on Insolvency Law. Indeed, one of us continues to attend Working Group sessions to this day.

3 This book treats lawmaking as a subset of normmaking, and focuses exclusively on transnational lawmaking. Transnational lawmaking refers to activities that produce laws for the world in varieties of hard and soft law as elaborated below and consistent with the expansive definition of law adopted in scholarship on transnational legal orders (Halliday and Shaffer 2015: Ch. 1). "[F]rom a socio-legal perspective, law establishes generalized normative

Invitations to UNCITRAL were wrapped in the diplomatic protocol characteristic of an inter-governmental organization (IGO). We were invited to observe the proceedings, but couldn't sit just anywhere. The location of seats had been pre-assigned and alphabetically arranged by delegation: the American Bar Association sent three participating delegates to UNCITRAL (one of them, Susan Block-Lieb); the American Bar Foundation ostensibly sent only one (Terence Halliday), although his pseudo-status as a delegate was a convenient fiction to regularize the observations of a nonparticipating social scientist.

This happenstance of alphabetical arrangement got us talking, mostly about what was going on around us. The UN chamber where we found ourselves was as large as a half a football field and maybe 50 feet tall. It contained semi-circular rows of desks and seats organized in parallel fashion to face a central dais with a large, raised desk where several seats faced the room as a whole. In the forward semi-circles sat the sixty state delegations that were current members of the Commission.[4] In the mid-section sat all other state delegations invited as observers, but which actually participated pretty much on the same terms as the UNCITRAL sixty. And in the longest arc of delegations in the back rows were the non-state observer delegations of professional associations, industry groups, international financial institutions, and other delegations from international organizations (IOs).[5] The chair of the working group, a Thai bankruptcy judge ceremonially appointed by acclamation of the group, was seated at the dais together with the working group secretary and several other international civil servants from UNCITRAL's Secretariat.

One by one, delegates to the working group raised their "flags" – the placards that identified the delegation they represented, whether the United Kingdom, Republic of Korea, Holy See, or International Bar Association – to speak about a text that had been prepared by the UNCITRAL Secretariat. Once recognized, the room was technologically enabled to permit delegates to interact in the six official UN languages[6] by pressing a button that activated earphones, the microphone to the front of their desk, and the services of the simultaneous interpreters who sat in the glass-enclosed booths forming a ring in a second story overloooking the proceedings from the back of the room. Although state delegations were seated in the front of the

expectations understood and used by actors within a particular context for purposes of constraining and facilitating particular behaviors" (Id.:11). Normmaking refers to all other activities that result in cultural prescriptions for social behavior.

4 UNCITRAL is an IGO, whose membership has changed over time: there were twenty-nine member states when UNCITRAL emerged in 1968, to thirty-six members in 1996, and its current sixty member states since 2003 (Chapter 2).

5 There are differing usages for the term "international organizations." In this book, the term designates all non-state organizations which embrace intergovernmental organizations (e.g., World Bank, International Institute for the Unification of Private Law), professional and industry associations (e.g., International Bar Association), clubs of nations (e.g., OECD), among others. When we seek to be more precise and refer to sub-sets of IOs, we explicitly label them as industry associations or inter-governmental organizations, as the case may be.

6 Arabic, Chinese, English, French, Spanish, Russian.

room and non-state delegations to the rear, the chair recognized all delegates' requests, one by one, in the order they raised their flags.

Delegates sought permission to speak on the lengthy pre-prepared text before them, often paragraph by paragraph, until the working group had commented on the draft in its entirety during the course of week-long meetings. After listening to the delegates, the chair would intervene to suggest his reading of the room, sometimes to remark that he thought that consensus had been reached; at other times, when consensus still eluded the group, he might offer a summary of the various positions that had been voiced. By the end of the week, the working group's secretary – a lawyer-international civil servant in UNCITRAL's permanent Secretariat – would publish her report on the group's meeting and the delegates' progress toward reaching consensus on their draft text. Her written report often combined the many interim oral summaries and conclusions of the chair.

In this way, we observed, delegations sought to reach consensus, which involved not voting so much as expressing views until no delegate wanted to voice further criticism. Consensus might take years on some portions of the text, but might be reached quickly on other paragraphs. The quasi-legislative process was both tediously slow and filled with the significance and symbolism of diplomatic agreement.

Hundreds of attendees from around the world circulated through the UN chamber during the working group's deliberations on corporate insolvency law. Many delegates were experts on corporate insolvency law: judges from France, Denmark, Thailand, and the US; practicing lawyers from North America, Latin America, and throughout Europe; government regulators and civil servants with expertise with the regulation of financial services, the drafting of corporate insolvency laws or the administration of national insolvency systems, whether from Poland, Canada, Croatia, China, Australia, Colombia, or Israel. Other delegates were not so much experts on insolvency law, as experts on the political processes of the UN – members of the national delegations to the United Nations who might be sent to observe the UN's Commission on International Trade Law one week and the UN's Atomic Energy Commission the next. Some delegates spoke, often and at length; most others were silent the entire week.

But speaking was not limited to the UN chamber itself. We also quickly learned that among the side benefits of UNCITRAL attendance were the lively conversations to be had at the coffee breaks and lunches that punctuated lengthy working group meetings, and the after-hour dinner parties and other social events organized to entertain delegates who, like us, found themselves located in either New York or Vienna twice a year for a week at a time. New York or Vienna law firms or professional associations put on cocktail parties or dinners in historic or gustatory sites. In addition, one of us was invited from time to time to observe expert working group sessions – informal meetings of a small group organized by the working group's Secretary at the conclusion of a working group meeting to assist her in converting a written report of the decisions reached at that meeting into revisions to the draft text for consideration at the next meeting.

Nevertheless, we were at UNCITRAL for different reasons. Block-Lieb, as a law professor and specialist in bankruptcy law, joined in the proceedings of the Insolvency Working Group as a delegate from the International Business Law Section of the American Bar Association. Halliday, a specialist in the globalization of law, was invited as a participant-observer thanks to the generosity and openness of the UNCITRAL Secretariat. Our fortuitous contiguity in the seating chart led to an interdisciplinary conversation that has expressed itself in a line of articles[7] on the road to this book.

Our integration inside the "black box" of global lawmaking permitted us to follow all its twists and turns in real time. No longer were we entirely reliant on published final outcomes, which are the most usual source of materials for writing on international law, or to retrospective reconstructions and their attendant fallibilities based on ex post interviews. We could observe in real time agenda setting and jump-starting, formal and informal proceedings, social occasions, written drafts, hopes realized, and hopes thwarted, without any of the biases attendant on reconstructing events once actors know the outcome of proceedings. In all these ways, we were both observers and participants embedded in a micropolitics on the writing of international commercial laws. We came to observe the practices that are a central finding of this book: *how* international commercial law is made influences *what* law is made.

PRAGMATICS OF GLOBAL TRADE AND COMMERCE

Why should the enormous energies of hundreds of delegates and delegations from state and non-state organizations incur the significant costs of creating commercial laws for the world?

Our immersion in UNCITRAL revealed more fully what international diplomats and discerning national policymakers acutely perceived: national economic fortunes and international competition turn, in substantial part, on the rules of the market and specifically on international commercial laws, which UNCITRAL was either writing *de novo* or rewriting for twenty-first century circumstances.

Consider three sets of market challenges.

A German car manufacturer with subsidiaries and assets in forty-five countries gets into financial difficulties and can no longer pay all its bills on a timely basis in Germany and twenty-five other countries across Europe, Asia, and Latin America. To save itself it needs protection from its creditors – the individuals, companies, and

7 (Block-Lieb and Halliday 2006; Block-Lieb and Halliday 2007a; Block-Lieb and Halliday 2007b; Halliday 2007; Halliday, Block-Lieb and Carruthers 2009b; Halliday, Block-Lieb and Carruthers 2012).

governments to which it owes money. Saving the business will require a restructuring of its finances and a reorganization of its operations and company group in order hopefully to survive this corporate crisis. How might it do this in an orderly way and re-emerge as a competitive multinational corporation? Transnational and national laws on corporate bankruptcy offer a solution.

Next, consider a Chinese manufacturer located in an inland city, Chongqing in China's west, which sends high-end electronic equipment worth $30 million to its distributor in another inland city, in Oklahoma City, in the middle of the US. The goods are loaded into a standardized container and put on a train to China's east coast. Later, the same container is loaded onto a ship, which makes the sea journey from China across the Pacific, where the container is unloaded at the Port of Los Angeles, loaded again onto a train, and shipped to Oklahoma City. Along the way, the goods in the container suffer $15 million of damage. Whose fault is it? Who pays? How much do they pay? Transnational commercial laws governing transport of goods by sea or otherwise offer answers for the parties involved in the commercial transaction.[8]

Finally, imagine a corporation in Brazil that has developed an innovative solar panel and wants to expand its business rapidly to capture market share. It needs money. It decides to borrow. Potential lenders want to be protected if the company gets into financial difficulties so they ask for property rights or security over assets of the company. What assets can the company use for security? Its buildings? Its manufacturing machines? Its intellectual property such as patents on the solar panel? The money that it is due to receive from buyers who have received the goods but have not yet paid? The personal assets of its owners? Secured transactions law is designed to make credit available to businesses to finance their operations and expansion.

Each of these situations is ubiquitous within and between national markets. Obtaining credit and shipping goods are daily practices of business enterprise. In regional economies and global trade, vast flows of capital fuel domestic and international commerce. A large proportion of this trade – from China to the US, US to Europe, Japan to Asia, to mention a few – crosses oceans and thus puts at risk the transport of goods in international waters.

A generic solution to these business challenges, believe the hundreds of delegates to UNCITRAL, can be found in the crafting and adoption of commercial laws that rescue companies, expand credit, and protect shippers of goods, to mention only several of the fundamental components of market activity. Commercial laws like

8 Although multilateral conventions exist to govern transport by sea, inland waterway and rail, the governing laws in China and US are styled as domestic legislation modeled after the conventions. For distinct political reasons in each case, neither China nor the US is party to the conventions themselves (see, e.g., Sturley 1991). Because we view these uniform national laws as a part of the transnational law governing liability for loss in transport of this sort, we leave aside this legal detail as otherwise unimportant to our analysis.

these, according to delegates, will remove obstacles, stimulate investment, spur market activity, enhance the wealth of nations and their peoples, and, implicitly, improve the quality of life worldwide. Put another way, markets matter, believe these lawmakers, because they affect individual lives, corporate behavior, national fortunes, and international relations.

And more pointedly, *law* matters for these markets and their expansion. This book might therefore be considered an encounter between *an economic sociology of law* (Swedberg 2003; Swedberg 2006; Frerichs 2009) or an empirical contribution to *international economic law* (Perry-Kessaris 2013). Our interior portrait of global economic lawmaking reveals the intricate interplay of economic lawmakers and how their actions aspire to shape a world of trade and commerce, of global finance and credit (Carruthers and Kim 2011).

But *law* can matter for *markets* both adversely and constructively. When does law present an obstacle to trade and finance, and when does it enable such commerce? In part, the answers respond to problems of diversity and problems of fit.

With respect to diversity, it is a too seldom examined premise of global lawmaking that extreme diversity in the rules of trade inhibits both domestic and international economic growth. There is a powerful impetus among global lawmakers to codify, simplify, and harmonize laws, thereby, they say, lowering the transaction costs of doing business and opening up markets by the reduction of uncertainties and risks.

With respect to fit, an asymmetry persists between law and politics, on the one side, and law and commerce on the other. Law and politics overwhelmingly remain dominated by the nation-state. Laws, legal institutions, and legal occupations primarily are creations of sovereign states. Trade and markets, by contrast, have overflowed national frontiers, spilling over into adjacent states and reaching those very far removed from them, not only in geographical terms but also into states whose norms for trade and commerce are deeply rooted in long histories of difference. The League of Nations and the United Nations signify only the most notable of endeavors in the last almost-century effort to elevate law and politics into a more symmetrical relationship with markets. One consequential, yet neglected, means of bringing transnational and national politics and laws into symmetry with economic activity have been global lawmakers such as UNCITRAL.

Which sharpens the question: Can a tiny UN entity such as UNCITRAL alter world commerce and domestic markets through law? Although this question has attracted far too little empirical examination, a retrospective on UNCITRAL's products since its founding in 1966 reveals that amid its several failures there are outstanding instances of global impact (Chapter 2). Some of this impact exists in the form of multistate treaties, such as the New York Convention on the Recognition and Enforcement of Foreign Arbitral Awards (which was drafted before UNCITRAL emerged but over which UNCITRAL now asserts authority) and the UN Convention on the International Sale of Goods (which was drafted by UNCITRAL). Both conventions have been widely adopted (by 157 and 85 states, respectively), and are the two most widely adopted treaties pertaining to the actions and behaviors of private actors (that is, conventions on international private law). UNCITRAL's model laws are also widely influential, including its Model Law on International Commercial Arbitration (implemented in seventy-five states), Model Law on Electronic Commerce (in sixty-nine states, and 145 jurisdictions overall), and Model Law on Cross-Border Insolvency (in forty-three states)(id.).

The potential market-shaping ripples of the three lawmaking episodes in this book point to far-reaching potential consequences of law in economic action over the next decades. If law matters for markets, and UNCITRAL's lawmaking matters in particular, this book demonstrates that *how* UNCITRAL's law is made affects *what* law is made.

A SOCIOLOGY OF LAW AND INTERNATIONAL ORGANIZATIONS

The issues of diversity and fit that pervade the "trade enabling commercial laws" that UNCITRAL's global lawmakers seek to produce raise two major sets of questions conventionally raised by lawyers and social scientists focused on the international.

1 *International Law*

Positivist theories of international law (IL) narrowly view IL as enforceable against sovereign states only, if at all, on the basis of their tacit or express consent – that is, only when framed as international or multinational treaties, international "custom," or "general principles of law."[9] In the latter half of the twentieth century and opening years of the twenty-first century, two significant turns occur in studies of international law and IOs' involvement in international lawmaking. We build on both.

First, there was recognition that not only were IOs extensively involved in the making of the conventional hard law of multilateral conventions (e.g., Szasz 1995a; Szasz 1995b), but also that IOs and transnational regulatory networks (TRNs) were increasingly engaged in normmaking of a softer variety, producing resolutions, standards, model laws, principles, best practices, legislative guides, codes, and so on (see, e.g., Abbott et al. 2000; Brummer 2015). Scholars began to study lawmaking by IOs that are IGOs, especially organizations affiliated to the United Nations (e.g., Alvarez 2005; Boyle and Chinkin 2007; Higgins 1963). Some of these studies

9 See, e.g., Statute of the International Court of Justice, Art. 38 (1945). Some self-described "enlightened" positivists in this arena accept the possibility that international custom may be impacted by the adoption of resolutions by the UN General Assembly and modern treaty-making practices (see, e.g., Simma and Paulus 1999), paving the way for subsequent research on international lawmaking.

mention UNCITRAL briefly (Alvarez 2005: 312-14); a very few focus exclusively on UNCITRAL (e.g., Gillette and Scott 2005a). Some of this commentary notes that the constitutions of a number of IGOs explicitly permit lawmaking (Alvarez 2005), and that IGOs increasingly take advantage of their constitutional mandates to provide inventive and creative ways to collaborate with lawmakers and assist states in international treaty-making and policy-making (e.g., Higgins 1994). Scholars also study standard-setting and quasi-regulatory activities of networks of regulators (Slaughter 2004) and even of private actors (Peters, Förster and Koechlin 2009). While it is still an issue for some IL specialists whether or not this IO activity constitutes the making of law per se, the recognition of IO involvement in production of law or law-like products is fully acknowledged.

Alongside the type of law or legal norm being produced, IL scholars began to attend to processes of international lawmaking. Alvarez (2005) details the treaty-making activities of a range of IGOs. Boyle and Chinkin (2007), similarly, "outline" a "variety of international processes" for "the negotiation and adoption of treaties, decisions, and soft law instruments of various kinds," including processes involving coordination with a wide range of non-state actors and "the use of consensus-negotiating techniques" (Boyle and Chinkin 2007: 41-93, 160-61). While international law scholarship generally remains intent on resolving *whether* IOs are actually making "law" in their terms, these scholars concomitantly pointed in a new direction of inquiry that dug more deeply into the *how* of international lawmaking.

It will immediately be seen that quite apart from conceptual specifications and judgments, normative and other judgments about law emanating from a global lawmaker rest on empirical foundations. Who sits at the lawmaking table? What qualities of deliberation occur inside the lawmaking chambers, in the corridors outside those chambers, and in distant government institutions, and far-flung congeries of social organizations and public opinion? And it is at this point that the second turn in IL/IO studies becomes particularly salient.

Second, while the first turn recognized the fact of IO activity and the need to inquire into processes of IO involvement in lawmaking in all its varieties, international law scholarship took another turn, most notably toward empirical inquiry, infused by social science sensibilities, methodologies, and theory, to move IL scholarship into a fully dynamic mode. Two leaders of this movement, Gregory Shaffer and Tom Ginsburg (2012), identify quickening waves of inter-disciplinary research over the past fifteen years on adjudication by international and regional tribunals, including the WTO,[10] on business regulation,[11] on norm production by

10 See, e.g., (Alter 2001; Helfer and Alter 2013; Stone Sweet and Brunell 1998; Hagan 2003; Meernik and King 2003; Meernik 2003). For commentary on adjudication in the World Trade Organization, see also, e.g., (Shaffer 2003b; Maton and Maton 2007; Colares 2009).

11 Mostly notably, the magisterial volume on *Global Business Regulation* by (Braithwaite and Drahos 2000).

policymaking IOs,[12] on private standard-setting,[13] on bureaucratic-like global governance by IOs,[14] and on global governance more broadly. In this rapidly expanding empirical enterprise, the mapping of global laws in all their manifestations is accompanied by an insistence that the behaviors that produce and result from these laws must be drawn into a dynamic concept of international law in engagement with IOs as they are understood by the sciences of social behavior.

Our book rides this wave, but in new directions. Rather than treat international tribunals or global regulatory bodies, we focus on a global lawmaking arena, specifically those focused on the production of international private law. Rather than take for granted that an IO produces a given type of lawmaking or standard-setting product, we problematize why global lawmakers choose one kind of "legal technology" over another. And, most importantly, rather than contribute to IL debates over *whether* IOs make international law or not-law, we examine intensively *how* such global norms are produced: we seek to unveil processes of global lawmaking.

Methodologically, this book rests on empirical foundations less common in IL or IO research. Rather than rely as outsiders on formal IGO or IO constitutions, by-laws, and legal products, we engaged in the lawmaking itself as participant-observer insiders. Rather than attempt a broad overview of regulatory bodies, which have contributed richly to the development of theory in IOs and IL, we undertook an intensive case study of a particular understudied species of IO, a global legislature engaged in international lawmaking. And rather than proceed retrospectively, by asking participants to reconstruct past behaviors and perceptions, we combined studies, observation, and analysis in real time, over many years, together with complementary interviews that sought perspectives both retrospective and prospective. Moreover, while our principal focus is one understudied UN commission, we sought variation within the UN's Commission on International Trade Law by studying three working groups that deliberated on different issue-areas and outside the Commission by studying its organizational environments, including not least its potential allies and competitors.

Theoretically, rather than privilege political science debates on IL and IO, which have contributed much insight on normmaking and lawmaking by international organizations, we develop a sociological theory of IOs. We adapt and reconstruct for the international the longstanding theory of social ecologies (see Chapter 1). We bring this new application of ecology theory into an encounter

[12] For examples, see, on gender violence (Merry 2006a), human rights (Simmons 2009), biotechnology (Pollack and Shaffer 2009), and corporate insolvency law standards (Halliday and Carruthers 2009; Block-Lieb and Halliday 2006).

[13] (Mattli and Büthe 2003).

[14] Cf. Barnett and Finnemore's work on IOs as bureaucratic entities including empirical work on three entities: the International Monetary Fund; the UN's High Commissioner for Refugees; and the UN's policies on genocide and peacekeeping within the Security Council and UN Assistance Mission for Rwanda (Barnett and Finnemore 2004).

with the currently emerging interdisciplinary theory of transnational legal organizations (TLOs)(Halliday and Shaffer 2015c).

All of these perspectives encounter the fundamental questions posed when social scientists ask *who governs*? What is common to otherwise conflicting schools of theorizing on international lawmaking is their manifest or tacit convergence on the exercise of more or less legitimate power and authority through lawmaking beyond the state. Theories of international political economy, world systems, IOs, hegemony, and counter-hegemony in the world system, of command and capitalist economics, of world polity and world society, of law and development all turn in substantial part on *who* they believe or demonstrate to be driving legal change through transnational lawmaking and whether these actors are perceived as legitimate participants in this sphere of activity.

Thinking about who governs can be sharpened by an overly stark but nonetheless useful contrast of polar opposite hypotheses. One hypothesis predicts that IOs are ciphers and proxies for the expression of raw economic or political power projected by dominant states. A contrasting hypothesis posits that IOs as arenas and actors are sites for interaction and emergent properties in which non-state actors and interactional processes contribute to deliberative outcomes not predictable, indeed, beyond those that follow from the raw economic and geopolitical power of states entering the legislative arena. Between these imaginary opposites lie variations emphasizing non-state actors, the epistemological power of professions, the legitimating cultures of world society, and the emergence of IOs as institutional actors of significance in their own right.

We therefore pursue the question of who governs, but with a much stronger emphasis on the interactional processes that add up to influence beyond the dominant states central to realist and structuralist views of global power. While our precise inside data demonstrate who chose issue-areas for lawmaking, who set agendas, who attended and spoke, who exerted more or less influence in various sites of interaction, who had resources and who provided resources, who struck the Big Deals, and whose interests ultimately were served by the lawmaking, we show that the *who* of lawmaking is inseparable from the *how*. The processes within this global lawmaking body, we demonstrate, allowed some actors to dominate while others remained subordinate, permitted some measure of consensus when dissensus seemed inevitable, enabled cooperation when competition threatened to be insurmountable, and permitted production of global norms when stalemate seemed imminent.

These processes display the surprising emergence of a tiny, resource-constrained IO as both an arena and actor whose impact on markets through law far exceeds its deceptive appearances of relative insignificance. Indeed, it may be that its shadowy impact follows precisely because its miniscule administrative apparatus and relative obscurity in a sea of highly visible IOs enable it to construct markets largely invisible to most market players themselves. This emergent reality in the world of affairs leads into lively contemporary engagements by scholars who labor at the intersection of law and markets.

2 *Markets*

A fundamental question brings into conjunction two extensive bodies of scholarship on economic sociology and the globalization of law: How do law and markets mutually constitute each other in a transnational world?[15]

Elsewhere, we observe a misfit between markets and political-legal orders (Halliday and Carruthers 2009; see also, e.g., Westbrook 2000). Economic activity increasingly spills over national frontiers. Yet politics remain deeply embedded inside nation-states.[16] Resolving the misfit between law and markets can occur in several places. Transnational recursivity theory (Halliday and Carruthers 2007b; Nourse and Shaffer 2009) proposes that in an interdependent world there is a proliferation of episodes of legal change, many directed to the construction of TLOs,[17] where the politics of fit occur simultaneously at global, transnational, national, and local levels. The fit between law and markets ramifies recursively through iterations of efforts to gain some symmetry between law and markets at each level and across levels of governance.

In this book, we open the black box of global lawmaking to examine the internal *processes* that shape the legal construction of transnational markets, as the dominant systemic form of global economic activity, beyond the local and national. These processes reflect, anticipate, and involve the national, local, and international.

They *reflect* current market practices, how markets are now operating for better or worse. They respond to supposed problems confronted by markets and to diagnoses and prescriptions offered by aspiring legal architects of markets. To a substantial degree, global lawmaking responds to deficiencies identified by diagnosticians in local and national settings, and to the compounding of those problems in international economic activities. Demands for international private law and legal change, in short, arise out of markets.

Yet it will also become apparent that the processes in which global lawmakers are embroiled *anticipate* subsequent iterations of implementation and normmaking. The global legal architects of markets are forward-looking insofar as they express through law enabling or constraining rules that will stimulate markets to function more propitiously, however they define "propitious." Global lawmakers are inherently prescriptive, imagining a future state of affairs where law will shape

15 For an insightful explication of the economic and legal as mutually constitutive, see (Perry-Kessaris 2015).

16 We are not among those who prematurely predict the demise of the state, but rather observe the complexities of its restructuring (Halliday 2012).

17 On the general theory of transnational legal orders (TLOs), see (Halliday and Shaffer 2015b). For the application of TLO theory in this book, see Chapter 1 and thereafter.

market behavior within and beyond nation-states and hoping to encourage markets and other actors to follow their lead.

Finally, consistent with the intuitions of IOs and ad hoc diplomatic conferences organized over roughly the past century and longer, our data demonstrate both the fact and the wisdom of processes that involve non-state organizations, a topic others also have addressed (see, e.g., Alvarez 2005: 154–56; Block-Lieb and Halliday 2016; Charnovitz 2006). UNCITRAL, like similar bodies, extends invitations to non-state delegations, encouraging their observation and participation in the making of international private laws that looked to alter these private behaviors. This reflection, anticipation, and involvement, thus, serve recursive ends.

Further, we reveal how these processes are both internal to UNCITRAL itself and external to UNCITRAL's political context. They are *internal* to the degree that there are micropolitics of interaction, negotiation, and association with the legislative arena that have far-reaching programmatic and symbolic effects. Processes of lawmaking are *external* insofar as the micropolitics inside UNCITRAL are nested within a wider politics of competition and cooperation among other IOs. We will elaborate a theory that UNCITRAL positions itself as an actor in an ecology of IOs (Block-Lieb and Halliday 2011).

These processes in turn are enabled by and reflected in the *formal* properties of IO products. The sociology of law and law and society scholarship have had, as a central *problematique*, the disjunction between law-on-the-books, or formal law, and law-in-action, or the behavior and practice of law. Overwhelmingly, the socio-legal enterprise has been directed at law's behavior and practice, at the moments when law is implemented and practiced by citizens and drivers and workers, by police and regulators, lawyers and accountants. Yet crafting the fit between law and markets also requires socio-legal attention to *lawmaking* as a process. And in the contemporary world that often involves global norm- and lawmaking (Halliday 2009). After all, the reflexive character of law, at once reflecting and anticipating future possibilities, arguably should be manifest in the lawmaking itself. Indeed, this is a central premise of transnational recursivity theory (Shaffer 2011).

Occasionally, sociologists have called for or advanced a sociological account of law's formal properties (e.g., Mallard 2014; Stinchcombe 2001). Braithwaite, for instance, forcefully maintains that global norms in the form of principles are far better suited to fast-moving areas of economic activity, where there are high economic stakes and quick-moving innovations, than bright-line rules, which are better suited to routinized behaviors that can easily be standardized across much of the world, such as traffic rules and regulations (Braithwaite 2002). The logic of critical discourse analysis (Blommaert and Bulcaen 2000; van Dijk 2003), if extended to law, would also propose that law's formal properties signal the constellations of power that are instantiated within it. Thus law's *rhetoric*, contained in seemingly technocratic and neutral legal language, if carefully dissected, reveals constellations of power, claims to legitimacy, and aspirations of authority (Halliday, Block-Lieb and

Carruthers 2009b). This book is, thus, also an extended study in which we emphasize the interplay of form and process in the legal constitution of markets, and the market constructions of law within and beyond the nation-states.

In so doing, we question a powerful operating assumption of world polity theory – that global norms will somehow emerge consensually out of global society and will do so without contestations at the heart of world culture (Campbell 2011). Our data reveal varieties of actors – states and non-states, professions and international financial institutions, industry groups, and regional bodies – disagreeing and maneuvering, disputing and settling, winning and losing, as each seeks to place its imprint on the global legal norms. Our data predict settled patterns of economic behavior for some economic actors, but also that institutionalization will evade others, whose actors are likely to suffer further turns in the recursive construction of legal orders.

Despite its invisibility and aura of technical deliberation, we also demonstrate that UNCITRAL's lawmaking arena is a site of struggles for influence and power. Consistent with our empirical observations, schools of sociological and political science theory on globalization and law variously contend that an international political economy pits powerful states and economic institutions against each other (Grieco and Ikenberry 2003; Helleiner 2009), that hegemons overwhelm counter-hegemons as they stamp their imprints on the weak (Darian-Smith 2013), that world systems are shaped by global centers that keep global peripheries enfeebled (Arrighi and Silver 2001; Wallerstein 1984; Wallerstein 2005), or that international financial institutions and private banks seek to align global markets with their ideological prescriptions (Morgan 2011).

Seldom do these grand theoretical characterizations obtain empirical grounding in the intricate and intimate unraveling of the sites at which struggles occur through years of intense interactions. Yet many of the actors integral to these theories can be observed in action inside UNCITRAL – the US and small African nations, the International Monetary Fund (IMF) and the Asian Development Bank, Germany and powerful financial associations, the International Labor Organization (ILO), and China. Distinct from this scholarship, which substantially is built on intuition and assertion, we carefully observe and examine *who* are the actors on this invisible global stage and *how* they are they exerting their relative degrees of influence in *whose* interests. We will demonstrate that *how* law is made in this global lawmaking body has consequential effects on *what* law is made.

Finally, it must be emphasized that this volume presents an empirical study that uses varieties of social science data in order to make sense of observable behaviors. Those observations are foundations on which to refine and build theory about lawmaking behavior. This book does *not* offer normative accounts of how IOs should behave, how markets should be constructed, or what forms and substance of law should shape global markets. We have no *a priori* commitments about whether more or less participation, more or less convergence, more or less law will be better for markets, market actors, or market outcomes. Even so, a theory of global lawmaking can be expected to show contingent relationships between lawmaking as a process and the effects of lawmaking. This book will show that the ways law is made affects what law is produced. Thereby it may provide evidence that normative commentators will wish to assimilate to normative arguments about global lawmaking and markets in the twenty-first century.

3 *Institutions*

We work at the nexus of fundamental questions – How does transnational law shape markets? How do markets shape transnational law? These questions are of such scope that they juxtapose the largest of social categories or phenomena – of global and national, of law and markets, of IOs and individual actors. What kinds of theoretical leverage are available to make sociological sense of this juxtaposition of law and markets?

One answer derives from institutional theory in sociology and political science. By pursuing social life through the theoretical framing of institutions, scholars seek to explain regularized practices and understandings in different spheres of social life, each of which has its distinctive logics, cultural rules and cognitive structures, organizing principles and distinctive organizational forms. This macro-sociological perspective paints with the broadest brush strokes distinctive properties of states, markets, religion, families, and politics, among others (Friedland 2012; Thornton, Ocasio and Lounsbury 2012).

Institutional theory offers rich conceptual and theoretical materials with which to approach the understanding of lawmaking for global markets.

We share with sociological institutional theory (Campbell 2004; Friedland and Alford 1991; Thornton and Ocasio 2008; Thornton, Ocasio and Lounsbury 2012) an affirmation of cultural contexts, discursive framing, and the pervasive influence of dominant ideas and paradigms in the determination of institutional logics and organizational forms. We concur that external influences and exogenous pressures shape institutional change. We also show that institution-building and organizational work involve active institutional entrepreneurs who diagnose problems, frame solutions and rhetorically construct futures (Battilana, Leca and Boxenbaum 2009; Rehder 2006). Our theory similarly rests on the premise that resources matter and control over resources influence the shape of institutional continuity and change. Not least we elaborate the significance of technologies and technology cycles in institutional change (Tushman and Murmann 1998).

In the application of institutional theory to globalization of law, we affirm that global institution-building and institutional change always involve an interaction, an engagement, a recursive dynamic between global centers of cultural production and material power and national or local centers of power (Halliday and Carruthers 2009). At these global-local intersections are actors shaping degrees of institutional convergence, whether these occur through bricolage or negotiation or resistance or rejection (Carruthers and Halliday 2006).

We share with historical institutionalism in political science the general thesis that long temporal shadows are cast through path dependencies where momentous events or policy decisions taken years or decades earlier continue to constrain subsequent institutional pathways, prospects, and options. And yet evolutionary, incremental change also can occur endogenously within institutions as actors find ways to work with the ambiguities, inconsistencies, and contradictions of rules that govern behavior (Hall 2010; Mahoney and Thelen 2010a; Mahoney and Thelen 2010b).

We share with rational actor variants of institutionalism the proposition that actors in institutions have degrees of freedom to exercise their cognitive capacities, mobilize their resources, engage in bargaining or coalitional maneuverings – that they are not simply unreflective recipients of norms that magically are diffused from a global center and to which they unthinkingly comply through imitation or normative conformity. And yet they are embedded in wider institutions, ambient cultures, and logics of action so that conscious choices about interests are in turn permeated by how interests and goal orientations come to be shaped by contexts and milieu.

By building upon these theoretical variants we heed the call for a "second movement" in institutional theory that is synthetic and open to complementary insights from its diverse schools of thought (Campbell and Pedersen 2001). We attend to interplays of exteriors and interiors, of exogenous and endogenous impulses for change, to structures and constraints in tension with active agents and innovators.

Yet our research reveals that institutional theory as it now stands exhibits a "missing middle."[18] Between the grand amorphousness of a market or state institution and a particular organization or individual embedded within that institution lies an intermediate zone of social interaction, a social space hitherto scarcely recognized in sociological studies of globalization but quite manifest to the actors in this zone. We show that social ecologies of IOs are active between the global institutions of law and markets, between the macroscopic aspects of institutions and their particular outworkings, and in the lived experiences of organizations and individuals.

By attending empirically to ecologies of IOs that shape the nexus between law and markets, we discover processes and features of social life in the international where institutional theory appears underdeveloped.

One key step is to discover the ecologies of IOs that forge the relationships between law and markets and to explicate in fine detail the cultural work that

[18] We borrow from Merry (2006a) her artful deployment of this concept in anthropological settings.

occurs when actors identify problems and draw boundaries around which actors will be considered legitimate participants in market-shaping lawmaking and which will be excluded.

A further crucial step focuses on competition – processes alluded to in some variants of institutional theory but weakly developed in others. Who are the IOs and other actors in the international social spaces who compete for primacy over which legal norms will prevail in global institutions and orders? How is that competition managed? And who prevails? How does competition relate to the possibilities of cooperation, of alliances and coalitions, of blocs and partnerships? Relatedly, but from another direction, our study shares with social movement approaches to institutional change in domestic markets an expectation of contestation and contentiousness that will drive market change through innovation and entrepreneurship (King and Pearce 2010). In our case, that change is driven through law, even as the law itself reflects shifts in economic institutions.

Relatedly, while the importance of resources recurs in many institutional theories, they seldom are systematically theorized, nor are satisfactory theories developed of the ways that actors compete for resources, or how their dependency on resources shapes interactions inside and outside ecologies of lawmaking.

Not least, while constructive attention has been focused on rules in the environments or interiors of organizations and institutions, this book will show how innovative technologies – in our case, legal technologies – become critical mechanisms whereby markets are enabled and ordered through law as law simultaneously constructs markets. Close attention to the sophisticated technical work of crafting legal technologies will reveal how lawmaking ecologies mediate between the most abstract and highest level institutional norms and practicalities of making them relevant to an enormously diverse world of states, organizations, and individuals whose behavior and practices are embedded in institutions, while also exercising sufficient agency to shape legal norms in ways consonant with their histories, ideal and material interests.

By discovering the ecological dynamics of IOs in the conjunction of law and markets, we attend to critical questions of institutional theory with some fresh angles of orientation.

AN ETHNOGRAPHY OF THE GLOBAL

At the core of this research enterprise is a "deterritorialized ethnography" of the global (Merry 2013). The research began and continued, as Merry specifies, as a "focus on a particular site," on a local stage where the global was performed in microcosm, in a situation where we could "observe interactions, who is present, who speaks, what is said . . . on forms of discourse and meaning, every day practices and habits, and systems of actors, networks and institutional frameworks" (Merry 2013:1–3). Yet our research design evolved as questions came more sharply into focus, as differences among UNCITRAL's working groups became more manifest, as the aftermath of working group products became manifest, and as access to multiple sources of data enriched the observations that accumulated in our initial site of UN deliberations.

1 *Design*

Commentators often repeated a similar gentle critique of our earlier writings on UNCITRAL's Working Group on Insolvency Law (Halliday, Block-Lieb and Carruthers 2009a; Halliday and Carruthers 2009). However fertile our data and findings on corporate bankruptcy law, what confidence could be assured that what worked for bankruptcy law could be said to work for other areas of international commercial law? That critique extended both to the global lawmaking itself and to iterations of implementation. We took the critique as well founded, especially since delegates to other working groups at UNCITRAL often told us that things were different in their groups. Insolvency should not be considered paradigmatic.

This book therefore reflects our decision, taken well into the research on insolvency lawmaking, to broaden the design to cover two additional working groups – the Working Group on Secured Transactions and the Working Group on International Transport. These were engaged in global lawmaking at approximately the same time (2000–2008) and we were able to obtain access to later deliberations of the Working Group on Secured Transactions, and to sources and delegates from all three working groups to observe points of contrast and comparison.

The groups varied in their products. The Insolvency and Secured Transactions Working Groups both produced legislative guides, which were intended to advise state legislators about how to craft statutes on these topics, whereas the Transport Working Group produced a multilateral convention consistent with the longstanding practice of inter-state agreements on transnational issues.

The groups varied in the distributive consequences of their lawmaking. The Transport Working Group negotiated among state and non-state actors over economic terms that had zero-sum effects. Better terms for some actors meant worse terms for others. By contrast, the Insolvency Working Group in principle generated soft law that could expand the "pie" for all actors, even if some might use that law to benefit over others. The secured transactions negotiations fell toward the middle of these two poles – a potential expansion of economic opportunities for all but in ways that directly affected benefits for some states and some non-state actors. These variations across the three episodes of lawmaking speak directly to the generalizability of this UNCITRAL-centered study for global lawmaking of several kinds.

The groups varied in the extent to which they were modernizing longstanding international trade law or venturing into creation of international law *de novo*. The Transport Group looked to supersede an earlier convention, The Hague Rules, that had governed more than 90 percent of the world's trade by sea and had been in existence since 1924. It also sought to provide UNCITRAL a second chance at this endeavor, since the Commission had in 1978 attempted to usurp The Hague Rules with its own Hamburg Rules, but the latter although entered into force govern only a few, mostly land-locked nations. The Secured Transactions Working Group also needed to address existing transnational law, such as the Cape Town Convention, which had been drafted by another global lawmaker, the International Institute for the Unification of Private Law (which occasionally is referred to as the Rome Institute and since 1965 as UNIDROIT). UNCITRAL endeavored not to supersede the Cape Town Convention so much as to supplement it with recommendations and commentary governing a far broader range of collateral and financial transaction. The Insolvency Working Group, by contrast, worked on a largely clean slate. Apart from UNCITRAL's own innovative procedural rules for dealing with corporate bankruptcies that crossed borders, no international law existed on corporate insolvency, although several international financial institutions, such as the World Bank and IMF, earlier had attempted to articulate general principles on the topic of business failure and reorganization.

The working groups also varied in terms of the likelihood that their proceedings would provoke conflict between UNCITRAL and other IOs. All three working groups potentially had other IOs as allies or opponents. This raised the prospect of potential conflict with international lawmaking organizations other than UNCITRAL, such as UNIDROIT, which had been created under the auspices of the League of Nations in the mid-1920s, and The Hague Conference on Private International Law, which had been around in one form or another since at least 1893. Other agencies of the UN, such as UNCTAD (the UN Conference on Trade and Development) and the World Bank, were also potential rivals whose interests required UNCITRAL's delegations and Secretariat to maneuver with care in volatile issue-areas.

Not least, the three working groups bore similarities and differences over who attended, who were the most prominent and active delegates and delegations, and whose interests emerged as dominant. By comparing and contrasting group dynamics it would also become apparent to us that all groups shared certain processes, whereas other processes arose in one or another working group but not all of them. We seek both to identify those common and differing processes and to consider why working groups should employ distinct methods of work. Why should global lawmakers differ when confronting market problems in contrasting issue-areas?

2 *Data*

Our data are comprised less of numbers and more of actors, their behavior, and their words – both spoken and written. Quantitatively, we tracked closely the participants in all three working groups – who showed up and who left – and for the Insolvency Working Group, who spoke, and how often. Qualitatively, we embedded ourselves, from beginning to end, in the Working Group on Insolvency and occasionally in the

Working Group on Secured Transactions and twice in the annual meetings of the Commission itself. This ethnography of the global involved daily attendance for one week in Vienna and one week in New York of all Insolvency Working Group sessions each year from 1999–2004; one of the meetings of the Commission one of us attended in Vienna was timed to observe that entity's reactions to the Legislative Guide produced by the Insolvency Working Group. We kept detailed notes about what was going on in the formal deliberative chamber, whether meetings of the Working Group or of the Commission, including the sequences or speech-turns of all speakers and the content of their speech. We analyzed draft and final texts prepared by the UNCITRAL Secretariat and the three working groups in our case studies. During breaks in these meetings, and in many sorts of informal settings, between 1999 and 2004 and thereafter we conducted hundreds of interviews, some structured formally, and others capturing informally an issue or comment of the moment.

There is some asymmetry in these data. While we participated and observed sessions from 1999–2004 in the Insolvency Working Group, and followed the iterations of its outcomes in subsequent years, we relied primarily on systematic interviews of delegates and members of the UNCITRAL Secretariat for the Secured Transactions and International Transport Working Groups. Fortunately, our intensive participation in the Insolvency Working Group informed much more precise and systematic subsequent interviews and analysis of the other two working groups between 2004–2012.

By working back and forth among varieties of data and different working groups we have been able to triangulate our findings in ways that provide a robustness and confidence that we have captured both continuities and discontinuities in the decision-making processes and lawmaking practices evinced by these hundreds of global lawmakers.

OVERVIEW

How law is made affects what law is made. The theoretical and historical underpinnings of our analysis together form the first section of the book. Chapter 1 explores the intersection of two broad theoretical frames. It elaborates the emerging theory of TLOs and its interplay with a new theoretical orientation focused on social ecologies of international organizations, especially those IOs engaged in international lawmaking. Chapter 2 applies these theories to UNCITRAL from the perspective of grand time, the emergence of a standing ecology of lawmaking IOs from the late nineteenth century to UNCITRAL's successful entry into this ecology in the mid-1960s through 1999 when the three issue-specific episodes of lawmaking we research most closely begin to unfold.

The second section peers intensively inside UNCITRAL's three lawmaking ecologies on insolvency, secured transactions, and international transport. The boundary work required to constitute lawmaking ecologies unfolds in Chapter 3, which demonstrates the determinative effects of agenda setting on actors and the ultimate products of each working group. A quantitative analysis of attendance and participation by delegates and delegations reveals internal contradictions between UNCITRAL's effectiveness, on the one hand, of drawing vital resources into its lawmaking activities while, on the other hand, potentially eroding its legitimacy through reliance on small selective circles of delegates in deliberations. The empirical inquiry then turns to analysis of adaptive strategies adopted in the lawmaking ecologies to solve potentially crippling challenges. Chapter 5 shows how UNCITRAL leaders coped with great difficulties posted by an enormous heterogeneity of delegates and delegations under conditions of institutional rigidity and time pressure. Informal methods of work circumvented debililitating organizational constraints. Manipulations of time relaxed temporal rigidities. By contrast, Chapter 6 demonstrates how the formal crafting of legal technologies simultaneously enabled consensus to emerge from conflicting interests within the lawmaking chambers and concomitantly to anticipate the degree of flexibility state lawmakers would demand as a condition of their convergence on UNCITRAL legal norms. These social, temporal, and formal strategems led to settlements on global norms through big deals in each issue-area. Chapter 7 shows that global laws for markets bear heavy imprints of power and influence, from the US in particular, and the Global North and some non-state actors in general. Yet the price of that dominance was to open up many of the norms to give discretion and flexibility to sovereign states. They tolerate some diversity in legal regulation of markets as a concession to the goal of settling on a single set of laws for the world.

The third section steps beyond the three issue-ecologies to contrast two sets of struggles confronted by UNCITRAL as an arena and an actor. Chapter 8 describes an unsettling proposal by France to change the decision-making rules and practices of UNCITRAL as an arena. The effect of this challenge would have been to lessen the influence of non-state delegates and delegations and probably constrain the lawmaking impact of the US. Since the recommended changes would likely deprive UNCITRAL of critical resources and effectiveness, the politics of deciding on what rules would govern lawmaking reveal the future conditions that UNCITRAL's core constituencies considered essential to its efficacy as a global lawmaker. Chapter 9 shifts the lens to UNCITRAL as an actor in relationship with other powerful IOs in its lawmaking ecology. By studying three paired rivalries with UNIDROIT, the World Bank, and UNCTAD, the chapter shows how jurisdictional settlements between rival IOs were attempted, but did not always succeed, through three types of "meta-texts."

We conclude by advancing in Chapter 10 a concept of inventive global governance. Drawn from both UNCITRAL's successes and challenges, we identify the modes of adaptation to the dynamics of its ecology. We juxtapose inventiveness realized, in seemingly successful adaptations, with inventiveness lacking, in challenges to the prospects of a legitimate and effective global lawmaker. We point to frontiers of imagination in global governance insofar as lawmaking for global commerce is attempted; here, markets and politics uneasily confront each other's logics in a world where TLOs seem steadily to advance.

Finally, given our interdisciplinary intent, readers may observe and perhaps be puzzled by use of numerous terms-of-art in this book. We draw your attention to our dual purpose in this volume. At one level we offer an analytically structured account of the emergence of UNCITRAL and its twentieth century lawmaking practices. At another level, however, we adopt and create concepts to generate theory that goes beyond UNCITRAL to other IOs and global lawmaking. This latter step intends that UNCITRAL become a springboard for new approaches to international organizations of many sizes, shapes, and purposes in global governance. The concepts and theory seek to enable us to transcend UNCITRAL's particularities to reach transnational phenomena of greater generality. Future research will specify the potential and scope of social ecology and TLOs in the understanding of global lawmaking, governance, and regulation.

1

Ecologies of International Lawmaking

Global lawmaking abounds. It comes in many forms and from many sources. Some is made in courts and court-like settings.[1] The International Court of Justice hands down decisions on public international law. The International Criminal Court advances the jurisprudence of crimes against humanity and genocide. The Appellate Panel of the World Trade Organization builds an increasingly dense law from international trade disputes.

Global law is also produced in administrative settings. Transnational regulatory organizations and networks of actors, sometimes of states, sometimes of non-state actors, formulate rules and frequently monitor practices from air traffic (IATA) to health emergencies (WHO) to intellectual property rights (WIPO). The World Bank and International Monetary Fund, together with regional development banks, present prospective nation-state recipients of loans and technical assistance with standards and codes for everything from anti-money laundering to financial system assistance. The International Organization of Securities Commissioners (IOSCO), the International Financial Consumer Protection Organization (FinCoNet), and the Financial Stability Board (FSB) coordinate financial regulators and their work, sometimes with the assistance of the Organization for Economic Cooperation and Development (OECD) and FSB, and the oversight of Clubs of Nations, like the G-20. The United Nations Commission on Elimination of Discrimination against Women regularly appraises countries against standards the UN has adopted, just as the international nongovernment organization (INGO), International Commission of Jurists, issues country reports of national compliance with global standards of legal protections, independence of courts, and access to justice.

[1] Some would argue that courts, whether international or domestic, do not "make" law. They instead "find" law that has been made in other settings. For now, we refer to the concept of "lawmaking" broadly to cover international activities that resemble judicial, legislative, or regulatory actions, as well as efforts by private actors to produce law-like texts for use in international settings.

Multinational corporations, too, have global lawmaking capacities through their company policies on food standards and treatment of workers. Groups of private actors – international professional associations like the International Bar Association, and international trade associations like the Commercial Finance Association – draft texts intended to influence litigation or contract practices.

We focus on the least visible of lawmaking institutions: international organizations that function more like legislatures. Unlike books on inter-governmental bodies such as the International Law Commission, which produce law-like texts to order the relationships among states,[2] this book intensively examines the institutional production of laws that aspire to order the relationships among private actors engaged in global commerce and trade. As an empirical investigation, this book penetrates the zones of invisibility that cloud the production of legal norms that govern international commerce and trade. By placing lawmaking under the social-scientific microscope, it seeks to unveil a genus of lawmaking that operates far below the radar of international media or the business press. This investigation asks: Who makes the legal rules for global commerce and trade? How does the lawmaking space itself become structured as a social entity? What are the interactional processes that enable the lawmaking space to settle into a relatively stable site of legal production?

Beyond global lawmaking arenas, this book uses an intensive empirical study as a springboard for the creation of a sociological theory of international organizations more generally. *Global Lawmakers* introduces an interactionist social ecology theory of global lawmaking in particular and global normmaking in general. It proposes that *how* global law is made significantly shapes *what* global law comes to shape international and national markets. The theory advances in two steps. First, it builds upon the emerging body of scholarship that conducts research and advances theory on the rise and fall of transnational legal orders (Halliday and Shaffer 2015a; Halliday and Shaffer 2015c). Second, it adapts and extends the longstanding sociological theory of interactionist social ecology to the international.

TRANSNATIONAL LEGAL ORDERS

Global lawmakers seek to create, to shape, to join, to understand, even to adapt or resist transnational legal orders. Put another way, the norm entrepreneurs and institutional entrepreneurs (Alford 2008; Battilana, Leca, and Boxenbaum 2009; Braithwaite and Drahos 2000) in global lawmaking bodies and other international organizations, together with their conferees in myriad production centers of global governance, seek to produce order through law. This production of law is directed to the general goal of creating a transnational legal order (TLO). In the issue-areas

[2] E.g., Reduction of Statelessness and other draft provisions like those on Most-Favored Nations Clauses – topics often referred to as involving "public international law."

we study, the progenitors of laws purport to solve fundamental problems of markets by smoothing world trade or to easing investment and lending or bringing order to capitalism's hard edges, such as the creative destruction that markets wreak on weak business firms.

Defining TLOs

The beginning point for TLO theory is a beginning point of all social theories – How to explain social order and change. How does it arise? What forms does it take? What processes govern its functioning? How does it change? When does it break down? There are many forms of social order – economic orders, political orders, religious orders. Each has its own logic,[3] its own means of establishing and maintaining order, its own means of adapting to changed circumstances in order to ensure its survival and vitality.

Following Halliday and Shaffer (2015a; 2015b), a transnational legal order has three interconnected properties.

It is *transnational* insofar as it produces order through means and with effects that transcend the nation-state. The transnational actors may be multilateral or intergovernmental bodies, such as the European Union or United Nations bodies or clubs of nations. Transnational actors may include networks of legal experts or multinational corporations or international NGOs or parliamentarians (Slaughter 2004) or activists (Keck and Sikkink 1998), all capable of acting collectively to produce law. They may be organized in transnational analogs to domestic parliaments, judiciaries and public administrations (Halliday and Osinsky 2006). What these diverse forms of social organization share in common are social relations and ordering enterprises that reach across national frontiers and exceed the jurisdictions of national legal systems and the powers of sovereign states.

A TLO is *legal* either insofar as its ordering norms proceed from law-producing institutions, such as international courts or global legislatures or international regulatory bodies; or the norms themselves are in legal form and thereby carry the rhetorical authority of "law"; or the norms are directed to legal institutions inside the state, whether nationally or locally. It will be seen that this expansive definition embraces the binding *hard* law that is the conventional province of international treaty-making and the terrain of the classical international lawyer, as well as the various sorts of *soft* law that may codify norms through nonbinding standards, regulations, model laws, best practices, and the like (Abbott and Snidal 2000; Shaffer and Pollack 2010). Both the hard and soft law in TLOs have recourse to legal institutions at one or another level of action, whether these are international regulatory bodies, national tribunals, or local municipal courts, to name a few.

[3] On logics of institutions and social orders there is a rich and variegated literature, which seeks to identify distinctive modes of thought and practice to institutions and orders. See (Alford and Friedland 1985; Friedland and Alford 1991).

A TLO brings *order* insofar as it produces norms which seek to create regularities and predictability in behaviors which themselves are expressed in discernible patterns. Following Luhmann (1985: 77), law creates "generalized normative behavior expectations," which in turn enable communication and interaction. A TLO represents an outcome socially constructed by local, national, and international actors functioning as norm entrepreneurs. In the ongoing construction of a global legal order to manage failing businesses, for instance, local lawyers and accountants advise debtors and creditors about the current norms that provincial or national laws, courts and out-of-court agencies will apply if a company goes into bankruptcy, and without saying so, will thereby be expressing the emerging consensus in global lawmaking that was set out in UNCITRAL's Legislative Guide on Insolvency Law. Hence, local professionals and global lawmakers alike insist that they are presiding over a legally constructed process that converts the potential chaos of every creditor scrambling to obtain whatever financial assets still exist in a failing firm into an "orderly" and predictable resolution of disputes over what creditors get priority in what distribution of assets.

It must be emphasized that a TLO functions simultaneously at multiple levels of action – global, regional, international, bilateral, and local. Indeed, it is a critical feature of TLOs that a fully defined TLO embraces at least transnational, national, and local levels of action, which distinguishes them from the international lawyer's treaty or convention. Put negatively, a set of global norms alone does *not* constitute a TLO. A universal consensus for a UN Commission to adopt a Legislative Guide on Insolvency does not amount to a TLO. It amounts only to a formulation of transnational norms. These may or may not come to be integrated into a global or transnational order and they may never be integrated into national and local norms. We distinguish ourselves sharply from accounts of the global or transnational that suppose that norms formulated to order behavior beyond sovereign jurisdictions thereby constitute anything more than what they are, i.e., global norms. We elaborate below that TLOs cannot be said to exist until other conditions of norm adoption have been satisfied.

TLOs vary in *legal* scope. It is possible that a TLO on corporate failures might focus entirely on how to liquidate (that is, sell in pieces or all at once) a failing business. Alternatively, a TLO on corporate failures might expand its scope to include both liquidation proceedings and restructuring mechanisms by which companies might be rescued from financial distress and given some prospects for reorganizing their management, operations, or financing to compete successfully in the market. It might be defined to include all collection laws, even those that apply outside the context of insolvency procedures and so one creditor at a time. Even further, a TLO on corporate failure might expand to encompass institutions inside the state, such as government "asset management companies" organized to buy and resell distressed debt, or outside the state, such as associations of insolvency professionals. Hence much of the dynamism in the lawmaking and implementation of TLOs turns on the breadth or depth of contours of their legal scope.

TLOs vary markedly in their *geographic* scope. An UNCITRAL Legislative Guide on Secured Transactions was designed by global lawmakers to apply to every country in the world. A European initiative on secured transactions law was directed at EU countries only. As Macdonald (2015) has shown, much of the dynamism of TLO expansions and contractions occurs precisely because competing producers of legal norms may bring claims of geographical scope into conflict with other. This volume focuses on several TLOs over which UNCITRAL intended to have global scope, but we shall see that in two of the issue-areas the prospectively global TLOs confronted regional TLOs that might inhibit the global geographic scope of UNCITRAL products.

The Recursivity of TLOs

Research on legal change in international contexts demonstrates that the rise and fall, adaptation and reproduction, of TLOs, has a strongly recursive dynamic (Halliday and Carruthers 2007b; Halliday and Carruthers 2009; Mallard 2014; Shaffer 2012). Recursivity theory posits that legal change in an era of globalization usually involves numerous iterations of lawmaking and implementation between the transnational and national, which is the conventional move of private international law, between the national and local, which is the longstanding province of inquiry by political scientists and sociologists of law (Liu and Halliday 2009), and between the global and local, which can increasingly be observed in activist practices and social science research on the ways that local actors circumvent their states to obtain transnational leverage and international bodies work around state authorities to reach directly more sympathetic local actors.

Accompanying these "vertical" levels of interaction are "horizontal" iterations of lawmaking and implementation. International bodies inside international lawmaking ecologies have experienced multiple rounds of interactional engagements in their various claims to lawmaking authority (Halliday 2009; Halliday and Block-Lieb 2013). Nation-states directly and recursively influence each other (Chorev 2012). Localities, too, have an impact on one another – across federal state lines or from province to province or from a locality in one nation-state to a locality in another, as did the Canadian province of Ontario and the Southern District of New York in the earliest years of transnational bankruptcy lawmaking.

TLOs appear and disappear, reproduce and adapt over time. Episodes of transnational law reform sometimes persist for years or decades between the onset of a lawmaking episode and the new equilibrium of norm settling and behavior that marks the end of the lawmaking process. This book follows the heuristic distinction between two types of circumstances that engender change and enable its settling: facilitating conditions and precipitating events (Halliday and Carruthers 2007b; Halliday and Shaffer 2015b).

Unlike much research on lawmaking in either global or national arenas, we do not accept explanations that focus only on lawmaking from "above," at an international level, which too often is the move from scholarship on international law. New episodes of TLO construction or destruction or adaptation frequently spring from "below" – from states, from sub-state or federal state initiatives, from non-state organizations, and even on occasion from individuals. Nor do we accept accounts of legal change that attend only to the first rounds of implementing new transnational norms, or find acceptable depictions of change that begin and end with the one-step move of diffusion from a global normmaking body to a nation-state, which too often is the move by sociological studies of world society and world polity. Not only does the construction of a TLO involve a series of interior cycles within and between actors at different levels of action, but research in many settings of lawmaking indicates that these cycles are driven by four mechanisms which recur repeatedly in the dynamics of TLOs.

Diagnostic struggles usually precede and accompany cycles of TLO construction and destruction as competing actors seek to frame a presenting problem in terms which privilege their preferred solutions. Thus, it could be predicted that the Asian Development Bank might consider the problems confronting the burgeoning capitalist economies of East Asia differently than the European Bank for Reconstruction and Development conceived of legal development in the former command economies of Central and Eastern Europe.

Actor mismatch designates struggles between lawmakers and law-takers when there is a mismatch between those actors sitting at global or national or local lawmaking tables and those actors absent from these forums but very present in practice. Where transnational lawmaking for TLOs excludes actors who have the capacity to resist or veto legal change in practice, then it is more probable that legal change will be resisted at national and local levels and thus remain unsettled.

Contradictions designate a process by which the substance and institutions that are formulated in global lawmaking internalize and express contradictory ideologies and institutional forms and logics that render unstable the political settlement that permitted promulgation of new legal products. These contradictions may be ideological or substantive and they drive repeated cycles of lawmaking and law implementation.

Indeterminacy describes the process through which various actors creating or implementing law at several levels of action cooperate or compete over the meanings of legal norms. In many situations, where vague or even inconsistent norms reduce certainty in legal meaning, a drive to obtain greater certainty may turn the wheels of law reform and implementation again and again until meanings settle (Pistor and Xu 2003; Block-Lieb and Halliday 2015). Yet a striving for determinacy may be a contingent and fraught process. In some circumstances it is clear that indeterminacy, indeed opacity (Mallard 2014), is a condition of settlement in global lawmaking. It may also be a condition that facilitates local adaptability (cf. Braithwaite 2002; Payne 2015). In either case, at every level of lawmaking and implementation interactional struggles arise to construct meaning.

Institutionalization of TLOs

If the beginnings of TLO construction can be identified in episodes of lawmaking that arise from facilitating circumstances and precipitating events, when can those episodes be said to end? What counts empirically as the institutionalization of a TLO in international trade law – or of law that governs and regulates economic behavior?

Following sociological convention, we consider norms institutionalized when understandings of how to act are taken for granted and ways of acting occur without question (Heimer 2008; March and Simon 1958). On the one hand, the norms about how to act are considered entirely legitimate and are accepted as general guides to behavior or even institutional logics. In the case of TLOs, these norms are expressly formalized at one or another level of action in legal codes, court rulings, contracts, and the like. On the other hand, actions by lawyers or accountants, or providers of capital, or managers of firms, or transporters of goods, or corporate restructuring specialists can be justified by appealing to those norms, but for the most part these actors proceed as if a given way of acting is entirely normal and not to be second-guessed or subjected to the need for regular justification. Each loan transaction, each contract for transporting goods to market, each corporate reorganization does not require reasoning or arguments *de novo* about how to proceed and who should do what. The terms of agreement, of course, will commonly be a matter for bargaining but the rules that govern the bargaining are not in question.

The degree to which a TLO is institutionalized is a function of two cross-cutting dimensions.

Normative settlement Norms settle when their meaning stabilizes and comes to be accepted as legitimate and an acceptable guide to action. The settling of norms within a TLO confronts two formidable challenges.

First, for a TLO to be fully defined, settling must occur in at least three levels of action – the transnational, national, and local – and in some contexts, regional levels, too. Research on global normmaking and national lawmaking demonstrates repeatedly that settling, if it does occur, may take many years and requires repeated cycles of lawmaking and implementation. In 1924 a diplomatic conference first set out The Hague Rules (formally, the International Convention for the Unification of Certain Rules of Law Relating to Bills of Lading), which by 2008 had been signed by over a hundred nations and governed trade in 90 percent of the globe; but industries and technology had developed in ways that undermined the usefulness of these rules and in that year, UNCITRAL promulgated a competing draft convention, the so-called Rotterdam Rules. At this moment, there is no settling on the Rotterdam Rules beyond a score of signatory nations. All that is clear is that international transport norms will remain unsettled in the near term (Block-Lieb and Halliday 2015).

Second, it cannot be assumed that if there is settling in global norms, national laws, and local norms or standards of practice, a TLO thereby can be said to be in place. It would be entirely possible for norms to be settled at the transnational or national or local levels of action, but for those norms to be discordant. In other words, some degree of concordance is required to reflect continuities of norm-meaning between global norms and national laws, or national statutes and local norms. In fact, discordance is common and comes in a variety of forms (Block-Lieb and Halliday 2015).

Alignment Since TLOs are erected to solve problems in a given issue-area, it remains open as to whether a given TLO or TLO in-the-making fully saturates or covers the issue-area. Studies of TLOs reveal that there are struggles over alignment. In one case, a TLO might correspond entirely to the underlying problems and the reach of its legal order embraces all dimensions of that order. In another case, a TLO may partition part of an issue-area so that it aspires to bring order to a subset of the problems. Competitive alignment can occur when the sponsors of several incipient TLOs confront each other.[4]

A fully institutionalized normative framework therefore can be observed where norms are settled and concordant at transnational, national, and local levels, and when a legal order is aligned with local behaviors in a stable manner, possibly as a result of negotiations with advocates of competing TLOs, with an underlying issue-area.

A fully developed account of TLOs, from their formation to institutionalization to their decline and fall, requires a socio-historical analysis that will cover years of legal change at every level of action and the cycles of engagement among them as normative settling, concordance, and alignment reach a new equilibrium of meaning and behavior.

This book does not purport to provide full accounts of TLO formation and institutionalization, but something more subtle and integral to a comprehensive account. On the basis of extensive empirical evidence on the inner workings of lawmaking for global governance, we show that global lawmakers at any moment are embedded in temporal and geographic self-understandings that invoke simultaneously a past and future in the present.

Looking back global lawmakers act in response to their perceptions and judgments about *prior* recursive rounds of lawmaking, earlier episodes of TLO construction, failures and successes at norm settling, alignment, and institutionalization (Block-Lieb and Halliday 2007b). Their mental maps offer guides based on an implicit and sometimes explicit "plausible folk theories" (Halliday 2014; Halliday 2015b) to explain why an earlier episode of TLO construction failed or why concordance did not occur between global norms and the nation-states and local actors to which they were directed. For instance, UNCITRAL's secretariat and latter-day

[4] It must be noted that there is nothing given about how the underlying terrain of the problem is demarcated. Like boundary work in ecology formation (see below), there is a politics of how the line around an issue-area is to be drawn. Similarities of processes and dynamics can be observed with the framing of TLO problem specification, and prescriptive responses, in many issue-areas (see Halliday and Shaffer 2015a, on meaning or framing).

lawmakers looked back on its 1978 Hamburg Rules for ordering global trade by sea and observed that they did indeed offer a set of global norms, but since their entry into force only a tiny number of states had acceded to the treaty on and these accounted for less than 2 percent of world trade. Neither industry nor powerful trading nations concurred with the norms. From this failure to institutionalize a TLO with wide geographical scope, UNCITRAL concluded that it should craft global norms that satisfied the major trading nations and key industries whose concurrence would be determinative of their successful adoption in law and practice.

Looking forward we find that global lawmakers in any given moment anticipate what iterations of negotiation would be required to attain settling of global norms, what concessions would be necessary to minimize impediments to national adoption of new rules for the world, and what the practitioners of law or accounting or business would likely accept as new standards for practice. This is not to say that all global lawmakers recognize consciously the consequences of actor mismatch, or the possibility that their diagnoses of the problem might be contested, or that political settlements might incorporate contradictions into global norms, or that complex drafting could produce inconsistencies or new concepts would contribute to ambiguities and confusion. We shall demonstrate the contrary was often the case. Yet the inner core of global lawmakers, who were most often veterans of transnational lawmaking, more often than not intuitively predicted what substance and forms of transnational laws would lead to attainment of their goals – the (re)formation of a TLO in their preferred image. An admixture of rational action, commitment to ideals of convergence, an internal legal epistemological commitment to textual clarity and consistency, an affective affinity for laws that look and feel like those to which they are accustomed, all intertwine in prospective orientations toward new TLOs.

We shall show that in the boundary-making moments of each of the three lawmaking enterprises we studied there was a debate about what *form* of legal norms would be likely to meet with adoption, and what *substance* would be acceptable to an eclectic community of nations, commercial actors, and professions, among others.

In short, in this book we do not provide socio-legal histories or tidy accounts of lawmaking episodes from beginning to end. Our attention is directed intensively to the moments of transnational lawmaking itself. Nonetheless, we insist that, at every moment of that transnational lawmaking, an "imaginary" of the entire episode, from onset of TLO construction to its possible institutionalization, captured the attention[5] of those lawmakers. Global legislators knew they were designing what they hoped would become TLOs of wide geographical scope and they applied to this task their own plausible folk theories of reconstructed pasts and "imagined futures."

[5] On studies of attention, see (Ocasio 2011).

We do not insist, however, that these lawmakers should be presumed to be perfectly rational beings that inhabit rational actor theory in political science. It will become clear that tactical and strategic calculations coexisted in the mentalities and interactions of delegates with unexamined assumptions about relationships between law and markets, with prejudices about which nations were most "advanced" and "modern," with tacit theories about law and development, with a priori notions about what kind of legal technologies produced what sorts of outcomes in radically different economic and political circumstances across the world. Feelings and emotions, politics and cultural distinctions, became salient in these social contexts where the core of inner lawmaking circles comprised no more than a handful or two of persons whose social and interactional skills mattered both as to the price of entry to the inner circles and the condition of continued residence in those micro-communities.

Despite its ambition as a theoretical framework for understanding a world of rising and falling legal orders, of complementary and competing TLOs, the theory of TLOs emphasizes more emphatically the *products* of lawmaking, its laws, texts, norms, than the social *processes*, the actors and interactions, that create and adapt those norms. An account of transnational *legal* orders must therefore be complemented by a social theory of actors and action, of structure and agency, of ideals and interests, of interactions and processes engaged in the production and reproduction of legal orders. The implicit theory inside the heads of the many transnational actors in this study points to one of sociology's most venerable theories: social ecology.

ECOLOGIES

This book asserts that global lawmaking should not begin with an IO as the unit of analysis, but with the sea in which it swims.[6] In the case of UNCITRAL, from its founding to the present, we argue that the organization cannot be understood without reference to other organizations in its sphere that variously compete, coexist or cooperate over different agendas or alternative working methods or varieties of products (Block-Lieb and Halliday 2013; Block-Lieb and Halliday 2016; Dezalay and Garth 2013). For working groups within UNCITRAL, as in other IOs, each area of trade law brings to the table a distinct array of industry and economic actors, states, professions, and inter-governmental organizations, among others. Working groups and UNCITRAL itself are situated in something bigger than this global lawmaking site. They exist in a context already rich with social organization that is manifestly discernible to its key players, indeed a social organization substantially constructed by the actors that constitute it. It is this greater whole in which any

6 This section presents a succinct version of a more technical article, which should be consulted for the elaboration of ecology theory for the international. See (Block-Lieb and Halliday 2016).

given lawmaking body must be dynamically understood. That greater whole is best captured by the sociological theory of social ecologies.

A long sociological tradition has offered theories of social space in which actors engage in activities – work, learning, residing – which bring them into patterned interaction with each other.[7] An entire school of sociology, the Chicago School, developed human ecology studies of communities early in the twentieth century and that tradition has continued to the present in research on diverse occupations and institutions, including professions, universities, states, and social movements (Abbott 2005; Fourcade and Khurana 2013; Freeman and Audia 2006; Liu 2011; Zhao 1998). A more extensive body of vibrant scholarship has developed in organizational ecology with particular reference to business firms (Freeman and Audia 2006; Hannan 2005; Popielarz and Neal 2007) but also on nonprofit organizations and professional associations. While much of organizational ecology is highly technical and relies on sophisticated analysis of large data sets of organizations within nation-states, core ideas of both qualitative and quantitative ecological analysis provide powerful tools for developing theories of global lawmaking organizations, even if there is some theoretical variation, even inconsistency, among ecological theories.

This book advances an interactionist version of social ecology theory that is suited to the vast complexity and dynamism of multilayered social spaces in international lawmaking and global governance (Block-Lieb and Halliday 2011; Halliday and Block-Lieb 2013). This sociological theory of the international stands on dual foundations. One emerges from the empirical sites themselves. As research-observers, listening carefully to what actors said and what they believed, and watching closely how they acted, we were impelled toward the theory that best fit with their logic of action. The other foundation rests upon a particular variant of ecology theory in sociology (Abbott 2016; Liu and Emirbayer 2016; Liu and Wu 2016),[8] as well as aspects of field theory, a widely deployed perspective drawn principally from the writings of French sociologist, Pierre Bourdieu.[9]

7 An instructive overview of these theories can be found in (Liu and Emirbayer 2016).

8 Another variant of ecology theory has been introduced to studies of international organizations, namely, the population ecology approach of (Abbott, Green and Keohane 2016). While we share aspects of the ecological approach introduced by Abbott et al., our variant of ecology theory differs insofar as we assume substantially greater agency to actors in the ecology, to the construction of the ecology itself as a bounded social space, and to relations among actors in the space. We relax the hard assumptions of population ecology and its limited view of actor agency in preference for the empirical realities of IOs as actors with creative capacities to adapt to environmental circumstances, a version of ecology theory that has affinities with constructivist theory of IO behavior.

9 Both field and ecology theory share a metaphorical conceptualization of social space. As Liu and Emirbayer (2016) argue, these theories converge in their views on structural isomorphism, temporality, and social psychology, but they differ in their treatment of power and inequality, endogeneity, and heterogeneity, among others. At the theoretical level, this book seeks to press toward a balance between structure and agency, and find places for rapprochement that draw on the strengths of both. For a technical analysis, see (Halliday and Block-Lieb 2014).

The fundamental elements of an ecology theory have been expressed as a set of actors who occupy positions or locations with processes that link actors to locations (Abbott 1988; Liu and Emirbayer 2016). To specify this abstract and compact formulation, we advance a conceptual approach to lawmaking social ecologies of IOs comprised of six elements.

Boundary Work

An ecology is a form of *bounded* social space.[10] Like any space, some actors are inside its often invisible boundaries and other actors are outside. For our purposes, any international lawmaking ecology is constituted by actors who construe a behavioral phenomenon as a problem that can be resolved through law. Lawmakers in the ecology seek to construct transnational legal orders that span frontiers, whether bilaterally, multilaterally, regionally, or globally.

Ecological theory does not accept that bounded spaces of social interaction occur "naturally" or "inevitably." They are cultural and social constructions that involve extensive and constant boundary work.[11] It is useful to distinguish among three kinds of boundary work (Liu 2010).

Boundary-making involves the deployment of symbols and construction of meanings that produce an in-group of actors who agree that they belong and an out-group of actors who do not share the same views or beliefs or attributes thought necessary for inclusion in the ecology. Actors within the ecology conventionally share an identity that differs from those outside.

Boundary-maintaining is a classic defensive strategy where actors inside an ecology resist any change to a status quo or settled ecological division of labor. These can be authorized by convention or binding legal provisions, such as licensing requirements for professionals. In fact, the evolving systems of professions have been conceived of as principally exclusionary enterprises.

Sometimes boundary work seeks neither to clarify nor solidify boundaries but to blur them. **Boundary-blurring** can be a deliberate strategem to permit adaptive flexibility as a basis for cooperation among the actors within an ecology. At one moment, for one purpose, actors in the ecology can ostensibly exclude issues or tasks from their activities, but do so ambiguously enough so that at another moment they may embrace tasks that previously were deemed inappropriate or beyond their capacities. Here, boundary-blurring is less a matter of insurgents seeking to expand

10 Throughout this book, we distinguish among several usages of the term "ecology." "Social ecologies" is a generalized phrase that refers to any kind of social organization through the metaphor of social space. We distinguish among four types of ecologies salient to global lawmaking.

11 There is an extensive scholarship on boundary-making and boundary work in several fields of sociology, much of it stemming from a seminal article by Thomas Gieryn (1983); see also (Gaziano 1996; Lamont and Molnar 2002).

the bounds of the ecology to embrace their issues and more a case of central actors in the ecology manipulating boundaries to leave options open. This blurring allows ambiguities to remain in an ecology for subsequent exploitation; it permits adaptive flexibility to embrace more or less territory as a subsequent issue-ecology arises (Liu 2008).[12]

Consistent with recursivity theory, much boundary work takes the form of diagnostic struggles. One set of actors seek to label a problem in one way that accords with their understandings of how institutions work or consistent with their interests, while other actors contest such a framing and diagnose the problem to be solved in a sharply contrasting way. Wherever there are ecologies whose actors are committed to lawmaking for solving of consequential problems, diagnostic or framing struggles will be observed.

The stabilization of boundaries for an ecology is one kind of *settlement* over which actors or ecologies have primary jurisdiction over underlying problems (Abbott 2004).

Actors

Ecologies are constituted of actors. "Actors" is a useful term of art since it is highly malleable and can embrace members in a social space that are collective actors or individual persons, official state delegates or delegations and inter-governmental bodies, non-state international industry or professional or civil society groups or local organizations from within a country. In both interactionist and population ecology theories and research, actors have been homogeneous – that is, an ecology of restaurants or universities or ethnic groups or law firms (Liu and Wu 2016). However, there is no theoretical reason to restrict the population of an ecology to one kind of actor and indeed some good reasons for extending the population of actors to all those who engage in a similar task, such as lawmaking, to solve a common problem.

Ecologies of international lawmaking usually involve varieties in classes of actors that share a common interest in a problem, but that vary markedly in their distributive and institutional interests, organizational forms, resources, and capacities. In each of the three issue-ecologies we study we find heterogeneous actors: states; intergovernmental organizations (e.g., International Maritime Organization, World Intellectual Property Organization); international professional associations (e.g., International Bar Association, International Federation of Insolvency Practitioners, *Comité International Maritime*); trade associations (e.g., International Chamber of Commerce, World Shipping Council, Commercial Finance Association); international financial institutions (e.g., European Bank for Reconstruction and

[12] A demonstration of the power of ambiguity and opacity in treaty-making can be found in Mallard's discussion of European nuclear proliferation negotiations (Mallard 2014).

Development); national organizations with international interests (e.g., Association of the Bar of the City of New York); eminent members of the legal complex (e.g., academics, judges, practicing lawyers), or accounting profession (e.g., restructuring specialists), among others.

Organizational actors in an ecology can vary enormously – by date of founding and thus their heritage, stature, and adaptability; size; financial and manpower resources; and whether they are generalists or specialized. They may differ in their orienting beliefs and their institutional logics (Thornton, Ocasio and Lounsbury 2012).

Again, there is nothing "natural" about which actors will be incorporated within an issue-ecology. Some may know nothing about it and remain outside. Some may know about an ecology's activities, but judge it to be of insufficient importance to warrant an investment of resources. Some may want to be inside but have insufficient resources to enable their participation. Some may wish to be inside the ecology, but those actors already inside work to keep them out.

In contrast to ecology theories where actors have little or no agency, because they are "selected" by their environment rather than shaping or adapting to it (Abbott, Green and Keohane 2016), or the over-socialized actors of earlier functionalist theory, or under-socialized actors of rational choice theory, interactionist ecology theory in the international lawmaking space grants significant agency to actors, insofar as it conceives of them as able to constitute themselves, to decide on courses of action, to frame problems and constitute the ecology, and to position themselves within it – all subject to historical and contextual constraints and structures both on the ecology as a whole and on given actors within it.[13]

Positions in Social Space

In social ecologies, actors metaphorically are distributed across the social space. The locations of actors in an ecology is an ambiguous concept, easily defined for a physical space, but difficult to define within the metaphor of a social space since location will vary by the criterion on which it is premised.[14] In Bourdieu's words, actors "are situated in a place in social space ... relative to other spaces (above, below, between, etc.) and the distance ... that separates it from them."[15] Actors must be mapped across that space in terms of their proximity to each other with respect to ranking principles that follow from the theory or can be observed in sites of empirical inquiry.

[13] On constraining institutional logics, see (Thornton, Ocasio, and Lounsbury 2012). On inertial attributes, histories and structure, that cannot readily be escaped, see (Barnett and Finnemore 2004; Stinchcombe 1963).

[14] Compare, however, use of smallest space analysis to map relations of individuals, specialties or occupations in studies of professions (Heinz et al. 1993); or of mapping symbolic objects as more or less distant from each other (Bourdieu 1984).

[15] Quoted in (Liu and Emirbayer 2016).

In international lawmaking ecologies, actors are located vis-à-vis each other in terms of the strength of their claims to legitimacy as crafters of global law in a jurisdiction of problem solving. Actors lie closer to the center of the ecology if they are taken for granted as legitimate, well-resourced, and effective lawmakers to solve a given problem through law. Actors lie closer to the periphery if their legitimacy or resources or effectiveness is susceptible to doubt and where they must therefore defend more energetically their rightness of fit in this space. Peripheral actors may be uncertain of their continued inclusion in the ecology and vulnerable to competition from outside the ecology. Much of the interaction among actors in a lawmaking ecology is implicitly and sometimes explicitly directed to obtaining greater centrality in the space or closer contiguity to like actors.

In an issue-ecology's spatial configuration, actors are arrayed according to their relationships with each other, some clustering together in tight alliances and continuing relationships, others scattered in relatively empty areas of the ecology with attenuated or weak relationships with other actors in the ecology. We shall show that these locations in the space may be divided by pre-existing cleavages, such as divides between the Global North and Global South, or by variations in legal families or positions in the global economy.

Resources

All ecologies, and actors within an ecology, require resources necessary for the ecology to exist and for actors within it to survive and thrive (Hannan 2005; Popielarz and Neal 2007). The specification of resources is quite open ended. To open up the concept of a lawmaking ecology in transnational and global spaces, we present a simplified inventory of resources that emerge from the empirical research and are consistent with earlier ecology theory.

We stipulate as resources any capabilities that actors in an ecology bring directly as delegates or delegations into the deliberative space, such as the chamber of a UN Working Group. These will be tangible and intangible. Again, it must be emphasized that resources are not simply given, but are made and unmade and often are manipulable, subject to creation and destruction, negotiation, and contest. Resources held by any actor and available to the ecology as a whole influence significantly the interactions that constitute the lawmaking process.

Tangible resources include money, space, and organizational infrastructure. Consider money and organizational infrastructure:

Money For delegations participating in international lawmaking, travel and accommodations are expensive. Traveling to and from the UN in Vienna and New York twice a year, with accommodations in expensive cities, takes a toll on the budgets of government ministries, even more if delegations seek to staff fully their quotas of four delegates in an UNCITRAL working group delegation. Add to that cost further travel or accommodation for participation in expert group meetings and time lost by lawyer-delegates from charging for normal professional services. Countries and ministries that can readily afford such costs obtain an immediate benefit for participation in global lawmaking.

Organizational Infrastructure. Global normmakers need places to meet, management personnel to prepare, staff, and facilitate meetings. Communication infrastructures can include transmission of reports, circulation of working documents, and the design and construction of websites. A global lawmaking body such as UNCITRAL possesses some of these resources, but we find that the actual practice of norm-production involves as much activity outside the UN facilities and infrastructure as within it. The capacities of the UN itself to provide infrastructure and the supplementary capacities of "reserve infrastructures" (Halliday, Powell and Granfors 1993) affect the resource capacities of UNCITRAL as an arena and the actors that congregate within it.

Intangible resources are no less significant, even if more difficult to measure. In global lawmaking they include expertise, reputation, rhetorical skills (e.g., linguistic, persuasiveness, clarity of expression, which can aid translators), relational skills (in establishing relationships, building alliances, ties, etc.), personal charisma, and time.

Time. States must make decisions about which multilateral or global normmaking enterprises are worth their while. Should the UK send its senior servants to Brussels or Vienna? Professors and lawyers must decide how much of their teaching, research, and client services can be sacrificed for the extensive *pro bono* activity necessary to exert influence. And law firms, universities, and INGOs must judge whether their underwriting of delegates has sufficient value to justify time lost to the requirements of each organization. Time can be gained and lost, expanded and contracted, manipulated and inertial (Chapter 5).

Technical Expertise. Trade lawmaking depends on highly technical mastery both of how the industry operates in fact and on the regulatory orders that exist or might be crafted to guide it. Depending on the subject matter, a premium is therefore placed on participation of the most important trade bodies, leading scholars, prominent judges, and experienced practitioners. Since the number of such people with international lawmaking experience is much smaller than might be supposed, competition for their services readily can break out, not least among actors vying for influence inside the ecology. Technical expertise can be constellated in the epistemologies and practices of professions (Abbott 1988; Halliday 1985), in the technicalities of government administration, and in the drafting expertise of international civil servants.

Legitimacy. Every actor in an ecology has legitimation warrants (Halliday 2007), and ecologies as a whole strive for legitimacy, not least UNCITRAL itself as a lawmaking actor and lawmaking arena or ecology (Block-Lieb and Halliday 2006). While a great deal of legitimacy can be generated inside the ecology, through the breadth of representation and fairness of its deliberations, surrounding ecologies also provide reservoirs of legitimacy: universities with scientific and epistemological warrants; other IOs which have established foundations on which to build; courts through the cases they have handled and the doctrine they have produced; private firms through their experience, market position, or prestige; and so on.

Resources are both material and ideal. While money and time are commensurable and appear fungible or zero-sum, ideal resources such as legitimacy and expertise draw on incommensurable ideologies, discourses, epistemologies, understandings, beliefs, and mentalities. Since law itself is a discursive rhetorical articulation of meanings and understandings, it can be expected that competition for ideal resources will loom large in lawmaking ecologies.

Every actor in a lawmaking ecology actively manages a portfolio of tangible and intangible, material and ideal, resources. This portfolio variously enables and constrains participation by a state delegation or a trade organization or any other actor in the ecology and indeed the viability of the ecology itself. Because resources are limited, access to resources cannot be taken for granted. As a result, it remains a challenge for any ecology as a whole to obtain sufficient resources that enable it to produce the laws that purport to solve a global problem.

Resource considerations matter constantly for all actors, especially those that suffer from scarcity of resources, and surprisingly, that scarcity does not always coincide with the relative wealth of an actor. Even wealthy actors may decide their priorities are elsewhere and divert resources away from lawmaking. In other cases, poor actors may call upon rich actors to underwrite their participation.

The proximity to resources affects location in the social space of the ecology and increases the potential influence of any actor in the ecology over the form and substance of the legal text(s) that emerge(s) from IOs in the ecology.

Interactional Processes

The variant of ecological theory we develop attends to two classes of interactional processes that explain the viability of an ecology and the position of any actor within it.

Relations among Actors

While theories of social space have, over the last century, identified various processes that constitute relationships in an ecology such as competition, cooperation, subordination (Hawley 1950; Liu and Emirbayer 2016; Park, Burgess and Mackenzie 1925 among many others),[16] we focus on a simplified triad – competition and cooperation, and their amalgam in the classic term, competitive cooperation.

[16] Varieties of ecology theory are remarkably open to varieties of processes. In one variant or another these have included competition, cooperation, subordination, assimilation, competitive cooperation, purification, symbiosis, accommodation, proletarianization, exchange, and selection.

Competition. Actors are fully aware that the outcomes of global lawmaking offer more or less competitive advantage to countries and industries; as a result, actors incipiently and sometimes overtly compete with each other to enter an ecology. Once inside the ecology, actors compete for recognition (e.g., voice, being heard), for influence (e.g., over the form and substance of laws being crafted), for prestige (i.e., imprints of impact acknowledged by others, such as their "principals," and audiences), and for capacities to shape and adapt to implementation of the global law. Actors compete for resources (e.g., between ministries within a country, between international organizations who seek cooperative relationships with the secretariats of global legislatures, for space in the lawmaking chamber) and the collectivity of actors may compete with other potential ecologies for continuing access to resources (e.g., UNCITRAL v. IFIs). Not least, actors compete over their respective claims to jurisdiction over the problem that brought them into the ecology at the outset.

Cooperation. Actors also cooperate.[17] Even if incipient competitors, they may find a higher interest in cooperating for a common good. We observe examples of complementarity (e.g., professional experts providing advice to states; industry indicating what is acceptable); formation of political alliances (e.g., delegations aligning with each other for greater influence); and concessions in bargaining (e.g., states or professions yielding on some interests in the greater search for consensus). Actors without certain resources are much more likely to cooperate with other actors who do have access to key resources. And, obversely, where an actor has exclusive access to a resource (e.g., a US delegation to the weight of US commercial power), then it may be more likely to shape cooperative relations on its terms, not least in a move toward centrality in the lawmaking ecology. Frequently this cooperation takes the form of an implicit exchange – of one set of resources for another.

Competitive Cooperation. "The ecological conception of society," state Park and Burgess (Park, Burgess and Mackenzie 1925: 559), "is that of a society created by competitive cooperation." Whereas actors may compete with little intention or practice of cooperation, whereas actors may cooperate with no intent or ability to compete, actors in incipient or actual competition may judge that their competition might be better moderated in favor of cooperation at a given moment on a given issue. That moment might be of long or short duration and the issue might be of broader or narrower range. Nevertheless, actors negotiate between themselves, or are drawn into wider ranging negotiations to cooperate (see Chapter 9), given the full awareness of all sides that competition and conflict might yield high returns but might also lead to consequences deleterious to all parties. For reasons of self-interest, prudence, calculations of risk, and cultural norms of collegiality or

[17] Readers will know of a massive literature on cooperation in the social sciences. Far beyond the purposes of this book, the scholarship on cooperation may fruitfully be brought into conjunction with twenty-first century formulations of ecology theory.

mutuality, competitive cooperation becomes an interactional process that leads to a dynamic equilibrium of social relations in an ecology.

Our view of processes therefore makes no *a priori* assumption, as do some theories, that global lawmakers exist in a space defined only or principally by relationships of domination or subordination. Instead we observe complex interplays of competition, cooperation, and competitive cooperation that lead to emergence of legal products. Power differentials exist and we shall map and reveal those differentials. But the interactionist variant of ecology theory we advance has more consistency with a negotiated order where diverse actors maneuver to limit a destructive competition and amplify prospective cooperation as a condition of producing a legitimate set of norms that have some reasonable probability of adoption by states and local actors which have the capacity to veto or negate them, as recursivity studies repeatedly demonstrate.[18]

We will elaborate how the tension between competition and cooperation commonly resolved itself in international private lawmaking ecologies; adaptive strategies of competitive cooperation permitted vertical and horizontal differentiation in the tasks, responsibilities, or the work of lawmaking and law implementation (Chapter 10).

Relations between Actors and Resources

Two salient processes order relations between actors and resources in global lawmaking: dependency and control.

Dependency. The sociological theory of resource dependence (Pfeffer and Salancik 1978; Scott 2004) posits that actors in an ecology must obtain and manage access to resources in such a way that the most vital resources on which they depend can be extracted in stable relationships and in sufficient volume. The issue-ecology of carriage of goods by sea, for instance, depends heavily on whether the lawmaking ecology, and its central actors such as UNCITRAL, can import resources from the maritime industry ecology, such as shipping, carrier and insurance actors. The failure of widespread adoption of UNCITRAL's Hamburg Rules, for example, was a constant reminder to contemporary global lawmakers that a lack of industry support may thwart the political engagement of large trading nations and, thus, doom lawmaking from the outset. The great success of UNIDROIT's Cape Town Convention, which drew the aircraft manufacturing industry into its standard-setting efforts, demonstrates how dependent an IO can be on the resources of an adjacent industry ecology and industry actors who will be critical to implementation of commercial norms in practice. Unlike resource dependence theory, however, the theoretical premise is not that actors in an ecology are determined or selected by

[18] The interactionist variant of ecology theory advanced in this book intersects and engages implicitly with recent theoretical moves in sociology such as relational (Emirbayer 1997; Liang and Liu 2016) and processual sociology (Abbott 2016).

external resource environments, but that actors exhibit perceptible autonomy in choices and actions required to ensure necessary resources for their viability.

Control refers to the degree to which actors in an ecology can establish claims of exclusivity to certain resources.[19] In principle, for instance, Germany or the US or India can claim exclusive control over the resources available to their governments and the capacities of their public administrations. Lawyers can claim exclusive expertise in governance through legal standards. Or insolvency practitioners can lay claim to practice experiences in restructuring failing companies. Often, however, control is contested. A delegate from a trade ministry responsible for state mediation between bankrupt companies and their creditors, and a bankruptcy lawyer from a boutique restructuring firm, and a restructuring specialist from a Big Four accounting multinational potentially compete for control of expert resources and so the ability to extract resources from their respective ministries or firms for global lawmaking.

Moreover, the two kinds of processes interact. Actors without certain resources are much more likely to cooperate with actors who have exclusive access to key resources. And, obversely, where an actor has exclusive access to a resource (e.g., a US delegation to the weight of US commercial power), then it may be more likely to shape cooperative relations on its terms, not least in a hierarchy of power.

These twinned sets of relationships – competition, cooperation, and competitive competition within a lawmaking ecology, and dependency and control within and between the lawmaking ecology and its adjacent ecologies – influence the viability of the ecology as a whole and the productivity of the ecology in a specific instance of lawmaking.[20]

Temporality

Social spaces are in motion. A social ecology may have a beginning, although these are rarely researched. And social ecologies may collapse, as boundaries dissolve, actors move into other ecologies, and resources disappear. In between beginnings and endings are constant changes within the ecology as the dynamic processes of competition, cooperation, competitive cooperation, and others unfold as actors relate to each other. And change in a dynamic world that contests globalization thereby ensures that proximate and remote ecologies will also be driving change within and among ecologies.

19 The concept of "control" tacitly or manifestly can be found across diverse and often discrete literatures, ranging from resource dependency theory to notions of jurisdictions in theories of professions.

20 In this chapter, we replace the concept of niches in some varieties of ecology theory with the concept of adjacent ecologies rich with resources. This move also relaxes the assumption of endogeneity that has provided unduly restrictive in contemporary versions of ecology theory (see Liu and Emirbayer 2016)

The probabilities of survival by individual actors in an ecology has been an important strain of research and theory on social spaces, generating such concepts as liabilities of newness or liabilities of ageing (Freeman, Carroll and Hannan 1983; Hannan 2005). We shall show how the fragilities an IO faces in its nascent beginnings and the inertia that can inhibit adaptability for venerable IOs both influenced ecological dynamics over more than a half-century of global trade lawmaking.

Moreover, entire ecologies might confront enormous pressures if they are not productive or if their products conflict with the influence of vibrant industry or political ecologies. A powerful state, such as the United States, might conclude that global lawmaking by global institutions will not work in its interests and thereby proceed through bilateral and multilateral treaties that bypass the community of nations and industry at work through legislative-like proceedings. Such a fear lay unexpressed but not unconsidered by more than one of the core actors in the international lawmaking ecology.

Not least, in the micro-interactions of actors within issue-ecologies (see Chapters 3 and 5) the manipulation of time becomes a tactic for turning a seemingly inelastic property of social interaction into a malleable property that can increase competitiveness, quicken productivity, and exclude rivals.

The recognition of temporality[21] therefore circles back to the dynamism of entire ecologies as they strive not only for some state of a moving equilibrium in processes and products, but as they recognize that their own boundaries and viability can rarely be taken for granted in a volatile world of scarce resources and conflicting interests.

In sum, (a) international issue-ecologies are problem-solving social spaces demarcated through (b) cultural and social boundary work by (c) actors in dynamic interaction who (d) structure their positions in the space vis-à-vis each other and (e) who seek to obtain resources necessary for the actors and ecologies to survive and thrive. These unfold (f) in temporal dynamics that are contextually and historically situated. Put another way, for an issue that both spans national frontiers and elicits law as a form of response, these elements offer a systematic theoretical framework that transcends issue-specificity, disciplinary particularities, and radically diverse actors.

VARIETIES OF ECOLOGIES

The power of the concept of an "ecology" lies significantly in its ability to be scaled broadly or narrowly, to be nested within or to nest other ecologies, to be examined

[21] A rich literature on social institutions, time, and temporality has developed in sociology and political science. See, for instance, (Pierson 2004; Sewell 1996; Zerubavel 2004). We build on this literature with a conceptualization of the micropolitics of time in this book (Chapter 5), and time and temporality more generally in global lawmaking (Halliday 2017).

as a single social space or to be seen a bundle or collection of ecologies – adjacent, overlapping, contextualizing whichever is the particular ecology of focus in a given empirical inquiry.

Yet this very powerful attribute of the concept also can be a source of referential confusion and even a kind of empirical *reductio ad absurdum* as the multiplication of ecologies salient to a particular issue ramify out across space and time.

Four Ecologies

In this book, where we are concerned with lawmaking for international commerce, we focus on four types of ecologies our research reveals as integral to international lawmaking processes and products: standing lawmaking ecologies, episodic lawmaking issue-ecologies, industry ecologies, and the organizational ecology of the UN.

Standing lawmaking ecologies (hereafter, standing ecologies) persist for decades or generations and are comprised of actors whose principal mission is lawmaking. In this book, we are focused on the lawmaking ecology committed to the development of international law to govern commerce and trade. Standing ecologies form around problem solving on the broadest scale, including the removal of the obstacles law creates for trade and development, or the unification of conflicting or confusing laws across international markets that might inhibit economic development. UNIDROIT, UNCITRAL, and The Hague Conference on Private International Law are the central actors within this standing lawmaking ecology insofar as they are the three IOs whose mandates expressly authorize wide-ranging potential jurisdictions of lawmaking on a variety of private law issues.

Episodic lawmaking issue-ecologies (hereafter, issue- or lawmaking ecologies) come together for a short time around a particular issue that focuses on resolving a problem that is defined rather precisely by actors. In this book issue-ecologies[22] are formed to solve three such problems: liability for carriage of goods by sea, saving failing businesses, and opening up credit flows to private actors engaged in commerce. The central actors in each issue-ecology vary by the salience of the issue to the actors but they include both state and non-state actors, as well as actors within the standing lawmaking ecology and the industry and organizational ecologies

Industry ecologies may be relatively young (electronic commerce) or longstanding (trade by sea). They comprise all those producers and consumers, and other market enabling actors (e.g., bankers, accountants, lawyers) involved in the production and consumption of specified goods and services in a particular segment of the market (see Chapter 3, Table 3.1).

[22] While this book focuses on issue-ecologies concerned with the production of law as a device for producing social order, in principle and in practice issue-ecologies can produce order through other means, including through economics, politics, religion, and other forms of creating social order.

Organizational ecologies are large complex organizations that encompass a wide spectrum of bodies salient to international lawmaking. Most salient to our case studies is the organizational ecology of the UN system, which encompasses actors from the office of the General Assembly and its Sixth Committee (on law), the UN Secretary General and Legal Vice-Presidency, UNCITRAL, UNCTAD, the IMF, and World Bank, all of which feature in this book.[23] These diverse elements of the UN are not adequately captured by the concept of bureaucracy. They are more productively understood as ecologies whose constituent actors are engaged in ongoing interactions of cooperation, competition, and competitive cooperation including struggles for control over dependable flows of resources. We shall show that all are drawn into competition over what sub-units will have jurisdiction over areas of lawmaking for commerce and trade.

It may be seen (Table 1.1) that these ecologies vary in terms of four properties.

(1) Do the ecologies deal with broad clusters of problems or focus on a quite particular problem? Some treat generic ordering problems of the widest scope. Others focus on narrow problems salient to particular actors.
(2) What form of order do actors in an ecology seek to produce? Transnational *legal* orders? An international *economic* order? A political or administrative or *bureaucratic* order that spans frontiers?
(3) Are the ecologies episodic or long-lasting? Some lawmaking ecologies have been in place for a century; others last for several years only.
(4) Who are actors characteristically found within an ecology? They might be states, intergovernmental organizations, businesses, professions, voluntary associations, or international organizations.

Adjacent Ecologies

There is an extensive and complex definitional literature on niches in certain variants of ecology theory (Hannan, Carroll and Polos 2003; Popielarz and Neal 2007). This literature overwhelmingly is drawn from studies of a single form of organization in a single market or community or state. In these contexts niches may be broadly understood as "the set of environmental states" in which this ecology of deliberating actors is situated and which are necessary for the survival of the ecology itself. However, we specify "environmental states" not as niches but as sources for resources in two senses. On the one hand, those resources may be available to actors

[23] The International Law Commission (ILC) is an organ of the United Nations and is positioned within this UN ecology, but overlaps very little with the *private* lawmaking focus of this book. Neither UNIDROIT nor The Hague Conference on Private International Law sits within this UN ecology, as each constitutes an independent intergovernmental organization, although both are focused on private lawmaking and figure importantly in the book.

TABLE 1.1. A *Typology of Transnational Ecologies*

	Problem	Form of order	Temporal span	Actors	Examples
Standing ecologies	Broad scope	Multiple transnational legal orders	Longterm	Global lawmaking IOs	Private international lawmaking
Issue-ecologies	Narrow scope	Single transnational legal order	Episodic	State Non-state	UNCITRAL WG on insolvency UNIDROIT WG producing Cape Town Convention
Industry ecology	Broad and narrow scope	Transnational economic order	Intermediate to Longterm	Firms Consumers Industry associations Professionals State regulators	Transport of goods by sea Rescuing businesses Commercial finance
Organizational ecology	Broad and narrow scope	Transnational political order	Longterm	Leadership bodies Constituent organizations Working units Administrative arms	UN

within the lawmaking ecology. On the other hand, resources can also be drawn from surrounding or adjacent ecologies, such an industry ecology (e.g., sea transport for goods, commercial finance), or the UN itself as an ecology of organizations and agencies. Hence the resources available to the lawmaking ecology constitute the sum of all resources available for actors inside that ecology plus those resources available from all ecologies intersecting, overlapping, or interpenetrating the lawmaking ecology.

This approach offers a very dynamic concept of "environmental states" for the lawmaking ecology, it escapes rigidities that follow earlier efforts at understanding linked ecologies (Abbott 2005), and it is well adapted to the empirical realities observed in the dynamism of international social spaces.[24]

In practice, the set of all intersecting ecologies for a given issue-area in a global context are almost limitless and thus far exceed our capacity in this book to theorize satisfactorily their relations within a given issue-ecology. This approach reflects both manifest behaviors we observe in global and transnational lawmaking and is consistent with two bodies of scholarly literature – one on principals and agents in political science and the other on states in sociology. All these inject degrees of contingency we observed throughout our fieldwork.

Actors' resources matter significantly in negotiations within UNCITRAL's working groups. Delegates speak with one or more languages and with more or less clarity. They evince more or less authority. Their delegations constitute more or less density and diversity (Halliday, Pacewicz and Block-Lieb 2013). They are more or less persuasive and more or less skilled in alliance-building or corridor negotiations. Hence the issue-ecology is being constituted day by day in actual negotiations as cooperation and competition and complementarity play themselves out.

However, it cannot be assumed, as principal-agent scholarship makes plain, that a given delegate or delegation can deliver resources from the delegate's state or non-state organization beyond those of the moment, whether these resources yield moneys for additional meetings; time away from the office for expert meetings; volunteer time for non-state delegates; expert drafting from professional bodies; ongoing communications by trade associations; law firm facilities for off-shore meetings; financial underwriting by an IMF or World Bank for poor states.

Further, social science scholarship on states demonstrates that because states themselves are internally fractured it is not clear that a delegation appointed by one ministry (e.g., the State Department, Foreign Ministry, Department of Trade and Industry, Central Bank) will be able to deliver any resources or even support for a product from other ministries (e.g., Justice or Finance). During the Asian Financial Crisis, the IMF and World Bank generally preferred dealing with the finance

24 See, e.g., the very sophisticated theoretical apparatus erected by Andrew Abbott in his study of linked ecologies (Abbott 1988). Yet Abbott deals here with two linked ecologies only within a single nation-state, whereas in the international lawmaking space the number of those ecologies will far exceed two and the multiplicity of jurisdictions challenges enumeration.

ministry within affected countries since they had closer ties with government finance officials and the finance ministry had more domestic power than the justice ministry (Halliday and Carruthers 2009). And even if ministries within states can deliver, there is no guarantee that legislatures will follow suit, as the US Senate has repeatedly shown in refusing to ratify international agreements that US delegations to UNCITRAL and other global legislatures have negotiated in good faith.

Even if states should be viewed as the ultimate "audiences" (Hannan, Carroll and Polos 2003) for adoption of lawmaking products, they may operate in interstate systems in which broad changes in markets or the international political economy may drain resources from adjacent ecologies (e.g., after a financial crisis) or where ideological shifts may drain the discursive foundations on which an issue-ecology initially framed the "problem" to which lawmaking was responding.

We shall demonstrate that these variations in resource mobilization within deliberations of actors in issue- and adjacent industry ecologies significantly influenced the behavior of actors in the lawmaking ecology. These variations constrained interactions, and thus influenced the form and content of their products, and the subsequent adoption of those products.[25]

ISSUE-ECOLOGIES AND TRANSNATIONAL LEGAL ORDERS

The nascent theory of international issue-ecologies and the developing theory of TLOs complement each other. This book explicates aspects of that complementarity and opens up avenues for exploration of their interplay.

Issue-ecologies encapsulate the social dynamics and modes of production in which local, national, and transnational actors engage each other in tasks. Issue-ecologies are not simply there. They are not merely arenas of struggles for survival. Issue-ecologies are problem-solving collections of actors seeking to produce solutions. When solutions are obtained through lawmaking, TLOs are an intended product of these interactions. TLOs are populated by problem-solving actors engaged in the production of legal norms, sooner or later in the form of texts. In a fully institutionalized TLO, these textually encased norms are variously incorporated into the behavioral orientations of states, commercial actors, and all those integral to local, national, and global markets. TLO theory attends closely to the texts that are produced, the relationship between these texts and the behaviors it seeks to alter, and the order this relationship can bring. Ecology theory, in turn, explicates the processes that enable this production. Each theory has powerful effects on the other. Indeed, processes integral to one frequently are constitutive of the other.

[25] For an influential treatment of resources that accords greater influence on actors outside an organization (or, by implication, outside an ecology) than on the adaptive capacity of actors' inside an ecology, see (Pfeffer and Salancik 1978).

Consider beginnings. While trade and market activity may proceed apace, more or less radical in its twists and turns, no lawmaking ecology takes form until a combination of facilitating circumstances or precipitating events turns the everyday ecology of market operations into a zone where certain actors argue that a problem exists and that its resolution requires new rules, laws, or regulations for the problem to be legalized in an orderly manner. That is, the emergence of an issue-ecology and the beginning of TLO formation or reformation may coincide. Creation of a TLO is a project that offers a *legal* solution to market disorder.

Consider boundary work. Part of the formative and continuing dynamics of an issue-ecology is the struggle among actors to define ecological boundaries in ways that privilege the status of one set of actors – those inside the ecology – versus another set – those absent or excluded from the ecology. This is a politics of meaning, a discursive politics, which frames issues in ways that legitimate one set of actors and delegitimate others. Framing is integral to the politics of TLOs (Halliday and Shaffer 2015a). To build a TLO, or adapt a TLO, or critique an existing or rival TLO involves negotiations among actors over the legal and geographic scope of the new or revised order. For instance, boundary work to include observers from road and rail transport industry associations in UNCITRAL's International Transport Working Group concomitantly informed debates over the legal and geographic scope of the Rotterdam Rules, calmed fears that UNCITRAL looked to undermine road and rail interests, and helped the eventual settling of norms within this new "maritime plus" TLO (Block-Lieb and Halliday 2015).

Consider competition and cooperation. TLOs involve actors at every level of action (international, national, and local), who in turn develop and implement legal norms and preside over their settling. In the recursive politics of the rise or reproduction or fall of TLOs, actors may compete with each other over who sits at the lawmaking table, which diagnoses of the problem will prevail, whether contradictory ideologies or organizations will be internalized in the norms themselves, or the organizations that convey them in practice. Actors compete over the legal and geographical scope of a TLO-in-the-making or unmaking. Precisely the same processes of competition, that may or may not be resolved in political settlements through cooperation, in turn permeate the rise and fall of TLOs as those that shape the interactions of actors within and between issue-ecologies.

Consider settling and institutionalization. An institutionalized TLO requires by definition that norms are settled and in concordance at several levels of action; that legal orders align legitimately with some underlying problem-space; that together these produce shared understandings of how to behave and behaviors that substantially express those norms. An issue-ecology likewise brings actors into a bounded social space, where inherent competition among them might be transformed into forms of cooperation or competitive cooperation, where positions in the space are substantially settled, and where adjacent ecologies supply resources adequate to actors and the ecology as a whole. Institutionalization may thereby constitute a feat of competitive cooperation. These states of affairs are interdependent. The settling of norms among actors in an issue-ecology can facilitate emergence of cooperative lawmaking. The emergence of the transnational norms in an incipient TLO can shape and reinforce relations among the lawmaking actors who also constitute the issue-ecology. An outbreak of intense competition in the issue-ecology may lead to withdrawal of support by some actors for a TLO to which they previously had been parties and indeed can precipitate efforts to produce a rival TLO. Such an instance might be exemplified by UNCTAD's efforts to resist UNCITRAL's Rotterdam Rules and to attempt to mobilize other actors around a rival Multimodal Convention.

Consider resources. Actors within an issue-ecology manage their use of existing resources and possibly also construct new ones. Normative concordance among local, national, and transnational levels of action may substantially turn on what resources will be mobilized to persuade legislators to adopt new laws, or professional firms to adapt their practices to new standards, or local judges can be trained to apply the new norms that TLOs convey. Adjacent ecologies can provide the fuel to drive adoption of new TLOs, or to deprive existing TLOs of the energy required for their survival.

A SOCIOLOGY OF INTERNATIONAL ORGANIZATIONS

There is no lack of rich theory on global lawmaking. While political scientists and legal scholars have dominated the field, in the last decade momentum has built for a sociology of the international. It ranges from a sociology of business regulation (Braithwaite and Drahos 2000) and economic governance (Morgan and Quack 2010; Quack 2010), to law and markets (Halliday and Carruthers 2009) and human rights (Boyle 2002; Halliday, Karpik and Feeley 2007; Merry 2003), among others.

We assert that global markets are constituted through law. We must then confront a fundamental question: How are the laws made that order global markets? This book offers a sociological answer. It seeks not to dislodge but to integrate rich theory from multiple disciplinary sources. In one sense the theory is open, since it can accommodate varieties of other theory. In another sense our theory is incremental, since it builds upon existing scholarship on TLOs and on international and transnational organizations and networks. And not least, the theory is empirically grounded, not only on our own primary research, but also on the research of others.

The interplay of IO ecology and TLO theory enables us to understand not only *who* governs, but *how* they govern. By rendering the invisible visible, our socio-legal inquiry seeks not only to expand scientific understanding of a complex world beyond the nation-state, but to open up awareness that consequential outcomes woven in the guise of technical commercial laws warrant the attention of publics of every kind whose ways of life are shaped by international trade, commerce, and finance.

2

The Emergence of a Lawmaking Ecology

A new international organization (IO) rarely enters an issue-area that is completely uninhabited by other IOs. If it proceeds deliberately, it will undertake a reconnaissance to discover what other organizational inhabitants already have staked a claim. If it hopes to obtain a foothold on the terrain of its choosing, it will likely avoid places where other IOs are already consolidated. It will seek to locate itself in a place where it does not invite intense competition. It will look for access to resources not already consumed by established occupants in the space. It may even seek friendly neighbors to shore up its vulnerabilities. In short, an IO's founders will proceed as if they are entering an ecology and they will avail themselves of the longstanding strategies that are inherent to ecological existence and sustainability.

In the mid-1960s there were already two notable IOs inhabiting an incipient ecology of transnational lawmaking for trade and commerce: UNIDROIT, an intergovernmental organization (IGO) created by the League of Nations and formally named the International Institute for the Unification of Private Law; and The Hague Conference on Private International Law, another IGO with beginnings in the late nineteenth century. There were two UN entities which conceivably might move into the trade lawmaking space: The UN's International Law Commission was established in 1947 for "the promotion of the progressive development of international law and its codification," a broad mission which was to be "primarily" focused on public international law but expressly was not exclusive of "the field of private international law."[1] And the UN created the United Nations Conference on Trade and Development (UNCTAD) in 1964 to address issues of trade and development, topics which might also have been construed to embrace lawmaking. By 1964, therefore, it was not at all obvious why another lawmaking IO was needed or wanted. Fifty years later all of UNCITRAL's original competitors still survive, but arguably UNCITRAL has come to dominate the international lawmaking space as

[1] Statute of the International Law Commission, Art. 1, ¶¶ 1 and 2.

the first among equals in the competition to produce transnational legal orders (TLOs) governing issues of trade, commerce, and their financing. How is this to be explained?

UNCITRAL was no exception to a pattern characteristic of ecologies. Its progenitors and their successors faced four fundamental problems of organizational viability. First, to enter an ecology-in-the-making UNCITRAL would need to show it belonged. And to show it belongs to an IO must be able to delineate boundaries with sufficient clarity to show it has jurisdictional claims inside the ecology in contradistinction, implicitly or explicitly, to those IOs that remain outside the ecology. Second, to survive in the ecology, it would need to avoid the liability of newness, or high probability of failure, that is common to all startup organizations (Hannan 2005). Third, once viable, could UNCITRAL simultaneously cope with competition within the ecology and adapt to changes in adjacent ecologies and wider geopolitical and economic contexts? Failure to escape the inertia or "stickiness" that attaches to the founding moment might render it vulnerable to altered contexts and make it marginal to changed environments. Intense competition might pose distraction or inspiration. Fourth, within the commercial standing ecology as a whole, could UNCITRAL ensure itself of a reliable flow of resources that could sustain its activities?

The founding and development of UNCITRAL in its first half century unfolded in grand time and in the context of epochal historical events: the founding of the United Nations; a Cold War that divided the world into competing geopolitical blocs and fundamentally different forms of economic organization; a New International Economic Order that accompanied the dissolution of European empires and the emergence of newly independent states in Africa, Asia, and Latin America; the collapse of the Soviet Empire and the transformation of its command economies; and the national, regional, and global debt crises which shook the financial stability of world trade and global markets. We find that these great movements and events set in motion facilitating circumstances for construction, deconstruction, and reconstruction of IOs and TLOs. Sudden jolts to world geopolitics, such as the fall of the Berlin Wall, or to regional economic stability, such as the Asian Financial Crisis, had an impact on entire ecologies of trade lawmaking organizations and their adaptations to sharply changing contexts.

Since lawmaking is a discursive enterprise, emerging ecologies of making law for markets drew into deliberations prevailing ideas about what can or should constitute the theoretical and normative interplay between law and markets. On the one side, notable nineteenth century legal theorists, David Dudley Field and Jeremy Bentham, argued for utilitarian, codified, and rationalized law to produce law that fit changing circumstances. Echoes of this logic would be observed in the legal realism of the 1930s, the pragmatism of Karl Llewellyn in the post-WWII period, and in law and development theory in the legal academy in the 1960s and 1970s. On another side, economic theory swung from celebrations of state intervention for Keynesian economic stability and state-led development through a New International Economic Order, to the latter day notions of an economic institutionalism, expressed in a Washington Consensus, which relied upon legal institutions to release private energies for economic growth and development. Law as both an expression of market practices and law as a instrument of market vitality was drawn more or less perceptibly into the work of constituting standing and issue-ecologies and their shaping of the legal products that emerged from their ever-expanding work.

Concomitantly UNCITRAL maneuvered in two global social spaces: both a standing international lawmaking ecology and a multiplicity of surrounding industry and organizational ecologies dedicated to the issues and problems in which UNCITRAL sought to promote legal order. UNCITRAL's maneuverings reveal a sustained attentiveness to its legitimacy and a creativity in its construction of a repertoire of legal forms or technologies. An IO's ecological viability and international authority ultimately rest on whether it can convince its constituencies of its "rightness" as a global actor. How this legitimacy is established and maintained, however, is not to be taken for granted. It is much too easy to segue from an already authoritative IO and presume its legitimacy. It is quite a bit more difficult to comprehend what is necessary to construct an IO's legitimacy, namely, to show how this legitimacy is built and is maintained. To take the more difficult path requires us to problematize UNCITRAL's legitimacy from the moment of its conception.

Like the standing lawmaking ecology as a whole, UNCITRAL also confronted the challenge of securing flows of other essential material and tangible resources, not least establishing and bolstering claims to expert authority. Lawmaking ecologies privilege legal knowledge, both as doctrine and practice. They rest on epistemological foundations. A TLO emerging from a lawmaking ecology is an order constructed by legal academics, judges, practitioners, and civil servants in ministries of justice, commerce, and trade. Yet this technocratic authority sits in tension with the democratic auspices of legitimacy central to institutions bearing the imprimatur of the United Nations.

Through each historical epoch, and a succession of ideas and ideals, we examine how the life course of UNCITRAL from its founding to a certain maturity sought simultaneously to cope with the vicissitudes of survival, to construct its legitimacy, to adapt to changing contexts within and beyond the international lawmaking ecology, and thereby to extend the scope of TLOs intended to reach farther and deeper into national and international trade and commerce.

UNCITRAL's founding as an IO simultaneously constituted the emergence of a standing international lawmaking ecology which would maintain some of its founding attributes for the following half century, an ecology, nevertheless, whose boundaries would shift, whose actors would diversify, and whose interactions within and outside the ecology would maintain salience despite volatile international contexts. Neither UNCITRAL nor the standing ecology can be understood without recognizing their dynamic interplay.

A PRELUDE[2]

From the mid-1800s until World War I, several movements pointed toward the later emergence of a standing ecology of commercial lawmaking IOs. The idea that IOs should work toward a codified unitary international law stimulated the formation of private advocacy associations of lawyers, academics, philosophers, traders, financiers, and commercial leaders in the late nineteenth and early twentieth centuries, such as the International Law Association (ILA) in 1873; *Institut de Droit International* in 1873; *Comité Maritime International* (CMI) in 1897; American Society of International Law in 1906; and the International Chamber of Commerce (ICC) in 1919 (Cutler 2003: 180–240; Dezalay and Garth 2013; Dezalay and Garth 1996; Lemercier and Sgard 2013). By the latter half of the nineteenth century, nation-states, including many of the Great Powers, were themselves convinced to attempt to bring order through the codification of international law, and diplomatic conferences on a range of public and private law topics began to be organized.

Throughout the nineteenth century, these diplomatic conferences were mostly ad hoc. One important early exception to this dissemblage involved the first convening, in 1893, of The Hague Conference on Private International Law, which looked to reach potentially all areas of private law by unifying the procedural rules applicable to resolution of cross-border disputes between private actors.

Despite its broad scope, The Hague Conference proved inadequate to order global trade. Although The Hague Conference sought to de-emphasize politics and legal difference by emphasizing neutral, process-oriented principles of technocratic lawmaking, a positioning which gave it generic scope over many areas of commercial and other private laws, its apparent neutrality ultimately proved illusory. Common law countries were reluctant to join in the conferences, which meant that the scope of the proceedings were largely Continental. In 1914, World War I brought its lawmaking to a standstill.

Reconstruction of the international order after World War I centered on aspirations of the League of Nations to bring order, peace and prosperity to a world subject to horrors previously unimaginable in "modern" Europe (Northedge 1986). Although it has largely been forgotten, the League had an interest in fostering trade and prosperity both to hasten recovery from the predations of wartime destruction and to forestall future conflicts (Potter 1922). Initially, the Assembly of the League of Nations was reticent to create any sort of formalized lawmaking organization within its auspices (id., at 253), but it quickly learned that it would be unable to address the

[2] For a more extensive discussion of the rise of lawmaking IOs in the mid-nineteenth to late-twentieth centuries, see (Block-Lieb and Halliday 2016).

breadth of issues on international law without assistance. By 1924, the League had organized two committees of experts and another international institute to assist it with lawmaking projects, but these, too, proved inadequate to the challenge (Block-Lieb and Halliday 2016).

On September 26, 1924, Italy proposed the foundation, in Rome, of an Institute to study and promote the unification of private law on an international basis, and by 1928 the Rome Institute was founded to unify private international law under the auspices of the League Assembly. From its first sessions, work proceeded on a wide range of procedural and substantive laws and by 1935 the Rome Institute had produced a draft convention on the international sale of goods and another on hoteliers' responsibilities. The outbreak of World War II brought the aspirations of the League of Nations and work of the Institute to a halt until a post-war world dissolved the League, formed a new multilateral United Nations, and left the Rome Institute an orphan – without institutional sponsorship or support (Block-Lieb and Halliday 2016).

THE VICISSITUDES OF FOUNDING

In contrast to the uneven success of the League of Nations to address issues of economic policy following World War I, the Charter for the United Nations explicitly charged the UN to achieve "international co-operation in solving international problems of an economic, social, cultural or humanitarian character,"[3] and empowered an Economic and Social Council (ECOSOC), comprised of fifty-four elected member states, to advance this mandate (Zamora 1995).[4] The UN Charter further authorized its General Assembly to encourage "the progressive development of international law and its codification,"[5] and to permit specialized agencies affiliated with the UN to put these goals into practice subject to coordination with ECOSOC.[6]

Although the founders of the UN envisaged ECOSOC as a global forum to resolve economic issues of global proportion, a deep divide nearly immediately confounded these aspirations, as the UN itself quickly became a stage for Cold War skirmishes to play out between the US and the Soviet Union and their respective allies (Wesson 1971). After the Soviets rejected the Marshall Plan, the US became reluctant to extend economic assistance through UN channels that were subject to Soviet obstructionism. Increasingly, the US reacted to these hurdles by bypassing the UN on issues of economic policy. The International Monetary Fund (IMF) and the World Bank similarly followed suit in establishing their operational independence from the UN, although the Bretton Woods

[3] Charter of the United Nations, Art. 1, ¶ 3.

[4] See also UN Charter, Art. 61.

[5] UN Charter, Art. 13.

[6] UN Charter, Art. 63, ¶ 2.

institutions had originally been established under UN auspices (Horsefield 1969; Kapur, Lewis, and Webb 1997).

In the ten years following the founding of the UN in 1945, a more complex international lawmaking ecology began to take shape, which led to the establishment of a tacitly agreed-upon division of labor and market segmentation among technical bodies. The UN General Assembly established the International Law Commission (ILC) in 1947 to work primarily on the codification of *public* international law (Rosenne 1960). This left potentially open a space for the Rome Institute to occupy – international law concerning the *substance* of private contractual interactions and trade law. In the late 1940s and early 1950s, the Institute energetically put its fingers on virtually every international and transnational initiative involving private law (Peters 2011).

Yet the UN seemed reluctant to adopt the Institute, as it had numbers of other League entities. By 1951, hopes that the Rome Institute might be incorporated into the UN seem to have cooled, when the country-members of the orphaned Rome Institute refounded it as a free-standing organization.

Curiously, this coincided with a re-awakening of The Hague Conference on Private International Law, which resumed meeting in 1951 for the first time since its inter-War sessions held in 1925 and 1928. As the ILC had deferred to its procedural work on private international law projects, The Hague Conference never challenged the ILC's claim to work in the area of *public* international law. Nor did The Hague Conference overtly challenge the authority of UNIDROIT to work on unification of substantive private laws.

By the mid-1950s, three IOs divided international lawmaking among themselves along three familiar boundaries. The ILC sat fully within the UN, but exercised jurisdiction primarily over *public* international law. The Hague Conference sat outside the financial and political protection of the UN, exercising jurisdiction primarily over questions of *private* international law of a *procedural* and jurisdictional nature. Similarly, the Rome Institute, also independent of the UN, had nestled itself into another corner of this emerging international ecology, content to work on the unification of *substantive private* law.

Ecologically, therefore, by the late 1950s there had formed an implicitly settled segmentation of the international lawmaking enterprise between a master division between public and private international law, and a subdivision between private *procedural* versus private *substantive* lawmaking. In 1958, the UN's ECOSOC expressly acknowledged the existence of this division of labor, of the work of the Rome Institute (which now called itself UNIDROIT) and The Hague Conference in these areas, and of the potential for "duplication and overlap," but ceded no more.[7]

7 UN Economic and Social Council, Co-operation between the United Nations and The Hague Conference on Private International Law and the International Institute for the Unification of Private Law, Resolution 678(XXVI) (July 3, 1958).

Instead, its Resolution committed merely to the "reciprocal exchange of information and documents in matters of mutual interest in order to promote co-operation and co-ordination" among the Council of ECOSOC and its "regional economic commissions," UNIDROIT and The Hague Conference on Private International Law.[8]

By the early 1960s, the authority that the World Bank, the IMF and the General Agreement on Trade and Tariff (GATT) exerted over economic and trade policy proved unsatisfactory to the growing number of developing and underdeveloped nations. Through the 1950s, many less developed countries grew increasingly unhappy with GATT's emphasis on trade in manufactured products and its lack of interest in commodity trade or in viewing trade, especially commodities trade, as a way to transfer wealth from rich to poor nations (Mingst and Karns 2007). Membership in GATT had been limited to twenty-three countries when it was created in the late 1940s; by the late 1960s, still only sixty-two countries were members. Developing countries were also frustrated with the unresponsiveness of the World Bank and IMF to issues of economic development and to the dominance of these institutions by developed countries, especially by the US.

Decolonization had altered membership and voting patterns in the UN, which is structured on a system of "one country, one vote," but not in GATT, the World Bank, or IMF, whose decision making weighted voting according to the financial strength of members. Developing countries turned to the UN to address their grievances about trade and development, proposing in 1964 an international conference to establish principles to govern international trade relations and trade policies. The UN should promote national economic growth and trade, said a large coalition of states with developing economies, a charge delivered to the UNCTAD, which subsequently became a permanent organ reporting to the General Assembly, with its own secretary-general[9] (Cordovez 1967).

The first UNCTAD session resulted in the creation of the Group of 77 (G-77) developing nations, and produced a report identifying a number of general principles to govern international trade relations and recommending a system of trade preferences for developing countries.[10] More importantly, UNCTAD was credited with causing an intellectual and political shift in thinking about development (Toye 2004). It framed trade issues in relationship to economic development and, for the first time in a global setting, established "the principle that a code of rules

[8] Id., ¶¶ 1. The motivations for the publication of this meta-text are not set out in any explanatory materials, but it seems likely that ECOSOC's work on the draft convention that would become the New York Convention was viewed by some as potentially likely to upset past work on arbitration by UNIDROIT and The Hague Conference, given that the diplomatic conference called to finalize what would become the New York Convention was held in 1958. See infra notes 113 - 114.

[9] See Establishment of the United Nations Conference on Trade and Development as an Organ of the General Assembly, A/1995 (XIX) (December 30, 1964).

[10] Joint Declaration of the 77 Countries (June 15, 1964).

on international trade should reflect the existence of basic differences of economic and social organization, economic development and bargaining power."

UNCTAD's focus on trade policy might have been seen to occupy the space for a UN agency on international trade, but its ability to promulgate legal texts was unclear (Chapter 9). Hard on the heels of UNCTAD's founding, the Permanent Representative of Hungary to the United Nations requested that the General Assembly consider creation of a United Nations commission on international trade law (Cohen 2011).[11] Said Hungary:

> Recently the United Nations has undertaken special efforts towards the development of international trade, having regards particularly to the general interest of the community of nations in the advancement of the developing countries. A thorough study of the legal forms of international trade, their possible simplification, harmonization and unification, would be well suited for this purpose.[12]

Rather than resurrect debates regarding the fairness or unfairness of then-current international policies on trade and economic development, Hungary centered its case for a commission on international trade law on the provisions of the UN Charter which required the General Assembly to "initiate studies and make recommendations" with the goal of "encouraging the progressive developments of international law and its codification."[13] Because UNCTAD's charge did not explicitly permit lawmaking, this requirement would go unmet without the creation of a new entity, implied Hungary.

Twenty years earlier the UN had created the ILC for the progressive development and codification of both public and private international law.[14] Hungary proposed drawing a boundary between its notional UN body and the International Law Commission by noting that the ILC had focused on *public* international law – that is, international law governing the relations between states and not that between private parties. While the ILC had the authority to enter *private international law*, it had not chosen not to cover these purely procedural issues.[15] Other IOs had made inroads in the field of private international law, but these generally did not encourage "the participation of representatives of the greatly interested States of

[11] Request for inclusion of an item in the provisional agenda of the nineteenth session of the General Assembly: Note Verbale from the Permanent Representative of Hungary to the United State, Official Records of the General Assembly, Nineteenth Session, Annexes, Annex No. 2, UN Doc. A/5728, reprinted in UNCITRAL Yearbook at 5 (1968–1970) [hereafter "Request for UNCITRAL"]. With this request, Hungary also filed a background paper to accompany the request for the creation of a law commission, and the Secretariat for the General Assembly followed with its own report.

[12] Request for UNCITRAL, supra note 11, at ¶ 2 of Explanatory Memorandum.

[13] UN Charter, Art. 13(1)(a).

[14] See Statute of the International Law Commission, Art. 1, ¶¶ 1 and 2.

[15] Request for UNCITRAL, supra note 11, at ¶ 1 of Explanatory Memorandum, citing GA Res. 174 (II), ¶ 2, Art. 1.

Africa and Asia."[16] Put another way, Hungary implied that an empty space remained in the ecology of international law and that this vacuum might be filled by a UN-related body focused on *private law* and *private international law* that confronted obstacles to trade and that would be legitimated by its universal representativeness of the world's nations.

The origins and motivations behind Hungary's initiative have never been discovered. Was it a clever move for the Soviet Bloc to take the side of developing nations? Was it a quiet deal in which the US found an unlikely ally to press the UN to reconsider conventions on private law, which it considered overly European in focus and approach? Was Hungary exercising some independence from its Soviet overlord? Whatever the motivation, however, the proposal required adept boundary work so as to forestall crushing opposition by established bodies at the moment of organizational creation.

In its lengthy background paper to the Sixth Committee of the General Assembly, Hungary elaborated its rhetorical framing to justify a new lawmaking IO under the authority of the General Assembly and its Sixth Committee, in relation to the ILC.[17] In discussing the prospects for the development of private international law within the then-current UN structure[18] and by non-UN entities,[19] Hungary's report concluded that new energy and a new organization were needed. Existing UN vehicles for lawmaking were overwhelmed with current projects for the progressive development and codification of public international law.[20] Academics criticized existing work on private international law as lacking in "direction, uniform organization and synthesis."[21] Hungary's Report concluded by arguing that the General Assembly should "find ways and means for systematically handling the problem of progressive development," which it argued existed "most forcefully in the field of international trade, the promotion of which primarily serves the progress of the developing countries and is thus in the interest of the whole community of nations."[22]

With its interests piqued by the Hungarian Report, the General Assembly requested that the Secretary-General submit to it a comprehensive report on the need for UNCITRAL.[23] In turn, the Secretary-General commissioned a report from Prof. Clive M. Schmitthoff of the City of London College, a prominent scholar on

[16] Id. at ¶ 2. See also (Honnold 1995: 1036) (contending that a "lack of wide participation in preparing the UNIDROIT Sales Conventions created difficulties of a . . . basic nature," which in turn "provided valuable lessons for the new UN Commission").

[17] Supra note 11, Background Paper at ¶¶ 1–39.

[18] Id. at ¶¶ 40–54.

[19] Id. at ¶¶ 58–68.

[20] Id. at ¶ 72.

[21] Id. at ¶¶ 69–71, citing and quoting Prof. Clive M. Schmitthoff.

[22] Id. at ¶ 75.

[23] UN Resolution 2102 (XX), available online at www.uncitral.org/uncitral/en/GA/resolutions.html.

the law of international trade and conflicts of law, who thereby became in effect UNCITRAL's founding institutional entrepreneur.

The Schmitthoff Report[24] surveyed then-existing work on the formulation of what he defined as "international trade law"[25] and identified four "main shortcomings" in the current state of international lawmaking on commerce and trade.[26] First, progress on the harmonization and unification of trade law had been slow. Second, developing countries had had only limited opportunities for participation in this process, although "those are the countries that especially need adequate and modern laws, which are indispensable to gaining equality in their international trade."[27] Third, it asserted that "[n]one of the formulating agencies commands world-wide acceptance; none has a balanced representation of countries of free enterprise economy, countries of centrally planned economy, developed and developing countries."[28] Finally, it found "insufficient co-ordination and co-operation among formulating agencies" which resulted in "a considerable amount of duplication."[29]

In short, through this amalgam of ideological appeal, pragmatic shortcomings, and an implicit theory of law and markets, Prof. Schmitthoff effectively demonstrated in his report to the Secretary-General that there was space for another IO, that it would focus on substantive matters critical to all nations,[30] that its work should build on but not duplicate the work of earlier IOs,[31] that it would be fully representative not only of rich and poor countries but also centrally planned with free market economies,[32] and that its goals, while lofty and by no means assured, could feasibly be achieved.[33] By carving out a particular jurisdiction for UNCITRAL, its foundations would be substantively and procedurally more secure than any of the existing bodies. By advocating cooperative and coordinating relationships

[24] Annexes to UN General Assembly Official Records, Agenda Item 88: Progressive Development of the Law of International Trade, Report of the Secretary-General, UN Doc. No. A/6396 (Sept. 23, 1966), www.uncitral.org/pdf/english/yearbooks/archives_e/A-6396-E.pdf [hereinafter the "Schmitthoff Report"].

[25] Id., at ¶¶ 10–13 (defining "international trade law" as "the body of rules governing commercial relationships of a private law nature involving different countries" and excluding "international commercial relations on the level of public law").

[26] Id. at ¶ 210.

[27] Id. at ¶ 210(b).

[28] Id. at ¶ 210(c).

[29] Id. at ¶ 210(d), citing (Gutteridge 1949: 183–84).

[30] Id. at ¶¶ 10–13 (defining "international trade law").

[31] Id., at ¶¶ 26-183 (detailing prior work of international and transnational IGOs, and of private, transnational NGOs).

[32] Id., at ¶ 208.

[33] Id., at ¶¶ 19–23 (describing three waves the "development of international trade law" beginning with the medieval lex mercantoria or law merchant, followed by national laws implementing this law merchant, and culminating in then-current work by IGOs and NGOs). For a more extensive laying out of this historical line of argument, see (Schmitthoff 1964).

with already existing lawmaking IOs, he offered an interactional template for relationships in an expanded lawmaking ecology.

In the end, the Schmitthoff Report recommended that the process of harmonizing and unifying trade law "should be substantially systematized and accelerated."[34] Given that its potential relationship with other international *private* lawmaking organizations, most notably UNIDROIT and The Hague Conference, could have created enormous threats to its nascent existence, the Schmitthoff Report proposed a specialized function for UNCITRAL. It argued that a UN body would be uniquely positioned to coordinate and implement the work of existing lawmaking IOs. This position might include technical advice and training in developing countries, but should also include the possibility of formulating new law, not least because a new UN-related lawmaking body alone would be fully representative of the world's nations on private international trade law. In this respect, Schmittoff played up the coordinating role, played down the innovating role, but nonetheless kept open the prospect of "formulation."[35]

As for the feasibility of these tasks, the Report admitted the difficulties that the new commission would face.[36] In an attempt to differentiate the new commission from The Hague Conference, the Report nonetheless noted that, because "the matters relating to the unification of the law of international trade are primarily of a technical nature," it should be easier to unify the law of international trade "than to unify the rules on such matters as family law, succession, personal status, and other subjects deeply rooted in national or religious traditions."[37] Recognizing the incentive for "unification at the lowest common denominator," the Report cautioned that any work should be preceded by "a thorough search for the right and ripe topics" involving "close collaboration between legal experts and trade experts."[38] Admitting that "[p]rogress in this field is bound to be rather slow," the Report argued that active involvement of the UN and "the sustained and continuing support" of its member states could accelerate things.[39]

Although the Schmitthoff Report had reviewed the work of dozens of IGOs and NGOs on topics of "international trade law" in making the case for a new UN commission on that topic, only three organizations commented formally on the call for creation of a new lawmaking organization within the auspices of the UN. The International Chamber of Commerce (ICC), an international organization formed in the late nineteenth century to represent business interests, submitted the resolution of its governing council "express[ing] the wish" that the procedural rules of the new UN commission would enable it "to associate the

34 Schmitthoff Report, supra note 24, at ¶ 212.
35 Id., at ¶¶ 211–224.
36 Id. at ¶ 222.
37 Id.
38 Id. at ¶ 223.
39 Id. at ¶ 224.

business community represented by the ICC on a world-wide scale with the commission's work on a consultative basis."[40]

Where Schmitthoff saw cooperation, UNIDROIT and The Hague Conference saw competition. UNIDROIT and The Hague Conference were quick to recognize the threat of a new IO in their lawmaking space, an IO moreover situated within a resource-rich UN. Seeing the new commission as a direct threat to its lawmaking jurisdiction,[41] UNIDROIT's Secretariat submitted to the UN Secretary-General a letter arguing that the "primary" task of any United Nations commission on international trade law should involve no more than "co-ordination and supervision."[42] In this view, the legal scope of the commission as a "formulating agency" should be limited to "exploring the possibility" of unification, "co-ordinating unificatory activities," "formulating guidelines," and "reviewing drafts" of other bodies. . . ."[43] In other words, UNIDROIT sought to define the "formulation" of trade law in terms of background research and administrative assistance but not in terms of actually drafting conventions or model laws. Indeed, UNIDROIT's Secretariat went so far as to propose "that the main seat of business of the proposed commission should be on the premises of the Institute," that is, of UNIDROIT in Rome, thus cementing "an informal link" between the two independent organizations.[44] Protecting symbolic space would be ensured by proximity in physical space – the very building occupied by UNIDROIT.

The Secretariat of The Hague Conference did not argue that UNCITRAL should not be allowed to "formulate" international trade law, but it did in effect press the case that the work and authority of The Hague Conference should not be diminished by UNCITRAL's creation.[45] While agreeing that a commission on international trade law should be created within the United Nations, it contended that the new commission "should provide for intimate contacts of a permanent character" with existing organizations "active in this field" because these existing organizations "could make a useful contribution to the interests which the United Nations is about to promote."[46] The letter detailed The Hague Conference's lengthy experience and expertise in "the technical, methodological and organization problems attendant upon the unification or codification of private international law."[47]

[40] UN Doc. No. A/6396, Add. II (Nov. 25, 1966)(appended as an annex to the Schmidtthoff Report).

[41] It should be noted that we use "jurisdiction" here not as a legal term but in the metaphorical sense in which it is employed in theories of professions and ecological theory. See (Abbott 1988) and the significant body of work derived from his theory of professions thereafter.

[42] UN Doc. No. A/6396.Add 1, Part A (comments to Schmidtthoff Report from International Institute for Unification of Private Law) at ¶ 12.

[43] Id. at ¶ 13.

[44] Id. at ¶ 16.

[45] UN Doc. No. A/6396/Add.1, Part B (comments to Schmitthoff Report from The Hague Conference on Private International Law).

[46] Id. at ¶ 15.

[47] Id. at ¶ 2.

Admitting that it had in the past failed to obtain the accession of a wide range of nations to conventions, The Hague Conference nonetheless questioned whether adding a more representative agency for law reform would alone result in accelerating the codification of international trade law. It further cautioned the General Assembly against believing that the creation of a UN-based commission on international trade law would provide a simple solution to the problem of accelerating the codification of law in this area since, it argued, codification requires both the formulation of international instruments, an activity best suited to academics, and their acceptance by national actors, a predominantly political activity.

This deft move thereby juxtaposed the *technical* foundation for international trade lawmaking with a *political* process, whether at the UN or within each states. The Hague Conference represented the former, a new UN commission the latter. Indeed, said The Hague letter, "work of this kind, in which scholarship is a vital and pervasive element, can best be pursued outside the larger political centres of the world."[48] In a further defensive protestation, the Secretariat of The Hague Conference on Private International Law differentiated between the unification of trade law in general, in which a new body might make a contribution, and "the unification or harmonization of rules governing conflicts of law,"[49] in which The Hague Conference was already the international leader.

When the Sixth Committee of the General Assembly took up the Schmitthoff Report for consideration, on December 2, 1966,[50] the main debate centered on whether UNCITRAL should be granted the ability to "formulate" law in this area. Several nations agreed with UNIDROIT's position that the new UN commission should not intervene except to encourage others to adopt existing conventions. France, a longstanding supporter of UNIDROIT, contended that existing institutions had been "slow but effective" and that their work should be expanded and strengthened. The United Kingdom, long reluctant to see expansive lawmaking bodies that might undermine its Imperial order, opined that UNCITRAL's "primary purpose" should be to coordinate existing institutions and promote existing laws, which it thought might "inject new sense of purpose and urgency to issues." Most delegations to the Sixth Committee nonetheless argued that the new commission should coordinate existing organizations, assist with the adoption of trade law products from other IOs, *and* be able to formulate its own agenda and work product.

The leading proponent of "formulation" was the United States, in a counterpoint to France, which prefigured a tension between states, political styles, and legal families that would recur fifty years later (Chapter 8). The US maintained that the new UN commission would "mark another step forward in the continuing efforts to establish a permanent regime of peace solidly based upon the

[48] Id. at ¶ 7.
[49] Id. at ¶ 4, n. 93.
[50] United Nations, General Assembly, Sixth Committee on Law, Debate concerning formation of UNCITRAL (Dec. 2–14, 1966).

rule of law."[51] The power to "formulate" uniform laws on international trade and commerce was a favorable development, remarked the US, as it reflected on the experience of its own uniform lawmaking under the auspices of the American Law Institute (ALI) and the National Conference of Commissioners for Uniform State Law (NCCUSL) to draft the US Uniform Code on Commercial Law (UCC).[52] Countries as diverse as Finland, Iraq, and Greece agreed with the US that, while UNCITRAL's coordinating function should be its "primary" role, the hands of the new commission should not be tied with an inflexible and limited agenda for reform.

The debate in the Sixth Committee effectively sought to find a way out of a legitimation paradox (Block-Lieb and Halliday 2006). Delegates sought to balance the need for broad representation with the fear that large numbers of delegates would render UNCITRAL unworkable. But, of course, limiting the membership in UNCITRAL left open complaints that geographic regions (North vs. South), legal families (civil vs. common law) or economic systems (capitalist vs. communist vs. statist), would be over-or-under represented. Delegates contrasted the prospective foundations of a new UN body with participation in UNIDROIT and The Hague Conference. For example, the Liberian delegate noted that "UNIDROIT had 43 members, 18 of which were from 'developing areas' but not all 18 were themselves developing countries; The Hague had 24 members and 3 were from Asia or Africa but all three were further advanced than most developing countries."[53] He argued that membership in the new commission should "enable the developing nations to help formulate the regulations governing the activities in which they were involved. Those nations would no longer have to accept and have their actions governed by rules in the formulation of which they had had no say."[54]

Proponents of UNCITRAL ultimately persuaded the UN General Assembly to establish its Commission on International Trade Law on December 17, 1966,[55] with the goal of "progressive harmonization and unification of the law of international trade." The Resolution granted UNCITRAL broad leeway both to promote international trade laws and to prepare them, even if the Resolution envisions UNCITRAL primarily as a coordinator of global law reform as much (and arguably even more than) as a source of global law (Faria 2005).[56]

[51] Id. (Dec. 7, 1966).

[52] Id. The reference at this point in the debate to its experience in uniform lawmaking opens up the conjecture that the US might already have been imagining the prospects of exporting its own commercial law via an international and legitimate global intermediary.

[53] Id. (Dec. 7, 1966).

[54] Id.

[55] Official Records of the General Assembly, Twenty-First Session, Resolution 2205 (XXI), A/RES/2205(XXI) (Dec. 17, 1966), http://daces.un.org/doc/RESOLUTION/GEN/NRO/005/08/IMG/NR000508.pdf?OpenElement.

[56] Resolution 2205 (XXI), supra note 55, at ¶ 8. Paragraph eight provides that UNCITRAL may proceed by:

The Resolution's sponsors defined this coordination function expansively by permitting UNCITRAL to "consult with or request the services of any international or national organization, scientific institution, or individual expert,"[57] as well as to "establish appropriate working relationships with intergovernmental organizations and international nongovernmental organizations concerned with the progressive harmonization and unification of the law of international trade."[58] The Resolution directed UNCITRAL to make incremental progress on the "progressive harmonization and unification of the law of international trade" standing, where possible, on the shoulders of earlier efforts of other organizations – international and national, governmental, intergovernmental, and nongovernmental, within the United Nations and outside it.

If its relationships to other IOs were carefully crafted – and skillfully blurred – in the Resolution, UNCITRAL's foundations of universal representation were far more precisely defined. The Resolution initially granted twenty-nine countries membership in the new commission and specified that seven of these countries would come "from African States," five "from Asian States," four "from Eastern European States," five from "Latin American States," and eight from "Western European and other States."[59]

(a) Co-ordinating the work of organizations active in this field and encourage co-operation among them;
(b) Promoting wider participation in existing international conventions and wider acceptance of existing model and uniform laws;
(c) Preparing or promoting the adoption of new international conventions, model law and uniform law and promoting the codification and wider acceptance of international trade terms, provisions, customs and practices, in collaboration, where appropriate, with the organization operating in the field;
(d) Promoting ways and means of ensuring a uniform interpretation and application of international conventions and uniform law in the field of the law on international trade;
(e) Collecting and disseminating information on national legislation, and modern legal developments, including case law, in the field of the law on international trade;
(f) Establishing and maintaining a close relationship with the United Nations Conference on Trade and Development;
(g) Maintaining liason with other United Nations organs and specialized agencies concerned with international trade;
(h) Taking any other action it may deem useful to fulfill its functions.

57 Id. at ¶ 11.

58 Id. at ¶ 12.

59 Id. In 1973, the General Assembly increased membership in UNCITRAL from twenty-nine to thirty-six members, and directed that these additional seven members to the young commission be drawn from each of the five regions that had been identified in its original resolution. The decision to increase UNCITRAL's membership preceded its production of any international instrument. The increase also preceded the General Assembly's 1974 pronouncement of a "New International Economic Order." By 1977, nine years after its creation, UNCITRAL decided to allow "non-member States" to "observe" its meetings and its working groups sessions, thereby effectively inviting all the world's nations to the deliberative body. Observer States are not entitled to vote, but since UNCITRAL endeavors to act consensually, without the need for a vote, this distinction mattered less than one would think. This arrangement held until 2003, when the General Assembly increased membership in UNCITRAL from thirty-six to sixty States.

At the moment of its founding, therefore, UNCITRAL's advocates had managed both to redefine boundary-markers of the ecology and to enter it. Through deft boundary work, UNCITRAL's advocates associated the new IO with bodies charged with public international lawmaking and with the facilitation of economic development through the development of trade policy – the ILC and UNCTAD, not least other UN agencies – and then differentiated itself from each of them. UNCITRAL's advocates aligned it with extant international private lawmaking bodies – UNIDROIT and The Hague Conference – but carved out separate territory on which to stake a distinctive claim, while all the time defining UNCITRAL's mandate with sufficient ambiguity to permit future encroachment on the domains of those bodies, should it so choose. UNCITRAL's sponsors concomitantly clothed the new organization in the garb of universal representativeness, thereby making a singular claim to an authority not shared by the European-oriented UNIDROIT and Hague Conference. UNCITRAL would be an organization of states, not of scholars, of all the world and not simply the imperial North. And with the United States as a principal supporter, and allies on both sides of the Iron Curtain, it maneuvered itself into a space where resources were likely to be abundant.

Once inside a standing ecology of international commercial and trade law, however, could UNCITRAL survive? And, if so, how? Would this new commission remain content with a purely coordinating and consultative role in the harmonization of international trade law? Could it exploit the ambiguity in its authorizing foundational mandate and expand its jurisdictional claims to lawmaking activity?

MANAGING THE LIABILITY OF NEWNESS

New organizations have a high mortality rate (Freeman, Carroll, and Hannan 1983). It is not improbable that IOs also suffer from a liability of newness. Compared to the ecologies that exist inside nation-states or communities, international social space is dynamic, fast moving, and sometimes chaotic. IOs move into ecologies where other IOs may be competitive and hostile, where resources are too limited to sustain all IOs that seek to occupy the space, where adjacent ecologies spark conflicts, where turbulent political and economic contexts may render them irrelevant or marginal.

At the outset, therefore, UNCITRAL confronted a conundrum. Should it make a quick start by focusing on the present landscape of problems, on existing or draft legal products, even though the IOs that initially had produced them were unrepresentative and indeed partly discredited by the debate over UNCITAL's founding? Or should UNCITRAL identify new problems, bring new resources to new global commercial law norms in unexplored issue-areas? In its first two sessions, the Commission made decisions on procedural rules and an agenda that would set the stage for the next thirty years of lawmaking.

In declining to adopt a formal definition of "trade law" to define the scope of its work,[60] at least at this early stage in its existence, the Commission refused to be boxed in by the narrow definition of "international trade law" proposed by the Schmitthoff Report. The Commission blurred its own boundaries, leaving open the possibility that some issues in international trade law might include both *private* and *public* law.

Yet the Commission chose not to venture into new issue-areas or open up new terrains of international commercial law but to concentrate its focus on the four areas of law the Schmitthoff Report had recommended: international sales; international transportation; international payments; and international arbitration. Each of these topics was highly technical, but on none of these topics would UNCITRAL write on a blank slate. Other IOs had already invested heavily in each, whether through international conferences or the promotion of multilateral treaties. In their discussion of this "programme of work," delegates acknowledged earlier groundwork by other lawmaking IOs. Yet, in doing so the Commission not so subtly delegitimized earlier efforts, as one after another delegate pointed out that a great number of countries had not participated in the creation of the conventions on international sales or international transport.[61] They looked to UNCITRAL for representation.

How then should UNCITRAL interact with existing IOs? Should it conclude formal concordats with UNIDROIT and The Hague Conference, among others? Openly compete with them? Ignore them altogether? The founding delegates decided cooperation through coordination "should be pragmatic and practical, and should continue to occur on an ad hoc basis," rather that attempting to work out a more formal agreement among organizations such as UNIDROIT and The Hague Conference.[62] Not only would this pragmatism enhance the nimbleness of a nascent IO as it sought to find its place among long-established lawmaking bodies, but it also gave UNCITRAL some degrees of freedom to maneuver among IOs and adapt its relationships with a given IO depending on the commercial law issue under consideration.

Although several delegates argued that the Commission should endeavor to minimize its review of pre-existing draft conventions, the Commission did the opposite and established Working Groups to prepare "uniform rules" on the international sale of goods, on time limits and limitations in the international sale of goods, and on shipping.[63] The Working Group on the International Sale of Goods,

60 Working Group, UNCITRAL Report on First Session (1970), UN Doc. No. TD/B/289, at ¶¶ 4–6; UNCITRAL Report on Second Session (1971), UN Doc. No. TD/B/C.4/86, Annex I. The Schmitthoff Report had defined "international trade law" as "the body of rules governing commercial relationship of a private law nature involving different countries." Schmitthoff Report at 10-13.

61 See UNCITRAL Report on First Session, supra note 60, at ¶¶ 4–6; UNCITRAL Report on Second Session, 60, Annex I.

62 UNCITRAL Report on Second Session, supra note 60. ¶¶ 144 and 155.

63 Id. at ¶ 183.

for instance, was asked to consider "which modifications of the Uniform Law on the Formation of Contracts for the International Sale of Goods, annexed to The Hague Convention of 1 July 1964, might render it capable of wider acceptance of countries of different legal, social, and economic systems and to elaborate a new text for this purpose."[64] In a word, UNCITRAL looked to revise a convention that had entered into force in the same year as UNCITRAL's emergence. It sought to remedy deliberative and representational deficits it observed in the products of other IOs, again implicitly contrasting their questionable legitimacy as normmakers for the world with its own universal representation of nations.

Not least, even in a world of nations divided into Cold War blocs, UNCITRAL aspired to decisionmaking that reflected neither blocs nor the arraying of votes. At its First Session, the Commission agreed that "its decisions should as far as possible be reached by way of consensus within the Commission," even if "recourse to votes might be necessary if no consensus were reached,"[65] a decision that would have longstanding repercussions for UNCITRAL's internal deliberations and its capacity to reach topics earlier thought to be too contentious for effective global lawmaking.

UNCITRAL took eight years to promulgate its first international instrument – the 1974 Convention on the Limitation Period in the International Sale of Goods. In the first fifteen years after its founding it produced a steady stream of laws for the world from each of its Working Groups. Although best known for its drafting of the Convention on Contracts for the International Sales of Goods (CISG), which it produced in 1980 and which has been adopted in eighty-six countries, including the US and, more recently, Japan,[66] UNCITRAL also promulgated its Arbitration Rules in 1976 and Conciliation Rules in 1980, both of which have widely shaped the practice of international dispute resolution and the promotion of international trade.[67] Similarly, in 1978 UNCITRAL promulgated its Convention on the Carriage of Goods by Sea (the "Hamburg Rules"), which was adopted by thirty-four countries and endorsed by UNCTAD, the Organization of American States, and the Asian-African Legal Consultative Committee.[68]

In each of these areas, UNCITRAL stood on the shoulders of earlier international instruments. For example, before commencing work on the international sales of goods, the Commission directed the Working Group to consider (and the Working

[64] Id. at ¶ 38, subpara. 3(a) of the resolution contained therein.

[65] Report of the United Nations Commission on International Trade Law on the work of its first session, Official Records of the General Assembly, Twenty-Third Session, Supplement No. 16 UN Doc. No. A/7216, ¶ 18 at 73 (1968).

[66] For a list of the eighty-six nations that have adopted the CISG, see www.uncitral.org/uncitral/en/uncitral_texts/sale_goods/1980CISG_status.html. Significantly, the United Kingdom has not adopted it.

[67] UNCITRAL's Arbitration Rules were updated in 2013. See UNCITRAL Arbitration Rules (with new Art. 1, para. 4 as adopted in 2013), available online at www.uncitral.org/pdf/english/texts/arbitration/arb-rules-2013/UNCITRAL-Arbitration-Rules-2013-e.pdf.

[68] For a list of the thirty-four nations that adopted the Hamburg Rules, see www.uncitral.org/uncitral/en/uncitral_texts/transport_goods/Hamburg_status.html.

Group considered at length) the texts of three earlier conventions: a 1964 Hague Convention on sales of goods; a 1964 Hague Convention on the formation of contracts in sales of goods; and a 1955 Hague Convention on international sales of goods.[69] These Hague Conventions had in turn been based on an earlier preliminary draft of a uniform law for the international sale of goods produced under UNIDROIT's sponsorship (Honnold 1959; Honnold 1979a). This pyramidal strategy was later viewed as instrumental to UNCITRAL's success (Block-Lieb and Halliday 2007a). A future General Secretary of UNIDROIT and one-time UNCITRAL lawyer opined that the convention of the international sales of goods "would not have been successfully completed had the ground not been leveled by the extensive work done by UNIDROIT in the preparation of The Hague Uniform Laws" (Faria 2005:270).

Before working on its Arbitration Rules, eventually promulgated in 1976 to govern procedures in commercial arbitration proceedings, UNCITRAL pointed to twelve different draft conventions or rules by the United Nations (and several regional economic commissions) on this topic.[70] One of these, the UN Convention on the Recognition and Enforcement of Foreign Arbitral Awards, also known as the New York Convention, had entered into force nearly ten years before.[71] Although UNCITRAL had no hand in drafting the New York Convention, it has nonetheless since the first sessions of the newly founded Commission claimed authority for encouraging and keeping official track of States' enactment of this text.[72]

69 Report of the Working Group on the International Sale of Goods, First Sess., UN Doc. No. A/CN.9/35 (Jan. 5–16, 1970), http://daccessdds.un.org/UNDOC/GEN/NL7/001/02/PDF/NL700102.pdf?OpenElement. See also Report of the Secretary-General: Analysis of Replies and Comments by Government on The Hague Conventions of 1964, UN Doc. No. A/CN.9/31 (1970) http://daccessdds.un.org/UNDOC/GEN/NL6/900//23/PDF/NL690023.pdf?OpenElement. The Working Group on Time Limits and Limitations, which ultimately produced the UNCITRAL Convention on the Limitation Period in the International Sale of Goods, also studied the 1955 and 1964 Hague Conventions. See Report of the Working Group on Time Limits and Limitations (Prescriptions), First Session (August 18–22, 1969), UN Doc. No. A/CN.9/30 (1970). For text of the 1964 and 1955 Hague Conventions, see www.cisg.law.pace.edu/cisg/text/antecedents.html.

70 Report of the United Nations Commission on International Trade Law on its First Session, *Official Records of the General Assembly Twenty-Third Session*, No. 16, UN Doc. No. A/7216, Pt. II, ¶¶ 30–33, at 80–81 (1968), www.uncitral.org/pdf/english/travaux/sales/limit/a7216-e.pdf.

71 Id. The New York Convention, to which more than 157 nations have acceded, was drafted by the International Chamber of Commerce (ICC) and the UN's Economic and Social Council (ECOSOC) in the mid-1950s, promulgated by the United Nations Conference on International Commercial Arbitration in 1958, and entered into force in 1959, seven years before the UN General Assembly established UNCITRAL. It is often considered the "most successful private international law treaty of the twentieth century" (Sanders 2001).

72 At its First Session, UNCITRAL's Commission "decided to direct the attention of the Member States of the General Assembly to the existence of the Convention and invite States to consider the possibility of adhering to it." Report of UNCITRAL on its First Session, supra note 60, at ¶ 33. To this day, UNCITRAL continues to keep track of the status of the New York Convention. In its description of the New York Convention, UNCITRAL claims ownership of the task of promoting the Convention as a "part of the Commission's programme of work." See www.uncitral.org/uncitral/en/uncitral_texts/arbitration/NYConvention.html.

Similarly, shortly after UNCITRAL's founding, the Commission created a Working Group on International Legislation on Shipping, a long-established field of international lawmaking. It directed the Working Group to consider earlier conventions, such as The Hague Rules of 1924,[73] and to "prepare a study in depth ... in the field of international legislation on shipping done or planned in the organs of the United Nations, or in inter-governmental or nongovernmental organizations."[74]

In each of these instances, UNCITRAL was both affirming the authority of the earlier global norms and easing global lawmaking initiative away from UNCTAD, ECOSOC, UNIDROIT, and The Hague Conference. In some cases, its impetus was an interest in solidifying the UN brand. It others, it expressed widespread dissatisfaction with the earlier norms, some of which had not entered into force precisely because aspects of the international community did not view their interests as having been represented in the negotiations that led up to their production. In both cases, UNCITRAL sought to accommodate the interests of developing countries, the Eastern European bloc, and common law jurisdictions, many of which had been absent in the drafting of earlier instruments.

This motivation was widely understood. One commentator explains that the 1964 Hague Conventions incorporating the Uniform Laws on International Sales and on the Formation of Contracts for International Sales "needed substantial revision before they could achieve world-wide acceptance" (Honnold 1979b).[75] Another commentator describes similar concerns regarding The Hague Rules on shippers' liability for cargo (Basnayake 1979).

UNIDROIT and The Hague Conference appeared to acquiesce in UNCITRAL's pyramidal strategies; both regularly participated in UNCITRAL meetings. Between 1968 and 2003, The Hague Conference missed only eight, and UNIDROIT only seven, annual Commission meetings. UNCITRAL also worked closely with UNCTAD, the UN organ charged with authority over trade policy. While UNCTAD's attendance record at UNCITRAL's annual sessions is spottier, each

73 International Convention for the Unification of certain rules relating to Bills of lading: Brussels, Aug. 25, 1924 (League of Nations Treaty Series, Vol. CCX, p. 157), reprinted in II *UN Register of Trade Law Texts* 130.

74 Report of the United Nations Commission on International Trade Law on the Work of its Second Session, UN Doc. No. A/7618. *See also* Report of the Secretary-General, A Survey of the Work in the Field of International Legislation on Shipping Undertaken by Various International Organizations and Co-ordination of Future Work in this Field, A/CN.9/41 (1970), http://daccessdds.un.org/UNDOC/GEN/NL7/001/04/PDF/NL700104.pdf?OpenElement.

75 John Honnold was Secretary-General of UNCITRAL between 1969 and 1974, had participated in the US delegation to the diplomatic conference that adopted The Hague Conference on international sales law in 1964 and in the drafting of the US Uniform Commercial Code in the 1950s. See Walter F. Naedele, Obituary, John O. Honnold, Jr. 95; a Penn law professor who played a role in twentieth century events (Feb. 4, 2011), http://articles.philly.com/2011-02-04/news/27100701_1_honnold-retirement-community-penn-law-professor.

year UNCITRAL forwarded a report to UNCTAD's Trade Board, which in turn "took note" of the report, often in general terms but from time to time with specific comments from delegates to UNCTAD or from UNCTAD itself. Thus, when UNCITRAL was "formulating" conventions built on the shoulders of existing IOs, it was also coordinating with these IOs, as its founding mandate had promised.

In short, UNCITRAL's Secretariat and Commission sought to manage relationships of interdependency with existing international lawmaking organizations by holding in tension, on the one hand, a reliance on their earlier products and continuing relationships, and on the other hand, a willingness to revise the products and expand their reach with the assistance of a broader and more representative cast of delegations. Essentially it converted the incipient competition displayed at the moment of founding into a competitive cooperation that enabled a standing ecology to persist and evolve. How adeptly, however, could UNCITRAL or its embedding ecology adapt to the exogenous impact of decolonization and its transformational impulses for global politics and markets?

THE NEW INTERNATIONAL ECONOMIC ORDER

UNCITRAL had its beginnings not only as the Cold War segmented the world into zones of command and capitalist economies, but as the retreat of European empires brought scores of new nations into post–War II political forums with increasingly vocal demands for economic justice and the redress of development-inhibiting residues of colonial economic orders. Law became embroiled in markets in ways scarcely imaginable to the lawmakers of The Hague Conference and UNIDROIT in earlier decades.

In the late 1960s and early 1970s, issues of economic and social development dominated the agenda of the General Assembly. Relations between the developed nations in the industrialized North and undeveloped, largely agrarian nations in the South continued to deteriorate within the UN. The less developed nations had found voice and political strength in the G-77, in the creation of UNCTAD, and also in the framing of UNCITRAL's purpose as more than the promulgation of international trade law. UNCITRAL, said developing and newly independent nations, should be producing global trade law that assisted less developed nations to grow economically.

Within a decade, the G-77 pressed the UN to promote a New International Economic Order (NIEO).[76] These and subsequent UN statements on NIEO constituted "an invitation and a challenge" to developed nations and IOs such as

76 The General Assembly memorialized the NIEO in a series of resolutions, including "A Declaration on the Establishment of a New International Economic Order" and "A Programme of Action on the Establishment of a New International Economic Order." See, e.g., General Assembly, United Nations, Resolution, Declaration on the Establishment of a New International Economic Order, UN Doc. No. A/RES/S-6/3201 (May 1, 1974).

the World Bank, IMF and GATT (Reubens 1981). The NIEO called for improvements in the economic development and welfare of less developed countries through reform in the areas of trade, finance, and technology transfers. Its "programme of action" confronted "fundamental problems of raw materials and primary commodities as related to trade and development;" it called for reform of the international monetary system and for efforts to be made to "encourage the industrialization of the developing countries," "to formulate an international code of conduct for the transfer of technology corresponding to needs and conditions prevalent in developing countries," and "to adopt and implement an international code of conduct for transnational corporations."[77]

Debates over the New International Economic Order "dominated and polarized" the UN during the 1970s (Mingst and Karns 2007). Developing countries made demands for institutional reform in the New International Economic Order. Developed economies, not least centers of former colonial empires, had moral obligations, it was argued, to support development in previously marginalized peripheral economies. Because their demands primarily focused on states' trade and financial policies, and not demands for law reform, most of these debates occurred within the General Assembly and UNCTAD.

UNCITRAL was also buffeted by this political, organizational, and economic turbulence.[78] In 1975 and 1977, the General Assembly called on the Commission "to take account of . . . the new international economic order."[79] The Commission responded with a question: What would be the subjects that "would be suitable for [its] consideration?"[80] The United Nations Secretary-General replied with a list of nine issues touching on trade policy.[81] But, admitted the Secretary-General, most of the "issues and policies" referred to in its report "are to a great extent of a political and economic nature and cannot be dealt with by a legal body such as the Commission."[82] In a word, he elevated UNCITRAL's own self-description as a technical rather than "political" body, a distinction more rhetorical than real, but nonetheless, as we shall see, of value to UNCITRAL as it sought to draw boundaries around what it could and could not reach in its agenda setting.

77 Id.

78 UN Doc. No. A/35/166 (Dec. 15, 1980). See also UN Doc. A/36/107 (Dec. 10, 1981); UN Doc. A/37/103 (Dec. 16, 1982); UN Doc. A/38/128 (Dec. 19, 1983).

79 General Assembly Resolution No. 3494 (XXX) (Dec. 15, 1975); General Assembly Resolution No. 32/145 (Dec. 16, 1977).

80 Report of the United Nations Commission on International Trade Law on the work of its eleventh session, Official Records of the General Assembly, Thirty-third Session, Supplement No. 17, UN Doc. No. A/33/17, ¶ 71, reprinted in UNCITRAL Yearbook, Part One, II, A (1978).

81 A generalized system of preferences, most-favored-nation treatment, trade obstacles, the need for uniform conflict of law rules and rules on arbitration and the enforcement of judgments, restrictive business practices and unfair competition, and general conditions, standard clauses and model rules. Id. at ¶¶ 7–64.

82 Id. at ¶ 65.

Although the Secretary-General's conclusions could have been read as constricting UNCITRAL to continuation of its prior work, the Commission chose not to interpret the report in this way. Instead, it created a Working Group on the New Economic Order, an adroit ecological move insofar as UNCITRAL signaled its alignment with shifting UN goals and the need to maintain access to UN resources in order to advance those goals. The Working Group proposed to the Commission five potential topics for consideration,[83] and identified one topic that should have priority.[84]

A new stream of products, tailored to the prevailing state-led model of economic development, began to come on line in 1987. They had in common the prospect that economic growth might be stimulated by legally-enabled partnerships between government and industry, most importantly through major infrastructure projects. The Commission promulgated its Legal Guide on Drawing Up International Contracts for the Construction of Industrial Works, followed in 1993 by the Model Law on Procurement of Goods and Construction with Guide to Enactment and in 1994 by the Model Law on Procurement of Goods, Construction, and Services, with Guide to Enactment. To reach these new issue-areas, UNCITRAL diversified its repertoire of legal technologies to include "soft" model laws and also "softer" legal guides. This broader range of products made it easier for UNCITRAL's lawmakers to reach consensus on legal norms while softer law also gave countries greater latitude to adapt global norms to varieties of local circumstances (see Chapter 6).

UNCITRAL reached more than new issue-areas. Its forays into law and development could be seen as the crossing of a well-demarcated boundary supposedly settled at the moment of its founding. Because procurement contracts often involve agreements between sovereign states and private actors, the topic of procurement extended its normal private law reach to cover what might have been considered an aspect of public international law.[85]

By tackling project finance and procurement, UNCITRAL stepped outside conventional interpretations of "law on international trade." In doing this, it both expanded its reach and redefined the label "trade law." First, project finance and procurement often do not involve "trade," in that the sale of goods between private parties from two different countries need not have been envisioned. Project finance concerns foreign investment in infrastructure projects. Procurement might involve goods, services, or construction, but the purchases are made by sovereign nations and, thus, not between private parties. When States enter into project finance or procurement contracts, public not private international law is triggered.

83 Id. at ¶ 31.

84 Id. at ¶ 31(4).

85 In the late 1990s, when reconstruction of command economies was now on the international development agenda, UNCITRAL returned to these topics, following in 2000 with a legislative guide on privately financed infrastructure projects (often referred to as "project finance") and in 2003 with model legislation provisions on this topic.

Second, with the topic of project finance and procurement UNCITRAL had moved away from its traditional reliance on conventions and model laws. The Legal Guide was not "law," in that it was not directed to domestic legislatures. Instead, the initial audiences were the private and public parties who negotiate, draft, and execute contracts for the construction of industrial works.

This double move coincidentally widened UNCITRAL's legal scope, its desired audiences, and its repertoire of legal technologies. UNCITRAL's work on private infrastructure and procurement succeeded in finding practical applications for the UN's highly controversial NEIO mandate as it concomitantly signaled an extension beyond UNCITRAL's four original issue-areas.

Although in theory this substantive expansion threatened to unsettle what had become a de facto division of labor among UNCITRAL, UNIDROIT and The Hague Conference, in practice UNCITRAL interpreted this new mandate narrowly. The NIEO Working Group at UNCITRAL fashioned an interpretation of the "new international economic order" that forestalled competition with UNIDROIT and The Hague Conference. The Working Group recommended only that UNCITRAL extend its mission over the "harmonization and unification of international trade law" to include a legal guide on drawing up industrial works contracts between public and private entities.

At the same time, UNCITRAL met the NIEO mandate creatively, by inventing new technologies for subjects on which a convention was thought to be impossible. Although in the past UNCITRAL had promulgated, besides draft conventions, model laws, model legal provisions and rules, in 1987 it produced a "legal guide" – the 1987 Legal Guide on Drawing Up Industrial Works Contracts; in 2000, it devised yet another legal technology – the legislative guide – and promulgated the Legislative Guide on Privately Financed Infrastructure Projects. Expanding the form of its products further enabled a more expansive substantive reach. UNCITRAL could further distinguish itself from UNIDROIT and The Hague Conference which remained locked into the production of conventions only, consistent with their longstanding practices.

This inventiveness cultivated a repertoire of formal possibilities for UNCITRAL that positioned it effectively to respond to the radical reformations of command economies in the 1990s, the information revolution, and quickening globalization of trade in the last two decades (see Table A.1 and Table A.2). Moreover, this newfound flexibility in products coincided with a now clearly apparent shift in rhetorical self-understanding. An organization founded to "unify" and "harmonize" international trade law now pivoted to a much less restrictive goal – to "modernize" it.

(RE)CONSTRUCTING MARKETS

While the fall of the Berlin Wall in 1989 represents a dramatic historical marker of an epochal turn in geopolitics and economic organization, in fact the contexts for the standing ecology of international private lawmaking had already been undergoing their own seismic shifts, an unsettling of global markets that continued through the Asian Financial Crisis in 1997.

Since international law purports to regulate commerce in goods and services that cross national borders, any significant shift in the world trading systems should in principle influence the IOs that claimed lawmaking jurisdiction over salient bodies of law. By the mid-1980s, the volume of global trade had caught back up to levels that had been interrupted by World War I and World War II. It continued to expand exponentially thereafter.

That trade expressed itself in growth in the number and complexity of multinational corporations; the global integration of banking and finance; the information revolution and the prospects of electronic commerce, innovative payment technologies, and pin-point communications; the invention and explosion of containerized transport of goods. Globalization during this period also brought a shift from the dominance of international trade in goods to growth in international foreign investment – a shift that paralleled and eventually exceeded the focus on trade in finished products because it included "trade" in intellectual property and services, including financial services.

Dislocating shifts in economic organization were punctuated by regional and national crises that in turn had global import. The fall of the Soviet Union led to the wholesale replacement of a half-century of command economies with wrenching marketization. Rapid privatization of state-owned enterprises and the opening of private markets threw millions out of work and shocked economies into deep retraction. The European Union accepted many of these countries, and their economies, into its fold, as did GATT and eventually the WTO. But this rapid move toward market economies and privatization also meant that new laws would need to be reformed and put in place quickly.

Economic and financial dislocations ricocheted across the world – in the debt crises of Ecuador, Argentina, and Mexico in Latin America and, most dramatically, in the Asian Financial Crisis beginning in 1997. When the Asian Tiger economies began to fold, initial fears by private and multilateral bankers of a regional economic collapse intensified into a near panic that Asia could bring down the entire world economy and lead it into recession or even depression. International financial institutions, prominently the World Bank and IMF, charged with a mandate for global financial stability, together with regional development banks, confronted high stakes challenges over how nations, regions and the world economy could be protected from uncertainties, instabilities, and panics.

A paradigm shift framed the world of pragmatic interventions by states and supra-state bodies into markets. The collapse of the Asian Tiger economies symbolized the end of an era in which state-led economic development had been championed for countries emerging from colonialism and the peripheries of the world economy. Whereas law had been marginal to state-led development, the new legal institutionalism in economic development theory become concretized in models of economic growth expressed through the Washington Consensus and the triumph of neoliberalism. Now economic growth would be driven by private market actors but only within institutions framed by law. IOs charged with maintaining financial stability, economic growth, and reduction of poverty would be drawn into the orbit of international lawmakers, on occasion with pretensions that they, too, belonged inside lawmaking ecologies.

Whether secular changes are measured in grand time or short-term shocks both sets of factors altered environments for UNCITRAL and the standing lawmaking ecology. If (international) commercial law was to keep pace with (international) commercial practices, then an enormous set of challenges confronted global lawmakers. If national and global market players were to leverage their burgeoning trade practices, then it was said that orderly governance of markets could stimulate expansion and guarantee some transactional certainty in the world economy. If the world economy was to insure itself against financial turbulence, then it required regulatory buttresses and emergency backup.

Each of the lawmaking organizations confronted these unsettling economic and political movements in its own way and adapted at its own pace.

For UNCITRAL, it became increasingly clear in the 1980s that its original mandate might no longer be flexible enough to cope with the dynamisms of national and global markets. Although the scope of UNCITRAL's lawmaking was somewhat hedged in its founding grant of authority, there was little doubt that its primary goal was to facilitate international trade by unifying and harmonizing the law that governed commerce. In justifying the creation of UNCITRAL in the late 1960s, the General Assembly had "*[r]eaffirm[ed] its conviction* that divergencies arising from the laws of different States in matters relating to international trade constitute one of the obstacles to the development of world trade."[86] Thus, the decision to establish a Commission, "which shall have for its object the promotion of the progressive harmonization and unification of the law of international trade," was based on a belief that "the extensive development of international trade" could best be furthered by removing "divergencies arising from the laws of different States" and "by harmonizing and unifying the law of international trade..."[87] Harmonization and unification of the law of trade would favor "the interests of all peoples" and "particularly those of developing countries" because "international trade co-operation among States is an important factor in the promotion of friendly relations and, consequently, in the maintenance of peace and security."[88]

The passage of time, however, had revealed that harmonization and unification were not so easy to achieve, whether in the drafting of the global norms or their

[86] G.A. Res. 2205 (XXI), supra note 55.
[87] Id.
[88] Id.

widespread adoption. Moreover, some areas of law seemed difficult to reach through a rigid multilateral treaty mechanism where exact wording on every provision was required to obtain "hard" unification. Some areas of law might be especially challenging because domestic law was either new or non-existent, so global legislators were cast upon their own devices. As a result, UNCITRAL searched for ways to escape further from the straitjacket of "harmonization" and "unification," even though its leaders had already shown considerable skill exploiting the ambiguities in its founding mandate. It did so by adding to its founding goals a much more flexible and adaptable mandate: modernization (Block-Lieb and Halliday 2007a). And the substantive path to this new goal presented itself through the issue of electronic commerce.

In 1978, the Study Group on International Payments, "a consultative body composed of representatives of bank and trade institutions," took on the issue of the legal implications of electronic funds transfers.[89] In cooperation with UNCITRAL, the Study Group recommended preparation of a text on the topic,[90] which led to UNCITRAL to produce its Legal Guide on Electronic Funds Transfers (1984).[91] This move opened up the much broader question of electronic transfers of non-financial data. Once electronic data were considered, why refer only to electronic data that served as the payment medium for effectuating a trade in goods? Why should there exist different standards for e-commerce as other electronic communications?[92]

The newness of transactions in and transmissions of electronic data challenged UNCITRAL's traditional focus on the harmonization and unification of international trade law. Since electronic data interchange (EDI) and e-commerce involved emerging technologies and markets, there existed few laws on these topics; the harmonization or unification of these laws was, thus, undoubtedly premature. More than side-step its harmonizing and unifying mission, UNCITRAL also did not limit itself to purely "international" e-commerce transactions or EDI transmissions. It took on the task of developing standards for both *domestic* and *international* electronic transmissions.

89 Note by the Secretary-General: Electronic Funds Transfers, UN Doc. No. A/CN.9/199, ¶ 1 (Apr. 29, 1981).

90 Note by the Secretariat: Electronic funds transfers progress report, UN Doc. No. A/CN.9/242 (May 6, 1983).

91 Draft Legal Guide on Electronic Funds Transfers: Report of the Secretary-General, UN Doc. No. A/CN.9/250 and Add. 1-4 (1984).

92 One of the reports on the draft Legal Guide on Electronic Funds Transfers makes this point directly:

> The problem [of the legal value of computer records], while of particular importance to international electronic funds transfers, is one of general concern for all aspects on international trade.

UN Doc. No. A/CN.9/221, quoted in Legal Value of Computer Records: Report of Secretary-General, UN Doc. No. A/CN.9/265, at ¶ 1 (1985).

As a result of the novelty of this technology and the means through which it sought to address this topic, UNCITRAL walked very gingerly into the subject of automatic data processing, computer records, and electronic communications. The preamble paragraphs of UNCITRAL's Recommendation (1985) to national governments on these issues makes clear that, although commercial practices associated with electronic communications were rapidly changing, domestic commercial laws had not. The Recommendations imply that this technology was poised to mushroom in importance and that international trade would be held back if commercial law was not brought up to speed with these developing commercial practices. The Recommendation urges governments to review their legal rules on these transactions, although not yet explicitly justifying this reform on the grounds that modernization fit within its mission.

By the mid-1990s, when UNCITRAL produced a model law on electronic commerce and followed this with a series of other related products,[93] the rhetoric of "modernization" was regularly deployed (Halliday, Block-Lieb, and Carruthers 2009b). The UNCITRAL Model Law on Electronic Commerce is intended "to enhance the needed modernization of legislation."[94] The UNCITRAL Model Law on Electronic Signatures "is designed to assist States in establishing a modern, harmonized and fair legislative framework. . . ."[95] The United Nations Convention on the Use of Electronic Communications in International Contracts justifies itself on the grounds that it "may help States gain access to modern trade routes."[96]

UNCITRAL thus reconceived its very mission and the means by which it carried out its central purposes, carefully acting so as not to jettison explicitly its founding mandate for harmonization and codification. It did so without consulting other international lawmaking IOs, or even the UN General Assembly. In restating its mission,[97] UNCITRAL extended its lawmaking jurisdiction and TLO aspirations

93 In 1996, UNCITRAL adopted a Model Law on Electronic Commerce with Guide to Enactment; in 2001, it promulgated the Model Law on Electronic Signatures with Guide to Enactment. Most recently, in 2005, the UN adopted its Convention on the Use of Electronic Communications in International Contracts.

94 UNCITRAL Model Law on Electronic Commerce with Guide to Enactment, at 67.

95 UNCITRAL Model Law on Electronic Signatures with Guide to Enactment, at 8.

96 United Nations Convention on the Use of Electronic Communications in International Contracts, at 7 ("*Convinced* that the adoption of uniform rules to remove obstacles to the use of electronic communications in international contracts, including obstacles that might result from the operation of existing international trade law instruments, would enhance legal certainty and commercial predictability for international contracts and may help States gain access to modern trade routes. . . .").

97 See www.uncitral.org. There, UNCITRAL describes its mission as follows:

> The core legal body of the United Nations system in the field of international trade law. A legal body with universal membership specializing in commercial law reform worldwide for over 40 years. UNCITRAL's business is the modernization and harmonization of rules on international business.

Id. at www.uncitral.org/uncitral/welcome.html.

well beyond its original mandate and, indeed, potentially created a conflict with goals to harmonize and unify international trade law as law reform intended to modernize might also "de-harmonize" outmoded laws.

UNCITRAL did not rely on the rhetoric of modernization solely to advocate "in with the new" legislation to the international community such as its work on electronic commerce. It has also advocated modernization as justifying a revision of existing commercial law, such as insolvency and secured transactions laws. "Out with the old" modernization constitutes a distinct law reform effort, one that may veer the farthest from UNCITRAL's original mission regarding the "progressive harmonization and unification of the law of international trade."

UNCITRAL similarly justified its work on proposals that sought to prevent another Asian Financial Crisis on grounds of modernization. In its 1999 Report on Possible Future Work on Insolvency Law, the UNCITRAL Secretariat noted that an important justification for authorizing the Working Group on Insolvency Law to begin its work on the Legislative Guide on Insolvency Law "was to modernize insolvency practices and laws"[98] by recommending to national actors that they reject their existing domestic insolvency laws in favor of more modern laws. "Out with the old" modernization is not limited to insolvency reform. A 2000 report on the then-current activities and possible future work of the Working Group on Secured Transactions justified authorizing it to begin work on the Legislative Guide on Secured Transactions Law on the grounds that "modernization and optimization of secured credit law can lead to expanded economic development and, therefore, promote the general welfare."[99] In every year since 2000, the Commission's yearly report to the UN General Assembly reaffirms "its belief that the progressive modernization and harmonization of international trade law" both "reduce[es] or remov[es] legal obstacles to the flow of international trade" and "contribute[s] significantly to universal economic cooperation among all States on a basis of equality, equity and common interest."[100]

[98] UNCITRAL, *Possible Future Work on Insolvency Law*, infra note 104, para. 2.

[99] UNCITRAL, Working Group on Secured Transactions Law, *Security Interests: Current Activities and Possible Future Work*, para. 45, UN Doc. No. A/CN.9/475 (Apr. 27, 2000) [hereinafter UNCITRAL, *Security Interests*], www.uncitral.org/uncitral/en/commission/sessions/33rd.html (follow "A/CN.9/475 - Security Interests - Current activities and possible future work" hyperlink).

[100] G.A. Res. 58/75, UN GAOR, 58th Sess., Supp. No. 17, UN Doc. A/RES/58/75 (Dec. 9, 2003), www.uncitral.org/uncitral/en/GA/resolutions.html (follow "A/RES/58/75" hyperlink). Similar language appears in the General Assembly resolutions to adopt the Commission's reports on sessions between 2000 and 2005. The reference to "modernization" does not appear in reports pre-dating 2000. The report reaffirms "its convictions that the progressive harmonization and unification of the law of international trade" would both "reduce[e] or remov[e] legal obstacles to the flow of international trade" and "contribute significantly to universal economic cooperation among all States on a basis of equality. . . ." *Id.* For a complete list of these reports of the General Assembly, see General Assembly Resolutions, www.uncitral.org/uncitral/en/GA/resolutions.html.

The broadening of UNCITRAL's goals to embrace modernization demonstrates not only a certain adaptive adroitness to its various organizational contexts, but also the rhetorical force of its repositioning. A notion of the "modern" is a social and cultural construction. As a concept, it appears self-validating. Inherent in its meaning are concepts of progress and development, of advancement and maturity. Paradoxically, part of its power lies precisely in its vacuity and opacity. It is relatively empty of meaning and may, thereby, be infused with content as circumstances require. For instance, modernization could mean something temporal (i.e., it is modern simply because it is different from something older or pre-modern). It could mean something comparative (i.e., this country claims to be "modern" in comparison to that country which is not). Or it could be functional (i.e., it achieves a function previously missing in a legal or economic system). We have seen that in practice UNCITRAL has used the term in two ways – "modern" means filling a gap in the law with contemporaneous content ("in with the new") or replacing former law ("out with the old") (Block-Lieb and Halliday 2007a).

But it should also be clear that the label of "modernity" veils an expression of power (see, e.g., Cohen 2011). Powerful countries in the international political economy adopt the label for themselves and then project their definition of modernity onto countries they label as not modern. In this sense, UNCITRAL's adoption of the label may be viewed as the appropriation of claims made by actors within UNCITRAL that they stand at the vanguard of development and, indeed, have the responsibility or even the right to make those claims pervasive throughout the less than fully "modern" world. This symbolic alignment of UNCITRAL with economic and political power thereby presumes an increased capacity to set global agendas and to earn the respect of global actors for the "modern" norms it produces.

The very ambiguity of the term "modern" may also serve a useful pragmatic function. UNCITRAL has long recognized the improbability of far-reaching unification of all private laws standing as obstacles to growth in international trade and commerce, particularly in contentious policy areas. But modernization might stand as a more plausible goal. If widely followed, the Legislative Guide on Insolvency is likely to be modernizing at least in its convergence on corporate reorganization as a policy goal. The vagueness of "modernization" as a goal allows global convergences around a set of variations on some global theme such that "modern" insolvency systems might variously approximate those of the United States, United Kingdom, Australia, Germany, or France, among others – all nations indisputably modern by their own claims and yet with perceptibly different choices and divergence on the options presented by the Legislative Guide. That even those countries that revise their corporate insolvency laws in reaction to UNCITRAL's guidance have not "harmonized" or more fully "unified" these laws would not prevent UNCITRAL from claiming credibly that its goal of "modernization" had fully been met.

As a rhetorical strategy and form of organizational adaptation, UNCITRAL's shift away from the goal of unification toward that of modernization simultaneously solved a number of ecological challenges, all of which enhanced its TLO-building capacities. Insofar as it was conducive to harmonization, modernization kept UNCITRAL faithful to the spirit of its original mission to facilitate global trade by reducing the divergence of national laws. Insofar as it sought to remain a central player in the ecology of global lawmaking institutions, modernization provided UNCITRAL the maneuverability to adjust to changing global agendas. Insofar as UNCITRAL endeavored to demonstrate its own relevance, and that of its parent organization, then modernization has enhanced its expansive reach. And insofar as it tolerates national diversity around overarching policy objectives, UNCITRAL could balance its deference to the global center with responsiveness to the global periphery, thereby satisfying divergent interests of its own member delegates and delegations.

Broadening Scope, Inventing Technologies

The rhetoric of modernization did more than authorize UNCITRAL to reach areas of law previously viewed as situated outside its original mandate or a bridge too far to reach with multilateral treaties. If UNCITRAL was to keep abreast of fast-changing trade practices and salient to leading edges of substantive legal development, then one avenue open for its leaders was to invent new, "modern" legal technologies. If UNCITRAL was to maintain or enhance the centrality of its position in the ecology of global commercial lawmaking, its Secretariat might do so by sharpening its competitive edge vis-à-vis other lawmaking IOs.

Until very recently UNIDROIT and The Hague Conference consistently retained exclusive normmaking through their signature technology – the multilateral treaty or convention (Block-Lieb and Halliday 2016). In the late 1990s, however, international financial institutions began to produce softer forms of norms. The European Bank for Reconstruction and Development (EBRD) produced a model law and then principles for secured transaction law in Central and Eastern Europe (EBRD 1997). The Asian Development Bank (ADB) produced standards for insolvency and secured transactions law (ADB 2000a; ADB 2000b). The International Monetary Fund published a small book on "orderly and effective" insolvency laws (IMF 1999), while the World Bank, too, produced "principles" and "guidelines" for insolvency and secured transaction (World Bank 2001; World Bank 2003).[101]

During this same period, UNCITRAL was confronted concomitantly with the limits of hard law norms, such as its conventions, with the broader possibilities of soft law norms, such as model laws and legislative guides, and with its own positioning in the wider ecology of global normmakers. From the mid-1980s, it sought to increase

[101] Since Abbott and Snidal (2000) first distinguished between reliance on hard and soft law in international governance, there has emerged a growing literature on the relative merits of soft and hard laws in international context, and especially where international agreement on matters of finance, commerce, and corporate governance is at stake. See, e.g., (Brummer 2014; Brummer 2015; Weiss and Kammel 2015).

its competitive edge by rolling out a series of new technologies, each different in form, directed to different audiences, and requiring a different politics of formulation and adoption.

If unification and harmonization represented a straitjacket for its goals, conventions shackled UNCITRAL to a technology with severe limits. A *convention* requires that multiple countries ratify a single standard. Conditions of formulation require zero-sum bargaining in order to reach agreement. The politics of formulation and implementation are time consuming and require painstaking negotiation consuming.[102] Countries generally may not alter any terms of the convention to suit domestic political, economic, and legal differences.[103]

While a *model law* sets a global standard, neither its conditions of formulation are as demanding nor its conditions of implementation as severe as a convention, because it may implicitly permit states to exclude or modify some provisions.[104] As an enhancement on a model law, UNCITRAL also created a new technology – a *guide to enactment* that sets out background information, explanations of decisions, and information on policy options that might enable legislators to make informed decisions.[105] UNCITRAL also created *legal guides* directed toward private parties and *practice guides* directed to courts and others interpreting UNCITRAL products.[106]

As UNCITRAL shifted its focus toward the "modernization" of trade law it invented new legal technologies that offered greater flexibility to reform a broader range of laws, especially with the benefit of time and incremental progress.[107]

[102] It can be argued that conventions are easier to "enact" because there may be no legislative process (Int: 2071, unpublished interview, on file with authors [hereinafter cited as "Int:"]).

[103] One senior official of UNCITRAL stated: "[T]he realities of many subjects are that you couldn't do a convention on them" (Int: 4003).

[104] *See* UNCITRAL, Working Group on Insolvency Law, *Working Paper: Possible Future Work on Insolvency Law*, paras. 162–68, UN Doc. A/CN.9/WG.V/WP.50 (Sept. 20, 1999) [hereinafter UNCITRAL, *Possible Future Work on Insolvency Law*]. There are also variations in the form of model laws. Contrast the Model Law on International Commercial Arbitration, which is a procedural instrument with tightly linked interdependent articles, and the Model Law on Electronic Commerce, which offers sets of principles with potential variations for satisfying them. UNCITRAL, *Possible Future Work on Insolvency Law*, id., paras. 165–66. A former Secretary of UNCITRAL observes that the Model Law on Arbitration now covers approximately one third of the world, something that would have been impossible with a convention (Int: 4003, 2071),

[105] UNCITRAL, *Possible Future Work on Insolvency Law*, supra note 104, para. 164.

[106] For example, UNCITRAL's Practice Guide on Cross-Border Insolvency Cooperation "provides information for insolvency practitioners and judges on practical aspects of cooperation and communication in cross-border insolvency cases." Available online at www.uncitral.org/uncitral/en/uncitral_texts/insolvency/2009PracticeGuide.html.

[107] Other scholars have argued the UNCITRAL acts "incrementally" and count this incrementalism as among its strengths. See, e.g., (Pottow 2005) (describing UNCITRAL Model Law on Cross-Border Insolvency as fundamentally procedural in focus and describing merits of process of incremental proceduralism). For an argument against such incrementalism, see (Levmore 2010).

TABLE 2.1. *UNCITRAL's Formal Technologies, by Decade*

	1970s	1980s	1990s	2000s	2010–2016	TOTAL
Conventions	2	2	2	3	1	10
Rules	1	2			1	4
Recommendations		2		1	1	4
Model Law Provisions		1		1		2
Model Laws		1	5	2	3	11
Legal Guides		1	1			2
Notes				1		1
Legislative Guides				3	4	7
Practice Guides	0	0	0	1	2	3
Reports	0	0	0	1	4	5
TOTAL	3	9	8	12	16	

Indeed, the implementation of a more expansive mission to "modernize" could only have proceeded on the basis of a broader repertoire of legal technologies.[108] The array of its products over time demonstrate that increasingly it relied on a wide repertoire of technologies to reach issue-areas that had long been regarded as beyond the reach of hard lawmaking in the global arena (Table 2.1).

Three Incrementalisms[109]

A comprehensive overview of UNCITRAL's products reveals a relationship among its more expansive goals, its widening substantive reach, and its elaboration of technologies. On close examination, a further pattern emerges, namely, that in a given issue-area, such as corporate insolvency, the technologies themselves may be arrayed in temporal sequences. Put another way, global development of international law proceeds incrementally.

A substantial scholarly debate weighs the merits of incremental reforms versus great leaps forward. For example, Oona Hathaway[110] argues for the benefits of incremental international lawmaking (Hathaway 2005):

> Rather than confront states immediately with a legal regime that couples challenging goals with strong sanctions for failure to meet them, states can be gradually led toward stronger legal rules. This can be accomplished by starting with relatively weak international rules backed by little or no sanctions that all states feel

[108] By "social technologies," social scientists refer to systematic social means of achieving a particular outcome. A legal technology is a refined social technology adapted to and employed in legal institutions (Halliday 2007). See also Chapter 6.

[109] This section draws from (Block-Lieb and Halliday 2007b).

[110] In this context, Hathaway constructs an integrated theory of international law, and observing that one method for mediating "conflict between commitment and compliance" with international law involves moving "states incrementally down the path toward stronger international rules with true enforcement provisions" (Hathaway 2005: 531).

> comfortable joining, but then gradually pushing states to accept successively stronger and more challenging requirements.[111]

The benefits of incrementalism are, perhaps by definition, only revealed over time. These benefits are also prominent when assessing how to tackle hard cases for global reform. Incremental development of global law is more often championed where law reformers possess limited authority (Cohen 2005)[112] and where the subject is either controversial or technical (or both).

Our empirical study of UNCITRAL's lawmaking over three areas of substantive law (insolvency, secured transactions, international transport) demonstrates that a dynamic model of incrementalism was employed by UNCITRAL and that this policy of incrementalism allowed it simultaneously to expand its ambitions, build legitimacy, and increase its access to other tangible and intangible resources.

UNCITRAL deployed incrementalism in three forms.

Pyramidal incrementalism occurs when an international organization deliberately drafts its norms by ostensibly standing on the shoulders of prior efforts of other IOs. UNCITRAL frequently positioned itself discursively by both endorsing the prior texts of other IOs and partnering loosely with other global lawmakers, including incipient competitors. For example, one commentator contends that the Convention on the International Sales of Goods "would not have been successfully completed had the ground not been leveled by the extensive work done by UNIDROIT in the preparation of The Hague Uniform Laws" and also that similar examples can be found in international transport and arbitration law (Faria 2005). Similarly, in its work on corporate insolvency law, UNCITRAL came late to the topic and it repeatedly insists in its working papers and published documents that it builds upon norms from the Asian Development Bank, IMF, and later World Bank (Block-Lieb and Halliday 2007a). In all these cases, UNCITRAL benefited from prior work, granted respect to other IOs in this issue-area, and appeared intent on turning potential competitors into interlocutors and allies.

Vertical incrementalism occurs when IOs dig more deeply in a particular area over progressive rounds.[113] UNCITRAL's vertical incrementalism is most starkly evidenced with the progressive hardening of legal technologies produced by

[111] *Id.*

[112] Amichai Cohen similarly describes agencies' slow progress in implementing international norms to domestic policy in this way:

> Revolution via bureaucracy will never be considered legitimate. In cases of persistent domestic opposition to the implementation of international law, agencies can only take small steps, constantly seeking to change public perceptions and ideas. Hence, when an agency uses its legitimacy to promote a specific policy, it usually does so through an incremental process of policy changes.

(Cohen 2005,:1107).

[113] Although we are the first to call this sort of progress "vertical incrementalism," we are not the first to note that the incremental development of international law may, and indeed perhaps should, take a path in which agreements slowly harden over time (see, e.g., Hathaway 2005:531).

UNCITRAL on electronic commerce. UNCITRAL's work in this area started quite modestly with its production of a two-page Recommendation on the Legal Value of Computer Records in 1985.[114] Eleven years passed before UNCITRAL promulgated a legal guide on the computerization of commercial practices, but since then UNCITRAL also issued two model laws and one convention on the topic, which build on the earlier recommendation and on each other.[115]

Horizontal incrementalism can be observed when an IO expands the substantive boundaries of the range of topics it seeks to embrace in successive rounds. Moving sideways along a topic's edges, an IO may expand the legal scope of its lawmaking. On three occasions, UNCITRAL began its work in an area of international commercial law by promulgating a convention – sales, transport, and payments.[116] Given the hardness of this sort of legal technology, one might have asked what sort of incremental progress could occur? But with each of these topics – sales, transport, and payments – UNCITRAL's incrementally progressed horizontally across the subject. With payments, UNCITRAL began by promulgating a convention on International Bills of Exchange and International Promissory Notes, then moved to related but not overlapping topics with later model law and conventions – international credit transfers, independent guarantees and stand-by letters of credit, and the assignment of receivables. Similarly, on the topic of international transportation, UNCITRAL first produced the Convention on the Carriage of Goods by Sea (1978)(the "Hamburg Rules"), and later promulgated the Convention on the Liability of Operators of Transport Terminals in International Trade (1991). The latter convention covered issues of liability that had not been addressed in the earlier convention; it also covered the liability of all transport terminals, and was not limited to the liability of terminals located at ports. The Convention on Contracts for the

114 UNCITRAL, *Recommendation on the Legal Value of Computer Records*, UN Doc. No. A/CN.9/265 (1985), www.uncitral.org/pdf/english/texts/electcom/computerrecords-e.pdf [hereinafter Recommendation]. The Commission prepared the Recommendation after considering several reports it had received on the topic. The first, a report from the Secretary-General of the UN entitled "Legal Aspects of Automatic Data Processing," (UN Doc. No. A/CN.9/254), "identified several legal issues relating to the legal value of computer records, the requirement of a 'writing,' authentication, general conditions, liability and bills of lading." *See* UNCITRAL Model Law on Electronic Commerce with Guide to Enactment 1996, With Additional Article 5 *bis* as Adopted in 1998, at 64, ¶ 125 (1999), www.uncitral.org/pdf/English/texts/electcom/05–89450_Ebook.pdf. The Commission also considered a report of the Working Party on Facilitation of International Trade Procedures (WP.4), which had been jointly sponsored by the Economic Commission for Europe and the United Nations Conference on Trade and Development, *id.*, and a report by the UNCITRAL Secretariat entitled "Legal Value of Computer Records" (UN Doc. No. A/CN.9/265).

115 UNCITRAL, Model Law on Electronic Commerce with Guide to Enactment (1996); UNCITRAL, Model Law on Electronic Signatures with Guide to Enactment (2001); United Nations, Convention on the Use of Electronic Communications in International Contracts (2005).

116 If UNCITRAL's claim to the New York Convention on the Enforcement of Commercial Arbitration Awards is to be given credence, there exist four substantive areas in which it followed this strategy.

International Carriage of Goods Wholly or Partly by Sea (2008)(the "Rotterdam Rules"), UNCITRAL's next work on this topic, significantly extended the substantive reach of these earlier products.

UNCITRAL's use of incrementalism not only increased its competitiveness inside the standing lawmaking ecology, but also enabled it simultaneously to expand its own jurisdictional reach, as well as that of the standing ecology. UNCITRAL's boldest projects – its efforts to develop international laws governing electronic communications and e-commerce, and to build and articulate a global consensus on, not simply the coordination of insolvency proceedings that transcend borders, but the substance of domestic insolvency laws – are its most recent efforts. UNCITRAL may not have been viewed as capable or qualified to take on global law reform of this magnitude without first having succeeding in promulgating conventions on international sales, transport, payments, arbitration and dispute resolution, and procurement and project finance.

Examination of multiple steps within a particular area of law reveals that incrementalism is not all of a piece. It involves not one but multiple strategies. Examining the entirety of its record of law reform, it is clear that UNCITRAL worked both vertically within issues to sharpen the focus, and horizontally to broaden the scope of the reach of its international instruments on a subject. Occasionally UNCITRAL worked pyramidally to build, not simply on its own work product, but on the shoulders of law reform efforts promulgated by other IOs, such as the United Nations, UNIDROIT, The Hague Convention, the World Bank, and the IMF In so doing it expanded the scope of the entire standing ecology, while seeking to maintain a delicate balance between maintaining competitive advantage and fostering the perception and sometimes actuality of cooperation.

Furthermore, each of the multiple incrementalisms has distinct logics of action. *Vertical* incrementalism follows a logic of "intensification of action." More intensive development of a topic can take several forms: a move toward more binding international instruments (e.g., from a set of recommendations or principles to a convention), an increased precision in the detail covered over successive rounds of normmaking, or a shift from procedural to substantive topics. *Horizontal* incrementalism follows a logic of "extensification of action." Here, the breadth of a topic or domain is widened. *Pyramidal* incrementalism follows a logic of "layering of action." It explicitly acknowledges that global normmaking frequently involves competition or cooperation among a variety of IOs, each of which may have offered one or another proposal for global norms. Indeed, pyramidal moves may be simultaneously competitive and coordinative. When successive products explicitly or even implicitly build on prior products, often produced by different international organization, then the subsequent steps toward an integration of products in a global consensus take on a pyramidal form. Multiplicities of building blocks are successively forged into more coherent products. And competition is deftly turned into competitive cooperation.

FROM EMERGENCE TO INSTITUTIONALIZATION

In the late nineteenth century a scattering of mainly European IOs and ad hoc conferences explored the promise that international law could be a palliative to international conflict and a lubricant for cross-national trade. A century later those inchoate origins had been transformed into stable ecologies of lawmaking for the entire world, most notably the standing ecology of IOs whose primary goals were the creation of international commercial law.

The emergence of this social space populated by three principal IOs, The Hague Conference, UNIDROIT, and UNCITRAL, exemplify the expansion of law in the international political economy and reveal the dynamics of interactions, settling, and adaptations of the ecology to the thought and practices, economics, and politics of a turbulent 150 years.

The long temporal span of lawmaking ecology formation can be construed in terms of large-scale institutional shifts in markets, states, and law. The increasing volume of trade among Great Powers in the second half of the nineteenth century, the political economies of imperialism, a first wave of economic globalization up to 1913, punctuated by the sharp break of WWI, efforts of the League of Nations to recover, only to be shattered by WWII, and the even more strenuous efforts to build post-War transnational economic and financial institutions, to forestall war, stimulate trade, and manage fiscal crises that spilled over national borders impelled legal responses. The collapse of European empires, the rise of scores of new nations as sovereign economic actors, and quickening globalization of commerce and finance in the last decades of the twentieth century all reshaped economic orders in ways that far surpassed the capacities of extant law to facilitate, regulate, or govern.

Sometimes lagging, sometimes leading, sometimes accompanying far-reaching economic shifts were new generations of political institutions designed to bind states into stable and peaceful international orders. The denouement of a Great Power orchestration of states in 1914–1918, and the ambitious if ultimately failed efforts of the League of Nations to forge a new set of transnational order of international relations, sunk into the cataclysm of WWII and the far more robust effort at post–WWII reconstruction by building new transnational political institutions, with states as their building blocks. The UN, in all its complex proliferation of agencies and organizations, has proved remarkably resilient as an organization of states beyond states, indeed as an enormous ecology of cultural, financial, political, economic, and legal entities in its own right.

Law itself as an institution was inextricably intertwined with these long-term institutional shifts. It was law in the latter half of the nineteenth century that was brought by market actors and championed by legal scholars to stimulate cross-border trade. The legal theories espoused by Jeremy Bentham or David Dudley Field or Max Weber insisted that simplicity, clarity, unity, rationality, utility of law would invigorate expansive markets and rationalize state administration and interstate cooperation. The League of Nations looked to law both to order peaceful relations among states and to energize trading relations across frontiers. The founders of the UN institutionalized law not only in its highest order normative codes, most notably the Universal Declaration of Human Rights, but in its establishment of international courts and the ILC to order relations among states, and later the founding of UNCITRAL to bring all states into alignment with industry to produce TLOs that would produce economic development and growth across the entire world.

This selective portrait of 150 years of lawmaking, and the intensive study of lawmaking issue-ecologies in the following chapters, show that paradigms and models[117] of law and markets, law and development, law and financial stability, legal institutions, and economic growth have bound together states, market actors, and legal actors in the work of legal production. Between the grand sweep of institutions over the *longue durée*, and the everyday practices of national lawmaking and economic activity, have emerged ecologies of lawmaking IOs drawn into sustained interactions on the shared premise that law matters for markets.

The formation and vitality of the standing lawmaking ecology can be observed in persistent boundary work. In order to enter a lawmaking space already populated by the ILC, UNIDROIT, The Hague Conference, and possibly, UNCTAD, UNCITRAL's founders framed its entry, and indeed the entire domain of "international trade lawmaking," by articulating distinctive grounds for its rightful belonging in the lawmaking space, by setting boundaries with enough precision to justify its presence and with enough ambiguity that it neither overtly competed with other IOs nor was excessively constrained in its future work. UNCITRAL's founders carefully constructed the boundaries and internal contours of the lawmaking ecology through a rhetorical positioning that narrowed UNCITRAL's mandate to the reform of "private laws" obstructing "international trade." They emphasized that UNCITRAL would focus on "technical" matters where it would play a "coordinating" role among IOs, yet sufficiently blurring boundaries to enable it to engage in "substantive" lawmaking as a "formulating agency."

The ambiguities inherent in these initial mandates would be later exploited for the considerably more expansive ambitions UNCITRAL's early competitors had originally feared. In moves familiar to historical institutionalists, UNCITRAL would widen its legal scope of aspirations from unifying and harmonizing law to law's modernization. This claim to "modernity" opened up expansive opportunities to pursue lawmaking wherever markets might demand or require "modern" regulation, a scope virtually without limits. Both the move to substantive lawmaking and modernization of laws widened UNCITRAL's landscape of activity and simultaneously expanded the present and future bounds of the entire standing ecology which could now predict a claim to lawmaking jurisdiction in any aspect of market activity.

[117] For a typology of ideas, paradigms, models, and programs, see (Campbell 2004: Chapter 4).

Boundary defense and maintenance can be observed from UNCITRAL's founding moments. While the ILC seemed not inclined to exploit its mandates that might take it into economic law, The Hague Conference and UNIDROIT fought diplomatically and not entirely successfully to preserve their bounds of lawmaking. Yet even UNCITRAL, we shall see (Chapter 9), found itself under threat and fought hard in the 1990s and beyond against new, powerful actors entering the commercial lawmaking space, most particularly the IMF, the World Bank, other regional development institutions, and even UNCTAD.

The never-ending protection of boundaries remains a continuing dynamic in the standing lawmaking ecology in part because exogenous shocks and shifting ideologies required continuing adaptations to ensure survival and relevance. Boundary work also reflects the ever-present search for resources to sustain and amplify its production of legal norms for markets. The three case studies will demonstrate how UNCITRAL constantly attended to its strategic need for critical resources. Where UNIDROIT failed to be assimilated within the UN, we shall see that UNCITRAL from its beginning and at the turn of the twentieth century sought to optimize its relationship with the resource-rich UN, a vast and variegated ecology in its own right. As it expanded its mission to modernization of laws necessitated by global commerce in the twenty-first century, UNCITRAL relied increasingly on industry ecologies as resources: to provide expertise, infrastructure, and other forms of tangible support. Significantly, its leaders worked diligently to position UNCITRAL in close proximity to certain states, most importantly the most powerful global trading nation – the United States. The complex and delicate relationships between the US and this UN body unfold in a relational tension as we observe how the US sought to use UNCITRAL to advance US global trade policy and UNCITRAL sought to appropriate US resources without being captured by US interests.

By expanding boundaries to embrace new issue-areas, by drawing in states at every level of economic development and from all legal families, and by situating itself in close proximity to supra-state, state and industry resources all confronted UNCITRAL with interactional challenges with other lawmaking IOs and actors and ecologies integral to its lawmaking work. Competition stalked UNCITRAL from its founding just as UNCITRAL itself appeared always to be searching for a new competitive edge. Competition for jurisdictional authority over problem and issue-areas, competition for resources, competition for positional centrality in the standing ecology – all threatened fractiousness and even dissolution of the standing ecology forged a half-century earlier.

In part, that interactional fragility was counteracted by cooperative relationships brought into the ecology from earlier and other interactional spaces. In part, it emerged through the community and collective identity of actors brought into close relationships over years of lawmaking deliberations (see Chapter 5). In significant part the centrifugal forces of competition were deliberately resolved through negotiated agreements, sometimes explicitly to recognize that cooperation among competitors could be sustained on particular issues for the benefit of all (see Chapter 7). Competitive cooperation, sometimes managed by short-term alliances, sometimes by long-term divisions of labor, sometimes through incrementalism enabled both standing and issue-ecologies, to persist and maintain production for years and decades.

A key factor in the viability of UNCITRAL and its embedding ecology has been the entrepeneurialism and inventiveness of economic lawmakers. UNCITRAL's redefinition of its identity as a modernizing body and its extension of reach into new areas of trade and and commerce were enabled by its elaboration of a repertoire of legal technologies. Armed with a variety of hard and soft law products, UNCITRAL could respond to great shifts in its institutional contexts by tackling once prohibitively difficult issues with the expectation that it could later broaden and harden its lawmaking. By proceeding incrementally, either horizontally or vertically, UNCITRAL bought for itself considerable flexibility to proceed as the complexity of issues or maturity of law permitted. At the same time the diversity of technologies served internal political purposes, permitting UNCITRAL's leaders and lawmakers to convert competition into mutualities of endeavor through manipulation of the formal properties of its legal repertoire (see Chapter 6). As an ecological move, the technologies gave UNCITRAL added leverage to lay claim to lawmaking jurisdictions at the expense of potential competitors, thereby also shifting their relative centrality as innovative organizations in lawmaking ecology itself.

In the last decade, increasing evidence accumulates that UNCITRAL's long-term partners qua rivals, UNIDROIT and The Hague Conference, are adopting its wide repertoire of technologies. Quite apart from potentially changing relationships among these three IOs dedicated to global lawmaking, a spreading adoption of soft law technologies enables the entire standing lawmaking ecology to prove its expansive adaptability to a widening terrain of market problems.

These ecological politics of UNCITRAL and of other lawmaking actors on the global stage were not and are not politics entirely for their own sake. It is true that organizational viability and centrality can become organizational imperatives on their own. Yet it is certainly the case that UNCITRAL's politics, like those of its potential competitors, were deployed to economic and legal purpose. From early indications in the later nineteenth century of lawmaking IOs that falteringly would be drawn into a collective enterprises, there took shape a purpose to produce a certain kind of *order* (i.e., unified or harmonized and later modernized) by a certain means (i.e., *legal*) in order to foster trade and commerce *transnationally* and *globally*. In short, the work of the lawmaking ecology has been directed to the construction of TLOs, transnational legal orders intended to stimulate trade and commerce.

Much of the politics in the lawmaking ecology turns on what kind of TLOs these would be. At stake was geographical scope – would trade be enhanced by a shift from an Euro-centric order toward a truly global order? At stake was also legal scope – how broadly could UNCITRAL and cognate IOs stake their claims to procedural versus substantive lawmaking? And, if substantive, how expansively would any of these IOs bring law to the farthest reaches of market activity.

UNCITRAL's history and the issue-areas examined in this book show that a politics of scope unfolded over time and issue. Incrementalism in its varieties and combinations became an integral factor in claims for scope, claims often at the expense of other IOs or even other forms of order. Moreover, while the creativity that led to a repertoire of legal technologies was certainly a means of ensuring competitive advantage over other IOs, that repertoire also expanded capacities for TLO-building into places previously thought resistant to the harmonization or modernization of law. Softer legal technologies enabled and expanded prospects for new and more ambitious TLOs.

In a certain sense, therefore, the very competition and cooperation integral to the standing lawmaking ecology pushed the entire enterprise of TLO construction much further than it might have advanced in the absence of those processes. Social processes engendered further legal ordering through an instantiated rhetoric of harmonization and modernization of international commercial law. Although we observe UNCITRAL's increasing centrality in the lawmaking ecology, there is also an overall enlargement of that ecology only partly enabled by increasing demands for international and transnational commercial laws and for the reform of national laws in coordination with these TLOs.

We have seen that both the architecture of TLOs and the social processes that shaped the international lawmaking ecology over more than a century were heavily inflected by geopolitical events and major economic shocks. The manifest failures of political and market orders led to demands for new legal orders that could prevent volatile finance and trade. That is, legal ordering itself was held to be a preventive measure by leading financial powers, their G-7 or G-22 clubs of nations, and the IOs they spawned and supported. From the turn of the twentieth century, therefore, a stimulus for TLO construction or reformation came from tacit theories of institutional weakness in markets, a weakness that might be repaired with TLOs on the laws governing commercial finance, corporate insolvency, trade by sea, electronic commerce, arbitration, and other topics.

Altogether these shifts led UNCITRAL and lawmaking ecologies into a conundrum. As the project of commercial lawmaking drew lawmaking IOs more fully into burgeoning world commerce, the deliberations of IOs were more fully open to the diversity of state and non-state economic interests, to incipient conflicts and contradictions between legal families, and to competition among professions. The stakes of lawmaking rose as the complexity of reaching consensus was compounded.

How then could UNCITRAL and its lawmaking issue-ecologies capitalize on opportunities and resources without falling prey either to stalemate or capture by the world's most powerful economic actors? The impact of these processes on legal outcomes requires an immersion into the interactional intricacies of lawmaking as it confronts quite particular problems of commerce and trade. We turn in the following chapters from the grand scale of standing ecologies of law and markets to targeted lawmaking in issue-ecologies that confronted specific problems in scattered terrains of national markets and international commerce.

3

Issue-Ecologies in Formation

Why does an IO initiate a new stream of work, a new topic for global lawmaking, a new organizational unit for lawmaking activity? It might act innovatively in order to protect or strengthen its dominance in a well-established arena. It might move pre-emptively to forestall potential rivals from moving into territory it seeks to claim for itself. It might proceed to ensure that powerful actors, whether states or non-state actors, continue to channel resources into this particular IO's coffers and chambers. It might take an incremental step forward to correct an earlier failure or maintain an already established momentum. It might widen its compass because new technologies give it the capacity to reach topics previously thought not feasible. It might be prodded into action by exogenous pressures – growing demands for modernized norms, shifting geopolitical pressures, changed ideologies, financial crises.

These questions must be addressed systematically by approaching UNCITRAL's lawmaking not as the experience of an single organization in an amorphous institutional environment to which it unreflexively conforms, but as an actor interacting within and among ecologies in dynamic relationship to each other. More precisely, a lawmaking issue-ecology represents a short-term temporal conjunction between two longstanding ecologies. On the one hand, we have shown in Chapter 2 that UNCITRAL is a centrally placed actor in a half century old ecology of IOs committed to solving problems of international trade and commerce through law. On the other hand, commercial issue-ecologies coexist relatively briefly in adjacency to longstanding industry ecologies. These industry ecologies have a dynamism of their own, persisting as bounded spaces in markets where their work reflects centuries or decades of endeavor to protect goods being shipped by sea, or to protect credit lent to borrowers, or to ensure orderly and fair ways of treating businesses when they fail. While these longstanding law and industry ecologies rise or fall or persist or adapt by their own logics, they do not encounter each other until events or opportunities convince norm entrepreneurs that a problem in one can be solved by an opportunity in the other, or vice versa.

The three issue-ecologies treated in this book represent that moment of short-term conjunction where for several years an ecology concerned with lawmaking in general and another ecology concerned with economic activity in general come into sustained interaction to solve a specific economic problem through law. This chapter therefore pivots toward answering the question: What explains the emergence of a specific issue-ecology formed to create a set of legal standards for the world?

An ecological framing of an answer to this question enables socio-legal observers of law and markets to sift through a welter of facts, events, problems, actors, ideas, organizations in each issue-area to formulate a coherent account of why the lawmaking took the form that empirical research discloses.

First, norm entrepreneurs, both individual and organizational, will seek to define and diagnose a a problem or challenge or shortcoming or barrier in markets that might be mitigated and alleviated by law. Second, actors then compete with each other to draw boundaries around the scope of the problem, the scope of the solution, and thereby the actors who will be considered legitimate participants in the lawmaking that fits the problem. Third, the onset of the lawmaking episode bring into lively engagement the four types of ecology identified in Chapter 1, namely, the standing lawmaking ecology dominated by UNCITRAL, UNIDROIT, and The Hague Conference, the industry ecology that identifies the issue in trade and commerce that industry actors want solved, and the UN ecology, whose vast interacting bundle of constituent agencies may offer cooperation or threaten competition. Fourth, at the early moments of an issue-ecology's formation, it can be predicted that there will be a push to obtain resources adequate to the task. Hence much of the boundary work, much interaction between adjacent ecologies, will be a scramble for resources, sometimes in direct competition with other potential centers of lawmaking generativity.

Indeed, it must be reiterated that one of the qualitative differences between a sociology of international lawmaking and that of national lawmaking is that the former cannot take for granted that a legitimate body, whether a legislature, court, or executive agency, will be the obvious locus of legal solutions to economic problems. A significant contribution of ecology theory to the international is that its openness to uncertainty about the legitimate locus of law for the world problematizes and then postulates a framework for abstracting meaningful explanations of why a given lawmaking ecology managed to assert effectively its jurisdictional claim to norm production in a given issue-area.

The nuanced empirical accounts of the three lawmaking episodes in this chapter reveal the strongly recursive properties of the issue-ecologies in the earliest stages of their lawmaking episodes. Like earlier research on global lawmaking (Halliday and Carruthers 2007b; Halliday and Shaffer 2015b; Block-Lieb and Halliday 2015), a close examination of the onset of lawmaking for carriage of goods, insolvency and secured transactions issues will show how a build-up of pressures in industries get precipitated into lawmaking action that brought state and non-state actors into rounds of diagnostic struggle and prescriptive outcomes, often prefiguring later indeterminacies and contradictions in the legal norms that were the price of the lawmaking endeavor at the outset and at its bid for consensus. In fact, we shall show that the prospect of settlement on a set of international norms, and even more, the probability of their ultimate adoption and implementation, pre-occupied actors struggling to shape an issue-ecology. Anticipation of future rounds of lawmaking, both incremental and adaptive, influenced definitions of the situation, actors invited or discouraged from participating, and the ever present bid for resources.

Issue-ecologies were socially housed in specific organizational sites, namely, UNCITRAL's working groups, and delegated lawmaking tasks by UNCITRAL's Commission. The formation of the three issue-ecologies must be set within the formal and real relationship between the Commission and these working groups. We then turn to examine the onset of lawmaking in the three working groups committed to solve imminent problems in the carriage of goods by sea, business failure, and insufficiencies of credit for market actors.

UNCITRAL'S COMMISSION AND ITS WORKING GROUPS

UNCITRAL's "governing council" is the Commission itself, whose membership is set by the UN's General Assembly on a rotating basis to ensure that a wide range of geopolitical and economic interests are represented within UNCITRAL. When initially created by the General Assembly in 1968, the Commission was composed of twenty-nine member states; that number was increased to thirty-six in 1976, and again to sixty in 2003.

Every summer, the Commission meets, generally for several weeks,[1] either in New York or Vienna (or, in its first few years, Geneva). Like UNCITRAL's working groups, UNCITRAL's Commission meetings are attended by a combination of state and non-state delegations.

A high percentage of member states attend Commission meetings. In 2000 through 2003, more than 90 percent of member states attended Commission sessions. Between 2004 and 2010, attendance ranged from 72 to 87 percent of the membership. Many other states attended as observers. Between 2000 and 2010 these ranged from 13 to 42 states, averaging approximately 27 per session. Thus, on average, delegations from member and observer state delegations attending the Commission together totaled a little over one-third of the world's states.

As with working groups, UNCITRAL allows non-state delegations to observe its Commission meetings. Non-state delegations' attendance also varies from session to

[1] If its work was incomplete by the end of its summer session, however, the Commission might decide to meet for a second time in a year, as it did in December of 2003 to resume discussions on the French Proposal and the Secured Transactions Working Group's deliberations on their draft Legislative Guide (Chapter 9).

session: between 2000 and 2010, between sixteen and thirty-seven non-state delegations have attended. UNCITRAL counts IGOs and NGOs separately and, as a result, makes clear that NGOs substantially outnumber IGOs at each such session.

While the Commission is formally charged as the governing decision-making body within UNCITRAL, in fact, stated delegates, the "real action" at UNCITRAL is "in the working groups" (Int: 6006).[2] From time to time, the Commission creates an additional working group, or reassigns the work of an existing working group, to take on an entirely new subject, and then mostly steps aside. With respect to working groups, the Commission is most proactive during the agenda-setting phase of UNCITRAL projects. The Commission's substantive input is most likely to "occur in the beginning" of a project when it decides "whether a topic should or should not be taken up" by UNCITRAL and, thus, whether a working group should be convened at all (id.). When it does this, the Commission generally also dictates a "mandate" for the working group, setting out both the form and expected scope of the group's work, as we show below. Thereafter, the Commission expects the working group to report to it on its progress on this mandate on an annual basis.

Although the principal engagement with working groups is in their formation and initiation of new programs of work, it should be noted that there is a rhythm to continuing interactions between the Commission and its working groups. Each working group "has to produce so there is something to show to the Commission each year" (Int: 2710). A working group's product may simply be a report of its progress on a draft. Once the working group's work on a legal text is done, the Commission is expected either to ratify the working groups' work product as the work of UNCITRAL as a whole, or to ratify the working group's work product as amended by the Commission, and then forward the ratified text to the Sixth Committee of the UN's General Assembly for its review and ratification. In either case, the "goal of the Commission is to make sure that the Sixth Committee has nothing to do" (Int: 6008).

After it sets a working group's agenda, the Commission often defers to its working groups (Int: 6002, 6006). For example, when the French and Australian delegates to the Transport Working Group complained to the Commission about the treatment of volume contracts in the emerging draft convention, "the Commission referred them back to the working group" (Int: 6006). Such deference can follow from the Commission's reluctance to upset a working group consensus that gets painstakingly constructed over many years. But this deference is also likely a function of the composition of delegations to the Commission. The Commission sessions "look like" working group sessions, "because the same people attend" the Commission as had attended the working group, although it is generally the "leading delegates from the working group that attend the Commission's annual meetings" (Int: 6008). This deference does not preclude the Commission from engaging in detailed review,

[2] This notation signifies an unpublished interview, on file with authors, that has been anonymized.

however, especially after a working group presented it with a final product. Sometimes the Commission's obligation to review and ratify final drafts, and its authority to ratify after making amendments to the draft, was construed by the Commission (or at least by the delegates in attendance at the Commission meeting) as an opportunity for a final "bite at the apple," as one of us observed first hand in the Commission meeting convened to review the "completed" Legislative Guide on Insolvency Guide. Yet this last-ditch expedient rarely succeeds.

TRANSPORTING GOODS BY SEA

The Pall of Failures

A long tradition marks the recourse to law as a means of resolving difficulties that arise in the transport of goods from their point of production across international waters to the point of consumption (Braithwaite and Drahos 2000: Chapter 17). A century-long history of that relationship juxtaposes an early long-standing TLO with a series of subsequent failed efforts to adapt to changes in industries and markets.

When the more than one hundred delegates met at UNCITRAL in New York, April 2002, a pall of failure hung over the proceedings. Repeated efforts over thirty years had been made to produce a new transnational legal order that would modernize the carriage of goods across oceans from one port to another. More than 75 years earlier, carriers and shippers had reached a "grand bargain" in the form of The Hague Rules, but over that span of time much about trade and seafaring transport had changed. Market and technical changes had made the need for reform apparent since the mid-1970s, but despite multiple efforts to reform and revise this convention, none had succeeded. The question before UNCITRAL was acute: Could it accomplish what other IOs, and indeed UNCITRAL itself, had not been able to manage over decades of effort?

Law on carrying goods over oceans seeks fundamentally to solve a problem of liability: If something goes wrong between the port at which the goods were loaded onto a ship and the port at which the goods are unloaded from the ship, who is liable for damage to the goods? The ship owner? The ship's officers? The ship's builder? The authorities responsible for navigation buoys and signals? The owner of the goods that are being shipped, whether the goods' seller or the buyer waiting for arrival of the goods at the other end of the voyage? The party that packaged, loaded, or unloaded the goods? Who can bring suit and who bears the burden of proof? In what courts should liability claims be litigated or arbitrated? Not least, who pays? Ship owners? Insurance companies? Shippers?

All these questions historically had pitted two principal sets of industry actors against each other: *carriers*, or the owners and operators of vessels; and *shippers*, the owners of the goods transported by sea. Carriers have an interest in minimizing their liability if ships are delayed, break down and founder, or if the goods are badly stowed.

Shippers have an interest in maximizing their compensation if the goods they load on ships in mint condition turn out to lose value or get destroyed during the voyage.

The transport of goods by sea is embedded in a wider web of transport. To get goods to docks for the sea transport leg, or to get goods from docks to the point of distribution, requires other forms of transport – by road and rail, by waterways such as canals and rivers, or by air. In principle, the law covering transport of goods by sea might either stand by itself as a segregated area of regulation, unrelated to whatever happened before or after goods arrived or departed from ports, or the law covering transport of goods by sea might be embedded in a broader legal scheme that covers the liability of goods from door (where goods were manufactured) to door (where goods are distributed for sale). If port-to-port, then only ships matter. If door-to-door, then ships and trucks and trains all matter and there could be a different transnational or national legal order covering each type of transportation. The industry interests at stake in transport of goods therefore include not only seagoing carriers and shippers, but potentially also trucks and railways and airlines. Hence, "everyone has their own unimodal scope of application they want to protect," said a specialist (Int: 6006).

Most actors involved in the transport of goods in most countries are private or state-owned enterprises. But the ability of industries to get goods to market safely and cheaply is also a macroeconomic problem for states. If a state has major seafaring industries, if it has a large ship-building, ship-owning, or sea transport sector, then it has an interest in protecting that industry from liabilities that would reduce competitiveness and profitability. If a state is a net exporter, because it manufactures goods, or grows or extracts commodities or other materials, and relies on carriers from other nations to transport these goods, then the exporting state will want its domestic industries to be protected from careless or inferior nautical carriers.

These national interests vary across levels of development and over time. While ship owners might have been located predominantly in developed nations in the nineteenth and twentieth centuries, the location of carrier nations has shifted. So, too, have national cargo interests as trading patterns and development levels have also changed.

Here, then, in principle, are the major actors in the maritime transport ecology (Table 3.1): the carriers by sea (ships); the shippers (manufacturers, freight forwarders); carriers by land, air, or inland waterway; and states. To these must be added the interests of the lawyers who practice maritime law and who preside over both the drafting of contracts of carriage and the rules governing their implementation in practice; and the insurers who issue contracts of insurance for both ship owners and shippers of goods.

These interests, in turn, frame the major fault-lines that have cut across the drafting of maritime law for the past century:[3] Will liability standards favor carriers or shippers?

[3] Since the middle of the nineteenth century, ocean liner conferences arose to contain competition and permit carriers to better "manage" the supply of ocean carriage (Faria 2009; Sjostrom 2004). Liner shipping brought order (or at least a predictable schedule) to the world of shipping, but it also enabled the proliferation of conferences throughout the world (id.). While shippers complained of liners' buildups in market power and threatened to bring suit,

TABLE 3.1. *Actors in Industry and Lawmaking Ecologies*

Working Groups	Transport	Corporate Insolvency	Secured Transactions
Industry and Lawmaking Issue-Ecologies	*Carriers* (Ship owners, ship operators) Shippers (exporters, importers) *Insurance* *Maritime lawyers/ law firms* *Freight forwarders* *Unimodal carriers* (Land, waterways, air) *States*	Corporations *Lawyers, legal academics, judges* *Accountants* Banks Trade Creditors *Labor* *States*	Banks Other Lenders Trade creditors *Lawyers, legal academics, judges* Business Debtors Consumers *States*
Standing Lawmaking Ecologies	General: *UNCITRAL* Specialized: IMO *UNCTAD* European Commission	General: *UNCITRAL* Hague Conference on International Law Specialized: *IMF* *World Bank* *Asian Development Bank* *European Bank for Reconstruction and Development*	General: *UNCITRAL* *UNIDROIT* Specialized: *World Bank* *IMF* *Asian Development Bank* European Bank for Reconstruction and Development European Commission

Note: Italicized actors are those that were present in UNCITRAL's Working Groups on transport, corporate insolvency, and secured transactions.

Will international conventions be confined to seagoing transport, or will they embrace land legs as well? To these relatively narrow questions add much larger questions of the relative market power of carriers, as well as questions regarding trade growth and economic development among shippers and, ultimately, nations. Will carriers continue to enjoy a stranglehold on the market for seagoing transport? Will shippers' interests in exporting and importing goods continue to be diminished by high costs of carriage or

investigations launched by the US and UK governments resulted in government supervision of conference practices and conference's exempt status under competition laws (Faria 2009), a status that persists in the US and only very recently was lifted by the European Union in 2008. With this market power, carriers negotiated contractual provisions widely exculpating their risk of loss during ocean voyages (Faria 2009; Yancey 1983). Conventions on international transport by sea were, from the start, aimed at regulating these contracts and thus this market power.

will trade flourish? This seemingly arcane area of the law therefore unfurls into a veritable cockfight for economic dominance in a global marketplace.

A post-WWI settlement sought to get beyond law that protected even the most reckless misconduct and defense of carriers in the nineteenth century (Faria 2009; Sturley 1991; Yancey 1983). The first international effort to standardize bills of lading and to create minimum mandatory loss liability rules, commonly known as The Hague Rules,[4] was drafted initially by the International Law Association (ILA),[5] revised by the *Comité Maritime International* (CMI),[6] and later formally adopted at an international conference sponsored by the Belgian government. Widespread adoption of The Hague Rules did not occur until after 1937, when the US Congress adopted its Carriage of Goods by Sea Act (COGSA), which closely resembles The Hague Rules (Sturley 1991). By the beginning of WWII most of the world's shipping nations had adopted The Hague Rules (Faria 2009: 287; see also Sturley 1991).

Shifts in markets and technology prompted extensive litigation in London over The Hague Rules, which in turn led interested actors to press for revisions to The Hague Rules, known in the industry as the Visby Protocol.[7] Also drafted by the CMI in the late 1950s and early 1960s, the Visby Protocol purported to "modernize" The Hague Rules but, covering only a handful of topics, the Protocol changed little. It largely reaffirmed the barriers to carrier liability set in The Hague Rules and its carrier-friendly provisions. It did not enter into force until 1977 and the thirty or so countries acceding to its terms are mostly also parties to The Hague Rules.

The rise of a developing nations' bloc in geopolitics, crystallized as the Group of 77 (G-77) in the 1960s, brought the long-established ascendancy of carrier nations under scrutiny. The UN's Conference on Trade and Development (UNCTAD) took up the issue of liner conferences in the late 1960s and early 1970s (Faria 2009). A liner conference is simply an agreement among carriers to provide scheduled services and rates for a particular trade route. Historically the conferences had acted as price-fixing cartels of carriers from Northern Europe including the United

4 Formally, the Brussel Convention for the Unification of Certain Rules of Law Relating to Bills of Lading (Aug. 25, 1924).

5 The ILA is a private organization founded in 1873 for "the study, clarification and development of international law, both public and private, and the furtherance of international understanding and respect for international law" (International Law Association Constitution, at ¶ 1).

6 The CMI, formed originally in 1897, was and continues to be a highly influential maritime international industry group whose full members included national associations, sometimes of maritime lawyers only and sometimes of several industry interests, and whose consultative members included insurance bodies and the International Chamber of Shipping. From the late nineteenth century, the CMI had significantly influenced private international conventions on the subject of international transport. After World War I it brought draft conventions to the government of Belgium, which would then convene a diplomatic conference to produce a multilateral treaty.

7 Protocol to Amend the Convention for the Unification of Certain Rules of Law Relating to Bills of Lading (February 23, 1968), https://treaties.un.org/doc/publication/unts/volume%201412/volume-1412-i-23643-english.pdf.

Kingdom since the latter half of the nineteenth century (Munari 2012), and were viewed by the latter half of the twentieth century as an important contributor to trade imbalances at that time (United Nations 1963).

UNCTAD promulgated its Convention on a Code of Conduct for Liner Conferences in 1974.[8] The Code enjoyed support among developing nations, in large part due to its market-sharing formula stipulating that, in trade between any two countries, 40 percent of the seafaring carriage should be provided by each country and the remaining 20 percent provided by "third party" carriers flagged by neither of the two trading nations. The Code of Conduct entered into force in 1984, despite opposition by the US, but was not viewed as effective in breaking the liner conferences. Important developing nations, mostly located in Latin America, declined to ratify the Code of Conduct, preferring to promote their own national carriers who, through regional market power, had succeeded in securing more than the 40 percent guaranteed by the Code. By 1992, the Code was largely abandoned.

Before UNCTAD had completed its work on the Code of Conduct, UNCITRAL in the late 1960s entered the maritime lawmaking arena for the first time to draft what were to become the Hamburg Rules. Unlike the CMI-sponsored Hague and Hague-Visby Rules, the UNCITRAL initiative was driven by the interests of smaller, shipper nations eager to get their goods to market on more favorable terms (Int: 6002, 6003; see also Faria 2009: 297). After ten years of deliberation, UNCITRAL succeeded in promulgating the Hamburg Rules in 1978.[9] At an international conference held in Hamburg to consider its terms, the draft convention was signed by sixty-eight of the seventy-eight states present, a little less than half of the UN member states at the time. Once again, this exercise of global normmaking produced only a pyrrhic victory for developing nations. The thirty-four contracting states represented about two percent of world trade (Int: 6005). This bloc of mostly African and smaller countries on other continents included no major international players, indeed "no significant maritime country adopted them" (Int: 6003, 6008, 6012). The Hamburg Rules entered into force in 1992, despite the absence of support from the US, France, Norway, Australia, and Canada, among others, who continued to look to The Hague Rules, the Visby Protocol, or some domestic variation of the two. By the 1990s, roughly 90 percent of the world's trade was still governed by The Hague-Visby Rules.

Not to be outdone by UNCITRAL, in the mid-1970s UNCTAD initiated an ambitious effort to rationalize transport of goods through a multimodal convention that would simultaneously apply a single comprehensive regulatory system to transport door-to-door and incorporate all modes of transport – land, sea, and air.

8 Code of Conduct for Liner Conferences (April 6, 1974).

9 Formally known as the United Nations Convention on the Carriage of Goods by Sea (March 30, 1978).

Pragmatically, this effort placed UNCTAD and UNCITRAL in direct competition, each seeking to modernize the law of international transport, each purporting to reflect the interests of developing countries. It also positioned UNCTAD to take on the CMI and UNIDROIT, each of which earlier had attempted to draft a convention on what was then referred to as "combined transport," although these other draft conventions "never went beyond the drafting stage" due to a lack of support from the US and other countries (Faria 2009: 302, n. 194).

The premise of UNCTAD's Multimodal Convention, said a skeptic, was that "sea transport was designed to operate against the interests of developing nations" (Int: 6003) and in favor of large, multinational multimodal operators.[10] UNCTAD aspired to a uniform system where "the carrier will be liable for the whole journey wherever loss or damage occurs. The advantage is that no one has to prove where it occurred. If the goods are lost or damaged, the carrier is liable" (id.). Although the logic of the impetus for a Multimodal Convention seemed unimpeachable, road and rail transport industries strongly opposed it (Int: 6002). Said one maritime specialist: "unimodal interests didn't want to give up their systems and take on a new system" (Int: 6006). In fact, said an international civil servant, unimodal "carriers of different sorts go crazy because they already have their own deals – they would lose all their bailiwicks and economic controls" (Int: 6008).

The Multimodal Convention required thirty contracting parties to enter into force, but only thirteen states acceded to its terms.[11] According to a maritime lawyer, "it never entered into force. It is not likely to. It has no real supporters. It is a convention that underwent a process and sat on the shelf. It didn't catch anyone's imagination" (Int: 6011).

Confronted with this succession of competitive failures, how can the initiation of yet another issue-ecology of lawmaking be explained? The explanations can be found in the perceptions of the primary actors at the center of the new normative order proposed by UNCITRAL. They articulate their diagnoses of presenting situations, their constructions of ways problems might be solved, in terms of shifts in both industry and law. Core players in the UNCITRAL reform initiative from the late 1990s to the roll-out of UNCITRAL's draft convention now referred to as the Rotterdam Rules[12] paint a portrait of cumulative changes in seafaring, communications, packaging, balances of market power, organizational fortunes, and legal regimes that required only a spark or two to precipitate concerted action.

10 United Nations Conference on Trade and Development, The Economic and Financial Consequences of the Entry into Force of the Hamburg Rules and the Multimodal Convention, UNCTAD Doc. No. TD/B/C.4/315/Rev.1 (1991).

11 United Nations Conference on Trade and Development, Convention on International Multimodal Transport, UN Doc. No. TD/MT/CONF/17 (Nov. 12–30, 1979 and May 8-24, 1980).

12 UNCITRAL promulgated the draft, formally named the UN Draft Convention on Contracts for the International Carriage of Goods Wholly or Partly by Sea, in 2009. Because the diplomatic conference convened to consider the draft convention was held in Rotterdam, the convention has come to be known as the Rotterdam Rules (Sturley 2009).

Facilitating Circumstances

From industry came far-reaching changes in shipping itself that altered exposure to liability and flexibility in agreements between shippers and carriers. In the past, when a ship left port, the shipowner could no longer instruct the ship's master, thus justifying the provision in The Hague Rules exculpating carriers' for loss due to the "act, neglect, or default of the master, mariner, pilot, or the servants of the carrier in the navigation or in the management of the ship" (Int: 6012). New technological advances in satellite-based communications now enabled shippers and carriers and ships' captains to communicate throughout a voyage. "Ship owners can communicate constantly" (Int: 6012). Ship owners could no longer credibly argue that they were not in control of the ship throughout the voyage.

How goods are packaged for shipment has also changed drastically. From the 1970s to the 1990s, major shipping lines significantly increased the proportion of goods that were shipped in containers from door-to-door.[13] Unless the buyer and seller were both located in ports, this meant that sea carriage increasingly was linked to carriage by rail, by road, or by air. A CEO of Maersk, a major shipping company, estimated that 30–40 percent of their goods included land and sea legs, not only from Rotterdam to New York but from Berlin to Detroit. Despite this change in economic relationships, liability regimes remained tackle-to-tackle (as with The Hague Rules), or port-to-port (as in the Hamburg Rules), rather than door-to-door (Int: 6002).

The balance of commercial power shifted over the twentieth century in the negotiations between merchants and ship owners. In the nineteenth and early twentieth centuries, several large carriers dominated the global market; moreover, several States exempted liner conferences from the application of their competition laws. By the latter stages of the twentieth century huge multinational shippers, such as Samsung, GM, Toyota, Ikea, Volkswagen, Lenovo, and Wal-Mart, had the economic power to negotiate deals with maritime carriers in favor of shippers. Although the liner conferences had historically looked to prohibit this sort of negotiation over rates for carriage, by the mid-1980s regulators in the US and Europe began to re-examine the immunities these conferences enjoyed from application of antitrust and competition laws (Clyde and Reitzes 2007; Fusillo 2003).

Deregulation in the mid-1980s provided shippers greater leverage in their negotiation with conferences, permitting "service contracts" between shippers and carriers in which a shipper "makes a commitment to provide a certain volume or pattern of cargo over a fixed time period."[14] Rather than rely on standardized

[13] Indeed, UNCTAD links much of the globalization of trade to the phenomena of containerization. See United Nations Conference on Trade and Development, Review of Maritime Transport, Ch. 1, Developments in International Seaborne Trade, at 22 (2013), http://unctad.org/en/PublicationChapters/rmt2013ch1_en.pdf.

[14] This deregulation came about through enactment of legislation in the US, namely the 1984 Shipping Act, §3(19). See also Ocean Shipping Reform Act of 1998.

rates for the number and size of packages to be carried, this new US law enabled shippers with bargaining power to break away from standard rate sheets and negotiate favorable deals with carriers in return for commitments to ship a specified volume of goods over a defined period (Int: 6012). "Rather than the carrier with his bill of lading telling the shipper to take it or leave it, the big shippers could dictate their own terms" (Int: 6007). With this deregulatory action, an age-old asymmetry in market power had been re-equilibrated. A new international convention might provide the occasion for law to catch up with market practices.

Deregulation of aspects of longstanding US shipping law led many to press for broader legislative reform. The Maritime Law Association (MLA) in the US mobilized in the mid-1990s to amend the US Carriage of Goods by Sea Act (COGSA). On the premise that COGSA, adopted in 1937, was "outdated" (Int: 6014), carriers set to work with the MLA to draft a new law. When representatives of the MLA took their draft law to Congress, they were told by Washington lawmakers "to bring us a deal between carriers and shippers or we won't do anything" (Int: 6014). A newly formed body to represent carriers, the World Shipping Council, therefore approached the National Industrial Transportation League, an industry association of truckers and railroads, and in early 2000 "we hammered out an agreement of what we would like to see – a negotiated carrier-shipper deal within the US. It was pretty clear that nothing would happen in Congress without both interests agreeing" (Int: 6014).

At the very moment of agreement between industry groups within the US, however, the initiative stalled. On the one side, the last two major US shipping lines, Sealand and American President Lines, were sold to foreign interests; as a result, there were few domestic advocates for carrier interests. On the other side, it was known by US reformers that international efforts were again gathering impetus and it seemed unwise for the US to proceed unilaterally when multilateral negotiations opened up a channel for the US to assert its imprint on a global set of rules (Int: 6014). Lawyer and industry activists in the US, turned their energies from Capitol Hill to Vienna, where UNCITRAL is headquartered.

International transport lawyers were also restive about the state of the law at the end of the twentieth century. The law seemed increasingly unsettled and non-uniform with a proliferation of overlapping conventions and weakly institutionalized TLOs, none of which commanded a preponderance of support. Said a CMI leader,

> The system was beginning to fracture with The Hague, Hague-Visby, and Hamburg Rules, as well as variations on those enacted by particular countries. So the view was that it wasn't very tidy and we were losing international uniformity. In shipping, international uniformity is a great mantra. You want to know wherever you are doing business [that] the same conditions apply.
>
> (Int: 6010)

Even worse, numbers of nations – Canada, South Korea, Liberia, New Zealand, Russia, and China – had either acceded to no treaty or revoked accession to The Hague Rules, instead having enacted domestic legislation that picked and chose from provisions of the conventions that others were bound to.

Reform seemed intractable. The two UN bodies with claims to jurisdiction over the topic of international transport had between them attempted three draft conventions, yet the preeminent convention continued to be The Hague Rules. It was also clear that reconciliation of the competing private interests of carriers and shippers was absolutely necessary to any resolution of competing economic and national interests on this front, but that sort of brokering would be difficult in the face of a long secular decline in lawmaking influence by CMI. Although the CMI had been a "driving force" behind The Hague Rules and the Visby Protocol (Int: 6010), by the late twentieth century it found itself "impotent" – without a diplomatic partner and unable to produce any international instrument for itself (Int: 6002). After World War II, Belgium "abdicated" its historic diplomatic role on issues of maritime law and policy in favor of the UN, most notably to the UN's International Maritime Organization (IMO). This left the CMI unable to call a diplomatic conference for any draft convention it might prepare, unless it could find another nation or IO to act as its sponsor. "The CMI lost its role. So the only possibility was for the CMI to liaise with another UN organ and to offer its services for the preparation of an international convention" (Int: 6012). "Unless it engaged the UN," said a CMI veteran, "it wouldn't get anywhere. … Without a partner, CMI could not have produced rules for seaway bills" (Int: 6002). Throughout its existence, the IMO, however, had nearly exclusively focused on issues of public international law.

Precipitating Events

Confluences of forces for change can occur over the longterm, sometimes intersecting, and sometimes not, until one or two precipitating events propel nations, industry groups, and norm entrepreneurs into a new episode of global normmaking. For the transnational law governing carriage of goods by sea, several events converged to precipitate concerted action by diverse interest groups, IOs, and states.

As the world's largest trading nation, the US exerted an out-sized impact on the new episode of transport reforms. However, the US government had made clear that it had no interest in an industry fight over a technical area of trade law. In the event, it was not Congress but the US federal judiciary that dramatically concentrated the minds of US maritime lawyers and the industry they represented. In 1995, the US Supreme Court handed down its decision in *Sky Reefer*,[15] regarded as "a terrible blow to the maritime industry by US lawyers" (Int: 6003). The effect of *Sky Reefer*

[15] Vimar Seguros y Reaseguros, SA v. M/V Sky Reefer, 515 U.S. 528 (1995).

was to "take cases out of US courts and put them in Japan or Hong Kong [or elsewhere] where there was no connection with the goods or [with] buyers or sellers but in the interests of those who owned the vessels" (Int: 6003). Exclusive jurisdiction clauses in carriage of goods contracts usually identified either New York or London as the forum of choice, but *Sky Reefer* meant that no one would choose New York law for fear that the clause would be construed to bounce the case halfway around the world. After *Sky Reefer,* parties were more likely to choose English law as governing the transaction. Industry actors feared that the Supreme Court's decision meant that "business would flow from New York to London as a consequence" (Int: 6011). US lawyers were determined to get rid of *Sky Reefer* but Congress had made clear to industry actors that the legislative channel was blocked. US reformers were also acutely aware that CMI had sprung into active reform deliberations in 1997 with the intent of crafting new global norms if only it could find a suitable diplomatic partner. *Sky Reefer* quickened the concern of US lawyers with CMI efforts.

Sky Reefer also created anxiety within international communities. The CMI feared US unilateralism. New US legislation would hasten the disintegration of international law, it was thought, by reinforcing a looming trend toward regional and even national solutions to long unresolved issues. Said a CMI official, "CMI considered this more disunification" (Int: 6002). While US domestic legislation would have solved domestic problems created by *Sky Reefer,* it would not have produced the same effect as a multilateral convention. Indeed, new US legislation would have detracted from the "degree of certainty" so craved by carriers (Int: 6014, 6002).

But CMI had an historical association less with the US than with Continental European and British maritime interests. Thus, a degree of regional rivalry had to be managed alongside the full recognition that no set of global norms stood a chance of widespread adoption if the US was not part of the multilateral settlement. "Unless the US is a party to a convention," stated a key CMI lawyer, "the prospects of other countries adopting it on a wide scale are much reduced" (Int: 6002). The failure of the US to adopt the Hamburg Rules served as a warning lesson to would-be reformers.

> The US was working on domestic legislation and the feeling was that if the US proceeded with a new act then the moment would be lost for an international agreement in this area. The US has so much of a history of using its rules internationally, forcing them on other countries, and the US is such an important international trade that it would shut down international efforts.
>
> (Int: 6006)

The gathering pace of change also concentrated the minds of US reformers, who had little hope for progress in Congress. Progress in an international arena would require new, more international alliances. "CMI was in the back of our minds ...

and we realized we needed action" if we were to be actors on the international stage (Int: 6014). For that to happen, the senior official in the US State Department division responsible for international private commercial law insisted that industry's voice had to be heard. State wanted no repeat of an academic-led delegation like that which previously had contributed to the failed Hamburg Rules (Int: 6005).

But industry involvement required more than an emancipation from academics. US carriers and shippers had to agree among themselves before the US could bring a unified voice to international negotiations. With the agreement in 2000 between the World Shipping Council and the National Industrial Transportation League, both industry groups could jointly approach the State Department and Department of Transportation and declare, "if the US is going to involve itself [in a new international convention], here is a way forward" (Int: 6014).

Convenors of the domestic US agreement immediately sent it to CMI, but by that time CMI's draft was almost complete. To meet UNCITRAL's urgency, and to insert the US fully into the intensifying international negotiations, the US State Department official proposed to UNCITRAL that if UNCITRAL didn't itself have the time, energy, or expertise to produce a draft maritime convention in short order, it should ask CMI to lay its draft on the table of UNCITRAL's newly formed Working Group on Transport (Int: 6005).

This flurry of action, thus, brought a new assemblage of actors into a new conjunction of industry and issue-ecologies. That convergence led to intensive interactions to orchestrate arrays of competitive and cooperative relationships between these ecologies, to demarcate the scope of issues to which they would attend and the actors they would include and exclude, and to obtain, combine, and control the resources key actors perceived critical to create a new legal order for carriage of goods by sea that would be widely adopted by industry, states, and professions.

Initializing a Transport Ecology

An intertwining of key actors in different ecologies brought into play a kaleidoscope of diagnostic framings of problems. Could actors find sufficient overlap and agreement in their problem-solving quests? Would they be able to forge cooperative relationships that ensured sufficient resources to bring a lawmaking project to completion while concomitantly overcoming incipient competition among several leading actors?

From the maritime industry, we have seen, came perceptions that unilateralism by powerful states, such as the US, and regional fragmentation from Scandinavia and elsewhere, would have "a disunifying effect" (Int: 6002). The multiplication of weak legal orders, it was said, impeded international commerce, erecting trade barriers, and increasing costs. But for CMI, as the most established representative certainly of the carrier side of industry, this was more than a matter of harmonization to produce smoother trading relations. CMI saw an opportunity to modernize international transport law far beyond the however laudable goal of modernizing bills of lading. When CMI surveyed members of national maritime law associations in 1999 to ask whether they had an interest in modernization or harmonization a consensus emerged that "it was time" for both (Int: 6007).[16]

Within the UN, both UNCITRAL and UNCTAD had claims to maritime lawmaking and both were potential partners with CMI. CMI had hoped that it might work closely with UNCTAD in the 1980s to bridge the gap between The Hague-Visby Rules, which were favorable to carriers, and the Hamburg Rules, which favored shippers. But UNCTAD would not meet it halfway, said CMI leaders. UNCTAD was at that time still optimistic that the Multimodal Convention and the Hamburg Rules might come into force and benefit developing countries, which were predominantly shippers. Why should it work to compromise those earlier efforts?

UNCITRAL, in the meantime, had been tracking developments within CMI. UNCITRAL's Secretary, who knew well the CMI President, attended some CMI meetings and was kept abreast of CMI's expanding ambitions for a new episode of maritime lawmaking. UNCITRAL's interests in picking up the baton of lawmaking leadership stemmed in part from its generic commitment to harmonization and modernization of international commercial law, whatever market issues might arise. Further, UNCITRAL could point to its own history – in the 1970s its unsuccessful but nevertheless plausible claim to a lawmaking role in the Hamburg Rules initiative for transport of goods by sea, and in the early 1990s in its forward-looking efforts to anticipate demand for law to govern electronic commerce. Maritime bills of lading presented an obvious starting point. But they did not take it very far, certainly not as far as CMI's members were seeking. Moreover, both industry actors and diagnosticians of legal orders governing international trade pointed out that many gaps existed in legal orders. Many countries did not have adequate or modern transport law that articulated with international trade. Conflicts and gaps between different legal regimes, between sea and land, and different forms of land transport, made carriage of goods across the world exceptionally complex at best and dislocated at worst.

The interests of the US transport industry and its maritime lawyers coincidentally were being reconciled on its national stage, within the US itself between potential industry rivals, and also internationally, as US lawyers contributed to CMI's evolving reform agenda.

Not content to wait for other actors to be first movers, CMI set up a steering subcommittee in 1998 to outline steps toward reforms that could replace Hague and Hague-Visby. An international subcommittee of CMI convened a series of meetings

[16] UN Doc. No. A/CN.9/476 (Mar. 31, 2000); United Nations Commission on International Trade Law, Thirty-third session, New York, Transport, at12–14 (June 12–July 7, 2000).

in 2000 to which is invited "different sectors of industry" to roundtable consultations on directions of change. To CMI's surprise, UNCITRAL's Secretariat informed CMI leaders and the UNCITRAL Commission that it was seeking authorization to set up a Working Group on Transport Law as early as June 2001 so that the Working Group could actually begin work in April 2002 in a new lawmaking venture (Int: 6002).

At this juncture it became apparent that the opening of a fresh lawmaking episode entailed a struggle to obtain resources and for leading actors to discover what kinds of cooperation might be possible among them. The norm entrepreneurs leading CMI, UNCITRAL, and the US, many already connected through their industry, professional, and academic networks, sought to create a new deliberative space or arena that in effect would constitute a short-term lawmaking ecology in which stable relationships could produce an outcome that had eluded the maritime industry for almost a generation.

Some rightly viewed UNCITRAL's rush as a sudden move to pre-empt its UN rival, UNCTAD. CMI leaders suspected, however, that this haste was also a bid for a larger slice of the UN budget and additional staffing allocations. With the support of the UN's chief legal counsel, Hans Corell (Int: 9123), UNCITRAL's Secretariat was at that moment seeking to upgrade its status within the UN system. By showing UN senior management that a critical industry in global trade was demanding law that fit twenty-first century commerce, UNCITRAL's senior staff could justify its institutional upgrading and its greater centrality to UN activity given the UN's growing intentionality of mobilizing law to solve global problems. UNCITRAL needed resources to match its ambitions and to align itself effectively with UN-wide shifts in ideology and orientation.

For UNCITRAL to satisfy its organizational impulses within the UN, rapid and effective action required one or more industry partners. UNCITRAL's Commission had already expressed reservations about a wide-ranging transport law initiative on grounds that the issues were "numerous and complex" and reform would "strain the limited resources of the Secretariat."[17] A mutuality of purpose offered to UNCITRAL all the expertise concentrated in CMI's membership, its longstanding lawmaking authority, and its pragmatic capacities to offer tangible support to lawmaking and the more critical subsequent phase of institutionalizing new legal norms in all the national sites of its member associations. A private-public partnership permitted UNCITRAL to work closely with an industry group of exceptional competence and an august past. An alliance with CMI empowered UNCITRAL to claim industry insight and proximity to the pragmatic challenges of contemporary trade by sea, without losing its access to developing nations' wide participation in the process of law reform.

[17] Op. cit., p.2.

UNCITRAL, in turn, offered CMI the auspices it had long lost. For decades, CMI had found no state or international organization to succeed Belgium as a reliable partner. Since neither the IMO nor UNCTAD would partner with it, CMI turned to UNCITRAL. A strong cooperative relationship with UNCITRAL offered CMI a new arena in which to marry its expertise and experience with the legitimacy and diplomatic heft of a long-sought UN partner. It could shed its reputation as "an old boys club" and become a global citizen (Int: 6008).

UNCITRAL agreed to partner with CMI, although initially UNCITRAL sought only narrow technical advice from CMI. CMI had made a small contribution to UNCITRAL's Model Law on Electronic Commerce (1996), ensuring that this Model Law might include fundamental documents of maritime trade such as the bill of lading in electronic form (Clift 1999). UNCITRAL's Working Group on Electronic Commerce viewed CMI's interest in bills of lading as a prominent example of electronic negotiable instruments, the creation of which could be facilitated by international legislation focused on e-commerce and electronic communications.

By 2000, UNCITRAL signaled it was ready to expand its lawmaking claims far beyond bills of lading, a move which coincided substantially with CMI's expansive vision. UNCITRAL's Secretary urged CMI to complete a draft treaty by the end of 2001 so it could be put on the table at the first session of UNCITRAL's newly authorized Working Group in early 2002 (Int: 6002).

An intersection of ideals (harmonization, modernization, reduction of commercial trade barriers) and interdependencies of interests (business pragmatics, national competitive advantage, an expanded footprint of lawmaking) and resources (money, staff, legitimacy, expertise, infrastructure) did not, however, demarcate the scope of jurisdictional claims to solve through law underlying industry issues. From the first moments of caucusing together in UNCITRAL's Transport Working Group, a large array of actors, led by a dominant few, sought to draw the substantive boundaries around which topics were to be drawn within the lawmaking ecology and which would be excluded. In so doing, these formative discussions substantially determined which industry and other actors would be welcome inside the lawmaking ecology and which would be quietly or explicitly excluded.

By inviting CMI to place a draft convention on the table at the first session of UNCITRAL's Working Group on Transport Law in June 2002, UNCITRAL appeared to surrender its lawmaking authority to the agenda setting of a private industry group, albeit an international nongovernmental organization. Indeed, both friends and critics of CMI and UNCITRAL later referred to the Rotterdam Rules as "the Son of CMI," "inspired by CMI," and described them as involving perhaps the most notable occasion on which UNCITRAL "out-sourced a major piece of work" to a private group (Int: 6002, 6010). How accurate are these attributions?

There is no argument that CMI's consultations with its members and other transport industries enabled it to identify the topics it and they thought important in a new international treaty. CMI presented six topics to UNCITRAL's Commission in March 2000.[18] The topics addressed what its constituencies considered the most pressing issues facing the maritime transport industry: inspection of the goods being transported and adequate description of those goods in the transport document; the contents and form of the transport document itself; the rights and obligations of the carrier of the goods; the rights and obligations of the company shipping the goods (including other non-carrier maritime parties, such as an intermediate holder or consignee); the delivery and receipt of the goods at the point of destination; the rights of disposal of certain goods (for reasons of safety); and the right to give instructions to the carrier.[19]

CMI's industry-led initiative had emerged over years of informal discussions with UNCITRAL's senior leadership. UNCITRAL's Secretary in the 1990s, Gerold Hermann, and his successor from within the Secretariat, former judge Jernej Sekolec, had engaged in continuing conversations with CMI in the later 1990s over the potential convergence between industry and UNCITRAL agendas. Sekolec, who became UNCITRAL's Secretary in 2001,[20] concurred with most issues identified by CMI. Yet he was reluctant to open up negotiations on perhaps the most distributive topic, namely, the liability of carriers for goods damaged or lost or delayed during their journey to market. Sekolec feared that UNCITRAL might be pressing too far into a contentious terrain that could lead to conflict and stalemate, a position with which the Commission initially concurred. As a "political move," UNCITRAL preferred to leave undisturbed the relevant liability provisions of The Hague Rules and Visby Protocol. CMI leaders strongly disagreed and insisted that "liability was integral" to carriage of goods by sea. If the maritime system itself was to be modernized, liability provisions needed reforming. "Either bring in liability," said CMI, "or it isn't worthwhile to do all this" (Int: 6012). As a price of cooperation, UNCITRAL's Secretary acceded and by 2000 a consensus was emerging within the Commission itself that liability must be inside the scope of the reform program.

Yet, the scope of reform ambitions laid out by CMI did not go far enough for the US. While several drafters of proposed US legislation had participated in CMI proceedings, the US sought to expand the lawmaking frontiers to include two issues it insisted were critical for its cooperation. The first was volume contracts, a significant US practice that allowed large shippers to negotiate separate deals or individual contracts with carriers (Int: 6010). The second was jurisdiction and arbitration. To counteract *Sky Reefer*, the US wanted provisions that would protect its juridical interests and provide some determinacy over the courts that would have jurisdiction over lawsuits resulting from maritime trade disputes (Int: 6010). Faced

18 See UN Doc. No. A/CN.9/476.

19 Id., at 4–8.

20 Within United Nations entities, the "secretary" describes the head of the organization. From 2001 to 2008, Sekolec held was the senior official at UNCITRAL.

with what was essentially an ultimatum, UNCITRAL's leadership and Working Group delegates agreed to extend the bounds of lawmaking to include both.

The boundary work, while intensive, nonetheless did not invariably lead to wider delineation of lawmaking domains. Two topics – rights to bring suit and assert freight charges – were both taken off the agenda (Int: 6010, 6012). Arguably the most controversial issue, which would endure through years of negotiations and beyond, led to an interim solution at the beginning of proceedings that amounted to boundary work of a different kind. That issue concerned the geographic scope of law to govern transport of goods from production to consumption.

We have seen that three fundamentally different approaches to geographic and market scope of the law would have far-reaching effects on who participated in the lawmaking, whether consensus would be possible, and, if so, what was the probability of implementing a multilateral treaty: a conventional port-to-port regime that focused on shipping vessels; a fully multimodal door-to-door regime that included every form of transport from point of production to point of distribution; and a limited door-to-door system that simplified carriage of goods without including all modes of transport.

Although CMI initially proposed a port-to-port regime, its initial draft contained a bracketed provision that, if adopted, would have shifted from this position, proposing tentatively a "limited network system," which would have expanded slightly on The Hague and Hamburg Rules' port-to-port or tackle-to-tackle approaches without going the full distance to a door-to-door or multimodal order.[21] The brackets suggest that there was some dissension within CMI itself, that a core group of CMI leaders wanted door-to-door coverage, but that some of CMI's national affiliates did not. Initially, "the UK shipping industry was against it. P&I Clubs,[22] the insurance industry, were also against door-to-door" (Int: 6012). Within UNCITRAL, too, some in the Secretariat feared the ambition of a door-to-door regime, as they anticipated the dangers of overreaching and repeating the failure of the Hamburg Rules. Whereas port-to-port seemed too conservative and out of synch with containerization practices in particular, a multimodal approach could stir massive opposition from many unimodal regimes, such as trucking and rail interests, not to mention the countries – and UNCITRAL delegations – firmly opposed to the

[21] UN Doc. No. A/CN.9/WG.III/WP.21, para. 49 (discussing proposed Art. 4.2.1 in initial draft as follows: "This [bracketed] article deals with ... [the problem of transport contracts that cover carriage of goods over both land and sea], and provides for a network system, but one as minimal as possible. The draft instrument is only displaced where a convention which constitutes mandatory law for inland carriage is applicable to the inland leg of a contract for carriage by sea, and it is clear that the loss or damage in question occurred solely in the course of the inland carriage.").

[22] "P&I Clubs" refer to the protection and indemnity associations, which work as informal cooperatives that underwrite P&I insurance on a mutual basis. See London P&I Club, website available online at www.londonpandi.com/.

dissolution of those existing regimes. But how could the Working Group draft something that sat between these two extremes?

To the surprise of core CMI drafters, however, UNCITRAL's senior officers wanted more than port-to-port. A veteran CMI leader told UNCITRAL's Secretary, Gerold Herrmann, that it was time to "kill our babies [CMI's Hague and Hague-Visby; UNCITRAL's Hamburg Rules] and make a new one together" (Int: 6012). Herrmann's successor, Jernej Sekolec, eventually agreed that if a new treaty could simplify carriage door-to-door, short of a fully-fledged multimodal system, then such a "flexible" approach would be attractive to UNCITRAL. This adept blurring of how far the UNCITRAL-centered transport lawmaking would reach seemed responsive to the practical realities of the marketplace. It also offered a way to get well beyond UNCITRAL's failed Hamburg Rules but at the same time to challenge UNCTAD's Multimodal Convention with something that was ambiguously enough defined at the outset of the lawmaking that was neither confrontive nor unduly restrictive.

Boundary work involves actors exerting influence and exercising power to shape an ecology around issues, around diagnoses of problems and prescriptions that solve the problems. If CMI channeled particular industry interests, how much did the most powerful state actor, the US, influence what actors would create what kinds of law on what issues?

CMI resisted the notion that the US through its CMI members was in control of the CMI drafting process. "To say the US brought across its own draft and handed it to the CMI is simply wrong," said one key CMI drafter (Int: 6002). The US had an indirect but tenuous effect in the late 1990s, insofar as MLA, CMI, and the US networks overlapped as some norm entrepreneurs had a common presence in multiple ecologies. But CMI's draft was already complete by the time US interests finally agreed in 2001 on draft legislation. As a result, some features of the US legislative agenda did get incorporated into the UNCITRAL agenda (e.g., volume contracts, arbitration and jurisdiction), but others did not.[23] Thus, although CMI brought the initial draft convention to the floor of Transport Working Group at its first session in April 2002, the Working Group's agenda had been negotiated among three main sets of actors, each of which had reached cooperative outcomes within their respective spheres: CMI, UNCITRAL's Secretariat, and the US delegation and its supporting non-state delegations.

Agenda setting and boundary marking characteristically focus on substantive topics. For IOs with diverse legal technologies, the earliest phases of a new lawmaking ecology are likely to include negotiations, even decisions, on which technology is best suited for the issues to be addressed. Since technologies affect what audiences,

[23] See UN Doc. No. A/CN.9/WG.III/WP.34, para. 10. For example, the US indicated publically that it supported "a door-to-door regime on a uniform liability basis as between the contracting parties, subject to a limited network exception," but not one that was fully door-to-door. Id. at para. 5.

what actors, what resources, and what interactions will feature in lawmaking (Chapters 6 and 7), this early decision is consequential.

On the issue of transport of goods by sea, consensus emerged seamlessly from the outset. The Secretariat never "thought of anything else but a convention. . . . There is no other way to harmonize." To "supercede" or to "integrate existing conventions" there was no alternative (Int: 6008). The US, too, wanted a convention to operate in a mandatory fashion, subject to the possibility of opting out provisions, such as exceptions that would allow parties to business transactions to contract out in private agreements. Further, a binding treaty would also have the salutary effect of overriding domestic law, including *Sky Reefer*. Shippers and shipper nations wanted a convention so they could lock in carriers (Int: 6005). Carriers, and carrier-centric nations, were prepared at the outset to trade away some of the advantages of earlier conventions if they could forestall threats of regionalism and its disintegration of harmonization that had compounded their costs of carrying goods. Only a convention could provide the needed certainty in international trade.

Despite these alignments of interests on form and substance of the lawmaking, the puzzle remains. Why did UNCITRAL, a multilateral organ of the UN, begin the proceedings of a working group with a convention drafted by a private group and, not any private group, but one that had variously been derogated as an "old boys club" (Int: 6008) and historically had been associated with carriers in the Global North against shippers and the Global South? Why did UNCITRAL take the risk of aligning itself with a single private interest group with a sectional interest?

The risks were clear, pointed out a longstanding state delegate to UNCITRAL. First, from its first session the work of the Transport Working Group would be perceived as connected to "an industry product." It could have looked from the outset as if UNCITRAL had been captured by a private sector body, albeit a peak association that embraced many countries in the world maritime and maritime insurance industries.[24] Second, the substance could convey the taint of being "pro-carrier." Shippers immediately objected that "this is not OK for us." Third, while CMI is near-universal in its membership of carriers, "not everyone in the universe is a carrier." Asian countries, Africa, Brazil, Argentina, India had no input in CMI's drafting until the first draft of the draft convention was placed on the table in 2002. UNCTAD, too, was highly critical that a non-state group associated with the carrier industry got this privileged status (Int: 6004), especially when UNCTAD might have been an obvious partner for UNCITRAL given their common UN pedigree. UNCITRAL stood to lose credibility, especially among developing nations. Right from the beginning, then, UNCITRAL potentially compromised its own identity as an arena for even-handed treatment of all UN states and the diversity

[24] We use the term here pejoratively in the sense employed by economic literature (Stigler 1971; Peltzman 1976; and others), although generally we use the term as defined by Ayres and Braithwaite (1992).

of private interests. UNCITRAL threatened to undermine its strongest warrant of legitimation – its universal representativeness of states and industry interests – by aligning itself so clearly with CMI.

UNCITRAL's Secretariat, of course, was not unaware of these risks but proceeded anyway. Why? First, UNCITRAL was in a hurry. It feared competition from other IOs, notably UNCTAD, and further fragmentation of the world system of trade by sea. It also feared that impatient US interests might re-ignite momentum for US legislation. Second, it had learned the lesson of the Hamburg Rules and UNCTAD's Multimodal Convention – if key industries and nations are not on board, if industry and lawmaking efforts are not aligned, products fail. By getting the world's carrier industry on board at the outset, by bringing the US to the table, and by signaling flexibility to non-carrier interests, it began with a head start. Third, carriage of goods by sea is a highly technical area within maritime law; maritime law is itself a tiny sub-specialty that combined private and public international law. UNCITRAL did not have the technical expertise, quite apart from many tangible resources, to go it alone. Beginning with a version that already got high technical grades from experts brought the legal experts onboard. Finally, since CMI itself knew well that its draft would be perceived as a carrier product, CMI needed UNCITRAL as much as UNCITRAL needed CMI. CMI, as the prime mover, already had tried "to move a little way toward the Hamburg Rules" and to anticipate the compromises that would be necessary for a UNCITRAL convention to be acceptable to carriers and shippers, the Global North and Global South (Int: 6002, 6006, 6008). Anticipating its critics, CMI had sought by wide-ranging industry consultations to transcend its own reputation as an organization that represented or favored carrier interests. Moreover, UNCITRAL had worked closely with private industry associations in other subject matter contexts and over time. Indeed, collaboration among state and non-state, public and private, actors had defined UNCITRAL's relatively unique method of work since its inception in 1966.

UNCITRAL therefore activated the transport lawmaking ecology in 2002 with at least two sets of pre-negotiated bargains in place. An industry consensus provisionally had been forged through CMI. Although a private association historically associated with carriers, CMI had repositioned itself by serving as a forum of its own, listening to the voices on other carriage of goods by sea actors in order to anticipate a wider compromise at UNCITRAL. A consensus within the most powerful trading nation similarly set the stage for a prospective global consensus. The US state delegation and US non-state delegations brought to UNCITRAL's agenda setting a bargain that had been struck in microcosm within the US: delegates included prominent figures on both the carrier and shipper sides of the carriage of goods industry, both government officials and industry specialists (Carlson 2009). This bargain inside the US among competing economic interest groups might thereby prefigure similar bargains in other states, regions, and the world.

By the second and third meetings of UNCITRAL's Working Group on Transport in 2002 and 2003, therefore, the contours of the lawmaking ecology were largely settled. The problem-solving net had been cast widely in response to significant shifts in market practices, to embrace issues that vexed industry, to meet the challenges and threats of powerful states or regional departures from global legal orders. Lawmakers staked expansive jurisdictional claims over substantive commercial issues and at the same time signaled that long-established formal properties of the multilateral treaty might require adaptations to better align lawmaking technologies with industry practices. Boundaries were set, boundaries were blurred. In so doing, the actors gathering in UNCITRAL's lawmaking arena implicitly disinvited industry groups, such as unimodal national and regional transport associations, which would have been vigorous opponents of threats to their established legal orders. Yet it was manifestly clear that actors drawn into the issue-ecology did so with clear understandings that they were pooling resources – of technical expertise with democratic representation of states, of money and organizational infrastructures. Bringing potential competitors into the same arena carried its own risks but the risks of debilitating deliberative conflict were mitigated by preserving ambiguity and delaying precise discussions of the most contentious matters.

CORPORATE BANKRUPTCY

It is a defining attribute of capitalist economies that businesses fail. Corporate bankruptcy law responds to this ubiquitous feature of markets by providing orderly means for all parties involved in a firm's business to handle their economic interests in the firm when it is in financial distress. When companies cannot pay their bills on time, or when their liabilities are likely to exceed their assets, their creditors become increasingly concerned about the loss of moneys owed them or of assets in the corporation that secure their loans. The further the company declines financially, the less likely it would be that all creditors get paid in full.

As financial collapse approaches, corporations essentially face two options. On the one hand, they can simply be liquidated: their assets are seized by creditors and sold off piece by piece, or, in more propitious circumstances, the company is sold as a going concern to another company. On the other hand, the company might be restructured financially and operationally. If it can reach agreement with its main creditors, and the law permits, managers can seek to turn the company around with the promise that this course of action in the long run will both preserve the business and yield more to the creditors. Often, this promise entails an agreement to pay creditors out of future revenue; sometimes it involves giving creditors an equity interest in the newly reorganized company. During the turnaround process, bankruptcy law may protect the company from arbitrary seizure of its assets by creditors, as seizure would also threaten a company's continued viability.

Bankruptcy law casts a long shadow over national markets. Collapse of too many private firms can lead to collapse of their banks, which in turn can put enormous pressure on a country's central bank. This domino effect is worsened when there exists no mechanism for addressing corporate financial distress. If firms cannot be restructured in an orderly fashion when they can no longer service their debts, then consequences can be severe for a nation and beyond. Corporate bankruptcy law, therefore, can be considered a bulwark of financial stability for a nation-state, the first domino in a sequence that can lead to financial crisis (G-22 1998a; G-22 1998b).

Corporate bankruptcy law has a particular salience for social scientists because all the interest groups in a market economy are brought together when a company might not be able to pay all its creditors in full (Carruthers and Halliday 1998). Managers who run the firm may come into conflict with owners of the firm: the latter may want new managers to bring a firm back from the brink of failure, whereas the current managers will want to hold on to their positions. Management may want to dismiss workers or reduce their wages, whereas workers will want to maintain their wages and their jobs. The state frequently is pitted against the firm because failing businesses may slow down or stop payments into state pension plans; even if payments continue, shifts in the market value of a pension fund may create added liability for a firm, which state actors insist on and the company may resist. Depending on the penalties for nonpayment, firms may also stop paying taxes. Bank creditors, who mostly lend on a secured basis supported by specific collateral, may come into conflict with trade creditors, who have supplied goods and services without collateral to back this debt. Customers may become creditors because they pay for goods they do not receive. A firm's bankruptcy therefore can produce a rush for the assets as parties try to grab whatever they can. It is a situation inherently infused with cross-cutting conflicts.

Corporate bankruptcy law therefore seeks to turn a disorderly scramble for the assets of a failing firm into an orderly process that is fair to all parties. What counts as fair will differ depending on the distributive aims of a bankruptcy law – regardless of how these priorities are organized, these provisions invariably privilege some creditors over others. Since failing firms frequently stop paying taxes or sending money to state pension funds, do states get taxes and pensions repaid before banks? Since banks have gone to the trouble of getting security for their loans, do banks get their secured assets out before trade creditors get paid anything? Since suppliers usually extend credit when they deliver goods or services, do these trade creditors, who are close to firms, get paid before more "distant" creditors? Do workers receive their unpaid salaries or vacation pay before other creditors, given that a reorganizing company will need to retain at least some of its workers? Corporate bankruptcy law reform within a country may therefore be seen as "meta-bargaining" over which interest groups in a market economy get priority.

In this meta-bargaining, national bankruptcy reforms potentially bring all economic actors onto the political stage: associations of bankers and the financial industry (e.g., American Bankers' Association, London clearing banks, credit unions), unions (e.g., AFL-CIO, Trade Union Congress), tax departments (e.g., UK Inland Revenue, US Internal Revenue Service), business associations (e.g., Confederation of British Industry, US Chamber of Commerce), government departments (e.g., trade and commerce, Environmental Protection Agency), consumer groups, guilds of managers and company directors (e.g., Institute of Directors, Consumers' Union), and, not least, professional associations of lawyers, judges, accountants, and insolvency practitioners – those experts who actually do the work of liquidation and reorganization (e.g., INSOL International, American Bar Association, National Conference of Bankruptcy Judges). Cross-nationally bankers' associations and government ministries exert disproportionate influence. Unions can be powerful in countries with strong labor movements and an allied political party (e.g., the Labour Party in Britain and the Democrats in the US). Almost always in advanced economies, professional associations exert powerful influence both because their expertise is intrinsic to lawmaking and their agreement affects implementation (Carruthers and Halliday 1998).

If national lawmaking is meta-bargaining inside the institutions of a nation-state, then global lawmaking for national bankruptcy systems takes places within issue-ecologies that transcend the state. Economic actors able to transcend or unify national groups, IOs with special interests in economic development and financial stability, and professions standing in close proximity to global standard-setting organizations, offer prospects for creating legal norms for failing businesses across the world.

A *Twenty-Year Quest*

The lawmaking ecology on corporate bankruptcies that emerged in the late 1990s brought to the global stage developments in legal thought and national lawmaking, market shifts, and state incapacities that had been building since the 1970s. Much of the impetus for regional and global reforms began with two landmark pieces of legislation, each of them resting on a new paradigm for state and market responses to companies in distress.

In 1978, the US Congress enacted a Bankruptcy Code, a major piece of legislation that unified three earlier acts governing discrete aspects of corporate bankruptcy. But the 1978 Bankruptcy Code institutionalized a paradigmatic shift in approaches to failing corporations. Rather than simply liquidating a corporation and allocating its assets to its creditors, jurisprudential theory in the US had moved from a liquidation to a rehabilitation model for treating businesses in distress. The theory proposed that if companies could be given a second chance, if they could be sheltered from creditors who sought to seize back their assets, if they had time to restructure their finances and company operations, then more jobs would be saved, more value would be preserved for creditors, and more stability would redound to markets.

The 1978 Code emphasized the rights of debtors (i.e., company managers and owners) by enabling failing businesses to seek court protection while business managers tried to restructure their finances and operations. This shift in paradigms and practice would ramify across the world in succeeding decades (Carruthers and Halliday 1998).

Shortly after US bankruptcy law was revised, the British government confronted a deep crash in the real estate market. Mrs. Thatcher's Government determined to "clean up" the market so it was "safe for investment" (Carruthers and Halliday 1996). In its far-reaching Insolvency Act of 1986, the Government sought to encourage reorganization of failing businesses where possible and to compel directors of companies to seek expert advice well before companies became technically insolvent.

By the mid-1980s it had become clear that the rise of multinational corporations (MNCs) posed an enormous problem when MNCs got into financial difficulty. A company-wide bankruptcy, spread across multiple national jurisdictions, each of which had different bankruptcy laws, would be exceptionally difficult to rehabilitate. If each country were to handle only those assets of the MNC that were inside its jurisdiction, an MNC likely would be dismembered and any prospect of saving the business would be lost.

Several national and international organizations sought to create norms and protocols that would enable courts in different countries to solve the coordination problem in order to save a multinational corporation (Halliday and Carruthers 2009, chapters 2–3). The International Bar Association developed a Model International Insolvency Code that might unify procedures across jurisdictions. While this failed to be adopted by any country, it informed other efforts. Some courts took matters into their own hands. In 1991, the federal bankruptcy court for the Southern District of New York coordinated proceedings in the massive collapse of the Maxwell Group with the English High Court in London. Another international agreement (often referred to as "protocols") emerged between the courts of Southern Ontario and the Southern District of New York. The International Bar Association in the early 1990s sought to systematize these instances of cooperation by drafting a Concordat to govern cross-border insolvency proceedings. At the same time, the European Union almost succeeded in adopting a convention to coordinate bankruptcies within Europe; although political back-biting had prevented finalization of the draft EU Convention on Cross-Border Insolvency, these debates involved political opportunism, not disagreements on the substance of the draft Convention (Moss, Fletcher, and Isaacs 2002).

By the mid-1990s, therefore, both industry and lawmaking bodies inside and beyond states converged in a recognition that some kind of transnational or international order would be required to solve the multiplying problems of domestic and cross-national corporate failures. Many solutions were on the table with their diverse alternative instruments to allow at least orderly cross-border insolvencies. All had failed except for ad hoc court-to-court cooperation, and that occurred only case-by-case in a very few jurisdictions (Halliday and Carruthers 2009: 38–69; Clift 2004).

Facilitating Forces

The collapse of the Soviet Union in 1989, and the rush of Western states and institutions to implant market economies in place of planned economies, thrust a new challenge on to the agenda of international lawmaking. The European Bank for Reconstruction and Development immediately recognized that the new market economies needed new laws to shape the market. Bankruptcy systems were understood to serve as bedrock legal infrastructures for open markets. The interest in bankruptcy reform was not just academic. Central and Eastern Europe were littered with unprofitable former state enterprises. New private firms were springing up, but no mechanisms existed to govern the possibility of failure, which frequently occurs in new businesses. This required more than a reform of pre-existing laws, believed IOs with reconstructive mandates. The more than twenty new markets in Central and Eastern Europe, as well as Central Asia, had a legal vacuum that intensified demands for erection of domestic bankruptcy systems.

What was occurring in Europe crystallized wider shifts in ideology and orientation. By this time, said a senior UN official, rich nations had grown weary of wasted bilateral aid: "The western world has grown disenchanted with giving direct financial aid [to developing countries]. It just sinks in the sand" (Int: 2065). But what alternatives were there to direct aid or sovereign lending? Modernization of legal regimes might serve as a type of development assistance, some argued.

In addition, the demand for insolvency law reform extended beyond a desire for structural reform in developing countries. The quickening pace of global trade beyond a nation's boundaries required "contractual discipline." Firms had to be able to trade over extensive geographical distances where parties to credit transactions were far removed, even unknown to each other. If globalization were to continue to expand, lenders and sellers required confidence that they would be protected if debtors failed to repay them. Both the European Bank for Reconstruction and Development and the Asian Development Bank (ADB) (See, e.g., ADB 2000a; ADB 2000b) constructed law-building programs on the premise that strong commercial laws and institutions backed up by a viable bankruptcy regime would stimulate the trade necessary to lift countries out of their economic demise.

Global and regional shifts in markets, the spread of MNCs, disillusionment with state-led development paradigms, and the rise of a new ideologies in law and economics coincided with UNCITRAL's twenty-fifth anniversary. To celebrate its past and envision its future, UNCITRAL organized a Congress in 1992 to imagine its work program for coming decades (UNCITRAL 1992).[25] Among many other economic issues confronting UNCITRAL's lawmaking mandate, a Luxembourg lawyer noted that the collapse of the Bank of Credit and Commerce International (BCCI)

[25] See also Proposals for Possible Future Work Made at the UNCITRAL Congress: Note by the Secretariat, UN Doc. No. A/CN.9/378 (1993).

had been particularly difficult to handle because of a "lack of harmonization in the field of bankruptcy" across the many countries in which BCCI operated. He asserted that, "in my opinion, it is imperative to take appropriate measures in order to remove discrepancies existing between the different countries" (UNCITRAL 1992). An American academic concurred: while he thought it impractical to try and harmonize bankruptcy laws across countries, he urged UNCITRAL to "seriously consider" work to deal with cross-border bankruptcies.[26] A Spanish law professor echoed the sentiment: "I understand the complexity [of bankruptcy law] and the reservations about it, but its vital international importance is such that we should at least identify and define a few areas of particular importance so that bankruptcy law can truly have an international impact."[27] A former Secretary of UNCITRAL, Kazuaki Sono, affirmed the recommendations of other speakers that changed patterns of commerce required UNCITRAL to "no longer be afraid of engaging in global public policy discussions" in such areas as insolvency and secured transactions.[28]

UNCITRAL's Secretariat heeded the charge immediately. It took bankruptcy law off UNCITRAL's "impossible list," as its Secretary, Gerold Herrmann, had once styled it, and identified a narrow issue – cross-border insolvency – on which the UN agency might work (Int: 4123). UNCITRAL formed a Working Group on Insolvency Law in 1993, which by 1996 had produced a Model Law on Cross-Border Insolvency.

The rapid progress and ultimate success of the Insolvency Working Group surprised everyone, not least its own members (Int: 2066). In significant part the lawmaking ecology's success stemmed from close partnership UNCITRAL's Secretariat had forged with two key industry groups: INSOL International, an international professional association, principally of accountants and restructuring specialists; and the International Bar Association's specialty committee on bankruptcy. UNCITRAL invited leading US, UK, and other judges with experience in international corporate bankruptcies to join a growing network of engaged experts. Together with state delegations, this aggregation of specialized professionals formed the deliberative core of the negotiations (Int: 2065). Arguably the principal achievements of the Model Law deliberations were not only its content, but also that it represented a successful foray into a new issue-area and the formation of a new lawmaking ecology of states cooperating with bankruptcy specialists across the world.

When UNCITRAL promulgated its Model Law on Cross-Border Insolvency, which the General Assembly ratified in late 1997, UNCITRAL's Secretariat and its insolvency lawmaking entrepreneurs had persuaded themselves that its success might be the first of many successive steps to build incrementally legal orders to

[26] (UNCITRAL 1996:158; see also Clift 2004) (discussing the influence of this intervention on at UNCITRAL Congress).

[27] (UNCITRAL 1996: 274).

[28] Id., 251.

refine corporate restructuring and state economic governance. While the Model Law properly focused on international commerce, norm entrepreneurs were persuaded that political upheaval and financial crises demonstrated the need for extensive reforms of *domestic* insolvency laws, not just coordination in the few cases in which the financial distress of MNCs bled from one border to another. On the heels of the Latin American and Southeast Asian Financial Crises, the international community, speaking through the G-22, reinforced the push for domestic reforms of corporate insolvency law as one of several steps to take in preventing subsequent financial crises.

By the late 1990s, the attitude of the UN to markets and trade had also changed. Once pre-occupied with security and state-to-state relations, UN Secretary General Kofi Annan began to emphasize the importance of building the rule of law, including better commercial laws, in developing countries (Int: 6530).[29] Increasingly, arguments were heard in the halls of the UN that improvements in the rule of law would allow for improved economic circumstances on the ground. Countries were asking the UN to assist them proposing structural reforms: "They feel they can prosper only if they can modernize their laws and practices" (Int: 6530).

This change in tone toward markets spilled over to lawmaking and UNCITRAL. Where once, said a senior UNCITRAL official, "we've been a side activity" where "we've traditionally had very little effect . . . [but] we now can expect more recognition and more resources" (Int: 2065), a view confirmed from within the UN Legal Department. An alignment with the restructuring industry and the hint of tangible resources to accompany the UN's paradigmatic shift toward institution building through law set the stage for a far more ambitious lawmaking program by UNCITRAL if it could claim for itself the right to be both an agent and arena for that program, a claim, we shall see, that was contested by a far more powerful actor on the international economic stage.

Precipitating Factors

If the national debt crises in Ecuador and Mexico had begun to quicken the impetus for reform of global bankruptcy norms, it was a regional crisis, the Asian

[29] The UN General Assembly has adopted a dozen resolutions affirming its commitment to concepts of "rule of law," see, e.g., UN, Declaration of the high-level meeting of the General Assembly on the rule of law at the national and international levels, UN Doc. No. A/RES/67/1 (Nov. 30, 2012). Although the phrase "rule of law" covers a broad range of issues, the General Assembly has emphasized the connections between "rule of law" and economic development in this way:

> the rule of law and development are strongly interrelated and mutually reinforcing, that the advancement of the rule of law at the national and international levels is essential for sustained and inclusive economic growth, sustainable development, the eradication of poverty and hunger and the full realization of all human rights and fundamental freedoms, including the right to development, all of which in turn reinforce the rule of law.

Id. See also (Rajah 2015).

Financial Crisis, that shifted the demand for global normmaking into high gear (Halliday and Carruthers 2009). The Asian Financial Crisis was acute because it involved some of the most economically advanced countries within Asia (e.g., Thailand, Malaysia, Indonesia, and South Korea). After WWII, these countries had exemplified what rapid economic growth might promise. If these countries could falter, and falter together, some fundamentals common to their markets needed close scrutiny. But a regional crisis signified much more – the prospect of not only a regional, but a global financial crisis. And this in turn implied that the international financial architecture might be more fragile than the managers of the world economy had assumed.

This wide-ranging collapse of *private* markets compelled many IOs to view financial stability in a new way. Unlike earlier financial crises, which had been triggered by public financial crises, this "market-driven collapse" required a re-appraisal through the new lens of the laws and institutions that governed private markets (Int: 2044). The G-7 and G-22, comprised of the finance ministers and central bank governors from the G-7 industrial countries and fifteen additional countries, quickly released reports on international financial stability (G-22 1998a). The G-22 pointed directly to law, and specifically to insolvency and debtor-creditor regimes, as a locus of financial vulnerability and urged the IMF, World Bank, and regional development banks to begin erecting new institutional bulwarks against private market collapses.

The IMF, World Bank, and ADB had been intimately involved in ad hoc rescues of countries battered by the Asian crisis. In Indonesia, South Korea, Thailand, and elsewhere, these international financial institutions compelled states to commit immediately to reforms of substantive bankruptcy law and institutions (Halliday and Carruthers 2009). But, complained a regional official, many of these changes were "hasty," "not well thought out," and "not very reflective of the laws of cultures in which they were being instituted" (Int: 2032), even if they shared some underlying fundamentals, such as mechanisms to rescue companies if at all possible.

The ideological shift toward privatization of economic activity that would be regulated by efficient economic law, and handled by institutions adhering to international standards for rule of law, brought a new set of actors into international commercial lawmaking. The central IOs in the standing lawmaking ecology settled in the 1960s became unsettled by unanticipated intrusions into their lawmaking territory by international financial institutions. While most IFIs became engaged in specific issue-areas, and not across the entire spectrum of economic law, three IFIs initiated lawmaking efforts for corporate insolvency law independently of UNCITRAL, UNIDROIT, and The Hague Conference in the later 1990s.

The ADB hired consultants to undertake consultations, conduct a survey, and write a report on eleven Asian countries. From this exercise came thirty-three standards of a robust bankruptcy system (ADB 2000a). The IMF Legal Department invited five international experts to help it create its own standards, which it published in a small book, entitled *Orderly and Effective Insolvency Procedures: Key Issues* (IMF 1999). In its turn, the World Bank Legal Vice-Presidency appointed a US bankruptcy specialist to spearhead the Bank's intention to create norms for insolvency and debtor-creditor regimes. The Bank's new hire in turn hired a small cadre of eminent academics from different jurisdictions as consultants and they began work on draft Bank principles.

There was much in common among the standards put forward by these international financial institutions. In substance, each followed fairly closely the normative core of "key principles and features of insolvency regimes" identified by the G-22 in 1998 (G-22 1998a). This commonality should have come as no surprise since a single professional association of insolvency practitioners – INSOL International – had, through its members, assisted the G-22, the ADB, and the World Bank in their deliberations. While INSOL members were not alone as technical advisors to the IFIs, the standards were in all cases drafted with the assistance of a small group of lawyers and academics who were most (or at least very) familiar with US and UK bankruptcy and reorganization law.

If the G-22 Report tentatively sketched topics without clear boundaries for insolvency lawmaking, it equivocated on precisely which organization(s) ought to have responsibility for drafting these standards, noting that "consideration should be given in the relevant fora to the development of additional means and incentives for encouraging the adoption of effective regimes" (G-22 1998a). The arena that would accommodate an issue-ecology dedicated to corporate insolvency law reform could not be determined by a sovereign authority, as can be usually taken for granted in domestic lawmaking. How then did UNCITRAL successfully claim jurisdiction over this area of work?

The ADB, IMF, and World Bank had initiated lawmaking or published sets of norms between 1998 and 2000. Yet each of these had significant legitimation deficits that detracted from the likelihood that any norms emanating from them would command assent from states across regions and with differing legal histories and levels of economic and legal development. But if these IFIs were not the right locations for consideration of national insolvency regimes, who was?

This question was taken up by Australia. In October 1998, Prime Minister John Howard commissioned a task force to advise on Australia's possible contributions to international financial reform.[30] The subsequent Report recommended that the UN's Commission on International Trade Law "undertake the development of an international model law on insolvency and participate in monitoring implementation"

[30] The Treasury, Government of Australia, Task Force on International Financial Reform (December 1998), http://archive.treasury.gov.au/documents/189/HTML/docshell.asp?URL=Index.asp. See also Conan Brownbill, Matthew Crooke and Andrew Sellars, Improving Global Frameworks for Corporate Reorganization: An Australian Perspective, Economic Round-Up (Spring 2004), http://archive.treasury.gov.au/documents/930/HTML/docshell.asp?URL=03_Global.asp.

of such a model law. UNCITRAL, according to the Task Force, had "a proven track record" in the form of its Model Law on Cross-Border Insolvency.[31] It was also broadly representative of a cross-section of nations with different cultures, of practitioners, and of judges and other national officials.

The UNCITRAL Secretariat was aware of the new urgency to reach far beyond what it had previously considered possible – the design of norms for an entire national corporate bankruptcy system.[32] International financial institutions had plausibly asserted that there was great demand for good corporate bankruptcy law in domestic markets; they showed it was "topical" and that indeed convergence might be possible (Int: 4005). If the IFIs set precedents, established building blocks, did "ground breaking work," then UNCITRAL might be well poised to take over leadership for the world (Int: 4120).

UNCITRAL's Secretariat knew it had a competitive advantage if it were to stand on the shoulders of the IMF, World Bank, and ADB. With the success of its Cross-Border Model Law, UNCITRAL could demonstrate its own track record for decisive action. It now could point to an earlier insolvency lawmaking ecology that was anchored to UNCITRAL's Working Group and it could properly boast it was the first global arena in which all states and non-state actors could convene to make insolvency law for the world's markets. Its industry auspices were strong. It had established close ties with INSOL, which had the "great advantage that it organizes things so well," and it had established good working relations with other key private groups, such as the International Bar Association and the international business wing of the American Bar Association (Int: 4123, 4002). UNCITRAL had garnered the confidence of the US and it had shown to skeptics that common and civil lawyers could find consensus despite their centuries of difference.

Not least UNCITRAL conveyed the aura of the UN, a reputation unsullied by the backlash against the IMF and World Bank interventions during the Asian Financial Crisis. Said one observer: "many countries resented the heavy-handed way in which the World Bank and IMF compelled them to make changes" (Int: 2032). The World Bank and IMF were perceived by many developing countries as "American controlled entities" and any norms they produced invariably would be perceived to favor first world countries (Int: 2043). The IMF Legal Department knew this and knew it needed the substance of its preferences adopted by a more politically acceptable international body. It thereby withdrew itself as a competitor to UNCITRAL. The World Bank continued to believe it could be the global leader, but had little ability in the short term to halt the march toward an UNCITRAL initiative, even if the

[31] Task Force Report, supra note 193.

[32] Such a system has several elements: (1) substantive and (2) procedural bankruptcy law; (3) often a specialized bankruptcy court; (4) a government agency for administration of bankruptcies; (5) an expert profession; and (6) in some countries an out-of-court mediation body. See (Clift 2009).

Bank's lead lawmakers harbored unstated ambitions that would later flare into open competition with UNCITRAL (see Chapter 9).

In 1999, Australia triggered the formal entry of UNCITRAL into the field by bringing a proposal to UNCITRAL's Commission that it should consider developing global norms for domestic bankruptcy systems,

> in view of its universal membership, its previous successful work on cross-border insolvency and its established working relations with international organizations that have expertise and interest in the area of insolvency.[33]

With this intervention, Australia recommended the development of a model law on corporate bankruptcy systems.

Agenda Setting

The beginnings of an alignment between industry and a loose clustering of lawmaking IOs, and the provisional identification of a core of topics to address fundamental economic problems which all acknowledged needed solutions, framed intensive discussions in 1999 and 2000 to chart more precisely the scope of lawmaking and to agree on which actors would be drawn into the lawmaking ecology.

In June 1999, the Commission, UNCITRAL's governing decision-making body, met, in part, to consider Australia's proposal on possible future work by UNCITRAL in the area of insolvency law.[34] The report of that discussion weaves back and forth between noting the considerable importance of the project to be balanced against the "fear that work might not be brought to a successful conclusion."[35] Like its first exposure to a new transport legal order, the Commission reacted cautiously. A proposal to scale back from Australia's proposal surfaced at the meeting: "[i]t was said that a universally acceptable model law was in all likelihood not feasible, and that any work needed to take a flexible approach that would leave options and policy choices open to States."[36] In the end, the Commission provided only the slimmest authorization to the Secretariat to prepare a "study" of "the work already being undertaken by other organizations and consideration of the relevant issues" and to present that study to a working group convened for a single, exploratory session.[37]

UNCITRAL's Secretariat followed up the June UNCITRAL Commission meeting and the Australian proposal with a working paper in which it put forward an extensive claim to UNCITRAL as the rightful locus for the lawmaking on corporate bankruptcy norms.[38] In classic incremental style, the Secretariat sought to turn

33 UN Doc. No. A/CN.9/WG.V/WP.50, at 3.
34 UN Doc. No. A/54/17 (May 17–June 4, 1999).
35 Id. at 43.
36 Id. at 43.
37 Id. at 47.
38 UN Doc. No. A/CN.9/WG.V/WP.50 (Sep. 20, 1999).

its potential rivals into partners by acknowledging the work of five other IOs (ADB, IBA, IMF, OECD, G-22, World Bank) by drawing them inside an ecology where they might work cooperatively. UNCITRAL's lawmakers asserted that there was "broad agreement on the key objectives" for an effective insolvency regime,[39] and then launched into a description of common issues in substantive law already flagged by the ADB and IMF as well as key institutional issues.

In contrast to the Commission's narrow conception of a program of work, which might also have the effect of inadvertently pushing IFI lawmakers outside UNCITRAL's ecology, the Secretariat presented a working paper with a boldly expansive agenda for the reconvened Working Group on Insolvency. Moving beyond the "key objectives" of a modern insolvency regime, which had comprised the lion's share of earlier IOs' reports on this topic, the Secretariat went on to identify in some detail the "core features" of liquidation and rehabilitation proceedings. It discussed the conditions under which bankruptcy proceedings ought to be commenced; the consequences of commencement (e.g., did it stop all claims by creditors); the role of creditors, insolvency representatives and courts (e.g., which could initiate actions); and the difficult issue of informal insolvency procedures (e.g., how much could private procedures achieve without the intervention of a court?). The report also tackled the form of possible future work. Should the Working Group aspire to write a model law or model legal provisions or should it more modestly aim at a product that was more open ended and flexible?

At a Working Group session convened in late 1999, delegates searched for common ground and identified flash points of potential conflict.[40] Interventions were wide ranging and exploratory, more conversational than the usual working group deliberations. Some key delegations, including the IBA and US, were "skeptical" that anything, especially anything ambitious, could come to fruition. "Maybe something will come out of Vienna," said a leading insolvency practitioner, "or maybe not" (Int: 2052). Even the Secretariat observed that the meeting was "very slow, and like drawing teeth." The prevailing sentiment seemed to be, "what the hell are we going to do?" (Int: 2066).

By the end of the meeting, however, the pall seemed to have lifted. The Secretariat was pleasantly surprised at how well the meeting went. The Group had identified a list of key issues on which agreement might be possible and it "looked like we can do something" (Int: 2006). Even if the bounds of work had not been precisely delineated at least centering topics attracted general support. Many of the delegates previously had worked together in deliberating on the Model Law. There was a level of comfort and camaraderie around the room. It was "easy to get agreement at a high level of generalization" (Int: 2066). Indeed, by the end of the session, delegates were expanding on the topics that had been provided to them

[39] Id., at 8.

[40] UN Doc. No. A/CN.9/469 (Jan. 6, 2000).

in the Secretariat's report. Emboldened by the consensus, the Working Group decided to return to the Commission and seek

> the mandate to prepare: a comprehensive statement of key objectives and core features for a strong insolvency, debtor-creditor regime, including consideration of out-of-court restructuring; a legislative guide containing flexible approaches to the implementation of such objectives and features, including a discussion of the alternative approaches possible and the perceived benefits and detriments of such approaches.[41]

But the World Bank complicated matters. At the time of UNCITRAL Insolvency Working Group's initial meeting, in December 1999, delegates were aware of the Bank's ongoing efforts but were unclear on the breadth of the scope of this project and how determined the Bank was to proceed unilaterally. How could UNCITRAL proceed if the Bank emerged as a direct competitor? The Bank's financial and infrastructural resources far exceeded those of UNCITRAL. Prudent politics and hesitation by the US delegation to proceed without knowing the Bank's disposition forced UNCITRAL to "mark time" for a year (Int: 4003). The Working Group committed in diplomatic language to "seek their collaboration in order to benefit from the expertise these organizations can provide and to build on their efforts."[42]

While the Working Group had committed not to meet formally until it knew how the World Bank intended to proceed, it feared a loss of momentum while it waited. It filled the vacuum ingeniously by joining forces with INSOL and the IBA to hold an informal Colloquium in Vienna in December 2000. The Colloquium was intended to chart more precisely the landscape of issues, to discern what this lawmaking ecology might include within its lawmaking jurisdiction and what it would exclude, and thereby to discover which actors elected to cooperate in a joint enterprise. This critical framing moment also provided a cautionary stocktaking of how much dissensus existed among actors with differing policy prescriptions and whether those differences could be surmounted or the issues themselves might be deferred for subsequent efforts.

The Colloquium revealed which actors would likely be central and dominant in the lawmaking. INSOL had prominent norm entrepreneurs as its lead delegates and a track record of cooperation and recognition by the G-22 in its report on international financial architecture (G-22 1998b). The IBA, too, had long been a player in international insolvency lawmaking. Their Committee J, which focused on insolvency matters, had drafted first a Model International Insolvency Code and later a Concordat to address coordination among insolvency proceedings pending in multiple jurisdictions (Halliday and Carruthers 2009). Although no country implemented the Model International Insolvency Code, more than several courts had expressly relied on the Concordat when approving protocols to govern coordination

41 Id. at 28.

42 Id.

in some financially significant cases, such as the spectacular collapse of the Maxwell Communications empire after its founder drowned in strange circumstances off the back of his yacht.[43]

The ADB and IMF placed their imprint on the Colloquium through their 1999 publications, which had converged on a rough consensus on the core issues of importance to institutions charged with financial stability. Draft World Bank *Principles* had been circulated to many delegates. But the IFIs were not entirely in accord and the brooding presence of US hegemony as the first state to adopt comprehensive rehabilitation reforms also met with reservations. When the World Bank first unveiled its long draft of principles in Sydney in November 1999 (World Bank 1999a), the ADB refused to co-sponsor or attend the event. The ADB simply "threw up its hands" when it saw the first draft of the principles as "much too long, much too complicated" and redolent with the "negative connotations" of the World Bank (Int: 2032). Pungently expressed by a Commonwealth expert, "the overwhelming impression I had," at first reading of the initial World Bank draft was, "hell, the Americans are coming. The world needs Chapter 11 [of US Bankruptcy Code] or we won't survive" (Int: 4120). Chapter 11, the provision of the US bankruptcy law permitting reorganization of distressed companies, was at the time controversial around the globe, not least because it allowed a debtor company's management nearly unfettered discretion to open proceedings and gain protection from creditors at their own discretion and timing, and, thereafter, to remain in control of the company's affairs without the supervision of a trustee or other insolvency representative. To yield too fully to the US as a first mover effectively threatened to put "the fox in charge of the henhouse," as many characterized the US debtor-in-possession system.

And while consensus could be found on many core topics, there were sharp policy divergences across national legal systems and legal families. Even INSOL and the IBA had quite different views about the relative powers of courts and out-of-court solutions to corporate failure. INSOL, like English and most Commonwealth lawyers and accountants, wanted to stay away from courts as much as possible and manage most restructurings in workouts with banks. The IBA's insolvency committee, dominated at this time by US lawyers, wanted an integral role for courts, even if preceded by out-of-court negotiations. It found on this issue an ally in the French delegate, who was himself a judge and frequently spoke at Insolvency Working Group sessions on the importance of judicial involvement to assure protection of the public interest in any insolvency process.

The relative importance of employees' claims in the order of distribution in insolvency was something on which the French (and other Continental) delegates

[43] For two of the decisions published in this case, see Maxwell Communication Corp pLC v. Societe Generale (In re Maxwell Communication Corp. pLC), 93 F.3d 1036 (2d Cir. 1996); Barclays Bank pLC v. Homan (In re Maxwell Communication Corp. pLC), [1992] B.C.C. 757 (Ch.)(Homan), aff'd, [1992] B.C.C. 767 (C.A.).

disagreed with other practitioners (with the exception of GRIP, the lone professional association centered in France). The IMF wanted to focus principally on substantive law and commercial companies. The World Bank's aspirations more broadly reached to state-owned enterprises and financial institutions, often dealt with outside corporate bankruptcy law, and certainly more politically fraught subjects.

More than simply a difference in substance, some delegates saw fundamental differences in underlying values and logics of institutions imbued by market values and those adhering to juridical standards. Said one delegate:

> there are countries that would be prepared to listen to what UNCITRAL recommends [but] who may have misgivings about the motives of the World Bank or IMF, countries which see the World Bank and IMF, rightly or wrongly, as bodies that are centered primarily on economics and global efficiency, whereas a body like UNCITRAL can get the mix right and also emphasize the need for fairness, for process, for social issues to be taken into account.
>
> (Int: 4120)

Framing and perception were important because the substance put forward by UNCITRAL, at least in the initial stages of its consideration of the Insolvency Legislative Guide, did not differ dramatically (or really much at all) from that found in the reports that had been issued by the ADB and IMF.

Faultlines began to open up on many topics that are integral to a comprehensive domestic bankruptcy system for companies. Would secured creditors, like banks, get the right to seize a company's assets outside bankruptcy law (favored by the British, parts of the Commonwealth, INSOL) or would secured creditors be compelled to be drawn inside bankruptcy proceedings (favored by the US, Canada, ABA, IBA)? Would out-of-court proceedings, perhaps coordinated by a central bank, get recognition as a legitimate restructuring option (favored by Britain, INSOL, ADB, and Australia) or would courts certainly be involved at some point (favored by the US, France, IBA, ABA)? Would control of bankruptcy proceedings be handled by private administrators and courts (favored by the British, French, INSOL) or by the managers of the failing company and creditors (favored by the US and ABA)? Would reorganizations of failing companies be possible with only limited court supervision (favored by Britain, Australia, INSOL, accountants) or would courts be integral to a workout (favored by France, other civil law countries, and the US)? Would all stakeholders, including the public interest, be acknowledged in corporate bankruptcies (favored by France, China and other civil law countries) or would they be confined effectively to private actors such as the best organized creditors and debtors (favored by common law regimes)?

Despite the prospects of vigorous debate and open difference, however, the boundary work of the 1999 Working Group discussions and the 2000 UNCITRAL Colloquium resulted in an agenda far beyond that initially envisaged by the Commission. The parameters revealed bold aspirations for an expansive and ambitious set of norms to shape a prospective TLO on corporate insolvency. If delegates earlier had been skeptical, unsure that the time was ripe, and if the Commission had been afraid to press too far at the risk of failure, by the conclusion of the Colloquium these doubts had been swept away.

The Working Group deliberately excluded some topics which it considered beyond its capacity to manage: bankruptcies of state-owned enterprises and financial institutions, which the World Bank had wanted on the agenda; the bankruptcies of corporate groups, the organizational form common to multinational corporations; the civil or criminal liability of company directors, which featured in English insolvency law and that of many Commonwealth countries; and most individual bankruptcies.

How it would treat the most contentious issues was left deliberately vague, not least how much the lawmaking collective would reflect the legal imprint of the world's largest economy. Perhaps most ambiguity that remained concerned not the bounds of the lawmaking substance but the form in which the norms would be conveyed. In 1999, the Secretariat put two principal options on the table: a model law, which had several variants, including perhaps a guide to enactment or explanatory texts; or a set of legislative principles or recommendations. Oddly, by the conclusion of the Colloquium, the options had opened up to include some combination of a comparative study or legislative guide or model statutes or even a "blueprint or route map." This uncertainty would fuel later decision-making debates about the degrees of discretion and sovereignty different forms of the norms would offer states (Chapter 6).

As the moment when an incipient lawmaking ecology became a more fully embodied interactional reality, the Colloquium revealed much to the lawmakers about resources, actors, and interactional dynamics.

By bringing in some one hundred and fifty delegates from forty-eight countries, and many non-state delegations, the adverse consequences of the legitimation paradox might have been predicted. Yet, said an official, "something happens in these Colloquia ... where there is a level of interest generated ... a spark in the atmosphere ... and people get carried along with enthusiasm" (Int: 2066). By the end, said an UNCITRAL official at the time, "it's clear to me that we all have an idea of what is possible," even if that doesn't "translate into exactly the same idea in everyone's mind" (Int: 2066).

The Colloquium had salutary effects beyond morale and aspirations. It offered a moment where UNCITRAL could simultaneously stake its claim to global leadership and convert potential competitors into constructive partners. For the IMF, at least, it constituted a place to consider whether a hand-off of the reform baton to UNCITRAL, which was much more legitimate as a global forum than the IMF, could be managed with confidence. It allowed UNCITRAL to display its unique strength vis-à-vis other more powerful IOs, not least by means of its ability to draw a wide range of nations and influential non-state organizations into a global quasi-legislature. The very fact of the Colloquium underlined UNCITRAL's claim to take over the leadership of this normmaking episode. It accomplished, said an official, yet another iteration of "redefining the possible" (Int: 2066). Its informal tone evoked a spirit of cooperation and engagement that in another setting might not have been possible among interest groups traditionally at variance with each other.

SECURED TRANSACTIONS

Shortly after UNCITRAL took on the carriage of goods by sea, and several years after its Insolvency Working Group had begun deliberations on a legislative guide, UNCITRAL embarked in 2003 upon an equally ambitious program – a set of global norms on secured transactions law.

Every homeowner is familiar with a mortgage. Banks are prepared to lend very large sums of money over long periods of time because if anything goes wrong the bank can seize the house. As a condition of the loan, borrowers have pledged their house as security. If the borrower stops paying, the bank takes back the house and realizes the security.

The principle of security as a basis for lending can be extended far beyond homes. Lenders, such as banks, may extend loans on the basis of both *immoveable* property (e.g., land, buildings, fixtures) and *moveable* property (e.g., inventories of cars, boats, and planes, chattel paper relating the sale of cars, boats, and planes). Lenders can take security on *tangible* assets (e.g., jewelry, art work, stockpiles of goods) and *intangible* assets (e.g., shares of stock, intellectual property rights, moneys owed for goods sold but not yet received, bank accounts).

The importance of secured transactions to trade has both a transaction-specific and market-wide significance. In any transaction between a lender and a borrower, the lender wants to be sure it knows what rights attach to the debtor's property – rights that others might already have in the property and rights available for the lender to obtain – because even unsecured creditors can force a recalcitrant debtor to pay its debts by forcing a sale of its assets. If the debtor has not paid several lenders, who should get paid first? If both lenders have rights in an asset, what priority does one lender have over the other when the borrower defaults? And in the final analysis, what rights do the various lenders have at the moment of insolvency, when almost certainly a borrower's assets will be insufficient to satisfy all lenders completely? Insolvency laws generally recognize the rights of secured creditors over unsecured creditors, but may differ on whether and the extent to which they require secured creditors to participate in an insolvency proceeding.

The availability of security may have a much greater significance for markets as a whole. Each country has a mix of security devices that are available to secure loans: some more, some less; some focused on immovables and little else; others permitting security rights in movables; sometimes only tangibles and other times both tangible and intangible property. It has become an article of faith within international financial institutions and global organizations that the easier it is for debtors to grant a security interest to its lenders, the more transparent various creditors' claims to the debtor's assets as collateral, the more credit (whether secured or unsecured) will be available for the economy. The greater the supply of credit, the more money businesses have to invest and consumers to buy. The logic is straightforward: better secured transactions law generates more credit which stimulates faster economic growth. And in times of financial crisis, having a secured transactions law on the books may clarify creditors' rights and remedies. Thus, this highly technical area of domestic commercial law in fact may have far-reaching implications for domestic markets and the global economy.[44]

There are three main parties of interest in a secured transaction: Secured lenders (also called secured creditors), borrowers (also called debtors), and the debtor's other creditors. Secured creditors often are banks or other financial institutions, especially when the secured lender agrees to provide the funding necessary to maintain a debtor's entire operations. When creditors provide operational lending of this sort, they may take a security interest in all or substantially all of the debtor's business to ensure repayment of the loan. In the event of the debtor's default, the secured lender might be allowed to repossess and resell the collateral on its own, or alternatively obtain the assistance of a receiver or court in accomplishing such a sale. In theory, the debtor's other creditors are aware of the infusion of funding on a secured basis, either because the secured creditor is required to provide public notice of its security interest, sometimes by means of a bureaucratic registration system similar to that governing land registries, or because the law presumes such knowledge in a tight-knit financial community.

Not all secured lending occurs in such a large scale, however. A great deal of lending is extended by suppliers and other trade creditors. A business may sell goods now and receive payment some time later. The time between sale, delivery, and payment for the goods effectively amounts to a loan. If the trade creditor feels insecure about the firm's ability to repay, the trade creditor can request a security interest in the goods sold to ensure repayment of the purchase price. The trade creditor may instead construct this transaction so that "title" to the good stays with the seller until the purchase price is paid in full. In countries that look to the economic consequences, rather than the formal structure, of the transaction, the law will be indifferent as to whether the debtor granted a security interest or the seller retained title in the goods. In both a secured transaction and a "retention of title" (or ROT) transaction, the debtor is entitled to possess and use the good while regular payments are made; if the debtor defaults, the good can be taken back or repossessed

[44] For a collection of essays examining and sometimes questioning this straightforward logic, see (Dahan and Simpson 2009).

by either a secured creditor or seller in a ROT transaction. But under many countries' laws, formal differences matter a great deal (Cuming 1997).[45]

Secured creditors and secured loans take many forms, but banks and other financial institutions often dominate domestic and international lawmaking efforts. Lenders are relatively easy to organize because their interests are focused and well financed. The American Bankers Association, the European Bankers Association, the Commercial Finance Association in the US (who represent asset-based lenders, both banks and finance companies), the Asset Based Finance Association in the United Kingdom, the International Factors Group in Brussels, and Factors Chain International are often present in secured transactions law reform efforts. Trade creditors may be less able to represent their diffuse interests effectively in any country, although they are not entirely unsuccessful. Some large industry actors can mobilize, especially where the law reform effort is tightly focused on the economic interests of a single industry. For example, although the interests of Boeing and Airbus may be diffuse as relates to secured transactions laws reform generally, their interests were sharply focused and well financed in the considering the Cape Town Convention on international interests in mobile equipment involving aircraft. Other trade creditors tend to find supporters in national and international chambers of commerce such as the International Chamber of Commerce (ICC), but the interests of the ICC are spread thin across numerous law reform projects.

Not least, there is a class of creditor frequently overlooked in purely market portraits of lending – the state. If the state is owed unpaid taxes, it has been acting as a creditor. If it is levying withholdings for workers' compensation plans, or demanding compensation for environmental clean-ups, it similarly acts as a creditor. Very often states claim a legislative priority for repayment, i.e., they will be paid first, over even secured creditors in many cases. For some delegates at UNCITRAL, the role of the state as a secured creditor became a critical issue because they considered UNCITRAL's overwhelming focus on private transactions to be unduly restrictive in the real worlds of credit in many countries.

Borrowers or debtors might be either individuals or corporations. Their interests are often unrepresented in law reform efforts, because their numbers and sheer heterogeneity make them extremely difficult to organize (Halliday, Block-Lieb, and Carruthers 2012). There may be consumer associations for individuals, but these

45 In some European and other civil law countries, for example, the formal differences between the two sorts of transactions can be powerful, depending on how the law protects the rights of sellers in ROT transactions. Even where secured transactions must be included in a public register to bind third parties, ROT transactions may not require such registration (since formally they are not secured transactions). Because formally the debtor does not have title to the good until after the purchase price is paid in full, the debtor may not be able to grant a competing security interest in the good that is the subject of a ROT transaction. Because formally the debtor does not have title to the good until after the purchase price is paid in full, the good may not become property of the debtor's insolvency estate.

rarely have deep pockets. Small- and medium-sized enterprises do not easily organize and, if they do, arcane topics like secured transactions are not high on their list of priorities and well beyond their competence. The ICC tends to represent the creditor and not the debtor interests in conversations about secured transactions law reform.

In any technical area of law, the legal profession has a singular expertise. The interests of lawyers in secured transactions law reform are strong, but tend to be focus along practice areas. Lawyers vary in their competencies in different forms of secured transactions. Since secured transactions laws in civil and common law countries tend to vary considerably, and indeed there is substantial variation even within common law jurisdictions, a potential competition springs up among lawyers not only within but also across jurisdictions on whose secured transactions law should permeate global norms.

UNCITRAL's aspirations are international and global. The norms that it promulgates for global adoption have distributional effects on the credit industries and professional services of those countries whose secured transactions law most closely approximates UNCITRAL's products. Global negotiations over secured transaction law, therefore, are not merely matters of theoretical agreement or technical elegance: they are potential contests among the credit industries of some nations (e.g., US, Canada, UK, and Germany), and some regions (e.g., North America, the European Union). There are also potential contests between types of law – between the forms and substance of civil law, which privilege formalisms over practicalities, and US, Canadian, and similar laws, which privilege practical substance over formalisms and favor detailed, very fact-specific rules within a more uniform, generic, functional approach to all secured credit.

Here, then, are several faultlines that cut across the world's credit markets. Across the creditor-debtor divide, in principle a tension exists between the ability of creditors to realize their security quickly and effectively, and the protections accorded debtors, especially consumers and small businesses, from creditor actions. In practice, however, the faultlines within UNCITRAL's Secured Transactions Working Group lay not between creditors and debtors so much as between different classes of creditors – between banks and finance companies, on the one side, and trade creditors and suppliers, on the other; between a deep faultline that pitted Continental forms of security rights against US secured transactions law, found in Article 9 of the US Uniform Commercial Code. While other developed nations have adopted secured transactions laws that resemble those of the US – notably Canada, New Zealand, and most recently Australia – in general the secured transactions laws of these countries more closely resemble US law as it stood fifteen years ago.[46]

[46] The US revised its Article 9 substantially in 2000; although the substance remained the same, its law became much more detailed and favorable to entities looking to securitize their payment streams for purchase in the capital markets. Because their economies are smaller and less likely to securitize payment streams, the revisions to US secured transactions laws adopted in 2000 have not been adopted widely.

Finally, an implicit faultline lay between those countries with significant infrastructure capacities to implement highly sophisticated variants of secured transactions and those countries where infrastructures were weak, including practicing lawyers and bureaucratic registration systems capable of specializing in the complex financial transactions.

A "Chaotic Environment"

At the beginning of the twenty-first century, UNCITRAL could look back on a disorderly array of possibilities for transnational norms that might govern secured transactions.

In the early 1980s, UNCITRAL itself had flirted with the idea of developing a model secured transaction laws for international consumption (Cohen 1998). A distinguished German scholar, Ulrich Drobnig, was asked to prepare a comparative study to investigate the possibility of a uniform law effort (McCormack 2011). At the time, Drobnig reported that he thought it was not only "desirable," but "possible," a recommendation he made to UNCITRAL. But, after debate, UNCITRAL concluded that "the world wasn't ready" for harmonization and set the project aside (Int: 6503, 6507, 8006). This had two effects. On the one hand, comprehensive efforts were abandoned by IOs in favor of specific financing techniques. On the other hand, in the vacuum created by UNCITRAL's reluctance to move at the global level, several regional efforts at harmonization got a head of steam.

Through the 1980s and 1990s specialized protocols tumbled into the public domain. The Council of Europe began work on a uniform retention of title regime in 1982, which it abandoned by 1986 (Int: 8006). In 1988, UNIDROIT promulgated a convention on international factoring and another on international financial leasing, which together are referred to as the Ottawa Conventions; the Ottawa Conventions entered into force in 1995 with ten or fewer contracting states.[47] In 1993, UNIDROIT announced its intention to work on a model secured transactions law; this work proceeded slowly for several years and then seemed to have been put aside when UNIDROIT began work on a draft Convention on International Interests in Mobile Equipment, and related protocols on aircraft equipment, railroad rolling stock and spacecraft (Cohen 1998). A diplomatic convention was convened in Cape Town, South Africa in 2001 to consider this draft convention and its protocols, where numerous countries signed what became to be known as the Cape Town Convention on International Interests in Mobile Equipment.[48] The Cape Town Convention entered into force in 2006, including now several protocols

[47] See UNIDROIT Convention on International Factoring (May 28, 1998), www.unidroit.org/instruments/factoring; UNIDROIT Convention on International Financial Leasing (May 28, 1988), www.unidroit.org/instruments/leasing/convention-leasing.

[48] See UNIDROIT Convention on International Interests in Mobile Equipment (2001, last update May 7, 2015), www.unidroit.org/instruments/security-interests/cape-town-convention.

on aircraft equipment, rolling stock for railways, and space assets. Currently, seventy-three states and the EU are bound to the terms of the Convention itself.

The Hague Conference on Private International law, which specializes in conflicts of law matters that cross legal jurisdictions, promulgated in 2006 a Convention on the Law Applicable to Certain Rights in Respect of Securities Intermediaries.[49] This convention provides conflicts of law and other procedural rules for sorting out multi-jurisdictional disputes involving securities intermediaries, some of which can involve secured transactions in securities, but has attracted only two or three signatories and seems to have stalled.

In 1994, the European Bank on Reconstruction and Development made the first effort to produce a comprehensive and coherent set of norms for Central and Eastern Europe – a Model Law on Secured Transactions. From its inception after the fall of the Soviet Union, the EBRD was given responsibility to assist the transition of Central and Eastern European command economies to market economies; it quickly became evident to the EBRD's governing board "that central and eastern European countries needed particular support in the strengthening of the legal framework for secured transactions" (EBRD Model Law, 1994:4). It observed that former command economies wanted law to handle credit transactions but when they or the EBRD looked across Europe, secured transactions law "was scattered in all sorts of places – case law, bits and pieces in other places" ... and "not a single west European country had anything" coherent (Int: 8007). US Article 9 was thought to be far too complex and English law was even worse, "scattered around many acts" (id.). Said one observer, "when you looked to any western European advanced economy with the question, 'how do you structure a deal?' you found it very difficult to discover [an answer] quickly or easily. You felt like entering a maze and you eventually got lost" (id.).

Advised by an English lawyer and a German practitioner, and supported by numbers of other specialists, EBRD staff drafted a model law that sought to condense in an abstract, concise, and readable way, basic principles of secured transactions law. This document, styled as "extremely good," by a Continental specialist, and "absolutely groundbreaking," by a subsequent Continental reformer, was intended to be "graspable" by civil lawyers (Int: 6502). It had influence on initial legislative enactments across Central and Eastern Europe and a more diffuse influence in the US, Canada, Australia, and New Zealand. But it was designed principally for Eastern European civil law countries, so it traveled less well in other parts of the world. Even in Central and Eastern Europe its drawback inhered in a specificity that was good for specialists but problematic for policymakers who had difficulty grasping the policy dimensions and implications of this arcane and technical law so

[49] See Convention on the Law Applicable to Certain Rights in Respect of Securities Held with an Intermediary (July 5, 2006), https://assets.hcch.net/docs/3afb8418-7eb7-4a0c-af85-c4f35995bb8a.pdf.

they could forge political consensus. EBRD therefore circled back and followed its Model Law with Core Principles in 1998 and later with more targeted instruments in its General Principles for a Charge Register in 2003 and a 2005 project on mortgages and securitization. Nonetheless, with its Model Law on Secured Transactions, EBRD set a precedent that some kind of comprehensive secured transactions protocol might be possible and practicable.

The EBRD was not the only regional IO focused regionally on secured transactions law reform. The *L'Organisation pour l'Harmonisation en Afrique du Droit des Affairs* (OHADA), an IGO of fourteen sub-Saharan African states, adopted in 1997 its Uniform Act on Security Rights, based mostly on French law. The governing body of the Organization of American States (OAS) adopted its Inter-American Law on Secured Transactions in 2002 and, in 2009, related Model Registry Regulations.

All these reform efforts were either focused on specific sorts of secured collateral or on specific regions of the globe. The quest for a statement of secured transaction norms that was both global in reach and general in application remained out of reach, but not because the international community thought the project unimportant.

After the Asian Financial Crisis, the G-22 had issued its reports on the International Financial Architecture (G-22 1998a). The international financial architecture to which the reports referred spanned a wide range of international economic law; in a small corner of this immense report included a global approach to secured transactions reform efforts. The Reports on Strengthening Financial Systems and International Financial Crises identified "debtor-creditor regimes" as potential antidotes to financial crises and facilitators of a rapid and orderly resolution of excessive indebtedness after the fact. Although the G-22 was somewhat ambiguous about the meaning of effective "debtor-creditor regimes," it did point to several "key features" of modern "debtor-creditor regimes," which were nearly all focused on "those laws that provide the framework for the extension of credit secured by the assets of an enterprise – both its movable property . . . and its real estate. . . ."[50]

As with the G-22's efforts to encourage the creation of international standards for corporate insolvency law, these reports called for action but did not specify who should take up the work. While the G-22 pressed for "technical assistance from both the IMF and the World Bank to encourage and facilitate improvement in the existing insolvency and debtor-creditor regimes,"[51] the ADB worked first to implement a plan of action. Agreeing that good insolvency and secured transactions regimes might have forestalled the crisis and could provide some protection from future crises, ADB developed a set of standards that it used both as a diagnostic instrument and normative criterion for national law. In a 150-page report released in 2000, the ADB made a case for the importance of secured credit, the policy issues

[50] G-22, at ¶ 2.5.2 (G-22 1998a).
[51] Id. at ¶ 2.5.3.

that lay behind legal frameworks, the several steps necessary to institute an effective secured transactions regime (ADB 2000b). For each of the four key steps in construction of a secured transactions regime (e.g., Creation, Publicity, Priority, Enforcement), the ADB's team created a set of standards and then appraised five Asian nations (i.e., India, China, Indonesia, Pakistan, Thailand) for the level of conformity to the standards (Asian Development Bank [ADB] 2000b).

The World Bank, too, included in its *Principles and Guidelines* (World Bank 2001) five principles relevant to a "legal framework for creditor rights," three of which were focused specifically on secured transactions: the need to adopt a law providing for the creation, recognition, and enforcement of security interests in moveable and immoveable, tangible and intangible property; the need to create an efficient and cost-effective means for publicizing these security interests; and the need to allow for efficient, inexpensive, transparent, and predictable methods for enforcing a security interest in property.

Unlike UNCITRAL's reform of the earlier Hague Rules, Visby Protocol, and Hamburg Rules, where a series of international conventions had overlapped over decades and had begun to compete with each other, the secured transactions legal orders were scattered across a variety of industry interests and across various regions of the world. Efforts to draw them into a global transnational legal order had come late in the day.

Facilitating Factors

The value of global agreement on secured transactions law was stimulated by commercial demand, at least as it was perceived by lawyer and lawyer-banker delegates.

Something like an international protocol will only make sense, stated a delegate, if "there is a semblance of demand, not just supply" (Int: 9030). And commercial demand was increasing as cross-border trade increased. Said one Continental delegate:

> If this [the Legislative Guide on Secured Transactions] translates into laws, this would be the best thing for small and medium enterprises. Take the case of a wine-maker in Bordeaux. He is planning to sell wine today in France. It is a predictable environment. There is no problem there. But if he looks outside France, to Spain or Germany, there are different rules and law. What are the means by which he can ensure he will be paid? Or how can the German buyer be confident that if he prepays he will get the wine? No one knows the answers. If I can convince the French and Germans that the rules will be identical, and without the need for x-thousand euros for legal advice, they will be more disposed to purchase, there will be more trust, more multiple relationships and dealings, etc. Our Legislative Guide would indicate exactly what they would get if anything went wrong. And with multiple countries, a Japanese purchaser will be in the same situation as a German purchaser.
>
> (Int: 6501)

Germany confronted issues regarding cross-border recognition of its retention of title security in business transactions with its neighbors. "German companies were selling to our national neighbors using retention of title and we found we had no security interest. So German banks and producers wept and cried. So they came to us [academics]. We said, 'life is hard!' Then I said, 'we have to do something and I suggested we do something at UNCITRAL'" (Int: 6509).

These examples pointed to "a slow growing problem in the deficiencies of international trade ... There was consensus that something needed to be done." The issue was how to do it without "destroying the market for finance in various countries" (Int: 6509).

Several leading delegates to the Secured Transactions Working Group observed that the US and some of prominent finance trade groups (e.g., the Commercial Finance Association), also saw that development of a global standard patterned closely on US law would benefit US competitiveness in international finance markets. The close relationship between the US delegation and CFA, said a delegate, occurred because "the CFA came and said [to the US State Department], we want to expand in international business. They wanted to expand internationally. They wanted more business – in Europe, Thailand, China" (Int: 6509). A mobilization on behalf of US finance interests worldwide would have a salutary benefit on its competitiveness in the legal services market, as well, one of the reasons that US private lawyers played an important role in deliberations within the Secured Transactions Working Group.

But there was broader interest in focusing on an international standard for secured transactions than simply from the United States. The variety of initiatives also had helped break an "unbreakable assumption" in many civil law countries that the law governing secured transactions had to be the law related to the location of an asset. This work on non-tangible assets showed that civil lawyers could imagine a law governing intangible collateral, and that it was not necessary to imagine tangible and intangible assets as apples and oranges, as forms of security that could not be brought onto the same plane (Cohen 1998). The relatively narrow UNCITRAL draft Convention on the Assignment of Receivables in International Trade, and the UNIDROIT Conventions on International Financial Leasing, International Factoring, and, perhaps most importantly, its (then) draft Convention on International Interests in Mobile Equipment, began to suggest that perhaps a unified set of rules might be possible for secured transactions (Int: 6501). Here there was something of an epistemic breakthrough, a cognitive recognition that a grand approach might after all be possible across legal families and types of security.

However, the narrowness of these earlier conventions signaled several potential problems, all political. Earlier conventions had emerged to govern transactions involving relatively narrow bundles of collateral, such as assignment of international receivables, in which there was a burgeoning international market, and security interests in mobile equipment, like aircraft, that was enormously expensive and almost guaranteed to cross borders. That these conventions had centered on specific sorts of transactions involving particular sorts of collateral was, in many ways, not simply a case of IOs taking small bites at a large apple. Interest group support was essential to the likelihood that a convention on such technical topics would ever enter into force. Focusing industry by industry on narrow forms of collateral – essentially creating mini-TLOs – allowed IOs to enlist the support of narrowly focused interest group interest, often industry specific. This strategy, if it was a strategy, had not panned out with the Ottawa Conventions, but looked enormously promising with UNIDROIT's Cape Town Convention on mobile equipment. Major industry actors, like Boeing and Airbus, wanted this convention to succeed. Could success in narrowly defined conventions on narrow topics of secured transactions law translate into success on a broader scale? No one was sure. But the prospect of a winner taking all, of a single IO emerging as the dominant player, of a comprehensive TLO that spanned forms of security, clearly concentrated minds in UNCITRAL's Secretariat.

In the late twentieth century, UNIDROIT had built its reputation for draft conventions on aspects of secured transactions law. By 2001, UNIDROIT had succeeded in convening a diplomatic conference on both the draft Cape Town convention and a related protocol on aircraft. Twenty-one nations signed the convention at the conference, with six additional nations signing shortly thereafter; signatories included the UK, France, China, US, Canada, a handful of European nations, and a wide range of emerging and developing nations, such as Ghana, Chile, Kenya, and Turkey. By many accounts, UNIDROIT was an obvious choice for a larger, more comprehensive project, especially since it had earlier begun work on a Model Secured Transactions Law. But UNIDROIT suffered from its historic reputation as a group of Continental academics that had emerged out of the League of Nations (Block-Lieb and Halliday 2016). UNIDROIT had expanded its membership only after UNCITRAL's creation by the UN General Assembly but more recently UNIDROIT's close embrace of industry actors, such as Boeing, did little to strengthen its claim of broad representation even if it did secure ample resources.

UNCITRAL could claim expertise in the area of secured transactions law by pointing to its draft Convention on the Assignment of Receivables in International Trade as precedent. This draft Convention provided a necessary step for the first truly global deliberative panel on secured transactions reform. But UNCITRAL's draft Convention was a narrower, more circumscribed instrument than a possible model law or legislative guide on secured transactions law; it did not involve tangible assets, where cross-national variation was so acute (Int: 6507). Nonetheless, the timing was nearly perfect. UNCITRAL's Commission was set to adopt this draft Convention in 2001, and send it to the UN General Assembly for ratification. UNCITRAL's Working Group on Secured Transactions, a collegial community of global lawmakers, had already begun to build mutual trust and cooperation;

the Insolvency Working Group had shown that a core group of delegates could continue incrementally from one project to another within the working group configuration (Cohen 1998).

Moreover, given the interdependency of insolvency and secured transactions law, UNCITRAL's progress with the Legislative Guide on Insolvency Law further increased confidence that a comparable project might come to fruition on secured transactions. The EBRD, ADB, and World Bank had closely linked their lawmaking on insolvency and secured transactions, so much so that at the ADB and World Bank the two initiatives has proceeded in tandem. If UNCITRAL could produce comprehensive insolvency norms that might lead to national convergence on insolvency regimes, then this too opened up the door to a secured transactions initiative (Int: 8006). If UNCITRAL could explode the assumption that insolvency law simply wouldn't yield to any possibility of a global consensus, then it might also lead the world to conclude that it was ready for a holistic regime for secured transactions.

Precipitating Factors

As UNCITRAL's leaders scanned the field of potential competitors they simultaneously feared a global disintegration of norms and a rival for production of a global standard. Said a leading delegate to Secured Transactions Working Group: "In early Working Group meetings we discussed the need to move fast because everyone is clamoring for a coherent protocol. The concern was a proliferation of competing models, dissipation of energy, and potential incoherence of regimes of credit" (Int: 9030).

When UNCITRAL looked to Rome, the seat of UNIDROIT, it observed that UNIDROIT's Cape Town Convention on mobile equipment financing (aircraft, railway rolling stock and spacecraft) got strong industry support and quick signatures from major nations, including the US (with Boeing) and France (with Airbus). The question was, given this success, could UNIDROIT use the Cape Town convention as a "launching pad" for something much more ambitious (Int: 9030)? It would have been difficult for UNIDROIT to build interest group support for a broader project, since the convention on mobile equipment had relied so heavily on industry groups – manufacturers and sellers of aircraft, railway rolling stock, and spacecraft – rather than financial interest groups writ large. But surely it would not have been impossible. And the Cape Town Convention's "insolvency exception" created a dangerous precedent for subsequent law reform efforts in this context (US DOS, Digest 2006).

UNIDROIT was not UNCITRAL's only competition on secured transactions law reform. As UNCITRAL warily observed the activities of the World Bank, it also saw "a threat" (Int: 8006). Although the G-22 had included secured transactions law reform in its wish list for raising the international financial architecture, it had identified the IMF and the World Bank as the likely locations for such law reform efforts. Both UNCITRAL's Insolvency Working Group and many Secured Transactions Working Group delegates knew full well that the World Bank had threatened to produce insolvency standards in competition with UNCITRAL and indeed had proceeded to develop its *Principles and Guidelines* in complete awareness of UNCITRAL's competing Legislative Guide on Insolvency Law. The *Principles and Guidelines* similarly covered topics of secured transactions law. Would the World Bank also claim this topic for its own? Would the Commission also ask the Secured Transaction Working Group to sit idly by while the World Bank determined how far it wanted to go on the topic of secured transactions? Said one official: as "the biggest organization of all it might claim everything" if it had decided to enter this domain. The World Bank had already developed one of its diagnostic instruments, a ROSC,[52] on insolvency and "ROSCs are used as a potential imperial move" by the Bank. If it did so on secured transactions, it might suck the oxygen out of the air for all other IOs (Int: 8006).

During the 1990s, the World Bank had moved into Central and Eastern Europe and turned not to the EBRD Model Law for its reference point but to the Central and Eastern Europe Law Initiative (CEELI), the American Bar Association's program in the region (Int: 9030). Earlier, the International Finance Corporation of the World Bank group had done work on a Model Law on international commercial leasing, which they brought to UNIDROIT. The potential for an alliance between the World Bank and UNIDROIT, combined against UNCITRAL, was also a possibility (Int: 8006).

Not least, Europe, too, was beginning to consider a European Union effort on secured transactions law. More than ten years after work by the Council of Europe on a convention on retention of title transactions had been shelved, the European Commission produced a draft report, which flirted on the edges with narrow issues of secured transactions law. In 1998 and 1999, the groundwork was also being laid for preparation for broader directives that were intended to cover "collateral takers" and "collateral providers" with the EU across a range of financial entities. The sounds of Brussels' murmurings reached Vienna. Roughly simultaneous with UNCITRAL's secured transactions work, the European Commission had embarked upon a major effort by distinguished European scholars, led by Professor Drobnig of earlier UNCITRAL discussions, to create a common framework for secured transactions in all EU countries, an initiative which offer a regional, then global, alternative to any product from UNCITRAL (Int: 6503, 9030).[53]

52 Report on the Observance of Standards and Codes, one of twelve World Bank diagnostic instruments used to evaluate the compliance of nations with the IMF/World Bank norms for financial systems.

53 Study Group on a European Civil Code and Research Group on EC Private Law, Principles, Definitions, and Model Rules of European Civil Law: Draft Common Frame of Reference, Outline Edition, Book IX, Proprietary Security Rights in Moveable Assets (2009), available online at http://ec.europa.eu/justice/policies/civil/docs/dcfr_outline_edition_en.pdf.

Competition among global lawmakers does not only arise from other IOs within a lawmaking ecology. It may also occur between adjacent lawmaking ecologies whose lawmaking overlapped, precisely the situation that confronted the insolvency and secured transaction ecologies. Relationships between insolvency and secured transactions law were reflected in the prospect of interdependency or competition between UNCITRAL's Working Groups on Insolvency and Secured Transactions Law. Insolvency is critical to secured transactions precisely because security interests might get undone in the context of an insolvency proceeding.

That the Insolvency Working Group had been at work for several years before the Secured Transactions Working Group had been authorized by the Commission to start its work presented some very real landmines in the secured transaction deliberations. By the time the Commission authorized the work of the Secured Transactions Working Group, the Insolvency Working Group had already set its agenda and made decisions about what would happen to security interests inside an insolvency proceeding. The draft Insolvency Guide contained recommendations that a secured creditor's collateral should be included within a debtor's bankruptcy estate and that, especially in the context of a company's reorganization, secured creditors should be stayed from grabbing these assets through foreclosure. While many countries paid lip service to the idea that secured debt could not be restructured in the context of an insolvency proceeding, the delegates to UNCITRAL's Insolvency Working Group had been convinced that this limitation made the success of reorganizations proceedings nearly impossible. Secured creditors, like the debtor's other creditors, most be included in a collective proceeding for there to be any chance of the firm's financial rehabilitation. These recommendations laid key groundwork for other provisions regarding the standard for confirmation of a plan of reorganization and the vulnerability of some security rights to avoidance actions in the context of insolvency.

The draft work on the Insolvency Legislative Guide would need to be finessed by the Secured Transactions Working Group if their efforts were to gain credence among banks, finance companies, factors, and trade creditors. Hence, UNCITRAL itself faced an internal challenge – to define the boundaries between its two working groups and to obtain consensus among specialists whose substantive and economic interests potentially put them in conflict.

By 2002 these converging pressures from outside and inside UNCITRAL had injected a sense of urgency into decision making by its Secretariat. Either an UNCITRAL initiative must begin immediately, or UNCITRAL would be sidelined as a promulgator of security norms not only in part by insolvency encroachments from within, but also in whole by initiatives emanating from Europe, the World Bank, or UNIDROIT.

Agenda Setting

Determined to move quickly, Jernej Sekolec, UNCITRAL's new Secretary, approached a leading civil law specialist on secured transactions to move temporarily to Vienna and produce a first draft (Int: 8007). This did not come about, but the invitation conveyed UNCITRAL's determination to move quickly while there was still an opening for its global leadership.

Who, then, set the agenda for the Secured Transactions Working Group? Did UNCITRAL start afresh or build incrementally on the work of earlier IOs? What topics were put on the table or taken off it? How was it decided what form would be chosen?

Two years earlier UNCITRAL's Commission had considered "work undertaken by other organizations in the field of security interests."[54] Unlike its consideration of the work of the Insolvency Working Group, the Commission did not have before it any proposal by a member state. And unlike the Transportation Working Group, it had no commitment of a private body to partner with UNCITRAL.

Instead, the Commission was asked to respond to an in-house report prepared by the Secretariat that proposed an UNCITRAL program of work. This Report noted that "a number of texts had been or were currently being prepared" by other groups and organizations, but also that empty spaces in the legal firmament where issues remained "unaddressed."[55] UNCITRAL should fill these gaps, the Report proposed.

Not surprisingly, an observer in the UNCITRAL proceedings from UNIDROIT dissented. UNIDROIT's representative to UNCITRAL objected to the claim that gaps existed, which UNCITRAL must fill. UNIDROIT had begun the very work that UNCITRAL now claimed. "[I]n 1980, after UNCITRAL had assigned low priority to the subject of security interests" with the Drobnig Report, UNIDROIT invested "significant resources" in the topic and "had become the premier organization to undertake and coordinate work in the field of secured credit law."[56] Indeed, in 1993 UNIDROIT "had started work on the preparation of a model law on security interests," although its efforts were suspended in 1995 in order to give priority to the then nascent Cape Town Convention."[57] But UNIDROIT had always intended, stated its delegate, that "once that work [on mobile equipment] had been completed, UNIDROIT could be expected to resume its work on the model law."[58] Hence, "UNCITRAL should not undertake overlapping work in the field of security interests." It should avoid "any duplication of efforts."[59] UNCITRAL should stand aside and allow UNIDROIT to resume its efforts.

Pressed to justify its incursions into what UNIDROIT claimed as its legal territory, others at attendance at the Commission meeting emphasized UNCITRAL's historic

54 UN Doc. No. A/55/17, at ¶ 455 et seq. (June 12–July 7, 2000).
55 Id.
56 Id., at ¶ 456.
57 Id.
58 Id.
59 Id.

role in the "co-ordination of the work of other organizations."[60] Characterizing itself "as the core legal body in the United Nations system in the field of the unification and harmonization of international trade law," the Commission "reaffirmed its mandate to monitor work carried out in other organizations."[61] It stepped back from the position that it alone should decide the workload in this or other areas of international trade law, and nonetheless agreed that "duplication could be avoided with a cautious, measured approach that would focus on particular types of asset."[62] After all, "the topic of security interests was so broad and the issues involved so complex that it would take work by several organizations to address all problems . . . ."[63]

To forestall an open conflict and the unattractive prospect to some delegations of two parallel tracks of lawmaking, the Secretariats of UNCITRAL and UNIDROIT sat down to negotiate a settlement. They agreed that UNCITRAL would proceed with a comprehensive lawmaking effort, but UNIDROIT would continue its trajectory of specialized products for particular areas of secured transactions law (Int: 6532). And, with this interchange, no further pubic conversation was had regarding the propriety of UNCITRAL's involvement in the writing of a legislative guide or model law on secured transactions law, either at this meeting or the Commission or at future meetings.

In preparation for the Commission's meeting in 2001, the Secretariat prepared a lengthy memorandum, which outlined the economic importance of secured lending, and the interrelationship between insolvency law and secured transactions law. It put on the table numerous issues on the creation, priority, and enforcement of security interests. It discussed security interests over specific sorts of collateral – namely, investment securities (on which the report notes that both the EU and The Hague Conference on Private International Law previously had worked), intellectual property rights (on which the World Intellectual Property Organization was likely to claim overlapping jurisdiction), and private international law (especially conflicts of law, a traditional concern for The Hague Conference on Private International Law) on secured lending. The Secretariat made far-reaching claims for the legal scope of its work, including investment securities and intellectual property.

The Commission demurred, drawing the boundaries of UNCITRAL's efforts less ambitiously, most particularly to ensure a carveout for other types of collateral because other IOs, and UNIDROIT in particular, had already treated them. These included aircraft and immoveables.[64] Complex financial instruments were also set aside, both because The Hague Conference had already worked on aspects of these issues and because the Commission feared opposition from the City of London

60 Id., at ¶ 457.
61 Id., at ¶ 458.
62 Id.
63 Id.
64 Id., at ¶ 354.

(Int: 9030). Intellectual property was a sensitive area because it potentially would bring UNCITRAL into conflict with the World Intellectual Property Organization.[65] "We had no interest ever in getting into IP qua IP," said a core delegate, so "a line was drawn." We didn't want "to invade [WIPO's] jurisdiction ... so we partly postponed it" for a later Supplement to the legislative guide (Int: 6510). The suggestion was made to limit the focus of the Working Group to "security interests in goods involved in a commercial activity," especially since such an initial focus "would not exclude the possibility of extending the scope of that work at a later stage," and the Commission agreed with this suggestion.

What form should this project take? Fear was expressed at the Commission's meeting that "a model law might be too rigid."[66] UNCITRAL had just promulgated its Convention on International Receivables, a project that had taken years to complete but on completion had inspired little in the way of excitement. This negative object lesson was imprinted on UNCITRAL's institutional memory. The experience of the EBRD, said a delegate, indicated "that the world is not ripe for a Model Law" (Int: 9030, 6502). And since "there was a certain reluctance against the whole project, [the Secretariat] wanted to lower expectations. A Model Law might have raised the bar too high" (Int: 6503).

Quick agreement developed within the Commission around a two-step format, like that adopted by the Insolvency Working Group – namely, the Secured Transactions Working Group should draft a set of "core principles for an efficient legal regime governing secured transactions," which would become a part of a legislative guide "containing flexible approaches to the implementation of such principles and a discussion of alternative approaches possible and the benefits and detriments of such approaches."[67] Precision died hard in this group, many of whom were used to drafting detailed bright-line statutory provisions, and so "it was further suggested that the legislative guide should also contain, where feasible, model legislative provisions."[68] A delegate from the US concurred that the "the politics were such that the world wasn't ready for anything stronger than a legislative guide" (Int: 6507). Put another way, "a legislative guide was chosen because it is the lowest level of consensus" (Int: 6509).

Thus, the decision to create a legislative guide was made by the Secretariat "on Day 1" as a prudent choice so that the Working Group's reach might not exceed its grasp (Int: 6510, 6502). It also represented a political compromise between a potential clash between two sharply divergent systems of secured transactions: Article 9 of the US UCC, which had a specificity and exactness more akin to a Model Law; and European codes, which had broad principles applied through rules. By combining commentary with recommendations, a legislative

65 Id., at ¶ 355.
66 Id., at ¶ 357.
67 Id.
68 Id.

guide permitted an amalgam of both precision and broad statements of principle (Block-Lieb and Halliday 2006).

If the Secretariat could not import a specialist lawyer to prepare a comprehensive draft, it took another tack. In March 2002, the Secretariat organized a Colloquium in partnership with a US trade association, the Commercial Finance Association, which had signaled its willingness to play a role analogous to CMI, INSOL, IBA, and the ABA in other working groups. The momentum of the Colloquium carried into preparation of a working draft to be placed on the table at the next meeting of Secured Transactions Working Group.[69] Chapters of the working draft were allocated to expert volunteers and compiled and integrated by the Secretariat for the Secured Transactions Working Group to consider at its first session in May 2002.

Unlike the Commission, the Secretariat's version was not modest in the scope of its substantive boundaries.

> In terms of scope of work, this draft starts from the working assumption that a guide should have as wide a scope as possible. The justification for this approach lies in one of the key objectives of any secured credit regime, namely the full utilization of assets for the purpose of obtaining credit, which requires a comprehensive regime in terms of assets, obligations and parties covered.[70]

Several core delegates wanted a very broad definition of the topic and "not to have exclusions at the beginning" (Int: 6509). For civil lawyers, in particular, "we have learned in the last two hundred years to have very general rules" (id.) Otherwise, many problems arise in domestic legislation as past practices, economic interests, and policy preferences differ from country to country (Int: 6503). But little else about the preliminary draft offered to the Working Group would have looked familiar to the civilians in the room.

The twelve sections of the draft covered key objectives; an introductory discussion of the sorts of financial transactions to be covered by a legislative guide; a statement of a guide's basic approach to secured transactions; publicity; filing systems; priority; the pre-default rights and obligations of the parties; default and enforcement; insolvency; conflicts of law rules; and transition issues.[71]

What the draft did not do, however, was acknowledge any of the products earlier promulgated by other IOs, most notably, the Model Law and later Principles of the EBRD. None of the delegates who came to form the inner core of the working group's proceedings give any credence to the notion that UNCITRAL was bound in any way by the multiple sets of extant norms crafted by international organizations, regional multilateral institutions, or domestic legislatures. Although the Report of the Secretary-General on Current Activities and Possible

69 UN Doc. No. A/CN.9/WG.VI/WP.3 (Vienna, Mar. 20–22, 2002).
70 UN Doc. No. A/CN.9/WG.VI/WP.2, at ¶ 5.
71 UN Doc. No. A/CN.9/WG.VI/WP.2 and Adds. 1–12.

Future Work on Security Interests[72] had earlier listed in detail these initiatives, it also pointed to significant problems, both inadequacies with many domestic secured transactions laws, which were viewed as insufficiently detailed, "'friction' resulting from the possibility that more than one country's law might govern," and a true conflict among these laws in the case of loss of security if collateral crosses national borders.[73]

Unlike the Insolvency Working Group, where delegates at the first working session had a template of prior protocols before them, the Secured Transactions Working Group did not. Unlike the Transportation Working Group, no "pre-deal" or draft instrument was put on the table either.

That this draft was potentially controversial became quickly obvious from a response written by the EBRD.[74] In this response, the EBRD offered both implicit and explicit critiques. First, it noted, a guide should stimulate change rather than sit on legislators' bookshelves. It "should not seek to impose solutions, even in matter of practical detail, where other approaches might be adopted."[75] With this comment it seems clear that the EBRD warned against including all the details of US Article 9 in an UNCITRAL legislative guide. Second, the response argued, a guide should not polarize civil and common law systems, and should be careful, by implication, not to "ostracize" some countries' choice of legal system. Third, the EBRD cautioned UNCITRAL's Secretariat that it should be more explicit about the distinction between a formal (i.e., a civil law) approach to secured transactions law and a more functional approach (like that adopted by the US in its Article 9 and Canada in its Personal Property Security Act). A functional approach to secured transactions law may, in the end, be more efficient, but, the EBRD argued, the "reform that entails adopting a functional approach also implies a major review of the law on obligations and property, and some fundamental changes in the approach to legal and practical issues."[76]

In toto, the EBRD commentary crystallized potential resistance to UNCITRAL's agenda that would run through deliberations and beyond completion of its legislative guide. To all intents and purposes, the preliminary draft appeared to

[72] UN Doc. No. A/CN.9/475, reprinted at UNCITRAL Yearbook 2000, Part Two, at 557–565.

[73] Id. at 565–566.

[74] UN Doc. No., A/CN.9/WG.VI/WP.4 (Apr. 24, 2002).

[75] Id. at ¶ 6.

[76] Id. at ¶ 9. The EBRD cautioned the Secretariat that its "stance on enforcement" of security interests in the event of default was also potentially polarizing. The US approach was to permit secured creditors to repossess collateral, without the involvement of courts, if the repossession could be accomplished without a "breach of the peace;" if peaceful repossession couldn't be accomplished privately, then, as a fall-back position, a secured creditor could seek enforcement through the courts. While this approach may have many benefits, the EBRD opined, it also may contradict "entrenched traditions and perceptions of the court's role" in a legal system, since in many countries, and most often in civil law countries, "there is a strong expectation of court involvement." UN Doc. No. A/CN.9/WG.VI/WP.4, at ¶ 15.

Continental and civil lawyers as an adoption in broad outline of US and perhaps Canadian law. Said one prominent delegate from the Continent:

> The USA and Canada effectively set the agenda. They already have a law; and their global trade was the largest; so when they deal with other countries, if the law is the same it is to their advantage. The UNCITRAL legislative guide follows the same pattern. You can sense it in the course of the meetings – they are pushing for their law . . . as far as possible they want UNCITRAL to conform to their own law. USA includes the American Bar Association and Commercial Finance Association.
>
> (Int: 6504)

Another civil lawyer had no doubt that the agenda was set by the Secretariat. And who pushed the Secretariat?

> I think it came from the Americans, the 'UCC Art 9 team' . . . The Secretary understood there was a need to reform secured transactions. They asked themselves, on what basis should we do so? What model should we promote? So, naturally, it looked to the US . . . When you look at the first draft submitted in 2002, it was really the structure of Article 9.
>
> (Int: 6506)

Said another civil lawyer from Europe:

> My personal opinion is that everyone [understood] that the benchmark was the UCC [US Uniform Commercial Code]. You could see this from the beginning. It was an adoption of the UCC re-drafted by the CFA.
>
> (Int: 6509)[77]

US delegates do not dissent strongly from this view, although the role of CFA is disputed. For one US delegate the initial dominance of the US and Canada was "purely a function of expertise . . . The US and Canadians knew what needed to be here" (Int: 6507).

Given the particularity of US secured transactions law in comparison to the widespread influence of English common law and civil law jurisdictions across the world, not to mention Islamic commercial law, why did UNCITRAL's Secretariat choose to align itself at the outset not with any of the other IOs which had extensive experience in the field, or with a civil law regime, but with the US bloc?

Several reasons suggest themselves. It was not at all clear that UNCITRAL's International Receivables Convention would succeed and, if not, UNCITRAL could not afford another failure with the Legislative Guide on Secured Transactions Law. Second, UNCITRAL's Secretariat did not have the in-house expertise to handle the technical intricacies of sophisticated secured transactions law. UNCITRAL therefore needed to form an alliance with experts who would produce.

[77] For a more extensive and nuanced argument on the connections between UNCITRAL's Legislative Guide on Secured Transactions Law and US Article 9, see (McCormack 2011).

The US bloc offered precisely this: its technical auspices had been demonstrated during work on the Receivables Convention. US and Canadian lawyers had a proven track record of industriousness and reliability. The US had just finished its own thorough revision of Article 9 in 2000; enactment and the latest modernizing amendments of Canada's PPSA had preceded this revision by only a few years. And as the world's largest economy, a partnership between UNCITRAL and the US also elevated the probability that a product would be forthcoming and that the US would affirm and disseminate it. The North American bloc therefore offered the Secured Transactions Working Group technical expertise, dependability, and influence. But could it convince the scores of global legislators from across the world, representatives of nations, industries, professions, and salient international organizations?

CREATING ISSUE-ECOLOGIES

To create an issue-ecology that produces effective international law is a formidable challenge of social organization. While generically analogous to starting a business, or beginning a family, or constituting a new independent state, or founding a voluntary association, the beginnings of an issue-ecology in international space compound such difficulties because international lawmaking issue-ecologies lie outside the institutional supports of shared laws or languages or interactional styles or regulatory orders that conventionally can be taken for granted within a state. Theoretical framing of this social task as an ecological process has a two-fold advantage: on the one hand, the conceptual vocabulary of social ecology brings to the international sphere a tested body of theoretical materials extensively elaborated over a century of applications to other forms of social organization; on the other hand, ecology theory offers a finite, compact, and interdependent set of concepts to make systematic meaning of the otherwise bewildering, fluid, cross-cutting, amorphous social relations that span any issue that is fundamental to markets, encapsulates in principle all law salient to that issue, and spans the entire world.

To create an issue-ecology that seeks to bring legal order to an underlying market problem, we have proposed, will involve the interplay of six elements integral to any ecological theory of the international: identifying and framing an underlying problem in activity; establishing claims through boundary work as to which actors will be legitimately tasked with resolving that problem through law; obtaining resources and managing relations with adjacent ecologies sufficient to sustain the lawmaking work; structuring interactions among actors in ways that surmount competition; distributing actors across the lawmaking space by the relative primacy of their roles and strength of their legitimacy; and situating that ecology in time, both the grand time of ecologies that contextualize this specific lawmaking task, and the time it takes for an issue-ecology bounded in task to produce its laws.

Whereas Chapter 2 drew a portrait of an ambitious standing ecology for all international commercial law, an ecology that would endure over decades, adjusting to long-term changing ideals and paradigms of law and economics, and adapting to epochal geopolitical shifts and economic transformations, Chapter 3 has tightly sharpened its focus to short-term lawmaking ecologies that worked for a handful of years to bring actors into temporary lawmaking encounters to produce a specific set of norms responsive to a strictly delimited issue or problem confronting international trade and commerce. These issue-ecologies emerged as distinctive forms of social organization, yet adjacent to an industry ecology and to the standing private international lawmaking ecology in which UNCITRAL, UNIDROIT, and the Hague Conference were centrally positioned. UNCITRAL, itself, is also partly nested within the UN's variegated ecology of administrative units, IOs, and agencies.

How then did these issue-ecologies of lawmaking for markets come into being? In what ways did the interactions at their moments of origin anticipate and potentially constrain the later work of actors intent on producing law for the world? Who led these ventures in social construction and how did they justify and circumscribe the breadth of their jurisdictional claims as lawmakers for global markets?

In conclusion we revisit the narratives of agenda setting in transport, insolvency and secured transactions lawmaking by analyzing the activities across all the emergent issue-ecologies to discern comparatively the social processes at work. We sharpen this processual analysis by identifying the many obstacles that stood between failure and success in ecology-building and law production (see Table 3.2).

Marking Boundaries

Like reform episodes for any legal change, international lawmaking actors struggle to diagnose a problem in a way that favors their interests and to frame that diagnosis in ways that lead to the prescriptions they prefer. At this point, the interests of particular actors can subvert the collective output of a lawmaking ecology. Premature or unthinking acceptance of a contentious prevailing ideology about markets or law can misdirect problem-solving solutions. Undue deference to the diagnostic framing of an issue by a powerful state or industry actor or IO can foster resentment or resistance among audiences and actors critical to ultimate implementation of norms.

Common to all the diagnostic struggles in transport, insolvency and secured transactions was acceptance of the fundamental paradigms of law and markets thoroughly institutionalized in the standing lawmaking ecology. With little dissent all actors at the formative stage of bringing the issue-ecologies into being accepted the verities that harmonizing and modernizing law for their respective issue-areas would yield economic benefits for capitalist markets. While the goal of unification of laws might have been contested, the idioms of harmonization and modernization were accepted as rhetorically self-justifying, especially when the lawmaking itself would reveal flexibility in the technologies of law that allowed states and industries degrees of adaptive freedom to fit local circumstances.

The misfits, lags, and gaps between the fit of law and markets in specific areas similarly revealed shared understandings of why lawmaking required a form of social organization focused on solutions. The maritime transport industry confronted the issues of out-of-date and fragmenting transnational norms for carriage of goods by sea. The industry that is centered on corporations in financial distress faced inchoate, conflicting, or counter-productive practices in markets across the world. The industry that provides credit based on security was similarly fragmented, fragmenting, conflicting, and outdated. Each industry actor found counterpart actors in law and IOs who shared framings conducive to reforms. Early consensus was found on industry demands for a worldwide unified legal order that could deal with the problems of carrying goods across oceans, a problem intensifying as seafaring trade continued to expand although old sets of rules no longer adequately kept pace with market changes. At the outset of lawmaking high level commitments were already shared on the demand for legal mechanisms to rescue failing companies, save jobs, preserve assets, or produce some order in the scramble to seize assets of a corporation approaching financial collapse. Consensus could be found on the general proposition that all business and states should have access to more credit within and across national borders.

Nevertheless, at more immanent levels of problem specification, actors pressing for a new lawmaking episode confronted challenges of how to ensure that critical problems were on the lawmaking agenda and how to rule out of bounds, at least for the moment, issues too marginal, or intractable, or too divisive. How was it possible to demarcate jurisdictional claims with sufficient precision to focus negotiations while keeping away insurgent or intransigent actors? And how could the early boundary work maintain sufficient ambiguity at the originating moment of lawmaking so that expansion or contraction of problem solving that would allow adjustments in mid-course to enable final consensus or stimulate creativity? At this foundational juncture lawmakers likewise faced the puzzle of finding that sweet spot on a continuum between a problem too small, in which case the lawmaking does little for market actors, and a problem too large, in which case the lawmaking itself would stall or otherwise subvert itself.

This boundary marking took several forms, including reassertions, extensions, exclusions, and blurring of boundaries.

The boundary-extending ambitions of UNCITRAL and the actors initially circling in its orbit can readily be observed in all three issue-areas – of getting beyond sea transport to include some aspects of land transport, of getting beyond narrowly defined topics of corporate insolvency law to entire insolvency and restructuring systems, of reaching far beyond one or another form of security to embrace all possible ways of taking security over diverse sorts of collateral. This ambitious boundary extending went hand-in-hand with boundary defending or maintaining. UNCITRAL defended its "right" to draft maritime law because it had precedent not only for maritime law (in its failed Hamburg Rules), but its initiatives in electronic transactions that might transform the historical reliance of sea transport on paper bills of lading. UNIDROIT asserted its jurisdiction over secured transactions law. UNCTAD insisted it had powerful auspices as an arena or core actor in international transport law, including that involving seafaring voyages. The World Bank signaled by indirection that the lawmaking territory it was staking out should not be seized by UNCITRAL or other contenders.

For UNCITRAL, and its claims to be the arena in which the ecology's work was housed, these reassertions and extensions of claims within an issue-area led to different combinations of incrementalisms (Block-Lieb and Halliday 2007a; Block-Lieb and Halliday 2007b). On insolvency, UNCITRAL's Working Group proceeded pyramidally, building on its own and other IO products, and horizontally, greatly expanding its substantive scope. On transport law, it proceeded simultaneously with all three incrementalisms, building selectively on past conventions, broadening out to topics not previously treated, and deepening its penetration in law and geography beyond ports. On secured transactions, it proceeded on the shoulders of earlier IOs and across issue-areas, to cover nearly as broad a range of topics as US Article 9, but as to both sorts of incremental progress the Secured Transactions Working Group was careful not to crow too loudly about its aspirations because full embrace of the breadth and temerity of these aspirations might well have scared off the room.

Boundary work may also involve boundary-blurring. Indeed, it is the boundary-blurring that may be the most intriguing tactic for subsequent negotiations, especially in the early phases of ecology formation. Repeatedly prime movers for lawmaking within UNCITRAL's arena presented proposals with wide legal and geographic scope that implied high ambitions for comprehensive TLOs covering large tracts of economic life. In each case, the most contentious of the issues were blurred at the outset. UNCITRAL's lawmaking entrepreneurs remained vague about how far they aimed to go beyond a port-to-port toward a door-to-door legal order; or how much intellectual property rights or equipment leasing or state property rights would drawn into a secured transactions legislative guide; or whether they would reach for state-owned enterprises, or financial institutions, or the liability of corporate directors in an insolvency or the responsibility of corporate groups for the debts of a subsidiary. Here UNCITRAL's boundary work corresponds to the value of opacity for enabling certain kinds of international diplomacy (Mallard 2014).

As theoretically salient as were its inclusions, the justifications and reasons this IO used to exclude potential topics from reform deliberations also demonstrates boundary work critical to the viability and productivity of the ecology. First, proponents for new law asserted a topic or form of product was a bridge too far and unlikely to be attained at all. Aiming for a unified TLO for transport of goods from door-to-door in a single comprehensive multimodal treaty simply exceeded the capacity of UNCITRAL lawmakers no matter how logical or rational or efficient it might be in principle. Second, there were deep divides between legal families, which justified sharp points of contention between them. Liability of directors for the failure of their captures would have pitted the common law world of the British Commonwealth against the US, Contintental Europe, and other regions, and any resolution of that conflict would be too taxing for an issue not fundamental to the overall philosophy of corporate rehabilitation. Third, deep conflicts would take too long to resolve, an argument implicit in the exclusion of door-to-door transport legal orders, in that a different cast of actors would be required to deliberate in such an endeavor. Similarly, if financial institutions were drawn into the insolvency lawmaking, central bankers, banking regulators, international banking associations would need to be invited into the lawmaking arena, but they would find much else on the agenda irrelevant or marginal to their interests. In two of these issue- areas, it was argued that domestic law was not developed sufficiently in an area to provide the needed building blocks for global lawmaking. While it made eminent sense to create international law for bankruptcies of groups of companies, an organizational form already ubiquitous in multinational corporations, domestic law in no country provided adequate models or experiences of corporate groups in insolvency regimes. We shall see below that relationships with other IOs and issue-ecologies determined a hands-off choice on certain topics.

Incorporating Actors

Initiating a lawmaking project in an issue-ecology requires first movers, norm entrepreneurs, activist IOs, or individuals with a reformist vision. Our ecological explanation of economic lawmaking therefore attends to the questions of who leads the drive to form an ecology? Where it will be housed? Which state and non-state actors will be drawn into the ecology or excluded from it? What IOs, states, or non-state actors will determine the parameters of problem solving through law? Here, too, contradictions can subvert the productive work of an ecology. If it is the US ostensibly leading the drive for lawmaking, then from the outset the work may be tainted. If it were to be led by the IMF or World Bank, it could carry the adverse sentiments against each in much of the developing world. If a given profession or a particular state appeared to be compelling the state and market actors to allow a biased imprint in the agenda setting, then the enterprise could be undermined from the outset.

The case studies have shown that impulses for lawmaking came from multiple directions. Always market actors, often through industry associations, pressed for problem solving through law. The International Maritime Association, the Consumer Finance Association, International Association of Restructuring Specialists, together with many others (see Chapter 4), led a drive for action. Always professionals, and legal professionals, were ubiquitous as would be anticipated in IOs committed to law as a means for producing economic order. Always one or another lawmaking IO saw underlying issues that they believed impeded economic activity.

They pressed for dedicated lawmaking to remove obstacles to trade, frequently with the expectation that the IO proposing new law would itself be the lead lawmaker or provide the arena in which lawmaking took place.

This chapter identifies strategies that UNCITRAL and its champions deployed to fortify UNCITRAL's claims to lawmaking centrality. First, UNCITRAL buttressed its claims by appeals to historical precedent. On insolvency, it pointed to its success on a narrow procedural product (the Model Law on Cross-Border Insolvency) and the epistemic community of lawmakers that had conjoined to produce it. On transport law, the Secretariat looked back somewhat ambivalently to its own efforts on the Hamburg Rules even if it had to concede its ultimate failure to build a global TLO based on its provisions. On secured transactions law, the Secretariat claimed it had been notionally imagining far-reaching global lawmaking since the 1970s. Second, if its precedents were weak here, UNCITRAL's Secretariat could reach back to the jurisdictional ambitions codified in its founding mandate. Harmonization clearly gave UNCITRAL ostensible authority to reach for a worldwide legal order. And it could appeal, third, to demands and needs of the market itself. Its work on insolvency had exposed it to the post-Asian financial crisis calls for a new international financial architecture and strong domestic debtor-creditor regimes. UNCITRAL also construed its bold claims on secured transactions as a response to the functional needs of credit markets in the early twenty-first century. Fourth, as the first among IO lawmaking equals (*primus inter pares*) in these issue-areas, UNCITRAL claimed a singular ability to draw not only every state in the world into its lawmaking, but also boasted a great and longstanding success at working productively with non-state and industry actors. Put another way, UNCITRAL made a persuasive case that it was the only transnational site where well-established practices of lawmaking smoothly integrated all state and salient non-state actors into the work of lawmaking for the world.

Securing Resources

Like any ecology, a lawmaking issue-ecology requires resources. What resources did norm entrepreneurs consider necessary to bring a new legal product to global markets? Who could supply those resources and how could that supply be stabilized and guaranteed? Paradoxes arise here, too. If resources are sought from within an issue-ecology, insufficiencies may result. If resources are drawn from adjacent ecologies, particularly from industry, all industry actors are not equal. Is the price of resource dependency therefore a relationship that excessively favors resource rich market actors? Too few resources and lawmaking will falter or shrink in its scope. Too many resources can lead to perceptions of a manifestly biased set of legal norms that are rejected by actors at the point of implementation.

The case studies disclose intensive efforts by UNCITRAL to obtain resources for its respective working groups, and for industry to supply resources for lawmaking in exchange for efforts it did not control. On UNCITRAL's side, the decisive and on occasion pre-emptive moves of its Secretariat and key members display a methodical effort to ensure it could guarantee its access to authoritative technical expertise for the duration of the lawmaking. Expertise inhered both in law, legal drafting, and legal practice, as well as in everyday economic activity where law might aid or inhibit commerce. At the conclusion of the lawmaking episode, UNCITRAL's reliance on industry would prove essential when lawmakers, far removed from actual market activity, depended on industry to mobilize and carry any future product into the markets where they had a significant presence. For each working group, UNCITRAL aligned itself with at least one energetic and resourceful private organization, which could provide infrastructure for communications and meetings and, if necessary, funding for travel and ancillary support. The leaders in each working group would leverage these relationships during lawmaking proceedings to overcome the temporal constraints that the UN and lawmakers themselves considered prohibitive (Chapter 5).

On the other side, UNCITRAL ensured at the outset that its claim to lawmaking jurisdiction had support from powerful state delegations, especially the US. In every case core delegates acknowledged that adoption of an UNCITRAL product depended heavily on adoption by the US and to obtain that adoption it was imperative to bring the US into proceedings at the outset. Thus, it is not surprising that in each issue-area the US had success in placing topics on the agenda that were of particular interest to US commercial interests, even if it would not get everything it wanted (Chapter 7).

Many actors in turn were dependent on UNCITRAL. The private associations of transportation industry actors, insurers, and maritime lawyers, bankruptcy lawyers and insolvency practitioners, and finance specialists all recognized that their power in global markets turned on partnerships with a supra-state organization that had international authority and the capacity to develop and promulgate global norms in a manner that was considered legitimate around the globe. That search for legitimacy brought CMI and international financial institutions to the UN trade law body. Impositions of rules by the IMF and World Bank, or efforts by the US to impose its domestic laws on those of other nations, were much less likely to be effective as unilateral assertions of power than norms created in a putatively representative global trade legislature precisely because such impositions generally were perceived as illegitimate.

UNCITRAL's claim to be the site of lawmaking and its leadership in all three issue-areas sprang from its singular success (Chapter 2) at combining three powerful legitimation mandates: its representation of all states in the world and its integration of expert and influential non-state actors into its proceedings; its procedural practices which treated all delegates and delegations in formal proceedings essentially as equals; and its effectiveness in producing quickening numbers of legal products in an expanding repertoire of technologies (Chapters 2 and 6). These distinctive qualities, even in the wider standing ecology of commercial lawmaking IOs, made UNCITRAL an invaluable resource for state and non-state actors with enormous fiscal resources, technical capacities, and infrastructures. The case studies show the IMF and World Bank, the US and France, the CMI and INSOL, all prepared to commit some of their resources in return for UNCITRAL's unique configuration of legitimation warrants.

Nevertheless, this very success at broad inclusiveness led UNCITRAL into a legitimation paradox. Technical expertise and democratic representation, both critical for legitimation of a lawmaking ecology, can engender sharp conflicts – of experts versus representatives, of closed-door technical drafting versus open negotiations on the floor of UN chambers. How, then, at this critical moment of bringing into being new issue-ecologies did UNCITRAL expect to avoid this legitimation paradox?

In the cases of insolvency and secured transactions, the proponents of new lawmaking efforts convened colloquia that drew diverse nations and industry groups into working group conversations. An even larger number of states sent delegations for deliberation on international transport law (Chapter 4). The possibility of drafting a binding convention itself drew participants. In each instance, diverse and strong industry interests were invited to the table. At the same time, UNCITRAL's Secretariat relied substantially and manifestly on a particular expert industry partner and aligned itself perceptibly with the interests of the US. Thus, one tactic for resolving the paradox was to offer critical narrow state and non-state interdependencies to a handful of key partners, while at the same time allowing a broad spectrum of state and non-state actors to participate and observe and comment on the deliberations.

But this potential solution of the diversity problem increased the risk of the opposite problem – that UNCITRAL would be seen to be captured or predominantly convinced by a given state or private body. Solving the problem caused by the heterogeneity of interests that endowed representational legitimacy on UNCITRAL threatened to come at the cost of delegitimating UNCITRAL's reputation for universalism by a manifest particularism (Cohen 2011).

Navigating the fine line between these two extremes concentrated the Secretariat's attention throughout the years of negotiations in all three issue-areas. In this launch phase, however, it was managed in some degree by a combination of techniques. First, timing mattered. Deliberative proceedings were delayed until UNCITRAL had hosted a colloquium that was broadly inclusive of attendees and free-wheeling in its topical considerations. Second, UNCITRAL's Secretariat made plain to all delegations that a first draft from a non-state body such as CMI necessarily would require much amendment to reflect the diversity of industry and state interests not necessarily considered by CMI itself. More subtly UNCITRAL could echo CMI's claim that CMI had itself acted as a kind of quasi-legislature that invited diverse industry interests into its formative discussions so that the draft brought by CMI to UNCITRAL's first maritime session might be seen as the product of industry-wide consultations, not as yet another carrier-centric body of rules. Third, the Insolvency Working Group showed that sets of norms emerging from IFIs nonetheless converged on key principles and thus UNCITRAL was not the creature of either the IMF or World Bank or US. But we shall see that these first steps to find a middle path that solved the legitimation paradox and avoided capture were not definitive. Tensions and conflicts persisted through proceedings and beyond their conclusion.

Managing Interactions

In contrast to many institutional theories of change, ecological theory begins with the premise that competition among actors invariably accompanies any effort to stake jurisdictional claims over issues. That competition ramifies through all elements of the ecology – competition over definition of the problem, framing of the solution, bounding the problem-solving space, obtaining scarce resources, crafting solutions, controlling the temporal flow of events. In those fragile and tenuous early moments in the formation of issue-ecologies, a measure of competition offers the benefits that can often be seen in markets, but too much competition risks escalation into conflict that precludes effective lawmaking. Hence a central problem for the norm entrepreneurs and central actors in an incipient issue-ecology is to forestall competition at the outset, or at least domesticate it productively by converting it into competitive cooperation, at least for the duration of the lawmaking episode.

The case studies exemplify three processes that fostered cooperation, mitigated competition, or converted competition into competitive cooperation, at least for a limited period on a limited issue. First, UNCITRAL and its advocates where possible built on cooperative relationships already established, most particularly with INSOL, the International Bar Association, and the US in the production of the Model Law on Cross-Border Insolvency. Converting one successful cooperation into the beginnings of another significantly smoothed the opening of the new lawmaking episode and gave experienced leaders the courage to widen their ambitions. Second, norm entrepreneurs pushing for the creation of new issue-ecologies gave vocal recognition to other IOs whose products had laid foundations for new lawmaking episodes. In a rhetorical politics of incrementalism, UNCITRAL's lead lawmakers acclaimed the IMF, Asian Development Bank, CMI, World Bank, among others for shoulders on which it would stand. Third, UNCITRAL's Secretariat and leaders in the newly forming or reforming working groups strived to draw potential competitors inside the deliberative community. Whether the principal potential rival was UNIDROIT for secured transactions, UNCTAD on maritime law, or the World Bank for insolvency law, UNCITRAL did not move until it had either come to an agreement with a prospective competitor or had sufficient confidence in its own enterprise to proceed in the face of potential competition.

TABLE 3.2. *Actor Strategies in Formation of Issue-Ecologies*

Challenge	Strategy
Marking Boundaries	• Finding common ground over problem-definition • Building on accepted paradigms for framing issues • Proceeding incrementally • Limiting scope on pragmatic criteria • Blurring contentious goals • Excluding issues likely to create stalemate
Incorporating Actors	• Avoid tainted deliberative sites or arenas • Justify the "rightness" of UNCITRAL as a deliberative site • Bring in actors with previous salient lawmaking credentials • Link actor problem-solving capacities to perceived market needs • Attract globally and regionally influential state actors • Attract industry actors critical to adoption and diffusion • Coopt potential competitors
Securing Resources	• Obtain drafting expertise from professional experts • Obtain commercial expertise from market players • Align with actors willing to offer financial or infrastructural support • Increase probability of adoptions by alliances with international industry and professional groups
Managing Interactions	• Build on already established cooperative relationships • Acknowledge and assimilate actual or potential competitors • Create partnerships with at least one powerful state & one influential non-state actor

While this did not always prove successful (Chapter 9), as UNCTAD's ultimate defection from the transport consensus and the World Bank's rupturing of cooperation on insolvency later showed, at the outset UNCITRAL tried to coopt potential critics or IOs which might form their own issue-ecologies and produce competing norms. These early moves also had the effect of bringing relational challenges inside UNCITRAL's working groups and thus converting potentially conflictual relations between with other ecologies or leading IOs in the standing ecology into an internal interactional challenge to be handled in a low-key manner so as to mitigate open and public discord.

It can now be seen that all these moves by lawmakers to draw boundaries, secure resources, incorporate actors, and forge cooperative relationships are more than the exertions of a single IO. Beyond the multiplication of dyadic interactions among actors lay the fundamental organizational task of aligning an industry ecology and a lawmaking ecology for a short time around a common task. Table 3.1 identifies all the usual actors in each of three industry ecologies. Each of these classes of economic actors in principle has an interest in the outcomes of economic lawmaking that alter the rules by which they produce and consume, trade, and compete.

The table demonstrates that most but not all the classes of economic actors were drawn into the respective lawmaking ecologies. This relatively strong goodness of fit ensured that most economic interests would be reflected in the lawmaking deliberations. The lack of perfect fit opens up the prospect of deliberative bias and actor mismatch, both of which could impair the likely institutionalization of new transnational legal orders. Finally, Table 3.1 indicates what will become increasingly clear: no longer did the dominant IOs in the standing lawmaking ecology control the production of law in specific issue-areas. Into those areas surged new IOs – regional governments, UN agencies, international financial institutions – that would demand not only their seat at the lawmaking table but some considerable deference to their ideal and material interests. How those new and powerful actors could be incorporated into the relatively successful alignment of industry and lawmaking ecologies created a continuing interactional problem in the years of lawmaking to come.

4

Delegations and Delegates

Susan Block-Lieb, Terence C. Halliday, and Josh Pacewicz[1]

The Cameroon delegation came day after day to Insolvency Working Group sessions, all four delegates, visibly attentive to the proceedings, year after year. They huddled together from time to time, but only once raised their flag to intervene in the twice yearly sessions that convened from 1999 to 2004. The International Insolvency Institute delegates flowed through the UN meeting rooms in Vienna and New York like a tide, constantly changing, often spilling over into the space of other delegations with their profusion of specialists from across the world. They spoke often, but with little cumulative impact. Indeed, on occasion, their interventions annoyed the room by raising a point that had been settled years ago. The Australian delegate always came and always alone. Now and again he made a comment, but mostly he sat and listened in his front row seat. When he did speak, the text of the Guide was likely to change. The US delegation, anchored toward the middle of the chamber, always filled its four allocated seats, usually with an amalgam of officials, judges, and private practitioners. Like the key French delegate, US delegates spoke early and often on every topic. China's delegation came in force, but delegates turned over at a high rate and rarely spoke. There were the desks of delegations full the first day of a five-day session, and vacant thereafter. And then there were those other desks, where the only sign of occupancy was a flag with a delegation's name but never a delegate.

As the global texture of transnational commercial laws grows increasingly dense, the questions raised by Braithwaite and Drahos (2000) and others take on renewed theoretical and pragmatic importance: Who makes the rules governing international commerce? The states at the center of the world's economy? Or, in a global market characterized by radical differences in economic power, are there opportunities for weak or poor states to advance their interests in global markets (Cohen 2008; Santos and Rodríguez-Garavito 2005)? How are business and other non-state stakeholders

[1] This chapter draws heavily on (Halliday, Pacewicz and Block-Lieb 2013).

integrated into the building of the global trade order (Bernstein and Cashore 2007; Black 2008)? In short, who are the global players who make commercial law for the world?

This question quickly devolves into complex empirical and theoretical considerations. Empirically, too little is known about the black box of lawmaking deliberation.[2] We seldom have precise details of who are the persons and the delegations that inhabit the physical space in which lawmaking occurs. A delegation might be analyzed from three angles.[3] First, what are the attributes of a delegation (a formal group given standing in IO deliberations) and the delegates (individuals) that comprise it? Second, how do delegates and a delegation participate in an IO's deliberations? And, third, what is the influence of delegation attributes and participation, or their probable impact, on the substance of global norms or the legitimacy of UNCITRAL?

This chapter focuses on the first and foundational question: the attributes of a delegation and its delegates. In this context, we proceed on the premise that delegations and their constituent delegates are the principal means by which states and non-state actors influence outcomes in lawmaking ecologies.[4] If they are not present, they can exert little influence. Two questions immediately arise: Who is present? And what does "present" mean? We ransack an original dataset on the identity and attributes of delegations and delegates, a complete attendance record for the three working groups in our study, to answer these questions.

Theoretically, UNCITRAL's working groups can be seen as issue-ecologies where actors seek to resolve economic and other problems through law. A lawmaking issue-ecology, we have argued, articulates actors from adjacent industry ecologies, with the standing lawmaking ecology, the UN itself as a complex embedding ecology, and states as actors in the world economy. That articulation is expressed through the presence and interactions of actors who link the ecologies by drawing a selection of representatives from those ecologies into a working group for a limited period of time.

By carefully analyzing delegates and delegations we can observe how the issue-ecology is constituted and the ways in which adjacent and embedding ecologies interact and intersect with the lawmaking enterprise. Hence, we examine which actors from other ecologies are drawn into the specific work of the issue-ecology, how the actors themselves constitute their delegations, and how attributes of delegations and delegates signify probable influence on the outcomes of the lawmaking.

2 But compare (Koppell 2010).

3 We focus here on a delegation's formal participation in legislative deliberations. See Chapter 5 for analysis of informal and behind-the-scenes participation in the politics of global lawmaking.

4 Of course, in theory it is possible to imagine hidden hands behind the scenes that manipulate a Secretariat without being present, but our extensive research on UNCITRAL provides no support for such a theory.

We demonstrate that there is a very considerable complexity in the interplay of delegates, delegations, and their respective and intertwined attributes. By unraveling this complexity, we can show which actors are central in the lawmaking space and which are peripheral. We identify with some precision the inner core of actors whose judgments shape the world of global trade through law.

The evidence on presence and participation of delegates and delegations sharpens further the hypotheses on who governs in commercial lawmaking for global markets. Although we postpone until Chapter 7 findings on influence in global lawmaking, the new methodology developed here goes far to predict which are the most powerful actors exerting influence on the rules that govern trade in these three issue-areas. The empirical findings to some degree erode a principal legitimation claim made by UNCITRAL. They indicate that it is not possible to extrapolate directly from the economic and geopolitical power of a state to its probable impact on lawmaking for global markets. And they reveal that the supposed rise of Brazil, Russia, India, China, and South Africa (BRICS) as a new complex of economic power in the world economy does not reveal itself in these arenas of global law- and market-making.

ATTENDANCE AND ITS MEANINGS

While the significance of delegates, delegations, and their attributes are not directly addressed in theories of IOs or global normmaking, it is possible to extrapolate from those theories to likely expectations about the participation of delegations and delegates and, thus, their probable impact.

We earlier divided theories broadly between those that emphasize the global economic and geopolitical power of states and those that also recognize the distinctive powers of IOs, epistemic communities, and international civil society (Introduction). For those theories of international political economy and world systems which emphasize the massive asymmetries in power between the global financial and trading hegemons and countries in the world's trade peripheries (Grieco and Ikenberry 2003; Helleiner 2009; Morgan and Quack 2010; Wallerstein 2005), it should follow that delegates and delegations from global centers of power will be present and vocal. On this ground, if UNCITRAL matters for global trade, then the nations at the center of the global trading system should seek to craft the legal order that governs international commerce. Similarly, realists generally emphasize the dominance of states and multilateral bodies heavily inflected by the interests of powerful states (Stone 2011; Waltz 1979). Viewed from this perspective, attendance and participation at UNCITRAL would disproportionately register states' intended influence over proceedings, and we would exptect powerful states and trading nations, such as the US, China, Japan, Germany, and others in the OECD club of rich nations, to be present and active, together with international financial institutions, such as the IMF and World Bank.

For theories that insist upon the rising influence of non-state actors it would be expected that a prominent role in UNCITRAL's proceedings will be observed from industry, the professions, labor organizations, and non-state civil society actors whose ideal and material interests are also at stake in the outcomes of global lawmaking (Cashore, Auld, Bernstein, and McDermott 2007; Held, McGraw, Goldblatt, and Perraton 1999; Meidinger 2001; Price 1998; Price 2003). Hence global policymaking to erect or reform TLOs will bring into the intimate ecology of UNCITRAL lawmaking the key industry associations, professionals with technical expertise and financial interests in issue-areas, and possibly international civil society groups anticipating the potential impact of global lawmaking on populations on whose behalf they advocate. Constructivist IO theory also would predict that UNCITRAL's Secretariat independently would exert influence, beyond that of its member states.

Both sets of theories hold implications for our assessment of delegations' capacity for participation and ultimately influence in global lawmaking.

For example, realist international relations theory, economistic international political economy theory, and world systems theory all emphasize the primacy of the state as the essential actor on the international stage and diminish to various degrees the autonomy or independent significance of IOs. In this view, the deliberative chamber merely reflects a microcosm of global *realpolitick*, of the concentration of wealth and economic power in the world economy. Delegations would be presumed to be more influential when their states are at the center of the world economy. Non-state delegations would be presumed to obtain a derivative influence when they, too, are centered in powerful states or their delegations are populated by the individuals from those states. Concomitantly, less powerful delegations and international civil servants in lawmaking IOs would be presumed to defer to the most powerful state and non-state delegations.

The second group of theories (constructivism, cultural IPE, global governance, professions) would argue, alternatively, that delegations have discernible properties beyond mere extrapolations from the power of the states sending delegations or hosting IOs. If the attributes of states are held relatively constant, such as the economic power of all G-7 states, these theories would predict that there will be consequential variations among the properties of state delegates and delegations, variations that result in differing participatory capacities and ultimately probabilities of influence. Similarly, they would predict that there will be similarities among the properties of distinct sorts of state delegates and delegations and, thus, that the wealth or economic power of the state sending the delegation need not limit the influence of the delegation. Moreover, constructivist theory would anticipate the prospect of emergence – emergent understandings of underlying problems, emergent sense-making about alternative approaches to problem solving, emergent social organization that blurs formal differences in types of delegations, and indeed some shifts in the authority and legitimacy of UNCITRAL itself as an actor and arena.

It is therefore necessary to isolate the properties of delegates and delegations and examine whether their variation, even within classes of states or non-state actors, suggests the possibility for differential effects on the outcomes of episodes of global lawmaking. An examination of these outcomes is left for subsequent chapters; here, we lay the foundations for later outcome analysis.

A NEW METHODOLOGY FOR SYSTEMATIC ANALYSIS OF DELEGATES AND DELEGATIONS

Since it is usually difficult to gain entrance to the internal workings of delegations in IOs, a first and generative step can be to analyze systematically data that often are available – those on delegations and delegates that are reported in official reports or may be obtained from secretariats of IOs on request. We present building-blocks for this analysis and demonstrate the possibilities for distinct and evocative findings from a methodical and close examination of attendance records.

Our systematic data on UNCITRAL's three working groups are drawn from three principal sources.

First, we analyze all data on attendance by delegates and delegations at the meetings of UNCITRAL working groups in our case study over the course of specified lawmaking episodes.[5] From 1999 to 2004, the Insolvency Working Group met eight times for a week at a time, usually twice a year, once in Vienna and once in New York at the UN. The Secured Transactions Working Group similarly met twice a year, in Vienna and New York, to work on a Legislative Guide on Secured Transactions Law from 2002 to 2007. The Transport Working Group met between 2002 and 2008. Initially, they met like the other working groups – twice a year for one week. In order to complete the project as its scope grew over time, the Commission decided to increase the time available for deliberations on international transport. For several of these years, the Transport Working Group sessions spanned two weeks, again twice a year, once in Vienna and once in New York.

For each meeting of each group we collected data on the type of delegation (e.g., state/non-state, advanced/developing/transitional country), the frequency of attendance, and the size of the delegation.[6] For each delegate, we recorded the frequency of attendance, and whether state delegates were generalist "diplomats," such as first or second secretaries from embassies or consulates in Vienna or

[5] Once the Transport Working Group promulgated the draft convention that would become the Rotterdam Rules, it was dissolved. The Insolvency and Secured Transactions Working Groups continued to engage in lawmaking projects on topics of insolvency and secured transactions law. Indeed, both remain at work on related projects, to date.

[6] These data are drawn from the official attendance records maintained by the Secretariat. However they are not perfect indicators of attendance because they reflect an amalgam of which delegations and delegates announce they will attend and which actually sign a circulating paper on the first day of week or two-week long meeting. After signing, a delegation might not further attend, yet the record will imply full attendance.

New York, or representatives of particular government ministries or the private sector with specialized knowledge or responsibilities in the subject area. For some delegates, we collected information on the occupation of the delegate and the government ministry from which state delegates are sent.

Second, between us, we attended and observed every session of the Insolvency Working Group, collecting systematic data on the frequency and order in which delegates spoke in these working group sessions, i.e., a record of "speech-turns." We attended occasional sessions of the Secured Transactions Working Group and none of the Transport Working Group sessions.

Third, we conducted extensive formal and informal interviews about the deliberative process over eight years with delegates from all three working groups and with UNCITRAL staff.

Making sense of attendance by delegations and delegates is not a simple matter. Two delegations, for instance, might attend a majority of sessions, but their profiles of attendance differ sharply. For example, one delegation may attend all consecutive sessions at the beginning or middle or end of deliberations and thereby build up incremental knowledge and experience about decisions and directions that form the basis for subsequent discussions and decision making. In another example, a delegation may attend a time or two, miss one or two sessions, return for a session, miss another, return again, and so on. The ability of these two delegations to engage in and influence debate in the legislative chamber would, we suspect, differ. In the latter case, the delegation may struggle to participate effectively. Even if it has taken extraordinary steps to inform itself of what transpired in their absence, its absences are likely to have diminished its integration into a normmaking community, and to have attenuated the ties and trust that frequently build up during extended negotiations. In short, temporal dynamics of attendance have consequences for participation and probable influence.

To some degree the attributes of delegations and delegates vary independently of each other. Because social relationships occur more naturally among individuals than among groups, the likely influence of a delegation depends importantly on the consistency of attendance by delegates within a delegation. For example, it is possible for a delegation (a formal group) to be present at every session, but for its constituent delegates (the people who comprise the group) to turn over completely. In that case, consistency of a delegation's attendance matters relatively little since each new delegate must begin learning from the outset and has little experience to draw upon, even if well briefed by a previously attending peer. Certainly, delegates that attend only infrequently will have more attenuated relationships with other delegates and the Secretariat. As a result, it can be expected that consistent attendance by delegations that also include delegates whose own attendance is consistent are most likely to exercise influence on lawmaking outcomes.

Further, the extent and contour of influence are likely to reflect *who* are the delegates within a delegation. We posit that influence is partly a matter of delegation size and partly of delegation composition. As to the latter, our observations at the Insolvency Working Group suggest to us that participatory impact relates to the backgrounds and life experiences of individual delegates who can speak with more or less authority based on their career trajectories and current occupational statuses. For example, the Insolvency Working Group deliberated on the contours of corporate insolvency law, a topic that involves detailed legal and financial considerations embedded in larger social and political decisions about which interests to preserve and which to jettison in the context of a firm's financial distress. There, delegates included not only legislators, civil servants, and judges, but also lawyers, accountants, and insolvency practitioners who had presided over everyday implementation of global norms. Each brought a distinct perspective to the legislative chamber.

Given the distinct messages emanating from this broad range of interested actors, we posit that a delegation might increase its impact if its membership were occupationally diverse, that is, if it were to include specialists from both the public and private spheres and state and non-state sectors. This would be most salient for state delegations, but it may also strengthen non-state delegations, where, for instance, a judge or law professor would complement the experiences of a private practitioner.

Closely related is an indicator of density. UNCITRAL permits each delegation to bring a maximum of four delegates. Size may serve as a rough proxy for the potential for influence. The more delegates on the floor, the more likely it is that a delegation's perspective is heard. Increasing the size of a delegation also means that it could increase its diversity, and the more consistently a delegation brings a more diverse group of stakeholders in lawmaking and implementation, the greater should be its probable impact. Yet size also is an imperfect indicator of the material conditions of participation in lawmaking. Larger delegations cost more. Size also signifies to some degree the domestic priority given an issue-area by a particular government.

These attributes of delegations and delegates may aggregate. For maximal impact, it might be anticipated that the delegations that combine attributes will magnify their influence. Consistent with this expectation, the strongest sort of delegation *qua* delegation[7] would be one that combined (i) high and consecutive attendance by the delegation with (ii) high and consecutive attendance of particular delegates and (iii) the conjunction of consistently attending delegates and delegations, (iv) occupationally diverse delegations, (v) and full or dense delegations. If each of these factors is independently important, influence might diminish as any of these properties is lost to a delegation.

Alternatively, some attributes of delegations and delegates may be more important than others. In particular, the size of a delegation may also be equated with a weight that works in tension with consistency of attendance. If consistency in attendance matters more than the size or diversity of the delegation in attendance, then we

[7] That is, holding constant the power of the state or non-state actor that sends the delegation.

would expect that small delegations consisting of a single delegate with near perfect attendance may exercise outsize influence.

Analysis of our findings follows these hypotheses of participatory capacity. We examine data in turn on (a) attributes of delegations, (b) attributes of delegates, (c) combinations of delegation and delegate attributes, (d) the density of delegations,[8] and (e) cumulative combinations of these factors.

ATTENDANCE PATTERNS

Delegations

We have noted that UNCITRAL invites three broad categories of delegations. At the core are the thirty-six (until 2004) and later sixty (2004 and thereafter) states that are members of the UNCITRAL Commission in a given year. By institutional design, official state delegations reflect the diversity of the world's regions and levels of economic and legal development. Under the terms of UNCITRAL's original mandate, member states are selected by lot, subject to "the adequate representation of the principal economic and legal systems of the world and of developed and developing countries,"[9] and additionally serve for staggered six-year terms.

UNCITRAL's Secretariat invites all other states that are members of the UN General Assembly to working group sessions as observer states. While in theory UNCITRAL might distinguish between the two, observer states attend and participate on exactly the same terms as UNCITRAL member states. In the Insolvency Working Group, for instance, approximately ten to twenty observer states attended regularly.

In addition, the UNCITRAL Secretariat seeks representation from international industry groups, multilateral organizations, and other trade bodies that have a putative interest in lawmaking for a given issue-area. Nongovernmental organizations accepting the Secretariat's invitation can attend working group sessions and participate effectively on nearly the same terms as state delegations. The Chair recognizes requests to intervene in the order in which flags are raised; in judging whether a consensus had been reached, however, the Chair may ignore non-state delegates' requests and suggestions unless seconded by a state delegation.

The data reveal a consistent pattern of attendance over the sequence of sessions held by all working groups: a very large number of delegations come at least once or twice, usually at the first two or three sessions of the working group. But only a small number of delegations attend with consistent regularity. For the Insolvency Working

8 Our data on occupational diversity is less systematic because records report delegates' titles and addresses, but not occupation per se. Often, occupation can be inferred from this data; in other instances, we were able independently to corroborate occupational inferences with information available in public records.

9 UN General Assembly Resolution 2205 (XXI), at Part II, ¶ 1 (creating UNCITRAL in 1968).

Group, 127 delegations attended at least once and 70 of these attended only twice; only 36 delegations attended more than half the sessions. We define delegations that attend more than 50 percent of the time as "high-attendance delegations." An even stricter criterion, attending 75 percent or more of the sessions, produces only 24 delegations in the Insolvency Working Group attending 7 or 8 of the 8 possible sessions. For the Secured Transactions Working Group, 161 delegations attended at least once, with 87 of these delegations attending only once or twice. Forty-two delegations attended more than half of the 11 Secured Transactions Working Group sessions; 19 delegations had near perfect attendance, attending 10 or 11 times. For the Transport Working Group, 149 delegations attended, but 49 of these came only once or twice. Fifty-six delegations attended more than half of these sessions (seven or more Transport Working Group sessions); 30 of these delegations had near perfect attendance (11 or 12 Transport Working Group sessions).

Who are the high-attendance delegations? Numerically and proportionately, Row A in Table 4.1 indicates that advanced economies and developing/transitional economies are about evenly balanced among the state delegations in attendance at the Insolvency Working Group (16 advanced to 13 developing/transitional), but that delegations from developing/transitional nations slightly outnumbered those from developed nations in the Secured Transactions (13 advanced to 18 developing/transitional) and Transport (19 advanced to 26 developing/transitional) Working Groups.

Moreover, for the Insolvency Working Group, most of the delegations from developing/ transitional countries attend five or six times and are thus concentrated at the lower end in the frequency of high-attending delegations. This is less true for the Secured Transactions and Transport Working Groups, where close to half of the developing/transitional high-attendance delegations are near perfect attenders. For all three working groups, the high-attendance delegations from developing/transitional nations come from all regions of the world but are disproportionately *big* economies and enjoy membership in the G-20, notably, Brazil, China, India, Mexico, Russia, and Turkey.

The high-attendance delegations that are non-state actors differ slightly among the three working groups. For the Insolvency Working Group, these high-attendance non-state delegations include international financial institutions, most particularly the International Monetary Fund and World Bank. UNCITRAL proceedings built on their prior lawmaking in the issue-area, but also these IFIs have a mandate generally to assess of the international financial architecture and, on a case-by-case basis, to evaluate and promulgate norms for insolvency systems across member countries. Significantly, the Asian Development Bank, which itself had produced regional norms and was quite visible at the earliest stages of the Insolvency Working Group, eventually withdrew, apparently because it thought the direction of proceedings were at variance to what its principal delegate thought salient to Asian emerging

TABLE 4.1. *High-Attendance Delegations*[a]

	State Delegations		
	Advanced Economies[b]	Developing/ Transitional Economies	Non-State Delegations
Insolvency Working Group	Australia (8), South Korea (8), Switzerland (8), Germany (8), Spain (8), Sweden (8), Canada (8), France (7), Austria (7), Italy (7), Japan (7), Singapore (7), US (7), Denmark (6), Ireland (6), the UK (6) **(16 Total)**	Thailand (8), Mexico (7), China (7), India (6), Russia (6), Philippines (6), Turkey (6), Brazil (5), Cameroon (5), Iran (5), Nigeria (5), Sudan (5), Turkey (5) **(13 Total)**	International Monetary Fund/IMF (8); International Bar Association/IBA (8); International Federation of Insolvency Professionals/INSOL (8); World Bank/WB (7); American Bar Association/ABA (7); *Le Groupe de Réflexion sur L'Insolvabilité at sa Prévention (GRIP 21)* (7); International Insolvency Institute/ III (7) **(7 Total)**
Secured Transactions Working Group	Austria (11), Canada (11), France (11), Germany (11), Japan (11), Korea (11), Sweden (11), Italy (10), Spain (10), US (10), Australia (6), Ireland (6), Switzerland (6) **(13 Total)**	Argentina (11), Mexico (11), Thailand (11), China (10), Colombia (10), India (10), Philippines (9), Poland (9), Russia (9), Turkey (9), Iran (8), Algeria (7), Czech Repub. (7), Peru (7), Brazil (6), Cameroon (6), Hungary (6), Lithuania (6), Tunisia (6) **(18 Total)**	American Bar Association/ ABA (10); Commercial Finance Association/ CFA (10);International Monetary Fund/ IMF (10); Center for International Legal Studies/CILS (10); International Chamber of Commerce/ICC (10); World Bank/WB (9); International Federation of Insolvency Professionals/INSOL (9); European Law Students Association/ ELSA (7); Max-Planck Institute for Comparative and International Law (7); City Bar of New York/ ABCNY (6) **(9 Total)**

	State Delegations		
	Advanced Economies[b]	Developing/ Transitional Economies	Non-State Delegations
Transport Working Group	Austria (12), Canada (12), Denmark (12), Finland 12), France (12), Italy (12), Japan (12), S. Korea (11), Spain (12), Sweden (12), Switzerland (12), Australia (11), Germany (11), Netherlands (11), Norway (11), US (11), Greece (10), UK (8), New Zealand (7) **(19 Total)**	China (12), Mexico (12), Russia (12), Brazil (11), Colombia (11), India (11), Senegal (11), Singapore (11), Thailand (11), Turkey (10), Venezuela (10), Cameroon (9), Czech Repub. (9), Iran (9), Tunisia (9), Algeria (8), Belarus (8), Kenya (8), Lithuania (8), Philippines (8), Argentina (7), Kuwait (7), Nigeria (7), Peru (7), Romania (7) **(26 Total)**	P&I Clubs (12); *Comité Maritime International*/CMI (12); The Baltic and International Maritime Council/ BIMCO (11); International Chamber of Shipping/ICS (11); Association of American Railroads/ AAR (10); International Association of Freight Forwarders Association/FIATA (10); International Multimodal Transport Association/IMMTA (10); International Union of Marine Insurance/IUMI (9); International Governmental Organization for International Carriage by Rail/OTIF (9), UNCTAD (8); International Chamber of Commerce/ICC (8) **(11 Total)**

[a] "High attendance" indicates a delegation that sent at least one representative to more than half of the UNCITRAL meetings (Insolvency = 5 meetings; Secured Transactions = 6 meetings; Transport = 7 meetings).

[b] "Advanced economies" as specified in the IMF Advanced Economies List: World Economic Outlook (Sep. 2011).

economies. Several professional associations maintain a consistent and visible presence, most notably the International Bar Association, International Insolvency Institute, American Bar Association, INSOL International, and the French *Groupe de Réflexion sur L'Insolvabilité et sa Prévention* (GRIP 21).

The Secured Transactions Working Group similarly include high-attending IFIs (IMF, World Bank) and professional associations (American Bar Association, INSOL International, Association of the Bar of the City of New York), but also included industry associations (the International Chamber of Commerce, the Commercial Finance Association), as well as think-tanks and academic institutes (Center for International Legal Studies, and the Max Planck Institute for Comparative Public Law and International Law).

The Transport Working Group did not include IFIs, which is not surprising since its deliberations were not financial in nature. Nonetheless, numerous other IOs attended with consistency. UNCTAD, the UN's Conference on Trade and Development, attended regularly. So did OTIF, the Intergovernmental Organization for International Carriage by Rail. International professional associations of lawyers attended regularly, most importantly, the *Comité Maritime International* (CMI). It was industry associations that predominated in the back rows of the Transport Working Group sessions, where the ICC and several professional associations of insurers, such as the P&I Clubs and International Union of Marine Insurance (IUMI), sat together. Shipping associations are among the high-attending delegations, including the Baltic and International Maritime Council (BIMCO) and the International Chamber of Shipping (ICS), as are other associations with broader interests in transport, such as the Association of American Railroads (AAR), International Association of Freight Forwarders Association (FIATA), and the International Multimodal Transport Association (IMMTA). Perhaps importantly, none of these organizations purport to represent shippers' interests, however, except perhaps the International Chamber of Commerce.

For the Insolvency and Secured Transaction Working Groups, non-state delegations are all based in countries with advanced economies. If these NGOs are aggregated with the state delegations also coming from nations with advanced economies, the numerical and disproportionate balance tips in favor of advanced economies (Insolvency: 23 advanced versus 13 developing/transitional; Secured Transactions: 24 advanced versus 18 developing/transitional). This pattern differs slightly in the Transport Working Group. The results are similar to those of the other working groups if an NGO's home office is considered, but the predominance of NGOs' representation of the interests of advanced economies may be less clear in the Transport Working Group. The CMI claims members from every continent. Arguably, BIMCO and ICS similarly claim to represent a broad range of shipping interests in transitional economies like China and South Korea. The Organisation for International Carriage by Rail (OTIF), an intergovernmental organization, is also unlikely to represent the interests of advanced economies alone. In addition, UNCTAD, another high-attendance delegation at the Transport Working Group, views itself as representing more the interests of developing/transitional nations than of advanced nations.

Do any delegations from states or non-state organizations stand out as high attenders over all three working groups, a pattern that might be expected if powerful states or non-state actors sought to shape contours of world trade beyond specific issue-areas? There is a core group of state delegations that attended more than half the working group sessions in all three working groups: Austria, Australia, Brazil, Cameroon, Canada, China, France, Germany, India, Iran, Italy, Japan, Mexico, Philippines, Russia, Sweden, Spain, Thailand, and the US. Whether from advanced or developing economies, these high attenders represent most of the world's largest economies. There are no NGOs that were high-attendance delegations in all three working groups, due to the lack of overlap in the three issue-areas covered. Yet several non-state delegations in common were observed in the Insolvency and Secured Transactions Working Groups (i.e., American Bar Association, World Bank, International Monetary Fund, INSOL International). Not surprisingly given that UNCITRAL is a lawmaking organization, state and non-state delegations are heavily populated by lawyers or law-trained specialists in every working group.

Delegates

Do the patterns of delegate attendance mirror those of delegations? And who are these delegates? It can be seen in Figure 4.1 that essentially the same overall pattern of attendance occurs for delegates as delegations: very large numbers attend at least once, sometimes twice, but a tiny number attend more than half of the time: for Insolvency, 27 delegates; for Secured Transactions, 30 delegates; for Transport, 50 delegates. Indeed, the number of high-attending delegates is significantly lower than the equivalent number of delegations. Even more dramatically, the graphs show that not much more than a handful of delegates attend virtually every session (Insolvency = 12; Secured Transactions = 15; Transport = 20). These graphs bring us much closer to delegates at the deliberative core of each lawmaking chamber.

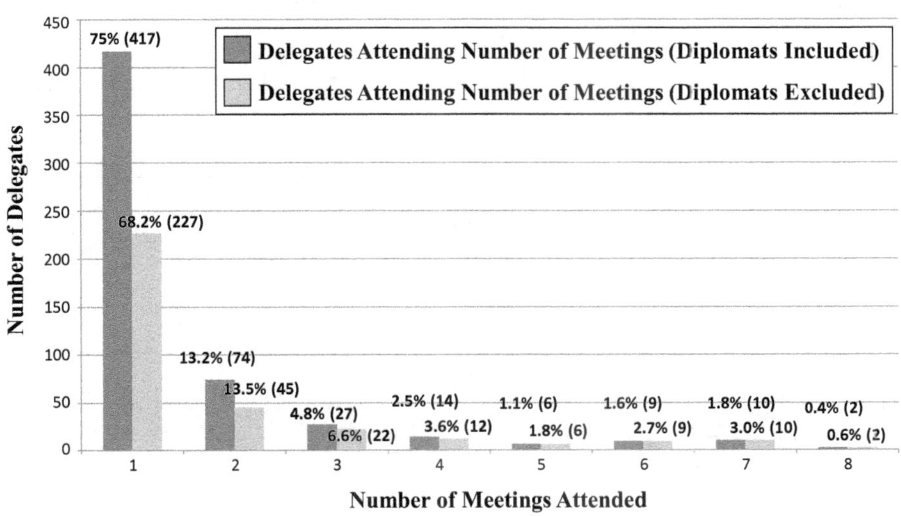

FIGURE 4.1A: Delegate Attendance, Insolvency Working Group (Total Delegates including Diplomats = 559; Without Diplomats = 333)

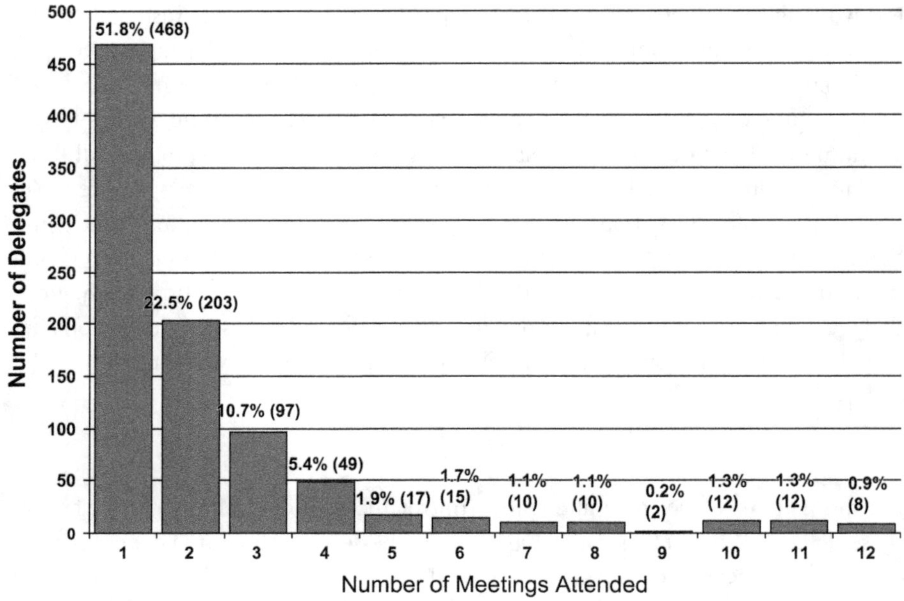

FIGURE 4.1B: Delegate Attendance, Transport Working Group (Total Delegates including Diplomats = 903)

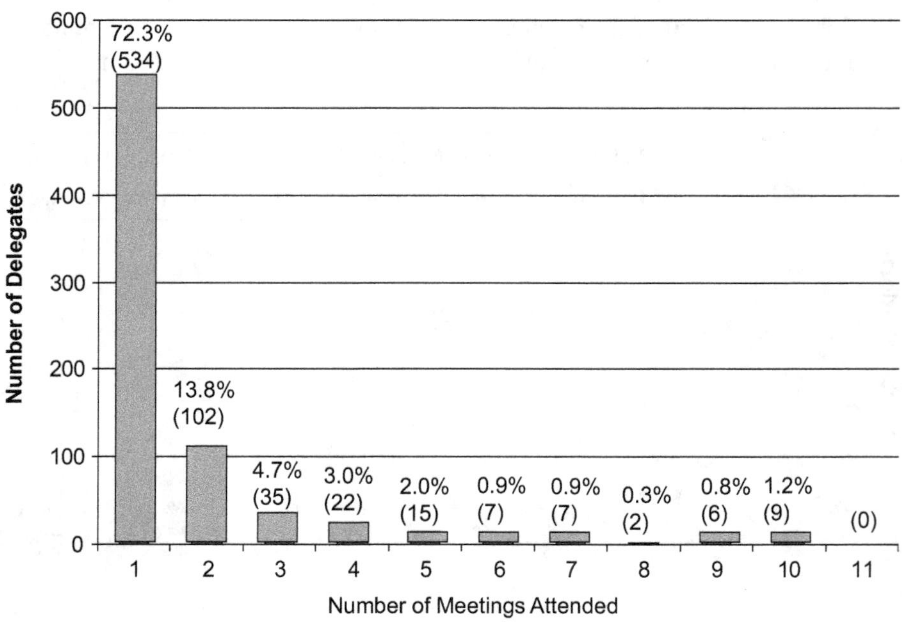

FIGURE 4.1C: Delegate Attendance, Secured Transactions Working Group (Total Delegates including Diplomats = 739; Without Diplomats = 473)

It is instructive to compare the numbers within and across working groups. Several hundred delegates attend at least once in all groups (Insolvency = 559; Secured Transactions = 739; Transport = 903). As Figure 4.1 demonstrates, however, the percentage of delegates that attend only once or twice is also very high in all three working groups (Insolvency = 80%; Secured Transactions = 84.5%; Transport = 74.3%). The sharp disjunction between those attending once or twice and those attending a majority of the time can also be seen when diplomats are deleted from the count. Even then data from the Insolvency Working Group (Figure 4.1A) indicates that 333 of 559 delegates attended at least once, as did 473 of 739 of delegates to the Secured Transactions Working Group.

All these figures replicate the same general finding: very large numbers come only once or twice; there is high cycling of delegates through many delegations; and the inner core of consistent delegates is a tiny proportion of all those who attend once or twice.

Who are the delegates that constitute the core group of consistently attending persons? From what corners of the world do they originate or do they represent?

For all three working groups, high-attendance delegates are overwhelmingly from advanced economies (Table 4.2). Several delegations had more than one consistent delegate. For the Insolvency Working Group, only the US had more than one high-attending delegate (4), but several professional associations also did so (International Federation of Insolvency Professionals (2), International Bar Association (2), International Bar Association (2), American Bar Association (2), *GRIP* (2)), as did the World Bank (2). In the Secured Transactions Working Group, three states sent multiple high-attendance delegates (US, Canada and Austria), and only one such professional association (Commercial Finance Association). In the Transport Working Group, there were seven countries that sent multiple high-attendance delegates (US, Spain, Italy, Denmark, Canada, Netherlands, Norway) and three such professional associations (P&I Clubs, AAR, BIMCO). In the Insolvency and Secured Transactions Working Groups, the single highest concentration of consistent delegates was within the US delegation (Insolvency = 4; Secured Transactions = 10). In the Secured Transactions Working Group, the US and Canadian delegations each sent an equally high number of high-attendance delegates (4).

If we combine state and non-state delegations and classify delegates by country of origin, the countries with the highest number of consistent delegates in the Insolvency Working Group are US (9 of 27, 33% of high-attending delegates), France (3), UK (2), and Canada (2). Citizens of the US (9 of 30), Canada (4), France (2), Austria (2) and Germany (2) predominate as high-attendance delegates to the Secured Transactions Working Group. And in Transport, US citizens predominate, not least because the US delegation sent eight high-attending delegates. However, there are a number of high-attendance delegates from non-state delegations to the Transport Working Group who are not US citizens. This compounding of delegates from state and non-state delegations is, thus, not present within the Transport Working Group.

TABLE 4.2. *High-Attendance Delegates*[a]

	State Delegations		
	Advanced Economies[b]	Developing/ Transitional Economies	Non-State Delegations
Insolvency Working Group	A. Sellars (Australia), J-L Vallens (France), S. Guido (Germany), M. Sigal (US), H. Burman (US), B. Lifland (US), T. Brozman (US), J. Matsushita (Japan), A. Drymala (Canada), L. Ghia (Italy), A. Markus (Switzerland), D. Moran Bovio (Spain), S-G Oh (S. Korea), R. Favier (UK) **(14 Total)**	W. Wisitsora-at (Thailand), J. Pinzon (Colombia) **(2 Total)**	N. Cooper (INSOL), R. Harmer (INSOL), B. Floyd (IBA), D. Glosband (IBA), B. Leonard (III), S. Block-Lieb (ABA), C. Redmond (ABA), G. Johnson (WB), A. Rouillon (WB), I. Didier (GRIP), M. Andre (*GRIP*) **(12 Total)**
Secured Transactions Working Group	M. Lukas (Austria), M. DesChamps (Canada), K. Sabo (Canada), C. Walsh (Canada), J. Riffard (France), D. Rehbein (Germany), M. Okino (Japan), R. Macdonald (Canada), N. Cohen (US), H. Sigman (US), E. Smith (US), L. Ghia (Italy); H. Burman (US), S. Niederberger (Austria), T. Jonsson (Sweden) **(15 Total)**	E. Belikova (Russia), B. Pasquali (Argentina), M. Sachova (Czech Rep.), M. Umarji (India), R. Manalo (Philippines), M. Kolibabska (Poland) **(6 Total)**	S. Weise (ABA), R. Kohn (CFA), G. Affaki (ICC), K. Karako (CFA), D. Morse (CFA), R. Palmieri (CFA), R. Harmer (INSOL), U. Drobnig (Max Planck), A. Rouillon (WB) **(9 Total)**
Transport Working Group	M. Carlson (US), P. Gatti (US), C. Hooper (US), S. Miller (US), D. O'Hare (US), M. Sturley (US), V. De Orchis (US), J. Lawrence (US),	W. Sa Leitao (Brazil), V. Sharma (India), S. Lebedev (Russia), L. Boumson	H. Hurst (P&I Clubs), S. Burgess (P&I Clubs), L. Warchot (AAR), K. Wilson (AAR), S. Larsen (BIMCO),

	State Delegations		
	Advanced Economies[b]	Developing/ Transitional Economies	Non-State Delegations
	D. Short (US), E. Sommer (US), R. Illecas (Spain), D. Moran (Spain), T. Arroyo (Spain), S. Zunarelli (Italy), C. Alvisi (Italy), .F Berlingieri (Italy), U. Rasmussen (Denmark), K. Christoffern (Denmark), T. Chatman (Canada), S. Halde (Canada), G. Van Der Zeigler (Neth.), Jan Boer (Neth.), Karl Gombri (Norway), I. Olebakke (Norway), P. Delebecque (France), T. Fujita (Japan), J Schelin (Sweden), S. Downing (Australia), B. Cherwenka (Germany), T. Mayer (Swiss), L. Eriksson (Finland), H. Talbot (New Zealand), D. Chong (Singapore), **(32 Total)**	(Cameroon), Q. Xu (China), P. Hron (Czech), A. Sogue (Senegal) **(8 Total)**	D. Chard (BIMCO), J. Moriniere (IMMTA), S. Beare (CMI), L. Howlett (ICS), G. Mutz (OTIF) **(10 Total)**

[a] "High Attendance" indicates a delegate who attended more than half of the UNCITRAL meetings (Insolvency = 5 or more meetings; Secured Transactions = 6 or more meetings; Transport = 7 or more meetings).

[b] *Source*: IMF Advanced Economies List, World Economic Outlook (September 2011).

Regional combinations are revealing, and roughly similar for all three working groups: there is a strong North American contingent (US + Canada), a strong British Commonwealth presence (UK, Canada, Australia), a strong EU contingent (UK, France, Germany, Italy, Switzerland, Spain), but relatively weak Latin American, Asian, Australasian, and African contingents. Rough balance can be observed between common law delegations (ABA, Australia, Canada, the US, UK, CFA, INSOL) and civil law countries (France, Germany, Japan, Switzerland, Spain, South Korea, GRIP 21, Colombia, CMI).

TABLE 4.3. *Summary of Delegation and Delegate Attendance Data*

	Delegations			Delegates		
	Attending at least once	Attending at least half of total sessions	Near perfect attendance	Attending at least once	Attending at least half of total sessions	Near perfect attendance
Insolvency Working Group	127	36 (A 16; T/D 13; NGO 7)	24	559	28 (A 14; T/D 2; NGO 12)	12
Secured Transactions Working Group	161	42 (A 15; T/D 18; NGO 9)	19	739	30 (A 15; T/D 6; NGO 9)	15
Transport Working Group	149	56 (A 19; T/D 26; NGO 11)	30	903	50 (A 32; T/D 8; NGO 10)	20

Radical drop-offs between delegations and delegates attending at least once, to those appearing at least half of their respective sessions, to those with near perfect attendance is demonstrated in Table 4.3. Arguably global trade law is most shaped by that combination of delegations and delegates with near perfect attendance.

Delegations Plus Delegates

The delegations with the highest capacity for influence at the deliberative core are likely to be those high-attendance *delegations* with high-attending *delegates.* Figures 4.2A and 4.2B compare side-by-side the frequency of high-attending delegations with their most consistent delegates for the Insolvency and Secured Transaction Working Groups.[10]

In the Insolvency Working Group, there were eight Working Group meetings, so a delegation or a delegate could attend a maximum of eight times. Figure 4.2A shows that eleven delegations (signified by the black horizontal bar) attend all eight sessions (Thailand, INSOL, Australia, International Bar Association, Germany, Switzerland, South Korea, Canada, Spain, IMF, Sweden), but in only three of these delegations is there a consistent single delegate who attends all eight sessions (signified by the gray horizontal bar) – Thailand, INSOL, Australia) (i.e., the gray bar). If we relax the criterion slightly we continue to see that only a tiny number of

[10] "A" refers to advanced economies. "T/D" refers to transitional/developing economies.

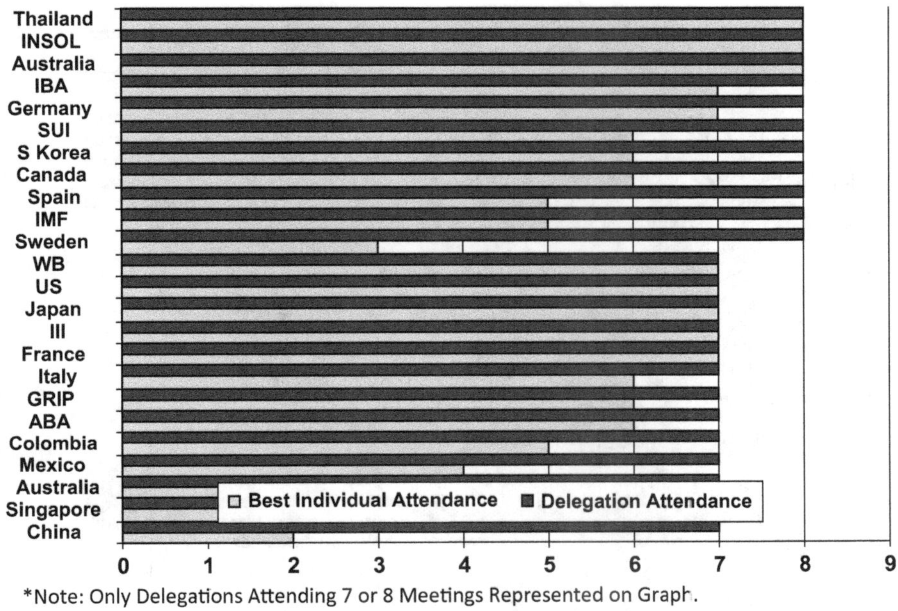

FIGURE 4.2A: Insolvency Working Group: Delegation Attendance and Attendance by Most Consistent Member of the Delegation*

delegations combine both high attendance and high consistency: Thailand, INSOL, Australia, IBA, Germany, World Bank, US, Japan, International Insolvency Institute and France attended either 8/8, 7/8, or 7/7 times.

Numbers of delegations have strong attendance records (Spain, IMF, Mexico, Austria, Singapore, China), but their delegates lack consistency in attendance. For China this is particularly noticeable as large numbers of individual delegates cycle through the Chinese delegation over the eight sessions. China's most consistent delegate attends only twice.

What are the attributes of these Insolvency Working Group high consistency combinations of delegates/delegations? Except for Thailand (and the consistent delegation for Thailand was the chair of the Insolvency Working Group), all the high-attendance delegations are from advanced economies. Moreover, four of the ten most active, consistent delegations are NGOs or international financial institutions.

A similar pattern holds for the Secured Transactions Working Group (Figure 4.2B). There were eleven working group sessions but no delegate was consistent in every working group session. Only 8 delegations had delegates that were present for ten out of eleven or ten out of ten times: Japan, Canada, France, Austria, Germany, US, American Bar Association, Commercial Finance Association. The delegations from Argentina, Thailand, and Mexico had near perfect attendance, but their most frequently attending delegate came 6, 5, and 4 times, respectively.

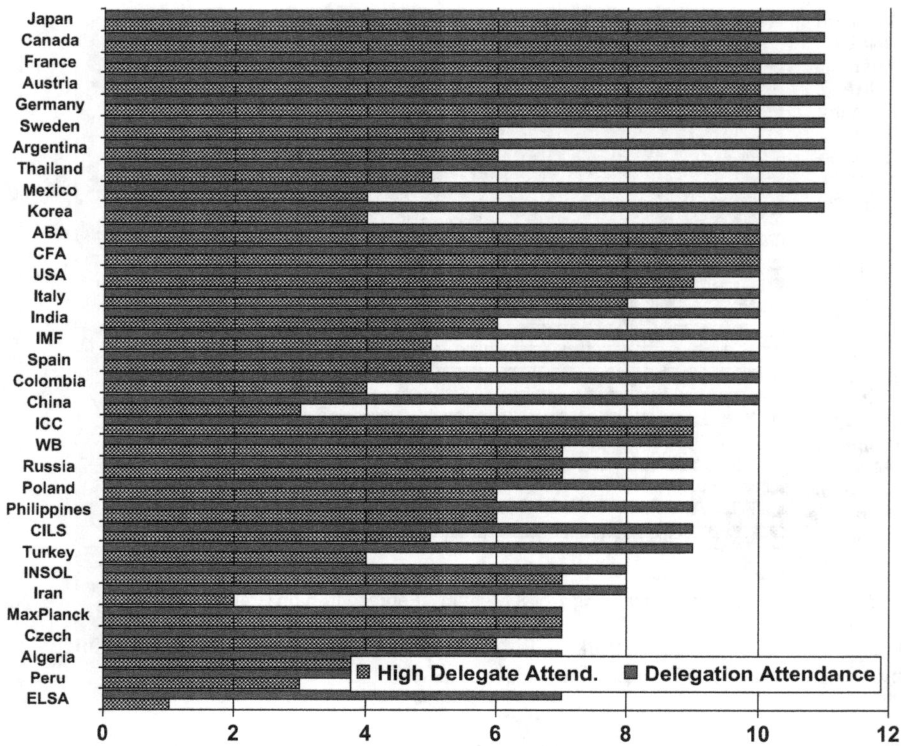

*Note: Only Delegations Attending 8, 9, 10, or 11 Meetings Represented on Graph

FIGURE 4.2B: Secured Transactions Working Group: Delegation Attendance and Attendance by Most Consistent Member of the Delegation*

High-attendance delegates in the Secured Transactions Working Group are more likely to come from state delegations and these state delegations are more likely to be from advanced economies. Only three such delegations are non-state actors – the American Bar Association, the Commercial Finance Association, and the International Chamber of Commerce.

Table 4.4 reveals a common pattern. It sets out for all three working groups the average number of meetings attended by the most consistent delegate, whom we call the "lead delegate," in those delegations with high attendance, that is, the attendance record for the highest-attending delegate within each high-attendance delegation. Consistent with Figures 4.2A and 4.2B above, the first two rows in Table 4.3 show that the attendance record for the lead delegates from advanced economies is substantially higher than that of lead delegates from developing/ transitional economies, but that advanced economies' lead delegate attendance is only slightly higher than lead delegates from non-state delegations to these working groups.

TABLE 4.4. *Average Attendance by Most Consistent Delegation Members among Highest-Attending Delegations*

	State Delegations		
	Advanced Economies[a]	Developing/ Transitional Economies	Non-State Delegations
Insolvency Working Group[b]	6.83 meetings	4.2	6.57
Secured Transactions Working Group[c]	8.3	4.7	6.3 (including think tanks) or 7.75 (excluding think tanks)
Transport Working Group[d]	9.61	5.23	8.00

[a] *Source*: IMF Advanced Economies List, World Economic Outlook (September 2011).
[b] Out of 8 meetings. Delegations attending 7 or 8 meetings included in measure.
[c] Out of 11 meetings. Delegations attending 8, 9, 10, or 11 meetings included in measure.
[d] Out of 12 meetings.

For the Insolvency Working Group, lead delegates from advanced economies' delegations attended on average more than 50 percent more often than those from developing/transitional economies (6.83 to 4.2 mean meetings), and lead delegates from NGOs attended, on average, at about the same rate as lead delegates from advanced economies' state delegations (6.83 to 6.57 mean meetings). The pattern for the other working groups is similar: the lead delegates from advanced economies' delegations attend nearly twice as consistently as those from developing/transitional economies (Secured Transactions Working Group: 8.3 to 4.7 mean meetings; Transport Working Group: 9.61 to 5.23 mean meetings); the lead delegates from NGOs attend almost as consistently as those from advanced economies (Secured Transaction Working Group: 8.3 to 7.75 mean meetings if think tanks are excluded from NGO count; Transport Working Group: 9.61 to 8.00 mean meetings).

Table 4.4 demonstrates that lead delegates often attend twice as many meetings as lead delegates from advanced economies. If lead delegates from delegations from advanced economies are aggregated with those from non-state delegations, the presence of lead delegates from advanced economies takes on outsized importance since all non-state delegations (and their delegates) come from advanced economies.

In sum, the combined data on high-attendance delegations and high-attendance consistent delegates indicate that a small number of delegations and delegates lie at the core of all three working group proceedings. These delegations have the highest likely capacity for influence over global lawmaking. While high-attendance delegations come from a wide range of countries, high-attendance delegates are more likely to come from advanced economies' and non-state delegations than from

TABLE 4.5. *High-Density*[a] *Delegations among High-Attendance Delegations*[b]

	State Delegations		
	Advanced Economies[c]	Developing/Transitional Economies	Non-State Delegations
Insolvency Working Group	Germany, Italy, Japan, S. Korea, Spain, Sweden, US (7/16)	Cameroon, China, Colombia, Russia, Sudan, Thailand (6/13)	IBA, III, INSOL, WB (4/7)
Secured Transactions Working Group	Canada, Germany, Italy, US (4/15)	Argentina, Thailand, Colombia, Philippines, Brazil, Cameroon (6/18)	ABCNYC (1/9)
Transport Working Group	Spain, Italy, Canada, US, Germany (5/19)	Senegal, S. Korea, Colombia, Venezuela, Cameroon, Nigeria (6/26)	(0/10)

[a] "High density" indicates those sending 3 or more delegates to meetings.
[b] "High attendance" indicates a delegation that sent at least one representative to more than half of the UNCITRAL meetings for this WG.
[c] *Source*: IMF Advanced Economies List, World Economic Outlook (September 2011).

developing/transitional economies' delegations. Since virtually all delegates from non-state delegations are themselves also from advanced economies, it can be argued that representation of the interests of advanced economies predominates in these working groups.

Density and Diversity in Delegations

We have identified high-attendance delegations, high-attendance and high-consistency delegates, and combinations of the two. However, delegations might strengthen their influence in ways other than through consistent attendance alone. A delegation might add depth to its bench by bringing several delegates to each meeting. These delegates might complement each others' experiences, skills, and perspectives. We define such a high-*density* delegation as a delegation that regularly sent three or more persons to each meeting.

The first row of Table 4.5 shows that approximately half of the high-attendance delegations to the Insolvency Working Group have a high density of delegates. High-density delegations are preponderantly from advanced economies (Europe, East Asia, US) and the professions (International Insolvency Institute, INSOL, International Bar Association), although four developing and two transitional countries also have high-density delegations.

TABLE 4.6. *High-Diversity Delegations*

	Advanced	Developing/Transitional
State	Denmark, Germany, Italy, Japan, South Korea, Spain, Sweden, US (8/16)	China, Colombia, Thailand (3/13)
Non-State	III, INSOL, World Bank (3/7)	

Note: "High Diversity" indicates a delegation containing a mix of public and private sector delegates that sent at least one representative to more than half of the UNCITRAL meetings (i.e. 5 or more meetings).

The second and third rows of Table 4.5 demonstrate that slightly different patterns exist in the other two working groups, where high-density delegations are less common overall. The high-density delegations that did attend these two working groups are equally likely to come from advanced economies and developing/transitional economies. With one exception, non-state organizations do not send high-density delegations to the Working Groups on Transport and Secured Transactions.

If a state delegation incorporates different backgrounds, skills, and experiences from different parts of the insolvency system – judges as well as practitioners, officials from lawmaking ministries or regulatory agencies as well as professors – it might arguably increase its authority in the deliberative process, enrich the discourse around normmaking, and become more persuasive. Our data enable us to specify the variety in backgrounds of delegates in high-density delegations only for the Insolvency Working Group. For simplicity, we divide high-attendance delegations into high-*diversity* and low-*diversity* delegations. We find (Table 4.6) that advanced economies are more likely to bring diverse delegations and that civil law countries do so more often than common law countries, except for the US. Several non-state delegations also have diverse delegations.

Cumulative Impact of Attributes

We hypothesized that a presence with the most participatory capacity and potential for influence may be one that combines all of these attributes of delegations and delegates. Comparable data were only available for analysis for the Insolvency Working Group. The findings are evocative. When we compare those delegations that combine high attendance with high delegate consistency and diversity we observe a striking convergence on a very small number of delegations and delegates. In Table 4.7, Column 1 (High Attendance, High Consistency), just ten delegations combine both. If we examine which of those delegations also have a higher density of delegates (Column 2), we see the same delegations (i.e., Germany, IBA, US,

TABLE 4.7. *Combinations of Delegate Attributes, Insolvency Working Group*[a]

High attendance + High consistency	High attendance + High consistency + High density	High attendance + High consistency + High diversity	High attendance + High consistency + High-attending delegate
Australia			Australia
France			France
Germany	Germany	Germany	Germany
IBA	IBA		IBA (2)
III	III	III	III
INSOL	INSOL	INSOL	INSOL (2)
Japan	Japan	Japan	Japan
Thailand	Thailand	Thailand	Thailand
World Bank	World Bank	World Bank	World Bank (2)
US	US	US	US (4)

[a] If we relax the criterion of selection (e.g., delegations with high attendance and high consistency of at least one delegates), we find: (1) most consistent delegate in a high-attendance delegation attended 6/8 times: Switzerland, South Korea, Canada; (includes 3 of high attendance delegates); (2) most consistent delegate in a high-attendance delegation attended 6/7 times: Italy, GRIP, ABA (include 5 of high-attendance delegates).

III, INSOL, Japan, Thailand, World Bank), with the exception of Australia and France who consistently sent just one delegate. Similarly, if we observe which high-attending/high-consistency delegations were also high-diversity delegations (Column 3), it can be seen again that the overlap is very substantial – indeed, 7 of the same 10 delegations. Finally, since we have identified the 27 highest-attending delegates, we can observe which coincide with delegations that score highly on other attributes. It will be seen (Column 4) that 16 of the highest-attending delegates are within this cluster.

Participation

Presence *per se* may not confer influence. It is conceivable that a delegate with a perfect attendance record, or a delegation with density and diversity, contributed little or nothing to deliberations. The Cameroon delegation attended diligently every day of every session at the Insolvency Working Group, but rarely spoke. Partial data permit no reliable conclusions, but they do raise important questions about the meaning of presence.

In four of the eight Insolvency Working Group sessions from 1999 to 2002, we coded every speaker in the formal proceedings of each session in the order in which they spoke (Halliday and Carruthers 2003). Each intervention or "speech-turn" is counted as one participation. We found that six of the ten high-attendance delegations whose delegates attended frequently and consistently were also the delegations with the greatest number of speech-turns. The delegations from France and the US intervened the most; together they account for almost one-quarter of the total interventions recorded. Otherwise, it was the professional associations that were both frequent and consistent attenders and spoke extensively; 26 percent of all speech-turns come from just four professional associations (International Bar Association, International Insolvency Institute, INSOL International, American Bar Association). Hence only six delegations accounted for more than 50 percent of all interventions.

Obversely, four of the delegations that attended frequently and consistently did *not* speak in the formal proceedings at anything like the levels that their delegation/delegate attributes might predict. Japan and the World Bank each contributed only 1 percent of the interventions and Germany and Thailand each contributed 0.2 percent. The Thai case is more complicated because the leader of the delegation chaired most UNCITRAL sessions and he is therefore counted in the 11 percent of speech-turns, but these were initiated from the podium and, thus, more likely to be procedural than substantive.[11]

Speech-turn data, of course, do not account for content or rhetoric. It is conceivable in principle that each intervention was purely confirmatory or vacuous or unpersuasive. Moreover, a delegate might not speak often, and yet convince the room with the power of their passion, the depth of their experience, or the logic of their argument. Nor do the data exhaust varieties of participation at working group meetings, many of which occur outside formal sessions. These include informal caucusing in corridors, attendance at expert group meetings at the invitation of the Working Group Secretary, annotations on drafts prepared by the Working Group Secretary, among others (see Chapter 5). Nevertheless, the conjunction of delegation attributes with delegation participation rates sharpens and narrows expectations about which delegations are more likely to have exerted most impact on the final product. Those were the US and France and the professional associations of lawyers and insolvency practitioners.

Moreover, the potential for influence by delegations from rich economies and of professions is multiplied by cross-overs. Rich countries obtain additional effective *de facto* representation when citizens participate in non-state delegations and the costs of those participations are externalized to the non-state bodies.

[11] While these data are provisional and suggestive only, our more consistent observation at Insolvency Working Group sessions corroborates these findings. Although it may have been possible that the pattern for the last four sessions of the Working Group were different, either because earlier activist delegates and delegations withdrew or had already achieved their substantive goals, or because some delegations came late or gained confidence or recognized the stakes of deliberations in the later sessions, we did not witness either sort of change in the pattern of speech turns.

Similarly, professions may be "double-represented" when they sit both in their non-state delegations and comprise one or more delegates in state delegations.[12]

These very limited data on actual speakers within the formal proceedings nevertheless set up a strong hypothesis that remains to be tested more widely: that the participating delegation/delegate combinations are an even smaller subset of effective participants in global lawmaking than the already tiny numbers of delegate/ delegation combinations in attendance.

THE INNER CORE

These data on delegations and delegates reveal an invisible component of a much larger whole – the inner core of deliberations in lawmaking ecologies. Concomitantly, they strengthen the accumulating evidence on who crafts the governing norms for TLOs-in-the-making.

The data and analysis indicate that the meaning of "presence" in a lawmaking arena is significantly more complex than might be supposed. By distinguishing between the attributes of delegations and delegations in attendance, and showing the complex relations between these attributes, we simultaneously unravel the complexity of attendance and offer methods for delegation analysis that may be applied to any international lawmaking organizations or IOs that rely on deliberative chambers and delegations for the formulation of global norms. This new methodology produces several provocative findings.

First, the actors who craft law for the world are a tiny subset of all the state and non-state delegations and delegates who at one point or another demonstrate sufficient interest in the lawmaking to attend working group sessions at least once. As few as ten (insolvency) and as many as fifty actors (transport) are architects of transnational legal orders.

Second, these inner cores of lawmaking are heavily skewed toward the Global North. Not only do states from advanced economies predominate but the non-state industry actors also are disproportionately located and centered in a tiny number of dominant economic powers. This is not to deny presence of state actors from developing and transitional economies, particularly in the transport lawmaking where we will show their presence was consequential. It is to affirm that in all three working groups high-attendance delegates from advanced economies significantly outnumbered those from developing and transitional economies, especially when delegates from state and non-state high-attendance delegations are aggregated. Delegations outside these inner cores did not for a moment miss the manifest interplay of numbers, diversity, depth, presence, and epistemic collegiality displayed by these few actors from the Global North.

12 We are indebted to Carol Heimer for this observation.

Third, professionals played outsized roles in the inner core of lawmakers. Delegations of professionals (International Bar Association, INSOL International, American Bar Association, International Insolvency Institute) to the Insolvency Working Group were arguably the critical technical drivers of that deliberative process. They attended consistently and with a large and diverse group of delegates; and, not least, they held the ear of the US delegation and, perhaps more importantly, the Secretariat. While one of the working groups saw only one high-attendance delegation of professionals (CMI at the Transport Working Group), high-attendance lawyer-delegates predominated in the Secured Transactions Working Group. And although lawyers may not have not been predominant in the Transport Working Group, their influence on the initial draft penned by CMI remained critically important throughout working group sessions.

Fourth, attendance data indicate that weak industry or economic actors seldom are present, certainly not to a degree that would give them decisionmaking influence. Trade creditors, small and medium businesses, and workers had no ostensible delegates or delegations in the insolvency lawmaking. Small and medium-sized shippers or businesses had representatives in the transport deliberations. Trade creditors, consumers, even financial institutions had no representation in the Secured Transactions Working Group.

There are several complicating findings. Although states at the center of the world economy are also predominantly those most present in deliberations, not all powerful, advanced economies were equally present as delegates or delegations. The US was first among equals, present in every working group and multiplying its presence with large diverse delegations and with cross-overs with US delegates in non-state delegations. However, Japan and China, two of the world's largest trading powers, were much less "present," either because their delegation was small and muted (Japan) or because their delegation was large but with a high and ineffective turnover of delegates (China). We shall show that both states exerted influence at one or two moments, but their power in the world economy in no way approximated their "presence" relative to the US in the shaping future markets through law.

Further, while much significance has been given to the rise of the BRICS in the world economy, especially the WTO (Hopewell 2013), the presence of the BRICS delegates and delegations in the three issue-ecologies signified much less participatory impact on the shaping of global markets through UNCITRAL's forms of legal norms. South Africa had no significant presence in any working group we studied. The other BRICS states all had high-attendance delegations in all working groups, but their participatory profiles diminished from transport, where they were most present, to secured transactions where Russia and India had high-attendance delegates, to insolvency where their presence was minimal.

These data generate puzzles. If only a tiny number of delegates and delegations were consistently present, why did so many other delegates and delegations cycle through working group sessions in Vienna and New York? Interviews with delegates indicate that some countries choose to expose a larger number of their officials to international negotiations as a form of socialization in global lawmaking and education on the substance of the law. That is, delegates are sent to learn, to ascertain the state of play, and to become aware of dominant ideas and paradigms on the intersection of law and markets, not to draft. This educative function might pertain more to the substance of the working group's deliberations, in that attendance could create incentives for casual attendees to learn about the topic in preparation for the meeting, or could represent an opportunity for attendees involved in legislative reform in their home state to compare UNCITRAL's work with that of their own.

At the same time, even brief and sporadic attendance might serve a scanning or oversight function. A quick appraisal of proceedings could enable even non-specialist diplomats at the permanent missions in New York or Vienna to prioritize their commitments to UN-related proceedings. It might also permit delegations to take the pulse of a working group and decide whether the subject matter area merits passive monitoring or active involvement, a critical decision when the cost of regular attendance is substantial for any country and particularly for a developing country. As in some domestic politics, by attending once or twice, delegations can discover whether other countries with similar interests or rival industry interests signal that a given issue-area is going to be consequential for future trade and commerce.

There is also the imputation, not always undeserved, that some countries use attendance at UN meetings as a kind of UN-tourism, a reward of a foreign trip at state expense for privileged officials. Or occasional attendance by diplomats already in place at permanent missions might signal to others – whether counsel to the United Nations or other political figures from the home state – that their position is an important one in that even this sort of casual attendance in the numerous UN-related committee sessions constitutes a "full-time job."

A related puzzle concerns those delegates and delegations that are high attenders and invest heavily in passive participation but remain silent throughout. While our data on vocal participation in formal meetings are limited, varieties of evidence show that some delegations diligently attend, including a small number from transitional and developing economies. An answer, which requires more intensive research, may come from scholarship on sense-making in organizations (Fiss and Hirsch 2005; Weick 1999). Participants enter a discursive or deliberative setting less to bring already clearly articulated interests to bear on negotiations and decision-making, and more to make sense for themselves of their own understanding of their circumstances or of ways of conceiving of goals and practices that are new or transformational. That is, their interests are not formed *a priori* because they are not aware of the stakes or of the alternative ways of framing and solving problems. Diligent presence in a global lawmaking arena offers an extraordinarily compact time in which state and non-state actors can make sense of problems they may now or will later perceive as they listen to alternative ways those problems can be addressed through law. This submersion in a discursive context simultaneously enables actors to map current configurations of already crystallized interests and to judge where they best fit in the deliberative space.

Also puzzling, and not able to be answered through attendance data, are the prospects of sporadic or infrequent or inconsistent delegates and delegations increasing their deliberative capacity through coalitions. For example, while most delegations from developing and transitional states were low attenders, it might take only one or two regular attenders to draw infrequent attenders into an effective coalition where numbers really did matter. We shall show that indeed such an occasion did arise in the Transport Working Group. That exceptional moment in fact raises the empirical question of why it did not occur more often in the other lawmaking arenas.

The attendance data offer a repeated series of static portraits of actors in attendance over successive six-monthly deliberations for a short number of years. Yet they also are highly evocative of dynamics in global lawmaking, most especially when viewed through the lens of IO lawmaking ecologies.

Lawmaking for global markets, we argue, occurs through interactions of ecologies. For our purposes, four ecologies are particular salient: the issue-ecology in which delegates draft laws; an adjacent industry ecology with economic interests in the way law shapes markets; a UN ecology, since multiple UN agencies claim jurisdictions over issue-areas where lawmaking is directed; and the standing lawmaking ecology of IOs dedicated over the longterm to production of private international laws for the world. The precise recording of attendance offers insight into the articulation of these ecologies by means of actors present in two or more of them. We have seen already a mismatch of representation between those within an industry and those in the issue-ecology. This mismatch immediately raises the plausible hypothesis that one or more industry actors whose interests are not directly represented in the lawmaking ecology will later be resistant to adoption of new laws that may not reflect their demands or needs. When the issue-ecologies are juxtaposed with the standing lawmaking ecologies, again it is noticeable that neither The Hague Conference nor UNIDROIT were high-attending delegates and delegations in any of the working groups. This reinforces the hypothesis that a division of topical labor had been negotiated among the leaders of The Hague Conference, UNIDROIT, and UNCITRAL, so that regular attendance either for lawmaking or monitoring was considered unnecessary. With respect to the UN as an enormous ecology of global governance, UNCITRAL attendance data show that the IMF, World Bank, and UNCTAD maintained high attendance in respective working groups.

Legitimacy, we have seen, is critical to the viability of any IO and to ecologies as a whole. The historical emergence of a standing lawmaking ecology required acceptance by powerful states that lawmaking for transnational relationships of private actors warranted dedicated organizations resourced over the longterm to problem solving through law. UNCITRAL's principal claim to enter that ecology in the 1960s, and its enduring claim, rested on its singular democratic legitimacy – that it alone of the lawmaking IOs invited all states of the UN into its organization, whether or not those states were rich or poor, powerful or weak, in Europe or in Africa. To a degree some attendance data support its expansive representativeness of states from many regions and levels of economic development. But when attendance data are subjected to the methodology introduced in this chapter, they can be viewed as undermining UNCITRAL's principal claim to democratic representation. The inner core of actors is heavily biased toward a few powerful states at the center of the world economy. That bias is intensified through the "double representation" of G-7 countries of delegates in non-state IOs. The reality of who does the actual work of producing global norms, therefore, fundamentally challenges UNCITRAL's claim to represent the world as a whole.

Yet another central pillar of UNCITRAL's legitimacy brings a potentially corrosive element to lawmaking for the world. Since the work of these issue-ecologies is to produce law, then professionals, and especially lawyers, exercise a powerful technocratic competency and authority. On the one hand, UNCITRAL has been enormously successful in attracting leading professionals into its lawmaking activities. On the other hand, that expertise and technical authority can create tension with democratic auspices. An inner core of actors heavily populated by lawyers, judges, and legal academics can imply that lawmaking behind UNCITRAL's closed doors is driven by experts, not policy makers. Experts have interests of their own in monopoly over work, as a long line of critical scholarship has asserted (Larson 1977). Legal experts are likely to bring into deliberations conflicts among legal families and ways of producing norms that reflect formal properties at which they themselves excel. In either case, the prominent presence of professionals potentially erodes a fundamental foundation of UNCITRAL's claim to representativeness even as it increases the probability of its effectiveness at production of legal norms.

The attendance data likewise evoke further questions about the material resources necessary for global lawmaking. Face-to-face deliberations are expensive for delegates and delegations. UNCITRAL's decision to break into six working groups that work throughout the year raised the financial stakes for many small nations and non-state associations. Meeting twice a year, once in New York and once in Vienna, might be affordable for one working group, but when this expense is multiplied by the six working groups within UNICTRAL, it can be prohibitive. Delegations with scarce resources and limited topical interest must choose between attending no sessions at all or coming often enough that they can resist draft laws to which they strongly object. In this participatory posture, limited attendance at working group sessions can enable a monitoring or protective brief. One UNCITRAL official recounted a particular working group session where only four or five delegations were speaking, time after time. Some delegations came to him and asked, "What about those who are just listening?" He replied, "If we go in a direction they don't like, then you will hear them. If things go in a wrong direction, they will speak out" (Int: 6132).

Nevertheless, the composition of high-attending delegations strongly suggests that the expense of global lawmaking may exclude large numbers of actors for whom those laws will be salient and, indeed, at whom those laws will be directed.

Even so, attendance is not simply a function of wealth. Many states with advanced economies did not send consistently high-attending delegations. This absence may reflect resource priorities, as was said to be the case for the UK's decision not to send substantial delegations to all working groups. Some states, such as Australia and France in the Insolvency Working Group, or Germany in the Secured Transactions Working Group, sent a limited delegation composed of one or two delegates who came with a protective brief to ensure that their own domestic legal orders would fall within the approved bounds of UNCITRAL's global norms. To fulfill these more limited purposes, influence would have been sufficient through sheer consistency of the attendance of a single authoritative delegate.

Two further sets of theoretical implications are evoked by these data. With respect to theories of IO politics, it is clear that the structural position of a state in the global economy is not sufficient to predict its active involvement in global lawmaking. Put another way, knowing *a priori* that a state is a powerful economic actor predicts only weakly that a given powerful state will be a central actor in economic international lawmaking. These hard data demonstrate that non-state actors, particularly professions, consider that the consequences of the lawmaking will matter for their industry and market interests and they must thereby invest in the construction of TLOs that reflect those interests. Yet it is also inescapable that the writing of laws for the world attracts the sustained involvement of a very small group of prominent actors in the international political economy.

Finally, the hard data on attendance set up expectations about recursive processes of lawmaking and law implementation in the settling of new legal norms and standards. A sharp mismatch between the universe of states and non-state actors with interests in an issue-area and the highly select minority of actual lawmakers immediately points to the possibility of laws being made by predominantly advanced economies, which thereafter are either rejected or ignored by the great majority of states with developing economies. The mismatch does not necessarily ensure rejection, as we shall show below, but it flags the prospect of low rates of adoption and thus the faltering of a TLO at the points of national and local implementation.

Likewise, the diagnosis of what problems in commerce might be remedied through law also becomes shaped by which actors are at the lawmaking table. Most of the nations in the Global South were either absent or silent. Hence ways of conceiving of increasing credit to borrowers or rescuing failing companies, or negotiating favorable transport liability levels are likely to be disproportionately construed in terms familiar to sophisticated actors in Frankfurt, London, and New York, rather than those directly salient to actors in Nairobi, Cairo, or Jakarta.

The very small numbers of lawmaking delegates and delegations might either resolve or intensify contradictions that erode lawmaking from the inside. If a small number of lawmakers overwhelmingly come from advanced economies and share common interests, then contradictions will occur less among those countries than between them and developing economies. In the chapters that follow, we show that even when the inner circle of lawmaking delegations and delegates appeared more homogeneous than the great spectrum of states and economies in the world, there nonetheless were several sharp disputes whose effective resolution would influence the probability of internalizing contradictions that could drive further cycles of reform within global and later national and local laws and practices.

Yet there is another side to the smallness of these inner circles. Rather than viewing them only as a collection of individual delegates or delegations, they can also be understood as the core of a deliberative community whose identity becomes interwoven with UNCITRAL's Secretariat as an emergent "us." These repeat players, we observe in key moments, take off their hats as delegates attending UNCITRAL sessions and put on hats to identify themselves as a part of an UNCITRAL team, with reciprocal ties to the Secretariat. Beyond an identity of delegates attending as representatives of state or non-state interests in UNCITRAL the lawmaking arena, and distinct from the notion of individuals sent to UNCITRAL as a part of a delegation but working "in their own capacity," they instead become constituents in the collective, mutually understood in terms of UNCITRAL as a lawmaking actor.

This emergent identity and sense of community became critical when working groups confronted the most divisive problems. Conflicts on some key issues would lead to "Big Deals" in working groups. And "Big Deals" were often forged outside the formal settings of lawmaking. It is to these informal politics that we turn.

5

The Informal Work of Lawmaking

In its longstanding effort to remove obstacles to global trade through proposals for reform or harmonization of private law, UNCITRAL's Secretariat and its most energetic sponsors well understood that institutionalization of transnational legal orders with an identifiable UNCITRAL imprint rested on a foundation of legitimacy. The formal constitution of UNCITRAL's global lawmaking body appeared to solve fundamental legitimation problems, but in so doing it led this IO into contradictions and paradoxes which threatened to subvert its efficacy and ultimately its legitimacy (Block-Lieb and Halliday 2006).

We saw in Chapter 2 that to enter into a standing lawmaking ecology, while differentiating itself from adjacent ecologies, UNCITRAL drew into its deliberations not only all states, but also a wide range of invited governmental and nongovernmental organizations: international financial institutions, professional associations, industry groups, and other stakeholders. While this inclusiveness radically reduced the probability of actor mismatch and misdiagnosis of underlying trade problems, it also multiplied the diversity of interests UNCITRAL sought to resolve, so much so that it threatened to problematize the consensual decisionmaking that had been a hallmark since emerging in the late 1960s. Broadly inclusive participation may have assisted UNCITRAL with its claims to global representation, but this numerosity also threatened to complicate its deliberations.

UNCITRAL ensured the formal equality of all participants in Commission and working group discussions and decisions, but the formalities that undergirded UNCITRAL's procedural claims to legitimacy concomitantly created deliberative rigidities and complicated its viability in its lawmaking ecologies. Although its expansive representativeness and its transparent and consensual decisionmaking processes smoothed its entry into the ecology, they also created the potential for at least three interrelated resource problems within UNCITRAL: financial, temporal, and infrastructural shortages.

These resource constraints start with the financial consequences of time-consuming decisionmaking. The more consequential the distributive implications of lawmaking, the more diverse the states and organizations seeking access to the deliberations, the more protracted the process. Because delegates and delegations incur heavy costs for regular and consistent attendance, the more protracted and costly the enterprise, the more likely it is that working group participation might be biased against poorer nations and weaker non-state and industry interests. In this way, the sheer breadth and cost of UNCITRAL's proceedings threaten to erode the legitimation warrants so painstakingly erected by this global legislature over half a century ago.

Time is an especially scarce commodity within this UN arena.[1] UNCITRAL's miniscule budget meant that the Secretariat's ability to work on any given product was limited. UNCITRAL staff consists of one Secretary for each working group, who acts as the primary reporter and researcher on the project, sometimes supported by a lawyer colleague, and two or three additional assistants. Because the Secretariat employs fewer than a dozen of its own staff, UNCITRAL could not have achieved a fraction of its historic output except through the assistance of volunteer delegates.

Time is also scarce for the state and non-state delegates who attend UNCITRAL working group sessions. We saw in Chapter 3 that state delegations may be comprised of as many as four individuals, some from the private sector and some from the public sector. While public-sector actors can view participation at UNCITRAL working group sessions as a part of their job description, their time was limited. When representing their country's position at UNCITRAL, some delegates continue to earn a civil servant salary. Nonetheless, public-sector delegates may have multiple obligations to tend to either at home or around the world. The same is also true of the delegates from the private sector. Private-sector delegates attend UNCITRAL working group sessions as public interest volunteers who incur costs related to their participation. While often reimbursed for travel expenses, they are not paid for the time spent in UNCITRAL deliberations. Private-sector delegates, thus, face monetized opportunity costs. Paying clients vie for the attention of private-sector delegates, such that every hour spent on assisting UNCITRAL may mean forgoing billable work for a paying client.

Finally, time is scarce for UNCITRAL working groups because there is limited space for working group deliberations. UNCITRAL's Secretariat, as a tiny body in

[1] The relationships between time, power, and resources have become a fertile area of writing in the social sciences as scholars articulate relationships between theories and methodology of grand time (*grande durée*) and events (*évenéments*) (Braudel 1996; Karpik 1993; Halliday and Karpik 2012), the sequencing of events (Abbott 2001), continuities, discontinuities and correspondence in political decisionmaking and efficacy (Pierson 2004), cultural constructions of the social through temporal dimensions (Zerubavel 2004), and the speed of legal change in its recursive cycles in the drive to normative settlement (Halliday 2017). This chapter explores frontiers in the manipulability of time as a form of organizational and ecology adaptations to resource constraints. We are especially indebted to Camilo Leslie for his perceptive suggestions and insights on the analysis of time in this chapter.

a vast UN bureaucracy and its wider ecology, has only a limited number of meeting slots available to it in its Vienna and New York sites because every other UN body is a potential competitor for those slots. In large part this is because official working group sessions must be simultaneously translated in the six official languages of the United Nations: English, French, Spanish, Russian, Chinese, and Arabic. Because UNCITRAL currently convenes six working groups that each meet twice a year for at least a week, UNCITRAL holds six working group sessions in New York and six in Vienna. The Commission itself meets for at least two weeks each summer, sometimes in New York and sometimes in Vienna. Moreover, there is no designated UNCITRAL space within the UN buildings in New York and Vienna. UNCITRAL competes for this space with other UN-affiliated entities, such as the United Nations International Atomic Energy Agency.

How, then, could UNCITRAL resolve the contradictions in its legitimation strategies, the resource constraints in its ecology, and the temporal pressures on its deliberations? In its issue-ecologies, UNCITRAL sought, imperfectly, to solve problems of constitutional and bureaucratic formality by cultivating a dual-tracked method of work: *informal* means of deliberation were layered upon and supplemented with *formal* rule-governed deliberations. A layering of informal and formal methods of work is effected in significant part through the transformation of time as a rigid metric or temporal constraint into a resource that is malleable and manipulable. By finding time in other places, UNCITRAL sought to circumvent the constraints of space and language.

UNCITRAL's informalities of work were more than efficient timesavers. By converting clock or calendar time into new constructions of temporal action, some individual and collective actors in global lawmaking also gained proximity and access to the lawmaking center. As a result, informal strategies of work held both the promise of responsiveness and the risk of capture.

We treat UNCITRAL's pastiche of informal methods of work in this chapter. In later chapters, we explore in greater depth its formal strategies: the decisionmaking and the range of rhetorical strategies it adopts when formulating commercial norms for the world (Chapter 6).

DELIBERATIVE RIGIDITIES

UNCITRAL's founding "constitution" authorized the formulation of a range of laws on international trade. Over time, the Commission expanded from twenty-nine to sixty formal commission members; it invited any UN member state to observe its sessions; it also invited select non-state actors to observe its deliberations and possibly represent industry and other interests (Chapter 2).

The Commission, as a representative body of the community of nations, predominantly was composed of diplomat-delegates who represented their country's commercial interests as a whole. They were expected both to set general working agendas and priorities across the entire field of trade law and to pass judgment on products that were often technically opaque and incomprehensible to all but trained specialists. To convert the Commission into a body of specialists in several arenas of global commercial lawmaking could overwhelm it with delegates technically sophisticated in one domain (e.g., arbitration rules) but completely uninformed in another (e.g., payment law). In effect, therefore, the Commission was well equipped to consider options for work at a high level of generality and it was less equipped to judge the relative merits and political settlements of a technical product from a specialized working group.

Even before expanding its membership and observers so extensively, the Commission, as a body of the whole, recognized that it was poorly suited to work on specialized technical subjects. Early on, it essentially turned amorphous issue-ecologies into bounded working groups to convene and produce reports for Commission approval.

Working groups seemed an optimal solution to UNCITRAL's technical challenges, but it needed to tread carefully along this path. Other international lawmaking organizations relied on small working groups of expert advisors to draft efficiently, but not every working group works according to the same strictures. In the lawmaking organizations that predated UNCITRAL – UNIDROIT, The Hague Conference, and the International Law Commission – working groups generally consist of a small number of technical experts sent as delegates from member states (Int: 9998). As a matter of long-term practice, these delegates work "in their individual capacity" and not as a political representative of their sponsor state (Block-Lieb and Halliday 2016). This allows experts to speak freely without the need to seek permission from political actors in the home state. But the circumstances of UNCITRAL's emergence created an imperative to alter the norm of comfort and clubiness that prevailed in these early global legislatures.

As a result, UNCITRAL working group formats intentionally set UNCITRAL apart from these antecedents. UNCITRAL's working groups are much larger and more overtly political. Since at least the 1980s these working groups have been open not only to all members states, but also to non-member states that seek access to working group deliberations and to non-state organizations that have been invited by the Secretariat.

Technically, both non-member states and non-state delegations are "observers" in the working group's deliberations, but rarely is this distinction enforced within the chamber. Certainly the distinction between categories of state delegations is rarely enforced. Since votes are not formally solicited, the distinction is almost irrelevant, although member states are by UNCITRAL custom seated at the front of the chamber and observer states seated to the rear. The distinction between state and non-state delegations is more palpable in working group sessions. NGOs sit behind delegations of observer states. Since the chair calls on delegations rather than delegates, each speaker's status in the room is made clear before any intervention begins. As with many international lawmaking organizations, the status of a non-state delegation "is an intermediate one between exclusion and full-participation as law co-makers" (Peters, Förster and Koechlin 2009).

To ensure participatory equality in formal working group sessions, so that small states got as much right to speak as powerful states, UNCITRAL adopted the norm that any delegate present in the chamber would be acknowledged by the chair in the order he or she raised a "flag" (the name of the delegation, which could be turned on its end so it was visible from the podium). Although an effective chair would ensure that speakers generally focused on a given article or section of a text in front of them, a sequence of speakers even on a narrow topic would not necessarily speak directly to the point of a previous speaker.

The result could be a series of scattershot interventions that made it difficult to work through complex differences of opinion and find mutually satisfactory resolutions. As one delegate put it:

> The protocol in [the working group] was that someone, the Chair or the Secretary, would watch for flags and make a list and the Chair would recognize particular countries in the sequence they raised their flags. That is very fair in one sense but it is idiotic. The first intervention might be the first sentence of a section. The second would be on the twelfth sentence. The third would have nothing to do with either. The fourth would respond to the first.
>
> (Int: 61c7)

An informal norm that frowned on one delegation intervening multiple times on the same point also worked against rapid back-and-forth exchanges to settle a precise point. The process was confusing to all but veteran participants in the room.

The clumsiness induced by this procedural norm also made it difficult to engage in technical drafting on the floor of the working group chamber. Drafting difficulties were compounded by a strength of the UNCITRAL staffing model, which recruited generalist lawyers to serve as secretaries of more than one working group, and its cognate weakness, which meant that delegates might have technical expertise on a topic beyond that of the working group secretary.

Further inhibitions to open participation were apparent in UNCITRAL's formal working group sessions. Many delegates found it intimidating to speak before a large audience where sophisticated specialists and IOs were observing and perhaps judging the quality of interventions. And for those delegates whose first languages were not translated into the UN official languages, and therefore were compelled to speak in their second or third languages, the challenge of linguistic mastery over technical legal subjects chilled many from speaking at length. Delegates from major trading nations such as Germany, Japan, South Korea, and Italy confronted hurdles not faced by those from Spain, France, or China. Depending on the delegate, these hurdles might be reflected in the frequency and types of their interventions.

Not least, time limits severely restricted the ability to negotiate policy and technical issues in formal working group proceedings. The newer the area of law and the greater its distributive consequences, the more severe were adverse effects flowing from the limits on time available to bargain and reach a political or technical settlement.

INFORMAL ADAPTIVE STRATEGIES

Over time, informal practices developed to dispel rigidities in UNCITRAL's deliberations. Although nowhere explicitly "authorized" in formal articles or other UN formal requirements, UNCITRAL's founding "constitution" and the subsequent evolution of its formal organizational architecture left ample room for imaginative officials and delegates to fill in empty spaces with innovative activities. UNCITRAL staff and delegates pragmatically sought to counteract impediments to their productivity by adopting these informal methods of work. Six adaptive organizational innovations served the pursuit of lawmaking by informal means: colloquia; expert groups; "off-shore" roundtables; inner circles and informal networks; corridor politics; and collegial and convivial events.

Colloquia

In the 1990s, UNCITRAL's Secretariat and delegates realized that neither the Commission nor its working groups were particularly suitable sites for exploration of new areas of international commercial law. In deciding what issues UNCITRAL could feasibly claim for itself, UNCITRAL's Secretariat sought constantly to negotiate between two threats – marginalization by competing organizations in the standing lawmaking ecology and over-ambition for itself. If UNCITRAL failed to push to new frontiers of international commercial law, then other global lawmaking bodies or even states might exclusively occupy the terrain. Yet if UNCITRAL broadly interpreted international commercial law to include topics that other lawmaking IOs had not themselves traversed, or, indeed, where there were few or no precedents in national law, then the risk of failure rose sharply. How, then, could global lawmakers assay the risk and decide what kinds of new ventures fell within its risk tolerance?

Long-range planning was not new for UNCITRAL. As early as 1978, the Commission had considered in its annual session the question of what to do next. At this juncture, the Convention on the International Sale of Goods, the Hamburg Rules, and the Arbitration Rules had been drafted; UNCITRAL had accomplished its initial "programme of work." What issues should now warrant its attention? Delegates suggested a wide range of ideas during the Commission's tenth session and asked the Secretariat to prepare a study report. With the benefit of hindsight, this process of strategic planning through a committee of the whole was less than ideal.

For example, the suggestion that UNCITRAL pursue the task of harmonizing secured transactions law had been raised in this setting, which led to commissioning a report by a noted expert at the Max Planck Institute on the feasibility of such a project, which led nowhere in the short term.

More than a decade later, the Secretariat returned to the topic of long-term planning and sought to improve on the process by organizing a "congress" in 1992, which it loftily announced would canvass "uniform commercial law in the twenty-first century." The Congress, which included not only delegates from Commission members and observer states, but also academics, practitioners, and other invited parties, succeeded in identifying broad ventures in new directions. One UNCITRAL Secretary opined that UNCITRAL's topical focus for the next twenty years had been prefigured by the generative discussions at the 1992 Congress (UNCITRAL 1992).

What the Congress could not so readily manage was careful exploration of the feasibility of producing international commercial law on a given issue for broad adoption. That kind of deliberation required tight focus on a particular topic by interested actors; a staffing of state delegations with delegates from ministries and the private sector with specialized state and private knowledge and interests; an awareness of industry and other non-state actors whose expertise and power would be critical for pragmatic solutions to problems in international commercial law; and a sense of whether political compromise and consensus could be forged around products to ensure timely completion of global standards and widespread enactment and implementation.

To achieve these practical political outcomes, the Secretariat and Commission opened the door to a new species of meeting – the colloquium. Perhaps not coincidentally, the first colloquium was proposed on the heels of the 1992 Congress. Several delegates had suggested that UNCITRAL address the vexing problem of coordinating bankruptcies of multinational corporations across national borders. Although the proposal had been general and ill-defined, in 1994 the first colloquium was jointly sponsored by the Secretariat and INSOL International and this persuaded the Commission to create a working group on insolvency.

Since 1994, UNCITRAL has held many colloquia, often before the Commission has authorized work on a subject or created a formal working group to take up the topic. The functioning of a colloquium is well illustrated by the Working Group on Insolvency's Colloquium held in 2000. The meeting in December of 2000 had both an immediate and longer context.

In 1999 the Commission had given the Insolvency Working Group a narrow mandate to consider whether a working group should be constituted to engage in deliberations on a project to set international standards on domestic corporate bankruptcy laws. The subsequent Working Group meeting in 1999 began to explore the dimensions of such a project, not least, whether it was "a bridge too far," since its ambition would much exceed what the Working Group had achieved with its

Model Law on Cross-Border Insolvency. The Model Law involved bread-and-butter UNCITRAL work, proposing a model law to coordinate insolvency proceedings pending in more than one country, but now it was proposed to tackle directly purely domestic law. While the Working Group was eager to proceed on this formidable task, the Commission was wary.

The Commission knew that other IOs had begun work and were producing global and regional standards on insolvency regimes. Already in 1999 the IMF and Asian Development Bank had published sets of norms (ADB 2000a; IMF 1999; UNCITRAL 1992). The most ambitious effort underway, however, was the World Bank, which had not yet produced its *Principles and Guidelines for Effective Insolvency and Creditor Rights Systems*.[2] Reluctant to proceed with the threat of potential competition from such a powerful unknown, the Commission urged the Insolvency Working Group to delay its work until after the World Bank had unveiled its product.

Loath to lose momentum, the Secretariat and its core band of supportive delegates decided to host a colloquium. Although it was not a formal working group meeting, it would be directed broadly by the Commission's earlier formal charge to explore options; since it was informal, the colloquium could abandon the usual procedural niceties of regular working group meetings, especially obligations of simultaneous translation, and could tailor the meeting to the core group's intentions to build support, add momentum, and expand the scope and form of the enterprise far beyond the Commission's restrictive mandate.

The Colloquium's organizers could draw upon the precedent of a longer context. In their opening remarks to the Colloquium, INSOL's President and UNCITRAL's Secretary could point to its "very successful" colloquium in 1994 which had provided the springboard for the production of the Model Law on Cross-Border Insolvency several years later. The 1994 Colloquium had shown that there was "a clear need" for UNCITRAL's involvement; it gave the Secretariat the courage to take insolvency off the "impossible list" and demonstrated that with outside pressure and inside support "modesty pays off."

Standing before the 150 "top people" from forty-eight countries who arrayed themselves in the large UN chamber in Vienna in 1999, UNCITRAL's Secretary, Jernej Sekolec, not only pointed to UNCITRAL's singular legitimacy as a global lawmaker, but also to its valuable partnership with the two co-convenors of the Colloquium – the two leading professional associations, INSOL and the International Bar Association, representing the essential professionals who preside over corporate insolvency worldwide, namely, accountants, insolvency practitioners, and lawyers. In his turn, INSOL's President opened by acknowledging UNCITRAL's "incredibly effective machine." Then, they got down to business.

2 Various versions of these norms emerged over time. See (World Bank 1999b; World Bank 2003; World Bank 2005).

For political and pragmatic reasons, the Colloquium sought to take stock of work already done, about to be done, and able to be done. A leading IBA insolvency specialist began by digesting the work of four other bodies – the G-22, IMF, Asian Development Bank, and UNCITRAL. He then challenged the assembly to set some boundaries: what UNCITRAL *could* do and what it should *not* do because the work was best left for other organizations. This conversation was not just an internal one. It also involved the leaders from the ADB, IMF, and World Bank, who contributed to a wide-ranging discussion on why a statement of international norms on the topic of corporate insolvency law would be valuable and how far these should reach into substance and procedural law, institutional reform, and private restructuring efforts. Vigorous debate and much maneuvering behind the scenes centered on an International Bar Association proposal emanating from the US that out-of-court restructurings should be on the Working Group's agenda. English bankers argued that bank-led restructurings should also find their place in discussions.

Participants debated the form of the technology that should be relied on to convey the norms that the Working Group might produce. UNCITRAL's Secretary wanted a text that would be flexible. The US State Department official wanted principles combined with black letter law. The Working Group's Secretary noted that half a dozen options were possible, ranging from a comparative "study" to a model law, or, perhaps, a new technology would need to be invented.

Under INSOL's deft leadership, the Colloquium appointed several "evaluators,"[3] who were distinguished insolvency specialists from around the world to offer a summary and synthetic report on discussions. These evaluators brought back to those in attendance at the Colloquium a list of eleven topics that they were convinced should form the core of an UNCITRAL product and would be "doable." They imagined a process that would include stakeholders from across the world, from different legal systems, different occupations, and business. The Secretariat would facilitate work by allocating tasks and coordinating the work of various expert groups. With these steps, they believed, the Working Group might produce a new international product on this topic in a mere two years.

The relatively free-wheeling, public-private collaboration in the Colloquium yielded more than its most optimistic organizers had imagined. UNCITRAL's Secretary concluded that the Colloquium had fleshed out the narrow mandate of the Commission. It had pointed in a clear direction, so that "we know where we are heading." And a pool of experts effectively was in place to provide technical assistance in an area previously thought to be an impossible reach for UNCITRAL.

[3] Ralph Zulman, a member of the Supreme Court of Appeal for South Africa, their highest appellate court; Clare Wee, the point person on insolvency law for the ADB; Justice James Farley, an eminent Canadian judge and judicial pioneer in bankruptcy law; Richard A. Gitlin, a leading US practitioner and former head of INSOL; and Judge Wisit Wisitsora-at, a noted Thai judge specializing in bankruptcy and corporate reorganziation.

Certain key delegates, initially skeptical on prospects, came away "more optimistic, positive" and ready to get down to drafting.

The Colloquium therefore accomplished several feats. It revealed what other IOs had done and found commonalities that would serve to forge influential alliances and incremental reforms. It served notice to the World Bank that UNCITRAL would neither wait indefinitely for its product nor be cowed into a subsidiary role. Indeed, the display of associational and expert support for UNCITRAL's initiative more than challenged the World Bank's assiduous effort to provide technical legitimacy for its own enterprise. In an effective "scoping exercise" of boundary-making, the Colloquium specified in broad brush strokes what could be the substantive core of a prospective set of norms where consensus might be imagined. Not least, the process of the Colloquium was itself a product. It re-kindled the sociability that had marked earlier deliberations on the Model Law on Cross-Border Insolvency and significantly expanded the reach of that circle to embrace new delegates and delegations. In this relaxed setting, the Colloquium began to knit together an ethos of the deliberative community that would prove essential to UNCITRAL's consensual lawmaking process.

Expert Groups

If the attributes of working groups and UNCITRAL staff worked against the prospect of timely consensual products, the work of the global lawmakers required another expedient. In response, informal expert groups emerged.

The very informality of these organizational entities meant that working group secretaries had much discretion over the role of expert groups and how they functioned (Int: 9000). Common to all three working groups were expert group meetings oriented toward or responding to the regular working group sessions. Small groups of Insolvency Working Group delegates tended to meet on the weekend after the week-long meetings in Vienna and New York. Secured Transactions expert groups met less predictably, sometimes after, sometimes before, and sometimes in between meetings. Transport expert groups met extensively, sometimes twice a year for a week or more, and toward the end of process, even while that Working Group was in session. These were endurance races.

Participation in expert groups was by invitation only. Working group secretaries chose whom to invite. Invariably, expert groups started larger and winnowed down over time. Delegates came overwhelmingly from advanced economies, mostly from North America and Europe. In the Transport Working Group, for instance, the most regular attenders were from China, Italy, Japan, Netherlands, Switzerland, Norway, US, Spain, and Sweden, together with a representative of CMI who was usually from the UK (Int: 6008). The expert group for Secured Transactions was predominantly a US-Canada caucus, with several delegates from each country, including two from non-state delegations, joined often by delegates from France (representing the International Chamber of Commerce) and India. In the Insolvency Working Group, US state and non-state delegates were the most consistent; they were joined regularly by the Australian delegate, the Colombian delegate, a World Bank official from Argentina, from time to time by delegates from France, Mexico, Switzerland, South Korea, earlier in the proceedings by the lead insolvency official at the Asian Development Bank, and later in the proceedings by various delegates from the IMF.[4]

Secretaries chose delegates who dependably and consistently attended working group sessions, who participated actively in those sessions, and who displayed technical expertise. Working group secretaries were encouraged by the UNCITRAL Secretary to make the expert groups representative of regions and legal systems, but this proved difficult. With rare exceptions, participants in expert groups had to pay for themselves, at least to stay on for an extra few days after a meeting or for travel and accommodations if meetings were held between working group sessions. Secretaries in the Working Groups on Insolvency and Secured Transactions also found it difficult to recruit civil law and Continental lawyers. Some attributed this to an affinity that common lawyers have with a politics that can include private parties involved in drafting statutes for parliamentary or regulatory bodies. One UNCITRAL official observed that common law lawyers like drafting and have a tradition of volunteerism (Int: 9000).

Despite the ease with which these groups were convened, working group secretaries appeared to be caught in a Catch-22 with expert group activities. On the one hand, since expert groups were entirely advisory to the working group secretary, they were never acknowledged as a source of authority in discussions with a working group. In some working groups, such as the Transport Group, the work of expert groups was well understood, with references to their involvement scattered through the public record; in others, the expert group flew somewhat under the radar. On the other hand, if the working group secretary had been fully transparent, then the compositional selectivity and potential bias of the expert groups would have been more evident. Because the expert groups existed in the shadows of the working groups, their opaque roles produced some unease among some delegations that knew about them but were not involved.

Whether unease was warranted, of course, depended on the role that expert groups performed. That, too, was undefined although a matter of tacit agreement between the working group secretaries and those who agreed to serve them. One participant in the Transport Working Group described its expert group activities:

> We had extensive expert groups – during and after sessions and they were often quite long. … The Working Group secretary did a first draft, invited responses

[4] Since no formal record is kept, we relied on interviews to assist us in compiling an imperfect approximation of who attended these discussions.

> [and asked for] proposed revisions. The Expert Group actually came up essentially with the final wording, although the secretary had the last say.
>
> (Int: 6006)

Another participant in the Transport expert group remarked:

> [The Secretary] would draft the changes, circulate them to the experts, and then go through the draft comma by comma. [The group was] all leading lights. They could also judge [when] what looked like a minor change might have all sorts of consequences. It was a very collegial experience.
>
> (Int: 6008)

A participant in the Secured Transactions expert group characterized its activities in another way:

> Fifty-five percent of the time, [the group] was producing texts before a Working Group meeting; forty percent was clarifying technical things, finding the right terms, cleaning up the text; and five percent was revising Working Group decisions and taking it back to the Working Group.
>
> (Int: 9030)

Taking the panoptic view across all the expert groups, it is clear they differed in their emphases. One might exercise an expansive function of preparing drafts for a secretary, which then went through quick iterations between the secretary and expert group before coming back to a working group. Another would react to first or later drafts produced by the secretary. All were concerned with clarifying and specifying discussions and decisions that emerged from working groups. All were involved in technical drafting. And all, indirectly at least, served as sounding boards and impromptu sites for the continuing professional education of secretaries who were not technical specialists.

The fundamental question, however, was whether expert group meetings were tantamount to "smoke-filled back rooms" where a small caucus of delegates made policy decisions. Some critics and even one or two participants assert that expert groups had policy influence. "Without any doubt it acted as a policy body," said one participant. "[W]e made decisions, not always coming back to the Working Group" (Int: 6501). Another participant considered that involvement in expert group drafting gave a "massive advantage" to the participant's delegation and interests (Int: 5803).

All working group secretaries and most participants contest the characterization of an "expert group as a 'smoke-filled room.'" "A smoke-filled room," said a regular attender to one expert group, "is where you introduce concepts that are foisted on the world. That didn't happen" (Int: 1000). The Secretary of his Working Group made "it clear all along that the expert group could only deal with issues raised by the Working Group" and it was very clear that if anything new arose in the expert group it had to be brought back to the Working Group (Int: 9011). A participant in another Working Group insisted that the secretary set the agenda and chose what to take away from the Working Group. Some participants in the expert group might have wanted it to act as a policy broker, admitted another, but the secretary "maintained control" and acted as "an honest broker" (Int: 9030). One Working Group Secretary asserted that, for the most part, the "main players" in the Working Group would "take off their country hats" and sit down and work through what the Working Group had considered in their capacities as individual experts.

We cannot arbitrate the extent of the policy influence exercised by the respective regular expert groups since, by definition, they functioned behind closed doors. It is clear from many of their members and secretaries, however, that expert groups are considered to be indispensable to compensate for UNCITRAL's scarcity of staff resources and time constraints. Effectively they multiply by 50 to 100 percent the consultations and deliberations of the Secretariat with delegates. They also offer a far more effective way of inserting technical expertise into deliberations than is possible in any of UNCITRAL's formal bodies. They might even provide an off-script private occasion to resolve conflicts or clarify ambiguities. And in the final analysis, all drafting comes in periodic iterations back to the working groups and in final form to the working groups and Commission for final approval. In principle, at least, this should provide a check on any transmigration of technical advice into policy decisions, a form of exercising professional influence well known in the politics of professionals (Halliday 1985).

On occasion, however, activities in expert groups became incendiary to certain delegations. In one instance, France agreed to participate in an expert group but its delegate asked that any papers considered by the group be sent to its Foreign Ministry. The Secretary cautioned that the documents were in "English only" since the practice of the expert group was to speak English and it was assumed, at least, that each participant was able to read or understand English. The French Ministry and delegation to the Commission "hit the roof" and insisted that since French was both an official and working language at UNCITRAL, all its working documents should be translated into French. UNCITRAL, said the Secretariat, was "stuck" since UNCITRAL "cannot afford to translate all expert group meetings into UN languages." This incident, bundled with some others, contributed to a French proposal to change fundamentally the way UNCITRAL went about its business, not least in the involvement of non-state actors or volunteers and in the procedures of its working methods (see Chapter 8).

In addition to the "standing expert groups," which fairly regularly met in coordination with topics under discussion in the working groups, the Secretariat on occasion convened special purpose expert groups. There were several examples of these special purpose expert groups scattered across the three working groups.

During discussions on the Legislative Guide on Insolvency Law, the Insolvency Working Group confronted a problem that had attracted the close attention of the IMF and New York office of the Federal Reserve (Int: 1973). When companies go into bankruptcy, their bankers can compare the client's loans to the client's bank deposit accounts; if the client has enough money in bank deposits to pay off the loan, the bank automatically pays off the loan in a process called a "setoff." Setting off creates a possible conflict among creditors because this practice effectively gives banks a first priority in the lineup of creditors wanting their loans repaid. But setoff holds a long and storied history in the common law, often equated to foreclosure on collateral. The importance of setoff had increased with reliance on derivatives and other financial contracts in the capital markets. Without the unfettered ability to set off between repurchase agreements, credit swaps and the like, argued bankers, the smooth functioning of the financial system on a day-to-day basis can be impaired.

The US had exempted these financial market transactions from the bankruptcy process since as early as 1984, and the bankruptcy laws in other developed nations had followed suit. But what about the rest of the world? The IMF argued that the Insolvency Guide should contain clear recommendations on the topic. The Working Group began working on draft provisions on setoff and the "clearing" of these financial market contracts, but the IMF was not happy with the wording of the protections given financial markets in drafts of the Guide. It therefore provided funding for UNCITRAL to convene an expert group of specialists to draft provisions that would be acceptable to US and IMF financial regulators. The specialized group consisted of delegates from the Insolvency Working Group, as well as some "outside" experts. It produced a document that came back to the Working Group and was eventually accepted by it.

This was only one of the specialized expert groups that assisted the Insolvency Working Group on their Legislative Guide. Mid-way through deliberations delegates suggested that the Guide should speak to the issue of what countries' laws should apply in an insolvency case. Conflicts of law is an especially complex and technical area nested within insolvency practice. The delegate from France was sympathetic to the project in principle, but raised concerns about the Working Group's expertise in this area. Moreover, he argued, The Hague Conference on Private International Law had for more than a century been conceded primacy of lawmaking authority on conflicts of law. For UNCITRAL to act unilaterally would be unduly competitive, even confrontational. Perhaps UNCITRAL should defer to The Hague Conference, it was argued. Rather than defer and hope that The Hague Conference took up this issue, however, the Insolvency Working Group agreed to convene a special expert group. In this gesture of cooperation among potential competitors, the Secretariat invited delegate-experts from the Insolvency and Secured Transactions Working Groups to meet for several days with representatives from The Hague Conference. Together this group hammered out provisions that would become the Insolvency Guide's recommendations on "applicable law."

The Transport Working Group likewise convened two special purpose expert groups, one on the vexed issue of whether UNCITRAL should aim for a multimodal or door-to-door convention; and another on carriage of goods by sea and electronic commerce (Int: 6002).

On several occasions, working groups overlapped in their deliberations and threatened to offer alternative global norms on related or identical issues. The potential conflict of issue-ecologies, where their boundaries of expertise blurred, might have led to competing norms. Since UNCITRAL could not afford to have dueling working groups that produced conflicting norms, it tried, in the first instance, to demarcate potential boundary disputes and resolve differences in overlapping interests by forming joint expert groups. At one point, delegates from the Transport Working Group joined experts from the Arbitration Working Group to resolve possible territorial disputes and conflicts of norms. On another occasion the Transport Working Group experts sat down together with experts from the Electronic Commerce Working Group to agree on language regarding "electronic transport records" that would eventually become part of the Rotterdam Rules.

A similar solution helped settle an incipient conflict between the Working Groups on Insolvency and Secured Transactions. Since insolvency law must always deal with creditors who have secured their mortgages and other loans in various ways, inevitably the Insolvency Working Group made decisions that might have preempted discussions by the Secured Transactions Working Group, whose proceedings lagged the Insolvency Working Group by a couple of years. That Insolvency had gone first created a tension within the Secured Transactions sessions, since the nearly inevitable "pro-debtor" tilt that would come with efforts to create international standards for a reorganization-friendly corporate insolvency law conflicted with the "pro-secured creditors" views of many of the delegations in the Secured Transactions Working Group. Boundary disputes and the possibility of conflicts between the two legislative guides would be unacceptable, so the Secretariat convened a joint session of the two working groups and asked delegates of both to hammer out jointly agreed recommendations in that setting. Long after these combined sessions had reached agreement, however, the deal started to unwind as delegates to the Secured Transactions Working Group began to want more specificity, in part to react to negotiations that were unfolding in that setting and in part because, on reflection, some things just seemed unclear. No one wanted to go back and hold an additional joint session of the two working groups, but pressure mounted. In the end, a special purpose expert group was convened. This was "intended to cool them down and get an agreement" (Int: 1000). Eventually the recommendations of the expert group came to a special joint meeting of the two working groups and they settled their differences in a cordial demarcation of boundaries and policy agreements.

Off-Shore Roundtables

The Transport Working Group began its proceedings with a methodical effort to work its way through the draft norms prepared for the first Working Group meeting by the International Maritime Committee (CMI). This article-by-article progress soon wearied certain influential delegations, which felt that the entire process was being "bogged down" by narrow technical matters when large policy differences had not been resolved (Int: 6006).

A threshold issue arose when it became increasingly apparent that the Working Group itself had not decisively agreed on the scope of its ambitions,[5] and so long as its own boundaries remained undefined, it was fruitless to try and resolve matters that presupposed a settlement over scope. Several core members of the Transport Working Group believed that UNCITRAL procedural norms and methods of work were not well suited to resolution of these big policy differences. The Working Group needed an informal setting where rules and principal-agent relationships were relaxed. Said a key delegate in the Transport Working Group:

> An unofficial group allows a faster exchange of opinions because it is less formal. A working group requires you ask for the floor, you speak, others speak – you have to speak officially. In informal gatherings the exchange is personal, unofficial, and therefore more frank. What some could not say as a delegate of their government they could say off the cuff because personally they agreed with a certain approach. [Informality] greatly facilitates problem solving.
>
> (Int. 6012)

Informal forums also had a relational value that flowed back into formal decision-making.

> Relationships between human beings are very important. . . . Relations get closer in unofficial meetings. You understand other people better informally. You trust others more. It facilitates an ambience among the people, which remains through into the next session. Those meetings had an impact beyond the subject matter discussed in the meeting. I have always considered mutual trust – you trust, you respect the knowledge of the other person, you listen with better attention – to be essential. We are not machines.
>
> (Int: 6012)

Spearheaded by the Italian delegate, a veteran Italian maritime lawyer, Francisco Berlingieri, the Secretariat agreed to a special format for informal discussion on how far the draft convention should extend beyond prior conventions' focus on liability from port-to-port or tackle-to-tackle. Berlingieri proposed approaching his own Ministry of Foreign Affairs to invite all delegations to send individuals to an informal meeting or "roundtable" away from Vienna or New York. The Ministry replied that it had no objection if the roundtable did not cost it anything. A London law firm volunteered its offices and some local financial support. The first of these meetings, in February 2004, included delegates from key non-state groups as well as core

[5] The issue concerned three different theories of scope which underlay already respective existing agreements on carriage of goods by sea: a contract theory (i.e., Hamburg Rules), an approach based on type of trade (i.e., liner vs tramp service trade), or an approach based on type of document (i.e., Hague Rules) (Int: 6012).

delegates from major delegations, including the US, Japan, Canada, and most European countries. In addition, a few specialists attended who had not been a part of the UNCITRAL deliberations.

Nevertheless, noted an organizer, "the optics were problematic." Some states, notably France and Germany, were uneasy about this kind of informality, where one or more persons drafted a position paper that was brought to an informal gathering of twenty to forty people conducted only in English. They thought that the roundtable could be considered "exclusive" – indeed, the attendees were overwhelmingly from advanced economies – and some delegations therefore simply "refused to play the diplomacy game" (Int: 6006).

To the satisfaction of its proponents, however, the roundtable did manage to identify core differences, reduce conceptual misunderstandings, and come to a settlement on a proposed solution. The agreement informally forged by the meeting was converted into a draft, which was then submitted to the Working Group Secretary and brought to the Transport Working Group at its next meeting. The Finnish delegate was chosen to introduce the draft on the floor of the Working Group and the "London delegates" who concurred swung in behind him (Int: 6006, 6005). Even one critic of nearly everything else about the Transport Working Group's policy decisions nonetheless felt able to applaud the value of the relaxed procedure in these off-shore roundtable discussions.

> I saw these as forums welcomed by everyone. They allowed more dedicated consideration in an informal situation. People didn't have to take positions. Discussions were much more frank. People spoke more freely and formed their positions in the course of the discussion.
>
> (Int: 6013)

Another major conflict spurred a second similar effort in February 2005. The US delegation strongly pressed for "freedom of contract" within the draft convention, that is, the ability to opt out of the generic terms of the convention to enable a particular shipper and particular carrier to agree on a volume contract whose terms they would negotiate (see Chapter 7). A second London conference essentially followed the precedent of the successful 2004 meeting and came to a similar conclusion – the outlines of an agreement were forwarded to the Working Group Secretary for debate at the next Working Group meeting.

A subsequent roundtable held in Barcelona in October 2007 differed from the London roundtables because its purpose was more to obtain political support for decisions already taken than to obtain settlements on matters still under contention. Smaller shipper nations from Africa, which had financial interests in the costs of getting their primary products to overseas markets, had been slow to be involved actively in UNCITRAL's discussions on this draft convention. All shipper nations had a financial interest in keeping the liability levels high for carriers that destroyed or failed to deliver goods to market. Proponents of the convention that was taking shape realized that if one political necessity for a successful convention was to keep on board the US, another was to have sufficient signatures from states to bring the convention into force. Smaller African states comprised a sizable bloc with a large number of prospective signatures and therefore needed to be wooed.

But the Africans had been absent from some of the Working Group deliberations and this was not a topic that could be learned by simply reading through the draft convention. Since they seemed to have "misunderstandings" about the agreements taking shape in the Working Group, and they were reluctant to part from their commitment to the Hamburg Rules, which strongly favored developing countries, the Secretariat and Chair of the Working Group invited ambassadors from several African countries and a number of experts to a meeting scheduled immediately before a Working Group session in Vienna. The Spanish law firm of the Working Group's Chair hosted the meeting and ensured that simultaneous translation would be available in French and English for Francophone African countries, not least Senegal, which had emerged as a leader of the African bloc (Int: 6008, 6012).

This "explanatory seminar" exceeded the expectations of the organizers. The two days of meetings allowed African officials to raise objections that could be answered by invited experts; the carefully selected experts in turn gave presentations to "clarify" the meaning and import of the draft convention. The net result persuaded several countries that the draft convention offered them more than the pre-existing conventions and led to the tangible result that thirteen African countries have signed the Rotterdam Rules.[6] Togo, a small nation on the east coast of Africa, and Congo, a much larger African nation but hardly a trade giant, are two of the three nations to have acceded to the terms of the convention (Spain is the other). Since twenty accessions are needed for this convention to enter into force, signature by this bloc of African countries may prove to be as important as signing by the US.

Inner Circles and Networks

Although "informal," the colloquia, expert groups, and roundtables had noticeable traces of formality, whether in the way participants were invited, or how their discussions were moderated, or in what were produced as outputs. The Secretariat also found even less formal ways to supplement its expertise, "multiply" time, and build support in anticipation of future working group meetings.

Working group secretaries functioned in a rather solitary environment. Although their offices clustered together in two corridors of a tall UN office building in Vienna, their jobs involved little mutual support and the ambience of the office suffered from a lack of esprit and conviviality. Working group secretaries found

6 The following African nations have signed the Rotterdam Rules: Cameroon; Congo; the Democratic Republic of Congo; Gabon; Ghana; Guinea; Guinea-Bissau; Madagascar; Mali; Niger; Nigeria; Senegal and Togo.

themselves thrust into areas of law where they were neophytes and where members of their working group more often than not had vastly more technical expertise in a given area of law than they did. Not only was this anxiety provoking, it led to a nagging sense of vulnerability about drafts and drafting when confronted with a legislative-type chamber packed with experts and scores of national delegations. Hiring addition staff was one potential solution to the problem, but not a tenable one since UNCITRAL finances were limited. If the Secretariat itself found no way to compensate for the isolation and vulnerability of its staff lawyers, and insufficient resources could be found in the UN system, then UNCITRAL's staff learned that it could look outside for help – to the working groups themselves.

Each working group secretary surrounded himself or herself with a congenial and expert inner circle from among working group delegates. The circle had no formal character or even discernible shape. It comprised a small number of trusted and responsive individuals, whether or not they came from state or non-state delegations. Individuals in the circles sometimes functioned as organizers or orchestrators of activities, such as colloquia or roundtables. Those delegates who were most useful on a day-to-day basis were quick to respond with comments on drafts from a working group secretary or to undertake drafting themselves. Not least, they served as sounding boards or advisors on difficult or technical or political issues. All assured a working group secretary, in effect, that drafts placed in front of a deliberative body of experts would have reached an acceptable threshold of competent drafting. And should drafting be subject to sharp attack in working group meetings, one or more of the inner circle quietly stood ready to spring to the defense of a working group secretary.

Who was in these inner circles? Usually the individuals were specialists from leading states and non-state actors. Their numbers were intentionally kept small, so small that these were just a subset of those who regularly participated in expert groups.

We have seen that working group secretaries enlisted individual non-state actors or a cluster of individuals or organizations at the agenda-setting stage (see Chapter 3). But secretaries did not discontinue these connections once the initial draft was set. Quite normally, when a working group secretary had a question on substance he or she called a trusted member of this working group cadre rather than reach out to another working group secretary. Small networks and clusters of specialized insiders were relied upon throughout working group sessions – in the mid-stream of proceedings and at their penultimate moment.

At the last stages of deliberation on the Legislative Guide on Secured Transactions, inner circles and networks were mobilized to bring the final product to fruition. The Secured Transactions Working Group had proceeded in bursts. The Working Group had begun by moving, chapter by chapter, through commentary and recommendations. When this seemed to get "totally bogged down," the Group switched to focus on the recommendations while keeping notes on how the commentary might subsequently need to be revised. When this process was completed, there was a lot of work to be done in revising the commentary, more work than the Working Group Secretary was likely to accomplish in the short time allocated to the project between Working Group sessions. The Secretary decided to distribute the work in order to complete the necessary work. He allocated each of the seven chapters of the draft Guide to members of the inner circle with the goal of bringing the commentary of each into line with the recommendations. For example, one member of the Canadian delegation took responsibility for the Introduction and Acquisition Financing; another tackled the section on Conflicts of Law; one of the delegates from the American Bar Association adopted the section on The Rights and Obligations of the Parties and also Enforcement; a member of the US delegation took responsibility for editing the sections on Third-party Obligors and Transition; a delegate from the Commercial Finance Association worked on the section on Priorities, while another member of the Canadian delegation edited the sections on Third Party Effectiveness and the Registries (Int: 9030). And at the very end, two delegates aided in the general smoothing of the Guide as a whole to find "a common voice" (Int: 6548). After several iterations of drafting by the inner circle, versions went back to the Working Group Secretary for editing and then to the Working Group itself.

Such networks were not always at the volition of UNCITRAL secretaries. In one working group, the notion of an "inner circle" was refined to include several such circles, each focused on a particular issue within the draft convention. This informal practice arose early on. After several sessions of the Transport Working Group, where progress seemed too slow to some delegations, delegations on one occasion took things into their own hands. The US head of delegation, Mary Helen Carlson, was reported to have said, "if we continue this way it will take another ten to fifteen years. People will lose interest, get transferred, we may have to take decisions over and over again" (Int: 6540). Said a member of the "inner circle," "to keep attention, to retain the chemistry among the people, you have to find a way to organize the discussion in a different way than the UN usually works. It needs to be more intensive" (Int: 6540).

In the face of opposition from the Secretariat, several delegations to the Transport Working Group found a way to speed up proceedings. In the words of a key delegate:

> By two to three years on the Rotterdam Rules we had gone one time through the whole draft. Between meetings people were not involved mentally. The subject matter was so complicated. It was an idea of Mary Helen's [the representative from the US State Department] that we have to organize the work differently. We organized correspondent groups – we cut the whole convention into eight or ten separate topics. We called for volunteers to organize a view on each of the topics between meetings. E.g., the Chinese had limitation of liability; Italy, liability;

> Swedes, shippers' obligations, etc. Our job was that when the subject was on the agenda for the next meeting to organize the Working Group. People were free to do it how they wanted it, e.g., first a study or synopsis of what had previously been said in meetings, but trying to find what people were thinking and a then a common denominator in order to arrive at proposals that could be offered by a couple of delegates. On the basis of detailed preparation, then there was discussion in the big room [of the Working Group].
>
> That had a tremendous influence. Without this way of organizing the discussion, it would not have been possible to get adoption within five to six years. The UNCITRAL Secretariat was fiercely opposed. They lost control of it . . .
>
> We organized our own website, sent out questionnaires, drafted proposal after proposal with comments, etc. It was all on the secure website. We worked in complete transparency. It worked: Each delegation that was responsible made proposals and . . . , during meetings themselves, the proposals often made by the coordinator of the group were more or less automatically adopted. It could only have happened because there was such hard work between meetings.
>
> (Int: 6540)

Corridor Politics

When working groups are in session in New York or Vienna, formal proceedings are embedded within informal corridor politics that buzz with activity among the most engaged delegations and delegates. Breakfast, coffee breaks, lunch, late afternoon drinks, and dinner each offer moments and sites where legislators make connections and solidify ties, set micro-agendas, clear up misunderstandings, resolve differences, devise tactics, and strike deals.

In the first several working group sessions of a new cycle of lawmaking, informal time enables introductions, most especially in coffee lines where sheer happenstance can bring into contiguity delegations unknown to each other. Since coffee breaks are quite flexible, both in their beginning and end, they can punctuate otherwise contested and even heated formal sessions with a chance for delegates to explain their positions to each other, and for temporary blocs of delegates to plan how to proceed. Often these tactics are processual. Once an orchestrator of a line of action has persuaded several delegates to follow a line, then the sequence of speakers may be determined, so that one country delegate opens proceedings in the next session, and others commit to fall in behind with supportive or amplifying comments.

An example from the Insolvency Working Group's 2000 colloquium shows how readily this can be stage-managed. The International Bar Association had introduced an idea that certain kinds of bankruptcies might be better handled with out-of-court agreements that were then confirmed *in toto* by a court. As the final panel of the Colloquium loomed, it appeared some notable delegates would disagree on grounds this approach would minimize the role of judges. The International Bar Association delegate, a New York corporate lawyer, spoke "backstage" to "line up agreement" among INSOL delegates and used the coffee break to persuade doubters that indeed judges were integral to the process. When the formal session resumed, several notable delegates were already primed to get on the record their support for the measure (Int: 1903).

The chairs of the Insolvency and Secured Transactions Working Groups took a more directive approach. If they believed that the formal session was deadlocked or misunderstandings hindered progress, they would call for a "consultation break" where delegates would retreat to the corridors or one of the vacant meeting rooms across the corridor to caucus intensively before the formal session was called back to order. Although some viewed the suggestion as one made with tongue in cheek, in fact UN interpreters were entitled by contract to regularly scheduled breaks from their simultaneous translation duty – a lengthy lunch, to be sure, but also two shorter coffee breaks, which were referred to as "informal consultation sessions" during which delegates were encouraged to consult but to do so "informally," that is, without the need for translation into the six UN languages.

Blocs of nations similarly used these intersessional moments to caucus. A European group might meet during lunch to try and harmonize their positions, while the Americans met for drinks to compare notes at the end of the day. Many African countries began to meet as a bloc halfway through the maritime negotiations. Because the UN offices in which UNCITRAL working groups met were situated in physically isolated locations in New York and Vienna, delegates often chose to eat in the subsidized cafeterias that the UN hosted.

Language facility makes a difference. Since no simultaneous translation occurs in the corridors or dining rooms, those delegates with mastery of more than one UN language have the distinct advantage to span language groups, which themselves often roughly reflect legal families. Whether career diplomats or academics, jurists or practitioners with international interests, many of the delegates were conversational in multiple languages. While only a few felt comfortable enough with one of the six official UN languages to intervene at the working group itself, most delegates could be coaxed into a more casual gathering between formal sessions and many could be heard to ask questions about some nuance of a recent floor debate. Some delegates spent close to as many hours in corridors and cafeterias, bars, coffee shops, and restaurants, as in the formal sessions themselves.

Collegiality and Conviviality

Veterans of UNCITRAL's working groups concur that informal evening occasions help convert dozens of disparate and unconnected delegates into a deliberative community. When evening events can spotlight an international association or a national firm, then benefits flow in multiple directions.

The Commercial Finance Association, a Chicago-based trade association, hosted sumptuous dinners during Secured Transaction Working Group sessions in Vienna and New York for delegates and their spouses. The International Bar Association frequently found a local law or accounting firm in Vienna and later in New York to co-host a cocktail party for all Insolvency Working Group delegates. The International Insolvency Institute similarly hosted what it called its "legendary dinners," where it entertained not only its own members who were attending Working Group sessions as delegates but also delegates from a range of state delegations in the hopes of encouraging them to join the "Triple I" or to speak at panel presentations at III meetings.

Nevertheless, the conviviality of dinners had a shadow side. Some dinners were by invitation only. Their composition did not mirror that of the working groups. English was the dominant if not exclusive language of sociability. In the shadows of the events were awkward conversations over "are you going," which referred less to conflicts in social calendars and more to whether invitations had been issued and accepted.

MAKING TIME

These informal practices allowed UNCITRAL to employ at least five temporal tactics: staging; compressing; expanding; segmenting and multiplying time (Table 5.1).

1. *Staging* time refers to influence on the moment of an onset of a lawmaking episode. Here actors may be able to speed up or slow down the temporal moment of beginnings to negotiations and lawmaking – to hurry when competitors threaten to pre-empt jurisdiction or to delay when prudence requires that some other event occur or set of norms be released before an actor proceeds with its own. We saw two examples of staging in Chapter 3.

For instance, in the late 1990s UNCITRAL sped up the onset of its lawmaking on secured transaction law when it became aware that UNIDROIT might claim exclusive competence over any global legislating on secured financial transactions. UNIDROIT had already had great success in developing new global norms on a narrow aspect of these international interests with its Cape Town Convention on mobile equipment. Energized by its success, UNIDROIT looked to pre-empt UNCITRAL's involvement in this issue-area. Anticipating this move, UNCITRAL sprang into action. To stake out territory before UNIDROIT had time to act, UNCITRAL organized a colloquium on secured transactions, which was co-sponsored by the Commercial Finance Association, and then "commissioned" the Secretariat to draft a report for presentation to it and to its standing Working Group. As a result of this quick sequence of events, UNCITRAL succeeded in blocking UNIDROIT and in repurposing a working group on international payments, which had just finished its draft convention on the assignment of receivables in international trade, as a working group on security interests.

TABLE 5.1. *Temporal Tactics in Global Lawmaking*

	Description	Instances
Staging **time**	Influencing the moment at which an episode begins.	Secured Transactions Working Group: Starting prematurely to head off UNIDROIT and European project.
Compressing **time**	Shortening the period of decision making.	Transport Working Group: Beginning with a draft convention by an industry group.
Extending **time**	Lengthening the period of decision making.	Transport Working Group: Met for one week twice a year, but then doubled meeting time to two weeks twice a year.
Multiplying **time**	Slicing decision-making episodes into finer tracks so there were more of them.	Transport Working Group: Creating parallel proceedings on eight separate tracks through Correspondent Groups.
Segmenting **time**	Dividing problem solving into successive lawmaking projects.	Insolvency Working Group: Beginning with a procedural product; Postponing deliberations on bankruptcy treatment of corporate groups.

By contrast, UNCITRAL's Working Group on Insolvency Law felt compelled to slow down the commencement of its deliberations on a legislative guide. Energized by their rapid drafting consensus on a Model Law of Cross-Border Insolvency, the Group had set their sights on making a quick pivot toward a much more ambitious effort of expansive legal scope. UNCITRAL's Secretariat organized a colloquium called to reconnoiter the prospects for a comprehensive legislative guide, which exceeded all expectations for prospects of international consensus. But UNCITRAL's progress was too quick for some. The World Bank signaled that it was drafting its own norms. Afraid that the World Bank might pre-empt or marginalize the much weaker UN body, UNCITRAL stalled its insolvency project for several months until it could take measure of how the "territory" of lawmaking might be divided between the Bank and UNCITRAL.

The power to alter staging in this and similar cases rests with the strong: high-impact delegations; the availability of resource-rich NGOs ready to offer extensive expertise; and an agile IO Secretariat with a broad repertoire of legal technologies from which to choose. Informal colloquia often figure prominently in staging time.

2. *Compressing* time is a tactic for shortening the period for a working group's decisionmaking. Here actors who control a calendar or who exert substantial power can reduce the amount of time available in order to inject urgency, to reduce the

probability of alternative agendas or solutions, and to exclude actors who are not at the center of communication networks or whose problems of collective action preclude rapid mobilization, or preserve resources.

One form of compressing time involves the "fast start." At UNCITRAL it was conventional to begin a new episode of global lawmaking with a colloquium at which issues were put on the table and an agenda was mapped out. Thereafter, a working group would divide up a lawmaking area into separate categories; discussions precede and result in drafting, followed by refinement and ultimately consensual acceptance of final drafts. But the Transport Working Group decided that any new convention, which in the past had taken six or more years to develop, might be marginalized or overtaken by regional fragmentation, or by the emergence of a radically new concept of governing carriage of goods from manufacture to market that was preferred by the UN Conference on Trade and Development (UNCTAD). UNCITRAL's Secretariat, with the support of some leading delegations, including the US, charged a private organization, CMI, the acknowledged leader of international lawmaking for carriage of goods by sea since the late nineteenth century, to kick-start proceedings by developing a draft treaty or convention that was placed on UNCITRAL's Working Group agenda at its very first meeting. Some delegates believed this potentially controversial move shaved years off negotiations. Another fast start was enabled when UNCITRAL's Insolvency Working Group divined, through a colloquium, that a surprising degree of consensus already existed across legal families on the core principles of bankruptcy norms for the world.

Another form of compression involves "overlaps" in meetings, or parallel tracks that occur with simultaneity. The Insolvency and Secured Transactions Working Groups twice held "joint" sessions, so that the two working groups could meet simultaneously and consider jointly language that was to appear in both the Insolvency and Secured Transactions Legislative Guides. Another example of working group meetings that accomplished twin purposes were sessions of the Transport Working Group to consider provisions on electronic bills of lading. Although these provisions are situated in the Rotterdam Rules, they codify ideas that originated in earlier sessions to draft a Model Law on Electronic Commerce. UNCITRAL's Working Group on Electronic Commerce worked collaboratively with the Transport Working Group, not in joint working group sessions, but in joint expert groups.

The power to compress time in UNCITRAL may depend on a coalition of strong delegations and a well-established non-state organization. The stimulus to compress time, however, may lie within the power of the weak, because if competing organizations or coalitions of states made credible threats to "exit" from the primacy of a given global lawmaking proceeding, then a prime adaptive response by the global body would be to speed up proceedings.

3. *Expanding* time involves lengthening the period of working group decision-making in calendar time from a three-year project, for instance, to five or six year

endeavor. This may result when issues are particularly divisive, sometimes to attenuate proceedings in the hope they will stalemate, sometimes to provide a more elaborate product with layers of norms or wider reach. Indeed, a large bloc of states may delay indefinitely the prospect of global consensus.

The absolute quantum of actual hours spent in deliberations in formal proceedings can be expanded, while holding calendar time constant. Leading delegations in UNCITRAL's Transport Working Group realized early on that annual formal meetings occurring one week in New York and one week in Vienna would be insufficient to handle the volume of work and intensity of negotiations required to get out a new multilateral treaty before it was pre-empted by competing efforts. Hard-driving delegations and the UNCITRAL Secretariat persuaded the Working Group and Commission that it must meet for two weeks, twice a year. By doubling its meetings, the Working Group looked to achieve in four years what might otherwise have taken twice as long.[7]

4. *Segmenting* time involves the temporal partition of global governance and lawmaking so that efforts are segmented and sequenced over several shorter lawmaking episodes (e.g., this current project; a next project; the next project after that). If negotiations prove particularly difficult on a topic, then tough issues can be excerpted from negotiations and held over for some future project. Deferral essentially transforms one block of lawmaking time into two sequential blocks. Segmentation often serves a strategy of incrementalism in global lawmaking (Block-Lieb and Halliday 2007b; Hathaway 2005).

Corporate bankruptcy laws had for decades been considered too challenging for international reform because bankruptcy law was thought to be too deeply entrenched in the particularisms of national legal cultures and economic histories. Rather than take on the full spectrum of issues that comprehensive national bankruptcy laws conventionally embrace, UNCITRAL began with a very small Step One – a procedural model law that would not bind countries but that would provide some rules about how a corporation's insolvency might be coordinated by companies, professionals and courts across national borders (Pottow 2005).

The relatively quick success of the Model Law on Cross-Border Insolvency emboldened UNCITRAL to consider a more ambitious Step Two. UNCITRAL's Insolvency Working Group decided to write a legislative guide to set international standards for domestic corporate bankruptcy law. In so doing, however, it deferred until Step Three a risky project where law was quite underdeveloped – how to handle corporate groups in financial distress. And it delayed further to Steps Four and beyond areas where controversy was likely to be even more intense (e.g., over whether company directors should be liable for the debts of their companies, and the cross-border coordination of insolvency proceedings for a group of corporations).

[7] In the end, the Group took six years to complete a broader convention than was initially envisioned.

The partition and sequencing of global norms resulted in multiple products, each building on the other, each punctuating time with periodic successes to maintain momentum and fuel normmaking ambitions.

Perhaps learning from the Insolvency Working Group, the Secured Transactions Working Group similarly segmented its work. Its Legislative Guide on Secured Transactions left behind unfinished work on intellectual property collateral, only to circle back and include this topic in a later supplement to its Guide. The Guide and its Supplement was thereafter followed by a Practice Guide on registries for filings to provide notice of security rights. Most recently, the Working Group has worked to translate the recommendations in the various Guides in to a Model Law on Secured Transactions.

Segmentation sometimes serves forces of reaction, because breaking a larger task in a finite period of time into many smaller products or decisions invariably amplifies the time for each and thereby extends the decisionmaking process. But it might also result from planning over the *longue durée*, particularly in colloquia that allow for a breadth in perspective. In either event, it is a risky strategy, in that segments left for later may never get resolved. This delay by segmentation can be a useful strategy of resistance by the weak (Halliday and Carruthers 2007a).

5. *Multiplying* time involves slicing decisionmaking episodes into finer tracks. This approach offers a creative adaptation for IOs with few or no options to extend time, or for IOs with severe constraints on the costs of deliberation. Time can be multiplied by creating parallel or simultaneous tracks so that different topics are allocated to different groups, or unofficial meetings (such as expert group meetings) are set to run on schedules that parallel official meetings, or deliberations in formal chambers are supplemented by deliberations in off-shore meetings.

Thus, an alternative way to interpret the actions taken by leaders within UNCITRAL's Transport Working Group, who realized that even with their fast start and expanded time schedule, any multilateral agreement would take many years to complete, is to view it as an adaptation by manipulating time. How? Divide the issue-area into multiple topics, each of which prefigured a separate section in a prospective treaty. Ask a country-delegation to lead an issue-area. Invite any delegates to join a network of persons to work on that topic. And give every network a deadline to produce a draft set of issues and lawmaking responses "off-shore." These off-shore groups met away from UNCITRAL's formal proceedings, but ultimately fed into formal deliberations and prefigured Working Group consensus on topics. The expert working groups organized by the secretaries for the Insolvency and Secured Transactions Working Groups discussed earlier in this chapter also served to multiply working group time by drafting proposals for working group approval.

The move to multiply time may present an opportunity for power to be exercised by large states or expert NGOs with the capacity to mobilize, or an opportunity for otherwise weaker players to shine in smaller informal grouping.

CLOSING IN: INFORMAL AND TEMPORAL ADAPTATIONS

The interplay of formalized rules of governance and methods of work with the informal politics and practices that developed within UNCITRAL reach to fundamentals as to how transnational legal orders are constructed and reconstructed. It is a formidable task to erect a TLO that is institutionalized across the world and integrates international, national, and local lawmakers and lawmaking bodies into a coherent system of organizations, institutions, rules, and standards. One challenge involves the construction and maintenance of an IO's legitimacy. Another challenge, often wrongly considered to be the only challenge, is obtaining consensus on laws within IOs and by state and non-state actors within global lawmaking arenas and after they conclude their work.

What effects do our data reveal for the impact of informal inventions on distributive effects for strong or weak state and non-state actors?

The informal adaptations varied markedly in the *distributive effects of informal adaptations*, especially through inclusiveness. Although the colloquia relied on invitations that might favor well known delegates and non-state organizations, they were the most expansive of the supplementary forms of meeting. By contrast, expert groups, inner circles, and networks favored the well-resourced, the experts and the English speakers that got involved. Off-shore roundtables and corridor politics, together with collegial events held outside formal working group meetings, might be more or less inclusive, depending on supplementary availability of resources (e.g., off-shore roundtables), language and cultural affinities (e.g., corridor interactions), and degrees of connectedness with central working actors (e.g., sponsored dinners). Additional conclusions can be drawn from the interplay of formal and informal social organization in this global lawmaking space in resolving these challenges.

There seems little doubt that the price of informality mostly reinforced a "smallness of global lawmaking" within UNCITRAL, albeit a smallness heavily tilted toward advanced economies, leading states, and resource-rich non-state actors in the global political economy. Informality was not the only way in which working groups reduced their numbers and increased access to the Secretariat. That UNCITRAL's lawmaking involved a "small world" of global lawmakers was also evident in the few powerful actors who advised and assisted UNCITRAL's Secretariat in setting agendas for the three working groups in our case studies (Chapter 3), and in the small number of high-attendance delegations populated with high-attendance delegates (Chapter 4). Each of these practices of contraction held the risk of undermining UNCITRAL's legitimacy.

On the other hand, there were substantial benefits from UNCITRAL's informal methods of work. It is very doubtful that lawmaking could have proceeded as expansively or rapidly or conclusively without the informal expedients of action. UNCITRAL's informal methods adopted a strategy geared toward making additional time for decisionmaking within a working group. Commentators note that consensual decisionmaking frequently fails (Boyle and Chinkin 2007). Failure is especially likely in a world of diverse stakeholders, and competing national and economic interests, legal traditions, and cultural foundations.

By finding ways to add time to lawmaking endeavors, informal practices conserved resources and aided in building consensus. While time in formal Commission and working group sessions was sorely limited, informal settings offered myriad additional opportunities for delegates to interact. Although working groups could only formally hold sessions during two weeks in a year, their delegates might interact informally during the remaining fifty weeks. The Secretariat also found that these informal meetings made working group sessions more efficient – each working group session took less time because problem solving was prefigured in expert sessions. Expert sessions ran more smoothly than working group sessions both because expert group sessions were small group sessions and also because these expert groups generally conversed in "English only."[8]

In addition, informal practices contributed to consensus-building because they brought parties closer together, not just intellectually but also socially. UNCITRAL's informal processes allowed it to build consensus in complex areas of technical commercial law, satisfying both the private interests of those likely to be governed by the new international standards and public interests of the diverse states involved in this global lawmaking. Colloquia allowed public and private delegates to brainstorm in UN chambers but without the formality of UN procedural rules. Expert group sessions ensured a place for the participation and not just the observation of technical experts. Coffee breaks allowed for questions to be asked and answered, and for conversation to explore a point in greater depth and focus than would have been possible with simultaneous translation of placards recognized by a working group chair. Epistemic communities bonded during, after, and in between working group sessions. From all of these emerged an inner community of actors who identified with UNCITRAL and shared with it an invisible collective identity.

What effects do our data reveal for the impact of temporal tactics on distributive effects for strong or weak state and non-state actors?

Different temporal tactics had differential distributive effects on actors' influence. Staging time, by influencing the moment at which lawmaking began, and compressing time, by beginning deliberations with a draft prepared with strong input from non-state actors, both were tactics of the powerful. Segmenting time, by dividing decisionmaking into sequential lawmaking episodes, and multiplying time, by slicing decisionmaking into parallel running discussion groups, had benefits for more marginal, less-resourced actors. If law production is broken into successive episodes, less well informed actors have a longer time for learning the policy options and salience for their interests; and less powerful actors have more time to

[8] The practice of speaking in official UN languages in formal working group sessions but "English only" in expert sessions behind the scenes is a longstanding one (Farnsworth 1972).

mobilize or cooperate with others similarly situated. If each lawmaking episode were to incorporate the informal networked parallel tracks utilized by the Transport Working Group, then the call for volunteer delegates to join groups, their smaller size, and their informal proceedings, could offer greater advantages to actors less assured to participate in formal sessions. Extending time, by lengthening the lawmaking episode, is more equivocal in its distributive effects. Longer time offers more temporal space for learning about interests, reflecting on options, and mobilizing by marginal groups. Yet longer time also increases costs.

What are the impacts of temporal tactics on ecological dynamics?

Staging and compressing time, both directed to when lawmaking begins and how quickly it proceeds, offer significant advantages to UNCITRAL in both issue-ecologies and the standing lawmaking ecology. By starting first, an UNCITRAL working group lays territorial claims for lawmaking jurisdiction that widen the legal scope of its boundaries. The early mover in ecological competition may thereby also garner additional resources from industry and states eager to be on the leading edge of lawmaking initiative. And by offering expertise and resources for fast starts, non-state actors assure themselves of centrality in the subsequent lawmaking episode. Finishing fast solidifies territorial claims. It enables the lawmakers in one ecology to assert that further lawmaking in another ecology is superfluous and costly.

Extending, segmenting, and multiplying time affect ecologies in more complex ways. Segmenting and multiplying time can offer more space for weak or marginal actors to enter the ecology and increase the prospects of cooperation and raise the probability of competitive cooperation within it. Moreover, by increasing the density of actors in the ecology its products thereby can be seen as more legitimate with a greater likelihood of being implemented. Multiplying time divides wider issues into narrower issues for parallel deliberations. By doing so, the range of differences is shrunk and the likelihood of mini-bargains increased. Extending time, however, involves the tying up of scarce resources in a particular lawmaking issue-ecology. This has trade-offs. By taking longer, and requiring more resources and infrastructures, UNCITRAL effectively reduces the number of issue-areas it can host at the same time. Or it may require UNCITRAL's agenda-setters to narrow each issue-area in legal scope so as to take on less demanding tasks with a larger number of simultaneous lawmaking episodes.

The inventiveness that has been observed in UNCITRAL's informal and temporal adaptations opens up the question of the *origins of invention*. Do they come from UNCITRAL officials, from the Secretariat itself? Are they rational responses to resource scarcity from the UNCITRAL Commission or the international civil servants that serve it?

The answers are complex and multi-faceted. We observe at least three adaptive moves. First, some adaptations are driven principally by the Secretariat, generally with informal consultations with core delegates. Staging time through pre-emptive fast starts in deliberations present one instance. Forming expert groups and inner circles are another instance because these are necessities for generalist working group secretaries. Second, adaptations arise from the "jointness" or cooperative circles that form between UNCITRAL staff and prime movers in state and non-state delegations. Together this inner core of officials and delegates hosted colloquia or initiated off-shore roundtables. Segmenting time by breaking lawmaking into smaller projects arose from an emergent consensus. Third, some adaptations occur from practices driven by delegates and delegations that are later acknowledged and adopted by the Secretariat and Commission. On occasion, an innovation by delegates was initially resisted by some UNCITRAL officials, but later embraced or at least accepted. Such was the case with the formation of topical networks to run informally and in parallel to the Transport Working Group. Altogether these adaptive moves reveal both an active community-of-interest that emerges in issue-ecology lawmaking and the several valences of action, they do not always begin and end in cooperation, which constitute the dynamics of law production in the ecology. Together these adaptations and inventions significantly affect the likelihood that new TLOs will be institutionalized in global, national, and local arenas of commercial behavior shaped by law.

But challenges persist. One such challenge is *settlement of norms*, not only in global lawmaking arenas but also in national legislatures and everyday practice. UNCITRAL's Secretariat sought to resolve private and public interests by bringing inside deliberative proceedings both the state actors likely to be responsible for enacting laws and representative of the industry actors who would need to comply with new laws and adopt them in everyday trade and commerce. By positioning the lawmaking ecologies to draw heavily on their adjacent industry-ecologies, in part by drawing representatives of both private and public interests inside the lawmaking process, UNCITRAL looked to increase the probability that consensus inside its deliberative chamber subsequently would produce assent to laws and norms that would be adopted concordantly across levels and sites of action. UNCITRAL sought not just concordant "law books" across national and local locations; it ultimately sought to assure institutionalization of changed behaviors on the ground with these aligned texts. If consensus could be forged among those most likely to adopt, or most able to veto, legal change just might take hold "on the ground" and inside the lawmaking arena within UNCITRAL, as well as in the texts UNCITRAL promulgated, thus, avoiding subsequent recursive cycles of reform.

UNCITRAL's informal politics sought to resolve problems of *alignment* between systems of laws and rules, on the one hand, and the challenges of trade and regulation of markets, on the other. From its earliest efforts to construct international laws, norms, and standards to govern private actors, UNCITRAL adopted a strategy perfected in the "private legislatures" that had promulgated the Uniform Commercial Code in the United States (see, e.g., Farnsworth 1972; Honnold 1979a; Honnold 1979b). Shortly before UNCITRAL was created, these uniform US commercial laws were first drafted by "working groups" of representatives from academic and professional organizations (i.e., the American Law Institute and the National Conference of Commissioners on Uniform State Law), and then offered to state legislatures for uniform adoption.

Socio-legal scholar Marc Galanter explains the logic of US commercial codification in this way:

> The drafting of the Uniform Commercial Code was a self-conscious attempt (by Karl Llewellyn) to synthesize formal law and commercial usage: the formal law would incorporate the best commercial practice and would in turn serve as a model for the refinement and development of that practice. The Code's broadly drafted rules would be accessible to businessmen and would provide a framework for self-regulation, which would in turn furnish attentive courts with content for the Code's categories. Thus the Code would serve as a vehicle for business communities to evolve law for themselves in dialogue with the courts, operating not as interpreters of imposed law but as articulators and critics of business usage.
>
> (Galanter 1981)

Ayres and Braithwaite (1992) would later term this model of lawmaking "responsive regulation," while others would view it as "capture," a term not altogether pejorative to them (Schwartz and Scott 1995; Scott 1994).[9]

UNCITRAL's informal methods of work find inspiration in this US model, and probably not by accident. When the United States sent its first delegation to UNCITRAL, in the late 1960s, it included in its ranks several academics who had been involved in the commercial uniform lawmaking project (Farnsworth 1972; Honnold 1979a; Honnold 1979b). Like these domestic "private legislatures" within the US, UNCITRAL ensured that non-state organizations representing industry interests, and the legal practitioners that served industry, sat alongside state officials so that the voice and demands of industry were heard directly.

Translating American ideals of private lawmaking to an international setting was not an idea that emerged first in the US. Karl Llewellyn's brand of "legal realism" (distinct from the "realism" of international relations) sought to build into the codification of private law room for incorporation and recognition of commercial practices. This inclusive reflex had its origins in nineteenth century Continental efforts to codify international law (see Chapter 2). Industry scions – bankers, traders, professionals, and other private actors – had been invited to the earliest diplomatic

[9] Ayres and Braithwaite readily concede that "policies that secure the advantages of an evolution of cooperation between regulatory agencies and industry are policies that also run the risk of an evolution of capture and corruption" (Ayres and Braithwaite 1992: 6), and spend several chapters in their book on Responsive Regulation developing proposals for mitigating this risk (id.: 54-157). Their differentiation of "good" and "bad" capture distinguishes them from that of Schwartz, Scott and other economic analyses of the interaction between private and public actors jointly involved in lawmaking.

conferences to reach international agreement on matters of private law (Block-Lieb and Halliday 2016). When the League of Nations put together a committee of experts to advise it on the possibility for reaching international agreement on uniform rules for bills of exchange and other payment measures, at least one member of the committee emphasized the importance of consulting "both lawyers and practical men of business (bankers and merchants) and to ask them to deliberate in common."[10] When UNIDROIT first began to meet to draft uniform laws on international sales, insurance, and copyright laws, the reports of its governing council similarly emphasized the importance of liaison with international organizations of private actors, like the International Chamber of Commerce and the *Comité Maritime International* (Block-Lieb and Halliday 2016). When UNCITRAL invited non-state observer delegations into its first working group deliberations, it was following on the heels of these earlier lawmaking IOs focused on promulgating international private laws.

The risks of this move likely were, thus, well known to UNCITRAL. The possibility that the presence of industry representatives might undermine the democratic legitimacy of the lawmaking chamber prompted UNCITRAL to take precautions when harnessing the expertise of these non-state actors in the room. Their interests might find representation in UNCITRAL's lawmaking arena, in the same way that the Global South found representation and both common law and civil law legal families found representation. But this representation was crafted with the intent that no single set of interests or regions or ideologies would overpower or capture the whole. Influence and access were carefully triangulated to put in place a system of checks and balances. Every delegation in attendance at UNCITRAL had equal access to the working group, at least in theory.

Much about the informal practices adopted by UNCITRAL may be seen as adaptive responses that simultaneously appropriated expertise to solve problems that industry and service professions had identified, while at the same time subordinating expertise to political scrutiny. NGOs were entitled to observe working group sessions, and even to voice concerns by intervening in these sessions in virtually the same way as state delegates could. But they could not vote (should voting become necessary). By custom, their interventions needed to follow a diplomatic protocol of deference to states. This deference involved more than reliance on polite language. A hierarchy of concerns was always woven into working group deliberations. Although a topic was important to NGOs, where states were unconvinced by what non-state delegates had to say, the issue would be dropped.

Nonetheless, our findings differ importantly from the conventional conclusion that "states retain a tight grip on the formal law-making processes" within IOs

[10] League of Nations, Economic Committee, Unification of Laws Relating to Bills of Exchange and Promissory Notes, Individual Report of Prof. Ch. Lyon-Caen, University of Paris, at 149 (Apr. 13, 1923).

engaged in global standard-setting (Boyle and Chinkin 2007: 95). It may be more challenging for states to constrain informal practices than those occurring within the public space of UNCITRAL's legislative chamber. The price of productivity achieved through informal innovations can be the constriction of active lawmakers to a tiny and tendentious few. It remains to discover whether UNCITRAL's formal procedural safeguards were sufficient to guard against a paradox of "smallness" in global lawmaking.

6

Creative Design in Legal Technologies

Conventions, rules, model laws, legislative guides, principles – global lawmakers generate substantive norms through a wide range of technical instruments. International organizations are producers not only of "software" – the norms that encapsulate laws for the world – but of "hardware" – the various instruments that have been created to convey norms.

Social scientists too readily take the formal products, the "hardware" that IOs rely on, as given. The products exist, it is assumed, so attention must be directed to the substantive and distributive content in the norms themselves. In this chapter we argue, by contrast, that a failure to understand the technical format in which norms are carried to the world leads to an under-estimation of how power is rhetorically inscribed and an over-estimation of the inertia built into IOs *qua* organizations.

By incorporating many states and non-state groups into its deliberations, by widening the range of actors in its ecology, UNCITRAL enhanced the legitimacy of its representativeness. Yet the legitimation paradox identified in Chapters 2 through 4 suggests that by solving one problem, namely, representation, it amplified another problem, namely, importing all the power differentials among states, all the variations in laws and policies, all the varieties of legal families and the many bases for competition or conflict into the deliberative chambers of the UN. The prospects of stalemate or capture or anodyne outcomes loom large.

If that conundrum were not enough, UNCITRAL itself was situated, we have argued, inside ecologies of international organizations, multilateral bodies, industries, and states, which threatened to siphon away resources and commitments, to spearhead incursions on UNCITRAL's notional policy terrain (Block-Lieb and Halliday 2011), and to inhibit whatever aspirations UNCITRAL's Secretariat nurtured for global leadership in the construction of transnational legal orders (TLOs)(Halliday and Shaffer 2015c; Shaffer 2012). To compete effectively in the lawmaking ecology, UNCITRAL thus also needed to confront these external challenges to its survival.

Meeting organizational challenges and adapting to temporal and resource constraints could be met, as we showed in Chapter 5, through informalities of process. The Secretariat and its circles of creative and supportive delegates could maneuver within or even step outside the formal structures that inhibited effective action. But each step took it closer to a line that might lead states or other IOs to question its methods of work.

These pressures led UNCITRAL's leaders to learn that the legitimation and ecological challenges of an IO could also be met through creativities of legal form and textual language (Halliday and Block-Lieb 2013).[1] An IO's products are not ontological givens but instruments that are negotiated, technologies that are invented or adapted, clusters of rules that are crafted and woven into varying normative tapestries, bodies of meaning that embody ideas and epistemologies, forms that carry differing legitimation mandates and ecological claims to centrality, texts that internalize legitimation warrants, and instruments that privilege certain professions.

Two kinds of micropolitics sandwich the formal product of a global legislature: the politics it *reflects*; and the politics it *anticipates*. The former encapsulates processes of global lawmaking, which responds to the challenges of legitimation, ecological conditions, and configurations of power that exist within UNCITRAL's lawmaking chambers and lawmaking ecologies more broadly. The latter is mostly an endeavor of norm implementation, which is expressed as an IO's efforts to ensure adoptions and changes in practice, to forestall adverse reactions of states to incursions on their sovereign concerns, and to maintain an IO's competitiveness in future normmaking endeavors. The politics of transnational lawmaking and law implementation, of course, have a recursive relationship to each other over the *longue durée*. Their interplay influences the probable emergence of a transnational legal order in an area of trade and commerce (Halliday and Block-Lieb 2014; Halliday and Shaffer 2015b).

Strategies of form often complement strategies of work. Apparently arid and technical rhetorical forms in which an IO's products are cast will reflect and shape centrality in the lawmaking space and the expressions of power that accompany core or peripheral locus in that space. Products of IOs bear the imprint of who produced them and how they were produced. They convey prospects for

[1] There is a variegated and evocative socio-legal literature on law and language (Mertz and Rajah 2014). It reaches to language in law school classrooms (Mertz 2007) and courtrooms (Drew and Atkinson 1979) to critical discourse analyses of parliamentary hearings (Rajah 2008; Rajah 2012) and to properties of global norms set by international governance organizations (Halliday, Block-Lieb, and Carruthers 2009a). There is, however, scarce empirical scholarship that analyzes the formal properties of legal rule-types as they both respond to interactional exigencies of lawmaking and anticipate the everyday challenges of law practice.

more or less settled and institutionalized TLOs that differentially benefit actors in national and local legal orders.[2]

We have shown (Chapter 2) that, since its founding, UNCITRAL has increased the number of law-like texts it produces and the diversity of forms these texts take. This inventiveness of form – especially the increasing breadth and variation among its soft law[3] technologies – holds implications for UNCITRAL's productivity, states' implementation of the texts once produced, and local actor's reliance on the texts once incorporated into domestic law. While these internal and recursive implications might be limited to the view of UNCITRAL as an arena, we also argue that the increasingly wide range of legislative technologies holds ecological implications for UNCITRAL as a global actor.

Form and content, product and substance, are not independent of each other. Nor can forms or technologies be understood as purely neutral instruments for conveying content. In this chapter, we show that legal technologies influence both the issues that can be reached by the lawmaking IO and the prospects that it can transcend the deep cleavages that transect differences in legal families and rifts and inequalities in the global political economy. In the next chapter, we delve further in the substance of the texts that emerged in an effort to search for connections between the deals that were struck and the tools that were relied on to construct this consensus.

While international law scholarship in general has focused on the distinction *between* hard and soft law, and particularly the distinctive set of qualities that enable "legalization" or "hardness" in international law (Abbott 1988; Abbott and Snidal 2000; Trubek, Cottrell, and Nance 2006), we look to distinguish *among* various soft laws and thus to articulate the qualities enabling and motivating "softness" in international law. While the array of potential products or instruments or technologies by an IO can be extensive and variegated, in this chapter we focus on the two contrasting technologies central to our case studies: one of conventions and two of legislative guides. This targeted analysis illustrates the significance of form for politics and politics for form. It reveals a tension among uniformity, complexity, and flexibility, which UNCITRAL navigates in the three case studies.

The chapter proceeds in four parts: Part I demonstrates empirically the claim that UNCITRAL has relied on an increasingly broad range of legal technologies, and especially soft law technologies. Part II distinguishes in broad brushstrokes among several sorts of soft law. Part III delves more deeply into the legal technologies

2 The emerging scholarship on TLOs points to the critical importance of framing (Merry 2015) and the nuances of discourse in shifting TLO frames (Lloyd and Simmons 2015). This chapter pushes forward this theoretical agenda by showing conceptually and empirically how the actual *form* of global norms can increase the probability of global normative consensus and the prospects that there will be concordance by state and local actors in the construction of a TLO (Block-Lieb and Halliday 2015).

3 We use the terms "soft law" and "soft law technologies" interchangeably to refer to "rules of conduct which in principle have no legally binding force but which nevertheless may have practical effects" (Snyder 1994). See also (Shaffer and Pollack 2010).

produced in our three case studies: the draft convention on contracts for the international carriage of goods (the so-called Rotterdam Rules); and the two Legislative Guides, one on Insolvency the other Secured Transactions Law. Finally, Part IV considers the implications of the wide range of choices among legal technologies for recursive and ecological processes that enhance or inhibit the prospects of institutionalization new or adapted TLOs.

INVENTING TECHNOLOGIES

Global lawmaking bodies in particular, and arguably IOs in general, generate at least two kinds of output. On one hand, there is the substance of the norms themselves. On the other hand, there is the form that this substance takes, or, put another way, the vehicle that conveys those norms. In the case of an IO engaged in lawmaking, that "vehicle" may be labeled a "product," an "international instrument," "hard law" versus "soft law," or any number of particular designations, such as a convention or model law or best practices (Abbott and Snidal 2000; Shaffer and Pollack 2010).

We refer to these vehicles, that is, the range of texts and other formal products of an international lawmaking organization, as *legal technologies*.[4] We refer to the form of these products as a "technology" both to convey that this structure involves more content than mere "packaging" (Murphy 2012), and is more complex than a simple "tool" or "technique" (McGinn 1978).

For an IO to create a new technology simultaneously implies that there is space within an ecology for that IO to exercise inventive creativity or to borrow creative inventions from elsewhere. It follows that technological inventions reflect and permit an emancipation of an IO from the dead hand of tradition or inertia as it also opens up new possibilities with all their potentialities, dangers, and unanticipated consequences.

For a global lawmaking institution such as UNCITRAL, all of these inventive capacities can add up to an enhanced adaptive capacity for the IO (Chapter 10). In a competitive ecology with scarce resources, an inventive IO can break out of antiquated practices that may render it increasingly irrelevant to a changing context. This inventiveness can increase the competitive advantage of such an IO by expanding the scope of its normative and lawmaking reach. In short, an adaptive lawmaking IO can diversify its products through the invention of new technologies, which not only enables an organizational response to historical changes in an ecology, but also offers at any one moment in time an enhanced range of technological solutions to demands for lawmaking.[5] Even more, insofar as technologies

4 For discussion and definition of the related concept of social technologies, see (Fourcade and Khurana 2013; Johnson, Dowd, and Ridgeway 2006; Sassen 2006: Ch. 10, n. 16).

5 The most sophisticated ecological theory of professions (Abbott 1988) investigates modes of establishing "jurisdiction" over areas of work. Yet its treatment of professional epistemologies points to, rather than explicates in precise detail, how epistemologies are encoded in the

themselves sort into sequences of complexity and sophistication, they may be arrayed over time in an unfolding of incremental lawmaking, each set of norms conveyed by technologies that rest upon more challenging politics and tighter strictures on the formal properties of the technology itself.

The history of UNCITRAL may therefore be understood not only as a sequence of contributions to substantive international lawmaking and the widening of the TLOs within its competence, but also as a history of technological invention to enable its survival and competitive advantage. What gave UNCITRAL the capacity to reach new areas of law? And what gave it a competitive advantage over other global legislatures and potential competitors?

A re-analysis of UNCITRAL's products since 1968 illustrates dramatically that its history has been punctuated by a steady invention or adoption of technologies (see Chapter 2, Table 2.1). In the 1970s it relied upon a traditional hard law technology, the convention, as did its potential competitors, the Hague Conference on Private International Law and UNIDROIT, as well as a minor technology, viz., rules. In the 1980s, it added model laws and model legal provisions to its repertoire; in the 1990s, legal guides and notes; and in the 2000s, practice guides and explanatory reports. By the mid-2000s, UNCITRAL held in its portfolio of formal products ten different technologies that it relied upon to confront a widening array of issues in substantive and procedural trade and commercial law.

The pattern that emerges from Chapter 2, Table 2.1 is one of expansion: both an expanding list of legal technologies and an expansion in the number of products emerging in each decade. While UNCITRAL relied on only two formal products during the 1970s, it had trebled the number of products by the 1980s, and now currently can choose among at least ten distinct legal technologies. Equally striking is the expanding number of products that UNCITRAL published in each decade. While it promulgated only three instruments during the 1970s (two conventions and one set of rules), it promulgated nine each in the 1980s and 1990s and twelve between 2000 and 2009. In the past several years, UNCITRAL has published an additional eleven products and several additional explanatory texts.

We also see patterns of consistency within each type of legal technology (the rows in Table 2.1), especially when similar technologies are grouped together. Most striking is the case of the convention – a stock in trade for any global legislature. Although it now chooses from as many as ten different sorts of legal technologies when drafting, UNCITRAL has consistently produced at least two conventions in each decade of its existence, with the period from 2000 to 2009 producing three such instruments. UNCITRAL has produced model laws and model legal provisions with nearly equal consistency in every decade other than its initial decade of work (the 1970s), although it produced more of these during the 1990s than in any other

precise terms and language of professional jurisdictional claims. This limitation may be reflected macrocosmically in interactionist ecology theory more widely.

decade of its existence: two in the 1980s; five in the 1990s; three during the 2000s and another one in the past two years. If recommendations and notes are similarly grouped together, two can be observed in the 1980s, one in the 1990s, one in the 2000s and one in the current decade.

UNCITRAL's expansion of legal technologies beyond conventions to other softer international instruments enabled its increasing productivity over time. Table 2.1 demonstrates that when UNCITRAL expanded its range of potential technologies it promulgated a far greater number of instruments, from three in the 1970s to twelve in the 2000s. The legal scope of issue-areas in which it worked widened from an initial four topics (sales, transport, payments, and arbitration) to roughly ten areas of focus (sales, transport, payments, arbitration and conciliation, procurement and infrastructure, electronic commerce, insolvency, secured transactions, micro, small and medium sized enterprises, and online dispute resolution).

Looking behind Table 2.1 to UNCITRAL's record of work – the periodic reports issued by the Commission and its various working groups – we find one possible explanation for the "softening" of its technologies: it takes UNCITRAL far more time to formulate a draft convention than a model law, a set of model legal provisions or certain other of the technologies it now holds at its disposal.[6] On average, conventions take about six years for a working group to write. Model law and model law provisions take on average less than half this time. To the extent that time is a proxy for cost, essentially UNCITRAL has expanded its repertoire to produce cheaper products. And lower cost also has implications for *who* is at the lawmaking table, and thus spills over into UNCITRAL's legitimation claim to global representativeness.[7] In addition, the quickening pace of production suggests that adoption or invention of new products may have a temporal logic that links productivity to resources. The more UNCITRAL can produce in a given period of time, the more competitive it may be vis-à-vis other lawmaking bodies in its ecology and the more compelling its case for enhanced resources.

What Table 2.1 does not answer is the puzzle of the diversity of UNCITRAL's soft law technologies: Why does UNCITRAL rely on a range of soft law technologies, rather than simply choosing between a hard law convention and a single sort of soft law, such as a model law? UNCITRAL's turn to a range of different soft

6 While this increase in the range of technologies available to UNCITRAL is partly responsible for the increase in the number of texts published over time, its increased productivity is also undoubtedly the result of its decision in the 2000s to double the number of its working groups.

7 Legislative guides are time-consuming technologies to draft. It took three years to draft the Legislative Guide on Insolvency Law; another four years was spent in writing an addendum on the treatment of enterprise groups. Five years was spent in writing the Legislative Guide on Secured Transactions Law, although a later addendum on the treatment of intellectual property collateral took only two additional years. A subsequent "guide" on registry systems involved another two years of deliberation. This comparison of convention writing to the preparation of a legislative or other guide looks at each product, independent of its substantive reach, the number of issues covered, or the number of pages written.

law technologies is not unique. UNIDROIT promulgated only draft conventions between its re-emergence after WWII until the 1990s, but since then has increasingly has relied on soft law formats such as model laws and principles (Block-Lieb and Halliday 2016); the International Law Commission similarly has begun to reframe much of its work product as "draft guidelines," "draft conclusions," and "draft principles," rather than "draft articles" for inclusion in a multilateral convention (Cogan 2014; Murphy 2013); the G-20 and the numerous lawmaking IOs and the transnational regulatory networks (TRNs) it relies on to build out the financial architecture project have put forward a wide range of high-level principles and other soft law technologies on financial consumer protection, financial inclusion, financial education, and other topics, but nothing "harder" (Block-Lieb and Halliday 2016); UNCTAD and other IOs focused on reforming sovereign debt lending and restructuring practices similarly have published principles on responsible sovereign lending and borrowing (UNCTAD).

That other lawmaking IOs have followed UNCITRAL's move in issuing a range of soft laws does not explain the breadth of this range. Each of UNCITRAL's various legal technologies has distinctive features, which suggests that these features enable UNCITRAL to tailor the product to particular circumstances. How can we understand UNCITRAL's reliance on and choices among such a wide array of soft law formats?

TECHNOLOGIES TO ENABLE FLEXIBILITY IN IO LAWMAKING

Although it would be conventional to do so, we do not distinguish among UNCITRAL's legal technologies simply on the basis of whether they would constitute "hard" or "soft" laws once implemented by state actors. The distinction between "hard" and "soft" international laws may be meaningful in other settings (see, e.g., Shaffer and Pollack 2010), but the distinction between hard and soft law provides little assistance in differentiating, not simply between conventions on one hand and all other technologies on the other, but among model laws, model legal provisions, legislative guides, rules, recommendations, principles, and so on.

We instead propose a concept of "flexibility" that looks to distinguish *among* the broad range of soft laws produced by UNCITRAL and, thus, to articulate the qualities enabling and motivating "softness" in international law and specifically in UNCITRAL's various legal technologies. This concept of "flexibility" looks to distinguish among the various legal technologies relied on by UNCITRAL with reference to their precision, obligation, and delegation, which inverts the classic analysis of the "legalization" or hardness of international law in order to view each concept through the lens of soft not hard law (Abbott et al. 2000; Abbott and Snidal 2000). Soft law technologies may differ in the degree of the precision of their recommendation; they may differ in terms of whether they rely on a language of obligation, that is, a language of prescription or of permission, and whether they are described as package deals that should be adopted wholesale; soft law technologies

TABLE 6.1. *Variations in Flexibility of Lawmaking Technologies*

General Categories	Variations	Features	Lawmaking Effects
Language of obligation	Framing as rule-like forms Use of prescriptive or permissive language Scope of provisions Structured as "package deal"	Looks like a "rule" Looks like a requirement or suggestion Breadth of coverage "Take it or leave it" vs "pick and choose"	Can focus, broaden or extend "obligation" of domestic legislatures to review and comprehend May limit discretion of domestic legislatures, courts, and other actors Affects level of domestic resources necessary for state lawmaking
Precision	Bright-line rules vs open-ended standards Defined terms Specific language Depth of analysis	Clarity vs vagueness Consistency and clarity in usage Ready for adoption and implementation Clarifies proposal with added context and deeper discussion	Can focus, narrow or broaden "obligation" of domestic legislature to review and comprehend Permits domestic legislature to delegate to adjudicators Affects level of domestic resources necessary for state lawmaking
Reservation of authority	Legislative guides Open-ended standards Default rules	Reserves authority for domestic legislature to enact or not Reserves authority for domestic courts Reserves authority for private actors to contract around	Delegates "obligation" of review and comprehension to specified domestic actors

may instead rely on distinct strategies for specifying a reservation of discretion favoring various third parties (such as reserving authority for domestic legislatures, domestic courts, or local actors). In the sections below, we describe each aspect of flexibility: obligation; precision; reservation of authority (Table 6.1).

Obligation

To address the most obvious difference between hard and soft international legal technologies, we accept that little of UNCITRAL's work product creates an "obligation" to which states are "legally bound" such that a failure to follow the UNCITRAL product would subject a state to international scrutiny. Rather than assess the obligation of the legal technology in question, we instead distinguish among technologies in terms of their "language of obligation." In other words, even if none of UNCITRAL's legal technologies were themselves to impose obligation, we nonetheless can distinguish among these technologies according to the extent to which they purport to oblige states in a way that resembles the obligations of legalized hard law.

This resemblance to obligation can come in several forms, including: (i) attention to the *framing* of nonbinding "recommendations" in formats that look like rules (and so are "rule-like") and (ii) attention to the *use of prescriptive* ("must," "shall" or "should") *versus permissive* ("may" or "can") *language*. The "bindingness" of a legal technology – even a soft law technology – might also get communicated in terms of the breadth of the issues purportedly covered and, thus, resolved by a text. We see breadth as a form of obligation in two ways. By covering a broader range of issues, (iii) the *scope* of a legal technology inhibits a state's flexibility in that even the softest legislative guide creates a purported obligation of attention, an obligation of review and comprehension. Moreover, there is less flexibility in a legal technology when (iv) it is offered as a *package deal*.[8]

Precision

We think of precision more broadly than simply the choice between *bright-line rules* and *open-ended standards*. With soft law technologies, precision also might be the result of *definition* (such as in a glossary), *specificity* (that is, language that states can adopt and enact wholesale) or *depth of analysis* (which might be offered in accompanying commentary that states can refer to and learn from when crafting domestic legislation).

Reservation of Implementing and Enforcement Authority

We view the "flexibility" of a soft law technology as also dependent on whether the text reserves authority to some domestic actor within the scope of a state's

[8] Many draft conventions offer a package deal in that they preclude variation among contracting states, or at least specify some particular articles that states may exercise reservation on accession. Some model laws are crafted to encourage states to enact implementing legislation that adopts the model law without modification; the model law is understood to present a coherent reform package. Other model laws and model legal provisions are crafted in menu style, offering each model provision as a recommendation that is independent of the other provisions. The bundling of the latter sort of provisions within a single model law is solely for convenience and, in this way, a model law may closely resemble a set of model legal provisions. A legislative guide might also look to bundle topics through a commentary that explains the connections among sets of recommendations intended to accomplish a particular policy goal. Even where the package deal is only loosely tied together through commentary there is an obligation of sorts to absorb the contents of the guide well enough to be able to sort among its various recommendations.

sovereign authority (that is, delegations to domestic legislatures, national courts, and local non-state private parties).

For example, the inclusion of open-ended standards in a legal technology might signal, not only a lack of precision, but also a reservation of authority for domestic courts. Open-ended standards are not simply poorly drafted rules; they intentionally leave final resolution of an issue to occur on a case-by-case basis after interpretation and enforcement is sought (Ehrlich and Posner 1974; Schlag 1985). Open-ended standards embedded in international legal technologies, thus, involve a reservation of authority for enforcement actors (often, domestic courts).

Alternatively, bright-line rules in a model law or a legislative guide can be viewed as reserving authority to domestic legislatures – the authority to enact implementing legislation or not, the authority to enact implementing legislation that deviates in some way from the IO's recommended text. Instead, the technology might reserve authority for private parties through "default rules" that private actors are free to contract around and opt out of. The terms of such a convention or model law or other legal technology apply only to those entities that do not enter into contractual arrangements to the contrary.

MANIPULATING TECHNOLOGIES

The three working groups produced two types of products – legislative guides (the Working Groups on Insolvency and Secured Transactions) and a draft convention (Working Group on International Transport Law). By examining closely each of these texts, we consider the precision, obligation, and reservation of authority within each. Comparison among the convention and legislative guides reveals the relative flexibility of the guides, but also "softnesses" within the hardest of the three legal technologies. Moreover, a comparison of the two legislative guides also reveals the capacity for variations *within* a type of technology, thereby further demonstrating the flexibility that skillful global legislators can exercise through adaptation and innovation

DRAFT CONVENTION: THE ROTTERDAM RULES

It would be easy to view the Rotterdam Rules as hard law given its status as a draft convention (that is, a multilateral treaty open for accession), but close examination of its language of obligation, the occasional imprecision of its language, and its implicit reservation of authority for domestic courts and private contracting parties reveals pockets of flexibility.

Obligation

Like any draft convention, the Rotterdam Rules will not constitute legally binding international law until it has entered into effect, and by its terms does not enter into effect until at least twenty contracting states ratify it and accede to its terms.[9] The convention does not allow states to make reservations, thus, on its face provides that states must decide between agreeing to be bound to the convention in its entirety or not at all.[10] By precluding reservations, the Rotterdam Rules would seem to be a tightly tied package deal.

Moreover, the substantive provisions of the Rotterdam Rules are mostly couched in imperative language that directs the obligations and liability of carriers, shippers and, in limited circumstances, other "maritime performing parties."[11] As an example, Article 11 provides that

> [t]he carrier shall, subject to this Convention and in accordance with the terms of the contract of carriage, carry the goods to the place of destination and deliver them to the consignee.

There are exceptions to this prescriptive language, however, and in practical effect these exceptions work to allow states to express their reservations about certain articles within the convention. Specifically, Chapters 14 and 15 of the convention, containing Articles 66 through 78, are optional, although purportedly drafted with the language of a mandate. In each of the two chapters, Chapter 14 (governing jurisdiction) and Chapter 15 (governing arbitration), a key provision specifies that the earlier articles of that chapter of apply only to those states that explicitly opt in to them.[12]

These choices to opt in or not offer flexibility in the package deal set out in the Rotterdam Rules. The optional chapters in the Rotterdam Rules on jurisdiction and arbitration were offered in order to resolve a particular political problem faced in the International Transportation Working Group (see Chapter 7): the US delegation viewed the jurisdictional provisions in Chapter 14 of the Rotterdam Rules as necessary to reverse, in at least a practical sense, their Supreme Court's decision in *Sky Reefer*[13]; but delegations from states belonging to the European Union were party to jurisdictional treaties that would have precluded their accession to the Rotterdam Rules if these jurisdictional provisions were a mandatory part of the package deal. Allowing states to choose whether the jurisdictional provisions in

9 Rotterdam Rules, Ch. 18, Art. 94.

10 Id., Art. 90 ("No reservation is permitted to this Convention.").

11 As such, the Rotterdam Rules constitutes a "persuasion treaty," in which nations make promises that can only keep if non-state third parties act or refrain from acting (Durkee 2016). It is not a resolution treaty involving states' agreement that they themselves will act or refrain from acting in a specific way (id.).

12 Id., Arts. 74 and 78 ("The provisions of this chapter shall bind only Contracting States that declare in accordance with article 91 that they will be bound by them."). Thus, the package deal offered by the Rotterdam Rules comes in four optional forms: (i) all of Chapters 1 through 18; (ii) Chapters 1 through 13, and 16 through 18, but neither Chapter 14 nor 15; (iii) Chapters 1 through 14, and 16 through 18, but not Chapter 15; (iv) Chapter 1 through 13, and 15 through 18, but not Chapter 14.

13 Vimar Seguros y Reaseguros, S. v. M/V Sky Reefer, 515 U.S. 528 (1995).

Chapter 14 and the arbitration rules in Chapter 15 permitted delegates to thread the needle and reach a cooperative outcome to a potentially competitive impasse.

Precision

Like most conventions, the Rotterdam Rules are overwhelmingly written with precise language that clearly specifies the terms on which contracting states will be bound.[14] An internal glossary defines thirty terms used throughout the convention.[15] Another provision specifies rules of interpretation that should govern.[16] Eight different provisions clearly demarcate the scope of the convention.[17] In the remainder of the nearly one hundred articles that comprise the Rotterdam Rules, the language is filled with the highly technical detail and internal cross-references that could only have been drafted by international commercial lawyers, and could only be found in a document meant to resolve commercial disputes involving actors from multiple industries from nearly any country around the world.

There is one issue on which the terms of the Rotterdam Rules are noticeably not very precise, and that is on the topic it refers to as "electronic transport records."[18] "Transport documents,"[19] another defined term within the convention, had historically been required to be in paper and in a very specific form. One of the Commission's motivating purposes in taking up the issue of international transport in the first place was the advice of the e-Commerce Working Group that this fixation on paper bills of lading and other transport documents was hopelessly old fashioned and in need of revision (Chapter 3).

But the International Transport Working Group faced a problem that crossed technical and political lines: How should the provisions of the convention on electronic transport documents get drafted at a time when no such documents yet existed? Specific requirements would be difficult to set out in bright-line rules because industry standards associated with electronic bills of lading or other

14 UNCITRAL did not prepare or otherwise agree to commentary to explain the terms of the Rotterdam Rules, although it and other lawmaking IOs sometimes couple a convention with commentary on the convention. See Roy Goode, Cape Town Convention and Aircraft Protocol Official Commentary (3d ed; 2013)(noting that it was "approved for distribution" by the UNIDROIT governing council pursuant to Resolution No. 5 adopted by "Cape Town Diplomatic Conference"); UNCITRAL Explanatory Note to UN Convention on Use of Electronic Communication in International Contracts, paras. 1–324, at 13–99 (2009)(noting that the commentary was prepared by the UNCITRAL Secretariat "for informational purposes" and "is not an official commentary").

15 Rotterdam Rules, Art. 1.

16 Id., Art. 2.

17 Three scope provisions provide that "contracts of carriage" are governed by the convention and specify that "contracts in liner transportation" and other transactions are not governed by its terms (Ch. 2, Arts. 5–7). A separate chapter specifies five additional "matters not governed by this Convention" (Ch. 17, Arts. 82–86).

18 Id., Art. 1(18).

19 Id., Art. 1(14).

electronic transport records had not been developed at the time UNCITRAL's Working Group was drafting the Rotterdam Rules.[20] The Working Group was concerned about squelching the flexibility that would be needed for industry development, but viewed provisions on electronic documents as a necessary part of the draft convention. As a result, the Rotterdam Rules are somewhat imprecise on the topic of electronic documents.

While normally the requirements specified in a convention are all contained within the terms of the convention, the provisions in Chapter 3 on electronic transport documents refer, at least in part, to standardized private contract terms and other documents that the Working Group hoped would be developed as industry practices developed over time. Thus, while Article 9 of the Convention specifies that the "use of a negotiable electronic transport record shall be subject to procedures" providing for details such as "the method for the issuance and the transfer of that record to an intended holder," an "assurance" that this record "retains its integrity" and the "manner in which the holder is able to demonstrate that it is the holder," the convention does not itself specify these procedures,[21] instead requiring only that these procedures "shall be referred to in the contract particulars" and that these contract particulars should be "readily ascertainable." In this way, the convention adopts a type of *default rule* that anticipates party autonomy to control specific provisions of the convention.

While Article 9 expressly delegates the drafting of the "contract particulars" of these procedures to private parties, it also specifies in only broad parameters how these procedures ought to work. In some instances, the convention looks solely for some agreement on such a procedure to develop, without specifying what it thinks those procedures ought to look like or accomplish. In other instances, the convention sets broad goals for the procedures (i.e., there should be an assurance that the record "retains its integrity"), implicitly leaving the work of judging whether these goals have been met to arbitrators or courts assigned the task of resolving disputes that later arise. These broad goals are, thus, *open-ended standards* through which the Working Group delegated to judges or arbitrators the task of developing these procedures in further detail.

The imprecision of the language in which the convention's provisions on electronic documents is drafted was, in other words, an important part of the consensus that was reached. Their very flexibility was the key to any resolution of this highly technical issue.

[20] For reference to emerging industry standards on electronic documentation of this sort, see Electronic (Paperless) Trading Systems: essDOCS Exchange Ltd, Bolero International Ltd and E-Title Authority Pte Ltd., Gard P&I Member Circular No. 07–15 (October 2015), www.gard.no/Content/20889007/MemberCircular_7_2015.pdf.

[21] Article 9 of the Rotterdam Rules, thus, closely resembles an "architectural recommendation," as defined below.

Reserving and Delegating Discretion

The articles governing electronic transport records provide an example of relaxed precision, but also a reservation of discretion for private actors to specify in their contracts the "particulars" of the enforceability of "electronic transport documents" – these provisions, as noted above, included both an open-ended standard and default rules that permitted parties contracts to govern these documents. The Rotterdam Rules' default rules on electronic documents are not the only reservation of authority for contracting parties. The most important of these provisions governing parties' ability to opt out of the specifics of the Rotterdam Rules are set out in Chapter 16 of the convention, which generally governs the validity of contractual terms. Although the Rotterdam Rules are intended to set mandatory obligations for contracts of carriage,[22] Articles 80 and 81 provide "special rules" for two sorts of contracts that are explicitly not mandatory: volume contracts and contracts involving the carriage of live animals and certain other goods.[23] Its provisions on volume contracts are an especially important part of the "big deals" struck by the International Transport Working Group, and the crafting of these provisions as default rules permitting parties to contract around the convention was an integral part of this deal (Chapter 7).

Article 80 broadly provides that "as between the carrier and the shipper, a volume contract to which this Convention applies may provide for greater or lesser rights, obligations, and liabilities than those imposed by this Convention."[24] In short, the parties to a volume contract are free to pick and choose among the Rotterdam Rules they like or dislike. Although generally contracts inconsistent with the convention are "void" – an unenforceable non-event – volume contracts, on the other hand, have free rein to alter the mandates of the Rotterdam Rules. With this provision, the six years of work on Rotterdam Rules might easily have been erased by the simple expedient of an agreement between private parties.[25]

Generally, the presence of default rules in any convention is controversial; parties' ability to contract around otherwise mandatory international legislation is viewed both as undermining the uniformity of applicable rules and undercutting the clarity and precision of the mandate (see, e.g., Gillette and Scott 2005; Stephan 1999). Deliberations on the volume contract provisions were no less acrimonious within

[22] See Rotterdam Rules, Art. 79 (clarifying the mandatory nature of the rules set out in the convention by specifying various terms in contracts of carriage that should be deemed "void").

[23] The term "volume contracts" is undefined but the convention restricts the format of these contracts. While they may be "individually negotiated," it is also clear that volume contracts might be formed on the basis of standardized contracts, so long as the "volume contract contains a prominent statement that it derogates from this Convention" and "prominently specifies the sections of the volume contract containing the derogations" and other process-related requirements are met (id., Art. 80(2)).

[24] Id., Art. 80(1).

[25] But see limits in id., Art. 80(2).

the Transport Working Group. Delegates from Australia, New Zealand, France and from the European Shippers Council thought the draft convention's provisions on volume contracts were too ill-defined and, as a result, too likely to be relied on strategically to allow powerful carriers to insist on standardized contracts taking away important protections (Chapter 7).

But the US delegation insisted that it needed to show its industry actors that these sorts of volume contracts, which were permissible under US law, would also be permitted under the new international regime that would get put in place with accession to the Rotterdam Rules (Chapter 7). Drafting these as "default rules" was a key component to any agreement on the treatment of volume contracts since, from the perspective of the US delegation, shippers with market power should be able to exert this power to their benefit. The mandatory aspects of the Rotterdam Rules were conceived of as shipper protections, so powerful shippers that didn't need these protections should be able to craft their own deals by contract (Chapter 7).

LEGISLATIVE GUIDE ON SECURED TRANSACTIONS

UNCITRAL's Legislative Guide on Secured Transactions is not a draft convention; nor is it drafted as a model law that would be binding as national law within those states that enacted legislation to implement its numerous recommendations. Domestic legislatures intent on following its direction would need to sift through nearly 600 pages of commentary, including nearly 250 recommendations, before enacting domestic legislation on the secured transactions as recommended in the Guide.[26] This Legislative Guide is not simply a soft law technology, but a complex and lengthy one.

What possible political and ecological advantages were gained with UNCITRAL's drafting of law for the world as a legislative guide, especially given that (with the benefit of hindsight) we can report that the Secured Transactions Working Group has subsequently succeeded in drafting a Model Law on Secured Transactions within three short years?[27]

Despite a state's lack of obligation in the Secured Transactions Guide, the Guide is drafted to rely on significant language of obligation. Its numerous recommendations look like model legal provisions; its scope is broad and connected together as a unified whole; there is little in the way of permissive language or options offered, with the exception of several provisions crafted as two optional approaches to the question of the treatment of "retention of title" (ROT) transactions. This language of obligation is coupled with language of precision, specificity and depth: bright-line

[26] The Working Group on Security Interests subsequently added to the Secured Transactions Guide (2007) with its Supplement on Security Rights in Intellectual Property (2010) and Guide on the Implementation of a Security Rights Registry (2013).

[27] UNCITRAL, Report of Working Group VI (Security Interests) on the work of its twenty-ninth session, UN Doc. No. A/CN.9/871 (New York, February 8–12, 2016).

rules prevail within the Guide; there are only a few open-ended standards. It is also coupled with language of obfuscation, which we view in part as intended to blur the influence of the North American, specifically the US, approach to secured transactions law.

This attention to the language and formal attributes of the Guide enabled the Working Group to reach consensus, despite grave dissensus on the treatment of ROT transactions. It also enabled the Group to move incrementally to its next steps: a horizontal move, toward supplemental work on security interest in intellectual property collateral and on registries for security interests; eventually, a vertical move, that hardened this soft law technology with seeming ease. The Working Group created time by segmenting and then sequencing lawmaking tasks.

As with the previous discussion of the flexibility of the Rotterdam Rules, we focus on the language of obligation, precision, and reservation of authority in the Legislative Guide on Secured Transactions.

Obligation

Legislative guides present a density and complexity of format that distinguishes this technology readily from either a draft convention or model law. The two legislative guides in our case studies combine lengthy "commentary" with a defining "glossary" of terms together with a collection of "recommendations."

A legislative guide is a soft law technology in that it imposes no obligation on states. The only obligation suggested is one of review and comprehension, implicitly pronouncing to states: "If you are thinking about enacting legislation on the topic covered by our legislative guide, and we really think you ought to, you should read this guide in its entirety and struggle with its contents – more than consider its recommendations, we think you should be guided by the debate set out in its commentary."

Despite the softness of this obligation of review and comprehension, legislative guides nonetheless adopt a language of obligation. In the Secured Transactions Guide, this language of obligation is accomplished by framing the "soft" text to resemble law-like recommendations, by employing prescriptive language, and by describing itself as a "package deal."

Framing. Legislative guides couple (lengthy and detailed) commentary with (specific) recommendations. The Working Group on Secured Transactions was explicitly aware that its recommendations "looked like" proposed legislative language and, thus, the articles of a model law or draft convention.[28] The recommendations made within the Secured Transactions Guide are especially "obligatory" for a legislative guide. Not only are these recommendations set apart within the body of commentary in the Guide, they are also reprinted as a body of recommendations

[28] UNCITRAL Legislative Guide on Secured Transactions, para. 80, at 28.

appearing as an independent Annex to the Guide.[29] Pulling the recommendations out from within the body of the text of the Secured Transactions Guide would ease the work of a domestic actor's review of the lengthy Guide, thus, save search time. At the same time, segregating the recommendations in a single (80 page) Annex would emphasize the significance of the Guide's recommendations as distinct from the commentary, and especially their language of obligation.

Prescriptive versus permissive language. In addition to this framing of its recommendations as obligatory in some sense, the recommendations found within the Secured Transactions Guide are drafted nearly exclusively in prescriptive language with an imperative or mandatory tone. The vast majority of the recommendations in this Guide begin with the chapeau: "[t]he law should provide" and then set forth in lettered subparagraphs a list of specific legal recommendations. That is, many of the numbered recommendations themselves subsume a number of substantive recommendations such that there are many more prescriptive recommendations than the 200 numbered recommendations suggests.

The Secured Transactions Guide also contains important permissive recommendations, however. Formally, these permissive recommendations are phrased in one of several ways. Some permissive recommendations simply indicate that one approach or another "*may* be implemented" through means that are identified in the recommendation itself.[30] Other recommendations set out the two acceptable alternatives in the disjunctive: For example, Rec. 69 of the Secured Transactions Guide provides that "the law *should either* specify the duration of the effectiveness of the registration of a notice *or* permit the registrant to specify the duration in the notice at the time of registration and extend it at any time before its expire."

Like in the Rotterdam Rules, the Secured Transactions Guide may speak with prescriptive language when offering options. A series of recommendations in the Guide are couched as imperative recommendations, in that they provide that "the law should provide" one thing or another, but then go on to specify "Option A" or "Option B" in the same detail that an imperative recommendation would take.[31] While such alternatives in a legislative guide present options to domestic legislatures, and should be viewed as a permissive recommendation, choosing between two options is less permissive than determining whether to adopt a single permissive recommendation, and for now we simply note the distinction without creating another rule-type.

One set of permissive recommendations in the Guide is important to emphasize, specifically Recommendations 178 through 202. These twenty-four recommendations constitute the core compromise embedded within the Secured Transactions Guide: these are the recommendations that present two alternative means by which

[29] Id., Annex I, "Terminology and recommendations of the UNCITRAL Legislative Guide on Secured Transactions," at 453.

[30] Id., Rec. 9,

[31] Id., Recs. 180, 185, 192, 199, 202, and 210.

domestic legislature could address the issue of acquisition financing through ROT transactions (see Chapter 7). Recommendations 178 through 202 offer two alternatives, referred to as Option A and Option B. The commentary accompanying these recommendations makes clear that the Guide "permits" both approaches and provides extensive discussion of the implications of this choice.[32]

As with the Rotterdam Rules, language of permission both signals and accomplishes compromise. These permissive recommendations were the key to the consensual agreement regarding the recommendations on ROT and acquisitive financing made within the Secured Transactions Guide.

Package deal. It would be hard to view anything as soft as a legislative guide as offering a take-it-or-leave-it package deal. And yet the Working Group's primary struggle – over how closely it should adhere to US law, and specifically what lawyers refer to as a "functional approach" to secured transactions laws like that which had been introduced in the US in the late 1960s and later followed in Canada, New Zealand and eventually Australia[33] – caused it to debate whether its detailed and prescriptively framed recommendations should be construed by states as a suggestion that the Guide offered a sort of package deal. Strong advocates of US Article 9 preferred the Working Group on Secured Transactions to produce recommendations that looked more like a model law, and thus could be imported in bulk into a country's statute book. Those who resisted either the US approach, or who wanted more recognition of existing secured transactions regimes and more discretion for legislatures in the adoption of norms, argued for a commentary that laid out different options for national lawmakers and reasoning as to which options might be justifiable. This struggle, in effect, became a contest over not only the content of the commentary and recommendations, but also how closely the two would be bound to each other in a formal document, such as the Legislative Guide itself.

The resolution of the struggle produced a "both-and" solution. While the body of the Secured Transactions Guide combines a lengthy commentary with specific

[32] Specifically, this commentary defines the concept of acquisition finance by explaining that a debtor might acquire particular assets either by borrowing (either from the seller or a third party) and securing the purchase price with the collateral acquired, or by structuring the acquisition as either a "retention of title transaction" or a "financing lease;" that some states take a pragmatic, functional view of the economic reality of the two sorts of transactions as indistinguishable, and thus apply their secured transactions laws to both sorts of acquisition financing transactions; it also indicates that other states take a more formal perspective on the significance of the structure and characterization of such transactions, and thus apply their secured transactions laws to the former and their ROT or leasing laws to the latter.

[33] The North American "functional approach" to secured transactions law is a reference to the legal notion that a law should have broad scope over all sorts of commercial finance transactions involving personal property collateral, regardless of their formal attributes, and a system of "notice filing" of these interests so that searchers might easily be made aware of the breadth of a lender's claim to collateral. Id., Introduction, para. 62, at 23. The Secured Transactions Guide refers to this legal notion as a "functional, integrated and comprehensive" approach to secured transactions laws.

recommendations, its recommendations are also restated as a stand-alone Annex to the Guide itself. The Annex, thus, closely resembles a detachable model law. The commentary then hedges on the importance of either:

> Although presented as recommendations and not as provisions of a model law, the recommendations in the Guide are often drafted with a high degree of detail and specificity. This does not mean, however, that States *must* enact a new law that is framed in such a manner. If drafting techniques in a State presume that legislative provisions are presented first by means of a statement of principle and thereafter by means of exceptions expressed in descending order of generality, this is the style it should follow in its new law. The Guide offers extensive commentaries developing the policy rationales for its recommendations so as to enable States to enact legislative that achieves their desired goals without having to adopt any particular drafting style.[34]

But, of course, even to suggest that states might read the Guide as requiring anything is to validate its language of obligation as purposive.

Precision

Most of the recommendations in the Secured Transactions Guide are drafted as bright-line rules. The clarity and specificity of this writing is then compounded in the Guide with the depth of analysis offered by the commentary preceding each set of recommendations.

Consensus and pedigree. Generally, the Guide's commentary is written as a comparative analysis of the world's secured transactions laws that does not identify any particular country or groups of countries except occasionally to differentiate between civil and common law approaches to an issue. In doing so it couples a *language of obligation* through which recommendations are drafted, with a *language of consensus and pedigree*. For example, the Secured Transactions Guide refers from time to time to issues on which it claims *universal* consensus exists. When discussing the technical rules associated with secured creditors' priority in commingled assets, the Guide provides that "States typically provide that non-possessory security rights in the same tangible assets that become commingled continue into the mass or product and have the same priority as against each other as they had prior to the commingling."[35] Occasionally, the Guide notes that the secured transactions laws in "many" states include a particular rule. And from time to time it refers to a *trend* in lawmaking, sometimes coupled with the rhetorical flourish that such a trend will brand a particular rule as "modern" or will be conducive to a "modern secured transactions regime." For example, the Guide notes that

[34] Id., para. 80, at 28.
[35] Id., para. 118, at 216.

> [o]ne of the key features of a modern secured transactions regime is that, regardless of the basis adopted for determining priority, priority will be determined by reference to objective facts ... This is the way that most States have modernized their regime of security rights.[36]

At other times, rhetoric emphasizing the *modernity* of a particularly rule is combined either with rhetoric explaining the consistency of the rule with financial or other business practices or the *efficiency* of that rule. At one point, for example, the Secured Transactions Guide remarks that "[m]odern secured transactions regimes not only reflect modern concepts of secured transactions law, but also accommodate modern business practices and take advantage of modern developments in State regulatory practices" and notes, specifically, "that a secured transactions law should not impede modern commerce." [37] Occasionally, the modernity of a rule is emphasized by reference to the fact that UNCITRAL or another international organization has adopted a similar rule in its earlier product.

The Guide sometimes validates a particular recommendation by reference to positions taken by other international organizations. For example, in discussing States' options regarding the drafting of a secured transactions law, the Guide notes that "[o]ne option is to adopt integrated legislation for both possessory and non-possessory security rights," which it notes is the approach "taken by the OAS Model Inter-American Law on Secured Transactions."[38] By relying on this sort of pyramidal incrementalism,[39] the Guide looks credibly to assert that the integrated, functional approach to secured transactions law is the "prevailing trend in modern legislation, at both the national and international levels" and then assert that the contrary approaches are "likely to result in gaps, overlaps, inconsistencies and lack of transparency, as well as in discontent in those sectors of industry that might be excluded."[40]

Obfuscation. At times, commentary in the Guide looks to obfuscate rather than clarify, but only with regard to the origins of its terminology or its recommendations. The Secured Transactions Guide is careful to state that it adopts terminology that "is not drawn from any particular legal system."[41] National secured transactions laws are rife with different terms that describe varieties of financing and acquisition mechanisms, and the Guide is also careful to define terms. In doing this, it may *adopt* terms that are well understood by industry actors,[42] it may *exclude* terms in

36 Id., para. 125, at 218.
37 Id., para. 119, at 60.
38 Id., para. 74, at 48.
39 See (Block-Lieb and Halliday 2007b) and pp.82–5.
40 Secured Transactions Guide, para. 75, at 49.
41 Id., at Introduction, para. 15, at 5.
42 The glossary in the Secured Transactions Guide *adopts*, defines and categorizes collateral in the same way as North American secured transactions law – goods, inventory, equipment, accounts and general intangibles; it adopts the term "control," which was first adopted in US secured transactions laws in 2000; it uses the North American term "proceeds" but relies on a definition of the term that is closer to Canadian than current US law.

order to create distance from a particular industry or national practice,[43] and it may *invent* terms in order blur the origins of its terminology.[44] It is also careful to build on precedent from within UNCITRAL's own historical trajectory of international lawmaking and thus attributes terms to earlier UNCITRAL conventions, such as the UN Convention on the Assignment of International Receivables and the UN Convention on the Use of Electronic Communications in International Contracts.[45] In so doing, the Guide amplifies the claims of UNCITRAL to be an emergent lawmaker that must be taken seriously as an actor and not merely an arena. Incidentally, this cross-referencing among UNCITRAL products helps build UNCITRAL's own rhetorical "brand" of legal concepts, which stake discursive claims to distinctive global lawmaking.

Put another way, UNCITRAL's distinctive terms and concepts help it define the boundaries of the TLOs where it seeks to place its stamp on legal systems and to define meanings within those boundaries. It is a "naming" strategy of social construction through language.

Reservation of Authority

Even more so than a model law, a legislative guide is intended by its drafters to reserve for domestic actors considerable discretion: discretion as to whether to enact implementing legislation, but also discretion to pick and choose among the various recommendations found in such a guide and even the breadth of topics on which a guide provides suggested resolutions. Although the Secured Transactions Guide framed its commentary with stand-alone recommendations, and although it frequently relied on prescriptive and imperative language in drafting these recommendations, the Working Group on Secured Transactions was clear in its choice among legal technologies.

Although it decided to work on a legislative guide, some within the Working Group hoped eventually to work on a model law. The extent to which the Secured Transactions Guide was drafted with language of obligation and precision signaled, we argue, the Working Group's interests in its eventual work on a model law on the same topic. Before moving vertically to harden its Legislative Guide into the

[43] The Guide's glossary *excludes* the US term "accounts receivable," relying instead on the term "receivable," consistent with terminology found in the UN Convention on the Assignment of International Receivables.

[44] The glossary *invents* an important cluster of terms that include "acquisition security right" and "acquisition secured creditor." These terms appear in no country's secured transactions law – they were invented expressly to bridge a rhetorical gap between the US concept of a purchase-money security interest and the European concept of a retention-of-title right and financial lease right and in so doing to create a neutral term deferential to no legal system in particular.

[45] The Guide's use of the term "receivables" presents one example; the terms "assignee," "assignor" and "assignment" present additional examples. Indeed, the Guide's Glossary cross-refers to the definitions for these terms in the Assignment Convention.

language of a model law, the Working Group first moved horizontally to supplement its transactional reach by also addressing intellectual property collateral and then again to clarify its recommendations on the form that a security registry should take.[46]

These horizontal incrementalisms presented important next steps for the Working Group. Although the Group would take an additional six years to complete these moves, this foundational work created deliberative efficiencies when shifting vertically: the drafting of a broad and deep Model Law on Secured Transactions is likely to be concluded within a short three to four years. The footprint of this Model Law holds important ecological implications for UNCITRAL.

LEGISLATIVE GUIDE ON INSOLVENCY LAW[47]

Because two of our case studies produced a legislative guide we can constructively contrast the two guides. While there is much similarity in both guides – both contain detailed glossaries, commentary that looks objectively to describe the state of the law broadly across legal families, regional divides, and economic disparities and hundreds of more specific recommendations – there is also a glaring difference between the them: although the recommendations in the Secured Transactions Guide are overwhelmingly drafted with prescriptive language that resembles a model law, the recommendations in the Legislative Guide on Insolvency Law present a much more diverse array of formal properties available for manipulation by UNCITRAL's lawmakers and norm entrepreneurs nationally and locally.

The content and structure of the Insolvency Guide further exemplify the flexibility of a soft law technology designed to facilitate consensus among a broad diversity of actors and interests in a contentious policy domain without insisting on uniformity. The Insolvency Guide is not just a soft law technology, but a softer legislative guide than that directed toward its cousin in law and legal practice. But if the Secured Transactions Guide was drafted to ease the way toward a Model Law on Secured Transactions, what possible political or ecological advantages were gained with the drafting of an Insolvency Guide that seems to avoid most language of obligation?

To some degree, the Insolvency Guide's failure to incorporate much language of obligation reflects the not insubstantial ecological and political concerns with any effort to set international insolvency law standards. These concerns were especially salient to the Insolvency Working Group whose efforts followed closely on the heels of similar work by the IMF and World Bank. These IFIs had been criticized for lawmaking as a conditional part of their lending in the wake of the Asian Financial

[46] See supra notes 26 and 27.

[47] This section builds upon (Block-Lieb and Halliday 2007a) and amplifies the analysis of formal properties in (Halliday, Block-Lieb and Carruthers 2009a: 157–9).

Frisis. If UNCITRAL sought implicitly to distinguish the legitimacy of its work, it would need to consider carefully states' sovereign interests in corporate insolvency law reform.

Unlike the Secured Transactions Guide, which marked its major political compromises with recommendations drafted permissively, the Insolvency Guide saved its strongest language of obligation for drafting its biggest political accomplishment – recommendations to guide domestic legislatures in adopting corporate insolvency laws that would enable and even facilitate reorganization and resuscitation of a business in financial distress. When Insolvency Working Group wrote on issues tangential to corporate reorganization, it drafted with a light touch, choosing among recommendations that varied between prescription and permission, constraint, and focus.[48]

In describing the extensive flexibility of the Insolvency Guide, we continue to refer to UNCITRAL's reliance on language of obligation, its precision, and its reservation of authority. These formal strategies demonstrate how the Insolvency Working Group and UNCITRAL's Secretariat together crafted a product that could bridge deep cleavages and wide variations in corporate insolvency law and policy across the world, avoiding both stalemate and ineffectual vacuity and thereby increasing the probability that a TLO based on UNCITRAL laws would eventually emerge.

Reservation of Authority

Legislative guides permit maximal reserve authority for domestic legislatures to reform national laws with degrees of freedom in their efforts to make them broadly consistent with international standards. While lawmaking IOs should in every instance move with care in purporting to "make" law for national actors, UNCITRAL knew that it should be especially careful in setting international standards for corporate insolvency law. UNCITRAL's corporate insolvency lawmaking initiative temporally followed similar efforts by the IMF, World Bank, and other IOs. That these earlier episodes of international lawmaking had been branded – by civil society, academic commentators, and important affected states – as assertions of authority by entities that lacked sufficient breadth of representation was well known to UNCITRAL's Insolvency Working Group. The effect of these earlier criticisms created an imprimatur of caution among delegates, including delegates from the wealthiest and politically strongest states.

But insolvency laws are, of necessity, mandatory: default rules that would reserve contractual authority to private contracting parties was out of the question. While delegation of authority to domestic courts appealed to some delegations, especially

48 For further discussion of these "Big Deals," see Chapter 7.

those that had sent delegates to the Working Group who were themselves judges adept in insolvency practice, other delegations had made clear their distrust of widespread and unfettered judicial discretion in insolvency settings.

In drafting recommendations on mandatory rules of insolvency law, the Working Group purported to create obligation in the Insolvency Guide, but only where uniformity of approach was necessary to its limited goals. As a result, the Working Group attempted a combination of clarity and ambiguity in its drafting.

Precision

Like the Secured Transactions Guide, the Insolvency Guide provides depth to the recommendations it offers by coupling these with extensive commentary on each issue-area and clarifying in a glossary numerous important terms used in the commentary and recommendations.

Consensus and pedigree. Commentary links recommendations to broad jurisprudential statements of principle (e.g., "it is desirable that the commencement standard is transparent and certain"[49]; "an insolvency law will need to clearly identify the assets" because this will produce "transparency and predictability";[50] "post-commencement finance is needed for a firm to continue operations and for reorganization"[51]). These overarching principles are meant to signal *international consensus*[52] on substantive grounds.

In other instances, consensus is identified, not based on substantive agreement on the "better" rule, but by "weighing" the relative sides of a debate to determine which side should be viewed as the "prevailing" view. Commentary may indicate universal consensus by stating that exceptions for banking and insurance companies from coverage by insolvency laws are "widely reflected in insolvency laws . . . ," or that insolvency laws "generally permit" an application for liquidation to be made by debtors, creditors, and government agencies. If universality cannot be claimed, the Guide relies on a *quantitative criterion*. The commentary persuades by stating that "many insolvency laws identify the minimum threshold of support required from creditors,"[53] or that a standard is "used extensively,"[54] or that the "most common approach" to application of the stay is that it begins at commencement of proceedings.[55]

49 UNCITRAL Legislative Guide on Insolvency Law, Part Two, I(B)(1) ¶ 21, at 45.
50 Id., II(A)(1) ¶3, at 75.
51 Id., II(D)(1) ¶ 94, at 113.
52 On parallel rhetorical constructions in global lawmaking by the IMF, World Bank and European Bank for Reconstruction and Development, see (Halliday, Block-Lieb and Carruthers 2009b)
53 UNCITRAL Legislative Guide on Insolvency Law, IV(A)(5)(g) ¶ 47, at 223.
54 Id., I(B)(2)(a) ¶ 23, at 45 (referring to the liquidity or cash flow test as "used extensively").
55 Id., II(B)(5)(c) ¶ 46, at 90.

It occasionally invokes the notion of a *trend*. On the highly contentious issue of whether secured property should be included in a bankruptcy estate, the world divides probably with a preponderance of countries in favor of its exclusion. Yet the move toward reorganization requires that secured property be brought the bankruptcy estate, even if only a minority of countries follows that principle. Although the Guide takes the minority view, it concludes that this view is "increasingly recognized" and that inclusion has economic advantages over exclusion.

It may weigh in on a debate by signaling in the commentary which approach has the better side of the argument (e.g., "it is increasingly recognized" that a certain course of action will have more advantages to the economy).[56] If it views two possibilities are both acceptable, the Guide may explicate how the two versions might be related to each other. For example, on the test for insolvency, it explains why a cash flow test might be acceptable, and goes on to note that a balance sheet test should not be used alone but only in combination with a cash flow test.[57]

Ambiguity. Countries may simply sit in disagreement on an issue. When the commentary addresses cross-national variation on an issue, it discusses this variation through comparative analysis. Even this comparative analysis tends to stick to general statements, however. It endeavors nearly uniformly to avoid identifying specific countries when discussing differing approaches to an issue. For example, on standards for commencing an insolvency proceeding, the Guide distinguishes between countries that employ a cash flow and a balance sheet test of insolvency without once mentioning which countries apply which test.[58]

And yet while the Insolvency Guide declines to be specific about the national origins of a particular approach, it is not vague about discussing the benefits and deficiencies of various alternatives, focusing both on juridical and practical advantages and disadvantages.[59]

Some of this obfuscation comes through the consistent use of precisely defined terms that, like the Secured Transactions Guide, may also *exclude terms* that are associated with one particular insolvency system, especially that of the US,[60]

56 Id.

57 Id.

58 Id. at I(B)(2)(a) and (b) ¶¶ 23–26, at 45–47.

59 Id.

60 Even though concepts of US bankruptcy law informed many of the debates over the Guide, the Guide generally does not adopt terms of art from the US Bankruptcy Code or practice. For example, the Guide addresses the treatment of contracts, but refers to the "continuation" of such contracts rather than to their "assumption," as is true under US law. As another example, the Guide recommends that a stay or moratorium of creditor collection activity ensue upon the commencement of an insolvency proceeding, but nowhere refers to this as an "automatic stay," a notable concept in US bankruptcy law. Terms too closely associated with one country, such as the US concept of "super-priority," or the English and European concepts of "retention of title," were also avoided.

invent terms to avoid aligning itself with one country and to provide universal umbrella concepts that transcend the practices associated with particular insolvency regimes,[61] or *launder terms* that might appear too derivative of one country's system.[62]

Obligation

Like the Secured Transactions Guide, the Insolvency Guide relies on recommendations to communicate a broad obligation of review and comprehension across numerous subject issues in corporate reorganization. Unlike the Secured Transactions Guide, the Insolvency Guide does not predominately speak in prescriptive or imperative terms. Instead, in order to emphasize the legitimacy of its project, the Group selected among a broad range of language or rule-types when crafting these recommendations.

UNCITRAL'S REPERTOIRE OF RULE-TYPES

A systematic analysis of the rule-types developed by UNCITRAL's drafters to provide degrees of flexibility and precision reveals that there are four main categories of rules that produce seven principal rule-types (Table 6.2). Each rule-type is illustrated by provisions in the Legislative Guide on Insolvency that embraces their full variety.

1. *Imperative recommendations.* These propose that national legislatures take a specific type of action whose content is expressly stated, and might be so precisely stated that it could be transposed word-for-word into a statute or model legal provision. For example, *imperative recommendations* take the general form: "There *should* be a rule [about the substantive entitlements of participants in

[61] For example, UNCITRAL's uses the term "insolvency representative," which corresponds with the usage of no legal system, yet it encompasses every configuration of insolvency actor in the world's insolvency systems, including both roles (e.g., trustees, liquidators, administrators, insolvency practitioners) and professionals (e.g., lawyers, accountants, bureaucrats). UNCITRAL's term "court" is also a universal defined to include any kind of supervising agency, including both administrative agencies and judicial decisionmakers. See id., Introduction, Glossary, at 7.

[62] Rather than adopt the US term of "adequate protection," the Glossary adopts the concept but with another term – "protection of value." In this case, commentary discussing "protection of value" includes in parentheses the statement that "(in some jurisdictions referred to as 'adequate protection.)." Id., Part Two, II(B)(7), at 121. Rather than referring to the US concept of "pre-packaged" reorganization plans, UNCITRAL adopts the phrase "expedited procedures," even though the underlying meaning is virtually identical. Similarly, retention of title transactions, which created a major sticking point for UNCITRAL's Working Group on Security Interests, are referred to only obliquely with reference to "third party owned assets," which are in turn defined to include, among other assets, those that are the subject of a retention of title transaction.

TABLE 6.2. *Lawmaking Effects of Rule-Types in Legislative Guides*

General Categories	Rule-Types	Rule Features	Lawmaking Effects
Imperative	Substantive	This substantive rule *should* be in the statute	Working group consensus most difficult to reach Offers little discretion to domestic legislatures If states implement, most likely to produce uniformity Most conducive to subsequent model law project (vertical incrementalism)
Constraining	Baseline	There *should* be a rule and it *should* have these minimal elements	Working group consensus less difficult to reach Offers more discretion for variation by domestic legislatures If states implement, then substantially likely to produce uniformity May be conducive to subsequent model law project (vertical incrementalism)
	Permissive	A statute *may* include rules with "X" or "Y" content	Working group consensus less difficult to reach Offers discretion for rejection by domestic legislatures If states reject, then uniformity less likely May be conducive to subsequent model law project (vertical incrementalism)
	Norms of minimalism	*If* there is a rule on this topic, it should have minimal provisions	Working group consensus least difficult to reach Offers greatest degree of discretion to domestic legislatures; "obligation" of review and comprehension shifted entirely to related commentary Least conducive to subsequent model law project (vertical incrementalism) Least likely to produce uniformity
Focusing	Architectural	There should be a rule on this topic but its content is unspecified	Working group consensus least difficult to reach Offers great deal of discretion to domestic legislatures; "obligation" of review and comprehension mostly shifted entirely to related commentary Great degree of discretion for domestic legislatures

(*continued*)

TABLE 6.2. (*continued*)

General Categories	Rule-Types	Rule Features	Lawmaking Effects
			Mostly not conducive to subsequent model law project (vertical incrementalism) Unlikely to produce uniformity
	Norm of disclosure	A rule should be clear, irrespective of content	Working group consensus least difficult to reach Greatest degree of discretion for domestic legislatures; "obligation" of review and comprehension shifted entirely to related commentary Least helpful in subsequent model law project (vertical incrementalism) Least likely to produce uniformity
Policy norms	Policy statements	A law should include certain policy objectives	Working group consensus least difficult to reach Greatest degree of legislative discretion; "obligation" of review and comprehension shifted entirely to related commentary Least conducive to subsequent model law project (vertical incrementalism) Least likely to produce uniformity

insolvency proceedings] that [contains particular substantive provisions]." One such recommendation reads:

> The insolvency law should govern insolvency proceedings against all debtors that engage in economic activities, whether natural or legal persons, including state-owned enterprises, and whether or not those economic activities are conducted for profit."[63]

Imperative recommendations speak directly and concretely to the content that a legislative provision should contain.

2. *Constraining recommendations* are not explicitly directive of particular legislative language, but they are conducive to convergence. Often they point in a direction and then give choices. There are three variants of these:

a. *Baseline recommendations* take the form – "there should be a rule on a topic, and it should include *at least* the following elements (with the implication that

[63] Id., Rec. 8.

other elements might also be included)." For instance, in the section on expedited proceedings, baseline recommendations set a floor or minimal standard for the commencement for initiating such proceedings:

> The insolvency law should specify that the following additional materials should accompany an application for commencement of expedited reorganization proceedings:
>
> (a) The reorganization plan and disclosure statement. . .
> (e) A financial analysis or other evidence that demonstrates that the plan satisfies all applicable requirements for reorganization; and
> (f) A list of the members of any creditor committee formed during the course of the voluntary restructuring negotiations.[64]

Baseline recommendations leave options open for domestic legislatures, and so closely resemble permissive recommendations. Unlike more open-ended permissive recommendations, baselines propose limits to what permissibly sits within international standards.

b. *Permissive recommendations* grant permission for a country to adopt one or another provision. They often take the form – "a country *may* adopt a rule on [X]" or "a country *may* adopt a rule that includes [X content], [Y content] and [Z content]." Sometimes, permissive recommendations detail the language that would implement the policy decision implicit in the recommendation, but they do not always do so. For example, on the protection of debtors and creditors when a stay is placed on creditors' efforts to collect on claims, the Insolvency Guide grants courts power in those countries that so choose and indicates what those powers might be:

> The insolvency law may provide the court with the power to:
>
> (a) Require the applicant for provisional measures to provide indemnification and, where appropriate, to pay costs or fees or
> (b) Impose sanctions in connection with an application for provisional measures.[65]

These sorts of recommendations enable UNCITRAL to acknowledge the acceptability of a strongly held preference by a nation-state, permitting it to give some guidance without endorsing the position for all nations.

c. *Norms of minimalism* take the form – "if there is to be a rule on a topic, or an exception to the rule on a topic, it should be *kept to a minimum*." Norms of minimalism accept the political or social need to deviate from the form of a rule that would otherwise be dictated solely by the dictates of insolvency policies, but caution that these exceptions often form a sort of slippery slope for legislatures. For example, the Guide provides that an insolvency law generally should provide

64 Id., Rec. 162.
65 Id., Rec. 40.

that "similarly ranked claims are paid *pari passu*,"[66] but also recommends that if the law deviates from this general rule by providing for statutory priorities or privileges to be accorded to unsecured creditors, it should "minimize" these priorities.[67]

3. *Focusing recommendations* sharpen the focus of any law adopted by a domestic legislature. They call attention to an issue, rather than look to constrain or limit choices. We identify two of these.

a. *Architectural recommendations* state that – "there should be a rule on [some specific topic of insolvency law]," but do not specify what that rule should say or otherwise provide advice on the content of such a rule. For example, Rec. 156 provides that "the insolvency law should establish the mechanism for approval of amendments to a plan that has been approved by creditors."[68]

b. *Norms of disclosure* indicate only that some rule "should be clearly and expressly set forth in the law" but again provide no detail on the content of such a rule. These norms of disclosure are almost uniformly couples with norms of minimalism. For example, the Insolvency Guide provides that "[c]laims superior in priority to secured claims should be minimized and clearly set forth in the insolvency law."[69]

Architectural recommendations in particular adapt to the internal politics of a Working Group where no consensus can be reached on the content of a rule but there is general agreement that a rule of some sort should be in place in a comprehensive statute.

4. *Policy recommendations* identify and affirm broad normative statements of insolvency law. These are the highest order recommendations in the Insolvency Guide. They are found uniquely in the list of "key objectives" found in Legislative Guides.[70] For example, in the Insolvency Guide, the "key objectives" of an insolvency law include (a) the need to provide certainty in the marketplace sufficient to permit economic stability and growth, (b) the desirability maximizing asset values and striking a balance between liquidation and reorganization, (c) the need to provide timely, efficient and impartial resolution of an insolvency proceeding, and (d) to establish a framework for resolution of cross-border insolvency proceedings.

[66] Id., Rec. 191.

[67] Id., Rec. 187.

[68] Id., Rec. 156. This architectural rule also acts as a sort of "table of contents," in that it goes on to provide a list of the topics that should be covered in the law it posits:

> That mechanism should require notice to be given to the creditors and other parties affected by the proposed modification; specify the party required to give notice; require the approval of creditors and other parties affected by the modification; and require the rules for confirmation (where confirmation is required) to be satisfied. The insolvency law should also specify the consequences of failure to secure approval of proposed amendments.

Id.

[69] Id., Rec. 188.

[70] Id., Rec. 7.

LEGAL TECHNOLOGIES AS POLITICAL DEVICES

An overview of UNCITRAL's products over the life of this global legislature reveals three long-term trends: the portfolio of technologies expanded in diversity from two in the 1970s to ten by the 2000s; the rate of production has increased in a secular upward trend; and the mix of hard and soft law technologies has given UNCITRAL's global lawmakers significant discretion in fitting a given product to an underlying issue of commerce or trade that might be integrated into a transnational legal order.

We have asserted that this range of formal products holds political implications for decisionmaking within an IO, for implementation of its product by states, including their domestic legislatures, and for the survival and competitiveness of an IO within a lawmaking ecology. UNCITRAL presently possesses a repertoire of legal technologies available to tackle varieties of legal issues, which gives it increasingly expansive geographic and legal scope in the prospect of spearheading TLOs.

Reaching Global Consensus

UNCITRAL's inventiveness produced a portfolio of legal technologies that go some distance toward solving its legitimation paradox. That paradox arose from UNCITRAL's highly successful effort to integrate all nations and many non-state interest groups in its deliberations so that it could claim unparalleled "legislative" and "technical" representativeness. Yet the internalization of vastly different state and private interests into the deliberations threatened conflict, stalemate, and low levels of product completion. Resolution of this paradox of representative legitimacy was enabled by flexibility within UNCITRAL's legal technologies: flexibility in the choice among conventions, model laws and legislative guide; flexibility among a wide range of rules or recommendations, regardless of the technology; and flexibility within a legislative guide between commentary and recommendation.

UNCITRAL's Secretariat and its core deliberative community found that the less discretionary a technology (i.e., with a convention), the greater the concerns about whether drafters lacked legitimacy in their deliberations. Delegations were composed of state and private actors – government lawyers sent from national ministries of justice or finance often sat side by side with industry representatives and members of international professional associations. This divergence of viewpoint slowed down negotiations; even after agreements in principle were reached, drafting got bogged down in minutae since every article, every comma, had to be vetted in terms of all possible implications.

By contrast, UNCITRAL found that the more discretion inherent in a technology, the less detailed and precise the language contained within it, the easier it was to negotiate. Model laws took far less time to negotiate than conventions. Rules and recommendations likewise saved time. And while legislative guides have been time consuming to negotiate, UNCITRAL learned that it might work on a far broader range of issues when drafting a legislative guide than a convention, and in either technology, when drafting flexibly.

It also learned that precision might come in the form of commentary, and that the decision between whether an issue would be addressed in the commentary or recommendations justified by that commentary might in turn provide flexibility within a legislative guide. Depending on the shifting sense of a working group, materials on which consensus could not be reached might be relocated from the recommendations back to the commentary; conversely, materials thought to be critical by influential delegations could be made more imperative by moving them from the commentary into the form of a recommendation. The content moves the formal locus where the micropolitics of working group negotiation permit. And, as such, the commentary allows room for defusing disagreement on an issue by reporting that dissent has been not only registered but also debated in an open setting. By including dissenting views in the commentary at length, even where the working group chose not to incorporate those views into its recommendations, delegations may be convinced that the process was fair and the content of the technology complete. Country delegates could signal to their ministries that national opinions were expressed and recorded.

Flexibility might also be exercised in terms of the language of obligation in which an article or rule or recommendation was drafted. Flexibility in the language of obligation often allowed UNCITRAL to reach consensus on difficult issues, albeit a consensus that left states recursive discretion: The main sticking points in the Working Groups on Secured Transactions and on International Transport (that is, acquisition financing and volume contracts) only got resolved by deviating from their usually prescriptive language and including instead permissive provisions. At other times, this flexibility allowed UNCITRAL to avoid or defer for future negotiations those potentially obstructive issues that might forestall a completed product. The Insolvency Working Group deliberately chose to avoid making a detailed recommendation on the treatment of employees' claims in an insolvency setting, and any recommendation whatsoever on the whether a company's directors and officers ought to be held liable for keeping a business up and running although insolvent. The Secured Transactions Working Group also deliberately delayed resolution of issues pertaining to security interests in intellectual property collateral and any detailed discussion of registry systems until after the Secured Transactions Guide had been published. Similarly, the International Transport Working Group intentionally stopped short of drafting a full-fledged multimodal transport convention, although many delegates might have preferred one and may yet prevail in the more extensive negotiations this would require.

Softer sorts of recommendations may signal areas of importance as to which an obligation of review and comprehension may be felt in subsequent episodes of global lawmaking. The Insolvency Working Group's reliance on constraining or focusing recommendations allowed more than empty gestures – remaining "nearly hands off" with architectural recommendations or a combination of norms of disclosure and minimalism in the Insolvency Guide, but also returning to some of the thorniest issues (such as corporate groups and director's and officer's liability in the zone of insolvency) with subsequent lawmaking projects. The Working Group on Secured Transactions similarly signaled that detailed agreement on international standards on the form of a registry system for security rights was one issue too many, but circled back to that issue after concluding the Secured Transactions Guide and a supplement to it on intellectual property collateral. So, too, the International Transport Working Group drafted as far as industry developments permitted on the topic of electronic transport documents, but left in the Rotterdam Rules sufficient flexibility for technical and contractual development within a fledging industry.

A further key finding indicates that the format of a legislative guide is itself flexible enough so that it can employ either a wide range of rule-types or hew more closely to imperative recommendations. This distinction between types of legislative guides may hold significance in terms of incremental effects and intentions. The Working Group's success in drafting the Secured Transactions Guide with mostly prescriptive language may have convinced the UNCITRAL's governing Commission to take up work on a Model Law on Secured Transactions, which is to date nearly complete; the Insolvency Group's failure in this regard may also explain the Commission's continuing reticence to accept the challenge to move toward a model law or convention on the topic of insolvency law.

The flexibility given by a combination of the formal elements and rule-types also enabled all three working groups to throw something of a veil over the obvious appearance of dominance by the US bloc, with this blurring of hegemony in turn assisting the groups to reach agreement. The Insolvency Guide rarely adopts a US position that is at odds with global norms, but simultaneously maintained sufficiently close proximity to US corporate reorganization law that UNCITRAL maintained the loyalty, and forestalled any prospect of withdrawal, by the US delegation and various non-state delegations representing the interests of American professionals, businesses, and financial institutions. As a result, many of the features integral to US corporate reorganization law, such as a debtor-in-possession, are permitted, not imposed, just as the centrality of courts in France or the powers of administrators in Britain or the locus of bankruptcy administration in the executive branch as in Colombia are authorized but not made mandatory. This result would not have been achievable except for the wide array of rule-types that the Working Group invented and used in the Guide.

In the other working groups this veiling of powerful actor interests was accomplished through invention of unique terms or concepts – i.e., "acquisition financing transactions," "maritime plus," "electronic transport documents," and "volume contracts." By differentiating existing legal practices from these new, inventive, modern commercial concepts, UNCITRAL could secure the active involvement and agreement of the US delegation but not drive away the others.

Driving Recursive Cycles of Legal Change

Despite the considerable effort required to draft them, not every convention enters into force, not every model law is implemented through adoption of domestic legislation, and not every legislative guide gains normative appeal. Many hoped that UNCITRAL's broad representativeness across geographic, economic, and political lines would mean that its legal technologies, regardless their form, would be more likely to enter into force or get implemented or followed than those produced by some less-than-global legislature.

To an important degree, the likelihood that international, national and local actors in a TLO settle in alignment on, and institutionalize, texts produced by a lawmaking IO depends on the representative and technical legitimacy of that IO. But as amply demonstrated by our case studies, law matters, too, and not just the substance of the international instrument but also the form in which the substance is cast.

The degree to which the formal properties of a legal technology encourage states to follow the norms set out in that technology, or permit states the flexibility to adapt to local contexts within the parameters of the norms, will affect the likelihood of future corrective or amending cycles of transnational lawmaking or the emergence of competitive norms that do permit adaptive flexibility. If a technology gives national legislatures ample room for maneuvering so they may readily adapt to local circumstances, and cycle quickly through amendments to fit a global standard to national and local consequences, then this will reduce the pressure from states to reform either the form or content of global norms. Conversely, if a product is broadly rejected by states, and thus fails to achieve widespread transnational legal order, or if market or technological or political upheavals unsettle pre-existing alignments, then there is an increased probability that the same or another IO will step into the legal void and draft an alternative text for global adoptions.

The form of the legal technologies that a lawmaking IO produces, and the language in which they are drafted, affect implementation and institutionalization of the law-like texts that get produced. Form also holds implications for likely reactions within a TLO to influences for unsettling and realignment.

First, the flexibility across different legal technologies may reflect more-or-less national obligation (or language of obligation) and more-or-less ability to reserve authority for domestic actors. Softer sorts of recommendations leave enormous space for domestic legislatures or private actors to exercise sovereignty or agency. Legislative guides reserve external political control for domestic legislatures. The flexibility in this technology means that domestic legislatures enjoy considerable freedom over the subject matter addressed by a guide; that guides often broadly cover a range of topics within an issue-area, offering specific recommendations rather than simply commentary, with many of the recommendations crafted using precise and detailed language means that this flexibility is fraught with international content. Domestic legislatures retain sovereignty over the subject area covered by a legislative guide, but if these domestic legislatures look to comply with the international standards set forth in a guide, if they take their obligation of review and comprehension seriously, they must read the recommendations and commentary carefully and often must read between these lines of text. Even multilateral conventions may be drafted to include permissive language, to open up the package deal or to fail to delegate implementation and enforcement obligations to third parties and even potentially to reserve discretion for domestic implementation agents (whether in the form of default rules or open-ended standards).

But, second, as much as flexibility in a soft law technology's language of obligation and reservation of domestic authority can provide recursive benefits, a lack of precision may well undermine these benefits. Uncertainty and lack of specificity can beget unsettling effects after a legal technology is implemented. Moreover, bright-line rules drafted with the assistance of a wide array of state and non-state actors might also provide some level of assurance to domestic legislatures that the legal technology has been thoroughly vetted, carefully prepared and comes with a stamp of approval. Maximizing domestic involvement and thus national sovereignty may be preferred on subjects of social, cultural, redistributive importance, but may not be preferred on all issues involving complex and technical commercial and financial regulation.

UNCITRAL's wide array of legal technologies may assist in the recursive project of juggling interests in preserving sovereignty, acquiring technical expertise, enabling transnational coordination and allowing for the involvement state and non-state actors with a range of experience and interest.

In this regard, commentary written to include both sides of an argument holds a significant didactic role to play outside UNCITRAL's legislative chamber. When it comes time to implement the recommendations set out in a legislative guide, the commentary can educate domestic lawmakers in that it identifies a international consensus where one exists, including especially on what issues should be addressed in legislation on a topic, as well as explaining the costs and benefits of various alternatives. Moreover, after implementation, a legislative guide may assist judges and other adjudicators when it comes time for them to interpret laws enacted to implement the guide, in that it may serve as a sort of "legislative history" and provide important background to explain choices made by these lawmakers (Int: 2071). UNCITRAL also promulgates guides to enactment alongside model laws in order to bridge voids between the lawmaking IO and adjudicators. Occasionally, even conventions may be coupled with official or unofficial commentary, although formal agreement can be complicated as a matter of international law.

Dynamics of Lawmaking Ecologies

As UNCITRAL invented technologies that left more discretion for national actors, or that were drafted with open-ended language, or with few details, it succeeded in promulgating a greater number of products. The quickening pace of production suggests that invention of new products has a temporal logic that links productivity to resources. The more texts promulgated by UNCITRAL in a given period of time, the more competitive it has been vis-à-vis other lawmaking bodies in its ecology and the more compelling its case for enhanced resources. Simultaneously, therefore, UNCITRAL's expansion of its technological offerings promised to solve two legitimation problems – the legitimation paradox that arises from universal representativeness; and the legitimation claim to effectiveness in prior norm production.

Its expanding list of technologies comes at some risk, however. UNCITRAL was created to promote the "unification and harmonization" of laws permitting or promoting international trade and commerce. The more discretionary the technology, the less likely it was to have a unifying or harmonizing effect on global norms. UNCITRAL resolved this legitimation paradox, partly, through adapting its mission statement to account for the need for "modernization" of global norms to address technical and market innovation and, partly, through embracing the incrementalisms through which it worked over the long arc of time.[71]

The politics of legal technologies therefore confronted three ecological challenges that were identified in Chapter 1. With respect to setting *boundaries*, it can be argued that the softer law technologies, certainly in the case of insolvency, enabled UNCITRAL to reach issues that previously had appeared so deeply entrenched in local cultures and histories that no meaningful global norms could produce convergence on norms that might govern a single transnational legal order. By manipulating the internal properties of the maritime transport convention, UNCITRAL managed to expand its legal scope not only from port-to-port but, under certain conditions, also door-to-door. As a result, UNCITRAL expanded the legal and geographical scope of the issue-ecology and its centrality in the lawmaking ecology.

With respect to *resources*, we have shown that a quickening combination of products that reaches areas of market regulation previously thought out of legal reach have kept resource-rich actors within UNCITRAL's political catchment area. As importantly, its wide range of legal technologies underwrites two different incrementalisms. The variety of technologies allowed UNCITRAL to "stand on the shoulders of giants" and engage in pyramidal incrementalism, whereby UNCITRAL could take products already promulgated by the IMF or World Bank or other IOs. Likewise, vertical incrementalism – the hardening of soft law – was enabled by

[71] For discussion of these incrementalisms, see (Chapter 2; Block-Lieb and Halliday 2007b).

UNCITRAL's portfolio of technologies that could permit a legislative guide in one round of normmaking to be "hardened" into a model law in the next round.

There may also be an ecological logic that inheres in commentary and other explanatory text that frames a technology. To facilitate adoption by national lawmakers, the commentary in a legislative guide or guide to enactment related to a model law makes overall claims about the importance of implemention for investment, economic development, and integration into the world economy. These claims assert more than the merits of the proposals explicated with the commentary: they also look to establish the effectiveness of substantive approach spelled out in the commentary and recommendations; the fairness of the deliberations that produced the commentary and recommendations; and the legitimacy of the lawmaking IO out of which these emerged. Because there exist multiple IOs engaged in the production of potentially interrelated and overlapping global norms, claims of expertise, representativeness, and transparency by one IO will be perceived and judged relative to those by the others. Explanatory text of all sorts provides an opportunity for an IO to engage in a rhetoric of self-validation (Halliday, Block-Lieb, and Carruthers 2009b).

With respect to *processes*, varieties of technologies become integral to the interplay of competition, cooperation, cooptation, and differentiation among global lawmakers. By diversifying its forms of legal texts, UNCITRAL could expand its substantive reach to compete effectively with other IOs, as it did in a threatening competition over a comprehensive secured transactions product with UNIDROIT. Its ability to integrate corporate insolvency norms into a legislative guide made it an effective competitor with the World Bank and its promulgation of principles at a higher order of abstraction and diagnostic instruments at a more detailed level. By manipulating the internal properties of legislative guides, UNCITRAL's deliberations managed to mitigate conflict and ensure a cooperative outcome. And by tailoring its instruments with care, UNCITRAL managed to differentiate itself, and thus forestall potentially crippling competition, from the World Bank on insolvency norms and from UNCTAD on norms governing unimodal train and truck transport. We return to these points of friction in Chapter 9, but for now emphasize that UNCITRAL's centrality in this standing ecology does not depend on the hardness of the technologies it promulgates. Enhancing its productivity by inventing new soft law technologies can underwrite its legitimacy and thus its survival.

* * * * *

Both for black-letter lawyers and many social science observers of transnational norms a close analysis of UNCITRAL's technologies and texts demonstrates that exercise of power and its accommodation should not be under-estimated in the seemingly neutral formalism of international instruments. Put another way, there are vastly more politics in the *form* of texts that inscribe global norms than is conventionally imagined. By scrutinizing the rhetorical structure of technologies in general and even variations in products using the same technology, it can be observed that a certain drama is uncovered in the seemingly dry concatenations of objectives and glossaries, commentaries and rules, preambles, and concepts.

As importantly for social scientists, whose theories of organizations can overestimate the degree of inertia in organizational life-courses or the degree of constraint supposedly fixed by path dependence, UNCITRAL's invention and manipulation of diverse legal technologies indicates its development of an expansive flexibility and adaptive capacity to changed circumstances in its standing lawmaking ecology and in the larger international political economy. Where adaptive capacities of international organizations have previously been focused on governance structures and internal procedures, we have shown that organizational behavior of a lawmaking IO may also be reflected in and enabled through the form of its texts.

7

Whose Global Norms?

If law is consequential for global markets, then actors with interests in that trade – material and ideal, substantive and technical, immediate and long term – will strive to shape law in contours consistent with their interests. We have shown in Chapters 3 and 4 that small numbers of well-resourced actors were centrally placed in issue ecologies to shape what issues were drawn into UNCITRAL's lawmaking arenas and which were excluded. Early deals took some issues off the table and excluded certain actors from the lawmaking. Other deals expanded or contracted the bounds of lawmaking. Many incipient conflicts, however, remained open for negotiation and resolution in the course of UNCITRAL deliberations, in some cases to the ultimate moments of decision making.

We demonstrated that a very small core of high-attendance delegations and delegates were consistently at the negotiating table in each issue-area (Chapter 4) and that this a tiny subset of delegates in addition had special access outside of formal meetings (Chapter 5). These delegates had capacities to channel extensive tangible and intangible resources into UNCITRAL as a lawmaking body. It should follow that the substantive outcomes, the imprints of power in the final norms promulgated by UNCITRAL, should disproportionately reflect the interests of these very few actors.

We examine this strong proposition by proceeding in three parallel steps for each issue-area. First, we identify the principal faultlines that implicitly or manifestly divided the actors in the lawmaking space. In ecological terms, we draw a verbal portrait of the ways that UNCITRAL's lawmaking arenas were divided not only in terms of centrality or peripherality in resources and participation but how the lawmaking space was criss-crossed by major faultlines that divided actors. Prospects of competition and even conflict created a significant challenge. The lawmaking capacity of the ecology can be assayed by the degree which those conflicts and competition could be turned into cooperation or competitive cooperation ultimately to be inscribed in legal norms for the world.

Second, we study the processes through which points of friction might be turned into instances of accord. Methodologically, and in order to cut through the enormous undergrowth of technical law, we focus on the "Big Deals" that delegates and delegations believed critical to overcome principal rifts. To settle on contested global norms required the extensive deployment of formal and informal tactics. We identify those tactics, most especially those that deployed the formal properties of legal technologies (see Chapter 6).

Third, we reach the question too often side-stepped in ecological or spatial theories of social action: which actors disproportionately placed strong imprints on UNCITRAL's global norms? From the vantage point of politics, this question can be seen in terms of power and influence. From the perspective of social interaction in ecologies, it must properly seen as a complex interplay of competitive and cooperative processes, of relations among actors, of emergence from the collectivity and community they created in the years of lawmaking they intimately shared.

Evidence from these empirical investigations becomes especially salient for predicting the fortunes of prospective transnational legal orders (TLOs). Insofar as UNCITRAL's lawmaking ecologies occur in a transnational sphere of norm-making, and at best reflect selective current or preferred norms of state and non-state actors situated in this transnational space, they do not in themselves constitute a TLO. However, the interactions that produced Big Deals, and the substantive, procedural, and formal properties of the legal norms in which those Deals were cast, have far-reaching implications for the probabilities that concordant norms will be adopted by state and non-state actors and become part of the mentalities of actors who are charged with implementing norms in localities worldwide.

Each lawmaking episode therefore also requires analysis of processes and outcomes affecting the probability that norms formulated by an IO will become truly global norms governing national and international market behaviors. If the Big Deals required norms to be crafted in vague terms, or if states are given varieties of options in order to reach consensus, then indeterminacies, inconsistencies or even contradictions may lead to further cycles of lawmaking at all levels to produce the certainty or predictability that businesses often covet. If actor mismatch in deliberations leads to the triumph of hegemonic actors in global lawmaking, and these are contested by state or non-state actors marginalized in the lawmaking, then probabilities rise that UNCITRAL's norms will be rejected or subverted at national and local levels. And if rigidities are built into the formal rhetorical expression of the global norms themselves, then they may be rejected by states on grounds of their irrelevance or lack of respect for sovereign discretion. In short, the dynamics of reaching Big Deals, and the substantive and formal properties of the Big Deals, cast long shadows over the probability that global legal norms will become concordant with national and local norms.

TRANSPORTING GOODS

Faultlines and Interests

A high percentage of the world's manufactured goods move through international waters at some stage of their transport from manufacture to markets. This is not simply a matter of conveying goods from one continent to another, across the Pacific or Atlantic or Indian Oceans. Often it is cheaper for goods to be moved within the Americas or Europe or Asia by ships that navigate international waters.

Sea transport has risks and potential costs – of goods that are damaged or destroyed en route, of schedules that are disrupted, of goods that are diverted and never arrive. TLOs that govern transport of goods are designed to assign liability for things that go wrong according to uniform and predictable rules. The assignment of liability to shipowners or operators, the ship's crews or builders, becomes a matter that is commercially and economically consequential. These liability rules affect the pricing of goods, manufacturers' competitiveness, competition among states, and ultimately, markets and economic development.

Classically, the deep divide of interests over transport of goods by sea pitted carriers (i.e., the owners and operators of seafaring vessels) against shippers (i.e., importers or exporters of goods by ship). As we observed in Chapter 3, carriers' market power has historically prevailed over shippers, with the effect that the contract terms offered by carriers were not subject to much negotiation or variation. Before international treaties on the topic, those terms might have exculpated liability altogether, or limited liability levels in ways that strongly favored carriers. Even after the entry into force of treaties to limit such contracts, states that had large fleets benefited over states that did not, creating an asymmetry in global markets that until recently worked in favor of the Global North and against the Global South.

Far-reaching transformations in industry and international trade in recent decades have blurred this divide. Huge multinational corporations like Samsung and Lenovo and Nokia and Amazon – shippers – may exert market power that can match or exceed that of carriers. While many of these multinationals are headquartered in the most powerful economic nations, however, their operations and chains of distribution are often scattered among many countries.

The carrier industry has also changed significantly over the past fifty years. The undisputed and unquestioned market power of liner conferences has subsided sufficiently for exemptions from competition law to get removed recently in the EU and elsewhere.[1] Carrier industries have also shifted their footprint on the

[1] The Hague Rules harmonized questions of liability for loss during carriage, but did not otherwise affect the market power of liner conferences, which until the early twenty-first century enjoyed wide exemption from national and transnational competition laws. Broad changes in regulatory approach occurred in both the US in the late 1980s and in the EU in the late 2000s. For discussion of these regulatory changes and analysis of their economic effects, see (US Federal and Analysis 2012).

global map, so that formerly powerful carrier nations, such as Great Britain, the US, and a handful of European nations, now have much diminished seafaring industries compared to China, South Korea, and Japan. Moreover, the residence and and political influence of a carrier has grown less clear since the early twentieth century because modern flagging practices mean that a carrier's owners might reside in one nation but they are governed by laws of another, such as Panama or Greece.

Most significantly, containerization of goods makes problematic any legal approach that seeks to render transport by sea as a discrete segment of an entire chain of transport of goods to market. Goods most often now are loaded into containers far from ports and stay in those containers as they move across land by road or rail, then by seafaring vessel, then back to rail or road transport, until they reach their final destination. This makes it very difficult to ascertain where damage or destruction of goods might have taken place. Containerization also created market incentives for integrated transport, which now often is carried out, or at least organized, by a single actor. This actor might be a single carrier who covers different modes of transport or a freight forwarder who arranges for transport by a series of traditional carriers. Such integration of varieties and sequences of transport permits the possibility of a single contract to cover the shipment of a container of good from Point A to Point B, even though Point A might be Witchita, Kansas and Point B might be Moscow.

Nonetheless, there remain deeply entrenched interests that can pit TLOs that govern transport by sea versus those that govern transport by rail or road or river or canal. While it might be rational and efficient in theory for a single legal order to cover the entire transport of goods door-to-door, longstanding industries and legal orders exist within countries and regions that have their own predictable legal standards and levels of liability. Hence any effort by one mode of transport (i.e., by sea) to develop a legal order that encroaches on or incorporates other legal orders (e.g., by rail or road) is likely to meet strong resistance. Not only do railways or trucking companies have economic interests at stake, but so, too, do freight forwarders, the industry that links one form of transport (e.g., sea) with another (e.g., rail and road). All of these interests could be expected to mobilize energetically to protect their market position, should it be threatened.

Historically, extensive insurance industries have also grown around transport of goods by sea. Sometimes they are cooperatives of carriers themselves. Sometimes they are private dedicated or generalist insurance companies. Some insurers specialize in providing coverage to shippers' interests, while others focus on insuring the ship and carriers' potential liability for cargo in the ship's hold. Generally, insurers' interests mesh with those of the industries they insure, but because insurance companies' perspectives exist as repeat players over multiple carriers or shippers, their focus can favor the longterm over the here and now.

We saw in Chapter 3 that at least three international organizations could claim authority for drafting of international trade law governing sea transport:

CMI (International Maritime Confederation), UNCITRAL, and UNCTAD. Since historically each of these had also been associated with a particular set of commercial interests (CMI with carriers; UNCITRAL and UNCTAD with developing countries), each came to the negotiations with a past, even if each also could argue that the past no longer adequately characterized their contemporaneous interests or capacities.

The large number and diversity of delegations that actively participated in Transportation Working Group sessions demonstrate both the distributive significance of transport law and the focus that diplomatic negotiations on an international convention can bring to bear. We reported in Chapter 4 a larger number of high-attendance delegations in the Transportation Working Group than in either the Insolvency or Secured Transactions Working Groups.[2] Moreover, unlike the Insolvency Working Group, there were more high-attendance delegations to the Transportation Working Group from developing and transitional economies than from advanced economies.[3] While this distribution of high-attendance delegations suggests the possibility that developing and transitional delegations were a strong source of influence in the Transportation Working Group, our data on high-attendance delegates complicates this story line (Chapter 4). The high-attendance delegates to the Transportation Working Group were overwhelmingly from advanced economies.[4] Moreover, not all economic interests were represented at International Transport Working Group sessions. There were multiple delegations representing the interests of carriers, of carriers' insurers, and of carriers' lawyers and other professionals. There were also high-attendance delegations and delegates there to ensure that the interests of rail and road carriers were preserved. None of the high-attendance non-state delegations or delegates expressly served the interests of shippers, however.

Chapter 5 further complicates the question of access to working group sessions by demonstrating a back door to the Secretariat through expert working groups and other informal meeting places. While the Secretariat strived to remain transparent about the occurrence of this informal work and to extend invitations to expert sessions that were representative of the interests involved, not everyone agreed that it succeeded in satisfactorily mirroring formal protections in informal settings (Chapter 10).

[2] In the International Transport Working Group, there were 56 high-attendance delegations, 45 of which were state delegations. The Insolvency Group saw 35 such delegations (29 state delegations), and the Secured Transactions Group 40 (31 state delegations).

[3] In the Insolvency Working Group, there were 16 high-attendance delegations from advanced economies and 13 from developing/transitional economies, while the high-attendance delegations to the International Transport Group more likely to come from developing than advanced economies (19 advanced; 26 developing/transitional).

[4] Thirty-two of the forty high-attendance state delegates to the International Transport Working Group were from advanced nations; the ten high-attendance non-state delegates were also all from advanced nations.

Big Deals

The Transportation Working Group deliberated for six years to write a convention containing roughly 100 articles. Consensus is difficult to achieve in any context, but it is especially difficult when writing a draft convention. Under international law, contracting states consent to the terms of a convention – all of them. In the negotiations to produce a draft, delegations must decide whether the benefits of the provisions they like outweigh the detriments of the provisions they don't like. In a convention on the carriage of goods by sea, bargaining may be zero sum. As a result, these were high stakes negotiations; the politics were sharpened because deals were likely to produce tangibly distributive outcomes along distinct economic interests. The influence of economic and national and political interests is often palpable on the face of Working Group texts. Even more, the bargaining, maneuvers of cooperation, and competition can be observed off-stage in the writing and rehearsing of the script later unveiled to the world.

The Rotterdam Rules are technically complex.[5] We focus here on the end result and not the details of these negotiations. In interviews, core delegates highlighted four Big Deals that determined the contours of the draft convention. Each of these Big Deals emerged from conflicting interests of vocal actors. Sometimes, these were one-off deals, and sometimes these were package deals that were balanced with negotiating outcomes of other deals. We review below the interplay of actors, interests and deals in each of these four sites of legislative bargaining.

Port-to-Port versus Door-to-Door

As seafaring transport containerized, the limited scope of existing transport conventions seemed antiquated. While containerized transport often involved transport organized from door-to-door, the Hague Rules governed the shipment only from tackle-to-tackle – measuring liability from the moment the goods were being loaded onto the ship to the moment they were taken off; drafted fifty years later than the Hague Rules, the Hamburg Rules covered from the moment that goods arrived in a departure port to the moment they left the arrival port, but no further.

In the actual behavior of market actors the contracts between carriers (ships, but also trains, trucks, planes) and shippers (manufacturers, distributors) were more adept than conventions in keeping pace with industry innovation. Some industry giants, such as the huge Danish shipping multinational, Maersk, had begun to take matters into their own hands. Maersk already had a contract it offered to shippers known as a combined contract "where the carrier accepted responsibility for the whole period – from inland receipt to inland destination," unless it could be proved that the damage had occurred on a specific leg of the journey and that mandatory law covering that leg superseded the combined contract (Int: 6002, 8003). Even if

5 See, e.g., (Carlson 2009; Faria 2005; Sturley, Fujita, and van der Ziel 2010)

carriage did not occur though a single carrier's door-to-door contract for carriage, freight forwarders might replicate this vertical integration through contract.

Pre-existing international agreements continued to complicate industry efforts to unify practices, however. A multiplicity of actual and rising TLOs threatened to subvert the certainties craved by carriers and shippers alike. An agreement governing all forms of transport was complicated by a patchwork of international and regional agreements, which had long set expectations within air, road, and rail transport industries in distinct ways. National and organizational interests had ossified around the complicated reality that each form of transport had learned to live with.

At the boundary-negotiating and agenda-setting phase of UNCITRAL's deliberations, CMI and the UNCITRAL Commission were a little uncertain about how far to push for a comprehensive solution that moved beyond port-to-port to a convention that extended door-to-door (Chapter 3). CMI proposed a bold advance beyond existing but old-fashioned rules. UNCITRAL feared heavy opposition from unimodal carriers, such as the European road and rail industries. The UNCITRAL Secretariat wanted to avoid opposition that might complicate negotiations and create stalemate, a potential recipe for failure on the heels of its earlier failure with the Hamburg Rules. UNCTAD clung to its preference for adoption of a single convention governing all modes of transnational transport, but was loath to cede jurisdiction over non-seafaring transport to UNCITRAL. UNCTAD's earlier Multimodal Convention had failed to enter into force, but its Multimodal Rules had been more successful; an UNCITRAL convention that extended beyond seafaring transport would threaten UNCTAD's multimodal claims.

National interests were also complicated. The US did not place the issue of the legal scope of the convention at the top of its declared package of "musts" from the negotiations. The German transport industry was divided and cautious, which created a similar impetus for caution in the German delegation. The Dutch delegate hoped that a solution at UNCITRAL might solve a high liability problem in transport law and practice in the Netherlands (Int: 6542). Still, the sense of CMI's suggestion on expanding the scope of the draft convention resonated within the Working Group.

But expansion of this substantive scope would require expanding the decision makers in the chamber. Core delegates recognized that not only were there incipient conflicts among sea, road, rail, and other transport interests, but international lawmaking bodies themselves, such as UNCITRAL and UNCTAD, were embedded in a lawmaking ecology. Shifting alliances between IOs, states and non-state actors could lead to deep rifts, conflict, or stalemate among coalitions for one or another solution to the door-to-door problem.

CMI's leaders, who were acutely conscious of the divisions in industry and among IOs, entered the UNCITRAL arena with a clever innovation that effectively blurred the boundaries between door-to-door and port-to-port regimes. The draft instrument put on the table by CMI at the first session of the Transport Working Group offered a limited door-to-door regime that retained and reformed the conventional elements of maritime transport law, but with some add-ons. CMI proposed that so long as there was a seafaring leg in the journey of goods to market, there might be circumstances in which the liability regime should extend for the whole journey. Put another way, CMI opened up the prospect of a transnational legal order centered on sea transport, but with the potential to radiate out to embrace other kinds of inland transport.

For carriers and some large shippers and for many national delegations this position held considerable appeal. It struck a mid-point between a fully multimodal approach, which had thus had far eluded global lawmakers, and the now antiquated port-to-port approach that inhered in the Hague Rules. Rail and road transport interests were unlikely to object to this arrangement if it didn't interfere with the protections they already enjoyed. But should UNCITRAL defer to all national protections, or just those set forth in international and regional conventions?

Innovators in the Transportation Working Group sought to negotiate this fine line, potentially a trigger for many kinds of opposition, by inventing the concept of "maritime-plus" (Fujita 2009). This new entrant to the vocabulary of international trade law had the double merit that it signaled to other transport national and transnational legal orders that a sea leg constituted a necessary condition of the new TLO, but that legs could be added, under non-threatening conditions, to unify liability rules for all parties across the entire trade route. To that new concept, UNCITRAL's lawmakers added another – "maritime performing parties" to distinguish between "performing parties" focused on the sea leg, and those focused solely on road, rail or air transport linked to the maritime portion of the transit. The draft convention thereby clearly demarcated between the two sorts of liability.

These innovations immediately raised two questions. Would a "maritime-plus" convention supersede other international or transnational conventions on transport of goods by air, rail, or road? And would the "plus" part of the new convention trump domestic law on liability for rail or road transport? In the end, the deal-makers decided it was prudent to defer to existing European-wide laws and similar multilateral conventions (Schelin 2009). But if there were conflicts between the Rotterdam Rules and the laws of a given state, the final deal concluded that a country ratifying the Rotterdam Rules would be agreeing in practice that UNCITRAL's "maritime-plus" regime would prevail over domestic law at any point where they disagreed (Art. 26).

This Big Deal satisfied many delegations. For some countries, such as the Netherlands, and even the US, the "maritime-plus" approach could solve problems that had defied national reforms. If the US Congress couldn't act, for instance, then UNCITRAL's lawmakers offered an international end run around the incapacities of domestic lawmakers. For others, the Rotterdam Rules' "maritime-plus" approach presented an efficient and elegant filling of a gap in international agreement on rules for liability in certain sorts of transport; rather than negotiate multiple treaties to cover varied forms of transport, the Rotterdam Rules would govern with uniformity. And for those already governed by an existing transnational agreement, such as delegates from states bound to the CMR Convention or COTIF, the Rotterdam Rules left the settled legal order alone (Schelin 2009).

Who was dissatisfied by this creative deal? Some states, especially vast states like China, Russia, Brazil and India, which had attended UNCITRAL working group sessions to draft a convention, they thought, which addressed only port-to-port transport, found that their domestic laws governing liability and limitation levels on land carriage or inland waterways were potentially subordinated to liability provisions in the Rotterdam Rules if, at some point in the carriage, there was a seafaring leg. There may also have been displeasure emanating from UNCTAD. Although UNCTAD delegates to UNCITRAL denied this, other UNCITRAL delegates thought that UNCTAD was unhappy with the scope of a "maritime-plus" regime in the Rotterdam Rules. Said one participant, "They want[ed] to preserve for themselves the entire question of transportation and its relationship with the Third World and the development of the trade" (Int: 8002, 6008). As written, the breadth of the Rotterdam Rules could substantially limit UNCTAD's involvement as a lawmaking body on issues of transport if the convention enters into force.

Contracting out of a Multilateral Convention

Earlier treaties on international transport had locked carriers and shippers into global rules that gave them no flexibility to opt out and bargain privately among themselves. The substance of the rules themselves offered no prospects for adaptive and innovative alternative ways for carriers and shippers to come to private agreements to address changing circumstances.

The US signaled right at the outset of negotiations that this had to change: the ability of shippers to negotiate the terms of a contract that would allow the parties to opt out of the convention was a deal-breaker. US shippers, especially large, volume importers and exporters, were already accustomed to US laws that enabled parties to contract around loss limitations on liability and other aspects of sea transport. The US delegation refused to be party to any UNCITRAL trade laws that did not contain what they construed as contractual freedoms. Unless the world adopted US practices, the US would not sign on to new global norms.

The US position immediately rang alarm bells among other delegates and delegations. The so-called freedom of contract touched on a fundamental issue of shifts in carriers' market power relative to shippers. Conferences of liner companies, which act as common carriers across oceans by offering scheduled services and published tariffs, held near monopoly power in the late nineteenth century. As a result, the contracts governing the terms on which these liners offered sea transport were often nonnegotiable, standardized contracts that contained provisions exculpating carriers from any liability for delay, loss or damage to goods in transit. Some national courts enforced these contracts; others invalidated them (Sturley 1991).

The resulting lack of uniformity undermined international trade, until diplomatic agreement on the Hague Rules in the early twentieth century.

For both carriers and shippers, the merit of a convention with fixed liability rates generally was to create a legal order providing the protection of certainty and predictability about the commercial viability of shipping goods to market across international waters. All parties from all nations, great or small, would be subject to exactly the same rules. Under the Hague and Hague-Visby Rules, however, shippers frequently asserted that these fixed rules favored carriers. By contrast, carriers and carrier nations described UNCITRAL's failed Hamburg Rules as too favorable to shippers. Whoever was favored, however, in either case levels were fixed, and all carriers and shippers trading under the mandatory rules of the convention were locked into the same rates once their countries ratified the convention.

Both carriers and shippers, particularly in the US, had begun to press against fixed rules. In the changing balance of power between carriers and shippers, the market power of large shippers had increased to the extent that they could negotiate better deals with carriers – and thus improve their competitive advantage – when these negotiations were legally permissible. Since the mid-1980s, US law enabled a carrier and shipper to opt out of the US Carriage of Goods by Sea Act and negotiate their own agreement, including agreements on liability limits. By 2003, the US delegation made clear to the Transport Working Group that UNCITRAL had to have something analogous in the convention if the US were to sign on to the final deals (Carlson 2009: 272). By throwing down this gauntlet, the US essentially put all other delegations and the UNCITRAL Secretariat on notice that it must not be ignored on this make-or-break interest.

Freedom to contract out of the convention was difficult to embrace for many delegations accustomed to nearly a century of conventions containing only mandatory terms. Some delegations – Australia, New Zealand, France, the European Shippers Council – did not want a shipper's ability to enter into a volume contract to step outside a convention's fixed liability limits because they thought carriers would exercise undue duress on shippers to opt out in order to sign contracts that would be to the carrier's advantage. In order words, they feared that the very provisions in earlier conventions that protected shippers could now be side-stepped to weaken shippers. The French delegate, for example, accepted big shippers might be in a position to negotiate at arms' length with carriers, e.g., "the Walmarts of the world" (Int: 6009), but worried that the volume contract provisions would benefit only these very large shippers. Small shippers might not be able to negotiate favorable contracts for themselves and, thus, wouldn't benefit and might even be competitively harmed by the contract provisions in a new convention. If the US were to prevail in including opt-out provisions in the draft convention, these delegations sought protections for the interests of small and medium sized shippers within these opt-outs.

For two years, quiet negotiations proceeded within "an informal drafting group composed of a number of delegations," ultimately coming up with a breakthrough brokered by Finland (Int: 6002, 8003). The breakthrough relied on yet another invention – the introduction of a new legal concept, "volume contracts." This innovation had the twin merits of avoiding terminology that was clearly associated with the laws of any given country and adding to UNCITRAL's growing lexicon of invented legal terms. The move reinforced the notion that UNCITRAL's forum and Secretariat were inventive lawmaking sites that could forge deals over and above laws that came from particular states.

Once the informal drafting group's proposal was brought back to the Working Group in 2005, it confronted the skepticism of delegates aligned with interests of suppliers, who continued to fear that powerful carriers had found a new way of weighting global trade law in their favor. CMI was therefore charged with the task of examining the draft set of checks and balances to be sure it would offer sufficient protection to weaker parties and exclude opting out altogether in some circumstances. Discussions continued through 2007. When CMI reported back to the Working Group, it didn't hide its awareness that there "were several expressions of sympathy" for the concerns raised by shipper interests. Nevertheless, CMI concluded that the concept of "volume contracts" opened the way to a deal that "represented the best possible consensus solution to address those concerns in a manner than preserved a practical and commercially meaningful role for party autonomy in volume contracts." CMI noted that while small shippers might be unable to negotiate a volume contract of their own, they might still find ways to strengthen their bargaining position. The assumption was that "small shippers will normally go to large freight forwarders who are very powerful" (Int: 6009). Or small shippers might band together for collective bargaining.

In the final deal, the Working Group adopted the "opt-out" provisions sought by the US and supported by the CMI Report. A separate article of the Rotterdam Rules permitted opting out of the mandatory liability levels, so long as various protections were offered vulnerable parties. Thereby, the Transport Working Group added a formal innovation to its new concept of volume contracts. Although nearly every other provision of the Rotterdam Rules contain mandatory provisions that are binding once a nation accedes to its terms, the provisions on volume contracts turn much of this convention into a set of "default rules" that, within limits, parties can contract around.

Critics remained, especially those that insisted that small shippers could be disadvantaged by the very presence of the provisions on volume contracts in the new convention. This victory for the US left a residue of resistance, especially from some European countries, most notably Germany, other countries, including Australia and New Zealand, and the European Shippers Council and UNCTAD. These sources of opposition sowed the seeds for continuing resistance to the Rotterdam Rules and intimated future recursive cycles of reform.

Paying When Things Go Wrong

Previous conventions on the transport of goods by sea set specific monetary rates for circumstances in which things went wrong. These conventions stated what kinds of situations would render a carrier liable, what sorts of defenses could be erected to protect a carrier against liability claims, and what the rates of successful liability claims should be. For example, the Hague Rules limit a carrier's liability for loss to "£100 sterling per package or unit," but specify that this limit is to be "taken to be gold value," which many argue means that the relevant limit is not £100 but the current market value of the quantity of gold that was the equivalent of £100 sterling in 1924 (Diamond 1988). A parallel limit under US legislation is "frozen" at $500 per package (id.), although case law on what constitutes a "package" for purposes of COGSA remains unsettled.[6]

Liability provisions therefore had direct economic effects on commercial parties, as well as on industries and nations whose carriers conveyed goods to market or whose producers or consumers relied on the goods getting to international markets at reasonable cost. Quite apart from the distributive implications of these rules, all parties to transport wanted predictability and certainty: "It is an allocation of risk and responsibility . . . You set up what each party is responsible for [and you have] clear agreement on liability levels; then both sides know where they stand" (Int: 6010).

Under the Hague Rules, carriers had sought – and sought successfully – to keep liability levels low, to limit the range of circumstances in which they could be liable, and to give themselves as many defenses as possible. The Hamburg Rules tended to favor shippers' interests and had increased liability limits and narrowed defenses as compared to earlier conventions.

Nations that aligned more or less with the interests of carriers tended to follow similarly predictable patterns in Working Group negotiations on this issue. Nations looking to protect shippers' interests also predictably argued to the contrary. Delegations from the United Kingdom, the Scandinavian nations, and the Netherlands were inclined to favor carriers' interests in lower liability levels and limited grounds for liability, while delegations from developing nations favored shippers' interests in increasing the amounts of these levels and the grounds for liability.

But matters were more complicated than this. Because both countries were also the largest importers and exporters of goods, the US and China were both carrier and shipper nations. How then could they decide on higher or lower liability limits, more or less defenses available to carriers defending against loss?

CMI also recognized that its reputation as a carrier-friendly organization had to be modified if it were to be positioned as an objective and influential player at the core of the negotiations. The CMI spent years preparing its Initial Draft for presentation

6 (Sturley 2009). See also, e.g., Maersk Line Ltd v. United States of America, 513 F.2d 418 (4th Cir. 2008)(holding that a large wheeled vehicle with an adjustable deck that is used to load cargo onto aircrafts – a K-Loader weighing over 30,000 pounds and lifting up to 25,000 pounds of cargo – was a "package" within meaning of COGSA).

at the first Transport Working Group session; it heard from a wide range of actors and interests during this period and worked to craft what CMI perceived to be a balanced position between carriers and shippers. Effectively, the CMI Draft prefigured a balance between carrier and shipper interests.[7]

The Rotterdam Rules' final outcome on liability represented "a lot of compromises" (Int: 6011) and "a balanced allocation of risk" (Int: 6002), said two core delegates. Each side gave some and got some. Carrier-friendly delegates managed to hold off most efforts by shipper-friendly delegates to impose absolute liability in which carriers were compelled to pay for damages without any need to prove they were at fault.

Carriers "were adamant [that] there must be a demonstration of a fault in the ways goods are carried" (Int: 6011), but ultimately accepted some small sorts of absolute liability under the terms of the new convention, thus diminishing the need and costs of subsequent litigation on these issues. For example, where there were errors in navigation, carriers had long been able to deflect liability by pointing to the crew. However, as part of the deal the carrier interests agreed this would no longer serve as a defense given the sophisticated geo-mapping devices now available and computer-aided means from communication between the ship and the home office. Carriers' absolute liability also applied to maintenance of the ship during the voyage (Int: 6012; Arts. 17 and 18). To avoid liability the ship owner must show that proper steps had been taken that a ship was seaworthy not only at the start of the voyage, but also throughout the voyage (Int: 6009; Art. 17(5)(a)). As a result, carriers would have to take on more liability in some areas, e.g., fire on board or negligence of the crew (Int: 6012). Importantly, the Rotterdam Rules now impose liability for delay on carriers (Art. 17(1)).

If carrier interests were persuaded to make concessions to shippers, then shippers also were persuaded to make concessions to carriers. Shippers would agree to provide proper documentation and correct information about the cargo (Arts. 28 and 29). Shippers agreed to absolute liability for shipping dangerous goods, such as explosives (Art. 32); this extension of liability was new and viewed by carriers as extremely important (Int: 6010, 6011). In this modern world of terrorism, carriers were keen to calm crews' fears. "Misinformation," said one delegate, "can have nasty effects on ship owners, especially if they involved dangerous cargoes" (Int: 6010).

If trade-offs between carriers and shippers potentially equalized their relative commercial advantages under the Rotterdam Rules, it was the liability levels that precipitated a last-minute bargain with significant distributive consequences. In the three preceding conventions, the Hague and Hague-Visby Rules subjected carriers to lower, and Hamburg higher, mandatory levels of liability. Early on in the Transport Working Group's deliberations, the US had signaled publicly that it

7 For other examples of ways that non-state or professional associations can prefigure political agreements later in state legislatures, see (Halliday 1987).

preferred loss-liability limitations to hold steady at the levels set in the Hague-Visby Rules. By 2007, the US, China, and other delegations had reached "provisional" agreement that the loss-liability limits could go as high as those set in UNCITRAL's Hamburg Rules, but "no higher" (Int: 6007).

Late in the negotiations, however, many African nations became aware that the liability limits had real effects on their costs of getting goods to market. Led by Senegal, some fifteen African delegations formed themselves into a bloc and shocked other delegations by seeking to drive a last-minute hard bargain. For these African delegations to support a convention that clearly promoted US interests in many respects, the African delegates insisted that liability limits needed to go higher than those set under the Hamburg Rules. Likewise, the Africans stated it was impossible for them to accept the position of China that it could go no higher than limits set in the Hamburg Rules. The Senegalese delegation "made a passionate plea" on behalf of the African bloc for higher loss limits, privately admitting to some delegates that, "if we just settle for Hamburg, it will look as if we didn't get anything" (Int: 6007).

This unanticipated and rare outspokenness by developing and poor nations confounded the powerful trading nations who previously had come to some kind of consensus at much lower liability limits. With the supposed consensus in tatters, the chair of the Transport Working Group called for informal negotiations outside the chamber between the African bloc and "big players" (Int: 6007). A meeting was called among the members of African bloc and the "big players" at a break at a Working Group session late in 2008. The group was told, "we need an agreement."

The US was forced to choose. Would the US side with China (and cap the loss limits at a level equal to those that had been set in the Hamburg Rules) or with the African bloc (and agree to higher limits)? The US struck a deal with the Africans.

Why did the US align itself with a small group of tiny economies with marginal impact on global trade? US delegates later stated that they had their eye on the long game. Time and again trade conventions emerged from global legislatures and failed to obtain sufficient accessions by states to come into force. Since accessions simply count the number of states that sign and accede to a convention, irrespective of their size, power or trading significance, the African bloc got what it asked for, not because the US didn't want the Africans to "come away empty-handed" (Int: 6007), but because the US and its allied delegations recognized that fifteen immediate ratifications by African nations could take the Rotterdam Rules a long way toward reaching the goal of twenty state accessions that bring a new trade order into being. For the US, this exercise in head counting essentially pitted China's single signature to the draft convention against Africa's fifteen.

Moreover, this bargain was bundled into a larger trade-off. The US led a deal with the Africans that if the US gave them what they wanted on liability limits, then the Africans must support the US on volume contracts. In fact, this bundling of deals included also a demand by the US and its allies that the African states accept the "maritime-plus" proposal for a door-to-door transport order where circumstances permitted. "The trade off was that the Africans would stop challenging volume contracts" and would stop challenging the limited network system crafted by the Working Group. As part of the deal, "no aspect of the compromise could be re-opened at the Commission" (Int: 6007).

France, Australia and China all complained bitterly about the terms for the bargain: the loss-liability limits were too high; protections for small shippers weren't explicit enough in the volume contract provisions. Nonetheless, the bargain held firm and the Working Group adopted the new "consensus."

Resolving Disputes

We have seen that a precipitant to UNCITRAL's activism on transport law was a US Supreme Court case – *Sky Reefer*[8] – that many viewed as opening up the prospect of judicial anarchy (Chapter 3). Disputes over liability for goods carried over oceans might be channeled to national courts with no history, no competency and no independence of judicial decision making in transport law, thereby throwing determinacy of case law into complete disarray. Not only in the US, but established carrier and commercial interests in other countries reacted with alarm to the juridical disorder that was sure to follow.

In fact, neither the Hague nor the Hague-Visby Rules included provisions on court jurisdiction or arbitration, relying instead on settled legal practices developed over decades and centuries by major ocean-trading nations. While the Hamburg Rules did contain provisions on these topics, its jurisdictional rules were controversial and in any event the Hamburg Rules governed little global trade.

Major carriers and shippers had strong preferences for courts in countries with longstanding maritime law institutions, with settled law and, therefore, with relatively predictable outcomes. Of course, for the most part these courts were *their courts* and thus they likely also had a substantial home court advantage. The prospect of litigating maritime disputes in the courts of countries where there was thin or no rule of law, and unpredictable political and economic influences on judicial decisions, could not be tolerated. Likewise, some major commercial interests in the established maritime transport industry looked to the certainty of procedures for international arbitration if the contracting parties agreed to be bound in this way.

The play of interests was further complicated by tensions between strategic and short-term interests of key actors and the wisdom of the longterm. When carriers were defendants, they preferred litigation or arbitration to be in a predictable location. When carriers were plaintiffs, they might instead prefer to have control over where a dispute would be heard in order to gain a home court advantage. Conversely, where shippers were defendants, they too preferred litigation or

8 Vimar Seguros y Reaseguros, S. v. M/V Sky Reefer, 515 U.S. 528 (1995).

arbitration in a predictable location; but if they were plaintiffs, their preference for control of the location of litigation might outweigh caution. Although carriers and shippers might agree in the abstract to uniform jurisdictional rules, in the heat of litigation arguments can lead to results that most regret.

The 1995 US Supreme Court's decision in *Sky Reefer* had stunned the US maritime industry. At best, the effect of the holding in *Sky Reefer* was to "take cases out of US courts and put them in Japan and Hong Kong where there were no connections with the goods or with buyers or sellers but where the interests that owned the vessels were located" (Int: 6003, 8004). As a result, liability and other maritime disputes could be settled in courts not only in New York or London, but also in any number of jurisdictions scattered around the world. At worst, cases might be channeled to Panama or other states where many ships were registered under flags-of-convenience. One solution within the US would be to remedy the *Sky Reefer* decision legislatively, but US congressional leaders had rejected proposals for reform.

Without any progress at home, the US delegation came to UNCITRAL to seek a transnational solution to US domestic law. Indeed, this compulsion to resolve legal and commercial uncertainty – and the losses to the US maritime bar – was a primary impulse for the US to press forward the quest for a new international convention on transport law.

While the topics of arbitration and jurisdiction were absent from the CMI's Initial Draft, a key delegate believed that "on Day 1 the working group consensus was that arbitration and jurisdiction had to be there" (Int: 6002). This desire provided an opening for the legal scope of UNCITRAL's global aspirations, since it might not have otherwise pressed the case for such procedural reforms.

However, by taking on a critical problem for the US, the negotiations on jurisdiction generated problems for delegations that were member states in the European Union. Since 1968, these member states were party to the Brussels Convention on jurisdiction over civil and commercial disputes within Europe,[9] which bound European member states to a result that didn't mesh well with a draft transport convention containing jurisdictional provisions. Delegations that were members of the EU found that their hands were tied, because they "could not speak on jurisdiction" (Int: 6005).

It became clear to the Working Group that if the US wanted to cover jurisdictional issues in the new UNCITRAL convention, it had to negotiate with the

[9] 1968 Brussels Convention on Jurisdiction and the Enforcement of Judgments in Civil and Commercial Matters. The 1968 Brussels Convention has since been supplemented or replaced by other European instruments, including the 2007 Lugano Convention [2007 Lugano Convention on Jurisdiction and the Enforcement of Judgments in Civil and Commercial Matters] and two EU regulations on the topic [Council Regulation (EC) 44/2001 of December 22, 2000 on jurisdiction and the recognition and enforcement of judgments in civil and commercial matters ("Brussels I Regulation"); Regulation (EU) No. 1215/2012 of the European Parliament and of the Council of December 12, on jurisdiction and the recognition and enforcement of judgments in civil and commercial matters (recast) ("Brussels II Regulation") (effective 2015)].

European Commission. But the European Commission was *not* a member of UNCITRAL. It was not a state, and so could not send a delegation as if it were. Furthermore, it had historically bristled at the idea of sitting in UNCITRAL in the rear rows of the UN chambers with the multilateral, commercial, and professional non-state organizations. As a result, the EU had not sent observer delegations to UNCITRAL, including to its Transport Working Group sessions.

As a result, the US was compelled to engage in informal side negotiations, meeting "commissioners from the European Commission privately for dinner and then for a subsequent drafting meeting that evening in a hotel lobby" (Int: 6005). The results of this "informal drafting group" were announced at a Transport Working Group session (Int: 6005). When delegations of states in the European Union heard about the deal negotiated behind their backs, "they were mad, both on the terms of the deal and in not having had a voice at the table" (Int: 6005). Surprisingly, the European Commission seems not to have consulted first with delegates from its member countries. European Commission and member states entered a complicated dance of dyadic and multilateral discussions with the US until they reached a deal among themselves. This deal, intended to prefigure a wider Working Group agreement, was brought back to the Working Group, which adopted it with hard feelings but few changes.

The jurisdictional provisions in the draft convention may have reversed the holding the *Sky Reefer*, but the draft convention did not insist that all litigation occur in New York or London or Paris. Indeed, it permitted court actions to be brought against carriers in a range of locations: either in the place of the carriers' domicile, in the port of loading or discharge, or in various places designated by the contract of carriage (Arts. 66 and 67).

Clearly, this failure of the US, Britain, and other longstanding carrier nations to perpetuate the geographies of dispute settlement in earlier legal orders did not solve decisively the problem created by *Sky Reefer*. To find some middle ground between reproduction of past practices versus the proliferation of dispute settlement in courts across the world, delegates came to a formal solution that potentially diluted the determinacy of the Rotterdam Rules. Countries retained the right to "opt in" to the new jurisdictional provisions, which would thereby be binding only on states that affirmatively agreed to their terms. Hence the deal on jurisdiction effectively created a mini-convention within the Rotterdam Rules that was "permissive" in its terms. A country might agree to be bound by the Rotterdam Rules but not accede to these jurisdiction provisions, or it might accede both to the Rotterdam Rules and the additional jurisdictional provisions. In this respect, the final document accommodated the interests of all actors, but at the price of permitting the prospect of two jurisdictional orders existing side by side.

In theory, the negotiated arrangement on issues of jurisdiction was distinct from any agreement on the subject of arbitration. But the US delegation felt strongly that it "couldn't lose in arbitration what [it] had gained in jurisdiction" (Int: 6005).

Like the jurisdictional issue, this negotiation was also complicated by politics. The commissioners from the European Union explained that the Brussels Convention did not cover arbitration and so representatives from the European Commission, who had come to assist behind the scenes with negotiations on the jurisdictional provisions in the Rotterdam Rules, could not address the topic of arbitration; nonetheless, delegates from member states in the EU *could* address this issue for themselves. This meant that in order for the jurisdictional and arbitration provisions to mirror one another, parallel negotiations had to take place. "When we spoke on jurisdiction, the UK wasn't in the room – the European Commission was. When we switched to arbitration, the UK was in the room and the EC wasn't" (Int: 6005). To address this complex of negotiations that managed the relationship of court dispute settlement versus private arbitrations, the Working Group struck a deal with two aspects.

First, in order to mollify states and industry interests that did not want to be bound by new provisions on dispute settlement in a transport convention, the Rotterdam Rules articles on arbitration would only come into play if countries opted in and adopted explicitly the provisions of this article. Thus, the formal solution on arbitration provisions in the Rotterdam Rules paralleled that for jurisdiction, in that countries would have to affirmatively choose to be bound either by the articles on arbitration or on jurisdiction.

Second, even if states did opt in to the arbitration provisions, the parties to an arbitration proceeding (e.g., a shipping company like Maersk or a manufacturer like Toyota) would also need to have agreed to be bound by the arbitration article in any contract they signed.[10] Arbitration is always a matter of contract.

At best, then, the deals over where disputes should be settled achieved the formal goal of drawing jurisdiction and arbitration provisions into the new treaty, but with sufficient flexibility for states to opt in or out of that particular provision. And even if they opted in on arbitration, the commercial parties to prospective disputes had complete freedom about where and how they would choose to arbitrate that dispute. In this respect, the opt-in, opt-out provisions bore some of the resemblance to discretionary provisions also adopted for volume contracts.

Whose Norms?

Core delegates, who crafted the final consensus document that became the Rotterdam Rules, expressed two strong, and seemingly countervailing, sentiments about the final product.

[10] But if parties wanted to extend this choice of forum clause to a third party – someone other than the shipper or carrier parties to the volume contract, such as a freight forwarder, for example, then the contracting parties had to ensure that the choice of forum clause or the agreement to arbitrate was on fair terms, recognized as enforceable under applicable law, and that the person to be bound was given timely and adequate notice (Art. 75).

On the one hand, UNCITRAL's Secretariat, leading industry interests, and some prominent states insist that it was "a fair compromise" (Int: 6005). "There are a series of compromises," said a prominent carrier industry leader. "We feel it balances interests. We gave up something – nautical fault – but we got containerization, electronic documents, which should benefit cargo" (Int: 6010). Others repeat the refrain of "balance," that it was a "package deal," a truly negotiated settlement where all parties-in-interest had to give and take.

Shippers got liability limits that were higher than all previous conventions. They also succeeded in removing antiquated rules that had insulated ships from responsibility based on a presumption that communication could not occur with the main office during a voyage; importantly, carriers accepted responsibility for delay in carriage, although the goods had not otherwise been damaged during transit. Carriers succeeded in imposing responsibilities on shippers, including for disclosure of dangerous goods and for enhanced documentation more generally.

But economic actors were not the principal negotiators in UNCITRAL's chambers; national delegations were. And on this score, there were clear prevailing influences. The US had come to UNCITRAL with a short list of deal-breaking expectations. This list was the result of a domestic political deal the US had managed between its own carriers and shippers before the UNCITRAL negotiations began (Carlson 2009). Early in deliberations, the US delegation had submitted its list of 10 "must-haves" into the record of proceedings, partly as a signal to the Working Group and partly as a signal to its own domestic audiences.[11] Volume contracts and jurisdiction and arbitration provisions were front and center on this list. In the end, the Rotterdam Rules do not diverge from the US's list of "must-have" topics. As one UNCITRAL official put it, "the US got all the big things they wanted and compromised on the rest" (Int: 6008).

Many other interests also aligned themselves with the UNCITRAL consensus. In addition to numbers of Continental states, the African countries signed the Rotterdam Rules, said an observer, because they are shipping countries trying to reform trade as a whole and the Rotterdam Rules helps produce a uniform system (Int: 6006). The International Council on Shipping, a shipowners' industry group based in London, "decided that the new regime must be prompted by the industry to avoid the risk of a proliferation of regional cargo liability regulations" (Int: 6011).

Importantly, UNCITRAL succeeded in keeping other potentially competing lawmaking bodies at bay. It persuaded the EU, ASEAN, ECOWAS and the Arab League to hold off on initiatives of their own to see what UNCITRAL would produce (Int: 6008). Its longtime potential rival, UNCTAD, was persuaded to join

[11] Note by Secretariat, Transport Law: Preparation of a draft instrument on the carriage of goods [by sea] – Proposal by the United States of America, UN Doc. No. A/CN.9/WG.III/WP.34 (Aug. 7, 2003).

the UNCITRAL lawmaking deliberations as an observer despite its well-known alternative approaches to legal convergence on carriage of goods by sea.

On the other hand, the deal making also produced casualties, which left several potentially troublesome delegates and delegations critical of the outcomes. Their disgruntlement could signify not only reluctance for their own states or industries to accede to the new legal order, but they also might form the nucleus of a bloc of opponents to the Rotterdam Rules that would consign the draft convention to yet another of the failures that UNCITRAL's Secretariat and prime proponents had been determined to avoid.

The Rotterdam Rules have not entered into force. States remain wary of signing on to it. China and Korea are reluctant to accede to the Rotterdam Rules because they do not accept liability limits higher than those set in the Hamburg Rules. For a time it appeared that the European Union itself might formulate a multimodal convention, and if this included short-sea carriage across the North Sea it would be directly competitive with the Rotterdam Rules (Int: 6006). This competition did not eventuate. Resistance has continued from the European Shippers Council, who purported to represent the interests of the small shippers fearing that the volume contracts provisions would make them vulnerable to pressure by more powerful carriers (Int: 6009). Freight forwarders in Europe, too, imagined increased pressure from shippers contracting directly with carriers and have not supported the new convention (Int: 6008).

And, despite the effort to integrate and possibly co-opt potential competitor UNCTAD, officials at UNCTAD remained staunchly critical of UNCITRAL's product. They both critiqued the Rotterdam Rules on their own account and offered a fulcrum around which opposition by other interest groups might muster. For instance, UNCTAD affirmed the criticism echoed even by some supporters of the Rotterdam Rules, namely, the interest group most benefiting from the Rules was not carriers or shippers or other commercial interests but maritime lawyers. Said a critic, "The great winner is the Union of Maritime Lawyers. … Every second line you think to yourself, it will depend on what the courts say. … Because of the complexity, wordiness, ambiguity, all the new features in terms of wording, structure, text, there will be a great need for litigation" (Int: 8005). Even a supporter of the Rules concurred: the language is "dense, lots of paragraphs and sub-paragraphs, and sub-clauses, and you have to go back and forth" (Int: 6011). Another veteran maritime lawyer acknowledged that "there will be a higher cost of litigation early on after adoption," but also argued that this is bound to be the case with a new convention that follows one which has been in force for eighty years (Int: 6012).

To some extent, the critique that the Rotterdam Rules are excessively complicated arose from drafters' decisions to expand its scope beyond the port-to-port or tackle-to-tackle limits of earlier conventions, not to mention the jurisdiction and arbitration provisions, and, indeed, the new legal concepts, such as volume contracts. The price of expanding the scope of a TLO includes the cost of renegotiating boundaries with existing legal orders, not least the national rail, road and freight regimes that have well-established practices that their beneficiaries will fight to defend. And, of course, a new set of legal standards always creates "liabilities of newness," since it confronts the classic problems of ambiguity and inconsistency that may take years to settle.

As of 2017,[12] the political fallout of the deals that produced the Rotterdam Rules continues. As promised, the African bloc signed the Rules at its launch event, and the Rules now have twenty-five signatories, including not only thirteen African nations, but also the United States, Switzerland and nine members of the European Union. Only three countries (Congo, Togo, and Spain) have more formally acceded to its terms, however, and the convention does not enter into force until there are twenty such accessions.

Political progress has been slow. Despite pressure to the contrary, in 2010, the European Parliament issued its recommendation that EU Member States should move "speedily to sign, ratify and implement" the Rotterdam Rules. Legislative committees in Denmark, Norway and the Netherlands have published favorable reports on the draft convention, also recommending accession. In the summer of 2013, the US State Department began its long process of review preceding a request for a vote on the new convention in the US Senate.

There is a widespread view that if the US accedes to the convention, then the probability will be high that the world will move away from the Hague and Hague-Visby Rules and toward a new "maritime-plus" transnational legal order. In that case, an epochal change will have occurred where the world concurs with a consensus forged around the core ten demands of the world's most powerful trading nation, albeit with discretionary powers granted to sovereign signatories and commercial actors as a price of its universal acceptance. But accession by the US is in no way certain.

As a result, the Rotterdam Rules remain more a potential for harmonization than a reality.

CORPORATE BANKRUPTCY

Interests and Divides

The financial collapse of a business potentially brings all economic actors into conflict. When a company has too little cash or too few assets to pay in full all of those to whom it owes money, affected parties compete to see which of them will get paid first or most or at all. Corporate bankruptcy law seeks to provide an orderly way of handling incipient conflict between the managers of a firm and its owners, between workers and managers, between financial institutions and trade creditors and other businesses that have extended credit to a firm, between the government

[12] Current as of July 12, 2017.

which may be owed taxes and workers whose pension fund is not fully paid up, between the business and the lawyers, accountants or insolvency practitioners whose expertise guides the rescue of the company.

Not only are everyday bankruptcies rife with conflicting interests, but the "meta-bargaining" over laws to govern business failures is also inherently conflictual since these laws can favor the financial interests of some economic actors over others (Halliday and Carruthers 2009). If this is true in national lawmaking, these conflicts and competition are only more evident in forums for global lawmaking.

We have shown (Chapter 3) that in 2000 UNCITRAL accepted a challenge previously on its "impossible list." With the support of professional associations, major trading nations and international financial institutions, it aspired to produce a comprehensive set of corporate bankruptcy norms that could be adopted with some variation in every country of the world. In so doing, the UNCITRAL Secretariat fully understood that they would confront intractable conflicts in the law and divisions among actors, organizations and states. Core delegates to UNCITRAL's Insolvency Working Group were also well aware that negotiations on insolvency law standards would be difficult to conclude in that insolvency laws govern "a zero sum game that cuts across every commercial issue and even the local culture" (Int: 2052C).

Since bankruptcy law always has distributive consequences, we ask: Where lay the principal faultlines? What processes enabled faultlines to be bridged, competitors to be turned into cooperators? And which actors prevailed?

Answers to this question have been anticipated in earlier chapters. Chapters 2 and 3 revealed that UNCITRAL won a very substantial victory by convincing the IMF, EBRD and ADB, potentially competitive IOs, to hand on the baton of lawmaking to this UN global legislature. UNCITRAL likewise achieved success by bringing into its lawmaking forum major trading nations, and from adjacent industry ecologies, the key international professional associations, international financial institutions, and, at least for a minority of sessions, a large number of developing and transitional economies.

Yet the inner core of lawmakers constituted a tiny fraction of all the potential actors with interests. In the Insolvency Working Group we observed (Chapter 4) that there were only ten delegations with high-attendance delegates. There were six states (Thailand, Australia, Germany, the US, Japan, and France), three professional associations (INSOL, International Bar Association, International Insolvency Institute), and the World Bank. Overwhelmingly the principal interventions were from advanced economies and the professions. The most numerous delegates were US citizens, who were either members of the US delegation or the delegations from International Insolvency Institute, American Bar Association or International Bar Association. We therefore would expect the global norms emerging from UNCITRAL to benefit powerful countries at the core of the world economy and the professionals – the lawyers and accountants – that preside over corporate bankruptcies.

Parenthetically, it should also be noted which actors were *not* present or present only infrequently. While periodically present in formal deliberations, participation by delegates from developing and transitional countries was inconsistent, even those delegates from high-attendance delegations. High-attendance delegations from developing and transitional countries instead seemed to prefer to send a round robin of delegates, different people to each working group session, which meant that none of these delegations had the benefit of participation through high-attendance delegates. The International Labor Organization attended once or twice, and only for purposes of making a single proposal to the Working Group. The International Chamber of Commerce attended only sporadically. Bankers' associations did not attend Working Group sessions at all.

In addition, economic actors have distinct interests in corporate bankruptcy laws, which can cut across national, organizational and professional divisions.

Secured creditors are those economic actors that have negotiated and extended credit to a firm on the basis of some security or collateral that the firm has offered the creditor, whether in machinery or inventory or cash flowing into the company or intellectual property or otherwise. Often these are banks. Because they incur additional transaction costs to obtain security, they expect to be at the top of the list of those paid first out of a bankruptcy estate and sometimes to be able to act outside bankruptcy law altogether.

Unsecured creditors are owed money by a firm, but the debtor has not promised to repay them out of specific assets. These may include the trade creditors and other suppliers who have sold raw materials or inventory or equipment to the debtor on credit, workers who keep the company's business running, banks whose loans were not (fully) covered by security rights. They may be resigned to receiving only a few pennies on the dollar from the insolvent bankruptcy estate. If this is a reorganization proceeding, these creditors are mostly interested in continuing to do business with the debtor after the plan is confirmed. Claims held by state taxing authorities and pension funds might be secured or unsecured; if unsecured, domestic insolvency law might require them to be repaid before other creditors receive anything.

Debtors, the firms themselves, want to survive either as a continuation of the previous going concern or at least for the assets of the business to be sold as an operational whole. Managers want some degrees of freedom and protection from creditors when the firm is in difficulty; they want to be able, both legally and practically, to reorganize the firm in ways that make business sense, perhaps with the assistance of expert professional advice.

There are also broader economic interests at stake. *Professionals* seek to maintain or extend their professional monopoly on the advice given to failing businesses. Attorneys and accountants may compete on this front; new entrants like turnaround specialists and investment bankers may also have an interest in whether a debtor is liquidated or reorganized in the event of financial distress. *International financial institutions* seek insolvency laws they view as likely to stimulate economic development and trade and forestall domestic or international financial instability, such as the Asian Financial Crisis. If they have participated in earlier drafts of global norms, these IFIs may also be concerned about their legitimacy in this role.

Historically, states in the world economy have differed in the ways they treat failing companies. To simplify greatly, insolvency laws have historically involved alignments between state and non-state actors on the one hand and types of creditors and debtor interests on the other.

Some states give secured lenders significant powers to act categorically and outside bankruptcy law when companies are in financial trouble, whereas others have insisted that these lenders must be brought inside bankruptcy law and cannot act without court approval. For instance, British Commonwealth, Continental and developing countries until the 1980s gave very substantial powers to secured creditors to act outside bankruptcy law and gave limited powers to debtor-managers. They facilitated liquidation rather than reorganization of companies. By contrast, in 1978, the US codified its preference for reorganization of financially troubled but viable businesses. This preference means that, under US law, secured creditors may not be able to repossess their collateral once a chapter 11 case starts, although secured creditors' claims enjoy the same property interests and priority claims to collateral inside bankruptcy as they would have in the absence of the bankruptcy filing.

There are also wide national differences in the treatment of other sorts of creditors. Some states extend substantial statutory protections to workers or taxing authorities, whereas others limit how much back pay for workers or unpaid taxes will be required of a bankrupt firm. Until recently, some Continental countries, especially France, gave employees a sort of absolute priority over other claims, making reorganization nearly impossible. And until recently nearly every country insisted on a high priority for tax and pension payments – some, like the US, still do, at least for tax claims, while others, like Germany and the UK, have agreed that tax and some similar claims ought not receive a priority distribution in insolvency cases so that reorganizations have a better chance of success. While US law continues to protect jobs and privilege employees' wage claims, it might also allow modification of labor contracts or termination of a private company's underwater pension plan in ways that could not be accomplished under other countries' laws.

In addition to broad differences in the content of the world's insolvency laws, domestic insolvency laws also administer their systems differently. British Commonwealth countries generally give accountants, rather than lawyers, professional jurisdiction over corporate bankruptcies, whereas the US law, especially after 1978, gives lawyers extensive powers. This cleavage between reliance on accountants rather than lawyers to guide insolvency proceedings is also suggestive of another historical distinction: British Commonwealth countries' reliance on accountants meant that courts' involvement in insolvency is often kept to a minimum. By contrast, Continental systems view bankruptcy as quasi-criminal and involve courts extensively. After 1978, the US system elevated bankruptcy referees to the status of bankruptcy judges (albeit without granting them the life tenure ordinarily conferred on federal judges), and required court involvement in a wide range of issues arising in a reorganization setting. While creditors' committees and other private actors hold substantial authority to negotiate chapter 11 plans and run chapter 11 cases under US law, courts are never too far in the background.

The historical trends (Chapter 2) and the delegate and delegation data (Chapter 4), together with several strains of international political economy and world systems theory, would predict the domination and prevalence of US interests. These theories might easily be relied on to predict emergence from UNCITRAL of a US-type bankruptcy system emphasizing companies' reorganization, giving managers substantial powers to restructure their business while protecting secured creditors' economic interests, ensuring that lawyers and courts are at the center of bankruptcy proceedings, finding ways for unsecured creditors to overcome their collective action problems, and reaching some sort of agreement in principle on distributions for taxes, pensions and workers' claims that still would allow for the reorganization of a company in distress. Global norms of this sort would enhance US competitiveness for at least its financial institutions and legal professions. It would encourage US multinationals and investors to locate overseas with confidence that their investments would be safe. In short, UNCITRAL could provide a means by which the US could push forward global norms for a transnational legal order centered on corporate insolvency law norms that advanced its financial and trade interests worldwide.

US interests in the emergence of a legislative guide resembling its own reorganization law were, moreover, consistent with the interests of the IFIs in the wake of the Asian Financial Crisis. Delegates from the World Bank, IMG, and ADB attended working group sessions with regularity, making it unlikely that the international standards drafted by UNCITRAL would conflict with these IFIs' structural reforms or geo-political interests.

Nor was the US alone among national delegations in promoting the advantages of reorganization over liquidation. Britain had revised its insolvency laws in 1986 and 2000, both times with reorganization in mind. Germany revised its insolvency laws in 1999, when it enacted its *Insolvenzordnung*, loosely modeled after US chapter 11. France, Japan and other countries also were interested in learning more about the possibility of a rescue culture; even Switzerland talked about encouraging a rescue culture after the embarrassing liquidation of its national airline, Swissair.

But openness to reorganization-friendly insolvency law reform is vastly different from agreement on a global set of legal norms that reflect details from US corporate reorganization law.

Divides and Deals

Although the Legislative Guide on Insolvency is an extensive document with nearly 400 pages and 200 recommendations, the incipient divides and efforts to bridge them can be captured in a handful of key areas.

Initiating Bankruptcy Proceedings

When and who should start a bankruptcy case sounds like a simple legal decision on which consensus might be reached, but even this question sits between difficult economic and social cross-currents. At a basic level, questions of initiation get at the "relative importance of liquidation versus reorganization," noted one participant. These issues can be "very, very difficult to resolve," because "in some countries the notion of recapitalizing the value of an insolvent business enterprise is not part of the insolvency culture." In the view of many countries' laws, "insolvent business enterprises simply get liquidated" by being broken into pieces and sold to any buyers in search of value (Int: 2052C).

Moreover, if a reorganization proceeding is to succeed, it matters *when* a case is initiated and who controls the initiation. Debtors may resist seeking bankruptcy protection, since a bankruptcy filing nearly always amounts to an admission of failure. A public admission of financial distress will be especially difficult when commencement of proceedings necessitates ouster of management from control. The stigma of bankruptcy remains strong around the world. US law allows management to stay in place because allowing managers to stay in their jobs during an insolvency case improves chances that the company is reorganized because they are likely to know more about the business operations than anyone else. In nearly every other country, management is removed because a company's financial distress is viewed as morally culpable behavior on the part of the company's officers and directors.

Counter-intuitively, debtors' and creditors' interests often overlap in this context. Secured creditors want to be paid as much as possible as soon as possible. They would prefer to avoid bankruptcy altogether, but if they can't prevent a filing, they want to control when proceedings begin, not least because they want to be sure the company's assets don't decline in value. Secured creditors may be indifferent between reorganization and liquidation, so long as they are paid in full, but unsecured creditors almost always prefer reorganization. Liquidation means that the debtor will go out of business; trade creditors know that in this context they will lose both a client and the money that the debtor owes them. Like debtors, then, unsecured creditors also prefer earlier rather than later commencement of a company's reorganization case because an earlier start to the case increases the probability that the business can be turned around and that they will paid more rather than less. After all, it often is unsecured creditors' money that is at risk in a bankruptcy case since these creditors have no collateral to support their claims.

All this presumes that the debtor and its creditors are acting in good faith. If creditors feel they have to push a debtor involuntarily into a bankruptcy proceeding, it is because they think something is awry with the debtor and they want a judge or trustee in bankruptcy or both to look into their suspicions of wrongdoing. But sometimes the perception that strategic incentives motivated a bankruptcy filing means that a court may need to assess the grounds for filing. Courts might also be involved in assessing the propriety of an application to commence an insolvency case because financial distress is viewed as a hair's breadth away from criminal conduct. If bankruptcy is quasi-criminal, courts will want to be sure that a debtor deserves to be before it.

Delegates on several sides of the commencement divide agreed to balance these interests. The Guide provides that an insolvency law should allow a *debtor*, that is, the firm's managers and owners, to initiate bankruptcy proceedings and get protection from creditors where it doesn't have sufficient cash flow to meet obligations.[13] It also provides that debtors' applications should either "automatically commence" a bankruptcy case or, if the judgment of a court is required, that judicial determination should occur "promptly" (Rec. 18). Together these recommendations would encourage debtors to file early to increase the likelihood of a successful reorganization.

To balance these powers given to debtors, delegates also authorized *creditors* to initiate bankruptcy proceedings, although on grounds requiring creditors to meet a higher standard of proof that the debtor generally wasn't paying its debts and not just that a few creditors had not been paid.[14] Virtually every country allows creditors to push a debtor into bankruptcy, and the Guide's recommendations are broad enough to resemble this global consensus.

Ensuring that the Legislative Guide allows debtors ready access to bankruptcy was critically important to US (and other) interests in enabling reorganization.[15] French, German and other Continental insolvency laws – and those of the many countries in their legal families – require their courts to assess the debtor's financial eligibility before opening proceedings. The Insolvency Working Group accepted this approach, too, largely in deference to the delegates in the Working Group who were judges and who couldn't conceive of balanced initiation powers that left them out.[16] Overall, therefore, the compromise amounted to a blend of global practices in advanced economies, but one that was centered on facilitating a corporate reorganization.

[13] Indeed, the Insolvency Guide goes as far as to provide that an insolvency law may set out a presumption of "cash flow insolvency" where the debtor fails in good faith to pay a single debt that has come due (Recs. 15, 17).

[14] Although some countries also enable state actors to push a company into bankruptcy, the Guide recommends that governments be allowed to do this only as creditors (e.g., for unpaid taxes) (Rec. 14, note 15) and not as a general tool for pressuring companies to comply with government directives.

[15] Since 1978, US bankruptcy law does not require debtors to establish or even allege their insolvency on filing, whether insolvency is defined on a balance sheet or cash flow basis; while earlier US laws might have required such a showing, companies had complained that debtors lost the opportunity to reorganize because they were caught up in expensive and lengthy trials to prove their financial status. So while the Legislative Guide on Insolvency Law refers to both sorts of financial standards, importantly, consistent with US law, automatic commencement is allowed under the Guide (Rec. 18(a)).

[16] Nonetheless, because the Guide specifies that this determination should occur "promptly" after a filing is made, the possibility that courts could judge a debtor's eligibility satisfied US interests in maximizing the probability of rescuing a business and reorganizing the firm.

Deepening the Asset Pool

The more a firm runs down, the fewer assets are available either to repay creditors or to finance a rescue of the business. Secured creditors have generally preferred to be able to reclaim their assets without going through bankruptcy, as they used to do in Britain and countries following UK law before 1985, because it is quicker and cheaper and their hands are not tied by legal restraints. Failing that, they prefer to see exceptions or bases on which escape is possible, so that at least some assets against which they have security are kept outside the "estate" that exists within the jurisdiction of the bankruptcy.[17]

Saving a business requires money. The deeper the pool of assets, believe the debtor's managers, the greater the likelihood that the reorganization will succeed. Unsecured creditors align with the debtors; they also understand that a large estate increases the probability of a successful reorganization.

Since the central thrust of the Working Group was premised on the goal to facilitate reorganization, and the ideology of reorganization was premised on the assumption that the more assets that are available, the more likely the reorganization will work, the settlement among delegates pushed in the direction of bringing all assets of any kind, including leases and contracts and the debtor's interests in third party owned assets, inside the pool of assets governed by the bankruptcy law. The provisions on the scope of an insolvency estate were hard fought.

Early on in Working Group deliberations US delegates emphasized the importance of including secured creditors' assets within the estate with a flexibility to alter the terms of their security if necessary. A US delegate stated "that if secured credit could not be altered, then this whole process [of drafting a Legislative Guide] was going nowhere" (Int: 2002). These remarks came not just from the US delegation, but also from various professional associations. The French delegate followed and immediately supported the US delegate. This position prevailed particularly over the mostly unspoken resistance of British practitioners whose practices gave secured creditors far more freedom to act unilaterally.

The ultimate compromise constituted a major win for managers and owners and advocates of rescuing rather than liquidating companies. But the Guide balanced this win with clear signals to secured creditors that its provisions would protect their financial interests. Several baseline rules provide ways for secured creditors to seek court approval to remove their collateral from the pool of assets in bankruptcy.[18]

While this distribution of benefits therefore adhered closely to the spirit of US law, it also followed trends in UK and Continental (French, German) bankruptcy systems and built upon precedent in the earlier UNCITRAL Model Law on

[17] If secured creditors cannot keep assets outside bankruptcy proceedings, then they press strongly for the value of their collateral to be protected from unwise or doubtful business decisions while a company is in bankruptcy.

[18] In the language of the law, they can obtain "relief" from a bankruptcy stay or moratorium if they can provide appropriate justification.

Cross-Border Insolvency.[19] The outcome was consistent with the 1978 US Bankruptcy Code, but also a growing consensus followed by other advanced economies and especially by the IMF and World Bank after the Asian financial crisis.

Checks and Balances in Bankruptcy Decision Making

Since almost by definition there is not enough money in a corporate bankruptcy to satisfy all parties that are owed money or have assets in the firm, *who* gets to make decisions about the business once it is in bankruptcy can be highly consequential. Said one participant in the deliberations:

> Who should run the insolvency proceeding? What role does the debtor have? What role do insolvency practitioners have? What role do bureaucrats and administrators have? Again, very different concepts in different countries
>
> (Int: 2052C).

Insolvency-related decisions could be made by the debtor's managers, by independent insolvency representatives (such as a trustee in bankruptcy or the like), by secured creditors who are often banks, or by groups of unsecured creditors like suppliers or even workers. Those decisions could diminish, preserve or enhance the property of the bankruptcy estate, including collateral assets of secured creditors. They could be made with or without the intervention of judges, and with or without the agreement of the general body of creditors.

In principle, secured creditors do not care whether the debtor's managers or an independent insolvency representative has primary discretion over business decisions, so long as the party in control is responsible for preserving the value of their collateral. Debtors' management have a strong preference to continue running the firm themselves, a practice referred to in the US as leaving the "debtor-in-possession."[20] Unsecured creditors tend to align with a debtor's managers – if

[19] One important exception is worth mentioning, at least parenthetically. While there is general agreement across national laws on inclusion of the substantial potential value of leases and contracts in the pool of assets, the Guide also strongly recommends following US law declining to enforce certain agreed-upon terms in these leases and contracts which are understood to limit this value. For example, important contracts or leases would be rendered valueless in bankruptcy if the agreement were to provide that a bankruptcy or similar event terminates the agreement (known as a "bankruptcy default clause"); similarly, a debtor would be unable to realize the value of a contract or lease if transfer of these rights is prohibited under the terms of the agreement (referred to as an "anti-assignment clause"). US law invalidates both sorts of contract clauses; the Guide similarly provides that bankruptcy clauses ought not be enforceable against an insolvency representative or the debtor, and that the invalidation of anti-assignment clauses is permissible.

[20] Not only is this beneficial to managers, who are unlikely to want to be displaced, but it may have benefits for early initiation of bankruptcy (as managers are unlikely to file early if they are instantly fired) and for the success of continued operations (because who knows the business better than those who have been running it?).

management is displaced, time will be lost learning the business and with it, the opportunity to reorganize – but not fully.[21]

Where a neutral insolvency professional is not appointed, and current managers continue to run a bankrupt firm, as is generally the case in the US debtor-in-possession (DIP) regime, unsecured creditors may not want to rely on the DIP alone to protect their interests. But unsecured creditors are often too numerous to join together to make effective decisions. They confront challenging problems of collective action. One approach, followed in the US, was to encourage formation of a creditors' committee – a small representative body of unsecured creditors funded by the estate so that the committee can effectively represent the interests of creditors. Secured creditors, debtors and professionals generally support this approach.[22]

The US bloc came to UNCITRAL at the outset of negotiations on the Insolvency Guide expecting to fight for US law and practice on the powers of managers. While some delegations from advanced economies saw the wisdom of leaving the "debtor in possession," their national laws often also required the appointment in corporate bankruptcies of a neutral insolvency representative like an accounting firm. Quite early in negotiations, the US bloc saw that insisting on a bankruptcy regime that closely followed the US "debtor-in-possession" approach would not be acceptable to most delegations. Quite apart from anything else, "debtors-in-possession" were too hotly contested by states with different bankruptcy systems. For UNCITRAL, embrace of the US DIP regime would appear to the rest of the world as though UNCITRAL itself were a cipher for US interests.

The deal that was deftly crafted contained a compromise wrapped in two types of rules. In a baseline recommendation, the Guide provides that at least three "different approaches" exist: (1) an approach that leaves managers in full charge of their businesses during bankruptcy proceedings; (2) one that appoints an insolvency representative to supervise the debtor left in possession; and (3) one that ousts the debtor from possession and replaces management with an insolvency representative (Rec. 112).[23]

21 Given that this same management presided over the failing company, unsecured creditors may well want supervision or approval of important decisions by a neutral insolvency professional. This supervision might also forestall future misconduct by managers, who could make decisions that benefit them at the expense of creditors.

22 Secured creditors do not usually oppose the formation of a committee since they are likely to protect their own interests and since the cost of the committee does not come out of their collateral. Debtors also generally support the formation of a committee as they may find it easier to deal with a single committee than a plethora of competing claimants, but they do not want too much interference from the committee in the running of the firm. As for the lawyers or accountants or investment bankers and other professionals that are integrally involved in bankruptcies, in general, they may favor formation of a committee since the committee may be authorized to expend estate funds to hire their own professionals, independent of those hired by the debtor.

23 A footnote to this recommendation clarifies that this "debtor-in-possession" approach may depend on the existence of "a well-developed court structure and the application of protections that operate to displace the debtor in certain circumstances," as more fully explicated in the related commentary.

The compromise meant that current practices in the US would not contravene international standards. At the same time a country might reject US practices, and yet comply fully with the Guide.

UNCITRAL's solution to the unsecured creditors' collective action problem displayed a similar compromise, again benefiting from the interplay of different types of rules. Delegates authorized the US approach and an alternative advanced by the Mexican delegation as a common practice throughout Latin America. The Guide offers a fabric of imperative, permissive and architectural set of recommendations that add up to two important outcomes: (1) states may choose to solve the collective action problems of unsecured creditors through appointment of a creditors' committee, but they are not required to do so and (2) if they do allow for the appointment of these committees, there are numbers of precise and directive provisions about how creditors' committees should operate.[24]

In addition, the Legislative Guide strongly affirms the worldwide movement, energetically pushed by the IMF and World Bank, encouraging the appointment of a highly qualified, professional insolvency representative whenever such a representative gets appointed (Halliday 2012). This movement got initial momentum from the 1978 US Bankruptcy Code and the UK Insolvency Act (Carruthers and Halliday 1998) in the Anglo-American world, and subsequently has become an integral component of the emergent transnational legal order on corporate bankruptcy.[25] By reaching this settlement delegates forestalled a potential jurisdictional struggle over monopolies erected by accountants and lawyers who have substantially divided bankruptcy work between them in most of the advanced economies. The settlement essentially bows to national preferences regarding which of these two professions should be relied upon to provide guidance in insolvency proceedings.

In sum, on checks and balances countries *may* follow US practices, and the Guide provides guidance on how to do so, but states are not told they *must* to do so in order to remain compliant with the global standards set out in the Guide. This flexibility enabled UNCITRAL both to acknowledge the influence of the US bloc, while at the same time gesturing to the rest of the world that neither UNCITRAL nor other countries are beholden to US norms.

New Money

Companies in financial distress are by definition short of cash. New money will very often be needed for continuing operations, for new investments to modernize equipment, for new management and consultants, and to buy out contracts of

[24] For example, how they should be constituted, what are their powers should consist of, and how they should relate to the debtor, the unsecured creditors they represent and other parties in a case.

[25] In a set of imperative recommendations, the Guide specifies the duties of insolvency representatives and suggests enactment of professional standards, yet gives maximum flexibility to countries over who should be invested with those powers (e.g., accountants, lawyers, specialized insolvency practitioners, or government officials) and precisely how these standards should be implemented (Recs. 115–125).

redundant personnel and expand into new markets. To attract vital new streams of cash and investment, incentives need to be found. Since 1978, the US provides assurances to new lenders, or old lenders providing new money, that instead of being at the back of the queue for repayment if the company fails altogether, the lenders offering new money will be paid at the front of the queue.[26] These rules predominately serve debtors' and unsecured creditors' interests in facilitating reorganization. Debtors have a strong interest in getting new money for operations. The unsecured creditors' financial interests are similar but they are not perfectly aligned since, if unsecured assets are offered as collateral for new money, and the company's turnaround fails, then the unsecured creditors will be left with fewer funds in the pool to satisfy their claims.

Delegates and delegations at the core of UNCITRAL's Working Group broadly agreed that reorganization needed access to new money and that new money needed new incentives. The US bloc and the IFIs clearly saw the tried and true methods practiced in the US as a model. Canada had for years followed the lead of the US. Delegates from France, Germany, and the UK were more cautious, mostly because they feared that the wrong kind of incentives might skew the law too far toward the interests of secured creditors and away from the interests of unsecured creditors. France was especially concerned that workers' claims would get undermined if these sorts of new loans were entitled to a stronger priority than employees.[27]

In the end, the deal hews quite closely to the US model. Recommendations enabling new money favored the interests of debtors and unsecured creditors but also protected the interests of pre-existing secured creditors who declined to provide fresh funding. Like US law, the recommendations strongly favor providing special protections to encourage lenders to provide fresh funds after an insolvency case is commenced.[28]

[26] Just how firm these assurances are is a matter of judicial discretion under US law. Court orders aren't needed to assure traders supplying goods to a chapter 11 debtor that they will share in the first round of distribution from the estate (together with lawyers and employees who work during the case), but are needed in most other instances. A US bankruptcy court might elevate some sources of new money so that they are first within the first-to-receive or to grant to these new lenders collateral that is otherwise free from grants of security; it might even grant a new lender a security right in collateral that already is encumbered with another security right and elevate the new lender above the old one, so long as there are "adequate assurances" that the collateral will be sufficiently valuable by the end of the case to repay both – either because the collateral will grow in value with the infusion of new funds or because the earlier lenders' claim is small by comparison to the collateral's value as a whole.

[27] There were, some delegates told us, all sorts of "myths" about how far US law could go to enable lending to an insolvency estate. "Is it really true, they say, that the DIP financer wipes out the liens of the pre-petitioned lender? ... There's so many misconceptions [about US debtor-in-possession financing]" (Int: Int: 2052B).

[28] The Guide specifies that new money should be protected with a priority ahead of ordinary unsecured creditors (Rec. 64). Importantly, the Guide provides that a court should be able to authorize fresh funding on terms that leap-frog over the priority of an existing security interest,

Approving a Reorganization Plan

What happens when most creditors want to approve a plan, but a small number of creditor hold out? Should the entire plan be held hostage to a tiny number of dissenters? Bankruptcy laws in general can respond to this hold-out incentive by binding dissenters based on the requirement that a specified super-majority of creditors favor the plan and the requirement that every creditor receives under the plan at least as much as it would have received in a liquidation. These two requirements sit at the heart of any reorganization law.

US chapter 11 provides additional measures for addressing the problem of the holdout. For example, US law accepts that the debtor can make distinct offers to different types of creditors. However, what happens when an entire class of creditors or claims votes against the plan? US law enables a court to override a class of creditors, a concept which US lawyers refer to as a "cram down." This concept was unknown, even alien, to many jurisdictions across the world. It seemed to run against the principle of consensual decision making. And it seemed to give a state institution or official, a judge, great powers over market behavior.

Under US reorganization law, debtors much prefer consensual reorganization in a spirit of cooperation. But debtors may push forward with a cram down because the alternative – liquidation and dissolution of the company – is even less attractive. Some trade creditors may view cram down as an acceptable last resort, especially depending on what other class of claims is getting crammed down. Some secured creditors may stand aside as another is crammed down, so long as that secured creditor is receiving payment greater than what they would have received in a fair sale of their collateralized assets.

These issues had clear distributive implications for deliberations at UNCITRAL, because they vested power in different corners of the financial network surrounding the firm. Cramdown also raised issues of political sensitivity because some delegations quietly worried that it might act as a back door for foreign investment – a way for foreign creditors to take over local businesses in financial distress by binding the local creditors as a "dissenting class of claims."

The final deal on approaches to hold-out creditors required the full array of rule-types to draft norms of wide applicability that offer states guidance on whatever policy decisions they might ultimately make but leave them substantial flexibility.

While the Guide ultimately moved in the direction of a growing global consensus, there is no doubt that these provisions were deeply influenced by laws and practices uniquely American in origin. The centerpoint of the US standard for confirmation – that every creditor should received at least as much in a plan of reorganization as it would have received in a liquidation of the debtor – sat at the

but only if (i) the earlier secured creditor consents or (ii) the debtor demonstrates to the court that it cannot obtain financing on any other terms and that the interests of the earlier secured creditors "will be protected" (Recs. 66, 67).

center of the standard for confirmation set out in the Guide.[29] The Guide was less directive on other aspects of US law. It did *not* contain an imperative recommendation on cramdown, but did permit it.[30] The Guide did *not* require courts to approve a reorganization plan, although they may – an exception that was crucial for some states, such as France, Germany and the UK, which often put judicial determinations at the center of their reorganization processes. But other states, such as Australia, which permits out-of-court agreements without judicial intervention, were keen to retain their flexible approach. The Guide was silent on other US practices. For example, it included no recommendation regarding whether a plan should be feasible or proposed in good faith, or whether debt for equity swaps should be permitted, criteria important under US law.[31]

In sum, the core elements of the Insolvency Guide followed the US. While the US bloc, the IMF and World Bank, and numerous other states and non-state delegations strongly supported the US approach, the Insolvency Guide did not require many of the most controversial aspects of US law, thus enabling significant room for maneuvering to countries with reorganization laws that deviate from US law and practice.

Prioritized Creditors

As a matter of public policy, all bankruptcy laws include a list of financial interests that are paid first – before unsecured, and sometimes even secured, creditors receive anything. These priority or privileged or preferential claims have significant distributive consequences for a company and an economy, as well as significant political consequences for domestic legislatures.

Earlier research on lawmaking in England and the UK (Carruthers and Halliday 1998) demonstrated that identifying the interests entitled to a priority in distribution from an insolvency estate often generates heated political debate. Historically, states have argued that unpaid and overdue taxes owed to the state by the company should be paid in full. Unions have argued that all unpaid wages and employment related claims should be paid in full, since workers are weak financial actors and shouldn't pay the price of poor management judgments. Professionals maintain that they shouldn't be required to offer expert services to a bankruptcy estate unless they are paid reasonable, market-rated fees and on a first priority basis. Suppliers and employees feel the same way about doing business with a company in an insolvency case. Debtors argue that the greater the number or value of privileged claims that a

29 Recs. 152(b) and 153(a).

30 Recs. 150–51.

31 Similarly, the Insolvency Guide avoided making recommendations regarding the exact period of time or number of creditors required for a standard set out in general terms to have been satisfied. For example, the Guide did not specify when a plan should be proposed in a reorganization proceeding, only that the law should clearly specify this time (Rec. 139). Nor did the Guide specify what proportion of votes are necessary for a class of creditors to approve a plan, although it did indicate that mechanisms should be put in place in a country's law to effect this (Rec. 145).

debtor must pay (or at least promise to pay) before a reorganization plan can be confirmed, the harder it is for the debtor to succeed in reorganizing. Unsecured creditors may share the view of managers, unless they themselves are entitled to some priority in distribution.

Recently, some states have pared back on privileges in distribution, including some (like Germany and the UK) that have agreed to give up the nearly hallowed priority enjoyed by governments for repayment of tax and similar claims in an effort to make more money available for corporate restructuring and thereby enhance the likelihood of success of corporate reorganization. Others (like the US and Canada) seem not to be able to resist the temptation to favor some creditors over others.

UNCITRAL's Secretariat and inner lawmaking core consistently argued that UNCITRAL is engaged in technical law reform, not substantive public policy debates. While this is clearly ingenuous – all the products of its Working Groups have distributive implications within countries and in the world trading and financial systems – UNCITRAL's position often succeeds in side stepping matters of national public policy that might sharply divide the world's nations and delegations. But priorities could not be avoided altogether in the Guide. Because priority claims generally need to get paid for a plan to be confirmed, priorities take money out of the pool available for distribution to unsecured creditors. Too many priorities, thus, make reorganization far more difficult to accomplish.

Delegates could agree that priorities should be kept to a minimum in any bankruptcy law (Rec. 187). Commentary in the Guide acknowledges that employees' wage claims and government tax claims are typically given priority in bankruptcy laws, but to reach common ground delegates took no view on the relative merits of these priorities, instead treating their existence and ranking as matters of "social policy." In addition to stating that these priorities should be kept to a minimum, the Guide also provides that any priorities should be clearly stated in the law so that back door politics is available for all to see (id.). Another recommendation reflected the consensus that priorities generally should not cut into secured creditors' collateral (Rec. 188).

The Guide's "light touch" on the topic of priorities was only partly explained by UNCITRAL's interest in avoiding issues of social or cultural importance. An imperative recommendation strongly condemning the presence of priorities in an insolvency law would have deviated from the US Bankruptcy Code, which includes eight different priority provisions. It would also have contravened laws in other states' that privileged certain creditors. A vague recommendation framed aspirationally and in terms of the importance of transparency allowed the Working Group to embrace the point that too many priorities can disrupt the chances of a reorganization without expressly confronting the US on the shortcomings of US law.

Courts

Countries across the world differ substantially over the need to involve courts in resolving a company's financial distress. At one extreme, depending on local law, courts may be involved throughout the case: a judge's approval may be needed to initiate bankruptcy proceedings (e.g., in France and Germany), to resolve disputes about whether a creditor should be entitled to relief from the automatic stay (e.g., in the US), or to confirm a reorganization plan (e.g., the US, France, and many others). At another extreme, courts may be irrelevant in all but exceptional circumstances. An administrator or other sort of insolvency representative may be vested with presumptive authority to run the case (e.g., the UK). Matters may be handled entirely within a state's bureaucracy (e.g., Colombia or Italy), or a central bank (e.g., the Bank of England's London Rules), or private actors, usually with the expert advice of accountants, may resolve matters largely among themselves (e.g., Australia).

Advocates for the centrality of courts argue that a public interest must always be considered and the court is the institution best positioned to express that public interest. Courts protect weak parties, it is said, and can break deadlocks or quicken proceedings. But courts also may be slow, expensive, incompetent or corrupt. In most countries, judges do not have training in matters of finance or possible not even in financial laws, and thus often lack the needed expertise or experience to handle a large corporate reorganization. And if the judiciary in a country is not independent from the other branches of government, judges can be subject to political and financial manipulation.

The role that courts should play in an insolvency proceeding ran through the Legislative Guide as a motif. The Working Group often bridged divides by drafting permissive recommendations, which simultaneously acknowledge the key role courts can play on an issue and, at the same time, accept an alternative approach that anticipates "automatic" results or defers to the autonomous discretion of an insolvency representative or creditor body.[32]

To some extent these alternatives reflected a compromise between different national systems. For example, US bankruptcy law provides that a bankruptcy case (whether liquidation or reorganization) automatically commences with the filing of a debtor's petition; in Continental Europe, by contrast, a debtor's petition is often merely an application that a court (and possible other judicial officers) are required to scrutinize before a case is opened. The compromise in the Guide accepted the wisdom of practices in both systems, providing only that an insolvency law should specify which of the two systems it looks to follow and, if judicial action is to be required, that a judicial determination of jurisdiction should occur promptly.[33]

[32] But not always. In drafting recommendations on "expedited reorganization proceedings" – or what in the US is referred to as a "pre-packaged plan" or a "pre-pak" – some delegates contended that courts need not get involved unless specific concerns of fraud or misconduct were raised. Although the arguments were forcefully made over several sessions, in the end the Insolvency Working Group insisted on expedited proceedings that were fully supervised by a court (Recs. 160–168).

[33] See Rec. 18. As another example, the Guide recommended the imposition of a stay "on commencement of insolvency proceedings," implying that it did not need express judicial

There was a quiet subtext to these compromises. Delegates reported an explicit interest in finding "a way open for a system that is not dominated by courts" because "courts' involvement can create expense and inefficiency" (Int: 5803). This emphasis on efficiency acted also as a diplomatic way to avoid mentioning the possibility of judicial corruption, a concern that delegates were unwilling to discuss openly because it would have meant pointing fingers at some judicial systems as more corrupt than others. But the need to protect against the possibility of corrupt judicial practices was quietly discussed at coffee breaks.

Big Deals or a Multiplicity of Small Gestures?

Leaving controversial topics off the table, and acceding to national interests through a flexible range of rule-types, limited the need to compromise on all but one or two big issues. As a result, deference to national delegations could come with accumulations of small gestures, and there were lots of these. Word choice mattered. The Working Group frequently debated whether to recommend that an insolvency law "should" or "may" provide something. Translations mattered to the Working Group, with more than several delegates multi-lingual. For example, the Working Group debated how best to translate the distinction between "should" and "may" into Spanish – should the Guide use the verb *deber* (to ought to) or should it simply use the subjunctive form of the verb *ser* (to be)? Moreover, the placement of language mattered. Language was added to the Guide's commentary almost any time a delegation asked. Moreover, the Working Group often moved language to the commentary from recommendations that were considered too controversial or too detailed. On several topics that were viewed as too controversial to reach agreement but too important to delete altogether, the Working Group inserted commentary into the Guide but without recommendations (e.g., treatment of corporate groups and of claims against directors' and officers' in an insolvency context). This commentary-only strategy allowed UNCITRAL to register several topics for future lawmaking episodes. Some would subsequently become supplements to the Insolvency Guide.

Whose Insolvency Norms?

The overarching ethos of corporate reorganization as an alternative to liquidation of financially distressed companies was the master normative thrust of the Legislative

action (Rec. 46), though it includes detailed provisions regarding the scope of "relief of a provisional nature" that "the court may grant" between the time an application for commencement is made and an order to commence proceedings is entered (Recs. 39–44). One further example provides two alternative methods: in one, courts are central and in the other, courts may be uninvolved. In one recommendation, the Guide specified the confirmation standard "where the insolvency law requires courts confirmation of an approved plan" (Rec. 152), and in another specified the basis for challenging a plan of reorganization where there is no requirement for judicial involvement in the confirmation process (Rec. 153).

Guide. UNCITRAL's Guide became the textual embodiment of a global consensus woven by powerful states in the Global North, reinforced by international financial institutions, and exemplified in everyday practice by delegates from the vocal professional associations.

The Guide's promotion of a rescue culture primarily benefited the economic interests of debtors and unsecured creditors. While there were no delegations expressly representing these industry interests, high-attendance delegations from the US, UK, Canada and other developed nations with a reorganization ethos pressed the cause of debtors and unsecured creditors. Delegations from the IFIs, who promoted a global rescue culture, also aligned with debtor and unsecured creditor interests.

Secured creditors' economic interests (or at least the economic value of these interests) were also protected by the Guide. This was done partly through the attendance and participation of delegations from the US and other reorganization-friendly nations, and from the IFIs and from international professional associations, but mostly through several sessions in which the Insolvency and Secured Transactions Working Groups worked together to develop uniform provisions for both legislative guides. In these joint sessions, delegates from both working groups negotiated and ratified proposed language – both commentary and recommendations – intended to insure that global standards for the treatment of secured claims in insolvency proceedings enabled the rescue of the debtor but also protected the property and economic interests of secured creditors.

Finally, there was the question of employees' interests. No delegations represented employees' interests who regularly attended Insolvency Working Group sessions, although an International Labor Organization delegate did attend briefly to propose that a fixed percent of every estate should go to workers. The Working Group rejected this proposal. Overall, the Guide did nothing to assist labor in obtaining privileged positions where they do not otherwise exist under national law. Indeed, the weak recommendations and lengthy commentary on the topic together suggested that employees' claims are best protected with a general social safety net.[34]

That the Insolvency Working Group agreed from the start that they would be advising national legislatures on how to implement a law that would enable corporate reorganization, thus, did not remove dissensus from the chamber. The US, UK, Canada, Germany, France, etc., each permitted corporate rescue, but did

[34] A possibly patriarchal argument can be made that employees' interests were being taken into account in that the Group's reorganization ethos allowed developing countries to use soft budget constraints in their economic management (Carruthers, Babb, and Halliday 2001), rather than driving firms out of business through strict liquidation laws. For example, once China's top leaders heard that bankruptcy law might be reformed in ways that allowed most workers to keep their jobs, their support for China's bankruptcy law reform improved markedly (Halliday and Carruthers 2009).

so through distinct national insolvency laws and practices. To some degree, these legal and political decisions were left intact in the Guide, if viewed through a wide lens. But a closer examination reveals a slightly different result.

On many topics, the US delegation sought and obtained recommendations in the Guide which reflected the details of US law and practice.[35] On many topics, the Guide provided that an insolvency law "should" follow a US approach.

But there are other aspects of US corporate reorganization law that the Guide did not strongly recommend. The Guide provided only that an insolvency law "may" follow other controversial US practices: (i) permitting debtors to commence proceedings "automatically," without the need for judicial intervention; (ii) permitting a debtor's management to "remain in possession" after commencement, without the appointment of a neutral supervisor; and (iii) invalidating contractual clauses that limit a debtor's transfer or assignment of a contract in bankruptcy.

By "permitting" US legal practices but not employing any stronger language of obligation, the consensus expressed in the Guide deferred to some degree to alternative insolvency regimes in France, Germany and elsewhere. For instance, delegations agreed that an insolvency law "may" require a court to assess a debtor's financial condition before authorizing the start of proceedings. Like France, the Guide permitted a process of court-supervised confirmation of a plan of reorganization; it also, however, permitted a process that enforces a plan of reorganization. Like Australia, and some other British Commonwealth countries, the Guide permits a process of that enforces a plan of reorganization based solely upon creditors' approval of the plan, like that in place in. Because countries like the UK and Canada generally rely on accountants to act as insolvency representatives (officials referred to in those countries as an administrator or trustee in bankruptcy), the Guide did not follow the US practice of requiring lawyers in these positions. High-attendance delegates from Canada and the UK persuaded the Working Group that qualified insolvency representatives or accountants would serve as competently as lawyers.

What of the interests of the countries that either did not attend at all or did not participate fully enough to make a difference (Chapter 4)? While there were high-attendance delegations from developing and transitional economies, there was only

[35] These include recommendations: (i) that defined the pool of assets subject to bankruptcy jurisdiction as broadly as possible; (ii) that included a stay to protect the integrity of this pool of assets that would arise "automatically," without the need for judicial intervention, on commencement of proceedings; (iii) that extended these protections to contracts and other intangible assets and invalidated contract terms (like a bankruptcy default clauses) that would undermine the breadth of this coverage; (iv) that broadly exempted capital market transactions from insolvency proceedings; (v) that permitted the debtor's continued use of estate assets during a case while a plan of reorganization was being negotiated, including terms on the debtor's use of "cash proceeds;" (vi) that encouraged lending to a debtor after an insolvency case had been commenced; (vii) that permit enforcement of a plan of reorganization, although a small percentage of creditors do not agree to its terms; (viii) that enable a fast track for confirmation for certain plans of reorganization.

one high-attending delegate from a non-OECD state, and his involvement was unique as the chair of the Insolvency Working Group. Some of the absent or low-attending delegations were from countries that already had adopted reorganization-friendly insolvency regimes at the behest of the IMF and the World Bank. Others had been integrated into professional and governmental networks, where US and practices in other metropolitan societies of the Global North were permeating the world. If developing and transitional nations had been intent on retaining alternative corporate insolvency norms and practices, advocacy for these alternatives was limited.

SECURED CREDIT

Faultlines and Interests

Trade floats on credit. Businesses seek credit to finance startups, to buy buildings or inventory or machinery, to keep the business afloat between the time a business ships products and buyers pay for them, to enable businesses to expand within a market or add new product lines. Lenders of money seek a return on their loans and assurance they will get their loans repaid. To increase the probability that they will be repaid, lenders may obtain property rights or some kind of security. Borrowers voluntarily grant security rights in collateral in order to signal their commitment to repayment; if the business doesn't pay back the loan in full and on time, the lender can seize property previously identified by the borrower as the lender's collateral and convert the seized property into cash so the loan is repaid.

Over time and place, lenders, borrowers and their professionals have become more and more creative about the kinds of security sought to support a loan. Real estate (referred to as immoveable property in civil law countries) provides widespread security for lending, but personal (or moveable) property also has economic value that might serve as collateral. In the twentieth century, not only has tangible personal property been used for security (e.g., works of art, equipment, goods delivered but not yet paid for), but intangible property has become increasingly important in many financial markets, so that future money flows (e.g., receivables, promissory notes), intellectual property (i.e., a patent, copyright or trademark) and even contracts or leases might also serve as collateral.

A plausible folk theory[36] developed in the 1990s with the logic that the more kinds of security available to a lender, the more money will be lent and thus the more trade will result, which in turn will stimulate economic development. From this vantage point, secured transactions laws facilitate lending that would not otherwise get extended; they enable businesses to grow that otherwise would languish; they create value and permit economic development that otherwise would remain

[36] On the concept and properties of plausible folk theories, see (Halliday 2015b)

unrealized. For countries in Eastern and Central Europe emerging from the command economies of the former Soviet bloc, and for developing countries the world over, this logic seemed unimpeachable. More legal means for obtaining security would stimulate trade and invigorate markets.

Since lending money is a core feature of capitalism in any of its forms, the stakes over the laws of secured transactions are potentially high. Secured transactions law has far-reaching distributive consequences, not only for categories of parties to the lending, but also for states with financial centers and with entrepreneurs seeking to enhance their global trade, for international and national financial institutions, and for other competitors in international trade and finance.

Secured lenders, broadly conceived, have three main interests: they prefer a greater variety of types of collateral against which they can lend so their lending can be expanded; they press for greater certainty that the law will protect their collateral; and they prefer greater flexibility in ways to act if the loan goes bad and the borrower defaults. *Debtors*, broadly conceived, want access to borrowed money, coupled with some flexibility and protections if they get into financial difficulty. And lenders who do not take security have a bifurcated attitude to secured lenders: if secured lenders help businesses expand, then *unsecured creditors* benefit from more opportunities to lend to a growing business; yet, if secured creditors tie up all the assets of a business in secured loans, then there will be less money available to unsecured creditors if loan defaults lead a business into bankruptcy.

Particularly important in the UNCITRAL negotiations was a special category of lenders – trade creditors who retain ownership of goods sold to a debtor after they have been delivered but before they have been paid for. In many countries, the sellers of goods protect themselves by shipping the goods to buyers but maintaining ownership or property rights over those goods until they are paid for. The legal concept of retention of title, very widely used in Continental trade, essentially keeps ownership in the hands of brick-makers or equipment manufacturers even when the bricks have been delivered to the construction site or the equipment is being used by a buyer. In principle, this retention of ownership means that, when the "buyer" fails to pay the purchase price, the bricks or equipment could be seized back or at least sold to others. Under US secured transactions law, this sort of conditional sale arrangement, like other forms of financing, is treated as "functionally" equivalent to a secured transaction and so governed by the same rules of Article 9 of the US Uniform Commercial Code.

The slow emergence of a global TLO in secured transactions (Macdonald 2015) reflects in substantial part the enormous variation across the world in the kinds of practices habitually undertaken within countries to finance trade. Many countries, for instance, have considered real property the principal form of security. Other countries, particularly with financial centers, widely loan on the basis of security over a wide range of tangible and intangible property, including property that doesn't even exist at the time the loan agreement is struck, such as inventory or accounts receivable that all parties understand will flow into and out of the debtor's business. In virtually all parts of the world, security laws have emerged as financial practices have evolved, with the result that they often are scattered in a variety of statute books across many different types of legislation.

We demonstrated in Chapter 3 that types of security and national and regional variations in TLOs intersected, most notably in a confrontation in principle and practice between blocs of nations led respectively by the US and Germany. The great divide at the center of UNCITRAL's Secured Transactions Working Group was the "huge conflict" over the primacy given to the comprehensive, coherent and all-embracing US approach to secured transactions laws, which looked to a single law broadly to cover any kind of transaction with the functional effect of a security right (Int: 9030).

On the one hand, "the US was pressing Article 9 [of its Uniform Commercial Code] completely," said a key non-US delegate (Int: 9030). Lined up alongside the US were other countries that had adopted substantially similar laws, most notably, Canada, but also Australia and New Zealand. The US bloc sought to bring as much secured transactions law as possible under the umbrella of a single unitary law. On the other hand, Germany did not want either a replica of Article 9 or a law that brought all security, including over property through retention of title, under a US-centric set of global norms. And, in between, there were numbers of other countries, such as India, Islamic states, much of Africa, that wanted global norms sufficiently flexible to permit "modernization and all its advantages except that it doesn't have to be done in the Article 9 way" (Int: 9030). From the perspective of Germany, the UK and many other countries, a range of statutes enacted to address variation in secured transactions and other financing devices could regulate security rights (Int: 6504).

This confrontation of major law and financial centers involved more than a struggle between powerful states over their competitive advantage in international finance. Both had strong allies in private industry. US banking interests and other lending associations stood to gain much from the globalization of Article 9-like law. European bankers, especially in Germany and Austria, sought to maintain their historic advantage in lending to businesses in Central and Eastern Europe. One delegate understood German bankers to dislike the UNCITRAL project because they viewed secured transactions law reform as "likely to undercut their market advantage" (Int: 6505).

Unlike other working group deliberations, this competition took center stage in the Secured Transactions Working Group sessions, not back rooms. It was expressed audibly, in a succession of interventions recognized in the order flags were raised. As a result, attendance mattered and the North Americans attended these sessions in force and with near perfect regularity. More than half of the high-attendance delegates came from either the US or Canada, whether state or non-state delegations are considered. This was a force to be reckoned with (Chapter 4). There were other high-attendance delegates from developed economies, including not only Germany but also several others (like Austria and Sweden) whose secured transactions law resembled those of Germany. But one important delegation was missing: The UK delegation, which might also have spoken convincingly against a functional approach to secured transactions law, had chosen not to participate in the Secured Transactions Working Group, claiming that its attentions were better focused on the Transport and Insolvency Working Groups whose deliberations were overlapping.

Divides and Deals

The politics over normative dominance in the Working Group on Secured Transactions, therefore, was less a matter of multiple small deals and more an instance of one very big deal that was expressed through subsidiary struggles. As a lead European delegate put it, there were "no Big Deals." There was "US Article 9, take it or leave it" (Int: 6509). Or as another eminent European delegate stated: the US "offered the big scheme," which rode on the premise that "our economy is terrific and if you are not on the program you are backward" (Int: 6503).

We approach these subsidiary struggles through three extensively debated issues that are fundamental to any system of security for lending.

Scope

The scope of a secured transactions law, and thus of efforts to reform secured transactions laws, can be characterized juridically either in the terms of the substance or form of these laws.

On the one side, the North American delegations and their "allies" argued for a functional approach to security, namely, anything that acted as a security interest should be considered a security interest, no matter how the parties had labeled the transaction or the sorts of personal property collateral it involved. If the transaction functioned as security devices, then it was argued, it should be governed by a single coherent, consistent legal instrument, such as a comprehensive secured transactions law. "The US," said a leading European delegate, "wanted a unitary system based on functionalism" (Int: 6501).

The US advocated in favor of a functional approach because this was a key component of the US Article 9 and its progeny in Canada, New Zealand, and Australia. This interest in functionalism was based pragmatically on historical US experiences with a patchwork of subnational laws enacted to address a plethora of transactions, many of which arose in order to avoid the constraints of the narrowly framed laws that previously had been enacted. From the point of view of recursivity theory, where indeterminacy and inconsistency of law is frequently a hindrance to the settling of legal norms, this perspective seemed pragmatically sensible.

On the other side, were those, like the German delegation, that pointed out that many forms of security had developed in many places over long periods of time in various contexts and it made no sense to disturb laws and practices that were already well settled. British secured transactions laws present the clearest example of this sort of divide and multiply approach to commercial finance. True, the law might not look like a Benthamite or Weberian rational legal code, and its various labels and locations might indeed be scattered across many laws within a country's legal system, but for reasons of tradition, predictability and political expediency, it was argued that the Working Group should not to try and force all square pegs into round holes. Similarly, the Germans and many other delegates from European countries "wanted to distinguish between secured transactions and those involving property" rights and ownership interests, including, most importantly, "retention of title transactions" (Int: 6501, 6503, 9030).

A balancing of interests and artful technical inventiveness helped bridge this divide. Although the Commission had initially envisioned a Secured Transactions Guide that narrowly covered only inventory and equipment, in the end the Working Group decided that this text should cover a wide range of transactional forms, to "ensure that all providers of secured credit are treated according to rules that produce functionally equivalent outcomes."[37]

Whose interests are favored by this sort of "functional" approach to secured transactions laws? In most respects, the Guide represents a victory for secured creditors because it covers an extensive variety of collateral and transactions. Debtors also, in principle, benefited from the expansive opportunities for borrowing governed by the Guide, should its norms get adopted in their countries.

For unsecured creditors, the outcome was more complex. Increased access to credit implied that businesses could flourish, which in turn would benefit the unsecured creditors who supplied these businesses with inventory, equipment and services on credit. But this growth potential might come at a price for unsecured creditors if things went awry. If the business became financially distressed and entered bankruptcy, then the greater the proportion of its assets that were secured, the less moneys might be available to pay off creditors without security since secured creditors nearly always enjoy a higher priority in distributions from a bankruptcy estate than do unsecured creditors.

Canadian delegate and law professor, Roderick Macdonald, created a solution to bridge the deep divide between the advocates of a functional big-tent approach and the keep-all-forms-of-law separate approach, most importantly, retention of title. Macdonald proposed that the debate applied only to what the Guide terms "acquisition financing transactions," a term he invented to refer to any transaction through which a debtor might acquire some asset from a seller.

When addressing "acquisition financing transactions" he argued, the Guide could tolerate two kinds of secured transaction regimes. On the one hand, following the North American approach, the global norms could take a *unitary* form whereby all types of collateral of any kind would fall within a single secured

[37] Legislative Guide on Secured Transactions, Purposes, Recs. 2–12.

transactions law.[38] On the other hand, to accommodate delegations resistant to the functional approach, the Guide would accept a *non-unitary* secured transaction bundle of laws in which retention of title, for instance, could coexist with all the other forms of collateral.[39] This compromise proved satisfactory to the civil lawyers in the chamber, including especially those from the German delegation that had fought hard against the Guide's embrace of a functional approach to secured transactions financing. Said a Continental lawyer, this would "preserve an alternative. The two [would] sit side-by-side – and countries can choose" (Int: 6503). Thus, the Big Deal in this Working Group, said another European, "was to provide an option: those for unity; and those who wanted to unify a regime but to keep the forms separate" (Int: 6501).

However, there was a legerdemain in this solution. While nations who opted for the non-unitary approach could keep retention of title laws separate from secured transactions laws, they nevertheless were encouraged through a set of conditional recommendations to create the rights in the same way as other security rights, to subject them to the same priorities and enforcement regimes, and, not least, that if a seller wanted to get back the value of goods subject to default they could not be seized but value would need to be obtained some other way (Rec 9(b)). In short, while retention of title could be retained, it now had to be subject to the same kinds of security steps as any other kind of security.

This prestidigitation proved sufficient for most of the Europeans to accept the Guide's overwhelmingly functional and comprehensive approach. While the Guide permits states to choose between a unitary and non-unitary approach to acquisition financing, it takes great pains to remove all functional difference from this permitted formal distinction. The substance and consequence of this treatment would be uniform, even if a country chose to follow the Guide's non-unitary approach. The distinction between the two sorts of regimes was, thus, largely rhetorical.

But this rhetorical distinction between secured transactions and other sorts of transactions was precisely the point that delegates from civilian legal traditions looked to emphasize. Argued one participant, the Guide was a success because "[y]ou *can* respect the form of the transaction where the seller is the owner. You *can* incorporate a wide variety of regimes across the world that take different forms" (Int: 9030). Form mattered to some delegates because form matters to many domestic legislatures, courts and lawyers. "Without this agreement, it would not have been accepted by India, any Islamic state, most of Africa, most post-socialist regimes. There would have been no take-up without this" (Int: 9030).

Transparency of Lending

In many countries and contexts, secured creditors face a transparency problem. How can trade creditors and other unsecured lenders know whether the debtor already

[38] Id., Rec. 9(a).
[39] Id., Rec. 9(b).

has granted a security interest in a piece of property to a previous lender? Indeed, how do creditors of any sort know whether they would be the first to be paid or the second, third, or fourth from the sale of an asset that secures their loans? Without that knowledge, they would be lending in a situation of considerable uncertainty, which, at the very least, substantially problematizes the pricing of their loans.

Secured creditors want at least two protections that render transparency in the kinds of security a business has already given to other lenders. They want to know *whether* other lenders have already taken security in the collateral in which they now seek security rights. And, because these interests often are respected in a first-come-first-served basis, they want to know *when* such security has been given.

A ready solution to this problem is creation of a publicly accessible register for all security rights. If the law requires that every secured creditor must file notice that they claim a security interest over specified assets of a business, then other lenders are put on public notice of this claim. The form of a registry of this sort was not uncontentious.

One sort of registry provides public notice of transactions. With transactional filings, the security agreement (or mortgage) is itself put on file for public viewing. Because these documents might take up hundreds of pages, this sort of registration can be costly. They might give the public access to more information than the debtor and lender may be comfortable in sharing. Moreover, transactional registries only look backward to provide access to what the parties already have agreed to, rather than an indication of the scope of what they might agree to in the future.

Another sort of registry more simply requires only the filing of a summary notice. Notice filing limits the information that must be included in public registries. This summary format both reduces the cost of a filing and limits the extent of information searchers can access publicly. Despite these advantages, notice filing also puts the onus on searchers to obtain further information from the parties identified on the face of this summary instrument.

Thus, if the notice provides too much information – how much money has been lent and at what rate – then it may provide more information than the company wants to competitors or to other lenders. If the notice provides only the bare minimum of information, then its very opaqueness may benefit the first lenders by discouraging others from providing credit to the same borrower. Finally, public registries of any sort have been controversial in some regions, particularly within Germany and other places in Continental Europe, which historically have questioned the wisdom or even the need for disclosure of lending practices given the small number of secured lenders within their borders and the ready availability of information through informal word-of-mouth. This kind of close-knit lending without public registration of any sort is also viewed as controversial, mostly on the grounds that it sets high barriers to market entry for outsiders, but also on the grounds that the greater transparency from public registries would aid unsecured creditors' decisionmaking.

In the ordinary course of business, unsecured creditors also would like to know whether other creditors have taken security in the assets of a business and, if so, the scope and terms on which security is claimed. Transactional registries provide more detailed information than notice filings, but unsecured creditors' preferences between the two sorts of registers are unclear.[40]

As to their preferences between transactional and notice registries, debtors are largely neutral; whether or not a security is registered by one means or another, the debtor businesses are still locked into repayment of one or another secured creditor under the rules set by secured transaction law for a country or jurisdiction.

There has been wide variation in requirements for registration across the world. The US Article 9 system requires public registration of secured transactions, but these are notice filings that identify the debtor and secured creditor and provide limited information about what assets are being secured, but say nothing about other details of the transaction.[41] By contrast, the UK requires transactional filings (when public registration is required at all), which means lots of paper gets filed but only after the transaction has been finalized. A number of countries, such as India, agree with the concept of a registry, pointing to widespread registration requirements around the world, but argued that registries should be differentiated by the kind of lending that was involved (e.g., a special registry for car loans). Some Continental countries, notably Germany, resist disclosure in a single register covering both security rights and retention of title. Said a European specialist at the core of negotiations, "Germans ... did not want to make public by registration a transaction involving ownership. The German market is idiosyncratic because it is opaque – when I transfer ownership [under German law], it functions as security although it is registered nowhere" (Int: 6501).

To bridge this divide, the Secured Transactions Working Group looked to split the difference between registration of transactional filings and no registration at all by providing that a security right is legally enforceable even against creditors who weren't parties to the security agreement "if a notice ... is registered in [a] general security rights registry" (Rec. 32). While the Secured Transactions Guide might be viewed as a compromise between several positions, in large part it deferred to US law. To Germany, and like-minded delegations, the Guide demands little in the way of disclosure, although it does demand at least notice that a secured lender has claims over a debtor's property without saying too much about what are those claims. And to countries that wish to maintain "a wide variety of

40 If a business enters bankruptcy proceedings, unsecured creditors may want to attack improperly filed security interests to enlarge the pool available for distributions to them, but a transactional filing is nearly impervious to these sorts of claims; notice filings open up the possibility that improper notice is subject to avoidance in an insolvency proceeding, but often encourage secured creditors to lay wider claims to a debtor's assets.

41 Indeed, the US approach is to allow a notice filing to be registered even before the parties have concluded negotiations, so that the putative lender's priority position is clear both to the lender and the world before the transaction is closed.

regimes . . . that take different forms," (Int: 9030) that too would be acceptable in UNCITRAL's Guide.

The Guide's architectural rules on public registries left for another day negotiations about just how these registries should work.[42]

Unilateral versus Collective Remedies

If a company in financial difficulty stops paying and defaults on its loans to a secured creditor, what actions does a secured lender want available to it? Before a company is insolvent or in bankruptcy, a lender is best positioned if it can quickly and inexpensively enforce its claim by seizing the assets and selling them. If this can be done without the involvement of courts, so much the better, since this sort of litigation is often costly and time consuming. Where secured creditors are allowed to act without judicial oversight, the argument runs, there would be fewer transaction costs and, as a result, the cost of lending should decrease.

Bankruptcy can put a halt to secured creditors' collection activity. If an insolvency law prohibits secured creditors' from simply grabbing assets out of the hands of defaulting debtors, it nonetheless will protect lenders' collateral value from diminishing during the insolvency procedure. Protecting against a diminution in asset value is not the same thing as ensuring secured creditors that they will be fully compensated for the time that bankruptcy can take, however. And so, even with these protections, secured creditors would prefer to be allowed to opt out of insolvency proceedings altogether, again arguing that the cost of lending will diminish if they are unfettered by the strictures of a bankruptcy court's jurisdiction.

Debtors and their unsecured creditors have different interests, depending on whether the consequences of default and bankruptcy are considered. Both sorts of actors benefit from the lower cost of credit that secured lenders argue is the consequence of allowing their unilateral action. At the same time, upon default, debtors and unsecured creditors may feel their fates left to the mercy of a secured creditor empowered to enforce its claim without the involvement of a court.

Unilateral actions by secured creditors were long associated with creditor-friendly British and Commonwealth practices permitting some secured creditors to act decisively in the event of a default, actions that were allowed to occur outside bankruptcy law and despite bankruptcy law. The English reform movement in the late 1970s and early 1980s strongly criticized the powers given secured creditors on grounds that they frequently destroyed businesses that could have been saved, if only the secured creditors had taken into account interests other than their

[42] See Id., Recs. 54–55. But UNCITRAL did not wait long to take up this issue again. By 2013, UNCITRAL had published its Guide on the Implementation of a Security Rights Registry (UNCITRAL Guide on the Implementation of a Security Rights Registry (2013)).

own (Carruthers and Halliday 1998). The English legislation of 1985, subsequently adopted in many of the near-fifty former British colonies, restricted this unilateral discretion and moved the UK approach closer to the US practices inscribed in the 1978 Bankruptcy Code.

Continental European insolvency laws generally favored secured creditors' interests, but often involved courts in this process. Because these laws often did not comprehend the notion of a debtor's reorganization, they may have permitted secured creditors' liquidation of collateral without the involvement of a trustee in bankruptcy or the court with jurisdiction of the bankruptcy proceeding. Nonetheless, European courts might well have been required to oversee secured creditors' enforcement of their priority positions. The notion that a secured creditor might repossess and sell collateral without court involvement was a concept nearly unique to North American secured transactions laws.

UNCITRAL's lawmakers again searched for a way to split the difference between historically creditor-friendly versus debtor-friendly laws and North American versus Continental approaches. On the one hand, the Secured Transactions Guide follows a widespread North American approach to repossession of collateral without court involvement. This was a "big breakthrough," according to many delegates (Int: 6510). Nonetheless, the Guide does not allow secured creditors unfettered discretionary enforcement, even permissively. In a series of imperative recommendations, it also conditions this process on fulfillment of a number of factors not currently present under US or Canadian law. These conditions lean toward a European approach to default, which seeks parties' consent and involves judges in policing this agreement. Members of the US delegation viewed these provisions as problematic.

> There is a rule [in the Guide] in the enforcement foreclosure area – you have to notify the borrower you are going to foreclose. There are eighteen sets of notices. We thought there were too many, too inefficient. We jokingly referred to it as a "notice to hide the collateral."
>
> (Int: 6510)

In addition, the two UNCITRAL Legislative Guides on Secured Transactions and on Insolvency Law jointly agreed on the treatment of secured creditors in an insolvency setting. These joint recommendations agree that a secured creditor's collateral should be subject to the jurisdiction of a bankruptcy court and to the restrictions of any stay or moratorium that exists under the insolvency law. Read together, the Secured Transactions Guide permits secured creditors freedom from judicial involvement in the event of a debtor's default (but not complete freedom), while the Insolvency Guide requires secured creditors' involvement in an insolvency proceeding involving the debtor. And, as noted earlier, the Insolvency Guide generally presumes judicial involvement in bankruptcy.

Whose Secured Transaction Norms?

Those standing close to the US Article 9, most especially the US delegation and US non-state delegates, such as the Commercial Finance Association, can point to a number of places where the Guide does not follow Article 9 as revised in 2000, nor even the Article 9 that previously was in place in the US since the late 1960s and subsequently adopted and adapted in Canada, Australia and New Zealand. In their view, the Guide diverges from US secured transactions law. Said one non-US delegate, "it brasses me off when people say the Legislative Guide is just Article 9. The US had to give up on a number of points" (Int: 9030).

Those standing farther away, and regarding the world either from a different region or the world as a whole, largely concur that the Legislative Guide on Secured Transactions seeks to formalize and propagate a set of norms that adhere most closely and most discernibly in their general contours and many of the particulars of US law, not to mention its form. Several non-US and non-North American delegates in the inner circle of global legislators expressed this view. When asked who came out ahead in the Working Group's deliberations, an eminent European replied:

> The US. They offered the big scheme and they had solutions for very, very many detailed questions . . . The American interest groups were very strong and numerous but of course they had the Uniform Commercial Code, Article 9, so what more could they want.
>
> (Int: 6503)

This European went on to say:

> [The delegates from the US] were the biggest players. But it was for a good reason. They have a good instrument on which they rely. And it was absolutely familiar to them. So it was a natural constellation for pro-American interests. They played their cards very well. Their delegations were very well prepared. They had their internal meetings. They lived in one hotel, and were not dispersed like others, [who were all] over the city of Vienna. Apparently, they met every evening or morning; they prepared well. They were excellently organized. So it was not so much [that they were organized] by the State Department, but just because they have a good instrument with which they are very well familiar.
>
> (Int: 6503)

Our review of the compromises inscribed in the Secured Transactions Guide supports both views. There is much about the Guide that closely resembled US Article 9 and the related Personal Property Security Acts that have been adopted in Canada and elsewhere.[43] Yet there were several aspects of the Secured Transactions Guide that complicate the simplicity of a hegemonic storyline.

[43] These include: (i) its overall functional scope; (ii) its focus on personal property and exclusion of real property mortgages; (iii) its focus on voluntary security rights, leaving involuntary liens

First, to describe the Guide as the product of North American domination of the proceedings is to imply that there was a unified North American position put forward in Working Group deliberations. When asked about just this, a member of the Canadian delegation replied: "Anyone who thinks that the Canadians and the US had the same position is dreaming in Technicolor."[44] There were many substantive issues on which the US and Canadian delegations disagreed, this delegate argued, since the North American approach is not a unified secured transactions regime.[45]

Second, the Working Group relied on a range of formal strategies when drafting the Guide, which also complicate the notion that the Guide merely restates US Article 9. The Secured Transactions Guide was comprised mostly of imperative recommendation (see Chapter 6), unlike the Insolvency Guide, which contains a mix of imperative, permissive, architectural and other rule-types. This insistence on imperative recommendations was a drafting decision implicitly adopted by the Secured Transactions Working Group, one that favored bright-line rules, offering no alternatives.[46]

and encumbrances to the subject of some other law; (iv) its coverage of many sales of accounts receivable and other payment streams, and of security rights in bank accounts, which many other laws consider mere rights of set off; (v) its insistence that security rights continue in the proceeds of collateral, notwithstanding a sale; (vi) its requirement that security rights be published, including especially through notice filings submitted in a public registry devoted exclusively to the registration of secured transactions; (vii) its acceptance of virtual forms of possession as relates to certain sorts of intangible personal property, which are referred to, as under US law, as "control" rights; (ix) its general trust in secured creditors' unilateral enforcement, without judicial involvement, of a right to repossess and subsequently sell collateral upon the debtor's default; and (x) its reference to secured creditors' enforcement rights as limited by a general obligation to act in good faith and in a commercially reasonable fashion. These issues included both fundamentals and technical details.

44 Citation attribution in files of the authors.

45 Importantly, despite broad statements reminiscent of US law that a secured transactions law should govern "regardless of the form of the transaction or the terminology used by the parties" (Legislative Guide on Secured Transactions, Rec. 8), the Guide also provides that security rights and ownership rights might be separately classified in distinct laws governing "acquisition financing" transactions (Rec. 9(b)). Similarly, despite broad statements that a secured creditor is "entitled to possession of a tangible encumbered asset" and can elect to obtain this possession without the assistance of a court, the Guide limits this right of self-help repossession to instances in which the debtor consents before default, in the security agreement and fails to object to the notice of repossession sent by the creditor (Rec. 147).

46 There was one notable exception to the general observation that the Secured Transactions Guide relies mostly on imperative recommendations. When the Secured Transactions Working Group declined to followed a functional approach to secured transactions laws to its logical conclusion, and agreed to permit either a unitary or non-unitary approach to acquisition financing, it adopted a formal strategy that had been relied upon both by the Insolvency Working Group in drafting their Legislative Guide and by the Transportation Working Group in drafting what would become the Rotterdam Rules. The Working Group drafted these provisions as permissive recommendations, although hidden in a conditional format that accepts both a Version A and Version B, each of which are laid out in technical detail.

Not all delegates were happy or content with this model-law-like Secured Transactions Guide, given especially its US-centric tone. At least three kinds of dissent emanated from those in the inner core.

First, there was the view expressed that secured transactions reform might take place in vastly different circumstances, with differing common and civil law heritages, where property rights varied in strength, where many forms of security were simply unknown, and rule of law too often was scarcely existent could not adhere to a single model. Given the possibility of such a varied set of background circumstances, some delegates complained that the Guide's imperative tone gave the impression that dropping a model-law-like set of recommendations into a statute book might alter national practices, an impression subject to legitimate question.

Second, there was a view expressed by more than one European delegate that their economies had succeeded without adopting the letter of US law. They had no desire to hand the US financial industry international standards that increased their competitive advantage, especially in regions previously dominated by major European financial centers.

Third, a view from the developing world pointed out a double irrelevance-in-the-making of a Legislative Guide on Secured Transactions Law composed principally of bright-line rules. In one respect, legislative drafting in some middle-income developing economies proceeded "on the basis of abstract principles" so that the facts-on-the-ground would be "governed by principles." This contrasted sharply with the form of US law, adopted in the Guide, "where the US thinks of every option and makes provisions for it" (Int: 6504). In another respect, many countries have long histories of dealing with property and property rights in very different ways, some of which continue into the present and would be either politically infeasible to change or undesirable given the legal uncertainty they could produce. Said one delegate from a middle-income state, the Legislative Guide might work well "where there is no law at present and so there is nothing to disturb." However, where there are long established practices, the recommendations in the Guide "might create difficulties given how well our law has settled ... If the Legislative Guide approach were introduced," what now works fine "would be disturbed" (Int: 6504).

The commentary in the Secured Transactions Guide allowed the Working Group a second opportunity to question US secured transactions law as setting international standards. This commentary sometimes undermined the US-centrism of the Secured Transactions Guide, and not accidentally. When the recommendation section of the Secured Transactions Guide was complete, the Working Group was faced with a set of rules without a workable commentary. The recommendations that the Working Group had settled on didn't match with the Guide's early commentary. The Working Group asked several core delegates to write a commentary for each chapter, but in the final event two delegates took the leading oar in polishing the final commentary – Roderick Macdonald from Canada and Richard Kohn from the Commercial Finance Association. Macdonald, a lawmaker with drafting credentials in common and civil law countries, and in advanced and transitional economies, had reservations about model-law-like imperative insistence of the recommendations that all countries, no matter what their histories or circumstances, shift to a "generic Article 9" system. As a result, he crafted his writing in the commentary to present a counter-narrative, where alternative courses of action were discussed with some appreciation of their merits, even if the imperative recommendations themselves leaned in a different direction. Said one delegate in the inner circle: "for a very careful reader, the commentary makes clear to a state reading it that there are alternative ways to getting to 'Go', other than the recommendations" (Int: 9030). Another inner circle dissenter from the "generic Article 9" quality of the recommendations stated, with similar import:

> during the discussion it became obvious that other solutions were in the air which could be discussed and which are successful in some countries . . . hence there is a general difference between the recommendations and the commentary.
>
> (Int: 6509)

As a result, the flexibility of the UNCITRAL text itself – a Legislative Guide on Secured Transactions Law – permitted both a main theme (i.e., the recommendations) and variations on the theme (i.e., the commentary) to coexist, potentially in creative tension. Dissenters from the form and content of some recommendations could find alternative authority for state lawmaking in the commentary. In this sense, with careful reading, the Secured Transactions Guide provided for countries with limited secured transactions law "a hornbook[47] for national legislators." They could "take the Guide as a hornbook on the issues and the options" (Int: 6509).

IMPRINTS OF POWER

The outcomes of UNCITRAL's lawmaking episodes are framed by two contrasting images of UNCITRAL. On the one hand, there is a deliberative process contained within a UN lawmaking arena where all the world's nations and most salient non-state actors are invited as delegates and delegations. This signifies universalism, diversity, and pragmatism in representation and provides UNCITRAL with a powerful mandate for global governance. Differences in power, wealth, location, legal heritage, resources, and capacities for action are all elided in a participatory process that treats every delegate and delegation in effect with procedural equality. On the other hand, the institutional resource dependency of UNCITRAL and the empirics of attendance and actual participation reveal a much circumscribed and narrower circle of lawmakers from a mostly unrepresentative selection of states. Asymmetries

[47] "Hornbook" is a term often used by lawyers to refer to a treatise or some other learned commentary on the meaning of law, and especially on the meaning of divergent case law arising in a common law setting.

of power, wealth, location, legal heritage, and resources potentially subvert UNCITRAL's potent claims to legitimate authority. Which of these images – or others – best reflects UNCITRAL's final products, the legal norms that are promulgated to the world?

Across all three arenas of lawmaking there is no doubt that the United States repeatedly emerges as the single most dominant actor, both as a state and as a leader of non-state actors. UNCITRAL's legislators always yielded to the key demands of the US, even if the US shared some its core demands with other countries, and the US bloc did not get everything it wanted. In fact, as a deliberative strategy, the US explicitly stated from the beginning its core demands in the transport lawmaking and implicitly joined a North American bloc with a general set of expectations for the outcomes of secured transactions lawmaking.

Getting to the Big Deals also demonstrates that it is the legal norms of the Global North that almost always prevail over the rest of world. Those norms originated from state and non-state delegates and delegations in the Global North, usually from North America and Europe, and always included influential international industry and professional delegations. Their pervasive influence frequently required a rapprochement between common and civil law traditions and at key points between particularly powerful states in the international political economy, most usually, the United States, France, and Germany.

The Global South – most of Latin America, Africa, South Asia, East Asia, and the Middle East – rarely made a substantive contribution with one major exception – the emergence of a bloc of small African nations in the transport negotiations. The African bloc held leverage because in jointly agreeing to sign the draft treaty they could assure economically powerful nations that their goal of accumulating the necessary number of signatures was numerically achievable. An effort was made by multilateral bodies such as UNCTAD to speak for the Global South and it failed.

UNCITRAL's Secretariat, Commission, and inner community of delegates within each working group exercised significant influence in their own right. This exercise of influence signals UNCITRAL's autonomy as a collective actor, rather than simply an arena for state action. Often, it was the UNCITRAL Secretariat's deliberative direction and strategic decisionmaking, coupled with the UNCITRAL methods of work, that enabled legal creativity and innovations of concepts and technologies to bridge deep divides between powerful blocs of opposing interests.

Not least, the prominence of professions, and the proportional dominance of lawyers, judges and other legally trained officials, ensured that the outcomes would be firmly anchored in law and legal institutions that were serviced primarily by lawyers. Yet even this professional project was mitigated by opportunities to circumvent courts or to permit private transactions or bureaucratic solutions that enabled private parties to side-line either lawyers or courts from time to time throughout the case studies.

Power and influence too often have been latent in ecology theory (Liu and Emirbayer 2016). A failure expressly to examine power would also weaken the value of interactionist social ecology approaches to IOs and global normmaking. This chapter intentionally considers and, thus, reveals that the imprints of power and tendrils of influence exercised in these issue-areas. Our findings resonate with complementary theoretical orientations. In the international political economy of lawmaking, it is the most powerful economy in the global center that dominates, yet it does not do unequivocally or without concessions. Moreover, the wider set of countries at the apex of the world financial system was not always aligned or active. Overwhelmingly, however, the three episodes of lawmaking confirm the general proposition that a relatively few countries in world economy exert disproportionate influence. And consistent with IPE's emphasis on powerful non-state actors, we find not only a prominent role for industry associations (Chapters 3, 4, and 5) but also the significant influence of international financial institutions (Chapter 9).

We can amplify the conclusion that the power of professionals, and most particularly, the legal complex, makes itself manifest at every point from initial drafts through expert panels, formal interventions and legal creativity. While world polity theory rightly predicts that professionals are among the primary conduits of norms across the globe, this chapter details how the core of those norms, or at least legal norms, are first forged under the strong influence and technical idiom not of economists or accountants, but overwhelmingly of legal professionals, who will later carry them back to domestic jurisdictions. A legal complex inside UNCITRAL's working groups is creating TLOs, and while lawyers and courts were not always privileged in these products it is legally crafted orders that emerge and these will be presided over for the most part by lawyers and judges. Trade and commerce, in this global order, is an economic enterprise situated inside a legal scaffolding.

Given that outcomes were not entirely predictable at the onset of the lawmaking episodes, influence and power must also be seen to reside in UNCITRAL itself. As institutional theory would predict, many actors entered UNCITRAL's lawmaking arena not fully or precisely aware of what were their economic or sovereign interests. For those who stayed, their interests were shaped and sharpened as faultlines became visible and deals to bridge those faultlines emerged. Yet the processes that enabled both Big Deals and a series of smaller ones exemplifies constructivist understandings of IOs as actors in their own right, who add value and stimulate emergence of ideas and norms, who create technologies and foster shared understandings that could not have been predicted from *ex ante* knowledge of the interests of any given state or non-state actor. Non-state actors and institutions exert influence in ways, therefore, that are not simply reducible to the *ex ante* interests of states. Indeed the global norms that emerged were very much a product of industry and international organizations, often conveyed by states, as they were of a distinctively Westphalian state itself.[48]

[48] This conclusion is consistent with the empirical findings of (Braithwaite and Drahos 2000) on global business regulation and (Shaffer 2003a) on the US and WTO.

Our identification of the forging of Big Deals and how they were forged offers specificity to institutional accounts of norms and practice we identified in the Introduction. We observed in the boundary work that accompanied agenda setting the discursive framings that often reflect what political scientists have characterized as path dependencies (Chapter 3). We observe here that some of the Big Deals bridged deep historical faultlines because evolutionary, incremental changes had already moved some common law countries toward each other and some civil law systems toward common law norms and practices. The deals forged consensus by building on already existing momentum. Construction of emergent norms depended frequently on the rhetorical work of legal entrepreneurs whose creativity permitted former competitors to see themselves in the future as variants of a legal order now subsumed under shared higher principles (Chapter 6). Although tangible material interests underlay such competition, for instance, between Germany and the US in European markets, intangible symbolic craft enabled rivals to settle at least for competitive cooperation. Inventiveness and negotiation centered on legal technologies became essential for the crafting of these deals. The creative design of these legal technologies allowed delegates to transcend difference to the extent they did.

Nevertheless, it is imperative to observe that answers to the question "whose norms?" must not be conflated with answers to the question "who benefits?" It can be argued that the bankruptcy norms will benefit all nations even if most countries were not active agents in the lawmaking. It might be argued that a single globally unified set of rules to govern transport of goods by sea will benefit trade for all nations, even if there are real prospects of disadvantages to many developing countries and small and medium businesses. If the theory that animated the secured transactions proves to be correct, then indeed investment will be attracted by prospects of security and economies will grow – but these tangible effects are, as of yet, mere suppositions and hopes to which some hold contrary views.

In part, the impact of norms crafted predominantly by the global center turns on the dynamics of emerging TLOs. We have shown in our case studies that the Big Deals and legal forms in which the norms were conveyed provided degrees of freedom for states (and in some cases economic actors) to exercise discretion in implementing the norms promulgated by UNCITRAL. The price of consensus not infrequently became openness or flexibility in the legal norms that got produced, an outcome enabled by the creative invention of rule-types that codified the varieties of difference and degrees of consensus in the lawmaking enterprise. Imperative recommendations drafted with a strong language of obligation were complemented by the incorporation of permissive and vaguely-phrased architectural recommendations in the same document.

Thus, at once, the lawmaking reached consensus by purporting to resolve global problems in lending, business rescue, and getting goods to market. In each of these issue-areas new TLOs began to emerge notwithstanding longstanding challenges of great complexity. This normative convergence reflected very heavily the imprint of the US and a small coterie of state and non-state actors in the Global North. Nevertheless, the price of consensus and convergence was concession – tangible concessions that ensured a degree of openness and adaptive capacity in order for weak states and subaltern actors to preserve a measure of legal, economic, and political autonomy.

Nonetheless, the inevitability of fully institutionalized TLOs in any of these issue-areas cannot be assumed by the big or small deals forged within UNCITRAL as an arena or by UNCITRAL as an actor. Recursivity theory sensitizes us to fragilities that remain below the surface of consensus. Seeds of resistance by sovereign states were sown in normative settlements made by few for the many, by the adoption of technologies whose complexities harbored inconsistencies and indeterminacies or whose law-like properties seemed to demand sovereign acquiescence whether or not its provisions were contextually relevant.

In sum, producing global norms to bridge deep divides was no small feat. That those norms bore the imprint of states, industries, and professions predominantly from the Global North appeared to be the price UNCITRAL had to pay to maintain its own standing among global lawmaking institutions. Whether that trade-off will produce new or reformed TLOs will unfold in cycles of lawmaking at all levels in coming years.

8

The Lawmaking of Lawmaking

Inside its formal operational parameters, UNCITRAL's Secretariat and delegates created informal methods of work to overcome inertial drag and resource scarcity (Chapter 5). In part this adaptive capacity flowed from what may well have been an historical accident. At the time of its founding, UNCITRAL's advocates ensured that not only would this new commercial lawmaking body promise the representativeness of a greater range of the world's states, but that it would also give other IOs a "right" to "observe" and "participate" in UNCITRAL proceedings. To assure the international community that UNCITRAL had access to the technical advice it would need to draft and promote global commercial laws, the General Assembly authorized the Commission to consult "experts." From its very first sessions, UNCITRAL interpreted this breadth of representation to include, not just a wide range of national interests, but also private interests or non-state actors that cover international industry groups and professional associations. By opening up its deliberations in its very first meetings to the International Chamber of Commerce, the International Maritime Committee, and the International Bar Association, among others, it signaled that this new lawmaking actor would also provide an arena for non-state actors to deliberate alongside states.

Who were these non-state actors? We have seen that across the issue-ecologies they included international financial institutions (e.g., IMF, World Bank), regional development banks (e.g., Asian Development Bank), clubs of nations (e.g., OECD), other standing lawmaking bodies (e.g., UNIDROIT, the Hague Conference on Private International Law), other UN entities (e.g., UNCTAD, International Law Organization), industry associations (e.g., the Commercial Finance Association, the European Freight Forwarders Association), and international professional associations (e.g., International Federation of Insolvency and Restructuring Specialists, called INSOL). Rather than a representative transnational government of states, UNCITRAL became a center of global governance where states, networks, clubs, international governmental bodies, trade groups, among others, sat side-by-side in lawmaking chambers practically as deliberative equals.

This expansive conception of representativeness solved important ecological problems. Non-state actors contributed heavily to the viability and productivity of lawmaking in the issue-ecologies. By giving non-state actors a place at the table, UNCITRAL drew in scarce resources of every kind – diagnostic intelligence on market failures, technical drafting expertise, volunteer labor, reserve infrastructures, money to underwrite travel by poor delegates to special meetings, ways to meet the challenges of time, and rapid response to the challenges of threats and crises. In so doing UNCITRAL leveraged its close relationships with industry ecologies and sought optimal degrees of freedom within the procedural rules conventional in its embedding institution, the United Nations. By drawing into the lawmaking body not only the world's most powerful states, but also global actors integral to international regulation and governance of markets, UNCITRAL signaled to all its constituencies, not least those within it, that this arena had authority to make laws and the world should take them as seriously as the delegations that implicitly acknowledged that authority. Non-state actors therefore became essential for UNCITRAL's operations, effectiveness, and centrality in lawmaking ecologies for global markets.

Incorporation of some non-state actors further helped solve relational challenges in standing and issue-ecologies. By welcoming potential competitors, like UNIDROIT and the Hague Conference, into its arena, UNCITRAL managed the territorial claims of these potential competitors even as the competitors could witness for themselves how far UNCITRAL's expansive inclinations intruded on their customary jurisdictions. Potential consumers of UNCITRAL's international products, the International Chamber of Commerce, International Maritime Committee, International Bar Association, or International Monetary Fund, among others, could observe, while they participated, that UNCITRAL would produce not just convergent laws governing international trade but laws useful to their industry, professional, and institutional interests.

This broad inclusion of non-actors also helped solve UNCITRAL's diagnostic challenges. The greater the diversity of actors in the room when drafting global commercial norms, the less likely it was that actor mismatch would result.[1] The resources offered to UNCITRAL by non-state actors multiplied the informal opportunities available to UNCITRAL as it sought to cope with resource constraints or formal UN rules on numbers of meetings, reaching consensus, and translation. As we have seen (Chapter 5), informal working methods significantly enabled by non-state delegates and delegations also allowed UNCITRAL to develop social substructures to support its legislative form. The limited resources of the Secretariat and the limits of a generalist model of working group secretaries found

[1] For more on the recursive dynamics of UNCITRAL's lawmaking, see Chapter 1.

"compensation" in their reliance on networks, inner circles, and expert groups. These inner circles presented working group secretaries with more than access to expertise. Informal methods of work provided working group secretaries with sounding boards, confidence builders, and reality checks. They provided secretaries with a community of professional access.

In this chapter, we show that the benefits endowed by non-state actors, and the Secretariat's initiatives and concessions around informal methods of work, led UNCITRAL into a contradiction of practices that eventually exploded into open conflict, albeit one couched in diplomatic nicety. On the one hand, the extensive embrace of non-state actors and a repertoire of informal practices had enabled UNCITRAL to produce rules for the world, despite its resource limitations and competitive pressures. On the other hand, these creative expedients of organizational adaptation led to shifts in UNCITRAL's internal balance of power in ways that arguably favored rich nations over poor nations, non-state actors over state actors, English-speaking delegates over non-English speakers, and "bottom up" styles of politics versus "top down" political practices.

In May 2007, France lobbed an incendiary proposal onto the agenda for the Commission meeting that summer, which fundamentally questioned the course of UNCITRAL's organizational evolution.[2] A French critique of participation by non-state actors and informal working methods centered on the very efficiencies that these methods facilitated for the Secretariat. Indeed, the use of informal methods underlies an enduring tension, or even contradiction, within UNCITRAL. While UNCITRAL's principal claims to legitimacy are centered on its representativeness of states and non-state interests, fair procedures, and effectiveness in earlier lawmaking projects, the informal methods achieve the last of these only by relaxing the first two. The unfolding and resolution of that conflict illustrate the contingencies of organizational adaptation and the challenges of balancing effectiveness without subverting UNCITRAL's long-crafted organizational identity.

THE FRENCH CRITIQUE

France's brief so-called "Observations" in mid-2007 challenged not only specific practices inside working groups, but also a lack of formalized rules to govern working group proceedings and all informal practices. While the UN General Assembly and other UN organs work within the confines of precisely stated written bylaws, said France, UNCITRAL possesses no such rules.[3]

France charged that the unregulated role of non-state actors within UNCITRAL opens it up to the potential for political mischief in several ways. First, it argued,

[2] Note by the Secretariat, Other Business: France's Observations on UNCITRAL's Working Methods, UN Doc. No. A/CN.9/635 (May 24, 2007).

[3] Id., ¶ 2.

UNCITRAL had gone too far in its inclusion of non-state actors in working group proceedings. The number of NGOs invited to participate in UNCITRAL working group sessions had steadily increased. France dates this expanded footprint to a shift in UNCITRAL's substantive focus,[4] when UNCITRAL extended "its scope of action beyond international trade law to domestic business law, for which non-binding instruments, such as legislative guides, are produced."[5] In other words, France objected to the opening of working group sessions to professional and trade associations, which it asserted began with the Insolvency Working Group's deliberations on the Insolvency Legislative Guide and continued with the Secured Transactions Working Group's deliberations on their Legislative Guide on Secured Transactions. Moreover, these non-state actors originally "had a stated interest in international trade."[6] Now these actors "are more obviously national in nature,"[7] referring specifically to "private associations."[8]

Second, France complained about the nature of the advice that these delegations provided:

> In practice the current role of private associations within UNCITRAL is far greater than that stipulated in the Economic and Social Council's framework-resolution, which is quite explicit on this point. These NGOs are active not merely in a consultative role, as provided for in the ESC resolution, or even in a higher advisory role, but in actually participating in the production of a standard-setting instrument.[9]

It viewed these non-state actors as participating on a "de facto equal basis with Member States."[10]

Viewed this way, decisionmaking within working groups had been compromised. France noted that the Secretariat constructed the list of non-state organizations issued invitations to working group sessions without active consultation or consent of states.[11] It also contended that "the Secretariat's excessive discretion can be seen in its active role in nominating the Chairman" of a working group from among the delegates members states have sent to the group, often without first consulting member states as a whole.[12] This objection was not just about the selection process because the position of a chair of a working group is not merely a honorary title.

4 Id., ¶ 6.1.

5 Id.

6 Id. Here, France singles out two general-purpose NGOs for praise: "In particular, the *Comité Maritime International*, a venerable institution responsible for the Hague-Visby Rules for maritime transport, and the International Chamber of Commerce, which publishes the Incoterms, the standards for international trade." Id., n. 5.

7 Id.

8 Id.

9 Id.

10 Id., ¶ 3, third bullet.

11 Id., ¶ 6.2.

12 Id., ¶ 5.1.

Chairs can and often do wield authority in running a meeting involving more than a hundred participants. While the chair's role in identifying delegations wishing to intervene in working group deliberations might involve nothing more than keeping an honest queue – a task that anyone seated in the room might audit – a chair also is expected to make a decision about when the working group has reached consensus. The best chairs guide the group to a consensual resolution of contested issues.

Because there is no clear definition of what counts as consensus within a working group, contended France, the power of the chair of a working group to propose a compromise held particular sway.[13] Moreover, the blurring of participants' roles in this regard might too easily influence the chair's decision. Because interventions may come from member states, observer states, and non-state delegations, the chair looks for a consensus among members and observers, state and non-state delegations. This center of gravity might differ substantially from what counts as a consensus if the count were of member states alone. Indeed, said France, working groups as a whole have gotten into the practice of exceeding the limits set in Commission mandates, implying that NGO influence went far beyond the limits of substantive agendas set by the Commission.

If these dilutions of member state influence were problem enough in formal sessions, France contended that problems were intensified in UNCITRAL's informal practices. The excessive influence of NGOs can be seen in the Secretariat's over-reliance on NGOs when organizing colloquia, asserted France, including the documents and presentations submitted at these "informal" settings. It viewed "a core of" NGOs as possessing "a key role" in those technical discussions and the drafting that results.[14]

In making this claim, France layered several complaints. It objected, first, that NGOs dominate conversation in these informal settings, both because so many of them are always in appearance but also because the use of English dominates in expert group sessions of Americans, Canadians, the British and Australians, and the occasionally brave users of English as a second language – a result that may be

[13] Id., ¶¶ 5.1 and 5.2. On the topic of the definition of consensus, France offered an array of possibilities:

> As commonly understood at the United Nations, a consensus on a proposal is achieved when that proposal has not been objected to by any delegation. Not any sort of objection prevents a consensus. It is generally agreed that the objection must be nullifying or fundamental in nature. Nevertheless there cannot be a consensus without the consent of all delegates. For UNCITRAL's legislative work, a consensus should be considered not to exist when
>
> - a simple majority of delegates supports a proposal and more than one other expresses a divergent opinion;
> - a proposal presented as a compromise by the chair of a working group has not received the approval of all its members;
> - a formal objection is presented by a delegation.

Id., ¶ 5.2

[14] Id., ¶ 3, fourth bullet.

"efficient" in one sense, since translation inevitably slows up the pace of debate and adds layers of expense, but also held the potential to narrow the perspective at these informal sessions and thus undermine the global representativeness more likely present in formal working group session.[15]

Language matters, and France complained about the predominance of English in informal settings.[16] While formal working group sessions are conducted in the six official UN languages, colloquia and expert working group sessions regularly are conducted only in English and regularly review documents prepared only in English, although the French delegation refers to General Assembly rules identifying both English and French as the UN "working" languages. The implication here is that France and other French speaking delegations are closed out of participating in these informal sessions because their delegates are not sufficiently fluent in English. There is also the diplomatic point of insisting that no one language should prevail over the other – even if everyone in the room is roughly fluent in English, to hold the conversation in "English only" in a UN setting is to waive an important diplomatic privilege, namely the privilege of simultaneous interpretation.

Covens of English speakers meeting informally to converse might not, on their own, present a danger of narrowing the point of view presented at more full-blown working group sessions, but the purpose of expert groups is often to assist the Secretariat in drafting. France complained about this drafting assistance, as well.[17] A working group may take an issue only so far, but then delegate to the Secretariat to "translate" their less-than-crystalline intent into prose for review at the next session. Because the Secretariat in turn relies on experts to assist in this drafting, this process might be viewed as thus permitting NGOs with two bites as the apple – a formal opportunity for comment in working group sessions and an informal opportunity in expert group sessions.

France also objected to experts' ability to submit documents for formal consideration in working group session, not because it was unclear who had drafted the language since often the fact that experts had written text was evident on the face of the submission, but rather because only state delegations should be allowed to submit documents in this setting.[18]

The several critiques of UNCITRAL formal and informal working methods added up to a general indictment of an internal UN politics that had diminished the power of states. The imprecision of UNCITRAL's methods of work, its reliance on English in informal settings, the Secretariat's control of the process through

[15] Id., ¶ 3, second bullet (referring to use of a "single language" in this context).

[16] Id., ¶ 4.1.

[17] Id., ¶ 3.1, fourth bullet ("Technical points are examined in greater detail by informal meetings, where a core of experts has the key role. These meetings, like the colloquia, are usually convened by the Secretariat.").

[18] Id., ¶ 3.2 ("[O]nly Member States and observing States (non-members of UNCITRAL), should be officially entitled to circulate *working* documents to be submitted for discussion by UNCITRAL and its working groups.").

which a chairman is selected and NGOs are invited to participate in the working group sessions: each objection might, on its own, constitute a minor infraction. But when these practices are aggregated into a bundle of complaints about non-state actors' role in UNCITRAL, they add up to a general challenge to the authority of state control over UNCITRAL policy and proceedings. France's concern was that private associations had wheedled their way into UNCITRAL's working group sessions and, more importantly, the ear and pen of the Secretariat. Positioned in this way, the concern was that these NGOs held importunate authority within UNCITRAL.

Put another way, France implied that the groundwork had been set for capture, not by any particular professional or trade association, but more problematically by all of them together. France, it seemed, wanted member states back in control of UNCITRAL.

THE FRENCH PROPOSAL

If this complaint about a dethroning of states as the dominant actors in global trade lawmaking constituted the heart of the French objections, what might be done about it? France proposed nine actions to remedy the ills it diagnosed with respect to the relationship between the Commission and its working groups, to working groups themselves, and to informal working practices.

In the first instance, France wanted powers restored to the Commission. It proposed that the Commission "give the working groups precise mandates."[19] It also proposed that the Commission keep a tight hold on this rein by requiring working groups to "resubmit to the plenary session or consult member states in writing if any change is envisaged to those mandates."[20] This indirectly would control the greater prevalence of NGOs in working groups and would reassert the Commission as the true province of member state authority.

It also thought that working groups needed substantial overhauling. France sought to constrain the involvement of NGOs in working group sessions. Definitionally, France first proposed to "establish an observer status for nongovernmental organisations" but also to clarify that these organizations and so presumably the rights of these organizations should "be divided into two categories, namely those institutions with a general interest in international trade, which may be granted permanent status, and those organisations with expertise on a particular topic, which may be approved only for the duration of the work on that topic."[21] By defining distinct categories of NGOs, France conceded UNCITRAL's openness to "institutions with a general interest in international trade," such as UNCTAD,

[19] Id., at ¶ 7(a).
[20] Id.
[21] Id., at ¶ 7(g).

UNIDROIT, and the Hague Conference.[22] But this openness should not, from France's perspective, extend to NGOs whose expertise was more limited. Under the French Proposal, these "private associations" would receive an inherently probationary and far more limited invitation to participate: once work on the narrow topic was concluded, these limited-purpose NGOs would no longer enjoy access until members states subsequently again agreed to their inclusion.

Indeed, France proposed more than a new typology of involvement. It also sought to formalize the terms on which NGOs were invited to observe and participate in Commission and working group sessions. It proposed that UNCITRAL "specify the rights of these non-state entities: to be consulted and speak at the start of a session in order to give their views on the topic under debate, but not to take part in the discussion or decision at the end of the debate; to circulate information documents but not working documents."[23] It proposed, in other words, to limit substantially the involvement of NGOs. While this document did not distinguish between commercial-law generalists and experts as to some specific issue-area, some sort of proposal of this sort was implicit.

This kind of two-tiered decisionmaking process had not been followed in UNCITRAL. While some states sent delegations made up of a wide range of actors – some political, some academic, some pragmatic, some with experience in an affected industry or as professionals or as judges – most delegations could not afford the expense of sending such a deep bench. Delegations from less developed countries may not even have had access to this sort of expertise across all six working groups. Excusing NGOs from the legislative chamber would inevitably mean that expertise would dissipate out the door. Not all state delegations would have the expertise to be able to resolve matters in these more formal working group sessions, but some would. And the delegations from states who could afford to send delegates with technical expertise would continue to hold advantage over those who couldn't. Asking NGOs to leave the chamber so that states could reach decisions without them would not have leveled the playing field in working group sessions.

Decision making, too, needed reassessment. France proposed to "reassert that no consensus exists when a simple majority of delegates approves a proposal, that a working group chair's compromise proposal must always be approved by the working group, and that a formal objection presented by one or more delegations blocks the consensus and must be reported in the minutes."[24] Member states should control decisionmaking within UNCITRAL, both at the working group and Commission level. One way to so would be to institute a new two-step process of debate and decision making: first, both state and non-state delegations might participate in debate on issues; but, second, at a subsequent decision-making session, non-state

[22] Id., ¶ 6.1, n. 5.

[23] Id., at ¶ 7(h).

[24] Id., at ¶ 7(f).

delegations could be excluded. Specifically, it proposed that the Commission "authorize a working group meeting to be held in camera if one or more delegations belonging to the group request it."[25]

Informal practices needed reining in and tightening up. France proposed that the use of colloquia be brought under tighter supervision of the Commission. The Secretariat should be required "to inform Member States in advance of the international colloquia it intends to convene on topics addressed by one or more working groups, and to provide Member States with all necessary information."[26] While in the past the Secretariat had "informed" member states of the colloquia it had organized through notice at sessions of the Commission and on the UNCITRAL website, rarely had there been a formal posting of agenda items or documents before colloquia.

Advance notice of colloquia was one thing, but the French delegation also sought a tighter and thus more formal connection between the Secretariat and these colloquia. While in the past colloquia had been viewed by all as brainstorming sessions at which participants attended informally and spoke freely, the French delegation proposed that the Secretariat "hold formal consultation with States whenever necessary" to keep them apprised of the goings-on at colloquia, "in particular if controversial points have been raised at colloquia or seminars."[27] Moreover, France wanted the Secretariat to "produce reports on the proceedings of these meetings."[28] In short, France wanted a complete formal record of these informal proceedings.

France also called for greater transparency on the conduct of "informal meetings of expert groups" by requiring Commission approval of these informal meetings between working group sessions.[29] As a practical matter, their proposal would limit expert groups sessions in two ways: by requiring these meetings to be set a year in advance, the Secretariat's spontaneity and so flexibility would be severely diminished; by requiring it to focus on the "balance" between formal and informal meetings, the Secretariat might need to consider not only the number of informal meetings but also the invitation list.

The French Proposal sought transparency in these informal settings, not simply by providing better notice of their existence. It also proposed that the Secretariat should "ensure simultaneous translation into English and French of the documents submitted to the expert groups" so that French-speakers could more effectively participate in this setting.[30] It also looked more generally to "apply the principle of

[25] Id., at ¶ 7(i).
[26] Id., at ¶ 7(b).
[27] Id., at ¶ 7(c).
[28] Id.
[29] Specifically, France wanted the Secretariat to "seek the agreement of the plenary session when the annual timetable of sessions is established, taking care to achieve a balance between these meetings and working group sessions." Id., at ¶ 7(d).
[30] Id., at ¶ 7(e).

parity between these two UN working languages in UNCITRAL's official activities," a diplomatic principle that it had in numerous UN settings fought hard to enforce.[31]

Although diplomatically phrased, together these proposals questioned the very foundations on which UNCITRAL rested. Opening UNCITRAL proceedings for observation to any interested state was consistent with UNCITRAL's long-standing practice of inviting non-state organizations to observe. From its first sessions, UNCITRAL had invited UNIDROIT, the Hague Conference, the International Chamber of Commerce, and other non-state actors to sit at the table and speak their minds. Although this openness was premised on the desirability of receiving "expert advice" in this setting, the French proposal questioned the legitimacy of the inclusion of "private associations" in UNCITRAL deliberations, as well as the legitimacy of informal UNCITRAL sessions. Moreover, by questioning the Secretariat's reliance on English in informal meetings, and by requesting clarification of the definition of consensus, France was picking up on arguments that had divided states in other UN organs and, thus, potentially pushed UNCITRAL's practices into a broader spot light.

WHY FRANCE? WHY NOW?

What prompted the French delegation to raise these concerns by means of a formal proposal to the Commission? Moreover, what explains the *timing* of the French proposal? At least five conjectures arise.

Reaching back years before the French proposal, to the emergence of the United Nations itself, a similar debate about nongovernmental organizations' access to the General Assembly and especially the UN's Economic and Social Council resulted in specific provisions in the UN Charter[32] and resolutions from ECOSOC[33] on NGO involvement in observing their decisionmaking (Durkee 2016). More recently, an incremental set of facilitating circumstances had brought the "problem" of UNCITRAL's consultation with non-state organizations into increasingly sharper focus for the French. A series of incidents within UNCITRAL, speculated a number of delegates, built up a sense of grievance.

All the working groups in the three lawmaking episodes had either begun or interspersed their work with a colloquium jointly sponsored by UNCITRAL and an industry or professional association (Chapter 3). Professional associations and trade groups sent delegates to each of these working group sessions (Chapter 4). Delegates from professional associations and industry groups also participated in expert group

[31] Id.

[32] Charter of the United Nations, Art. 71.

[33] See Resolution of the Economic and Social Council of the United Nations, Consultative relationship between the United Nations and nongovernmental organizations, UN Doc. No. 1996/31 (July 25, 1996), http://esango.un.org/paperless/Web?page=static&content=resolution.

sessions (Chapter 5). Although NGOs' participation in working group sessions was observable to the state delegations in attendance, their participation in expert working groups was less transparent. UNCITRAL's Secretariat broadly extended invitations to participate in expert group sessions, with an interest in both expertise and diversity, but in the end NGOs' attendance in expert sessions was more concentrated than in formal working group sessions and subject to fewer restrictions.

UNCITRAL's working methods, thus, involved a sort of mingling of interested parties that was unheard of within Continental Europe, and delegates speculated that France's proposal to formalize the lawmaking process was the result of its discomfort with the observation, access, and behind-the-scenes participation of private parties to a process that felt, at least to Continental sensibilities, somewhat seamy. One UNCITRAL participant speculated that the French proposal reflected their reaction to a way of doing public policy that might have felt problematic.

> [Some] government [officials are] uncomfortable speaking to their constituents. They don't want them in the door. These officials think that private groups will look over our shoulders about other things.
>
> (Int: 5188d)

Continental policymakers "want governments dominant, not to have to listen to private groups ... Who are you to tell us what is right or wrong?" (id.).

It surely did not help that UNCITRAL's informal working methods could accurately be described as American working methods. The US Uniform Commercial Code had been drafted in the mid-twentieth century by law professors (the American Law Institute) and practitioners linking arms with state politicians (the National Conference of Commissioners on State Law). Virtually no other country drafted legislation through a "private legislature" of this sort (Gillette and Scott 2005b; Schwartz and Scott 1995). Viewed from the perspective of this historical background, the French proposal had the potential, intended or not, to create a wedge between the US delegation and those who were suspicious of US methods of legislating, suspicious of US professional associations and suspicious of the US in general. While some argued that the "US had to work hard" at UNCITRAL (Int: 5188b), harder than it might have to work at UNIDROIT or the World Bank, if the French had their way and the French proposal gained momentum within UNCITRAL, the US would have been forced to work even harder to achieve global norms to its liking.

Some thought that France simply wanted to slow things down so that states could find the time to take stock of UNCITRAL proceedings. France's critique fell in the final stages of negotiations in the Transport and Secured Transactions Working Groups where NGOs had played a prominent role. Did the French proposal signal that France was considering making a formal objection to the draft Secured Transactions Guide or the draft convention on contracts for the carriage of goods by sea? The Commission was scheduled to consider both of these for approval later in the year the French proposal arose, but deliberations had been contentious and consensus was fragile at best. The French delegation had voiced concerns about the speed at which these proceedings developed and that working groups seemed to evade the Commission's directions, saying "you need to consult" – "they felt the show was running them" (Int: 6530).

The timing of the French proposal might also have been framed by the forthcoming change in the Secretariat's leadership. Many of the complaints raised in the French proposal were pointed directly at the Secretariat. UNCITRAL's Secretary, Jernej Sekolec, was due to retire in the following year (Int: 2008). A critique of practices that intensified under his tenure might influence the choice of his replacement or at least serve to obtain commitments that the new Secretary would restrain or scale back the role of NGOs, informal work practices, or US-type politicking.

Many delegates and some Secretariat staff told stories of incidents in working groups and expert groups that explained for them why the French finally lost patience with UNCITRAL's habitual work practices. In one incident, it was whispered that a working group secretary had invited France to participate in a working group session "and they nominated someone who spoke French only ... He asked for the documents, we sent them in English, he said but he wanted them in French – and things went from there" (Int: 6530). In another incident, one private association substantially exceeded the permissible number of delegates over the course of deliberations in the work group throughout a notable week – while there may not have been more than four delegates on any given day, there were nearly a dozen delegates from this organization over the week, spilling over into the space of adjacent delegations, and straining administrative efforts to ensure that there were sufficient seats for these observer-delegates. The problems caused by this influx involved more than simple housekeeping matters. Although some of the individual observer-delegates had attended none of the previous working group sessions, they nonetheless questioned recommendations that had existed in the document under consideration for some time, using language that might not have been perceived by state delegations as sufficiently diplomatic. On other occasions, delegates from non-state delegations substituted for delegates from state delegations and vice versa. Seats that had been changed after a coffee break seemed to violate the protocol of the chamber. The agency of delegates that had switched seats, and the relationship between states and non-state delegations, was blurred by abrupt transitions like these.

Whatever had motivated the French proposal, there was no turning back. Each of the complaints would need to be addressed in turn by the Commission.

THE COMMISSION'S RESPONSE

Despite the fundamental implications of France's critique and proposal, the Commission reacted rather mildly in its first response in July 2007.[34] The proposal had been submitted roughly six weeks before the Commission's annual meeting was

[34] UN Doc. No. A/62/17, Part I, ¶¶ 234–241.

scheduled to take place – barely enough time to translate the French proposal into the five other official UN languages so that Commission delegates could read and absorb it. The US delegation "handed out" a written response to the proposal at the beginning of the Commission's annual session,[35] which given the timing was available to read in "English only." Delegates from the US "did lots of politicking beforehand, trying to line up other delegations" (Int: 5601), and succeeded in organizing an informal meeting of delegates before the Commission's formal debate began. Ironically, this meant that Commission delegates held "an informal meeting about how there should not be informal meetings" (Int: 5188a), and almost inevitably little was accomplished in this setting. Half a day of formal debate on the proposal ensued.

France spoke first. In explaining its motivation in making the proposal, the French delegate wondered aloud whether the "fortieth anniversary of the Commission" might not be a useful occasion for considering "the role of non-State entities" within UNCITRAL. More directly than it had in its written submission, France proposed to the Commission that limits be placed on the involvement of the NGOs.[36]

Delegations entered the debate in quick succession. "Germany supported France unequivocally" (Int: 5811b). Several African countries spoke about the difficulties they experienced in participating at UNCITRAL (Int: 5188e), and the need for additional funding to support greater participation (Int: 5188b). Other countries responded cautiously to question the French proposal. Several delegates, several from Scandinavia, spoke of the need for technical advice and expert groups, arguing that "UNCITRAL couldn't operate without them" (Int: 5188e). But "quite a few countries, such as, Australia, held the view that ... yes, yes, there must be rules" (id.). Throughout this discussion, the US delegation held back since its memo was already on the table (Int: 5188c). Also silently in attendance were representatives from UNIDROIT, the International Monetary Fund, and other IOs. Said one observer, there were "quite a few bodies" seated in the back rows of observer delegations (Int: 5188a).

The Secretariat's formal report on the Commission's session recounts aspects of the floor debate, albeit in the cool passive voice of a UN report, devoid of specificity about sources for any given opinion. While delegates are reported as commenting that "any input aimed at maintaining the tradition of excellence of the UNCITRAL and ensuring its effectiveness should be welcomed," they are also reported as reluctant to embrace any effort to limit NGO involvement, emphasizing

35 This informal document was undoubtedly similar to the US proposal subsequently placed in the UNCITRAL record on this debate. See UN Doc. No. A/CN.9/639 (Nov. 22, 2007).

36 UN Doc. No. A/62/17, Part I, ¶¶ 234–241 (proposing "that a clearer distinction should be made between the phase of negotiation, during which non-governmental organizations might make useful contributions, and the phase of decision making, in which only member States should take part").

that the nature of UNCITRAL's work on international trade lawmaking – that is, private lawmaking – "required expert input from professional associations outside governments who had insight into the areas of law being considered for work by the Commission." Others delegates suggested that rules might nonetheless be drafted to "guarantee transparency in the selection of such organizations and to clarify the advisory nature of their role," perhaps on the theory that a little transparency never hurt, unless of course there was something to hide.[37]

A tenuous resolution emerged from proceedings. While several delegates emphasized the positive aspects of UNCITRAL's efforts "to seek commonly acceptable solutions ... that were acceptable to a broad spectrum of countries" – noting that this sort of consensual decisionmaking avoided both "quick results through voting" and "entrenched disagreements"[38] – several argued that further clarification of the concept of consensus would not diminish these benefits.[39] Some delegates went as far as to express sympathy for the desire for broader use of French and other official UN languages.[40]

Ultimately, the delegates determined that "a comprehensive review of the working methods of the Commission might be timely," and requested that the Secretariat "present a compilation of procedural rules and practices ... regarding the work of the Commission" for its next meeting.[41] It was a classic strategy – delay, deliberate, report back, delay further – which allowed the Secretariat both an opportunity and a means for response.

THE SECRETARIAT REACTS

France's critique barely concealed a direct attack on the Secretariat's adaptations to compete with other IOs and amplify the impact of a resource-poor IO. If NGOs had overstepped their limits, this laid responsibility on the doorstep of the Secretariat, which had invited NGOs to participate, encouraged their involvement in brainstorming and drafting at colloquia and expert drafting sessions, and carefully listened to and read the responses prepared by these private associations. Placed on the defensive by France, indeed, stung by its open critiques, the Secretariat poured enormous effort into a justification of its current practices.

Not be outdone in the formality of the French proposal, which went to the core of UNCITRAL's way of doing business, in a few short months, the Secretariat

[37] Id.

[38] Id., ¶ 235.

[39] Id., ¶238 (commenting on the benefits of such an exercise as "regarding the possibility of better reflecting the views of minorities and the criteria to be applied by chairpersons in assessing the level of consensus or in recognizing the exceptional circumstances where voting might be unavoidable").

[40] Id.

[41] Id., ¶ 236. See also id., ¶ 241.

prepared a "note" on "UNCITRAL's rules of procedure and methods of work" that stretched to over 100 pages.[42]

At its heart, the Secretariat's Note was a legal document written with a socio-legal sensibility. For each topic, and there were many, the Secretariat looks first to determine whether there exists a General Assembly procedural rule on the issue, next to assess what practices in the General Assembly and other UN organs say about how these rules of procedure have been followed outside UNCITRAL, and finally to consider UNCITRAL's own practices on the topic. Like a learned treatise on the law, nearly every sentence is supported by reference either to a procedural rule or by-law or to a report or other UN document. True to its law-and-society sensibilities, the Note cites both to "rules on the books" and evidence of practices "on the ground" in UN offices of all sorts.

Although the Note nowhere refers explicitly to the French proposal, each of its points implicitly responds to a French criticism. However, the Note is not structured as a direct point-by-point response to France. In fact, many of the topics covered in the Note went well beyond the French proposal, perhaps to anticipate other arguments that might arise or to bury France's concerns in a welter of other, and minor, considerations.[43]

1. *Texts governing UNCITRAL procedure and methods of work.* The Note observes that while the General Assembly is, as France notes, governed by written bylaws, the General Assembly did not impose its procedural rules on UNCITRAL; nor did it otherwise impose on UNCITRAL specific requirements regarding its organization or method of work. Instead, we are told, at its initial sessions, UNCITRAL "set general parameters for its working methods,"[44] which it has reviewed and revised from time to time, but "has not adopted a formal set of its own rules of procedure."[45] In addition, we learn that the General Assembly's "hands off parenting" of UNCITRAL was not unusual in the UN. UNCTAD and the International Law Commission, for example, had negotiated their own bylaws internally; once created by the General Assembly, the UN governing body had removed itself from administrative details such as the internal procedural rules that governed the decisionmaking in these other IOs.

[42] UN Doc. No. A/CN.9/638, A/CN.-/638/Add1, A/CN.9/638/Add2, A/CN.9/638/Add3, A/CN.9/638/Add4, A/CN.9/638/Add5, and A/CN.9/638/Add6 (Oct. 17, 2007). In a background section, the Secretariat distinguished generally between "rules of procedure" and "methods of work," noting that the French proposal had raised objections only to the latter. UN Doc. No. A/CN.9/638.

[43] For example, the Note considers at length issues relating to the agenda and organization of the Commission's work, UN Doc. No. A/CN.9/638/Add2, which is nowhere addressed in the French proposal.

[44] A/CN.9/638/Add1, ¶ 15. The Note traces UNCITRAL's authority to delegate to working groups as flowing from various General Assembly rules of procedure and legal opinions issued by the General Assembly Office of Legal Affairs.

[45] Id., ¶ 10 ("Instead it has taken decisions on its procedures as needed and has applied the Rules of Procedure of the General Assembly with flexibility.").

2. *Drafting Processes*. The Secretariat's Note carefully traces the origins of the drafting practices complained about in the French proposal and finds a long pedigree for current processes. For example, the Note indicates that UNCITRAL has relied on working groups since its first session;[46] and that, on the suggestion of the Secretary-General, the Commission had determined in its second session to make provision, "where necessary, to obtain the services of consultants or organizations with special expertise in [the] technical matters dealt with by the Commission."[47] It also indicates that, although working groups have prepared most of UNCITRAL's texts, the Commission has long authorized working groups to request that the Secretary-General prepare studies and other documents,[48] and, moreover, that working groups frequently began their work based on preliminary drafts prepared by the Secretariat,[49] although it was "common for the Commission and its working groups to authorize the Secretariat to have recourse to assistance of outside experts in the its preparatory work."[50]

Although the Note finds consistency in UNCITRAL's methods of work since these initial sessions of the Commission, it also finds that the Commission reconsidered its methods of work from time to time. In 1978, at a time when UNCITRAL had completed its initial "programme of work," the Commission appointed a working group to reconsider things. Similarly, after the General Assembly increased UNCITRAL's membership in 2001, the Commission again reconsidered its methods and future "programme of work."

The Note finds that these moments of procedural introspection led to adaptations and innovations. Since 1980 the Commission has relied on "full-membership working groups," which means that every member state was, in theory at least, a member of every working group.[51] Similarly, in 2001, the Note remarks that the Commission "increased the number of its working groups from three to six, working in parallel, with the corresponding shortening of the duration of the working group sessions from two weeks to one week."[52] So that the group's compressed work week might be made all that more efficient, "the Commission also invited delegations to

[46] Id., ¶¶ 16 and 22. See also A/CN.9/638, ¶¶ 13–15 (indicating that, at its first session, "the Commission established sessional and intersessional working groups" and citing A/7216, ¶¶ 45 and 52).

[47] A/CN.9/638, ¶ 16. For the report of the Secretary-General on organizations and method of work, see UN Doc. No. A/CN.9/6.

[48] A/CN.9/638/Add1, ¶ 33.

[49] Id.

[50] Id., ¶38 (citing to six unspecified examples of such authorization).

[51] A/CN.9/638/Add1, ¶27.

[52] A/CN.9/638, ¶ 22. This shortening of working groups' work weeks required some rejiggering of the schedule for these sessions and the Note indicates that the Commission clarified, in 2001, that working groups should "hold substantive deliberations during the first eight half-day meetings," and spend the last session of the work week agreeing to a "draft report" of the work accomplished. Id.

resort to informal consultations prior to actual meetings."[53] By 2003, the Commission settled on the current schedule of two one-week long work week per working group each year.[54]

Thus, the Note argues that since its inception the Commission has worked through the expedient of working groups and agreed to delegate at least preliminary work to the Secretary-General, UNCITRAL's Secretariat, and other "consultants or organizations."[55] It also argues that these practices were pragmatic rather than strategic decisions by the Commission: the "breadth and complexity of the Commission's responsibilities" necessitated year-round work on multiple technical topics with a limited financial budget.[56]

3. *Languages*. The Secretariat devotes an entire document to the vexed and visceral topic of language.[57] Language has been a touch point within the United Nations since its inception. The Note concedes that, in 1946, at the first session of the General Assembly, "Chinese, French, English, Russian and Spanish were to be designated the official languages, and English and French the working languages, in all organs of the United Nations, other than the International Court of Justice."[58] It goes further, indicating that amendments to the General Assembly's rules of procedure later added Arabic to the list of official languages, and Spanish, Russian, Chinese, and Arabic to the list of working languages.[59] As a result, the General Assembly rules of procedure no longer distinguish between the UN's official and working languages.

Nor is language a problem limited to formal UN sessions. Earlier, in 1993, the UN Office of Legal Affairs issued an opinion viewing "informal meetings, consultations and negotiations" as sitting outside these formal rules of procedure,[60] prompting the General Assembly to adopt in 1995 a resolution questioning the frequent practice of holding "low-cost informal meetings."[61] Later, a report issued in 2002 by the Joint Inspection Unit within the Secretary-General saw the "pragmatism" of encouraging reliance on "one language" as potentially also limiting the participation of Member States, "particularly developing countries," and "other stakeholders."[62] Members of the UN System Chief Executives Board for Coordination nonetheless have "expressed the view that a degree of flexibility"

53 Id., ¶ 22.
54 Id., ¶ 24 (although it also indicated that a working group might, if needed, pull and week of work from another less busy working group).
55 A/CN.9/638, ¶ 16.
56 Id., ¶¶ 14–24.
57 A/CN.9/638/Add6 (Oct. 18, 2007).
58 Id., ¶ 3.
59 Id., ¶ 4.
60 Id., ¶ 11.
61 Id., ¶ 12.
62 Id., ¶¶ 13–16 (referring to a 2002 report by the UN's Joint Inspection Unit).

should direct "the choice of languages for certain types of meetings so as to ease the burden" on interpretive and other staff.[63]

The Secretariat's Note ends ambiguously on the question of language. The UN as a whole continues to struggle with the question of when informal meetings held in "one language," presumably English, are efficient and when such meetings work to silence delegations (whether state or non-state delegations) from full participation. Nonetheless, its unstated conclusion is that pragmatism should triumph over principle if anything is to get done.

4. *Decisionmaking processes*. The Note refers briefly to the election of officers, whether chair or rapporteur, to the Commission and its various working groups. While responsive to the question of the source of the Commission's authority to appoint such officers, the Note is not responsive to the criticism that the Secretariat solicits candidates for these positions without first seeking advice from member states.[64] Similarly, the Note does not speak to the role of the chair in assessing whether consensus exists, except in regard to the range of meaning it provides to the term.[65]

The Note does, nonetheless, speak at length on the topic of consensual decisionmaking, its importance and meaning.[66] It notes that the Commission determined at UNCITRAL's first session "that its decisions should as far as possible be reached by way of consensus, but in the absence of a consensus, decisions should be made by a vote as provided for in the relevant rules of procedure of the General Assembly."[67] Despite this agreement, the Note indicates, "a formal vote in the Commission took place only once."[68] Instances that fall just shy of voting are also reported, such as "explicit reservations made to the content of the decision [that] did not block the adoption of the Commission's decision by consensus,"[69] as well as instances in

63 Id., ¶ 17.

64 The Note has only this to say on the topic: "Before a working group's session, the Secretariat might facilitate consultations among States members of the Commission as regards the candidature of the position of a chairperson." UN Doc. No. A/CN.9/638/Add2, ¶ 36.

65 UN Doc. No. A/CN.9/638/Add4, ¶¶ 16–24.

66 UN Doc. No. A/CN.9/638/Add4.

67 Id., ¶ 6. The Note also indicates that representatives of the Sixth Committee "welcomed" this decision on the grounds that "the consensus method was conducive to achieving a larger cooperation among countries having different legal, economic and social systems and would ensure that the uniform rules derived from the work of the Commission were generally acceptable." Id., ¶ 7. It also refers to UNCTAD's reaction to this determination as supportive in that "it would not be conducive to the formulation of a unified law if some provisions or instruments were approved by a small majority." Id., ¶ 9.

68 Id., ¶ 3 (indicating that this vote occurred at its 11th session, in 1978, regarding the motion to "reopen the consideration of the Commission's recommendation to the General Assembly that it should defer the transfer of the Commission's secretariat to Vienna for a period of three years," and that as a result of the voting "the Commission decided not to reopen the consideration"). See also UN Doc. No. A/CN.9/638/Add.3.

69 UN Doc. No. A/CN.9/638/Add4, ¶ 11.

which the Commission did not take a vote on substantive matters even in the absence of consensus.[70] As for the precise definition of "consensus," the Note remarks that the UN Office of Legal Affairs has "repeatedly" noted in its legal opinions "that there is no definitive or authoritative interpretation" of the term "consensus,"[71] but that "consensus is generally understood to mean adoption of a decision without formal objection and vote" and that such a result is possible "only when no delegation formally objects to a consensus being recorded, though some delegations may have reservations to the substantive matter at issue or a part thereof."[72] This definition, the Note argues, is distinct from the concept of unanimity,[73] although only procedurally since it is also clear that a member State "may insist on its Charter-given right to exercise its vote."[74]

Although the Note is silent on why UNCITRAL embraces consensual decision-making so firmly, interviews suggest that UNCITRAL's motivation is at least partly explained by an interest in distinguishing itself from its close cousin in trade policy within the United Nations: UNCTAD. The UN Conference on Trade and Development previously held a legislative mandate as an important part of its mission, but some would argue that they "messed it up" by "politicizing the process" (Int: 6530). Whereas UNCITRAL tries to reach decisions based on consensus among delegates, UNCTAD engages in "bloc-voting" – they have an annual plenary meeting at which issues are discussed and debated; to reach a decision, delegates "break into blocs, confer, then come back together, and read out their positions," but few decisions emerge because the process is so "confrontational" (Int: 6530).

The Note nonetheless speaks directly to the suggestion made by France that working groups should, at least on occasion, work in closed sessions. While "United Nations practice as regards private [or closed] . . . meetings has evolved,"[75] the Note makes clear that the Commission has never made the "decision to hold private meetings."[76] Again, an indication that the Commission has never followed a practice put forward in the Proposal proves only that the proposal is a new recommendation rather than that it finds fault with the Commission's failure to follow a procedure rule or clear practice. The Note leaves criticism of this proposal implicit from this lack of precedent. If few follow the practice, what would justify its adoption?

70 Id., ¶ 12.

71 Id., ¶ 20.

72 Id., ¶ 21 ("Thus a reservation made formally at the time of decision making, while indicative of a qualified assent, does not prevent the adoption of the consensus text in question.").

73 Id., ¶ 22 (noting that unanimity requires "complete agreement as to substance and a consequent absence of reservations," but that "there are numerous occasions where States make declarations or reservations to a matter at issue while not objecting to a decision being recorded as taken by consensus.").

74 Id., ¶ 23.

75 A/CN.9/638/Add1, ¶ 7.

76 Id., ¶ 8.

5. *Non-State Actors' Involvement.* The Note also responds to the complaint that UNCITRAL's inclusion of non-state actors in working group session had changed over time, especially more recently. Although the French proposal refers to the involvement of "private associations" as having increased after the Insolvency Working Group completed their deliberations on the Model Law on Cross-Border Insolvency, the Secretariat found a long history of UNCITRAL's consultation with non-state actors.

In its resolution creating UNCITRAL, the General Assembly refers explicitly to UNCITRAL's relationship to non-state organizations.[77] It confers authority to "coordinate" the work of trade lawmaking organizations and encourage "cooperation" among them[78]; to "collaborate, where appropriate" with these organizations "in preparation and promotion of the adoption of new international instruments"[79]; to establish and maintain close collaboration with UNCTAD, and to maintain relationships with other relevant UN organs[80]; to consult with or request the services of any international or national organization, scientific institution, or other experts;[81] and to establish appropriate working relationships with intergovernmental organizations and international nongovernmental organizations concerned with the progressive harmonization and unification of the law of international trade.[82]

The Note provides details of UNCITRAL's practices consistent with this authorization. The Commission invited to its first session a wide range of "specialized agencies, international and regional intergovernmental organizations, and national, regional and international nongovernmental organizations,"[83] a practice that has continued over time.[84] And while the Secretariat has invited various organizations to sessions of the Commission or its working groups, the Note emphasizes that there exists "no practice of issuing standing invitations."[85] Still, the Commission has

77 General Assembly Resolution 2205 (XXI).
78 Id., ¶ 8(a).
79 Id., ¶ 8(c).
80 Id., ¶ 8(f) and (g).
81 Id., ¶ 11.
82 Id., ¶ 12.
83 Id., ¶ 22 (listing the Food and Agriculture Organization, Inter-governmental Maritime Consultative Organization, International Bank for Reconstruction and Development, International Civil Aviation Organization, International Labor Organization, Council of Europe, European Economic Community, Organization for Economic Cooperation and Development, Organization of American States, Afro-Asian Organization for Economic Cooperation, European Insurance Committee, Inter-American Institute of International Legal Studies, International Chamber of Commerce, and the National Association of Credit Management as having been invited to its first session).
84 Over its first, second and third sessions, the Note remarks, the Commission opted for a "flexible approach as regards working relationships and collaborations with international organizations," which has been "repeatedly endorsed" by the Commission and the Sixth Committee. Id., ¶ 25.
85 Id., ¶26 (meaning that "to be able to attend a session an organization must receive an invitation from the Secretariat"). But see id., ¶ 29 ("Although the Commission decided not to draw formally any distinction among organization attending its sessions (such as between

"repeatedly recognized" that the participation of non-state organizations "was crucial for the quality of texts formulated" by it,[86] and that the General Assembly has concurred in this assessment.[87]

Despite this clear practice, the Note concedes that there is no formal agreement on the scope of observers' rights in either the General Assembly or its subsidiary organizations, including UNCITRAL,[88] other than that they do not have the right to vote.[89] Formal rules on this involvement may be absent, but practices are consistent. The Note reports acceptance of observers' rights of access to a wide range of settings and to documents, as well as rights to make and reply to statements, to submit proposals, and to circulate documents.[90]

BACK AND FORTH AT THE COMMISSION

The Secretariat filed its Note in November 2007 in time for the Commission's resumed Fortieth Session in December 2007,[91] but the Commission did not resolve the Proposal at either this session[92] or at the three annual sessions that followed. In all, the Proposal was considered over a two and a half year period during five different Commission sessions.

It seems clear that initially the Commission was delayed by the sheer quantity of paper produced by the Secretariat. Was it accidental that its 100-page long Note was filed just one month before the December session? The issues were complex and

permanent, temporary or functional observers), in accordance with General Assembly resolution 2205(XXI), for example, UNCTAD may be considered to be the organization enjoying permanent observer status with UNCITRAL … [and] Unidroit and the Hague Conference may fall into the same category.").

86 Id., ¶ 30.

87 Id., ¶ 32.

88 Id., ¶¶ 33–35.

89 Id., ¶36.

90 Id., ¶¶ 41–59.

91 Typically the Commission meets for two weeks once a year. When it met for two weeks in July 2007, for its Fortieth Session, the Commission had left unfinished its approval of the Legislative Guide on Secured Transactions Law; the Commission also agreed to reconsider issues pertaining to its methods of work that had been raised by the delegation from France.

92 A brief several paragraphs appear in the Commission's report on its meeting at this "resumed" Fortieth Session. Report of the United Nations Commission on International Trade Law on the Work of its resumed fortieth session, ¶¶ 104–106, UN Doc. No. A/62/17 (Part II) (Jan. 8, 2008). These paragraphs report no new arguments – some delegates "expressed the view that the elaboration of new rules of procedure for UNCITRAL would not be necessary," while others express support for "introducing more clarity." Id., ¶ 104. Some cautioned the Commission against "entering areas, such as the possible definition of consensus, where its decisions might impact other bodies of the General Assembly." Id. In the end, the delegates agreed that full review was "premature," id., ¶ 105, and that the Commission should "continue reflecting on practical ways to facilitate the participation of representatives of developing countries and nongovernmental organizations from those countries in the work of UNCITRAL." Id., ¶ 106. To assist in this regard, the Commission asked the Secretariat to prepare a document "distilling" relevant information from its previous note. Id., ¶ 107.

went to the heart of UNCITRAL's mission and historical practices. Delegates clearly understood that UNCITRAL's effectiveness and its very legitimacy had been questioned by France, that the Secretariat had been forced to explain itself and had responded with what at least on cursory review appeared to be a strong rebuttal.

If, indeed, the US was the hidden target behind France's broadside, then it was not surprising that the US entered the fray directly. The US delegation filed its own "observations" on the French proposal.[93] This document was much shorter and far more accessible than the Secretariat's Note; in seven pages, it tersely summarized the Note, agreed with the Secretariat's conclusions, and concluded that UNCITRAL's "current methods [of work] are sound and should be continued."[94] Involvement by the US delegation meant that political wrangling complicated resolution of the French proposal. To the extent that delegates expressed support for the French proposal at the resumed meeting in late 2007, they phrased theirs as support for greater transparency and clarity and not for the specific suggestions that had been raised with the Proposal.[95] Most delegations preferred not to choose sides between the US and French positions.

In preparation for the Commission's 2008 session, the Secretariat met the request for further clarification of UNCITRAL's working methods by submitting a second, shorter report with the Commission, which largely summarized its earlier Note.[96] The Secretariat also invited other states to submit to the Commission written observations regarding the Secretariat's two reports, and a number of states filed short documents commenting on UNCITRAL's working methods, including Australia (member state), Turkey (observer state),[97] Spain (member state),[98] El Salvador (member state),[99] Malaysia (member state),[100] and Belgium (observer state).[101]

All of these documents were phrased in elegantly diplomatic language that complimented the Note prepared by the Secretariat and the opportunity for reaching greater clarification of UNCITRAL's working methods. Without expressly

93 Note by the Secretariat, UNCITRAL Rules of Procedure and Methods of Work: Observations by the United States, UN Doc. No. A/CN.9/639 (Nov. 22, 2007).

94 Id., ¶ 21.

95 Report of the United Nations Commission on International Trade Law on the Work of its resumed fortieth session, ¶ 104, UN Doc. No. A/62/17 (Part II) (Jan. 8, 2008).

96 UN Doc. No. A/CN.9/653 (Mar. 19, 2008). This Second Note divided discussion among three topics: decisionmaking in the Commission (consensus; voting; other methods); status of observers (attendance by non-member states and inter-governmental and nongovernmental organizations; observers' participation, election as officers; submission of written proposals by observers; circulation of drafts to observers for comment) and preparatory work by the Secretariat (future work; work programme). It broke little in the way of new ground, in less than 20 pages summarizing and referring to the research and arguments raised in the Note.

97 UN Doc. No. A/CN.9/660.Add1 (June 3, 2008)(comments received from Australia and Turkey).

98 UN Doc. No. A/CN.9/660.Add2 (June 6, 2008)(comments received from Spain).

99 UN Doc. No. A/CN.9/660.Add3 (June 10, 2008)(comments received from El Salvador).

100 UN Doc. No. A/CN.9/660.Add4 (June 20, 2008)(comments received from Malaysia).

101 UN Doc. No. A/CN.9/660.Add5 (June 20, 2008)(comments received from Belgium).

criticizing it, these submissions provide little support for the positions that had been put forward in the earlier French proposal, with the exception of one intervention agreeing that perhaps on occasion consensus had been found to exist although the working group's discussion had been divided.[102]

And although Germany, Nigeria and Kenya had spoken in the previous Commission meeting to support the French proposal (Int: 5188b), by 2008 none of these delegations chose to file more formal written statements of support.

France submitted its own clarifying, second document.[103] But this sur-reply added nothing of substance to the debate. It avoided refuting assertions made by states in their submissions. Mostly, it repeated arguments that had been raised in the earlier document.

The sum of these many written comments seemed to encourage delegations to speak freely at the Commission meeting held in July 2008.[104] On decision-making, delegates at the Commission agreed that "consensus should remain the preferred method," but that efforts to settle "the exact meaning" of the term should be viewed with "utmost caution" since efforts at definition "might have an impact on the work of other bodies of the General Assembly."[105] As to the role of observers, the "broad openness of the Commission and its subsidiary bodies to observers from State and non-State entities was widely recognized as a key element in maintaining the high quality and the practical relevance of the work of the Commission."[106] While there was agreement that "non-State entities should not participate in decisionmaking" or voting, and that only member States should vote, there was less clarity on whether observer States should be considered in determining whether consensus had been reached in a working group or at the Commission.[107] As for the Secretariat's practice of involving non-state entities in the preparation of drafts, the Commission expressed its general agreement "that it was particularly important for the Secretariat to preserve the flexibility necessary to organize its work efficiently, including through recourse to external expertise" so long as these practices were transparent.[108] On the topic of the languages in which expert group meetings were held, the Commission agreed "that every effort should be made to provide simultaneous interpretation" if this could be done "within existing resources."[109]

102 But see UN Doc. No. A/CN.9/660.Add1 (June 3, 2008)("Australia has been concerned that, on occasion in certain Working Groups, consensus has been deemed to have been reached when the room was clearly divided on the decision in question.").

103 UN Doc. No. A/CN.9/660 (May 28, 2008).

104 Report of the United Nations Commission on International Trade Law on its Forty-first Session, UN Doc. No. A/63/17, ¶ 376 (June 16–July 3, 2008).

105 Id., ¶ 377.

106 Id., ¶ 378.

107 Id.

108 Id., ¶ 379.

109 Id.

The broad contours of the Commission's position were now clear. To the extent that the French proposal sought clarity on issues no one seemed to disagree with – that UNCITRAL should seek to achieve consensus; that while member states could seek a vote on issues, consensual decisionmaking should be preferred; that only state delegations could participate in such a vote – the Commission agreed that the Secretariat should provide greater clarity. To the extent that France sought a declaration that informal meetings should be conducted only if they could be held in multiple languages, the Commission diplomatically agreed in principle, but only if this would not require additional financial resources; since financial resources always had been limited, in practical effect this meant that informal meetings would continue to be held in English only.

Notwithstanding these face-saving victories, the Commission eviscerated the heart of the French proposal during this short debate. France had objected to the "unrestricted access of observers to the working groups,"[110] and had complained that "the distinction between States members of the Commission and observers has become blurred."[111] It sought procedural rules limiting observers' opportunities (i) to speak at working group and Commission sessions and (ii) to circulate written documents for working group consideration "unless this is specifically requested by the working group in question."[112] The Commission wanted no part of this. Delegates affirmed that the "broad openness of the Commission and its subsidiary bodies to observers from State and non-State entities was widely recognized as a key element in maintaining the high quality and the practical relevance of the work of the Commission."[113] Nor did delegates share France's vision of the Commission as functioning solely through its member states. France sought affirmation that "observer states should not be entitled to vote,"[114] but the Commission could not reach agreement on this point.[115]

DENOUEMENT: NEW GUIDELINES

France sought not only changes in procedure and the distribution of power at UNCITRAL, but also a formalization of UNCITRAL's operating practices. UNCITRAL's governing Commission agreed with the desire to put practices down

[110] Note by the Secretariat, UNCITRAL Rules of Procedure and Methods of Work: Comments Received by Member States, UN Doc. No. A/CN.9/660, ¶ 1 (including supplemental comments received from France)(May 28, 2008).

[111] Id., ¶ 4.

[112] Id.

[113] Report of the United Nations Commission on International Trade Law on its Forty-first Session, UN Doc. No. A/63/17, ¶ 378 (June 16–July 3, 2008).

[114] Note by the Secretariat, UNCITRAL Rules of Procedure and Methods of Work: Comments Received by Member States, UN Doc. No. A/CN.9/660, ¶ 4 (including supplemental comments received from France)(May 28, 2008).

[115] Report of the United Nations Commission on International Trade Law on its Forty-first Session, UN Doc. No. A/63/17, ¶ 378 (June 16–July 3, 2008).

in writing. It charged the Secretariat to produce brief guidelines for "chairpersons, delegates and observer and by the Secretariat itself."[116] The Secretariat produced a draft,[117] formally solicited written comments on the draft guidelines,[118] and organized an "informal" meeting of delegations to review them over the two-day period preceding the 2009 Commission meeting.[119] This intersessional politicking appeared designed to ensure that Commission delegates would be word-smithing the Guidelines rather than debating their underlying precepts at the full Commission meeting, and the report of this session indicates that the plan worked. Delegations announced that they had reached agreement on revisions to the Guidelines, with paragraphs of revised language read into the record.[120]

By the summer of 2010, it was all over. The final Guidelines are brief, spanning less than two pages in length and containing fifteen numbered paragraphs of guidance.[121] They are divided into three subject matter areas: decisionmaking by the Commission and its working groups; the status of observer delegations in these sessions; and working methods of the secretariat. They were adopted in full with no additional debate.[122]

[116] Id., ¶ 381. While a proposal to create a working group on working methods also had been proposed at this session, this proposal was not adopted; "there was support for holding informal consultation instead." Id., ¶ 380.

[117] Note by the Secretariat, UNCITRAL Rules of Procedure and Methods of Work, UN Doc. No. A/CH.0/676 (Mar. 31, 2009).

[118] Note by the Secretariat, UNCITRAL Rules of Procedure and Methods of Work, Comments received from Member States and interested international organizations, UN Doc. No. A/CN.9/676/Add1 (Apr. 28, 2008)(submitting comments from Iraq, a member state); id., UN Doc. No. A/CN.9/676/Add2 (June 5, 2009)(submitting comments from France, member state); id., UN Doc. No. A/CN.9/676/Add3 (June 12, 2009)(submitting comments from the US, member state); id., UN Doc. No. A/CN.9/676/Add4 (June 17, 2009)(submitting comments from Turkey, observer state, Palestine, entity with observer status, and several interested international organizations – International Maritime Organization, International Civil Aviation Organization, Islamic Development Bank, and Organization for Economic Cooperation and Development); id., UN Doc. No. A/CN.9/676/Add5 (June 24, 2009)(submitting comments from Singapore, member state); id., UN Doc. No. A/CN.9/676/Add6 (June 25, 2009)(submitting comments from New Zealand, observer state); id., UN Doc. No. A/CN.9/676/Add7 (June 29, 2009) (submitting comments from European Commission, intergovernmental organization); UN Doc. No. A/CN.9/676/Add8 (July 2, 2009)(submitting comments from Belgium, observer state); id., UN Doc. No. A/CN.9/676/Add9 (July 13, 2009)(submitting comments from Jordan, observer state). See also Note by Secretariat, UNCITRAL rules of procedure and methods of work, Proposal by France, UN Doc. No. A/CN.9/680 (June 5, 2009).

[119] Report of the United Nations Commission on International Trade Law at its Forty-Second Session, UN Doc. No. A/64/17 (June 29–July 17, 2009). Reports indicate that this informal meeting was simultaneously translated into the six official UN languages. Id.

[120] Id., ¶¶ 382, 384–397.

[121] The brevity of the final Guidelines should be compared to the draft submitted in the previous session, A/CN.9/676, which was thirteen pages in length, and the Secretariat's Note, A/CN.9/638, 638/Add.1, 638/Add.2, 638/Add.3, 638/Add.4, 638/Add.5, and 638/Add.6, which together comprised 100 pages of commentary.

[122] Report of the United Nations Commission on International Trade Law at its Forty-Third Session, UN Doc. No. A/65/17, ¶¶ 302–305 (June 21–July 8, 2010). See also id., Annex III, pp. 101–102.

What did the Guidelines ultimately provide?

On "decision-taking" within the Commission, the Guidelines provide that "decisions should be reached by consensus as far as possible," that voting "as provided for in the relevant rules of procedure of the General Assembly" should take place "in the absence of consensus," but that "voting is to be regarded as an exceptional procedure," having "only once" occurred in the Commission "on a procedural matter."[123]

Although the Guidelines make clear that only member states make decisions on behalf of the Commission,[124] they also indicate that non-member states and other observers possess limited "rights" of participation. We are told that "non-member States are entitled, when they so request, to attend the sessions of the Commission and its working groups as observers and may participate in the collective effort to achieve a generally acceptable text."[125] While they can observe and participate, they cannot vote,[126] "they cannot object to a decision being recorded,"[127] and they "do not participate in the decision-taking."[128] These same limits hold true for non-state observers.[129] Although the Guidelines specify that sessions "are open to representatives of international governmental and non-governmental organization,"[130] they permit observation by only those organizations "invited by the Commission"[131] and specify the parameters for such invitations by distinguishing between "United Nations organs and specialized agencies brought into relationship with the United Nations," who are "permitted to participate in the sessions and the work of the Commission and its subsidiary organs,"[132] and "other international organizations" and "non-governmental organizations with which UNCITRAL entertains a long-standing cooperation."[133] This latter category is only able to participate if they "have been invited"[134] based on a request by "the Commission or its subsidiary organs."[135] The Secretariat may "take the initiative to invite an organization on the basis of its assessment of the relevance and potential contribution of the organization concerned to the proceedings of the relevant session," or an organization may itself "request" that it be invited to a session, but before an invitation is extended on this

[123] Id., Annex III, ¶¶ 2, 4.

[124] Id., ¶ 1 ("The views of non-member States and observer organizations are for the benefit of member States who may take such views into account in determining their positions on the issue to be decided upon.").

[125] Id., ¶ 5.

[126] Id., ¶¶ 1, 3.

[127] Id., ¶ 5.

[128] Id., ¶ 7.

[129] Indeed, the Guidelines provide that the limits "particularly" apply to nongovernmental organizations. Id. ("Observers, in particular non-governmental organizations, do not participate in the decision-taking.").

[130] Id., ¶ 6.

[131] Id.

[132] Id., ¶ 8.

[133] Id., ¶ 9.

[134] Id.

[135] Id., ¶ 10.

basis the Secretariat must "inform the member States of the Commission" and "where an objection is raised, the decision will be taken by the Commission."[136]

The Guidelines also remark on the "working methods of the UNCITRAL Secretariat." This portion of the Guidelines both grants authority to the Secretariat and imposes obligations on the Secretariat to provide specified information to member States. The Guidelines authorize the Secretariat to "make either oral or written statement at any time to the Commission or its subsidiary organs concerning any questions under consideration."[137] They specify that the Secretariat "formulates its proposals to the Commission or its subsidiary organs under its own responsibility" so long as consistent with "specific instructions received from the Commission or its subsidiary organs" and "the policies express in relevant General Assembly resolutions and decisions adopted previously by the Commission."[138] They further provide that "the Secretariat may have recourse to the assistance of outside experts from differing legal traditions and affiliations,"[139] although of course "the Secretariat is not bound by the advice of such experts."[140] The Guidelines also specify the disclosure expected of the Secretariat regarding both the "results" of colloquia "organized or co-organized by the Secretariat"[141] and the conduct of "expert group meetings."[142] Moreover, the Secretariat "is committed to endeavour, resources permitting," to provide translation and interpretation of expert group meetings "as appropriate,"[143] although nothing is specified in the Guidelines regarding interpretation and translation of colloquium.

WHAT CHANGED?

Did France's proposal alter UNCITRAL's methods of work? Reduce the discretion of the Secretariat? Enhance the power of states? Limit the ubiquity of non-state delegations? Constrain US influence? Rein in the widespread use of informal methods of work?

The formal answer can be summarized in Table 8.1 by a comparison of the original French proposal and the final Guidelines.

Although Table 8.1 might be read to suggest that France got most of what it was looking to accomplish with its proposal, this would view the proposal as nine equally important suggestions for change and note that in only two instances did France

[136] Id.

[137] Id., ¶ 11.

[138] Id., ¶ 12.

[139] Id., ¶ 11 (so long as this recourse fits "within the limits of [the Secretariat's] available resources," the Secretariat "shall decide on the appropriate form that the assistance of outside experts may take depending on the needs of the Secretariat").

[140] Id., ¶ 12.

[141] Id., ¶ 15 (also requiring such colloquia to be "widely advertise, particularly by posting relevant information concerning such events on the UNCITRAL website").

[142] Id., ¶ 13.

[143] Id., ¶ 14.

TABLE 8.1. *Comparison of French Proposal to Subsequent UNCITRAL Guidelines on Methods of Work*

French Proposal	UNCITRAL Guidelines
Provide formal mandates for working groups	No reference to working group mandates
Give advance notice to member states on international colloquia	Advertise widely prospective colloquia on the UNCITRAL website
Consult with states and report on colloquium proceedings	Report results of colloquia to the Commission and working groups
Seek approval from Commission for informal meetings of expert groups	Inform member states about expert group meetings on request
Mandate simultaneous translation into English and French of the documents submitted to the expert groups	Endeavor to provide translation and interpretation of expert group proceedings in official UN languages, resources permitting
Formally define a consensus decision-making rule	Maintain UNCITRAL's longstanding practice of reaching consensus
Classify observer delegations into two categories	No classification
Specify types of involvement by non-state delegations	Maintain current practices of involvement by non-state delegations
Authorize exclusion of observer and non-state delegations from working group proceedings under specified conditions	No reference to exclusions of any class of delegations

come up empty. But throughout the Commission's deliberations on the proposal, France emphasized that its primary complaint was with the access that non-state private associations enjoyed to the UNCITRAL Secretariat and to Commission and working group sessions – and indeed the parity that these observer delegations appeared to enjoy with the member state delegations in some settings. France sought with its proposal to limit the rights of these observers – in particular, the non-state private associations – not only in formal sessions but importantly also in the informal expert group sessions. Viewed from this perspective, the French achieved little more than a Pyrrhic victory. France prevailed in its quest for formality – for a written statement of UNCITRAL's methods of work – but this formalism did not limit observers' access to Commission and working group sessions. Instead, ironically, it assured this access.

Importantly, there were limits to the formalisms France accomplished. The Guidelines did not implement France's effort to impose procedural formalities at UNCITRAL. There would be no temporal or spatial distinction between where and when experts, other non-state organizations, or observer states could observe and comment on the deliberations of member states. There is no Guideline authorizing member states to request closed sessions.

Nor did the resulting formalism limit the Secretariat's behind-the-scenes reliance on expert advice from private associations. Again, if anything, it expressly specified the Secretariat's right to seek this advice. To the extent the Guidelines imposed limits on the Secretariat's reliance on colloquia and expert group sessions, these limits involved minor obligations to provide member states with notice of their occurrence. But obligations of disclosure were a small price to pay for clarifying the propriety of the Secretariat's "recourse to the assistance of outside experts from different legal traditions and affiliations."[144]

FOUR IRONIES

There are at least four ironies that underlay UNCITRAL's resolution of the French proposal.

There was, first, an *irony of form*. The French proposal complained that "UNCITRAL does not have its own rules of procedure,"[145] and with this statement objects to the lack of transparency that inheres in the Secretariat's interactions with non-state entities, especially private associations. The French proposal sought the clarity and predictability that formal rules, or at least a formalized statement of practices, can provide.

In its first line of defense to the French proposal, the Secretariat drafted an extensive Note. In its Note, the Secretariat conceded that "the Commission has not adopted a formal set of its own rules of procedure" but did not agree that this lack of formal bylaws meant that the Commission was lawless. In response to the contention that UNCITRAL's failure to spell out its procedures in black and white rules permits obfuscation and ad hoc methodologies, the Note carefully picks through the decisions made by the Commission in each of its forty or so sessions and finds consistency and clarity in its review of these practices. In doing so, the Secretariat develops a common-law trail of the Commission's decisionmaking.[146]

This was a classic debate on form – rules versus standards, civil codes versus common law pronouncements. To the French, formality brings clarification and rationality but, to the Secretariat, formality spells rigidity and inflexibility. France – the source of the Napoleonic Code – sought predictability through the expedient of a single formal statement of UNCITRAL's working methods. The Secretariat prepared a common-law response to this civil-law challenge. It responded with a treatise of the common law of the Commission.

Thus, ironically the Guidelines provided France with the formal statement of working methods that it had sought, but this formality worked to ensure experts' access to the Secretariat, as well as to the Commission and its working groups.

[144] Id., ¶ 11.
[145] A/CN.9/635, ¶ 2.1.
[146] A/CN.9/638, ¶ 10.

The Guidelines also formalized the Secretariat's role within UNCITRAL as autonomous. In putting pen to paper, the Guidelines formalized what had formerly been merely informal practices. The Guidelines, thus, lent legitimacy to the very practices that France sought to call into question.

Second, there was an *irony of politics* in the resolution of the French proposal. France objected to the informal politicking that took place behind the scenes at UNCITRAL – during colloquia and expert group sessions, in particular. Perhaps the French delegation thought that member states were unaware of these practices and that states would object to the interactions once revealed. On the contrary, states did not object. Instead, they referred to UNCITRAL's involvement with non-state organizations as not only longstanding but critical to its success in formulating global norms on technical topics of trade and financial law. Importantly, the fingerprints of non-state organizations are entirely absent from this debate. The Secretariat writes a lengthy Note and invites comment. States submit written comments at two distinct stages in the debate – member states and observer states; states from distinct legal families, economic circumstances, and geographic locations. Not one state objects to NGOs' involvement in UNCITRAL decisionmaking. When the Secretariat requests commentary from non-state organizations, several submit comments that are literally devoid of comment. Despite this silence, the result was clear: "The French mission was completely isolated on this. They had no other supporters" (Int: 6531).

Third, there was an *irony of process*. Although the French proposal objects to non-state entities' access to the Secretariat in informal colloquia and expert group sessions, the Guidelines seem to have been hammered out in just such an informal setting. The Secretariat submitted multiple formal documents to the Commission in response to the French proposal – the Note, in two versions, and a draft set of Guidelines. While states submitted formal written comments in advance of Commission sessions, and commented orally in floor debates during formal sessions of the Commission, it seems clear that delegates rolled up their sleeves in informal drafting sessions before and after the Commission's forty-second session. France's objections to informal meetings between the Secretariat and private organizations of experts were resolved in informal meetings between the Secretariat and motivated delegations from member and observer states.

Fourth, and most important, there was an *irony of outcome*. Senior staff at UNCITRAL agreed that in the two or three years after responses to the French proposal were settled the Guidelines had not "had any practical effect" in the end (Int: 6531). Although the Guidelines permitted states to enforce a tighter leash on the number or identity of private associations invited to participate in Commission or working group sessions, they still "don't really comment" (Int: 6531). The Guidelines had "led some states to ask about whether organizations from their region could attend" various sessions, but "in practice it hasn't changed anything" because rarely do these additional organizations seek access. As for NGOs' participation in discussions or decisions, the Secretariat is now more careful to "remind observer organizations of their status" (Int: 6531). The Secretariat also reminded these organizations "systematically that they are expected to contribute expertise and views but not to interfere with decisionmaking, which is in the hands of states" (Int: 6531). In practice, little had changed, although perhaps these "organizations might be a bit more mindful or cautious as to how their interventions are received" (Int: 6531).

META-BARGAINS

France's observations on UNCITRAL's working methods presented a crisis of several sorts. Its objection to the unfettered involvement of observer delegations (whether delegations from states that were not members of UNCITRAL or from non-state entities, including especially private associations) threatened to bar non-state members from participation in sessions of both the Commission and its subsidiary working groups. Its claim that chairs shut down debate by declaring that consensus had been reached, and its related request for clarification of the concept of consensus, threatened to open an issue that had festered throughout subsidiary organs of the General Assembly. Its insistence that even informal meetings should be held in French and perhaps other UN languages similarly poked at issues that had plagued both the collegiality of meetings with UNCITRAL and more broadly throughout the UN and the increasing costliness of translation for these meetings. Finally, its objections to the Secretariat's reliance on NGOs for advice, for drafting assistance, and for financial support in co-hosting colloquia and other informal meetings, threatened to undermine methods of work that had produced many global norms for the forty years of UNCITRAL's work to date.

If France's primary goal was to limit the involvement of non-state entities, especially NGOs representing the interests of specific national, professional, or industry interests, then it failed. UNCITRAL's Guidelines for the Preparation and Conduct of Meetings now specify that "sessions of the Commission and its subsidiary organs are open to representatives of international governmental and non-governmental organizations invited by the Commission."[147] While the Guidelines state that observers "do not participate in the decision making" of the Commission, no one had claimed to the contrary.[148] More importantly, the Guidelines etch in stone the rights of NGOs to observe at and advise the Commission and its working

[147] Guidelines, ¶ 6. See also id., ¶ 10 ("In addition, the Secretariat may be requested by the Commission or its subsidiary organs to invite a specific organization to the relevant session. It may also receive a request from an organization to be invited to a session, or it may itself take the initiative to invite an organization on the basis of its assessment of the relevance and potential contribution of the organization concerned to the proceedings of the relevant session. In such cases, the Secretariat shall inform the member States of the Commission. Where an objection is raised, the decision will be taken by the Commission.").

[148] Id., ¶ 7.

groups. The Guidelines expressly provide that, "within the limits of its available resources, the Secretariat may have recourse to the assistance of outside experts from different legal traditions and affiliations." While the Guidelines make clear that the Secretariat is not bound by this expert advice, no one had made such a claim.

In the first instance, then, France's proposal may be viewed as a two-pronged, albeit thinly disguised, confrontation with the US. France clearly observed what was apparent to most other delegations in the working groups: the US saw UNCITRAL as a vehicle to advance US law, US lawyers, and US trade competitiveness. The US came to UNCITRAL deliberations both well-prepared and well-staffed (Chapter 4). The US was the only country or bloc that came to UNCITRAL with a coherent global trade policy to strengthen its position in the international political economy (Chapter 6).

The efficacy of the US at UNCITRAL, however, could not be reduced to the attributes of the US itself as an economic and geopolitical power. Its effectiveness in driving much of its trade policy through UNCITRAL, and institutionalizing US interests in global commercial law, derived in considerable part from the emergence of a politics inside UNCITRAL that mirrored the politics of Congress and other US lawmaking bodies at the state and local levels.

Like some liberal democracies, US legislative politics involve broad participation of politicians and officials from government ministries. Unlike many other democracies, including France, the US polity is extraordinarily porous and open to the direct involvement of business and civil society actors, so much so that non-state actors in the US are accustomed to bringing already drafted laws to their legislators as an initial step in the lawmaking. Bargaining goes on far beyond the floor of the House of Representatives and Senate and the House and Senate committees on various specialized subjects.

The very informality and multiplication of sites for politics at UNCITRAL reproduced in broad outline a politics with which the US delegation was thoroughly familiar and which France was not. US-style politics inside UNCITRAL necessarily involved non-state actors from professions and industry and required constant informal consultations at diverse sites of social interaction. In the first instance, then, the French proposal was directed against the US, its putative dominance, and a style of politics that empowered or at least enabled such dominance.

In the second instance, the clash of informal and formal politics continued a much longer struggle over who should make commercial laws for the world – states or lawyers or industry? From the second half of the nineteenth century, lawmaking and standard-setting bodies began to emerge in Europe, some academic, some centered on an industry or commerce more generally, some in ad hoc conferences of states. Initially on the European stage in the nineteenth century, subsequently through the interwar initiatives of the League of Nations, and later in the United Nations and beyond, the relative influence and lawmaking roles of non-state actors went through one permutation after another, and, indeed, UNIDROIT, the Hague

Conference, and UNCITRAL each represents a distinctive structural permutation and political arrangement. This century-and-a-half long endeavor to resolve lawmaking practices for interested parties became acutely internalized inside UNCITRAL because all the actors, all the parties with their varying permutations of political process, were brought into an issue-ecology – the lawmaking of a working group. Thus, the melding of formal and informal processes within UNCITRAL's working methods represented a microcosm of a macrocosmic structuring and restructuring of lawmaking politics that has a long lineage and whose respective resolutions were represented in the very organizations that constitute UNCITRAL's delegations.

In the third instance, the struggles between UNCITRAL's informal working methods and France's formal alternatives reprise the scholarly and pragmatic debate over the relative power of states vis-à-vis the multilateral bodies they create. Do those bodies remain entirely a servant of the states that created them, a mere convenient administrative cipher through which states drive their preferences, or do they emerge as actors in their own right?

Although realists would view UNCITRAL as merely an arena for interaction among state actors, the Guidelines codify potentially expansive claims for the independent, autonomous role of the Secretariat in the formulation of global norms on trade and finance. The Guidelines stand as a testament to the authority of the Secretariat as an actor distinct from the states that are members of the Commission. Although the Guidelines provide that "decisions of the Commission are taken by members States of the Commission," they also formalize the role of the Secretariat as an independent actor in the workings of the Commission by specifying that the "Secretariat may make either oral or written statements at any time to the Commission or its subsidiary organs concerning any question under consideration," that the "Secretariat may have recourse to the assistance of outside experts from different legal traditions and affiliations," and that the Secretariat "shall decide on the appropriate form" of this assistance "depending on the needs of the Secretariat" and not the concerns of member states.[149] In a strong statement of the independent authority of the Secretariat, the Guidelines also provide that the Secretariat "formulates its proposals to the Commission or its subsidiary organs under its own responsibility."[150] The Guidelines are clear that the Secretariat's authority to formulate proposals is subject to limits: they must be in "accordance with specific instructions received from the Commission or its subsidiary organs" and must bear "in mind the policies expressed in relevant General Assembly resolutions," as well as "decisions adopted previously by the Commission."[151] Nonetheless, the Guidelines leave the Secretariat a wide degree of discretion within these parameters.

[149] Id.
[150] Id., ¶ 12.
[151] Id.

These struggles over the politics of work by UNCITRAL reach to the viability of the entire international lawmaking ecology. To adopt the French proposal might well have led simultaneously to twin resource constraints. On the one hand, by limiting or excluding activist non-state delegations, it would also have deprived UNCITRAL of the tangible and intangible resources those delegations and their industries brought to that setting. With a much more constricted role, arguably powerful non-state actors would look to other forums where their expertise, infrastructures, and legitimacy might be more effectively deployed. On the other hand, France's proposals would have placed more substantial administrative demands on UNCITRAL, including travel and translation, which had resource implications for an already resource-poor organization.

These threats to resource capacity might have been met in other ways. UNCITRAL might have turned from reliance on its working groups to the UN as an institution. Yet the probability of obtaining significant capacities for continuing its informal working methods were low within a UN where competitions for resources were constant and resource commitments were uncertain. It is true that UNCITRAL managed to upgrade its status within the UN early in the new millennium and this gave it capacities to increase the number of its working groups and so the reach of its intellectual influence. But those capacities reached more to staff than working methods. France and other states might have offered resources in lieu of those that could be lost by adopting France's proposals, but that offer was never made, and it would have stirred another ferment of inter-state competition.

Effectively, UNCITRAL had orchestrated over decades a policy of *inclusion* that set few boundaries between delegates enmeshed in deliberations within its lawmaking ecology and actors in a salient industry ecology. All states, all non-state actors with demonstrable interests and resources, were admitted to working group deliberations. Hundreds of delegates and delegations took advantage of this relatively expansive policy of admission. With admission came resources and the prospect of effectiveness, not least the promise that norms adopted by UNCITRAL would be enacted by states and adopted by commercial actors, that TLOs in concept would become TLOs in practice, that norms would alter behavior, that law would shape markets.

None of this is to say that France was mistaken about the thumb on the scale that UNCITRAL's informal methods of work potentially offered to economic powerhouses inside this global legislature, whether this power is dressed in the garb of a state or non-state delegation. Indeed, our evidence shows that apart from the colloquia, which are broadly representative, all other working methods tended to be partly selective and partly self-selective in the delegates that attended. Usually, these were a subset of the very few delegates we previously identified as core participants in working group proceedings and, as such, they were overwhelmingly from a small number of advanced economies, and, in the case of the Insolvency and Secured Transaction Working Groups, from common law legal systems, and even North

American countries. The price of resources and efficacy that were obtained by inclusion of non-state actors into formal and informal working methods often intensified and compounded the paradox of smallness – that in this global arena, a tiny number of delegates presided over global lawmaking. This was the tradeoff, the meta-bargain among states and non-state actors, that brought to an end this internal episode of lawmaking on UNCITRAL's practices of lawmaking.

9

Rivalry in the Ecologies

Lawmaking ecologies are comprised of varieties of actors, each of which has its own goals, its own resource challenges, and its own vulnerabilities to competition and rivalry. If struggles in the ecology are not only for survival and existence within the bounds of lawmaking bodies, but also over which IO will emerge ascendant in the competition for lawmaking primacy, then the prospects of conflict and struggle, of bargaining and negotiation, of competing norms, will be high. The stakes are nothing less than promulgation of the world's gold standard for TLO construction in international and regional trade and commerce.

The dynamics of relationships within a lawmaking ecology can be discerned most acutely by scrutinizing emergent rivalries between those lawmaking IOs at sharpest contention with each other. In each of the three lawmaking episodes, UNCITRAL's stature and claims as a lawmaker with jurisdictional primacy in areas of commercial law came under challenge. For each lawmaking episode this chapter therefore examines paired rivalries between UNCITRAL and the World Bank in corporate insolvency law, UNCITRAL and UNIDROIT in secured transactions law, and UNCITRAL and UNCTAD in transport law.

Each rivalry among incipient competitors led to meta-bargaining[1] over which IO or global legislature should take the lead in drafting and promulgating rules for world commerce. In each case, the meta-bargaining led to the formulation of meta-texts. These texts served not to convey the norms themselves, but to order the relationship between rival claimants to lawmaking authority worldwide. The chapter demonstrates that three sorts of meta-texts were generated by rivals to manage prospects of debilitating conflict: (i) *organizational* meta-texts that set out the relationship among several IOs with potentially overlapping jurisdictional claims; (ii) *substantive* meta-texts that describe the relationship among

[1] For the concept of meta-bargaining, see (Carruthers and Halliday 1998) on bargaining over master rules to govern everyday bargaining in economic activity.

potentially overlapping primary texts; and (iii) *counter* meta-texts that expressly critique the substance of one or more primary texts and implicitly critique jurisdictional claims.

The meta-texts thereby articulate past, present and future relationships between both the proliferation of texts produced by lawmaking IOs and, most importantly, the processes of cooperation, competition, or conflict to govern future relationships among powerful IOs in the lawmaking ecologies. Concomitantly, the meta-texts sometimes clarified and sometimes blurred the boundaries between the IOs. They expanded, reduced, or maintained jurisdictional claims to lawmaking territory. In so doing they expressed implicitly or explicitly the contours of TLOs imagined by the IOs.

A "TURF WAR" ON COMPETING INSOLVENCY STANDARDS

Insolvency's Backstory

Before UNCITRAL began work on developing international standards on corporate insolvency law, alternative primary texts already existed. Chapter 3 described the sequence of events preceding UNCITRAL's work on the Legislative Guide on Insolvency Law: the Asian Financial Crisis had prompted the G-22 to issue an expansive report on the need to raise the level of the financial architecture; the IMF and Asian Development Bank wrote reports in reaction, but these were unlikely to result in corporate insolvency law reform anywhere, given their brevity and, in the case of the ADB report, regional focus; the World Bank stepped into this fray and, by 1999, had published a preliminary, draft version of its *Principles and Guidelines for Effective Insolvency and Creditor Rights Systems*.

None of these IFIs were global lawmakers. Unlike UNCITRAL, which devoted itself nearly exclusively to the production of international instruments and other law-like global norms, the IMF, ADB and World Bank were primarily financial institutions – they lent funds consistent with their particular missions. Nonetheless, these IFIs had increasingly found themselves engaged in the drafting of legislation, both as a consequence of the Washington Consensus and implementation of their policies of conditionality in the wake of the Asian Financial Crisis (Chapter 2; see also Block-Lieb and Halliday 2013; Halliday, Block-Lieb, and Carruthers 2009b).

It must have surprised World Bank officials when UNCITRAL's governing Commission decided to hold an exploratory working group session in the winter of 1999 on the topic of insolvency law reform. Some members of the Insolvency Working Group "wondered whether UNCITRAL was essentially laundering the World Bank approach" (Int: 9021). But UNCITRAL's decision to enter this fray had been based on a proposal initiated by Australia – admittedly, an unlikely entity to take on the Washington Consensus. The notion that the US had masterminded this sequencing seemed unlikely to most delegates, since the US Treasury Department had itself suggested that the Bank's Legal Vice-Presidency respond to the G-22 mandate.

But interactions with UNCITRAL were headed within the US, not by Treasury, but through the State Department. The State Department's section on international private law had been headed for years by Harold Burman, who was no stranger to international lawmaking organizations, having been involved for many years in deliberations at UNIDROIT, the Hague Conference, UNCITRAL, and other IOs. He had led the US delegation that had negotiated UNCITRAL's Model Law on Cross-Border Insolvency and brought this same group to deliberate on what would become the Insolvency Guide. Under Burman's leadership, the US delegation to the Insolvency Group included key actors in the field, most notably the most famous face of the bankruptcy court in New York City, the Honorable Burton Lifland, and two experienced practitioners from global law firms, Simpson Thacher and Davis Polk.

To lead its new insolvency initiative, the World Bank had hired a New York lawyer from another prestigious law firm, Weil Gotshal, named Gordon Johnson. Weil Gotshal lawyers had been involved in every important corporate reorganization case in the United States since the US Bankruptcy Code was enacted in 1978, but the lawyer that the Bank had hired was relatively inexperienced as compared to those sitting in the US delegation. Although Johnson had received post-graduate training in comparative law at the London School of Economics, and had been involved in the IBA and INSOL in their efforts to promote the harmonization of corporate insolvency law, his practice experience was comparatively slim compared to the substantial depth of experience in the US delegation to UNCITRAL's Insolvency Working Group.

At the Commission's annual meetings in 1999 and 2000, delegates discussed Australia's proposal (Chapter 3). They raised questions about whether UNCITRAL should get involved in this work, given similar work on this topic within the IBA, ADB, IMF, and World Bank. In 1999, the Commission authorized an exploratory working group session. Still unready to commit to this project by its annual meeting in 2000, the Commission authorized an informational colloquium to be co-hosted by the international professional association, INSOL. The Commission had been convinced that UNCITRAL might play an important role on the topic, but cautioned the working group to sit back until the World Bank first had published their Principles and Guidelines.

The Commission dragged its feet in giving final approval to the project because the World Bank's project remained unfinished in early 2001. Under Johnson's direction, the Principles had grown substantially. They now included recommendations and commentary on, not just on topics of corporate insolvency law, but also general collection law and the laws governing secured transactions and their enforcement, as well as larger governance questions concerning various insolvency institutions. Two annexes were added on bank insolvency and restructuring, and systemic insolvency and crises.

The breadth of the Bank's Principles and Guidelines was partly a function of the its commitment to the Washington Consensus[2] and partly the result of what its President at that time, James Wolfensohn, referred to as a Comprehensive Development Framework.[3] It was also related to the breadth of reforms that had been proposed by the G-22 in the wake of the Asian Financial Crisis (Chapter 3).[4] It was finally a function of the "mental ecology" that the Bank's point person on the issue, Gordon Johnson, envisioned as distinguishing this project from the work of earlier IFIs. Compared to the IMF's report, which seemed focused more on emergency reaction, the Bank Principles took the broader view of "a longer infrastructure project" (Int: 2004C). While the ADB Report was more attentive to substantive law than institutions, the Bank Principles took a "more systems-oriented approach" that emphasized "adequate institutions, regulatory institutions, commercial institutions" and "a more holistic view of commercial relationship from the beginning of the credit relationship" (Int: 20054c).

The World Bank finally published its "draft" Principles and Guidelines on the web in April of 2001. Within months of the Principles' unveiling, UNCITRAL's governing Commission held its annual session, where delegates persisted in calling for UN involvement. The Commission reconvened the Insolvency Working Group and invited the World Bank, IMF, ADB, and European Bank for Reconstruction and Development (EBRD) to attend working group sessions, confident that these IFIs shared its pyramidal vision for progress. At the moment of agenda

2 A focus on law and the significance of law to economic development and sovereign borrowers' creditworthiness grew among the IFIs in the late 1970s and early 1980s, and as a result the World Bank's policies of conditionality broadened to include structural conditions. With the Washington Consensus that emerged among IFIs during this period (Williamson 1990), structural adjustment programs (SAPs) – policies of conditionality keyed to structural reforms – conditioned World Bank and IMF loans on law reforms modeled on privatized and deregulated market (Krever 2011). During this period, the Bank prompted law reform based on a neoliberal diagnosis of the issues creating obstacles to development: structural reform of a wide array of legal topics included laws on banking, insurance, securities, commercial corporations, trade practices, and property law (Ofosu-Amaah 2002). After the fall of the Berlin Wall, Bank loans throughout Eastern and Central Europe looked to promote economic liberalism (id.).

3 In the late 1990s, World Bank President James Wolfensohn had promulgated a series of memoranda detailing his vision for the Bank's mandate, which he described as a Comprehensive Development Framework (Ofosu-Amaah 2002; Wolfensohn 1997). This CDF looked "holistically" at governance institutions and regulatory frameworks (id.).

4 The Washington Consensus should have been chastened by financial crises in Asia and Latin America in the late 1990s (Krever 2011). Instead, the Bank spun these financial crises as the result of an absence of the rule of law and as further justification for law reform initiatives. To support its work on law reform, the Bank pointed to the new financial architecture called for by the G-22 and its 1999 report on the Asian Financial Crisis (Halliday and Carruthers 2009; Sheng 2009). The G-22's architecture project covered a wide range of laws and regulations governing banking, securities and capital markets, corporate governance and accounting standards, but also corporate insolvency and creditors' rights regimes (Chapters 3 and 7).

setting, it appeared that all contending IOs had deferred to UNCITRAL's effort, including the World Bank (Chapter 3).

From the moment delegates settled into their seats at UNCITRAL working group sessions, observers from the World Bank sat at the rear of the chamber with the non-state delegations. The Bank's Principles and Guidelines informed deliberations, as did the earlier reports that had been issued by the IMF, ADB and EBRD, but they did not serve as a template for the discussions. Although the Bank might have thought it that would have the stage to itself, said one delegate, "now it has to fit in and adapt" (Int: 2101).

The Illusion of Collaboration

This apparent bargain fell apart at a critical point in 2003. The illusion of collaborative work was shattered at an international conference hosted at the headquarters of the World Bank in January 2003. Those in attendance at the conference learned that the Bank quietly had continued to work on its Principles and Guidelines with the assistance of its task force of academics and practitioners and, more importantly, that it intended to seek approval of the revised Principles from the Boards of the World Bank and IMF. With this endorsement, conference organizers made clear, the Principles would set the international standards for corporate insolvency law sought by the G-22 in its 1998 report and would form the basis for the Bank's Report on the Observance of Standards and Codes (ROSC) on the topic.

At the January 2003 conference convened in Washington, the Bank confronted UNCITRAL with rival products (its revised Principles and Guidelines, and its Insolvency and Creditor Rights Standard for ROSC Assessment) and a public claim to be the predominate source for international standards on the topic of corporate insolvency law. Each of these texts contained both substantive recommendations for international standards on corporate insolvency laws and extensive description of the context of the drafting of the Principles and Guidelines, on one hand, and the Legislative Guide, on the other. This contextual material also implicitly made a case for the legitimacy of each IO, the WB, on one hand, and UNCITRAL, on the other (Halliday and Block-Lieb 2013).

Participants' reactions to the assertion of authority ranged from a characterization of the conference as involving a "scrap" between the World Bank and UNCITRAL, and outright anger at the Bank's "pure power play" (Int: 2055B). A delegation from a leading state viewed the "weakness" of the World Bank's approach as a matter of process not substance in that "they are not fully enough consultative or participatory to draw in such a diversity of nations to consider national variation" (Int: 1947). Delegates from the IMF made it clear that the Fund "was not in favor of two competing products;" the Fund's lawyers thought that "the US could never go along with a product that is so secretive and private, as the World Bank approach has been" (Int: 1950). Delegates from international professional associations similarly didn't like the idea of the Bank "going it alone" (Int: 1951). UNCITRAL's Secretariat viewed the vague "air of conflict" that had characterized its previous interactions with the Bank turning, with this conference, into an outright "turf war" (Int: 4003).

Although the US delegation favored UNCITRAL's endeavor, its position at the World Bank conference was complicated. After making a few phone calls, US delegates learned that "someone" at the World Bank had convinced "someone" at US Treasury that the Bank's Principles and Guidelines should be preferred over UNCITRAL's ongoing work on the Legislative Guide. But this put Burman, the US delegation's lead negotiator and a diplomat within the State Department, in the difficult position of having to convince the Treasury official that State's opinions on the matter conveyed more heft than Treasury's. Getting Treasury to back down was likely to be difficult. Could some face-saving compromise be brokered?

Several possibilities presented themselves. First, UNCITRAL and the World Bank might have divided their normative domain by allocating to the Bank a focus on high-level principles and leaving for UNCITRAL the work of filling in gaps with the sorts of detail that would benefit domestic legislatures and justice ministries. Second, the Bank could claim jurisdiction over governance issues associated with insolvency institutions, consistent with the Bank's holistic Comprehensive Development Framework, while UNCITRAL claimed authority over legal substance. Finally, these IOs could divide their authority by highlighting their divergent areas of expertise: UNCITRAL could promulgate prescriptive norms, whether as principles or rules, and the Bank could integrate these norms into its diagnostic ROSCs, which informed technical assistance and guided law reform efforts within nation states.

The Bank objected to all these proposals. It opted for a zero-sum strategy of "winner takes all." From the Bank's perspective, UNCITRAL held no enforcement authority, had access to limited financial resources, and no personnel on the ground other than several international civil servants located in Vienna. The World Bank, on the other hand, had substantial material resources, an extensive network of specialists on the ground throughout the globe, and member states from 187 countries. It also famously held the ear of the US government, especially in its powerful Treasury Department. Why should the Bank defer to standards set by a small, poor, technical deliberative body working far away in Vienna?

UNCITRAL's Secretariat resisted being bullied into capitulating. Its work, which had begun in earnest in 2001, was nearing completion by 2003. Its Legislative Guide on Insolvency Law was more than the product of a widely representative and deliberative body. As compared to the Bank's Principles and Guidelines, the Legislative Guide focused narrowly on issues of corporate insolvency law (and its Secured Transactions Working Group had devoted several years to producing a separate Legislative Guide on that related topic of law). While rarely straying from the topic of corporate insolvency law, the Insolvency Guide telescoped from broad statements of principle to precise statements resembling, at times, model statutory provisions, coupling both sorts of recommendations with background commentary and statements of purpose (Int: 4002). Despite this variation in specificity, on most issues the Insolvency Guide provided more detail than the Bank's Principles.

Deference to the Bank would involve more than a loss of the fruits of the Working Group's several years of effort. Unlike the Bank, which had the financial wherewithal to put together a team of paid consultants, UNCITRAL had relied on teams of volunteers to work on the Legislative Guide. State delegates who came from various ministries of justice might view their UNCITRAL work as a pleasant part of their employment status, but practitioners, judges and academics attended UNCITRAL meetings in their free time. While most received reimbursement for their travel and lodging, many delegates ran from the room at the conclusion of the day in order to take care of professional responsibilities between working group sessions. If the Bank could seize work away from UNCITRAL at the last minute, who would take the time to roll up their sleeves and work on UNCITRAL projects? UNCITRAL's longstanding methods of work were as much at risk as its subsequent product.

Fractious Meta-Bargaining

Intense negotiations ensued between in-house counsel for UNCITRAL and the Bank, but things had gone too far for anything short of a written set of "Points of Understanding" regarding the two organizations' responsibilities. Bank officials took a hand at drafting a memorandum of this sort, but this initial draft ruffled feathers at UNCITRAL. Delegates learned about its details when the working group resumed sessions in New York in 2003. As deliberations proceeded over the week, delegates remained "agitated and angry" at the proposed resolution (Int: 1970).

Late in the 2003 working group sessions, UNCITRAL's Secretary produced his own draft agreement for the Bank's consideration. In it he proposed that UNCITRAL would accede to the force of the Bank's Principles, which largely were consistent with the Legislative Guide, so long as the Bank agreed that these Principles were fully consistent with the recommendations and extensive commentary in the Legislative Guide. This face-saving proposal was difficult for the Bank to turn down outright, but the Bank continued to insist that it be allowed to prepare its own Technical Paper on the relationship between the Principles and the Legislative Guide.

Suspicions about the content of this yet undrafted Technical Paper stalled UNCITRAL's full endorsement of the compromise that had been crafted. Some delegations balked at the prospect of UNCITRAL's recognition of the Bank's Principles on the grounds that their support for UNCITRAL had been premised on the precise opposite – "they wanted a product *not* developed by the Bank" (Int: 1970). Others feared alienating the Bank too fully, since UNCITRAL did not possess the capacity to disseminate its product without the Bank's assistance. They understood that UNCITRAL "doesn't have the resources to go out and sell.

If you can get an aid organization to essentially promote the product, then in theory that is good" for UNCITRAL (Int: 1970).

While the US delegation and the many senior North American participants sent to represent various non-state delegations protected UNCITRAL from the full force of the Bank, ironically, UNCITRAL couldn't fully rely on these partners. It could not make an enemy of the Bank and easily survive and thrive as an IO in the fields of commercial lawmaking where the Bank had an interest.

But UNCITRAL had a strong ally in the IMF. The IMF favored UNCITRAL's Legislative Guide, mostly as a result of UNCITRAL's widely participatory, transparent and deliberative process. The Fund had been "burnt politically" in the past, as a result of its insistence on structural reforms as conditions to its balance of payments lending in the context of the Asian Financial Crisis (Int: 4008). If the Fund were to refer to international standards as "a stick" it looked to wave in the context of future lending, it understood that the stick would have to be the product of a legitimate process (id.). Moreover, in making proposals for legislative reforms, the Fund preferred to point to precise recommendations like those in the Legislative Guide, rather than the Bank's Principles, which were "so vague and general" (Int: 2351B).

The IMF's position in the dispute between UNCITRAL and the Bank was difficult, however. Its close association with the Bank required a gentle touch. Siding with UNCITRAL against the World Bank might be viewed as favoring a sister-in-law over one's own brother.

UNCITRAL delegates sought to convince officials at the US Treasury that the World Bank was not, as they claimed, "the only game in town" (Int: 1971). One UNCITRAL delegate garnered a meeting at Treasury and used the time to describe the working group's extensive output and the advanced state of the draft Insolvency Guide; at the same time, another delegate similarly briefed the general counsel of the NY Federal Reserve Bank (Int: 1958).

UNCITRAL's Secretary called on the UN Vice-President for Legal Affairs to intervene. This led to a meeting between the UN's general counsel and the acting general counsel of the World Bank, as well as a subsequent meeting organized by the UN general counsel among UNCITRAL's Secretary and the Working Group's Secretary, the IMF's deputy general counsel and a senior Bank official. The latter meeting led to a timetable and an outline of an agreement under which (i) the Bank would produce a document detailing differences between its Principles and the recommendations in the Legislative Guide, (ii) a joint expert group would review this work in time for a presentation at a working group session in the Fall of 2003, and (iii) by late 2003, the Bank would prepare a commentary on its Principles, to which (iv) the UNCITRAL secretariat would respond. All of these documents would allow the Bank to take its revised Principles to its Board by late 2003.

This agreement involved more than simply a roadmap for combining the two extant documents. In this version of their Points of Understanding, language also was exchanged regarding future interactions between the IOs. It specified that the two organizations would "promote active collaboration and partnership among other international institutions and organizations, maximize resources, avoid duplication, promote complementarities and ensure development of the best possible products ... " (Int: 1973).

The US government sought peace. It wanted a single text that reflected a resolution of the dispute between the Bank and UNCITRAL, that garnered the approval of the IMF, and that reflected a concord between the US Treasury Department and Department of State. Trade interests had been impaired by the failure to reach a conclusion; countries felt "whiplashed by different IFIs – the EBRD and World Bank;" a third text from UNCITRAL would have compounded confusion (Int: 4004B). By early 2004, things were still up in the air. A senior official at the IMF "got fed up and twisted arms and got a deal done" (Int: 2100B).

An Organizational Meta-Text

Confronted with divergent primary texts and the possibility of non-uniform national adoptions across the world, powerful states and the highest legal officers of the UN, World Bank, IMF, and UNCITRAL negotiated an agreement both to rationalize their respective roles and the two products they had produced. This negotiation was codified in an organizational meta-text. This meta-text combined the work of the two IOs and led to the development of a distinct primary text – a "unified standard" that both merged UNCITRAL's Legislative Guide and the Bank's Principles and Guidelines and established a tenuous partnership for future work on the topic of corporate insolvency lawmaking.

In the end, a memorandum among the Bank, the Fund, and UNCITRAL was signed agreeing to the preparation of a unified standard that would incorporate (i) the World Bank's Principles, with no technical paper or comparative commentary, and (ii) UNCITRAL's Legislative Guide on Insolvency Law, together with (iii) some complementary material from the Bank on issues that sat outside the work of UNCITRAL's Insolvency Guide, plus (iv) a ROSC diagnostic instrument that would be keyed into the recommendations in UNCITRAL's Legislative Guide (Int: 2100B; 4008B; confidential memorandum dated March 25, 2004). While earlier versions of the Points of Understanding had referred to the interactions of the World Bank and UNCITRAL, the final version spoke only in terms of the unified standard that would be prepared by the two IOs. The final deal was reported to the Insolvency Working Group in the spring of 2004,[5] and later blessed by the Commission in their annual summer meeting that year.[6]

Agreement on the form of the unified standard did not fully conclude the situation, however. The merging of the documents took until the end of 2005 to

[5] UN Doc. No. A/CN.9/551, ¶ 21.

[6] UN Doc. No. A/59/17, ¶ 54.

complete, as each IO fought rear guard battles over the form of the "unified standard" (Int: 5503). Things were not fully resolved until a change in leadership at the Bank "brought a change in tone" a "giant shift in attitude" and, thus, the prospect of a "framework that preserves the integrity of both documents" (Int: 5504).

These negotiations resulted in a document posted on the World Bank website on December 21, 2005.[7] The site explains that insolvency and creditor rights is one of twelve areas on which the World Bank and the International Monetary Fund conduct "assessments" based on "standards," and that the "Insolvency and Creditor Rights (ICR) Standard for ICR ROSC assessments" is based on "two complementary texts," the World Bank Principles for Effective Insolvency and Creditor Rights Systems and the UNCITRAL Legislative Guide on Insolvency Law, which together "represent the international consensus on best practices" and "set forth a unified standard for ICR systems." The Bank's website provides hyperlinks to its Principles and Guidelines (both the 2001 and 2005 versions), UNCITRAL's Insolvency Guide, and a separate document called the Creditor Rights and Insolvency Standard (the "ICR Standard").

The ICR Standard meshes the Bank's Principles and Guidelines and UNCITRAL's Legislative Guide into a single stand-alone diagnostic document, distinct from both antecedents. Although it provides on a cover page that it is "based on" the Bank's Principles and on the recommendations found in UNCITRAL's Guide, the ICR Standard does not summarize these documents. Instead, it combines key portions of both – that is the Bank's principles (but not the commentary contained with its Guidelines) and UNCITRAL's recommendations on insolvency law (but not the commentary contained in the Guide).

Nevertheless, this digest of the work of the Bank and UNCITRAL is intertwined according to the logic of the Bank's Principles, not those of UNCITRAL's Legislative Guide. A "table of contents" lays out the four subjects contained in the Principles and Guidelines (creditor rights; risk management and corporate workout; commercial insolvency; implementation – institutional and regulatory frameworks), although the Insolvency Guide was focused exclusively on "commercial insolvency." An "introduction" follows, explaining the substance but mostly the context of the ICR Standard. This introductory text emphasizes the representativeness of the Bank's deliberations (Halliday, Block-Lieb, and Carruthers 2009b), as had earlier versions of the Bank Principles and Guidelines, and provides limited mention of

[7] The ICR Standard was initially published in 2005, but the Bank and UNCITRAL both have supplemented the documents underlying this standard. UNCITRAL supplemented its original two-part Legislative Guide with additional commentary and recommendations on the treatment of enterprise groups and on directors' obligations in the period approaching insolvency. The Bank amended its Principles and Guidelines in 2011 and 2015 to add principles on the insolvency treatment of enterprise groups and on secured transactions and creditors' rights more generally. It also revised recommendations on the insolvency treatment of financial contracts to include references to UNIDROIT's Principles on Close-Out Netting.

UNCITRAL's deliberations. Indeed, in noting that "the Bank staff and experts, in collaboration with the Fund and UNCITRAL staff and experts, have prepared the unified Standard for Insolvency and Creditor Rights Systems," the introduction mentions but minimizes UNCITRAL's distinct "governance processes and structure" involving "a total of 87 states, 14 intergovernmental organizations, and 13 nongovernmental organizations"(ICR Standard at 4). Rather than focus on the distinct processes through which the Bank's Principles and UNCITRAL's Guide where promulgated, the introduction emphasizes the work of staff and experts to combine the two products.

The ICR Standard intersperses the Bank's principles with correlative recommendations from UNCITRAL's Guide but, whenever possible, prioritizes the Bank's Principles. The Bank places itself before UNCITRAL at every location, beginning with the title page. Because the Guide's recommendations are included according to the order of the Bank's principles, the recommendations are confusingly included out of sequence. The Standard is structured so that national readers are forced to cross-refer to UNCITRAL's Guide if a complete statement of the recommendations is desired. The commentary that explicates UNCITRAL's recommendations, as well as the commentary from the Bank's Principles, is altogether absent from this document.

From all appearances, the ICR Standard is a Bank-orchestrated product. While UNCITRAL staff were central to its preparation, it appears on the World Bank's website, together with hyperlinks both to Bank's Principles and Guidelines and UNCITRAL's Legislative Guide. Although UNCITRAL frequently endorses the work product of other IOs, there is no reference to the ICR Standard on UNCITRAL's website.

MULTIPLYING NORMS, DIVIDING TERRITORY: SECURED TRANSACTIONS

Before UNCITRAL began work on developing international standards on secured transactions law, several IFIs were at work drafting and setting international standards for secured transactions laws, including both the World Bank and the EBRD. Regional efforts had also begun, including draft model laws produced by the Organization of American States (OAS) and *l'Organisation pour l'Harmonisation en Afrique du Droit des Affaires* (OHADA), and a working group convened by the European Commission to examine the possibility of converging the laws governing commercial finance throughout the European Union.

UNCITRAL's most direct competitor, however, was another global lawmaker, UNIDROIT. From the first Commission meeting in which UNCITRAL proposed working on a comprehensive legislature guide on secured transactions, UNIDROIT had vigorously objected (Chapter 3). But by the time the UNCITRAL working group began deliberations in earnest, UNIDROIT decided to retreat from direct competition on a comprehensive set of norms and to intensity its focus on the Cape Town Convention and related protocols on leasing.

This division of labor stood undocumented until completion of both the Secured Transactions Legislative Guide and the Cape Town Convention, when an implicit challenge arose again between the global quasi-legislatures. Although UNCITRAL, UNIDROIT and other IOs had managed to avoid collision in their overlapping efforts to formulate global norms for commercial finance, there remained the prospect of incipient confusion for states when they were faced with an increasing number of international instruments on varieties of secured transactions. Quite apart from the complexities of reconciling these often arcane sets of global norms, the confusion they could induce increased the risk that states would simply ignore all the global norms and the prospects for convergence or economic development they promised.

Over a period of fifteen years, therefore, UNCITRAL and UNIDROIT, together with the Hague Conference, maneuvered around each other, aware of each other's products, wary of each other's intentions, and yet unresolved in their future relationships, not least insofar as these might impair the prospect of worldwide adoption of their respective sets of norms. The resolution of the unstable relations among IOs and products alike led to a new kind of meta-bargain through a new kind of meta-text.

UNIDROIT's Backstory

UNIDROIT was officially inaugurated in 1928 as an international organization that fit within the auspices of the then newly created League of Nations (Peters 2012; (Block-Lieb and Halliday 2016). The Rome Institute (as UNIDROIT was known at the time) existed as an intergovernmental organization associated with the League of Nations for only a few years. By 1939, its sponsor, Italy, had withdrawn support from the Institute and from the League of Nations. The League of Nations ceased to exist in 1946, with the United Nations established to replace it.

Various League of Nations organizations continued to exist as UN-affiliated entities, but the Rome Institute was not similarly embraced within the UN family. This rejection of sorts did not result in its demise. Both the Hague Conference on Private International Law and UNIDROIT were (re)incorporated in 1951, but as stand-alone international organizations. Thus, although there was no UN entity devoted to the codification or development of (substantive) international private law or (procedural) private international law during this post-War period, none was proposed until UNCITRAL's creation in the late 1960s.

UNIDROIT's independence might have brought political advantages, but its orphan status meant that UNIDROIT could not rely on financial support from the UN or any other international organization. While in theory nothing would have prevented member states from making financial contributions both to

UNIDROIT and to the United Nations (which would, in turn, funds UNCITRAL and other UN-affiliated entities), in reality funding and attention spans are limited. UNIDROIT therefore developed partners who would assist it both financially and intellectually in its lawmaking projects, most importantly, the aeronautical industry in its drafting of the Cape Town Convention on Security Rights in Mobile Equipment and its related protocol on aircraft equipment.[8]

Conflicting Claims

UNCITRAL had studied the possibility of drafting a model secured transactions law in the early 1980s and, based on a report it had commissioned, rejected the idea (Chapter 2). Relying on UNCITRAL's abandonment of the issue, UNIDROIT took up the work of secured transactions law reform by carving this enormous issue into bite-sized pieces – one form of transaction, one type of collateral, at a time.[9] By the late 1980s, UNIDROIT had promulgated two draft conventions on factoring and commercial leasing, which would become the Ottawa Conventions on these two topics.[10] It next began work on what would become the Cape Town Convention on security rights in mobile equipment in the early 1990s.[11]

When it started work on what would become the Cape Town Convention, UNIDROIT's governing council explored the idea of building on the expertise it had been developing on the topic of secured transactions law. It put together a Restricted Working Group "to study the desirability and feasibility of the preparation of a model law in the general field of secured transactions" (UNIDROIT Report of 72nd Session 1993; Peters at 47), which later published several draft reports on the topic. These preliminary reports differed from that prepared by Dr. Prof. Ulrich Drobnig for UNCITRAL roughly a dozen years earlier. The UNIDROIT reports, prepared by Prof. Ron Cumming from the University of Saskatchewan, viewed the project as both feasible and timely. In the dozen years that had passed since Drobnig's earlier conclusion that this area of law was not ripe for harmonization, Canada's provinces had adopted "personal property" security laws modeled on US Article 9. Pressures for greater globalization of finance had proceeded apace, including pressures for "modern" secured transactions laws. In addition, the fall of the Berlin Wall had prompted demand for widespread reform of private law

[8] UNIDROIT's aircraft protocol to the Cape Town Convention enjoys wide accession; while the rail and space asset protocols to the Cape Town Convention have not yet entered into force as of yet, this failure is less an indication of international opinion than that they have only recently emerged.

[9] For more detailed discussion of UNIDROIT's emergence and adaptation over its nearly one hundred years of existence, see (Block-Lieb and Halliday 2016)

[10] *See* Ottawa Convention on International Factoring (1988), and Ottawa Convention on International Financial Leasing (1988).

[11] *See* Cape Town Convention on International Interests in Mobile Equipment (2001).

regimes throughout Central and Eastern Europe, including interest in the adoption of "modern" secured transactions laws.[12]

Founded in 1991, the EBRD had spearheaded work on this topic within Europe. Among the EBRD's earliest law reform projects included promulgation of a draft Model Secured Transactions Law. In addition, the International Bank for Reconstruction and Development (which is a part of the World Bank Group) exported a similar fervor for secured transactions law reform to other Continents.

UNIDROIT's Study Group viewed these developments as indications that comprehensive secured transactions lawmaking for the world was now plausible. Its interest in work on a generalized secured transactions law caught the attention of the EBRD, which in turn commented favorably on the preparatory work that had been commissioned by UNIDROIT's governing council.[13]

Ultimately, UNIDROIT's governing council decided to hold off on this larger project pending completion of what would become the draft Cape Town Convention, but not because they did not think secured transactions reform was premature or problematic. Instead, the council considered there were too few UNIDROIT delegates available to work on both projects at the same time. Priority was accorded to the convention project, which had been further along and which attracted the attention of industry actors with extensive resources, UNIDROIT's own solution to a resource scarcity endemic to its free-standing status as an autonomous lawmaking body.

Nevertheless, the Study Group's work, and the interest it raised within the EBRD and World Bank, led UNIDROIT's Secretariat to recognize there was a threat of overcrowding of IOs and lawmaking initiatives on secured transactions. In late 1994, UNIDROIT's Secretariat hosted a meeting that focused specifically on "the International Organizations currently involved in the preparation of legislation in the field of personal property security," and looked to "permit an exchange of information" to "avoid[] unintended prejudice" (UNIDROIT 1995). This continued a practice initiated in the 1950s in which UNIDROIT organized regular meetings among international organizations engaged in the unification of private law (Matteucci 1956). Subsequently, annual coordinative meetings among the heads of UNIDROIT, UNCITRAL and Hague Conference – the "Three Sisters" of international private lawmaking – were informal affairs, often tucked between

[12] See, e.g., UNIDROIT, Restricted Working Group, Some Preliminary Considerations with a View to the Drawing Up of a Check List of the Issues to be Addressed in a Possible Future Model Law in the General Field of Secured Transactions (Ronald C.C. Cummings, Univ. of Saskatchewan)(Oct. 1994), www.unidroit.org/english/documents/1994/study72a/s-72a-01-e.pdf.

[13] See, e.g., UNIDROIT, Comments on the UNDIROIT Project for Drawing Up A Checklist of the Issues to be Addressed in a Possible Future Model Law in the General Field of Secured Transactions (John L. Simpson and Hendrick Röver, EBRD)(Nov. 1994), www.unidroit.org/english/documents/1994/study72a/s-72a-03-e.pdf.

UNIDROIT's observations at UNCITRAL sessions, UNCITRAL's participation in UNIDROIT meetings, or participation by either at meetings in The Hague.

The 1994 gathering records a presentation of many lawmaking projects by the IOs in attendance, including UNIDROIT, UNCITRAL, the Hague Conference, the EBRD, and World Bank, as well as several international NGOs (i.e., IBA, ICC and CMI).[14] Malcolm Evans, then UNIDROIT's Secretary-General, called the meeting to order by encouraging those in attendance to "pool their resources" given difficulties lawmaking organizations had faced in promoting the harmonization of private law.[15] Resource maximization would come from two sources, argued Evans and other participants in the meeting.

First, Evans articulated "a perception of the need for co-ordination between the various regional efforts that had taken off in this area of the law in recent years," noting both the work of the EBRD in Central and Eastern Europe and of the IDB "in a number of Latin American countries but also in Bangladesh, Bulgaria, and Sierra Leone." He was explicit that the "goal of this co-ordination" was, from UNIDROIT's perspective, to avoid "unintended prejudice to the efforts underway to develop a new global regimen for the secured financing of mobile equipment."[16]

Second, Evans emphasized the need to attract the "attention" of industry actors. Perhaps conceding indirectly that UNIDROIT's two Ottawa Conventions, one on international factoring and another on international commercial leasing, had been a disappointment,[17] he argued that he was more and more convinced that the efforts of IOs in drafting international instruments of this sort "should be founded right from the outset on the perceived needs of the business practice so as to ensure that ... these same business circles would see it as being in their interests to bring the necessary pressure to bear on governments to implement them as speedily as possible."[18]

[14] Participants in the meeting included not only the Secretary-General of UNIDROIT, Malcolm Evans, but also two representatives from the European Bank for Reconstruction and Development (EBRD), John Simpson and Hendrick Röver, who perhaps not coincidently, earlier had commented on UNDROIT's preliminary report on secured transaction law reform, as well as representatives from the Hague Conference on Private International Law (M. Pelichet), the World Bank's International Bank for Development (IDB) (H. Flesig and N. de law Peña), UNCITRAL (S. Bazinas), the International Bar Association (M. Gioscia), the International Chamber of Commerce (Roy Goode), the Committee Maritime International (R. Herber), and the American National Conference of Commissioners on Uniform State Law (C. Mooney, Jr.).

[15] Id., ¶ 4, at 2.

[16] Id.

[17] Evans explicitly emphasized his point with reference to the two international instruments on multimodal transport promulgated recently by UNCTAD. One, the convention, had produced "disastrous results" because adopted only by a few land-locked countries, whereas the Rules, had "enjoyed enormous success," which he attributed to UNCTAD's partnering with the International Chamber of Commerce in their drafting (id., ¶ 6 at 3).

[18] Id., ¶ 6 at 2.

There was also an implicit competitive edge to the explicit focus on transparency and cooperation. Participants each implied in their admonitions against duplication of effort that other IOs should keep their distance and not compete or overlap in their lawmaking endeavors. These tacit commitments to cooperate may have convinced UNIDROIT's Governing Council that its decision to put work on a general secured transactions law aside until work on the mobile equipment convention was complete would not be viewed by other IOs as disinterest in working on a model secured transactions law.[19] Its claim was recorded in its report and posted on the UNIDROIT website for all to read.[20]

Thus, when UNIDROIT decided in 1995 to focus on international interests in mobile equipment and to postpone any further work on a model law of broader scope, it had no intention of abandoning the general secured transactions project altogether, but simply to proceed incrementally. In the 1994 meeting among lawmaking IOs in the issue-area, UNCITRAL was both aware of the claim and had agreed to work around UNIDROIT's project without "duplication of effort."

UNIDROIT's decision to delay in writing a model law on secured transactions law was, with the benefit of hindsight, ill timed. UNIDROIT may well have thought that a gradual incrementalism would lead it eventually to a grand set of norms, especially as UNCITRAL had, in the early 1980s, itself considered the possibility of such work and decided against it.

But UNIDROIT could not have foreseen the Asian Financial Crisis or the structural reforms on insolvency and debtor-creditor laws that the World Bank, IMF and other IFIs would insist upon in the context of providing balance of payment and other emergency funding to save several South-East Asian economies. It could not have foreseen that UNCITRAL would succeed in completing its Model Law on Cross-Border Insolvency by 1999, and on the basis of this success convince the US State Department and IMF and others in the international community that it should work on setting international standards for corporate insolvency laws. No one could have predicted that UNCITRAL's work on what would become the Legislative Guide on Insolvency Law would succeed – there was too much dissensus in insolvency laws around the world. Nor could UNIDROIT have foreseen that the US delegation would begin to ponder if the time was not ripe for a similar Legislative Guide on Secured Transactions Law, in effect, to rethink UNCITRAL's decision in the early 1980s not to take on a comprehensive secured transactions program of work.

By 2000, when UNCITRAL had finished working on a convention on the assignment of international receivables but UNIDROIT remained fully immersed

[19] Indeed, the UNICTRAL representative at the 1994 meeting explicitly remarked that he "did not see any potential conflict with a model law that UNIDROIT might decide to prepare in the field of secured transactions" (Id., ¶22, at 8).

[20] A copy of the report of the 1994 meeting is available online at www.unidroit.org/english/documents/1995/study72b/s-72b-01-e.pdf.

in the Cape Town project, UNCITRAL moved swiftly to pre-empt UNIDROIT from returning to its work on a comprehensive model law on secured finance. That UNCITRAL's governing Commission was more likely motivated by the progress its Insolvency Working Group was making on an Insolvency Guide than an interest in beating UNIDROIT to the finish line was hardly the point (Chapter 3). Clearly, those in power at UNCITRAL felt no obligation to defer to UNIDROIT's earlier claim to global leadership on comprehensive lawmaking.

Oddly perhaps, the World Bank remained perfectly silent about UNCITRAL's ambitious secured transactions reform agenda. Although the Bank's Principles and Guidelines covered not just insolvency law but also creditors' collection rights, including a handful of principles about modern secured transactions laws, the World Bank did not object to UNCITRAL's work that would become the Secured Transactions Legislative Guide. During deliberations of the Secured Transactions Working Group, the World Bank sat quietly, observing from the back rows. Much later, in 2015, the Bank would amend its ROSC to account for the international standards on secured transactions law developed by UNCITRAL, but this revision waited until UNCITRAL had nearly completed its work on a draft Model Law.

Toward Coordination

When UNCITRAL's Commission considered a proposal in the early 2000s to re-convene the Secured Transactions Working Group and begin deliberations on what would become the Legislative Guide on Secured Transactions Law, UNIDROIT strenuously objected (Chapter 3). From UNIDROIT's perspective, leadership in this issue-area rightly belonged to UNIDROIT based on preliminary work that it had done six years earlier.

Thus, before Germany and other national delegations objected on substantive grounds to aspects of the Secured Transactions Guide, UNIDROIT raised jurisdictional objections to UNCITRAL's proposal. In theory, UNIDROIT might have laid claim to creation of new products in any of insolvency, transport or secured transactions lawmaking programs since its mission extended to the unification of all private law. But UNIDROIT's claim was not simply that secured transactions law fit within its mission, but instead that its claim to this topic previously had been vocalized, recorded, and temporarily suspended, without any indication it had been abandoned altogether.

On its side, UNCITRAL's governing Commission supported its right to work on secured transactions law reform by pointing to precedent: it had previously produced a draft convention on Assignment on International Receivables, which intersected with the Ottawa Convention on Factoring. UNIDROIT had not objected to UNCITRAL's work on the convention on International Receivables; why should its belated claims to all of secured transactions law merit objection at this point? Moreover, UNIDROIT's work on the Cape Town Convention had taken on a life of its own. While initially framed as a convention to address the difficulty of financing aircraft, UNIDROIT had become enmeshed in additional protocols involving international interests in rail cars and space assets. Discussion of the inclusion of international interests in agricultural equipment was also heard. If the world was to wait for UNIDROIT to finish these earlier projects first, decades of opportunity costs would mount.

In addition, UNCITRAL pointed to the ongoing efforts of its Working Group on Insolvency Law, which had already made preliminary decisions about the need to include security rights in any insolvency estate. UNCITRAL's work on a legislative guide on secured transactions law could take advantage of the substantial overlaps in the two topics. Delaying work on recommendations on secured transactions laws until after UNIDROIT finished its Cape Town project would leave security rights at a substantial disadvantage.

By the time the US delegation proposed the formation of a new Working Group on Secured Transactions Law at the annual meeting of UNCITRAL's Commission in 2000, the determination to work on another legislative guide at UNCITRAL was far advanced. UNIDROIT's complaints, while heard, were virtually ignored by the Commission and later by the newly formed Working Group on Secured Transactions Law.

Confronted with this pre-emptive move, UNIDROIT stepped aside. It intensified work on what would become the Cape Town Convention, an achievement that vindicated its capacity to craft international conventions. In fact, the Cape Town Convention is often referred to as one of only several successful substantive commercial law treaties, with the CISG as the other (see, e.g., Coyle 2011). But after reinforcing its auspices as a specialist lawmaking body in secured transactions, it was too late for UNIDROIT to move back to secured transactions law reform more generally.

UNCITRAL never delayed for a moment its efforts to draft a Legislative Guide on Secured Transactions Law. It commenced work on a Secured Transactions Guide in 2001. The Guide's publication in 2007 would be followed, in quick succession, by a supplement to that Guide on security rights in intellectual property in 2010, a separate Practice Guide on implementation of a security rights registry in 2013, and its current work on a Model Secured Transactions Law (which has been finalized by the Working Group but not yet ratified by the General Assembly). In 2013, the World Bank convened a Task Force to consider how best to weave UNCITRAL's Secured Transactions Guide into its ICR Standard, a task that it concluded in 2015.

In the meantime, UNIDROIT continued its line of discrete lawmaking in the secured transactions field. Its Cape Town Convention and a related Protocol on Aircraft Collateral entered into force in 2008. Protocols on rail and space assets followed in 2007 and 2012. While UNIDROIT would drop its claim to "ownership" of a model law on security rights outside the scope of its Cape Town "brand," it later followed its Ottawa Convention on Financial Leasing with work that culminated in a 2008 Model Law on Leasing.

Nevertheless it was UNIDROIT's work on the 2008 Model Law on Leasing that triggered rounds of meta-bargaining between UNCITRAL and UNIDROIT. Delegates to UNCITRAL's Secured Transactions Working Group had quietly monitored UNIDROIT's Cape Town project, but largely ignored UNIDROIT's Model Law on Leasing. Quite incidentally a member of the US delegation read the Model Law and was surprised to find an obvious inconsistency (Int: 9999). While UNCITRAL's Guide would have treated as a security agreement a "lease" that functioned as a financing transaction, UNIDROIT's Model Law did not distinguish between a "true lease" and a "lease functioning as a financing transaction," which meant that the Model Law was, at least, "potentially inconsistent with the Secured Transactions Legislative Guide" (id.). A quick fix was proposed to the Model Leasing Law, but this inconsistency pointed to a wider prospect of other inconsistencies, confusion and conflicts among the stream of secured transaction projects flowing out of both private lawmaking bodies.

In 2007 and 2008 the Secretariats of UNIDROIT, UNCITRAL, and the Hague Conference (The Hague Conference, UNIDROIT and UNCITRAL 2012) convened several "coordination meetings" to confront the current multiplication of norms and prospects of conflict in the future. They recognized forthrightly "that they could have done a better job of coordinating their work effort" in the past (Int: 9999) and that now there was a pressing need to do so. UNCITRAL's Secretary asked several individuals to work on a "quick agreement" and the project was mentioned at several subsequent annual meetings of UNCITRAL's governing commission, but the drafting seemed to be given a low priority "because there was always something more important to do" (Int: 9999).

Two US delegates. Neil Cohen, a law professor from Brooklyn Law School and a frequent member of the US delegation to UNCITRAL, and Steven Weise, a practitioner but also a leader of the American Bar Association's Section on Business Law and a member of the ABA's delegation to UNCITRAL, forged an agreement that ultimately obtained joint approval by the secretariats of all three lawmaking bodies.[21]

A Substantive Meta-Text

The joint text, entitled "UNCITRAL, The Hague Conference and UNIDROIT Texts on Security Interests" had the ostensible purpose, not to mitigate competition or set boundaries between the IOs, but rather to assist national legislators in navigating among the eleven international instruments promulgated by the three IOs. A Preface details the history of its drafting. An Introduction notes that the three

[21] Although UNCITRAL rarely mentions countries let alone individuals, a footnote to the Preface of this joint document mentions, by name, "Neil Cohen (Professor, Brooklyn Law School) and Steven Weise (Partner, Proskauer Rose LLP, Los Angeles, California)."

IOs "regularly coordinate their activities" both "to assure the integration" of the "instruments that they sponsor" and also to "avoid overlap and inconsistency." The Introduction recognizes that the work of these IOs overlaps,[22] and admits that this overlap may create the potential for confusion (especially on the part of "policy-makers and legislators who have not actively participated in the preparation of the instruments"). In order to allay this possibility for confusion, the "joint document" looks to summarize the instruments, shows how they complement one another, and "provide[s] a comparative understanding of the coverage and basic theme of each." A General Summary lays out in tabular form the eleven instruments covered by the Joint Document and provides a one or two sentence summary of the purposes of each. The Summary Charts and Detailed Charts that follow provide more detailed information, in matrix form, on the connections and distinctions among these eleven instruments. The Summary Chart summarizes the scope of these instruments; another set of eleven Detailed Charts provide information on each of the eleven international instruments.

This joint document is not explicitly articulated as an organizational meta-text. Nowhere does it invoke an explicit agreement to cease or redirect secured transactions work. Nor does it attempt to justify the eleven international instruments that are discussed as following a unified philosophy of reform. Instead, the "joint document" looks backward to rationalize the work of the Three Sisters on topics related to secured transactions law.

Yet there is little doubt that the document serves as a mapping enterprise in that it refers to territorial boundaries claimed by the lawmaking IOs while essentially dividing the labor of global lawmaking among them. Emphasizing the consistency of their past work, the unmistakable implicit message of the "joint document" is that the three global lawmakers will continue to work in a coordinated fashion to develop modern secured transactions law reform proposals and, where possible, their future relationships will be interdependent and complementary rather than competitive and inconsistent.

PERSISTENT RIVALRY: INTERNATIONAL TRANSPORT LAW

The UN Commission on Trade and Development (UNCTAD) had long competed with UNCITRAL for primacy as an international lawmaker on the issue of international shipping. While UNCTAD and UNCITRAL had mostly worked together to produce the Hamburg Rules on maritime transport contracts, UNCTAD had alone drafted the UN Convention on Liner Conferences without UNCITRAL's

[22] Id., at 1 ("Many instruments promulgated by the three organizations concern or directly affect transactions creating rights in movable assets (whether tangible or intangible) to secure obligations and similar financing transactions. . . .").

involvement[23] and the UN Convention on Multimodal Transportation.[24] Later, UNCTAD collaborated, not with UNCITRAL, but with the International Chamber of Commerce (ICC) to draft Multimodal Rules providing proposed standardized contract terms to resolve many of these issues.[25]

Thus, when UNCTAD in 2002 raised objections in early sessions of UNCITRAL's Transport Working Group, it was not complaining about UNCITRAL's partnership with the International Maritime Committee (CMI). UNCTAD had itself partnered with CMI. UNCTAD's objections concerned the scope of UNCITRAL's work, not its choice of partners. Its objections were, thus, jurisdictional. UNCTAD objected to the potentially door-to-door scope of the draft conventions and made its objection known by means of a sustained critical commentary on the draft convention put on the table by the CMI at UNCITRAL's first Working Group meeting.

Ignored by the International Transportation Working Group, in 2003 UNCTAD persisted in its claims for lawmaking jurisdiction by unveiling findings from a survey it had undertaken of governments about their preferences for transport law on the carriage of goods (Chapter 3). UNCTAD asserted that states' preferred a unified multimodal approach to the carriage of goods from manufacture to market, precisely the approach that earlier had been championed by UNCTAD. But again the International Transport Working Group largely ignored UNCTAD's claims. Indeed, despite UNCTAD's submission of extensive texts articulating how the draft UNCITRAL convention would subvert the interests of developing nations' small shippers, a bloc of African nations, historically aligned with UNCTARD, ratified UNCITRAL's Rotterdam Rules. From this point on, the decades-long competitive cooperation between UNCITRAL and UNCTAD broke into open conflict.

UNCTAD's Backstory

When 120 states gathered in Geneva to participate in the UN's initial Conference on Trade and Development in mid-1964, delegates primarily focused their attention, not on substantive trade issues, but on the "institutional question," that is, whether then-existing trade institutions, especially GATT, should be responsible for carrying out the policy recommendations made by the conference or "whether new machinery within the United Nations should be set up" (Cordovez 1967: 282). The developing nations in attendance presented a united front that formed the Group of 77, which eventually was joined by delegations of socialist countries. Although the

[23] UNCTAD's Convention on Liner Conferences has narrowly entered into force, but its practical influence waned substantially in light of industry developments (Chapter 3).

[24] The Multimodal Convention had been drafted to work together with the Hamburg Rules, but unlike the Hamburg and Liner Conference texts, the Multimodal Convention never entered into force (Chapter 3).

[25] That UNCTAD turned its back on UNCITRAL to craft the Multimodal Rules was understandable in that, unlike the Multimodal Convention, these Rules were crafted to interact with provisions of the Hague and Hague-Visby Rules (Chapter 3).

West nonetheless held firm in their opposition to the G-77's proposal, by December 1964, the UN had established UNCTAD as "an organ of the General Assembly" to be convened "at intervals of not more than three years."[26]

The first actions of UNCTAD's Board of Trade and permanent Secretariat involved the creation of committees to address specific areas of trade and development, including a Committee on Shipping in April 1965.[27] Although the Prebisch Report had identified shipping as an impediment to trade based on *economic* considerations (i.e., the cost of maritime freight and insurance), the Board quickly turned its attention to the *law* governing international transport by sea.[28]

UNCTAD's shift from consideration of the economic implications of seafaring trade to questions of international legislation on shipping was complicated for two reasons. First, UNCTAD's competence to draft an international convention was unclear. Second, if Hungary thought that the UN should create UNCITRAL (Chapter 2), did this not imply that UNCTAD did not itself possess the authority to formulate international legal texts?[29]

Potential jurisdictional disputes between UNCTAD and UNCITRAL were resolved initially by a classic division of labor: The Conference viewed diagnosis of the "commercial and economic" problems associated with international transport as fitting within its economic bailiwick and it handed off the work of legislative

[26] UN Doc. No. A/1995 (XIX), Art I. Membership in the Conference was open to all members of the General Assembly (id., Art. 1), but the G-77 looked to ensure numeric superiority in this context. The Resolution provided for fifty-five members in the Board, and specified that these members would consist of 22 from the countries listed in Annex A (Asia and Africa), 18 from Annex B (Western Europe and the United States), 9 from Annex C (Latin America) and 6 from Annex D (the Soviet Union and other socialist economies) (id., Art. II, para. 5). This formulation was intended to ensure regional diversity in the Board's decisionmaking, and particularly that developing nations would enjoy a voice on the Board, despite their relatively weak economic authority.

[27] Although shipping was not among the three committees identified in the General Assembly Resolution establishing UNCTAD, a early report by the Secretary-General of the Conference (even before its creation as a permanent UN organ) had identified "the mounting burden of external payments for maritime freight and insurance" as an important part of explaining developing countries' growing trade imbalances (Prebisch 1964)

[28] Members of the Board advised that "international legislation on shipping" be addressed at the second session of the Conference and asked the newly formed Committee on Shipping to make recommendations on the topic. Official Records of the General Assembly, Twenty-first Session, Supplement No. 15, part two, annex A, decision 34(IV)(proposal of representative of United Arab Republic); Official Records of the General Assembly, Twenty-second Session, Supplement No. 14, part one, para. 18 and annex I, decision 39(v)(September 1967). The UNCTAD Secretariat commissioned a report on "International Legislation on Shipping," which was prepared by a noted academic and barrister, T.K. Thommen, for consideration by the Conference at its second session in early 1968 (Thommen 1968).

[29] UNCITRAL's express authority to "further the progressive harmonization and unification of the law of international trade" by "preparing or promoting the adoption of new international conventions, model laws and uniform laws" (Chapter 2) complicated the scope of UNCTAD's claim to "initiate action" for the "negotiation an adoption of multilateral legal instruments in the field of trade" (GA Resolution 1995, Art. II, para. 2(e)).

drafting to the newly created UNCITRAL. Essentially, therefore, UNCTAD and UNCITRAL divided work on international shipping legislation depending on professional expertise. UNCTAD, whose Secretariat was composed primarily of economists, took up the preliminary policy work, assessing issues from economic and commercial perspectives. UNCITRAL, whose Secretariat consisted of legally trained international civil servants, worked on drafting a multilateral treaty to implement these policy recommendations.

But the division of labor between UNCTAD and UNCITAL wasn't quite so simple. UNCTAD would supplement UNCITRAL's work on the Hamburg Rules with draft international shipping legislation of its own. In 1970, the UNCTAD Secretariat published a report entitled "The Liner Conference System." In 1972, it published a second study on liner conferences, entitled "The Regulation of the Liner Conference System – A Code of Conduct." Within months of this second study, UNCTAD's Working Group on International Shipping Legislation completed a draft convention on the topic.[30] Between 1973 and 1980 UNCTAD was involved in negotiations resulting in the UN Convention on International Multimodal Transport of Goods.[31] While UNCTAD did not formally concede the failure of its Multimodal Convention to enter into force for nearly another twenty years, in 1986 UNCTAD's Committee on Shipping instructed UNCTAD's Secretariat to "elaborate model provisions for multimodal transport documents"[32] and the Secretariat would later draft Multimodal Transport Rules with the assistance of the ICC.[33]

As the Washington Consensus reordered the work of the IFIs and other IOs in the late 1980s, as the Berlin Wall fell and the international community rose to replace socialist structures with laws and institutions framed by a vision of political and economic liberalism, UNCTAD's Marxist origins felt anachronistic to the Conference and its governing Board. Similarly, UNCTAD's focus on facilitating trade by and between developing nations had been undermined by the emergence of the World Trade Organization (WTO) and the demise of the GATT in 1995. If UNCTAD was understood as a temporary vehicle for trade negotiations pending creation of a truly international trade organization, then the creation of the WTO could have been viewed as the beginning of the end of the Conference.

[30] By 2003, 78 countries had ratified the Liner Convention. Although the Liner Conference entered into force in 1983, having secured the needed 24 accessions representing more than 25 percent of the world's liner tonnage (with 56 country's accessions representing 28.6 percent of this tonnage). Its influence was short lived, however. The shipping industry's increasing reliance on containers and other changes in the liner shipping system meant that by the early 1990s application of the Liner Convention had begun to decline (UNCTAD 2004).

[31] This convention was adopted in 1980, but ultimately only 10 countries adopted its terms, substantially fewer than the 30 ratifications needed for it to enter into force.

[32] UNCTAD Resolution 60(XII), Nov. 1986.

[33] These are standard contract terms for incorporation into multimodal transport documents, and do not have the force of law. The UNCTAD/ICC Rules for Multimodal Transport Documents came into force in January 1992.

Although these world events raised questions about UNCTAD's place in the trade and development ecology, they did not cause UNCTAD to fold its tent. During the 1990s, UNCTAD would substantially rethink its *raison d'etre* and methods of work. "After the collapse of the Soviet Union, UNCTAD discovered the market place" (Int: 8004). How shipping conventions fit into this new economic ordering and what UNCTAD's role would be in the crafting of these international instruments became increasingly unclear, however.

Between 1987 and 1996, UNCTAD's Conference and their Board on Trade and Development would put aside further involvement in shipping related issues,[34] but UNCTAD's Secretariat continued to promote the topic. And yet the Secretariat's work on international transport no longer fit within the jurisdiction of any of UNCTAD's inter-governmental entities. Without authority from the Conference, there was little of substance that the Secretariat could accomplish.

By 1996, UNCTAD was no longer formally engaged in the making of international shipping legislation. Informally, however, this work had continued in fits and starts. In the late 1990s, UNCTAD's Secretariat tried to resume interest in shipping legislation and start talking to various industry groups. The Conference authorized its Commission on Enterprise, Business Facilitation and Development to conduct a series of expert meetings on transport and trade facilitation (UNCTAD IX, 1996). "CMI set up a subcommittee to consider reform of the law on carriage of goods by sea. It was then hoped that CMI would cooperate with UNCTAD. But that didn't happen" (Int: 8003). These expert meetings did not result in the production of a text because the UNCTAD Secretariat was negotiating like an entity with leverage. "UNCTAD wouldn't meet us halfway, partly because they were nearing the needed twenty countries for entry into force of the Hamburg Rules" (id.). When CMI stopped talking to the UNCTAD Secretariat, CMI turned to UNCITRAL (Chapter 3).

Estrangement

Thus, when in 2000 UNCITRAL's Commission authorized its Secretariat to work in collaboration with the CMI, UNCTAD qua UNCTAD had not been engaged in lawmaking on international transport for nearly a decade. UNCTAD's Secretariat couldn't quite let go of the topic, however. The UNCTAD Conference agreed to allow the Secretariat to send an observer to UNCITRAL's sessions,

[34] In 1987, the Conference did not place shipping on its triennial agenda, although this topic had been on its agenda from UNCTAD's beginnings in 1964 (UNCTAD VII, 1987). By the next Conference meeting, the Committee on Shipping had been dissolved and replaced by the Standing Committee on Developing Services Sector, with shipping, ports and multimodal transport included in the form of a sub-committee (UNCTAD VIII, 1992). In the next Conference meeting in Midrand, the Standing Committee on Developing Services Sector was also abolished (UNCTAD IX, 1996). Transport issues were reduced to an agenda item of the Commission on Enterprise, Business Facilitation and Development.

but did not recreate its earlier Committee on Shipping or otherwise formalize UNCTAD's work on transport.

UNCTAD's Secretariat participated in UNCITRAL's Transport Working Group sessions with little firm support from national delegations. The relationship between the two IOs was described by many as "a turf war." Most viewed the "UNCTAD/UNCITRAL rift" as traced back to UNCTAD's earlier work on the Multimodal Convention, "which went nowhere" (Int: 2010).

> They had produced a Multimodal Convention in 1980, which dealt with themes and areas that were also the subject of this convention. The Multimodal Convention can be described as unsuccessful. It never entered into force. It is not likely to do so. It has no real supporters. It is a convention that underwent a process and sat on the shelf. It didn't catch anyone's imagination. And then the Rotterdam Rules came along, brought in by the CMI. They took on an energy of their own, especially once it was apparent that the US was [committed to the project.] ... Once the US was on board, there was a lot of energy behind the project and it started to go. UNCTAD must have seen this as another nail in its coffin.
>
> (Int: 6011)

Others wondered whether UNCTAD had hoped to be involved in UNCITRAL deliberations "as a joint process," and when that didn't happen, got discouraged (Int: 6014).

Few leading UNCITRAL delegates viewed UNCTAD's participation in the deliberations as convincing or important. While UNCTAD sometimes could "rally developing countries'" delegations, most questioned whether "they were very influential" in the end (Int: 6014). Participants reported that UNCTAD's delegate "registered disagreement but didn't make a central impact"; the objections that were raised weren't "given a lot of weight" and were viewed as "more disruptive than anything else" (Int: 6011). "UNCTAD got involved in nitpicking" (Int: 2010). Its delegate "would take the mike for extended periods to lecture people," but make "minor academic arguments" that some found "misleading" (Int: 9001).

Eventually, some delegates noted, "the French complained about the NGOs saying too much" but everyone understood that this was "mainly because UNCTAD talked too much" (Int: 8001). "The non-governmental observers were warned by the Secretariat that we were to intervene only when there was a particular point of view of our organization. Not to intervene at large;" NGOs were told that "it was the governmental representatives who have to decide policy" (Int: 8003). The chamber heard that non-state delegations should be "seen but not heard" (Int: 8001). After that, "things may have changed a little. UNCTAD backed off a bit and other NGOs spoke less, which was unfortunate" (Int: 9001). Several delegations remarked on a moment, not quite at the end of the six years' of work, when UNCTAD's delegation left the UNCITRAL chamber, never to return. What explains this sudden leave-taking?

There are two stories that Transport Working Group delegates tell in describing why UNCTAD's delegation left the chamber. Several think that the UNCITRAL Secretariat was asked by the French delegation to ask the UNCTAD delegate "to quiet down" (Int: 8001). This request escalated and eventually, as detailed in Chapter 8, the French made a proposal that looked to alter UNCITRAL's methods of work.

Another delegate describes UNCTAD's sudden absence as a question of agency. Chapter 7 describes the deal that was struck between the US and a bloc of African countries late in the Working Group sessions. This delegate describes the effect of the deal that was struck as undermining UNCTAD's place in a "law and development" ecology, and put it this way:

> In the moment that the African countries joined themselves and presented papers by themselves and began to negotiate directly with other countries, at that moment UNCTAD's reason to be in the room evaporated.
>
> (Int: 8002)

UNCTAD departed from the deliberations at UNCITRAL with several meetings left in the Transport Working Group's deliberations. Once it left UNCITRAL's lawmaking forum, UNCTAD became, in the words of one delegate, "a strong enemy of the Rotterdam Rules" (Int: 8006). After it left, UNCTAD led what some referred to as a "rearguard action" against the new convention (Int: 9001). It ceased looking to convince delegations in attendance at UNCITRAL Working Group sessions, and began looking to convince a broader, more international audience that the Rotterdam Rules held dangers for the developing world and should be ignored.

UNCTAD's delegate to the UNCITRAL Working Group began "fighting tooth and nail – actively trying to get nations not to sign or ratify" the convention (Int: 9001). UNCTAD's Secretariat drafted a memorandum summarizing its critique of the Rotterdam Rules and disseminated this report as a part of its annual Review of Maritime Transport in both 2009 and 2010 (UNCTAD RMT, Chapter 6; Int: 2009). Although the Review of Maritime Transport notes that "the UNCTAD secretariat has been participating in the relevant UNCITRAL working group meetings as an observer and has provided substantive analytical comments for consideration by the working group throughout the drafting process," its conclusion is blunt: despite UNCTAD's participation, the draft convention fails to protect the developing countries' interests; "many aspects of the new Convention appear potentially problematic, in particular from the perspective of small and medium-scale shippers in developing countries" (id., at 124).

A Counter-Text

The RMT's five pages constitute a counter meta-text. Like the unified standard jointly issued by UNCITRAL and the World Bank, and the joint document issued by UNCITRAL, UNIDROIT and the Hague Conference, UNCTAD's RMT Report constitutes a meta-text insofar as it seeks to transcend or limit one or more IO's texts in counter-point or mutual adjustment. Unlike the other meta-texts, UNCTAD's Secretariat wrote with gloves off. This unilateral statement of UNTAD's Secretariat was not the product of negotiation or compromise.

The RMT Report critiques the Rotterdam Rules and advises developing countries not to accede to its terms. The reasons for this criticism are couched in technical legal rationale. The Report reviews (i) "the rules on burden of proof" in the new Convention, which it asserts are "more advantageous to carriers than those in the Hague-Visby or Hamburg Rules," (ii) the rules governing "the obligations and liability of the shipper," which it notes are mandatory and "not subject to any monetary limitation," and (iii) provisions permitting carriers "to deliver the goods without surrender of a negotiable transport document," about which it warns (id., at 129). The Report also criticizes provisions in the Rotterdam Rules enabling "volume contracts" on the grounds that small shippers and consignees "might find themselves bound by contractual terms effectively set unilaterally by one of a small number of large global liner-carrying companies" (id.).

Overall, the Report opines, these provisions will undermine uniformity in international shipping legislation, although elsewhere it notes that "the regulation of liability arising in connection with the international carriage of goods by sea has, over the past decades, become increasingly diverse" (id., at 124). The Report warns that the "the complexity and considerable scope for interpretation inherent in the Convention means that extensive litigation may be required to gain a clear understanding of the new rules." This position is contradicted somewhat by other portions of the Report noting that currently "no uniform international liability regime is in force" on multimodal transportation; as a result, "the international legal framework is particularly complex, as liability continues to be governed by existing unimodal conventions, and by increasingly diverse national regional and subregional laws and contractual agreements" (id.).[35]

This "rearguard action" was not limited to publication of the RMT Reports in 2009 and 2010. After UNCITRAL's governing Commission and the UN's General Assembly ratified the Working Group's draft convention, which set the stage for a diplomatic conference in September 2009, another UN entity picked up on themes put forward by UNCTAD's Secretariat. ECOSOC's Economic Commission for Europe (UNECE), through its Inland Transport Committee's Working Party on Intermodal Transport and Logistics, submitted its own counter meta-text on the Rotterdam Rules.[36] This Working Party Report prompted eight former delegates to

[35] UNCTAD's website provides a shorter report on the Rotterdam Rules, which hyperlinks to UNCITRAL's website and another website dedicated to the Rotterdam Rules, as wells as UNCTAD's writings on the topic. Although these writings are critical of the Rotterdam Rules, on its face the UNCTAD website appears neutral.

[36] UN Doc. No. ECE/TRANS/WP.24/123, paras. 36–43.

UNCITRAL's Working Group to publish their own report in reaction – Francesco Berlingieri, Philippe Delebecque, Tomotaka Fujita, Rafael Illescas, Michael Sturley, Gertjan van der Ziel, Alexander von Ziegler, and Stefano Zunarelli.[37]

The timing of these counter texts was not purely coincidental. Reports in mid-2009 were likely timed to influence countries attending the diplomatic conference convened to sign what became known as the Rotterdam Rules. UNECE's focus was more regional and especially pointed toward influencing the European Parliament's consideration of the Rotterdam Rules in 2010. In the end, "lobbying" by UNECE and UNCTAD didn't succeed. The European Parliament ultimately recommended in favor of member states' accession to the Rotterdam Rules.[38]

Despite this lack of success on UNCTAD's part, members of the UNCITRAL Secretariat reported feeling chafed by these texts and public performances. "UNCTAD needs to be reminded that the General Assembly has adopted the Convention and thus other branches [of the UN] shouldn't attack it."[39]

Although counter meta-texts issued by UNCTAD and UNECE failed to prevent countries from signing the Rotterdam Rules and failed to convince the European Parliament to recommend against Member States' adoption, UNCTAD's Secretariat continued to promulgate additional counter meta-texts.[40] Since then, Congo and Togo acceded to the terms of the Rotterdam Rules, joining Spain's earlier ratification. Legislative action within the US Congress and several European Parliaments leave industry actors hopeful that the Rotterdam Rules will eventually enter into force (Chapter 7).

Nonetheless, public debate on the Rotterdam Rules still simmers. Immediately following UNCITRAL's release of the draft Rotterdam Rules, delegates referred to the reaction of UNCTAD representatives as fighting "tooth and nail" against the draft (Int: 9001). At a conference of the CMI held in 2011 in Marrakesh, former UNCITRAL delegates from Italy and Sweden questioned the interpretation of the Rotterdam Rules put forward by a former delegate from UNCTAD. "One of

37 UNECE Informal Doc. No. WP.24/No. 2, "An attempt to clarify certain concerns that have emerged," (August 14, 2009). This "clarifying report" was prepared by eight individuals as their "personal views," although the report also notes that the authors "are former delegates of Governments that have attended the sessions of the UNCITRAL Working Group on Transport Law" (WP.24/No. 2, at 1). It responds, not just to the Working Party Report, but also to counter texts promulgated by several non-state actors: the European Shipper's Council, a Working Group on Sea Transport of FIATA and the European Association for Forwarding Transport Logistic and Customs Services-CLECAT (id.).

38 In a report issued late in 2009, the European Parliament recommended that EU member states should move "speedily to sign, ratify and implement the UN Convention on Contracts for the International Carriage of Goods Wholly or Partly by Sea, known as the 'Rotterdam Rules,' establishing a new maritime liability system" (European Parliament Report on Strategic Goals and Recommendations for the EU's Maritime Transport Policy until 2018 (2009/2095(INI)).

39 Cite on file with authors.

40 Most recently, the UNCTAD Secretariat contributed a similar report to the UNECE Expert Group on the Rotterdam Rules. UNECE Informal Doc. No. WP.24/No. 2 (Nov. 2, 2011).

TABLE 9.1. *From Meta-Bargaining to Meta-Texts*

	Dispute	Ecological Move	Meta-Text	Resolution
UNCITRAL v. WORLD BANK	Normative primacy	Competition to Cooperation	Organizational	Sequencing primacy
UNCITRAL v. UNIDROIT	Substantive jurisdictions	Competition to Coexistence	Substantive	Dividing primacy
UNCITRAL v. UNCTAD	Substantive norms	Competition to Conflict	Counter	Contesting primacy

the professors disagreed with the reading of the convention and [UNCTAD's former delegate to UNCITRAL] responded, 'Are you calling me a liar?' He said, 'You are not leaving me much of an option'" (Int: 9001). Five years after this exchange, UNCTAD's website continues to incorporate the meta-textual rejoinders it first published on the Rotterdam Rules.[41]

META-BARGAINS AND META-TEXTS

A meta-bargain is a high order resolution of an incipient competition between IOs aspiring to lawmaking primacy in an issue-area of global commerce and trade. The meta-bargain alters interactions among IOs in ecologies insofar as it settles or seeks to settle potential disputes in order to turn competition or conflict into competitive cooperation. But not all meta-bargaining succeeds and cooperation does not always ensue. The three instances of rivalry among leading lawmaking bodies reveal differing ecological processes and the meta-texts that emerge (Table 9.1).

A Reconciliation of Rivals?

In the case of the insolvency rivalry, UNCITRAL as a global lawmaker, and the World Bank, as an international financial institution, confronted each other in what became a naked competition for primacy in setting "the Gold Standard" for corporate insolvency regimes. From the initial Colloquium on prospects for insolvency standards to years after UNCITRAL had completed its Legislative Guide, the two rivals, sometimes quietly and sometimes openly, constructed their competing bids for normative primacy and institutional centrality. Expressions of high emotion,

[41] Although UNCTAD's website refers to UNCITRAL's Rotterdam Rules in straightforward terms that neither speak in favor of or against the draft convention, it also hyperlinks to its reports of 2009 and 2010 on the draft, which critiqued the draft convention in detail and the policy decisions it promotes. See UNCTAD, The Rotterdam Rules, http://unctad.org/en/Pages/DTL/TTL/Legal/Rotterdam-Rules.aspx.

metaphorical allusions to "war," and countervailing claims to legitimacy all reflected an intensity far beyond the cool calculations of purely rational actors.

Nevertheless, powerful actors in the lawmaking ecology and adjacent ecologies refused to allow the conflict to continue and pressed both sides to find grounds for cooperation. After several false starts, UNCITRAL and the Bank were pressed by the US State Department, the IMF, and the UN Under-Secretary of Legal Affairs, among others, to find a way to convert the rivalry into complementarity. UNCITRAL and the Bank did so by issuing an organizational meta-text that codified in print and online the complementarity of the IO's normative products. In practice, the agreement amounted to a sequencing of primacy. UNCITRAL's Legislative Guide presented an extensive statutory-like presentation of norms that readily lent itself to adoption by national legislators. The Bank's Principles conformed with these. But more importantly the Bank and IMF together conformed UNCITRAL's Guide to the diagnostic and implicitly normative instrument the Bank and Fund employed in their national assessments of conformity to Insolvency standards through periodic national reviews in the financial surveillance program entitled Reports on the Observance of Standards and Codes. While it oversimplifies this effort to turn competition into competitive cooperation, the relationship between UNCITRAL can be understood as a complementarity of international master norms in statutory form from UNCITRAL, which are specified by the IMF and World Bank in diagnostic instruments for implementation in national settings.

In the case of the secured transactions rivalry, UNCITRAL and UNIDROIT, as global private lawmaking bodies, had long taken account of each other, indeed, from the moment of UNCITRAL's unwelcomed entry into the standing lawmaking ecology in 1966. Each global body had eyed both a comprehensive set of international norms, surely the apex of lawmaking aspirations for an IO in this issue-area, and various more circumscribed areas for lawmaking for particular industries or particular types of lending. Each had broached the bold vision of a comprehensive product and each had backed away from it. But each was fully aware of the incipient rivalry as to which IO would take the lead. When the rivalry broke into the open in the early 2000s, the dispute was over the scope of substantive responsibility for lawmaking.

Their meta-bargaining led to a dry meta-text which turned competition into coexistence by dividing the territory of lawmaking among them. Although the substantive meta-text was construed as guide to ease the confusion of national lawmakers, in fact it can be read as a settlement among IOs as to who had already normatively mapped a particular issue-area, where terrain was still unmapped, and how a comprehensive set of secured transactions norms that had been drafted by UNCITRAL might fit together in the pastiche of targeted norms previously produced by the other trade lawmaking legislatures. The meta-text, in short, became a technical formula for substantive coexistence and cooperation.

Similarly, the rivalry between UNCITRAL and UNCTAD had decades-long roots, although both UN agencies had worked together in the past. In the issue-area of carriage of goods by sea, their conflict centered on contrasting substantive solutions to very real barriers to ease of transport from manufacturing to market. In one sense that rivalry lay in their constituencies: UNCTAD had long been a UN-designated champion of developing countries; UNCITRAL wavered over its two episodes of international lawmaking on seafaring carriage between emphasizing the interests of developing nations (in its Hamburg Rules) and accommodating the interests of both the leading carrier and shipping nations and industries (in the Rotterdam Rules).

In another sense, the rivalry between UNCITRAL and UNCTAD arose from idealistic versus pragmatic approaches to politics and existing TLOs. Rationally, UNCTAD's preference for a single multimodal TLO from door-to-door across the entire world made eminent sense as the most efficient kind of legal order, but this position faced the potential of enormous opposition from entrenched unimodel, national and regional TLOs. Pragmatically, UNCITRAL's legislators sought to push a unified system as far as politically feasible, without generating backlash likely to subvert its normative product. The result was a highly complex multilateral treaty from UNCITRAL and open conflict from a repudiated UNCTAD. The result was also a degree of indeterminacy in the articulation and implementation of UNCITRAL's lawmaking as a fractiousness continues to disturb an equilibrium of relationships in the ecology where a settlement remains elusive.

The move from competition to conflict found its expression in UNCTAD's counter-text. Initially expressed through memos and oral interventions during UNCITRAL proceedings, the counter-text became the rallying point for critique of UNCITRAL's product and for substitution of an alternative product. Rather than sequencing or dividing primacy in the lawmaking ecology, UNCTAD and UNCITRAL broke into open conflict where they contested primacy. UNCITRAL's success in producing the Rotterdam Rules and obtaining many initial signatures to the convention, and UNCTAD's uncertain successes in persuading Europe to follow its lead, make the contest uneven. But the episode remains instructive insofar as it demonstrates that coexistence in a lawmaking ecology is by no means inevitably harmonious and that cooperation sometimes is won and sometimes lost.

Processes in TLO Construction

It can now be clearly seen that rivalries within and between ecologies amount to a politics of TLO social construction. The prize for all lawmaking IOs is to be the primary progenitor of transnational and global legal norms in a given issue-area. The goal is to emerge as the central and dominant actor in a space inhabited by many others, some of which are possible rivals. In recursive cycles, those norms emerge from states, non-state and supra-state actors, and they in turn offer norms to be adopted in national and local contexts to guide behavioral change.

The struggles over secured transactions lawmaking indicate a pattern until the late 1990s of accumulating mini-TLOs on circumscribed topical areas. The incipient conflict over which global legislature should produce a comprehensive secured transactions set of norms, therefore, was also a conflict over the configurations of TLOs within the bounds of all secured lending. Would a complementarity of mini-TLOs coexist? Would they be superseded by a single mega-TLO? Or would pragmatics yield some kind of negotiated order where specialty and general TLOs could coexist as an outcome of explicit meta-bargaining. The solution became possible once leaders of the three global quasi-legislatures saw their mutual advantages to aligning their respective endeavors through recognition and negotiation.

A similar pattern emerged in the insolvency space. Once the IMF and Asian Development Bank ceded TLO construction to UNCITRAL, the politics in the insolvency ecology essentially pitted two claimants for comprehensive TLOs against each other. Unlike the secured transactions negotiations, there was no substantive division of labor possible because UNCITRAL and World Bank norms substantially covered the same topics.[42] The sequencing of primacy between prescriptive and diagnostic forms of insolvency norms therefore created a mutuality of purpose and endeavor in which the recursive process of global, then national lawmaking, might unfold in cycles of TLO implementation.

The politics of the international transport lawmaking ecology unfolds historically and into the present as a now unsettled multiplicity of TLOs, adjacent to each other and incipiently competing with each other. The Hague and Hague-Visby Rules continue to govern trade in the maritime industry ecology, but their historic ascendency has been undermined by industry changes. The Hamburg Rules have played a limited role, nearly from their inception, because countries that have acceded to the Hamburg Rules are for the most part economically unimportant to global trade by sea. UNCTAD's Multimodal Convention was marginal, never having entered into force. Now the Rotterdam Rules are championed by UNCITRAL's advocates within the maritime industry, but until they enter into force and with the backing of countries with significant global trade they remain less significant than the now fading Hague-Visby Rules. Even so, the unresolved tensions between extant lawmakers in this issue-area – especially between UNCITRAL and UNCTAD – cloud probabilities that UNCITRAL's new global norms will align and settle as convergent norms governing transport of goods by sea worldwide.

[42] At an earlier stage it might have been possible for UNCITRAL to have focused on substantive and procedural law and the World Bank on institutions to implement the law. Bank officials rejected this potential division of labor.

10

Inventive Global Governance

The hidden logic of survival for IOs engaged in global governance through law rests ultimately on adaptation.[1] If IOs are to thrive in ecologies, they must adapt constantly to each other and to the environs that supply or deprive them of critical resources. If norm entrepreneurs are to champion new transnational legal orders (TLOs), compete with existing TLOs, and fend off threats from proponents of insurgent TLOs, then they will be constantly in motion, adapting to changing exigencies, circumstances, and events.[2] And, to be effective, adaptation over the longterm, as contexts and circumstances change in unanticipated ways, demands invention. Hence, global lawmakers that construct markets through law vindicate their enterprises to the degree they display inventive global governance.

We now invert the lens of orientation toward the ecologies introduced in Chapter 1. We began by asserting that a spatial theory of IOs looks to the space itself, to the sea in which IOs swim, as a shift in perspective away from the dominant focus on single normmaking IOs. This shift moves inquiry from individual IOs alone and beyond detailed accounts of multiplicities of actors coming together on one or

[1] The centrality given adaptation as a key ecological process varies significantly across schools of ecology theory. For population ecologists, there is no adaptation by individual actors in an ecology; they are merely selected out of existence by competition or niches that cannot support them (Hannan and Freeman 1989; Hannan 2005; Freeman, Carroll and Hannan 1983; Freeman and Audia 2006). In other ecology theory adaptation is explicitly identified as an ecological process but it is not given theoretical primacy (Park, Burgess and Mackenzie 1925; Hawley 1950). Nevertheless, in any ecology theory that gives degrees of agency to actors in a given social space, the reality of adaptation is present, even if not explicitly given conceptual primacy (cf. Abbott 1987).

[2] The concept of adaptation is ever-present in TLO theory, but implicitly so. Insofar as actors are creating ecologies or positioning themselves within those ecologies, their practices of framing, efforts at settlement and alignment, are all instances of adaptation as a deep processual undercurrent. Indeed, insofar as TLOs rise and fall, the social processes that generate their emergence or decline or relations with other TLOs may also be said to comprise degrees of adaptation (see Halliday and Shaffer 2015: chapter 14).

another issue,[3] to theoretical formulations that assimilate them both. We conclude by adopting the lens of an IO seeking to swim in that sea of IOs we identify as ecologies. While this lens focuses on a particular actor, it looks outward to a lawmaking IO's embedding, embedded, and adjacent ecologies[4] to encapsulate its efforts to adapt and invent, to survive or thrive, with more or less capacity and facility. In that sense our perspective is adaptive-actor oriented. We reiterate that UNCITRAL, like any normmaking IO, is neither an entirely free agent nor a hapless Darwinian product of social selection. Heavily constrained by the past, by access to critical resources, by geopolitical and economic events far outside its control, this IO nevertheless retained degrees of freedom to maneuver and adapt, to invent and sometimes shape its present and future, its own fate, and those of ecologies in which it swam.

In these adaptive maneuvers, the inventiveness[5] of an IO is directed toward two ends. On the one hand, an IO will strive for ecological positioning, whether it involves pioneering through the creation of an ecology *de novo*, or boundary work to justify its fit or enhance its relative status within an existing ecology, or indeed working jointly with other IOs to ensure the continuing viability of the ecology as a whole. On the other hand, inventiveness of a lawmaking IO very often will be deployed in bids to forge TLOs and its centrality to construction of those orders. A lawmaking IO may push either to produce a new TLO, or to become a leader in the normmaking of a developing or established TLO, or to defend the existence of an established TLO when confronted with forces of competition, disintegration or dissolution.

By investigating carefully a particular IO's adaptive and creative capacities in its ecological surrounds[6] we can conclude that not all of its adaptations worked in ways that enhanced its interactions with issue-ecologies or its formation of TLOs, nor in ways that inevitably ensured its centrality in the standing lawmaking ecology. Indeed, the logic of this chapter displays UNCITRAL's mixed record of navigating the complexities of invention – adaptations realized and adaptations failed.

3 (Braithwaite and Drahos 2000).

4 For further description of the four ecologies in which UNCITRAL is an actor or arena (UN as an ecology, standing international lawmaking ecology, adjacent industry ecologies, and issue-ecologies), see Table 1.1.

5 Although inventiveness or invention might be thought to be subsumed within adaptation, there are at least two benefits to be gained by giving it a specific conceptual designation. First, there are forms of adaptation that do not require invention. They may depend simply on diffusion, on borrowing for a new context what has been observed in another. This is a leading assumption of processual links in world society theory of globalization (Dobbin, Simmons and Garrett 2007; Johnson, Dowd and Ridgeway 2006; Meyer 2010). Second, an explicit focus on creativity and invention will generate research on varieties of ways that innovative frontiers can be found in social organization, discourse and texts, interactional processes, meaning-making, and legal technologies, to mention but a few (Bowman and Hodge 2009; Chorev 2012; Dezalay and Garth 2013; Gaziano 1996).

6 See Introduction, for discussion of generalizability of empirical findings on UNCITRAL.

Yet UNCITRAL's case also impels us to consider the conditions under which it was more or less adaptive and to introduce inventive possibilities from other settings that might increase probabilities that new or reformed TLOs are institutionalized worldwide. Not least, we consider what lessons UNCITRAL's ecological actions might hold for IOs that appear as weaker actors in ecologies populated by the powerful.

ADAPTATIONS REALIZED

An analytic appraisal of UNCITRAL's dynamic history of international private lawmaking and its sustained efforts to build TLOs can be reprised as an amalgam of adaptations contingently available to any lawmaking IO, certainly of transnational and global markets, and conceivably of other institutions as well. Adaptations vary in sequence and significance. Some adaptations and inventiveness come at the expense of others and indeed explain why other inventions failed or were not considered. Nevertheless, it will be seen that adaptations realized by this inventive IO indicate not only its particular ecological adeptness, but signify actions available to many or any IOs intent on articulating norms for the world within their respective social spaces.

Shaping Boundaries Within social ecologies, boundary work[7,8] involves a representation of meaning, a justification by an IO that an ecology should be created for some purpose, and, correlatively, that a particular IO should be included in the ecology where it might survive and flourish.

A slow-developing and inchoate ecology of international lawmaking IOs emerged out of sporadic, if *ad hoc,* initiatives in the nineteenth century. These were shaped into something approximating an ecology by the League of Nations. Broad contours of public and private international law were acknowledged and reflected in organizational initiatives, even if international lawmaking focusing specifically on obstacles to trade lagged until the advent of post-WWII UN innovations and reactions to earlier efforts.

By the 1960s, jockeying among longstanding, recent, and insurgent IOs revealed a politics of boundary work, not least precipitated by the norm entrepreneurs who advocated the entry of UNCITRAL into the space already occupied by the International Law Commission, the Hague Conference on Private International Law, and UNIDROIT (Chapter 2). At this (re)defining moment UNCITRAL's boundary work had two dimensions.

Boundary-making UNCITRAL's advocates depicted international lawmaking as a terrain divided between the public and private, between the substantive and

7 For general theory on boundary work, see (Abbott 1995; Lamont and Molnar 2002).

8 For a sense of the heterogeneous settings in which boundary work can be observed as a meaning-making process, see (Gaziano 1996; Mennicken 2010; Wouters 2008).

procedural, between Euro-centric and truly global, and between those IOs that functioned as genuine creators of new law and those that coordinated the efforts of others.

Advocates for a new IO in this space demanded historical (re)interpretation of the successes and, more pointedly, the failures of already extant lawmaking IOs with the not very subtle message that even if other IOs were already occupying space within a lawmaking ecology, they were not doing so very productively. Having mapped the terrain of international law, UNCITRAL's proponents then inserted UNCITRAL into purportedly unoccupied territory, viz., not public but private, not procedural but substantive, not Euro-centric but global jurisdictions.

Boundary-blurring[9] At its point of origin, when any new organization is most vulnerable, UNCITRAL's sponsors anticipated counter-attacks on what might reasonably have appeared to actors in an already incipient ecology as an organizational insurgency. UNCITRAL's advocates were therefore distinctly vague about how directly they would confront or replicate the functions of UNIDROIT or the Hague Conference, among others. UNCITRAL's champions played on ambiguities in their drafting language about UNCITRAL's intentions to engage in UNCITRAL-driven initiatives, whether on previously neglected topics or on topics where there had already been international effort, and whether UNCITRAL would undertake lawmaking in its own right rather than acting to promote work previously completed by IOs already present in the loosely bounded standing ecology for international lawmaking.

Framing Claims Ecologies are social constructions that rest on discursive foundations, especially in a global world of contested ideologies.[10] IOs and their champions not only point to regions of normmaking around which can be drawn meaningful boundaries, but also stake their claims to inclusion in the ecology by the ways they formulate their goals and express to the world their reasons-for-being. These processes are conventionally understood as exercises in framing,[11] certainly in the construction of TLOs.[12]

While UNCITRAL was successful in staking its claim to lawmaking for all member states of the UN, namely, by asserting that its geographical reach would be truly global, and by re-assuring existing IOs that UNCITRAL would confine itself to a particular type of lawmaking, namely law governing private transactions that presented obstacles to trade and economic development, the very scope of its

9 On ambiguity, opacity and indeterminacy in the setting of discursive and social boundaries, see (Mallard 2014).

10 The discursive foundations of social space are not sufficiently developed in either field or ecology theory. See (Liu and Emirbayer 2016). For constructive ways forward offered by institutional theory, see Introduction.

11 On framing in global settings, see, for instance, (Cameron, Lawson and Tomlin 1998; Dobusch and Quack 2013; Jönsson 1995; Merry 2006b; Shaffer 2001).

12 (Halliday and Shaffer 2015: 481–485).

claims at its founding moment in the mid-1960s confronted it with an impossible mandate – *to unify* laws on given topics for the world as a whole. It hedged this most challenging of goals by accompanying it from the earliest days of its existence with a less demanding but still formidable goal – *to harmonize* laws, which might liberally be interpreted as reducing some but not all of the heterogeneity of laws for the market across the world.[13]

Even this pair of goals, however, proved constricting within a short time. Its most adroit adaptation to fast-moving changes in markets and to demands from potential client-states (e.g., the US) and to powerful IOs in the global economy (e.g., IMF, World Bank) was to adopt in the 1990s an expansive, indeed boundlessly expansive, goal to *modernize* laws and to make this a governing frame in the standing lawmaking ecology. Ultimately, other IOs in the lawmaking ecology adopted this same expansive *raison d'etre* for creating global norms.[14] This frame had extraordinary rhetorical force that could be mobilized on its own terms or in combinations with its earlier goals. For instance, with the Rotterdam Rules UNCITRAL combined modernization with unification. With its efforts to set international standards for corporate insolvency law, it combined modernization with a nod toward harmonization at a high level of abstraction. With its work on secured transactions law reform, it combined modernization with a strong push for some point between harmonization and unification.

Even more fundamental was the implicit discursive move that trade and commerce were more likely to be facilitated by a transnational *legal* order[15] than by other ways to order market relations, whether through informal or business-led logics of interaction or public policy orders that would not have put market transactions in the hands of lawyers and judges. It must be reiterated that for UNCITRAL this fundamentally legal means of creating market order was not simply order for its own sake. UNCITRAL's ideals, expressed in different ways and with more or less emphasis at different times, ultimately were directed to economic development. Economic development, it was maintained, required a lowering of legal barriers and reduction of costs in commerce across state borders. One means to this end was the regulation and integration of markets through law.[16] Later, UNCITRAL's ideal for promoting economic development was widened to a mission of stabilizing the international economic order, whether through the building of the NIEO or the prevention of financial crises or, more generally, with reference to the orderly conduct of economic relationships among private market actors.

13 (Block-Lieb and Halliday 2007a).

14 (Halliday, Block-Lieb and Carruthers 2009b).

15 On the definition of a transnational legal order, see (Halliday and Shaffer 2015:7–21).

16 UNCITRAL's focus on reforming laws that obstructed trade and so economic development was, from its emergence at least, coupled with that of its companion organization, the UN's Conference of Trade and Development (UNCTAD). UNCTAD looked to approach these same issues of trade and development from the perspective of economic policy.

UNCITRAL's normative economic goals were complemented by ideals of global governance. One ideal reflected the UN principle of providing formal equality to all states in decisionmaking for the world. While the principle was practiced in the UN General Assembly of one state, one vote, UNCITRAL adopted this idea of universal equality and also engaged in consensus-based decisionmaking that only rarely involved voting by delegations. A related ideal insisted that global governance required the representation of states from all levels of economic development and from all regions of the world. This appropriation of the ideal of universality expanded further to encompass representation of non-state actors with economic and legal interests, even if principled incorporation of those interests were driven substantially by pragmatic concerns.

Within this double framing of market behavior as a goal-driven enterprise requiring *legal* order, and what for a time was UNCITRAL's pioneering focus on the mix of unification, harmonization, and modernization of legal norms, UNCITRAL used varieties of boundary work. It established lawmaking claims in a range of issue-ecologies, but sometimes abandoned or delayed such claims in other contexts in order to find new issue-areas in which its legal norms might be directed.

Two such processes were apparent in working group agenda-setting efforts in maritime, insolvency and secured transactions law. In the insolvency and secured transactions lawmaking, working groups engaged mostly in *boundary extending*,[17] by pushing more widely on the frontiers of an expansive issue-area than even the UNCITRAL Commission had expected or explicitly authorized.[18] In transport lawmaking, the working group extended the boundaries of their work beyond previous conventions on the topic, but it very deliberately signaled its intent to be *boundary constricting*,[19] that is, it explicitly ruled out a jurisdictional claim to govern transport that would bring it into direct conflict with established rail, road, or inland waterway mode of transport in Europe and elsewhere (Chapter 3).

The secular drive to convert economic, political, and commercial orders into *legal* orders was reflected in efforts by UNCITRAL as a whole, and by some

[17] Boundary extending is a variant of boundary-making in which boundary work by normmaking actors is directed to the widening or broadening of already legitimated boundaries.

[18] Where these working groups engaged in boundary-constricting moves, they did so temporarily. For example, the Insolvency Working Group could agree only on commentary on the topic of corporate groups in Parts I and II of the Insolvency Guide, but then went on to draft a supplemental Part III to the Guide focused exclusively on this topic. Similarly, although initially the Secured Transactions Working Group stopped short of making recommendations on collateral consisting of intellectual property, it later worked to produce a supplement to that Guide that covered that issue extensively.

[19] Boundary-constricting moves in the opposite direction to boundary-extending. As Halliday and Carruthers demonstrate, professionals and other actors may choose deliberately to exclude certain kinds of work or jurisdiction which could harm professional projects (Carruthers and Halliday 1998). A similar strategy was adopted by UNCITRAL (Chapter 3) to exclude actors whose interests could forestall lawmaking consensus on carriage of goods by land.

of its working groups, to amplify the scope of prospective TLOs. Strategies of amplification took at least five forms.

First, regional norms might be universalized, as the United States and Canada sought in the universalization of the broad thrust of the secured transactions law of both countries.

Second, a potential fracturing of global TLOs into coexisting regional TLOs was countered by a universalization not so much of a given country's legal order but more of a legal order that would transcend any particular current or prospective regional order. This was certainly a goal of the Transport Working Group, which was driven by a pragmatic fear that world trade by sea would be carved up by competing or incompatible sets of rules as ships crossed one or another invisible line at sea.

Third, a nascent commercial practice, such as electronic commerce, might be identified as undeveloped terrain that was ripe for new legal order. Yet, despite the failure of UNCITRAL to craft a TLO on electronic commerce, and certainly to obtain concordant norms across states, nonetheless, the foray of UNCITRAL into this lawmaking later proved a stepping-stone toward a new transport TLO many of whose global norms now incorporated forms of electronic contracting that up-ended millenia of tangible bills of lading as requisite proof of ownership in transport of goods by sea, and now permitted digital equivalents of such documents.

Fourth, UNCITRAL was pressed by conjunctions of national demands (e.g., for ways to mitigate adverse economic and social effects of failing companies) and national solutions (e.g., of domestic legal orders that purported to solve or the inherent problems or soften the adverse effects of businesses in distress) to internationalize local orders by making them transnational. Hence, the apparent success of the US in developing a legal order, through their US Bankruptcy Code (Chapter 11) and Uniform Commercial Code (Article 9), that dealt less harshly with casualties of hard budget constraints, provided a convincing *raison d'etre* for a global lawmaker to adopt, with variations, what apparently worked in some very influential markets across the globe.[20]

Fifth, UNCITRAL amplified its mandate by extending the definition of its lawmaking mandate to provide transnational commercial law instruments to be implemented not only between states but within them. The legislative guides for insolvency and secured transactions did not claim to solve cross-border disputes. They did provide means by which UNCITRAL expanded its normative influence by offering nation-states bundles of law-like norms that, in part or whole, could be adopted by national legislatures in filling voids in local law and practice.

Notably, UNCITRAL's working groups and even its Secretariat deployed innovations used creatively by UNCITRAL in its positioning vis-à-vis potential competitors. Where UNCITRAL's Commission both authorized and set boundaries for activity, working groups read these rhetorical frames as providing some freedom of

[20] (Carruthers, Babb and Halliday 2001).

action. For instance, the Insolvency Working Group took creative liberty with the blurred authorizing language from UNCITRAL's Commission to far exceed what commissioners initially had granted.

These strategies of amplification were not confined to UNCITRAL's competitive advantage in either the issue-ecologies it housed or in the standing ecology in which it coexisted. By adopting the goal of modernization, and pursuing that goal through a repertoire of technologies that enhanced the reach of lawmaking into markets, UNCITRAL indirectly extended the potential legal scope of the entire standing ecology of lawmaking IOs. Other lawmaking IOs in the ecology responded by also widening their horizons.

Manipulating Technologies Whether to survive and flourish in an ecology, or to emerge as a leader in TLO construction or defense, an IO can resort to borrowings or adaptations or inventions of new products. These products may differentiate it from competitors and prove more adaptive for entire ecologies in their relationships with adjacent ecologies.

UNCITRAL's inventiveness manifested itself in two ways: a repertoire of technologies[21] for the packaging and delivery of trade law norms; and varieties of rhetorical forms in which the technologies themselves were crafted. Both types of inventions were enabled by sophisticated norm entrepreneurs and legal experts who were drawn inside the inner core of UNCITRAL's deliberative community.

VARIETIES OF TECHNOLOGY To quicken the pace of production, to reach issue-areas previously viewed as unreachable by hard law treaties, and to embrace the diversity of markets and law, UNCITRAL developed across its history legal technologies that enabled it to attain goals of harmonization and modernization (Chapter 2). These technologies included as of 2017 (i) conventions (that is, multilateral treaties), (ii) rules, (iii) recommendations, (iv) model laws and model legal provisions, (v) legal guides, (vi) notes, (vii) legislative guides, and (vii) practice guides and other explanatory texts (Chapter 6).

This array of means to different ends gave UNCITRAL an unusual degree of flexibility to adapt competitively to new circumstances. It enabled UNCITRAL to strive to occupy a central place in a global lawmaking ecology and to offer products conducive to solving the enormous challenge of TLOs with normative concordance among international, national, and local levels of norm adoption and behavior.

One side of inventiveness addressed the demands of sovereign states that they retain degrees of freedom over how much national and local variation they could inject into transnationally and globally promulgated norms. A technology that allowed states only the discretion to adopt all or nothing of a set of global norms could create tensions with sovereignty and practicality. Negotiation of a single set of

[21] On the concept of social technologies, see (Fourcade and Khurana 2008; Johnson, Dowd and Ridgeway 2006; Sassen 2006).

standards both acceptable to the whole world and coincidentally of maximal pragmatic payoff in local conditions often presented insuperable difficulties. Negotiation of more flexible technologies was far easier and so ostensibly more productive.

The other side of inventiveness concerned domestic audiences for IO products.[22] Domestic lawmaking and practice rest upon many institutions. Audiences for domestic lawmaking could range from executive and legislative branches of the state, to courts and arbitration practitioners, and to private parties, such as business firms and professionals engaged in commercial transactions, among others. Each of these audiences might reasonably expect norms to be in forms that best fit their domestic institutional functions and their logics of decisionmaking and implementation.

The portfolio of technologies it adopted or invented over decades gave UNCITRAL adaptive flexibility to fit circumstances and audiences as they varied across issue-areas, time, and place. Not least, this portfolio or repertoire of legal inventions increased the probability that a fully institutionalized TLO might emerge because international norms reflected national and local interests in lawmaking. Flexible international norms concomitantly permit normative concordance without locking all lawmakers at every level into a bright-line legal straitjacket.

Two effects followed, both of which enhanced UNCITRAL's position in global lawmaking. On the one hand, UNCITRAL could now reach and colonize regions of market activity, such as bankruptcy law, previously unordered by transnational law. On the other hand, UNCITRAL obtained a quickened capacity to craft norms that might adapt rapidly to changing markets, thereby lessening the mismatch between legal and economic orders that stalks global governance and regulation of markets more generally.[23]

Significantly, these two sides of inventiveness had repercussions for the entire international lawmaking ecology. Certainly they enabled UNCITRAL to compete within the standing lawmaking ecology, but as importantly, they empowered the ecology as a whole because they demonstrated its flexibility and productivity to reach previously intractable or newly emergent issues. Thus, in recent years not only have technologies diffused to some degree across IOs in the lawmaking ecology, but the ecology as a whole now offers an extensive repertoire of formal devices, ranging from the form of a nineteenth century treaty to the IMF and World Bank's diagnostic Reports on the Observance of Standards and Codes with many technologies in between. The collective message is clear: Law can reach a wider range of trade and market challenges through construction of flexible *legal* orders that confront disorder or problematic existing orders in problem areas within and beyond the state. This flexibility maximizes sovereign states' involvement as partners in the constructing and implementing of TLOs.

[22] See Table 6.1.

[23] See (Westbrook 1996).

RHETORICAL PROPERTIES Just as lawmaking IOs might choose a particular technology to produce some legal order in a given issue-area, so too adroit drafters can invent and manipulate the formal properties of any given technology to effect political purposes in the deliberations over global norms and in their reception and implementation in national and local contexts.[24] Much of this rhetorical dexterity can be observed in the texts produced by IOs in the lawmaking ecologies.[25]

In a close rhetorical analysis of two of UNCITRAL's legislative guides and one convention, we have shown that the internal *forms* in which norms are cast can serve multiple aims in the institutionalization of TLOs and the ecological standing of the IOs that cooperate and compete in TLO dynamics. For instance, in a legislative guide, four sets of rhetorical properties could serve diverse political purposes (Chapter 6). The opening formulation of *objectives* articulates high order norms sufficiently abstract to embrace global variation in extant legal systems, but sufficiently balanced to signal the broad contours of norms in a national statute that would adhere to transnational norms. The politics of naming are reflected in an artfully crafted *glossary* where terms are defined in ways that purportedly transcend particular legal family traditions, thereby again signaling universalism, and as importantly, where terms closely associated with a particular legal tradition are effectively laundered by invention of a new term so as to liberate the legislative guide at its outset from its association with a particular country, especially an incipient hegemon. In the body of the guide, *commentary* in each chapter can serve to acknowledge that several plausible approaches to solving problems through law could be observed in the world, but that UNCITRAL justified its preferred solution with reasoning it lay bare. And most apposite for lawmaking itself, UNCITRAL's text presented large numbers of *recommendations* that served the practical needs of legislative drafters. To avoid normative straitjackets that would likely increase the probability that national lawmakers would reject outright transnational norms, UNCITRAL also developed a *repertoire of rule-types* that adjusted the form of a recommendation to degrees of consensus in the transnational lawmaking and to prospects of adoption and local needs for adaptation.

The combination of a portfolio of technologies, each of which contains an amalgam of rhetorical devices, allows the inventive IO and resilient lawmaking ecologies to resolve the potential contradiction between expansive normative ambitions for TLOs in issue-areas previously thought intractable for global governance. Varieties of technologies and multiple rhetorical properties give IOs enormous flexibility in the application of TLO norms to the particularities of national and local contexts.

[24] A scholarship on the rhetorical and discursive properties of legal texts as technologies of governance is burgeoning in several directions. Cf. (Alkoby 2008; Halliday, Block-Lieb and Carruthers 2009b; Hülsse 2008; Merry 2003; Payne and Samhat 2004; Weiss 2003).

[25] (Halliday, Block-Lieb and Carruthers 2009b), op.cit.

A recognition of UNCITRAL's technical innovations should not lull the critical observer into an illusion that the idioms of legalism are thereby apolitical. In fact, a distinctive feature of professional power is that professionals gain enhanced efficacy by converting political issues into what they style as technical issues.[26] Rather than compete in political arenas where professionals will often be far weaker actors than other claimants to influence, legal and scientific and other professionals wield far more influence when they can convince critical audiences that an issue should be delegated to technical experts. Even more, if expert professionals can then wield their technical power by creating new technologies and new techniques to solve problems, they can increase their bold claims to be ceded technical authority.

Frequently protestations were made within UNCITRAL's formal proceedings that it was a technical body and therefore policy or political issues were outside its mission and mandate. We have shown, by contrast, that an interactional micro-politics accompanied all the lawmaking episodes and that distributive politics were implicitly or explicitly implicated in lawmaking whatever the purported technicality of the issue-area. Even further we have shown that politics can be enabled by technicality. To construct TLOs previously thought beyond the reach and capacity of global lawmaking, and to increase the probability of normative penetration inside states, instrumental technologies were crafted sometimes to direct their messages to domestic legislators, or regulators, or judges, and always to reach across the diversity of the world's legal families and states.

Creating Legal Concepts Lawmaking IOs confront a double-edged challenge to institutionalize TLOs for the world. On the one hand, many current terms or concepts that are familiar in metropolitan societies or legal systems are either unfamiliar to other legal communities or, worse yet, carry adverse connotations of dominance or auras of colonialism or hegemony. On the other hand, the daunting task of finding common ground among the world's nearly 200 states, multiple legal families, and multiplicity of markets and interests opens up space for new concepts able to transcend difference.

UNCITRAL's lawmakers displayed features of both (Chapters 6 and 7).

First, relabeling established concepts that are not country-specific or particular to a given legal family. In several cases, UNCITRAL delegates and Secretariat staff found alternative terms to those that otherwise would appear too closely associated with a given legal system.

Second, inventing new legal terms of concepts. In two cases, a critical breakthrough in a deadlock among contesting blocs of delegates at UNCITRAL working groups was enabled when inventive delegates created an entirely new concept that either embraced seemingly conflicting approaches (e.g., unitary or non-unitary

[26] On the idiom of legalism and capacities of professionals to coopt policy issues into matters they assert are properly sites for the assertion of technical authority, see (Halliday 1982; Halliday 1985).

forms of acquisition financing) or escaped pigeon-holing by contesting interests (e.g., the concept of "maritime plus").

Mobilizing Resources Both theoretical expectations and empirical observations place resource dependency and resource mobilization[27] at the operational core of IO existence and efficacy (Chapter 1). The heuristic adopted in this book distinguishes between the intangible and tangible resources that individual IOs and lawmaking ecologies strive to obtain in their drive to be progenitors of TLOs. Among the *intangible* resources, three were critical for UNCITRAL's viability and centrality in standing and issue-ecologies.

LEGITIMACY Authoritative pronouncements of legal norms rest on foundations of subjective acceptance.[28] That is, global norms should appear to prospective audiences as right, fair, defensible, and persuasive if they are to be adopted widely. In the best-case scenario for an IO, the norms it propagates are taken for granted as the way to proceed. Over the fifty years of UNCITRAL's existence in standing and issue-ecologies, it has rested its legitimacy[29] on a three-fold foundation: (a) Universal representation of (i) all states, varieties of legal families, regions, degrees of economic development, and (ii) all salient interests of professions, industries, and interested IOs; (b) Procedural fairness in the comportment of its participation and decisionmaking; and (c) Effectiveness of its previous track record in the production and adoption of norms for the world (Chapters 2, 3, and 4).[30] Much of UNCITRAL's success in building legitimacy rested on its pragmatic move to create mutually cooperative relationships with adjacent industry ecologies and to exploit its competitive advantage over free-standing IOs through UNCITRAL's distinctive ability to cloth itself with universally legitimated UN values and standards. We shall see, however, that this three-fold set of legitimation warrants brought its own contradictions.

TECHNICAL EXPERTISE If an international lawmaking ecology arrogates to itself the prospect of TLO norm development across a wide spectrum of commercial and market activity for all the world, then it cannot possibly incorporate within itself an

27 Resource dependency theory elevates the external conditions of organizational existence whereas resource mobilization theory, particularly in studies of social movements, places greater stress of the capacity of actors to find and deploy resources. An interactionist ecology theory has a greater affinity with resource mobilization theory. See further (King and Pearce 2010; Pfeffer and Salancik 1978; Sherer and Lee 2002).

28 See (Suchman 1995) on subjective properties of legitimacy.

29 We do not seek to arbitrate here amongst the many themes and variations in the massive scholarly literature on legitimacy in IOs. For useful theoretical formulations and empirical studies, see (Barnett 1997; Bodansky 1999; Cashore 2002; Clark 2005; Finnemore 2009; Franck 2006; Suchman 1995). See also the complementary three-fold analysis legitimacy in transnational global governance by Quack (2010), which adds expertise to inclusiveness and procedural fairness.

30 For legitimacy of global deliberative bodies most proximate to UN deliberations, we draw upon the elegant conceptualization of Ian Hurd substantially grounded in his studies of the UN (Block-Lieb and Halliday 2006; Hurd 1999; Hurd 2008).

array of technical expertise[31] that mirrors the macrocosm of economic activity. Moreover, if an IO of member states seeks both to reflect market demands and possibilities and to stimulate market activity within and beyond national frontiers, then the inclusion of market actors will be more likely to solve problems of diagnosis and actor mismatch that can bedevil national and local implementation of transnational and global norms.[32]

UNCITRAL very early in its startup phase made several moves to solve this problem. It implicitly reached back to nineteenth century ad hoc efforts of industry actors themselves to create transnational commercial law.[33] It found a way for its issue-ecologies to incorporate industry actors into cooperative deliberations on equal terms, in effect, with states. And it drew professionals, especially lawyers, into the technical machinery of drafting prospective norms – and thereby their international and national communities into implementation of norms (Chapters 2, 3, and 4). In both cases it created symbioses with adjacent ecologies rich in technical and pragmatic resources. These, too, carried risks.

TIME Global lawmaking is costly. One principal cost is time – time available to a Secretariat, time slots for meeting rooms and translators, time forgone for private actors who would otherwise be charging clients for long hours of expert advice, time salient to the civil service and political delegates with their domestic priorities and responsibilities. Time also has competitive significance – IOs faster to move into lawmaking areas, IOs quicker to produce norms, states and industries that act expeditiously to adopt norms and integrate them into market behavior – all these provide more or less competitive advantage for survival and positioning of an IO in a global normmaking ecology.

Yet time appears to be rigid, lacking the fungibility of money and resisting manipulation. We have shown that in fact UNCITRAL found multiple ways for the issue-ecologies it hosted to convert seeming rigidities into manipulable resources that quickened production and enhanced competitiveness.[34] Five instances of temporal inventiveness can be observed in efforts at *staging* time, *compressing* time, *expanding* time, *segmenting* time, and *multiplying* time (Chapter 6).

More conventionally, an IO depends upon *tangible* resources. Two have been particularly salient for UNCITRAL (Chapter 2).

MONEY In addition to expanding its budget within the UN, by upgrading the status of UNCITRAL in the hierarchy of UN units, UNCITRAL obtained supplementary

[31] Technical expertise also lends authority to lawmaking over and above the specifics of the drafting itself (Halliday 1985; Karpik 1990).

[32] See (Carruthers and Halliday 2006), on negotiating globalization via a narrow pipeline substantially presided over by legal experts.

[33] (Block-Lieb and Halliday 2016).

[34] On social meanings and manipulations of time, see (Abbott 2001; Halliday 2017; Zerubavel 2004).

financial support for particular events (e.g., IMF funds for bringing developing countries to informal meetings, etc.) (Chapters 5 and 8). Perhaps most importantly, it obtained services that are conventionally monetarized in the form of expertise volunteered by professionals, industry associations, and industry employees.[35]

ORGANIZATIONAL INFRASTRUCTURES Earlier research on the influence of national professional associations demonstrates how they can leverage their meager resources as voluntary associations by drawing upon the "reserve infrastructures" of their members.[36] That is, they discover what organizational capacities are controlled or accessible by delegate-members and externalize infrastructural demands to those members. UNCITRAL did so, for instance, by permitting or acceding to delegates' willingness to offer infrastructure to support some lawmaking efforts, including by meeting at law firms which voluntarily hosted events, or by relying on an industry association to provide an online communications infrastructure, or by requesting that states sponsor certain events.

Essentially, therefore, UNCITRAL's civil servants and allied sponsors ensured that the Commission as a whole, and each of the three working groups we studied, drew on adjacent ecologies that were rich in the resources vital to UNCITRAL's viability and productivity. Resource-rich actors – states, professional associations, firms, expert individuals, industry groups – underwrote lawmaking enterprises in which they had immediate interests. In this respect UNCITRAL drew heavily on resources controlled by adjacent industry and inter-governmental ecologies.

Diversifying Processes The classics of ecological theory identify processes in domestic social organization that can be adapted to contemporary international and global arenas.[37] There is *competition*, even conflict, among states, IOs, industries, and professions in the founding and persistence of ecologies, and for the positioning of actors within ecologies and the relationships of one ecology to another. There is also the prospect and actuality of *cooperation*. And there is not infrequently a shift to *competitive cooperation* where otherwise zero-sum or distributive rivalries can be converted into common public or private goods. In both cases power is exercised in ways that can lead to super-ordination or subordination. And in both latter cases, there are outcomes that can be expressed through vertical or horizontal differentiations of activities or responsibilities that lead to negotiated ecological orders in which tendencies toward disintegration can be countered by integrative processes.

Our research has identified the interplay of these processes in two settings.

35 The significance of volunteer commitment of time and expertise, i.e., resources committed without direct monetary cost, can be observed in the dangers presented by the French proposal, which would have changed methods of work and decisionmaking in UNCITRAL to marginalize volunteers (Chapter 8).

36 (Halliday, Powell and Granfors 1993).

37 (Liu and Emirbayer 2016).

INTERNAL PROCESSES Within UNCITRAL's own proceedings three processual moves forestalled otherwise prohibitive impediments to effective consensual outcomes. First, UNCITRAL's working groups overcame the deliberative rigidities built into UN rules, practices, and facilities by means of informal adaptive practices, whether by staging colloquia to set agendas, or forming ad hoc expert groups to assist in drafting, or organizing off-shore roundtables to resolve thorny problems, or benefiting from inner circles of willing volunteers and topical networks for between-session discussions, or encouraging corridor politics, or building community and rapport through social events after hours (Chapter 5). Second, like many IOs, UNCITRAL's delegates and delegations reached decisions through a process of consensus, which relied more on the sense of a working group chair taking the pulse of sentiment in the deliberative chamber than on the formality of vote-counting and its potential for manifest divisiveness (Chapters 2 and 9). And, third, each UNCITRAL working group co-opted or aligned itself with leading industry groups and adjacent industry ecologies to ensure its pragmatic relevance and to appropriate current and future resources for lawmaking and law implementation (Chapter 3).

EXTERNAL PROCESSES The most fundamental of processes that permit moving equilibria among actors in an ecology is that of competitive cooperation. In the standing ecology for international lawmaking, UNCITRAL worked assiduously from its founding to turn its potential rivals into allies, albeit always aware that competition might break out as IOs and circumstances changed.

One repeated tactic to turn competitors into cooperators was deploying the language and logic of incrementalism.[38] Repeatedly telling other IOs, and their constituencies, that UNCITRAL was building on their prior and pioneering efforts, that UNCITRAL was expanding frontiers that previously other IOs had opened up, created a narrative of temporal unfolding in which powerful IOs, such as the IMF or World Bank or UNCTAD, might see themselves as collaborators in a common enterprise of benefit to them all.

A related tactic, tried by UNCITRAL's rivals at its birth, and deployed repeatedly by UNCITRAL to the present, has been to try and convert rivals into partners, albeit cooperative competitors, through a division of labor or differentiation of function. The lawmaking ecologies as a whole, we have seen (Chapter 8), each resolved strong conflicts by actors reaching a settlement[39] in the form of horizontal differentiation, or a division of labor among different actors with different capacities and focus. Sometimes this took the form of temporal sequencing of products, as in prior work by

[38] See (Block-Lieb and Halliday 2007b). On incrementalism in insolvency and law reforms more generally see (Hathaway 2005; Pottow 2005a).

[39] On settling of meanings of legal norms, see (Grattet and Jenness 2001). On settlement in professional jurisdictions, see (Abbott 1988). On settling and settlement in the institutionalization of transnational legal orders, see (Block-Lieb and Halliday 2015; Halliday and Shaffer 2015b).

UNIDROIT subsequently built upon by UNCITRAL. Sometimes this took the form of specialization of function, as in UNCITRAL's lawmaking priority in the Insolvency Legislative Guide and the World Bank and IMF's use of those norms in their ongoing diagnostic instruments for financial stability in their member countries. Sometimes the settlement occurred in textual concordats, as in the rationalization of secured transaction texts agreed upon by UNCITRAL and UNIDROIT (Chapter 9).

Not all of these efforts to convert competition to cooperation were immediately or ultimately successful. Some resisted, as we observed with the World Bank for a time on the insolvency lawmaking. Others agreed to divide issue-areas and seek to initiate complementary TLOs, as appears to have been the case with UNIDROIT and UNCITRAL on secured transactions issues. Periodic meetings among senior officials at UNIDROIT, the Hague Conference for Private International Law, and UNCITRAL have had the goal, among others, of avoiding outright confrontation, duplication of effort, or multiplication of competing norms in rival incipient TLOs. The implicit intent, in theoretical terms, is to establish in the international lawmaking ecology relatively stable moving equilibria[40] of relationships, and to ensure the relevance and viability of lawmaking ecologies as a whole.

Inventing Production Multipliers Like a domestic legislature, a global lawmaking IO renders itself vulnerable to critique, at best, and to the ebbing away of tangible and intangible resources, at worst, if it cannot point to its productive value. For any issue-area susceptible to ordering through law, then, a basis of entry by a new IO into an existing ecology, or for the marginalization or expulsion of an IO from an ecology, turns on whether it is productive for classes of actors critical for its organizational existence.

UNCITRAL's politics from the 1960s to the present demonstrate that both its rhetoric and its actions rested on types and rates of norm production and acceptance.

Expressed negatively, UNCITRAL justified its own claims for entry into the trade lawmaking ecology with its not so subtle claims in the mid-1960s that IOs currently in the incipient ecology had limited success. Large areas that were open for lawmaking were entirely uncultivated, and where lawmaking was in process the rates of production and were low (Chapter 2).[41]

Expressed positively, perhaps mindful of the vulnerability of unproductive IOs and even entire international lawmaking ecologies, and aware its resource dependency on adjacent ecologies, UNCITRAL sought to increase its rate of production through: (i) invention of new technologies that are less time consuming to produce (Chapter 6); (ii) doubling the number of its working groups (Chapter 2); (iii) allying with state and non-state partners who would enable fast starts to lawmaking and resources to permit quick finishing (Chapter 3); and (iv) managing

[40] The search in sociological and ecology theory for a dynamic concept of order remains contested, as Abbott (2016) demonstrates, without however offering a convincing alternative to his critique of concepts like social equilibrium.

[41] See also (Block-Lieb and Halliday 2016).

incrementalism so it could get a fast start and collateral resources for production of norms in their various forms (Chapter 3).

These effects were iterative so as to produce virtuous cycles: more production could garner more resources; more resources could quicken the pace of production. UNCITRAL seemed to adopt the strategy that faster rates of production increased ecological competitiveness.

Again, the consequences were not limited to UNCITRAL itself. They were slowly transformative for entire ecologies. Faster rates of production by UNCITRAL impelled other IOs in the standing lawmaking ecology to reconsider their mix of products and pace of production. In fact, they had the contradictory effect of bringing new classes of actors, not least the World Bank, IMF and other development banks, into the lawmaking ecology. They solidified symbiotic ties with industry ecologies for future projects. Arguably, increased production also lifted the profile of the UN (and, by implication, the whole UN ecology of actors) as an institution salient to the rule of law, markets, economic development and world trade.

Attuning Adaptations to Changing Contexts Both the inventive IO within an ecology and commercial lawmaking ecologies in all their variety maintain currency by attuning various forms of social organization toward changes that alter supplies of resources or salience to powerful constituencies and that might thus invigorate potential competitors. A global lawmaking body, as actor and arena, enhances its ecological advantage to the extent that it scans accurately the perturbations in its environs and their constructive possibilities or adverse effects. For IOs intent upon erecting or protecting the TLOs in which they are leading actors, leadership also requires creative imaginings of openings for *legal* orders that previously were disordered or ordered by other means.

A simplifying heuristic for analysis of contexts, environments, and adjacent ecologies distinguishes between facilitating circumstances, often unfolding through grand time, and precipitating events, frequently tinted with surprise.[42] UNCITRAL's adaptations can be observed in both.

Facilitating circumstances unfold over the longer term in slowly and even imperceptibly altering contexts and environments. In such changing circumstances, IOs may be rendered out-of-date or opportunities opened up for the founding of entrepeneurial IOs or ecologies, both of which compete with existing social organization of the transnational. We observe pressures for new commercial lawmaking episodes stimulated by (i) industry changes (e.g., containerization, new forms of financing), (ii) market shifts (e.g., in the balance of power between carriers and shippers), (iii) pressures arising from domestic law reforms (e.g., COGSA, Article 9, and Chapter 11); (iv) shifting concepts of international law and the ordering capacities of law; and (v) the fall or rise or inertia or competitiveness of IOs in an ecology or

[42] (Block-Lieb and Halliday, 2015: chapter 3; Halliday and Shaffer, 2015: chapter 1, 31-37).

of adjacent ecologies (e.g., failures by UNIDROIT and HCCH to adapt; questions raised about IFIs policies of conditionality) (Chapter 3).

Precipitating events act as triggers for onset of new lawmaking episodes. We have documented the impact of (i) epochal geopolitical shocks (e.g., the fall of the Berlin Wall and collapse of the Soviet bloc); (ii) wholesale and rapid transitions from command to market economies (e.g., Central and Eastern Europe, Vietnam, China); (iii) debt crises (e.g., 1990s national debt crises, Asian Financial Crisis); and (iv) dramatic political or legal events in powerful countries (e.g., *Sky Reefer* ruling by the US Supreme Court; success in revision of US Article 9) (Chapter 3).

By taking an actor-adaptive orientation toward the issue- and standing ecologies, it is clear that UNCITRAL is not a fully autonomous actor immune from contexts, whether these are industries or markets, the UN or world geopolitics. In fact, the emphasis of adaptation and invention presupposes the constant challenge for UNCITRAL to wrestle with its contexts, to obtain scarce resources, to situate itself in already extant discursive universes, to co-opt states and industries into believing that UNCITRAL's *legal* initiatives are enabling paths for state and market development. All UNCITRAL's adaptive strategies are therefore constrained significantly by its structural locations and institutional contexts. Like any IO, UNCITRAL is not only *proactive* but *reactive*. Like other IOs, and especially small and resource-poor organizations, it responds to shifts in politics (e.g., Cold War) and markets (e.g., containerization), to ideational movements in understandings of law and development (e.g., NIEO), to changes in ways the UN regards itself and is regarded by others (e.g., the UN as a champion of the rule of law). Not least it is responding to the realities of international political economy, and to the power of the US in the world economy and the Global North in setting terms of trade, at least until the rise of China (Chapter 2).

More than reactivity, UNCITRAL's inventiveness occurred in conditions that enabled or cultivated adaptive responses. Its entry onto the world stage in 1966 was enabled, in large part, by the world's most powerful state, a state moreover, that had a high regard for legal regulation of markets, a low regard for the lawmaking IOs currently in place, and which sought a new lawmaking arena in which the whole world might be incorporated. Growing restoration and expansion of international trade stimulated a demand for some kind of commercial order beyond a *lex mercatoria* or patchwork of rules created by sovereign, regional, or economic blocs. Following WWI, law too was rising as an ideology of international order – in human rights, codified in the UN Universal Declaration of Human Rights; in economic development driven by the state-led New International Economic Order; in property rights, and the institutions and law necessary to effectuate and enforce those rights; and rule of law, more generally, as a philosophy of governance to be adopted by the great international institutions, ranging from the UN and IMF to the World Bank and regional development banks.

At its founding and thereafter, UNCITRAL benefited from manifest deficiencies in other lawmaking IOs – of UNIDROIT and the Hague Conference, because their dated composition, methods of work, and limited products left them behind a world outstripping their capacities; and later of the IMF and World Bank, which had ventured into lawmaking, but found themselves impugned by their proximity to the US and by the coercive conditionalities they exerted against developing and transitional economies. As a low profile and perhaps even weak institution, UNCITRAL was sheltered from the opprobrium that had been directed at others. And as a creature of the UN, UNCITRAL had auspices, access to resources, and deliberative practices accepted by the world as the best of imperfect alternatives.

Conditions for UNCITRAL's adaptive successes flowed from adjacent industry ecologies, which solicited *legal* solutions to market problems. The actors in these industry ecologies were prepared to enter into partnership and invest resources in UNCITRAL's lawmaking initiatives. UNCITRAL formally incorporated every category of state into its Commission and working groups, and practically acknowledged sovereign discretion in many of the products it offered. Without these conducive conditions UNCITRAL's inventiveness would have been stifled, possibly precluded.

Not least, UNCITRAL's successes stemmed from adroit blurring of its properties both as an actor and agenda. As an actor, we have seen, UNCITRAL could express an identity or unity of interests whether as a Commission of sixty member states, as a body of UN officials, as a community of core officials and delegates, or as a working group expressing itself as a collectivity. As an arena, UNCITRAL drew diverse state and non-state actors into a space where deliberation and lawmaking might occur. It could act adaptively and nimbly as an authoritative actor because its core leadership was small, but yet it could legitimately claim the whole world participated in its creative arena. It could function effectively as an arena because it attracted delegates knowing that their lawmaking could and would be carried to the world by a nimble actor.

ADAPTATIONS UNREALIZED

Intensive study of UNCITRAL in its standing and episodic lawmaking ecologies also reveals that this global body, and quite possibly the standing lawmaking ecology as a whole, engaged in tradeoffs and missed creative opportunities that may have subverted aspirations for leadership in TLO construction and defense. This is *not* a normative argument. It is an empirical account of tensions and contradictions, choices about resource dependency and resource allocation, and costs of constraints or choices that counteract any hint of triumphalism by UNCITRAL's champions. These under- or unrealized adaptations further demonstrate that dominance or centrality in a social space cannot be taken for granted, and that such centrality demands continuing renewal by IO leaders.

UNCITRAL's unrealized possibilities for adaptation and invention, and analysis of its failures, offer a set of hypotheses, more generally, on IOs' failures to achieve their own goals as they aspire to leadership for lawmaking and normmaking in global arenas.

Deliberative Exclusion Global governance offers the prospect of drawing all interested state and non-state actors into a collective decisionmaking process that does more than offer merely the possibility for universal representation.[43] UNCITRAL's form of global governance provided an arena in which states and inter-state bodies, networks and epistemic communities, international NGOs and businesses could all be drawn into a deliberative community. Yet the pragmatic and legitimating accomplishment of bringing a diverse amalgam of actors into a lawmaking forum may fail to be realized when the universal inclusiveness of state and non-state delegates and delegations does not convert into deliberative inclusiveness within *de facto* circles of decisionmaking. Similar participatory challenges bedevil many IOs whose formal methods demand longstanding, active involvement and reward participation by experts over generalists.[44]

At its founding, UNCITRAL distinguished itself from other dedicated lawmaking IOs by seeking to incorporate the full diversity of states into its deliberative chambers. It went much further by drawing in non-state organizations, civil society, and other IO interests, especially to specific issue-ecologies (Chapter 2). This blend of states and non-state organizations underlined UNCITRAL's legitimation warrants[45] and increased the probability of behavioral conformity by states and market players with the legal norms UNCITRAL's lawmakers would ultimately produce.

Yet we have demonstrated empirically that the core decisionmakers in UNCITRAL, that is, those who were deliberating most intensively at decisive moments, did not include anything like the full spectrum of states. Both the composition of its inner circles of decisionmakers (Chapter 4) and the realities of informal politicking (Chapter 5) reduced the number of core lawmakers to a small and sometimes tiny subset of actors. Moreover, those actors more often than not were situated in the center of world finance, trade, or geopolitics. They reflected the interests of the strong, not the weak, the global center, not the global periphery.

Perhaps, more seriously, our analysis of the speechturns in formal sessions of UNCITRAL (Chapter 4) showed that the vast majority of delegations spoke scarcely at all. Their presence signified representation. But their silence raises doubts about the breadth of interests incorporated in the resulting texts.

The demonstrable phenomenon of small groups spearheading decisionmaking over rules for the world certainly served the purposes of cost-effectiveness, efficiency, and flexibility in deliberation. In so doing, however, this phenomenon also raises questions about whether the texts that emerged reflect the preferences of those less engaged in the decisionmaking core. The absence of demonstrable influence by this "silent majority" might undermine widespread adoption and implementation of the norms promulgated by UNCITRAL, as well as perceptions of the legitimacy of the

[43] (Black 2008; Börzel and Risse 2010; Bowman and Hodge 2009).

[44] (Bernstein and Cashore 2007; Bodansky 1999; Seabrooke and Tsingou 2009; Shaffer 2001; Skelcher and Torfing 2010).

[45] On legitimation warrants, see (Halliday 2007).

lawmaking IO and its methods of work. It would be wholly inaccurate to say that UNCITRAL (whether as an IO, or through its Secretariat), or the leading delegates in particular working groups, deliberately set out to exclude parts of the world or certain voices from deliberations. Yet the silent acquiescence of many UNCITRAL delegates leaves it unclear whether the norms promulgated by UNCITRAL reflect truly global thinking or the diversity of interests in world commerce and trade. UNCITRAL's practices, therefore, inadvertently demonstrate that informal methods of work that creatively solve deliberative rigidities might also deprive it of a key resource.

There is a more subtle form of exclusion that cuts across the divides of Global North and Global South. Global governance confronts extreme linguistic diversity. This is more than a matter of hearing and speaking. Perhaps more importantly in technical lawmaking, it is a matter of conceptualizing, of encapsulating norms and ways of ordering commercial life through law in linguistic terms that never translate perfectly. The UN confronts this challenge by translating many formal proceedings into the six UN languages of English, French, Spanish, Chinese, Russian, and Arabic.

Nevertheless, we have observed a double language barrier. In formal deliberations, those whose languages are not among the six UN official languages confront a barrier to participation on the floor of the chamber. Sophisticated academics, lawyers, and diplomats from outside those six language groups, not least from leading states in the global economy (e.g., Germany, Japan, Brazil), must participate in their second and third languages, and almost certainly not in the language they use in their everyday dealings with corporate insolvencies, financial transactions or maritime trade. Even when speaking in one of the six official languages, persons educated in English or French, for instance, may be participating in their second language. The problems that result from linguistic barriers may be compounded in the informal deliberations that prove so critical in the production of global norms. The French proposal, which stemmed in part from linguistic exclusion in some informal proceedings (Chapter 8), emphasized the dominance of English in these settings, and hence the disadvantages to legislators whose second or third languages are other than English. The dominance of English as a legislative language may, thus, reinforce other dominances, as the French undoubtedly perceived.

Asymmetries Uncorrected Enormous asymmetries of power exist in global geopolitics and the international political economy, including asymmetries in global trade and finance.[46] Such asymmetries also have existed in laws governing world trade, some reaching far back into the history of Rome or Islam, some stemming from colonial impositions, some from voluntary and involuntary adoptions euphemistically described as legal transplants.

[46] This imbalance is central to world systems theory (Wallerstein 1984; Wallerstein 2005; Wallerstein 2002), international political economy (Helleiner 2009; Cohen 2008) and counter-hegemonic theory (Santos 2006; Santos 2000).

The silence we observe by many UNCITRAL delegates might be construed as a reflection of the enormous asymmetries of power that UNCITRAL sought to internalize within its chambers – the asymmetries in political influence, economic heft, expertise, and industry power, all drawn into one issue-ecology of lawmaking at a time. Occasionally, a delegation from outside leading circles in the Global North or world financial centers could turn the working group's debate and alter the substance and form of norms (Chapter 7). But these were few in number, and generally took the form of convincing more powerful delegations that certain practices in the global periphery worked well enough and should not be pushed outside the bounds of new global norms.

The asymmetry of power within UNCITRAL's deliberations may have encouraged the least powerful delegations simply to listen rather than participate, as well as permitting the most powerful delegations to pronounce rather than listen. These powerful delegations described their "modern" and "advanced"[47] practices and prescriptions as exemplars of laws on the books. As a consequence, a history of success in contests among economic heavyweights often served as the sole indicia of global best practices. Rarely did working groups look to cultivate or create structures in which they might hear and absorb national or local functional equivalents to high-level objectives of normative orders. Nor did they seek an understanding of the cultural and institutional conditions under which norms generated from a transnational organization might have any prospect of adoption by the actors that would implement those norms in altered practices (Chapters 3, 4, and 5). Unlike the work of some global lawmakers, UNCITRAL often dispenses with the "scientific" background work of uncovering, studying, and comparing all existing laws on an issue, often on the grounds of achieving greater efficiency. But cutting this initial diagnostic step may serve more to concentrate power than to level it.

Lost Creativity It is an implicit and surely unconscious conceit of IOs dominated by high-attending powerful actors from the Global North that the sources of creativity in the globalization of laws reside predominantly in the Global North.[48] While it is surely the case, as we have demonstrated, that a great deal of creativity in commercial lawmaking did come from Canada, the Netherlands, the United Kingdom, or the United States, among others, it remains open whether the silence of non-participatory actors will deny lawmakers the very knowledge fundamental to their global aspirations.

Failures to hear from weak states and industry actors decrease probabilities that proposed global norms will work in the particular circumstances of states with limited institutional capacities, weak civil services, scarcities of professional expertise, limited effective professional regulation, and challenges of corruption or

47 On this self-validating rhetoric of justification for IOs and global lawmakers, see (Halliday, Block-Lieb and Carruthers 2009b).

48 (Halliday 2015).

particularism in its various manifestations.[49] Who better knows the domestic challenges and limitations of law-taking and implementation in a given national and local setting than delegates from those countries. Who better knows the value of new laws for small- and medium-sized businesses than representatives of those businesses? Without that knowledge – the conditions under which proposed norms might work, or the likely anticipated and unanticipated consequences of adopting such norms – then global lawmakers fly blind, hoping rather than ensuring a reasonable probability of behavioral change.

As a result, there is an increased likelihood of lost creativity – the loss of creative options proffered by marginal or peripheral states in the world economy. Assuming political will, delegates from those states know best what imaginative adaptations or measures might yield results consonant with the broad objectives of global lawmakers. National actors accustomed to act with weak domestic infrastructures, poor communication capacities, ill-trained or ill-equipped personnel, pervasive corruption or civil unrest are also accustomed to creative adaptations to survive institutional incapacities and the frustrations of everyday work and life.

Weak Empirics Global governance frequently is built upon plausible folk theories rather than empirically verified foundations, or, in their absence, a rhetorical testing of unstated or unexamined premises.[50] Global lawmakers may proceed on the basis of common assumptions, assumptions that may be both unquestioned and unexamined. Global lawmakers might also proceed in ignorance or willful failure to examine evidence salient to their lawmaking.[51] Without solid evidentiary or reflexive foundations, there is an increased likelihood that prevailing ideologies or pocket theories will produce norms that fail when confronted with the realities of practice.

Clearly, the absence of well-attested empirical evidence could not be a necessary condition for global lawmaking. This would be a counsel for inaction in many issue-areas. Yet a rush to craft a TLO based on a theory promulgated by a very few prominent or notable actors, without any search for evidence or testing of a logic of reasoning in debate, could lead to poorness-of-fit in many local circumstances. A failure to test claims that a new convention or legislative guide will produce

49 A thorough and thoughtful analysis of the cluster of problems relating to local implementation of global norms can be found in (Andrews 2013).

50 This critique converges with the scholarship on the sociology of ignorance in making public policy and elsewhere. See (McGoey 2012).

51 Precisely this critique was made by a distinguished national reformer and global delegate in UNCITRAL's drafting of global norms on secured transactions law. There is no convincing evidence, he asserted, that providing greater security for loans either stimulates inflows of credit to a country or stimulates commerce within a country. Nor is there evidence that drafting a single comprehensive secured transactions TLO, or consolidating multiple narrow TLOs into one broad TLO, yields demonstrable economic benefit. Yet UNCITRAL's working group proceeded without opening up a discussion of whether its premises were well-founded. In fact, none of UNCITRAL's lawmaking efforts involved any evaluations of (a) available empirical research on actual laws-in-practice or indeed practices themselves, or of (b) rigorous appraisals at the level of argument and critique of the underlying theories which drove the lawmaking.

certain desirable outcomes opens the lawmaking enterprise the accusation that it serves unarticulated interests that may be entirely estranged from the pragmatics of everyday commerce and law. If it is the case that TLOs have increased probabilities of being institutionalized and effective when they are premised on the best diagnostic evidence and tested theories, then the short-term advantage to rapid closure of global normmaking based on plausible folk theories may lead to a long-term disadvantage in the commercial efficacy of misconceived theories.

Contingency Fallacies UNCITRAL's leaders believed that competitive advantage for UNCITRAL as an arena and actor required a track record of effectiveness. Looking back, they sought to learn why some finished products were not adopted widely by states or implemented by regional or local practitioners. Looking forward, they were mindful that resources might be contingent on demonstrated uptakes by states and other actors of the norms under development. Despite this self-conscious counting of treaty accessions and statutory adoptions, UNCITRAL and prominent actors in its issue-ecologies stop short of analyzing rigorously and systematically the conditions that are likely to impede either adoption of norms or changes in behavior such norms are intended to effect.

Working groups remain trapped within epistemologies that deny a contingent basis for the erection of effective TLOs. The seduction of hegemony, whether of finance or legal thought, is the wishing away of all the messiness of social, cultural, political, and other variations in the states where global norms were directed. If hosts of lawmakers imagine that a single set of best practices or bright-line rules will fit Fiji in the same way as Norway, or Somalia as in Israel, they may be deluding themselves.[52] If it is the case that one-size-does-not-always-fit-all, and that uniformity is not always important to the resolution of the problem at hand, then it becomes necessary for lawmakers to identify a range of possible solutions and the conditions under which some forms and substance of norms will work and other conditions that require adaptive variations in the forms and possibly the substance of applicable norms.

This limitation circles back to failures in formal representation and participation, to inadvertent exclusions of weak actors, to diminished participation by certain language groups, to over-reliance on folk theories based on a little more than plausibility. It also amounts to a critique of an understanding of law that is autonomous or detached from the cultures and social institutions in which it exists. The critique reaches to a fundamental epistemological and methodological issue for UNCITRAL, and many other global legislatures and lawmaking IOs. The critique centers on repeated failures to ask and to identify the conditions under which certain norms will fit or not fit, work or not work.[53] It thereby also reaches to the lively debate over

[52] For a generalized critique of this thinking, see (Andrews 2013). For specific application of this critique to global regulation by the World Bank and IMF, see (Halliday, Levi and Reuter 2013).

[53] Elaboration of this point can be found in (Andrews 2013).

functional equivalents in transnational lawmaking and degrees of freedom that must be given to local lawmakers if transnational or global norms are to be authoritative and effective.[54]

Two sets of questions immediately arise from this analysis of non-adaptive or unadapted responses to lawmaking challenges. Where is the locus of adaptive failure? And what explains such failures?

This book proposes that global lawmaking and governance must focus on the interplay of ecologies and actors. Consistent with this proposition it should be observed where adaptations do and do not occur. In one respect, adaptations apply to the standing international lawmaking ecology as a whole. The standing ecology is premised on the master principle that *legal* order has salience for private market behavior. It is the common interest of principal actors in this ecology, including UNCITRAL, UNIDROIT, and the Hague Conference, and those new lawmaking IOs that have edged inside that ecology such as the World Bank and ADB, that law can be seen to work for markets and economic and financial institutions. Hence the entire ecology rises or falls depending on its demonstrable efficacy, on the order-producing effects of its legal products, on the flexibility and adaptability of its technologies to all corners of the world.

In another respect, adaptations apply to the lawmaking delegates in each issue-area. It would be entirely possible to imagine that the lawmakers in one issue-ecology formulate norms that appropriate local knowledge, recognize contingencies of implementation, insist on scientifically defensible empirical foundations, whereas the lawmakers in another issue-ecology do not. Failures also arise out of the ways that states and non-state organizations populate their delegations. Delegations with non-experts, or with infrequent attenders, or with high turnovers, or with little breadth of practical coverage, or questionable status vis-à-vis their sending countries or organzations all diminish their likely impact on global lawmaking.

In yet a further respect, it can be imagined that UNCITRAL as an arena that houses lawmaking ecologies might suffuse its deliberative chambers with modes of participation that encourage or discourage some kinds of adaptations and not others. Certainly UNCITRAL as an actor can convert its dual actor-arena identity so that when it interacts with a World Bank or UNIDROIT it will selectively deploy adaptations in a bid for cooperative outcomes even with competitive IOs.

What then explains failures to adapt? Why does inventiveness falter or creativity get squandered? Often it is a result of tradeoffs by the IO itself. Much of UNCITRAL's inventiveness involved expansion of boundaries and technologies. Adaptation through expansion created a number of attendant risks.

54 For a critique of the IMF and Financial Action Task Force global regulatory regimes that may be generalized to other lawmaking and global regulatory IOs, see (Halliday, Levi and Reuter 2013).

There were risks related to its *internal workings*: Expansion means more work. In order to accomplish all this work, UNCITRAL may take short cuts (Chapter 4); it may be increasingly tempted to rely on non-state actors from adjacent industry ecologies more than on state actors; it may rely more on the economically and politically most powerful states than on those states who have less experience in IO lawmaking.

There were *recursive* risks, as well: States may understand themselves to have an "obligation of review and comprehension" as to the soft laws increasingly produced by UNCITRAL, but given the growing number of these products and their increasing complexity, states may get overwhelmed and simply ignore the legal texts that get produced or the processes through which they are produced. This reaction will always negatively implicate UNCITRAL's legitimacy claims, but is especially problematic in those issue-areas in which "uniformity" or rising above some floor of internationally established problematic practices is in some sense viewed as important.

There were also *ecological* risks: The global lawmakers and lawmaking IOs that share this space may understand themselves to have an "obligation of coordination and minimization of overlaps." UNCITRAL's expanding boundaries may be viewed as pushing other IOs aside, and thus as imperializing within the lawmaking ecology. More than "taking" work from other lawmaking IOs, its boundary expansion and manipulation of technologies might also be viewed as "making" work for the other IOs that need, at very least, to keep track of UNCITRAL's work product in order to keep that expansions in check.

Sometimes failures resulted from the dynamics of the ecologies themselves. For an entire ecology to be adaptive in rapidly changing worlds, it may need to move fast, show results, produce evidence that benefits justify the risks. An insistence on immediacy of outcomes may, in turn, work against struggling with the complexities of a highly heterogeneous world.

Failures might also result from *epistemological traps*. Although industry actors were drawn into all UNCITRAL's lawmaking efforts, it is lawyers and judges and legal academics who ultimately preside over the conversion of economic and financial outcomes into means effected through law. By successfully incorporating highly sophisticated academic and practicing lawyers and even domestic lawmakers into proceedings, an imperative, positivistic view of law and social order prevails. The drafters of the law find difficulty in reaching outside their powerful but epistemologically tinted views of economic behavior.

That failure is indirectly abetted by the paucity of empirical research on the recursivity of lawmaking and law implementation across the full diversity of the world's states and markets. Compounding these gaps in knowledge are failures by social scientists and interdisciplinary scholars to examine the logics and test the empirical assumptions of theories driving global lawmaking.

Other pragmatic considerations help explain missed adaptations. Regional and global IOs confront the daunting task of making sense of extraordinary complexity as compounded by rapid change. There is cognitive efficiency in simplifying assumptions and plausible folk theories. They lend meaning to otherwise debilitating cognitive noise and they justify action for the lawmakers and their constituencies in digestible bites.

Not least, lawmaking ecologies and the actors in them justify their activity by demonstrable outputs. A new legislative guide or draft treaty represents an ostensible product, just as a new law on the books in a domestic legislature represents some sort of response to demands or ideals of certain interest groups. Even accession or adoption of laws can be and is counted by policymakers and social scientists alike. By contrast, demonstrating that global norms influence everyday practice is a far more difficult outcome to document. Hence it is a rational strategy by IOs to pay the price of short-term failures in adaptation because long-term consequences will be far removed in time and place.

INVENTIVE LAWMAKING FOR TRANSNATIONAL LEGAL ORDERS

Inventive adaptations enabled UNCITRAL's global lawmakers to enter, form, and shape ecologies whose work was to produce legal norms for international commerce and trade. That lawmaking and law production propelled UNCITRAL into bids for leadership in the formation and reformation of TLOs. UNCITRAL's adaptive limitations point to the challenges confronting TLO construction given that the process of lawmaking required enormously diverse actors to reach consensus on norms that would effectively order economic behavior in an issue-area for every market worldwide. To extrapolate these findings we take two further steps. First, we consider under what conditions in transnational lawmaking will lower the probability of TLO-building. Second, we turn to theories and practices of recursive global lawmaking and regulation to identify mechanisms that may increase probabilities that such lawmaking will become institutionalized in TLOs.

Although UNCITRAL may not be typical of all lawmaking IOs, its adaptive struggles indicate conditions under which the probable impact of its norms on TLOs may be more limited than its leaders and norm entrepreneurs might have predicted. We must subject to more empirical research the propositions that TLO-building will be more impaired: (a) the larger the number of interested parties "on the books" that did not participate "in action" of the deliberations; (b) the greater the asymmetries of power involved in assimilating inputs from the range of settings toward which the norms are addressed; (c) the greater the degree to which technical expertise is relied on in the lawmaking rather than democratic processes; (d) the less creativity salient to national and local adoptions is brought to the lawmaking table; (e) the weaker the empirical foundations of decisionmaking, and (f) the less specified the contingencies under which substantive, procedural, and formal properties of norms will be salient in given settings.

Research and theory on legal change in global contexts point to practices that foster TLO building in diverse contexts. These construct "if, then" scenarios that affect the impact of IOs as they erect governance institutions

Recursive Diagnostics TLOs rise and fall through iterations of interactions among actors at all levels of governance – from the global (e.g., UNCITRAL) or transnational (e.g., EU) to the national (e.g., China), from the national (e.g., India) to the local (the state of Kerala or Mumbai), and so on. The probabilities that new norms settle at all levels are influenced by four mechanisms.[55]

All law reform proceeds on the presumption that law offers a means for solving some problem. How that problem is construed, however, requires a diagnosis. The medical metaphor immediately connotes the possibilities of misdiagnosis or conflicting diagnoses. Moreover, if economic stakes are high, and if laws matter, then *diagnostic struggles* propel into motion the wheels of lawmaking. If TLOs are erected to solve problems of commerce and trade, how those problems are construed will influence significantly how solutions are crafted. If lawmakers seek to lower the risk of misdiagnosis, they will explicitly ask: Are there competing diagnoses of problems? Who advances those diagnoses? What are their respective justifications? What kind of evidence can be produced to support a given diagnosis? A decision to proceed on the basis of a given diagnosis would present a considered foundation for normmaking, in full awareness that competing diagnoses, if held by actors with influence, may later lead to faltering construction of a TLO or to rival TLOs.

Research indicates that global lawmakers may not include in deliberations all actors responsible for the transmission or implementation of the resulting product. *Actor mismatch* spells danger for lawmakers because it increases the risk that actors who are not included in lawmaking sites, and who are potential veto players in national or local normmaking, or potential veto players in the translation of norms to practice, ultimately will be determinative as to whether global norms become local norms and norms become practice. The greater the degree of actor mismatch, the greater the probability that TLOs will fail to institutionalize. It follows that the more IOs can identify and redress actor mismatch in the process of global lawmaking, the more likely it is that normmaking will facilitate norm adoption.

New legal norms may not settle because global lawmakers build *contradictions* or contradictory ideologies into the norms as a price of consensus. In soft law recommendations they may seek to implement norms through multiple state agencies and organizations whose interests, norms and practices also diverge. Contradictions or fractures within the norms therefore can occur at all levels from the global to the local. The ultimate effect will be to inhibit convergence and quite possibly to induce indifference. If the destabilizing effects of contradictions on norms are to be minimized, then lawmakers will be acutely attentive to whether differing ideologies or theories of legal change have in fact been resolved in an authentic and real consensus.

[55] (Halliday and Carruthers 2007b; Halliday 2009; Shaffer 2011; Levy 2010). For a more critical reading of recursivity in the construction of TLOs, see (Payne 2015).

Energetic debates over principles versus bright-line rules or of hard law versus soft law technologies in global lawmaking signal that the form of norms, especially in their global formulations, matter significantly for adoption and implementation.[56] An enormous body of scholarship approaches this challenge to the concept of *vagueness*. Transnational recursivity theory views vagueness as a mechanism that can subvert concordance on transnational, national or local norms and slow the stabilization of legal meanings essential to the order expected of laws' practitioners and subjects. In fact, there are two dangers. Too much rigidity in global laws may aggravate discontinuities and gaps between the global and local, such as the universal extension of bright-line rules to many, perhaps most states, where they are ill-fitted to local circumstances and contexts. Too much flexibility, on the other hand, may offer an openness to local adaptation that is so wide that the harmonizing goals of global legislators are frustrated. If the risks of vagueness and flexibility are to be balanced by an openness to local adaptations, then global lawmakers will seek formal strategies to avoid the twin dangers of excessive rigidity and indeterminacy.

Iterative Lawmaking The empirical study of transnational and global legal change demonstrates repeatedly that effective changes at any level – transnational, national, local – will involve multiple iterations of lawmaking, law implementation, responsive adjustments to the lawmaking, further adaptations in law implementation, until some kind of settling or moving norm equilibrium is reached.[57] Yet lawmaking IOs very often are structured to produce an initial set of norms for the world but have not constructed institutional capacities to manage subsequent iterations. If the pragmatics of institutionalizing TLOs require repeated iterations of feedback from the realities of practice back to global lawmakers, then inventive global governance will require greater attentiveness to local creativity manifest in the application of global norms, and global creativity in adaptations to the multiplicities of local innovations across world markets.

Institutionalizing TLOs at all levels so that concordant norms and clear jurisdictions ultimately yield "new normals" in legal and commercial behavior is a formidable task. Transnational and global lawmaking IOs may therefore be confronted with tradeoffs: whether to expend resources on declarative lawmaking on a broader scope of issue-areas or to increase institutional capacities for TLO-building through iterative cycles of global-local encounters, but at the cost of tackling fewer issue-areas.

Contingent Implementation The critique of one-size-fits-all global standards, while widely accepted as a lawmaking trap, nevertheless has not changed many of the foundational assumptions in lawmaking IOs about the institutionalization of global legal norms in local settings. Lawyer-driven products not surprisingly adopt

[56] Important writings, from those on the rule of law (Waldron 2011) to those on development (Andrews 2013), emphasize the value of flexibility in local adaptations to particular circumstances.

[57] See (Andrews 2013; Block-Lieb and Halliday 2015).

epistemologies consistent with juridical traditions, such as legal drafting and legal interpretation – the core of what makes law a distinctive form of ordering social behavior. The corresponding weakness of this epistemological emphasis lies in the encounters of law with culture, institutions, entrenched behaviors, local customs, and practices. Since global lawmakers by definition embrace the totality of world cultures, the entirety of state or economic institutions, the extraordinary diversity of local customs, then the potential clash between pristine concepts of law-on-the-books and the messiness of everyday law-in-action confronts global governance through lawmaking with a seemingly unresolvable challenge.

Since social scientific epistemologies are highly skeptical of universal conformities built on global norms, and yet can recognize the impracticalities for IOs to treat every national and local circumstance as different and thus requiring endless tailoring, a grounded (i.e., empirically based) theory takes a middle position. In this theory, contingencies of TLO institutionalization must always be specified. A contingent theory for the institutionalization of a TLO in insolvency or secured transactions or transport law would thereby take the form, "x" law is designed to solve "y" problems that will work in "z" circumstances.

A radically simplified contrast illustrates the point. In Society A there is an enormous black or gray market, weak state regulatory capacity, a tiny commercial bar, a judiciary that has low competency or integrity or both, widespread corruption, and limited customary experience in using formal law to structure commercial relationships or resolve disputes. In Society B the market is highly formalized, the state infrastructure reaches seamlessly to geographical borders of the state and penetrates deeply and effectively into social and economic life, the bar is sophisticated and extensive, the judiciary has high probity and competency, corruption is low, and formal law conventionally regulates commerce.

It is entirely improbable on its face that global laws and institutions designed for Society B will fit in Society A. It follows that if global lawmakers are to create or reform TLOs that take root in all territorial soils, then law reformers will build contingent models that specify in what circumstances what norms are likely to work. It further follows that this difficult and different approach to global lawmaking will yield more thoroughly institutionalized TLOs when lawmakers work cooperatively with social science and policy specialists on the cultural and institutional attributes of societies that will condition normative concordance and convergence. Increased cooperation will compound and possibly slow the tasks of global norm production, but arguably increase the probability that configurations of global legal norms will be well adapted to identifiable configurations of states and societies.

Functional Equivalents One approach to ensuring more aligned national settling on global norms has been to allow degrees of freedom for the local to find its own variations on the theme of the global. In some regional contexts, such as the OECD's convention on bribery, this occurs when a transnational body promulgates general objectives but encourages states to meet those objectives with creative alternatives best fitted to state and local circumstances.[58] Thus, Society A would take the overarching objectives of UNCITRAL's lawmaking on insolvency and propose that it could be practically implemented through local measures despite the absence of a large sophisticated bar, a history of formal legal ordering of economic activities, and a judiciary accustomed to dealing with large, complex multinational corporations, and in conscious recognition of social shame experienced by public admissions of business failure or of the historic insignificance of courts as centers of power in a polity or economy. Assuming there is political will, therefore, the prospect for sovereign states to exercise their inventiveness in adjustment of global standards to particular circumstances is likely to increase the probability of normative convergence and real change in practice. At once – and awaiting empirical verification – this may increase respect for sovereignty, recognize that few outsiders know a society's social circumstances as well as its own citizens, and foster creativity.

Norm Pyramids We have seen that the repertoire of legal technologies adopted or invented by UNCITRAL vary in their formal properties, not least in their levels of abstractness or specificity. If the institutionalization of a new TLO will occur in widely diverse national circumstances, then it follows that the forms of norms may need to be sufficiently flexible to cater to that diversity. These norms would be designed in ways that recognize clusters of national cultural and institutional configurations and would permit creative co-production of national and local norms and practices through functional equivalents.

UNCITRAL has developed what might be called norm pyramids.[59] In the norm pyramid of the Legislative Guide on Insolvency, legal standards are expressed in degrees of generality. Eight high level objectives provide maximal opportunity for local creativity and variation. Architectural recommendations provide broad bounds for local adaptations. Imperative recommendations provide less room for maneuvering. High-level objectives or principles offer the greatest opportunities for creative solutions, for adoptions and adaptations, for inventions and creative options, in national and local norms and ultimately practice. States with severe incapacities or ill-fitting institutions gain degrees of freedom to find their own levels in the hierarchy of generality or specificity in a norm pyramid.

This move offers more than feedback. Indeed, it may qualitatively differ from the kind of law-in-action, law-on-the-books interaction well understood in socio-legal scholarship. Feedback implies a response to a change initiated elsewhere. Creativity generated by national and local actors implies that the "somewhere else" has itself already been incorporated into inventive approaches to shared goals of global governance.[60]

58 See (Waldron 2011; Braithwaite 2002).

59 See (Braithwaite and Drahos 2000), as well as Braithwaite's writings more generally on national and international regulation.

60 (Halliday and Shaffer 2015c: Chapter 14).

Therefore we return to the earlier analysis of how global norms themselves are formulated. Once creative adaptation is admitted as a component of iterative global governance, then invention from below can become an integral element of normative design that infuses global lawmaking bodies and IOs with far more information about the probabilities of reformed global governance than will be the case when global lawmakers comprise only a handful of delegates from a tiny number of states or one side of an industry.

* * * * * *

Global lawmakers create commercial law for the world. They are doing so more expansively than ever before. Their ambitions potentially affect every market actor in the world, from the largest multinational corporations to mom-and-pop microenterprises. They do so in ecologies of lawmaking which themselves are embedded in adjacent industry and proximate ecologies. Until now they have proceeded invisibly, making consequential decisions by means and through practices unobserved by those they influence.

By opening itself to social science investigation, UNCITRAL has opted for a transparency that concomitantly reveals its inventiveness and adaptability, yet also lays bare its continuing struggles for competitiveness, legitimacy, and effectiveness. UNCITRAL has, thus, provided a rich empirical site to address simultaneously the fortunes and pathologies of global governance. This site permits both observations of solutions to the intractabilities of global governance of trade through law and of the challenges of holding in creative tension the search for universality in a world of endless particularities.

Appendix

TABLE A.1. *UNCITRAL Work Product (1974–2017) by Subject Matter Area and Legal Technology*

Year	UNCITRAL Work Product	Subject Matter	Legal Technology
	International sale of goods		
1974	Convention on the Limitation Period in the International Sale of Goods	International sale of goods	Convention
1980	Convention on Contracts for the International Sale of Goods	International sale of goods	Convention
1983	Uniform Rules on Contract Clauses for an Agreed Sum Due Upon Failure of Performance	International sale of goods	Rules
1992	Legal Guide on International Countertrade Transactions	International countertrade	Legal Guide
	International Arbitration/Conciliation		
1976	Arbitration Rules	Arbitration/ conciliation	Rules
1980	Conciliation Rules	Arbitration/ conciliation	Rules
1982	Recommendations to assist arbitral institutions and other interested bodies with regard to arbitrations under the UNCITRAL Arbitration Rules (with revisions in 2010)	Arbitration/ conciliation	Recommendations

(continued)

TABLE A.1. (*continued*)

Year	UNCITRAL Work Product	Subject Matter	Legal Technology
1985	Model Law on International Commercial Arbitration (with amendments as adopted in 2006)	Arbitration/ conciliation	Model Law
1996	Notes on Organizing Arbitral Proceedings	Arbitration/ conciliation	Notes
2002	Model Law on International Commercial Conciliation with Guide to Enactment and Use	Arbitration/ conciliation	Model Law
2006	Recommendations regarding interpretation of Article II(2), and Article VII(1), of the Convention on the Recognition and Enforcement of Foreign Arbitral Awards (New York Convention 1958)	Arbitration/ conciliation	Recommendations
2010	Revised Arbitration Rules	Arbitration/ conciliation	Rules
2013	Revised Arbitration Rules (New art. 1, para. 4)	Arbitration/ conciliation	Rules
2014	Rules on Transparency in Treaty-based Investor-State Arbitration	Arbitration/ conciliation	Rules
2014	Convention on Transparency in Treaty-based Investor-State Arbitration ("Mauritius Convention")	Arbitration/ conciliation	Convention
	International Transportation of Goods		
1978	Convention on the Carriage of Goods by Sea (the "Hamburg Rules")	International transportation	Convention
1982	Unit of Account Provision and Provisions for the Adjustment of the Limit of Liability in International Transport and Liability Conventions	International transportation	Model Law Provisions
1991	Convention on the Liability of Operators of Transport Terminals in International Trade	International transportation	Convention
2008	Convention on Contracts for Carriage of Goods Wholly or Partly by Sea ("Rotterdam Rules")	International transportation	Convention
	International Payments		
1988	Convention on International Bills of Exchange and International Promissory Notes	International payments	Convention
1992	Model Law on International Credit Transfers	International payments	Model Law

Year	UNCITRAL Work Product	Subject Matter	Legal Technology
1995	Convention on Independent Guarantees and Stand-by Letters of Credit	International payments	Convention
2013	Recognizing and Preventing Commercial Fraud: Indicators of Commercial Fraud	International payments	Report
	Procurement and Infrastructure Development		
1987	Legal Guide on Drawing Up International Contracts for the Construction of Industrial Works	Project finance/ procurement	Legal Guide
1993	Model Law on Procurement of Goods and Construction, with Guide to Enactment	Project finance/ procurement	Model Law
1994	Model Law on Procurement of Goods, Construction and Services, with Guide to Enactment	Public finance/ procurement	Model Law
2000	Legislative Guide on Privately Financed Infrastructure Projects	Project finance/ procurement	Legislative Guide
2003	Model Legislative Provisions on Privately Financed Infrastructure Projects	Project finance/ procurement	Model Law Provisions
2011	Model Law on Public Procurement, with: Guide to Enactment (2012); Guidance on Procurement Regulations (2013); and Glossary (2013)	Project finance/ procurement	Model Law
	Electronic Commerce		
1985	Recommendation on the Legal Value of Computer Records	Electronic data	Recommendations
1996	Model Law on Electronic Commerce, with Guide to Enactment	E-commerce	Model Law
2001	Model Law on Electronic Signatures, with Guide to Enactment	E-commerce	Model Law
2005	Convention on the Use of Electronic Communications in International Contracts	E-commerce	Convention
2007	Promoting Confidence in Electronic Commerce: Legal Issues on International Use of Electronic Authentication and Signature Methods	E-commerce	Report
	Insolvency		
1997	Model Law on Cross-Border Insolvency, with Guide to Enactment (1997; revised 2013)	Insolvency	Model Law

(continued)

TABLE A.1. (*continued*)

Year	UNCITRAL Work Product	Subject Matter	Legal Technology
2004	Legislative Guide on Insolvency Law	Insolvency	Legislative Guide
2009	Practice Guide on Cross-Border Insolvency	Insolvency	Practice Guide
2010	Legislative Guide on Insolvency Law, Part Three: Treatment of Enterprise Groups in Insolvency	Insolvency	Legislative Guide
2011	Model Law on Cross-Border Insolvency: The Judicial Perspective	Insolvency	Report
2013	Legislative Guide on Insolvency Law, Part Four: Directors' Obligations in the Period Approaching Insolvency	Insolvency	Legislative Guide
	Secured Transactions		
2001	Convention on the Assignment of Receivables in International Trade	International payments and secured transactions	Convention
2007	Legislative Guide on Secured Transactions	Secured Transactions	Legislative Guide
2010	Legislative Guide on Secured Transactions: Supplement on Security Rights in Intellectual Property	Secured Transactions	Legislative Guide
2011	Joint UNCITRAL, The Hague Conference and UNIDROIT Texts on Security Interests: Comparison and Analysis of Major Feature of International Instruments Relating to Secured Transactions	Secured Transactions	Report
2013	Guide on Implementation of Security Rights Registry	Secured Transactions	Practice Guide
2016	Model Law on Secured Transactions	Secured Transactions	Model Law
	Online Dispute Resolution		
2016	Technical Notes on Online Dispute Resolution	Online Dispute Resolution	Notes

TABLE A.2. *Status of UNCITRAL Conventions and Model Laws, 1974–2017*

Year	UNCITRAL Work Product	Legal Technology	Status[a]	Number of States[b]	Comments
1974	Convention on the Limitation Period in the International Sale of Goods	Convention	Entered into force	30 countries as unamended/ 23 countries as amended	Amended by Protocol of April 11, 1980
1978	Convention on the Carriage of Goods by Sea (the "Hamburg Rules")	Convention	Entered into force	34 countries	Endorsed by UNCTAD, AALCC, and OAS
1980	Convention on Contracts for the International Sale of Goods	Convention	Entered into force	85 countries	US acceded in 1988, Japan in 2009; UK has not
1985	Model Law on International Commercial Arbitration	Model law		76 countries, including additional subnational jurisdictions	
1988	Convention on International Bills of Exchange and International Promissory Notes	Convention	Not yet entered into force	5 countries (10 are needed)	US has signed but not acceded to convention
1991	Convention on the Liability of Operators of Transport Terminals in International Trade	Convention	Not yet entered into force	4 countries (5 are needed)	US has signed but not acceded to convention
1992	Model Law on International Credit Transfers	Model law			EU directive based on Model Law on Int'l Credit Transfers issued January 27, 1997
1993	Model Law on Procurement of Goods and Construction, with Guide to Enactment	Model law, with guide to enact-ment		See below	

(*continued*)

TABLE A.2. (*continued*)

Year	UNCITRAL Work Product	Legal Technology	Status[a]	Number of States[b]	Comments
1994	Model Law on Procurement of Goods, Construction and Services, with Guide to Enactment	Model law, with guide to enact-ment		30 countries	
1995	Convention on Independent Guarantees and Stand-by Letters of Credit	Convention	Entered into force	8 countries	US has signed but not acceded to convention; in 1998, UNCITRAL endorsed ICC's International Stand-by Practices, ISP98
1996	Model Law on Electronic Commerce, with Guide to Enactment	Model law, with guide to enact-ment		69 countries, including additional subnational jurisdictions	
1997	Model Law on Cross-Border Insolvency, with Guide to Enactment	Model law, with guide to enact-ment		43 countries, including additional subnational jurisdictions	Including US, Canada, UK, and Australia
2001	Model Law on Electronic Signatures, with Guide to Enactment	Model law, with guide to enact-ment		32 countries, including additional subnational jurisdictions	Not including US, but including UK
2001	Convention on the Assignment of Receivables in International Trade	Convention	Not yet entered into force	1 country has ratified; 3 others have signed but not ratified	5 actions required before entry into force; only Liberia has ratified
2002	Model Law on International Commercial Conciliation, with Guide to Enactment and Use	Model law, with guide to enact-ment and use		16 countries, including additional subnational jurisdictions	

2005	Convention on the Use of Electronic Communications in International Contracts	Convention	Entered into force	Signed by 20 countries; acceded to by 7	3 actions required for entry into force; US has not signed this convention
2008	Convention on Contracts for the Carriage of Goods Wholly or Partly by Sea ("Rotterdam Rules")	Convention	Not yet entered into force	Signed by 25 countries, including US; 3 have acceded	20 actions required for entry into force
2011	Model Law on Public Procurement	Model Law		23 countries	Used as a benchmark by: African Devel. Bank; Asian Devel. Bank; EBRD; Inter-American Devel. Bank; OECD, World Bank
2014	Convention on Transparency in Treaty-based Investor-State Arbitration ("Mauritius Convention")	Convention	Will enter into force as of Oct. 18, 2017	Signed by 19 countries (including US and UK); 3 have acceded.	3 actions needed to enter into force; US has not ratified this convention
2016	Model Law on Secured Transactions	Model Law			

[a] The legal status does not fully signify impact. Countries may adopt or adapt principal provisions of UNCITRAL legal norms into their domestic laws without explicitly acceding to a convention or explicitly adopting a given UNCITRAL Model Law. Further research is needed to document these levels of impact.

[b] Id.

References

Abbott, Andrew. 1988. *The System of Professions: An Essay on the Division of Expert Labor*. Chicago: University of Chicago Press.

1995. "Things of Boundaries." *Social Research* 62:857–82.

2001. *Time Matters: On Theory and Method*. Chicago: University of Chicago Press.

2004. *The System of Professions: An Essay on the Division of Expert Labor*. Chicago: University of Chicago Press.

2005. "Linked Ecologies: States and Universities as Environments for Professions." *Sociological Theory* 23(3):245–74.

2016. *Processual Sociology*. Chicago: University of Chicago Press.

Abbott, Kenneth, and Duncan Snidal. 2000. "Hard and Soft Law in International Governance." *International Organizations* 54(3):421–56.

Abbott, Kenneth W., Jessica F. Green, and Robert O. Keohane. 2016. "Organizational Ecology and Organizational Strategies in World Politics." *International Organizations* 70(2):247–77.

Abbott, Kenneth W., Robert O. Keohane, Andrew Moravcsik, Anne-Marie Slaughter, and Duncan Snidal. 2000. "The Concept of Legalization." *International Organization* 54(03):401–19.

Alford, Robert R., and Roger Friedland. 1985. *Powers of Theory: Capitalism, the State, and Democracy*. New York: Cambridge University Press.

Alford, Roger P. 2008. "The Nobel Effect: Nobel Peace Prize Laureates as International Norm Entrepreneurs" *Virginia Journal of International Law* 49:61–153.

Alkoby, Asher. 2008. "Global Networks and International Environmental Lawmaking: A Discourse Approach." *Chicago Journal of International Law* 8(2):377–407.

Alter, Karen J. 2001. *Establishing the Supremacy of European Law: The Making of an International Rule of Law in Europe*. Oxford: Oxford University Press.

Alvarez, Jose E. 2005. *International Organizations as Law-Makers*. Oxford England; New York: Oxford University Press.

Andrews, Matt. 2013. *The Limits of Institutional Reform in Development: Changing Rules for Realistic Solutions*. New York: Cambridge University Press.

Arrighi, Giovanni, and B. Silver. 2001. "Capitalism and World (Dis)order." *Review of International Studies* 27:257–79.

Asian Development Bank (ADB). 2000a. "Insolvency Law Reforms in the Asian and Pacific Region." in *Law and Policy Reform at the Asian Development Bank*. Manila: Asian Development Bank.

2000b. "Secured Transactions Law Reform in Asia: Unleashing the Potential of Collateral." in *Law and Policy Reform at the Asian Development Bank*. Manila: Asian Development Bank.

Ayres, Ian, and John Braithwaite. 1992. *Responsive Regulation: Transcending the Deregulation Debate*. New York: Oxford University Press.

Barnett, Michael, and Martha Finnemore. 2004. *Rules for the World: International Organizations in Global Politics*. Ithaca: Cornell University Press.

Barnett, Michael N. 1997. "Bringing in the New World Order: Liberalism, Legitimacy, and the United Nations." *World Politics* 49(4):526–51.

Basnayake, Sinha. 1979. "Introduction: Origins of the 1978 Hamburg Rules." *American Journal of Comparative Law* 27(2 & 3):353–56.

Battilana, Julie, Bernard Leca, and Eva Boxenbaum. 2009. "How Actors Change Institutions: Towards a Theory of Institutional Entrepreneurship." *The Academic of Management Annals* 3(1):65–107.

Bernstein, Steven, and Benjamin Cashore. 2007. "Can Non-State Global Governance Be Legitimate? An Analytical Framework." *Regulation & Governance* 1(4):347–71.

Black, Julia. 2008. "Constructing and Contesting Legitimacy and Accountability in Polycentric Regulatory Regimes." *Regulation & Governance* 2(2):137–64.

Block-Lieb, Susan, and Terence C. Halliday. 2006. "Legitimacy and Global Lawmaking." in *Fordham Law Legal Studies Research Paper No 952492*: SSRN.

2007a. "Harmonization and Modernization in UNCITRAL's Global Legislative Guide on Insolvency Law." *Texas International Law Journal* 42(3):481–514.

2007b. "Incrementalisms in Global Lawmaking." *Brooklyn Journal of International Law* XXXII (Symposium on Bankruptcy in the Global Village – The Second Decade.):851–903.

2011. "Social Ecology, Recursivity and Temporality: A Sociology of Global Law-Making." in *American Sociological Association Annual Meeting*. Las Vegas, NV.

2013. "The Ecological Politics of International (Trade) Law-Making: From the League of Nations to the United Nations." in *Law and Globalization in a Comparative Perspective: The Interwar versus the Post–Cold War Periods*. European Center for International Relations, Sciences-Po, Paris.

2015. "Settling and Concordance: Two Cases in Global Commercial Law: Corporate Bankruptcy Law and International Trade by Sea." Pp. 75–113 in *Transnational Legal Orders*, edited by Terence C. Halliday and Gregory Shaffer. New York: Cambridge University Press.

2016. "Contracts and Private Law in the Emerging Ecology of International Lawmaking." Pp. 350–99 in *Contractual Knowledge: A Hundred Years of Legal Experimentation in Global Markets*, edited by Grégoire Mallard and Jérôme Sgard. New York: Cambridge University Press.

Blommaert, Jan, and Chris Bulcaen. 2000. "Critical Discourse Analysis." *Annual Review of Anthropology* 29:447–66.

Bodansky, Daniel. 1999. "The Legitimacy of International Governance: A Coming Challenge for International Environmental Law?" *American Journal of International Law* 93(3):596–624.

Börzel, Tanja A, and Thomas Risse. 2010. "Governance without a State: Can It Work?" *Regulation & Governance* 4(2):113–34.

Bowman, Diana M., and Graeme A. Hodge. 2009. "Counting on Codes: An Examination of Transnational Codes as a Regulatory Governance Mechanism for Nanotechnologies." *Regulation & Governance* 3(2):145–64.

Boyle, Alan, and C.M. Chinkin. 2007. *The Making of International Law*. Oxford: Oxford University Press.

Boyle, Elizabeth H. 2002. *Female Genital Cutting: Cultural Conflict in the Global Community*. Baltimore: The Johns Hopkins University Press.

Braithwaite, John. 2002. "Rules and Principles: A Theory of Legal Certainty." *Australian Journal of Legal Philosophy* 27:47–82.

Braithwaite, John, and Peter Drahos. 2000. *Global Business Regulation*. New York: Cambridge University Press.

Braudel, Fernand. 1996. *The Mediterranean and the Mediterranean World in the Age of Philip II*. Berkeley: University of California Press.

Brummer, Christopher. 2014. *Minilateralism: How Trade Alliances, Soft Law, and Financial Engineering Are Redefining Economic Statecraft*. New York: Cambridge University Press.

2015. *Soft Law and the Global Financial System: Rule Making in the 21st Century*. New York: Cambridge University Press.

Cameron, Maxwell A., Robert J. Lawson, and Brian W. Tomlin. 1998. *To walk without Fear: The Global Movement to Ban Landmines*. Oxford: Cambridge Univ Press.

Campbell, John. 2011. "On Terence C. Halliday and Bruce G. Carruthers, *Bankrupt: Global Lawmaking and Systemic Financial Crisis* What Does Bankrupt Tell Us about World Polity Theory and Comparative Political Economy?" *Socio Economic Review* 9(2):376–80.

Campbell, John L. 2004. *Institutional Change and Globalization*. Princeton: Princeton University Press.

Campbell, John L., and Ove K. Pedersen. 2001. "The Second Movement in Institutional Analysis." Pp. 249–82 in *The Rise of Neoliberalism and Institutional Analysis*, edited by John L. Campbell and Ove K. Pedersen. Princeton: Princeton University Press.

Carlson, Mary Helen. 2009. "U.S. Participation in Private International Law Negotiations: Why the UNCITRAL Convention on Contracts for the International Carriage of Goods Wholly or Partly by Sea Is Important to the United States." *Texas International Law Journal* 44(2 & 3):269–76.

Carruthers, Bruce G., Sarah L. Babb, and Terence C. Halliday. 2001. "Institutionalizing Markets, or the Market for Institutions?: Central Banks, Bankruptcy Law, and the Globalization of Financial Markets." Pp. 94–126 in *The Rise of Neoliberalism and Institutional Analysis*, edited by John Campbell and Ove Pedersen. Princeton: Princeton University Press.

Carruthers, Bruce G., and Terence C. Halliday. 1996. "The Moral Regulation of Markets: Professions, Privatization and the English Insolvency Act 1986." *Accounting, Organizations and Society* 21(4):371–413.

1998. *Rescuing Business: The Making of Corporate Bankruptcy Law in England and the United States*. Oxford: Oxford University Press.

2006. "Negotiating Globalization: Global Templates and the Construction of Insolvency Regimes in East Asia." *Law & Social Inquiry* 31(Summer):521–84.

Carruthers, Bruce G., and Jeong-Chul Kim. 2011. "The Sociology of Finance." *Annual Review of Sociology* 37(1):239–59.

Cashore, Benjamin. 2002. "Legitimacy and the Privatization of Environmental Governance: How Non-State Market-Driven (NSMD) Governance Systems Gain Rule-Making Authority." *Governance* 15(4):503–29.

Cashore, Benjamin, Graeme Auld, Steven Bernstein, and Constance McDermott. 2007. "Can Non-state Governance 'Ratchet Up' Global Environmental Standards? Lessons from the Forest Sector." *Review of European Community & International Environmental Law* 16(2):158–72.

Charnovitz, Steve. 2006. "Nongovernmental Organizations and International Law." *The American Journal of International Law* 100(2):348–72.

Chorev, Nitsan. 2012. "Changing Global Norms through Reactive Diffusion: The Case of Intellectual Property Protection of AIDS Drugs." *American Sociological Review* 77(5):831–53.

Clark, Ian. 2005. *Legitimacy in International Society*. Oxford: Oxford University Press.

Clift, Jenny. 1999. "Electronic Commerce: The UNICTRAL Model Law and Electronic Equivalents to Traditional Bills of Lading." *International Business Lawyer* 27:311–15.

2004. "The UNICTRAL Model Law on Cross-Border Insolvency–A Legislative Framework to Facilitate Coordination and Cooperation in Cross-Border Insolvency." *Tulane Journal of International and Comparative Law* 12:307–45.

2009. "International Insolvency Law: The UNCITRAL Experience With Harmonization and Modernization Techniques." *Yearbook of Private International Law* 11:405–24.

Clyde, Paul S., and James D. Reitzes. 2007. "Market Power and Collusion in the Ocean Shipping Industry: Is a Bigger Cartel a Better Cartel?" *Economic Inquiry* 36:292–304.

Cohen, Amichai. 2005. "Bureaucratic Internalization: Domestic Governmental Agencies and the Legitimization of International Law." *Georgetown Journal of International Law* 36(4):1079–144.

Cohen, Edward S. 2008. "Constructing Power through Law: Private Law Pluralism and Harmonization in the Global Political Economy." *Review of International Political Economy* 15:770–99.

2011. "Normative Modeling for Global Economic Governance: The Case of the United Nations Commission on International Trade Law (UNCITRAL)." *Brooklyn Journal of International Law* 36(2):567–604.

Colares, Juscelino F. 2009. "A Theory of WTO Adjudication: From Empirical Analysis to Biased Rule Development." *Vanderbilt Journal of Transnational Law* 42(2):383–439.

Cordovez, Diego. 1967. "The Making of UNCTAD: Institutional Background and Legislative History." *Journal of World Trade Law* 1(3):234–328.

Coyle, John. 2011. "Rethinking the Commercial Law Treaty." *Georgia Law Review* 45:343–407.

Cuming, Ronald C.C. 1997. "The Internationalization of Secured Financing Law: The Spreading Influence of the Concepts UCC, Article 9 and Its Progeny." Pp. 499–524 in *Making Commercial Law*, edited by Ross Cranston. Oxford: Clarendon Press.

Cutler, A. Claire. 2003. *Private Power and Global Authority: Transnational Merchant Law in the Global Political Economy*. New York: Cambridge University Press.

Dahan, Frederique, and John Simpson. 2009. *Secured Transactions Reform and Access to Credit*. Cheltenam: Elgar Financial Law.

Darian-Smith, Eve. 2013. *Laws and Societies in Global Contexts: Contemporary Approaches*. New York: Cambridge University Press.

Dezalay, Yves, and Bryant G. Garth. 1996. *Dealing in Virtue: International Commercial Arbitration and the Construction of a Transnational Legal Order*. Chicago: University of Chicago Press.

2013. "The Reinvention of the Lex Mercatoria on the Transatlantic Marketplace by 'Merchants of Peace': Parallels and Contrasts with International Justice and Human Rights." in *Conference on Law and Globalization in a Comparative Perspective: The Interwar versus the Post-Cold War Periods*. European Center for International Relations, Sciences-Po, Paris.

Diamond, Anthony. 1988. "Liability of the Carrier in Multimodal Transport." in *International Carriage of Goods: Some Legal Problems and Possible Solutions*, edited by Clive M. Schmitthoff and Roy M. Goode. Trowbridge: Centre for Commercial Law Studies.

Dobbin, Frank, Beth A. Simmons, and Geoffrey Garrett. 2007. "The Global Diffusion of Public Policies: Social Construction, Coercion, Competition, or Learning?" *Annual Review of Sociology* 33:449–72.

Dobusch, Leonhard, and Sigrid Quack. 2013. "Framing Standards, Mobilizing Users: Copyright Versus Fair Use in Transnational Regulation." *Review of International Political Economy* 20(1):52–88.

Drew, Paul, and Maxwell Atkinson. 1979. "Order in Court: The Organisation of Verbal Interaction in Judicial Settings." Atlantic Highlands, NJ: Humanities Press.

Durkee, Melissa J. 2016. "The Business of Treaties." *UCLA Law Review* 63(2):264–321.

Emirbayer, Mustafa. 1996. "Manifesto for a Relational Sociology." *American Journal of Sociology* 103:281–317.

Faria, José Angelo Estrella. 2005. "The Relationship between Formulating Agencies in International Legal Harmonization: Competition, Cooperation, or Peaceful Coexistence?" *Loyola Law Review* 51 (2):253–86.

2009. "Uniform Law for International Transport at UNCITRAL: New Times, New Players, and New Rules." *Texas International Law Journal* 44(3):277–320.

Farnsworth, E. Allen. 1972. "UNCITRAL: Why? What? How? When?" *American Journal of Comparative Law* 20 (2):314–22.

Finnemore, Martha. 2009. "Legitimacy, Hypocrisy, and the Social Structure of Unipolarity." *World Politics* 61(01):58–85.

Fiss, Peer C., and Paul M. Hirsch. 2005. "The Discourse of Globalization: Framing and Sensemaking of an Emerging Concept." *American Sociological Review* 70(1):29–52.

Fourcade, Marion, and Rakesh Khurana. 2008. "From Social Control to Financial Economics: The Linked Ecologies of Economics and Business in Twentieth Century America." *SSRN eLibrary*.

2013. "From Social Control to Financial Economics: The Linked Ecologies of Economics and Business in Twentieth Century America." *Theory and Society* 42(2):121–59.

Franck, Thomas M. 2006. "The Power of Legitimacy and the Legitimacy of Power: International Law in an Age of Power Disequilibrium." *The American Journal of International Law* 100(1):88–106.

Freeman, John H., Glenn R. Carroll, and Michael T. Hannan. 1983. "The Liability of Newness: Age Dependence in Organizational Death Rates." *American Sociological Review* 48(5):692–710.

Freeman, John H., and Pino G. Audia. 2006. "Community Ecology and the Sociology of Organizations." *Annual Review of Sociology* 32:145–69.

Frerichs, S. 2009. "The Legal Constitution of Market Society: Probing the Economic Sociology of Law." *Economic Sociology European Electronic Newslaetter* 10(3):20–25.

Friedland, Roger. 2012. "Review Essay: The Institutional Logics Perspective: A New Approach to Culture, Structure, and Process. Patricia H. Thornton, William Ocasio and Michael Lounsbury (2012). The Institutional Logics Perspective: A New Approach to Culture, Structure, and Process. Oxford: Oxford University Press." *M@n@gement* 5:583–95

Friedland, Roger, and Robert Alford. 1991. "Bringing Society Back In: Symbols, Practices, and Institutional Contradictions." Pp. 232–63 in *The New Institutionalism in Organizational Analysis*, edited by Walter W. Powell and Paul J. DiMaggio. Chicago: University of Chicago Press.

Fujita, Tomotaka. 2009. "The Comprehensive Coverage of the New Convention: Performing Parties and the Multimodal Implications." *Texas International Law Journal* 44:349–73.

Fusillo, Mike. 2003. "Excess Capacity and Entry Deterrence: The Case of Ocean Liner Shipping Markets." *Maritime Economics & Logistics* 5(2):100–15.

G-22. 1998a. "Report of the Working Group on International Financial Crises." Washington, D.C.: World Bank & International Monetary Fund.

1998b. *Summary of Reports on the International Financial Architecture*. Washington, D.C.: World Bank & International Monetary Fund.

Galanter, Marc. 1981. "Justice in Many Rooms." *Journal of Legal Pluralism* 13(19):1–47.

Gaziano, Emanuel. 1996. "Ecological Metaphors as Scientific Boundary Work: Innovation and Authority in Interwar Sociology and Biology." *American Journal of Sociology* 101(4):874–907.

Gieryn, Thomas F. 1983. "Boundary-Work and the Demarcation of Science from Non-Science: Strains and Interests in Professional Ideologies of Scientists." *American Sociological Review* 48(6):781–95.

Gillette, Clayton P., and Robert E. Scott. 2005a. "The Political Economy of International Sales Law." *International Review of Law and Economics* 25(3):446–86.

2005b. *The Political Economy of International Sales Law*. New York University.

Grattet, Ryken, and Valerie Jenness. 2001. "The Birth and Maturation of Hate Crime Policy in the United States." *American Behavioral Scientist* 45(4):668–96.

Grieco, Joseph M., and G. John Ikenberry. 2003. *State Power and World Markets: The International Political Economy*. New York: Norton.

Gutteridge, H.C. 1949. *Comparative Law: An Introduction to the Comparative Method of Legal Study & Research*. Cambridge: Cambridge University Press.

Hagan, John. 2003. *Justice in the Balkans: Prosecuting War Crimes in the Hague Tribunal*. Chicago: University of Chicago Press.

HagueConference, UNIDROIT, and UNCITRAL. 2012. "UNCITRAL, Hague Conference and UNIDROIT Texts on Security Interests."

Hall, Peter A. 2010. "Historical Institutionalism in Rationalist and Sociological Perspective." Pp. 204–24 in *Explaining Institutional Change: Ambiguity, Agency, and Power*, edited by James Mahoney and Kathleen Thelen. New York: Cambridge University Press.

Halliday, Terence C. 1982. "The Idiom of Legalism in Bar Politics: Lawyers, McCarthyism, and the Civil Rights Era." *American Bar Foundation Research Journal* 7(4):913–88.

1985. "Knowledge Mandates: Collective Influence by Scientific, Normative and Syncretic Professions." *British Journal of Sociology* XXXVI:421–47.

1987. *Beyond Monopoly: Lawyers, State Crises, and Professional Empowerment*. Chicago: University of Chicago Press.

2007. "Legitimacy, Technology, and Leverage: The Building Blocks of Insolvency Architecture in the Decade Past and the Decade Ahead." *Brooklyn Journal of International Law* XXXII (Symposium on Bankruptcy in the Global Village – The Second Decade. 3.):1081–102.

2009. "Recursivity of Global Normmaking: A Sociolegal Agenda." *Annual Review of Law and Social Science* 5:263–90.

2012. "Architects of the State: International Financial Institutions and the Reconstruction of States in East Asia." *Law & Social Inquiry* 37(2):265–96.

2014. "Plenary Lecture – The Inexorability of Globalization? Fragments of a General Theory of Legal Change." At *25th Anniversary Congress, International Institute for Sociology of Law*. Oñati, Spain.

2015a. "Pathologies and Prospects of Global Governance." At *International Panel on Social Progress*. Istanbul, Turkey.

2015b. "Plausible Folk Theories: Throwing Veils of Plausibility over Zones of Ignorance in Global Governance." Workshop on *Monitoring and the Politics of Ignorance. Graduate Institute of International and Development Studies*, 20 May, 2015, Geneva, Switzerland.

2017. "Time and Temporality in Global Governance." Pp. 305–24 in *Regulatory Theory: Foundations and Applications*, edited by Peter Drahos. Canberra ACT: Australian National University Press.

Halliday, Terence C., and Bruce G. Carruthers. 2003. "Globalizing Law: Political Influence in the Legal Construction of Markets by the UN." At *American Sociological Association Annual Meeting*. Atlanta, GA.

2007a. "Foiling the Financial Hegemons: Limits to the Globalisation of Corporate Insolvency Regimes in Indonesia, Korea and China." Pp. 255–301 in *Globalisation and Resistance: Law Reform in Asian since the Crisis*, edited by Christoph Antons and Volkmar Gessner. Oxford: Hart Publishing.

2007b. "The Recursivity of Law: Global Normmaking and National Lawmaking in the Globalization of Bankruptcy Regimes." *American Journal of Sociology* 112(4):1135–202.

2009. *Bankrupt: Global Lawmaking and Systemic Financial Crisis*. Palo Alto: Stanford University Press.

Halliday, Terence C., and Gregory Shaffer. 2015a. "Researching Transnational Legal Orders." Pp. 475–528 in *Transnational Legal Orders*, edited by Terence C. Halliday and Gregory Shaffer. New York: Cambridge University Press.

2015b. "Transnational Legal Orders." Pp. 3–72 in *Transnational Legal Orders*, edited by Terence C. Halliday and Gregory Shaffer. New York: Cambridge University Press.

(Eds.). 2015c. *Transnational Legal Orders*. New York: Cambridge University Press.

Halliday, Terence C., Josh Pacewicz, and Susan Block-Lieb. 2013. "Who Governs: Delegations and Delegates in Global Trade Lawmaking." *Regulation & Governance* 7:279–98.

Halliday, Terence C., and Lucien Karpik. 2012. "Political Liberalism in the British Post-Colony: A Theme with Three Variations." Pp. 3–55 in *Fates of Political Liberalism in the British Post-Colony: The Politics of the Legal Complex*, edited by Terence C. Halliday, Lucien Karpik, and Malcolm M. Feeley. New York: Cambridge University Press.

Halliday, Terence C., Lucien Karpik, and Malcolm M. Feeley (Eds.). 2007. *Fighting for Political Freedom: Comparative Studies of the Legal Complex for Political Liberalism*. Oxford: Hart Publishing.

Halliday, Terence C., Michael J. Powell, and Mark Granfors. 1993. "After Minimalism: Transformations of State Bar Associations from Market Dependence to State Reliance, 1918–1950." *American Sociological Review* 58(4):515–35.

Halliday, Terence C., Michael Levi, and Peter Reuter. 2013. "IMF Assessments of Anti-Money Laundering and Combating the Financing of Terrorism In the Context Of the Financial Action Task Force Standards, Methodology and Practices." Pp. 1–130. Center on Law and Globalization, American Bar Foundation: International Monetary Fund.

Halliday, Terence C., and Pavel Osinsky. 2006. "Globalization of Law." *Annual Review of Sociology* 32:447–70.

Halliday, Terence C., and Susan Block-Lieb. 2013. "Global Duelists: The Recursive Politics of the Text in International Commercial Law." Pp. 77–97 in *Sociolegal Approaches to International Economic Law: Text, Context, Subtext*, edited by Amanda Perry-Kessaris. London: Routledge.

2014. "Issue Ecologies in Global Lawmaking." in *Working Papers, Center on Law and Globalization, American Bar Foundation*. Chicago: American Bar Foundation.

Halliday, Terence C., Susan Block-Lieb, and Bruce G. Carruthers. 2009a. "Attaining the Global Standard." Ch 4 in *Bankrupt: Global Lawmaking and Systemic Financial Crisis*, Terence C. Halliday and Bruce G. Carruthers. Palo Alto: Stanford University Press.

2009b. "Rhetorical Legitimation: Global Scripts as Strategic Devices of International Organizations." *European Socio-Economic Review* 2009:1–36.

2012. "Missing Debtors: National Lawmaking and Global Normmaking of Corporate Bankruptcy Regimes " Pp. 236–79 in *A Debtor World: Interdisciplinary Perspectives on Debt*, edited by Ralph Brubaker and Robert M. Lawless. New York: Oxford University Press.

Hannan, Michael T. 2005. "Ecologies of Organizations: Diversity and Identity." *Journal of Economic Perspectives* 19(1):51–70.

Hannan, Michael T., Glenn R. Carroll, and Laszlo Polos. 2003. "The Organizational Niche." *Sociological Theory* 21(4):309–40.

Hannan, Michael T., and John Freeman. 1989. "*Organization Ecology*." Cambridge: Harvard University Press.

Hathaway, Oona A. 2005. "Between Power and Principle: An Integrated Theory of International Law." *The University of Chicago Law Review* 72(2):469–536.

Hawley, A.H. 1950. *Human Ecology: A Theory of Community Structure*. New York: Ronald Press

Heimer, Carol A. 2008. "Thinking about How to Avoid Thought: Deep Norms, Shallow Rules, and the Structure of Attention." *Regulation & Governance* 2(1):30–47.

Heinz, John P., Edward O. Laumann, Robert L. Nelson, and Robert H. Salisbury. 1993. *The Hollow Core: Private Interests in National Policy Making*. Cambridge, MA: Harvard University Press.

Held, David, Anthony McGraw, David Goldblatt, and Jonathan Perraton. 1999. *Global Transformations: Politics, Economics and Culture*. Stanford: Stanford University Press.

Helfer, Laurence R., and Karen J. Alter. 2013. "Legitimacy and Lawmaking: A Tale of Three International Courts." *Theoretical Inquiries in Law* 14(2):479–504.

Helleiner, Eric. 2009. "Division and Dialogue in Anglo-American IPE: A Reluctant Canadian View." *New Political Economy* 14(3):377–83.

Higgins, Rosalyn. 1963. *The Development of International Law through the Political Organs of the United Nations*. New York: Oxford University Press.

1994. *Problems and Process: International Law and How We Use It*. Oxford : New York: Clarendon Press; Oxford University Press.

Honnold, John. 1959. "A Uniform Law for International Sales." *University of Pennsylvania Law Review* 107(3):299–330.

1979a. "The Draft Convention on Contracts for the International Sale of Goods: An Overview." *American Journal of Comparative Law* 27(2 & 3):223–30.

1979b. "The United Nations Commission on International Trade Law: Mission and Methods." *American Journal of Comparative Law* 27(2 & 3):201–11.

1995. "International Unification of Private Law." Pp. 102–04 in *United Nations Legal Order*, edited by Oscar Schachter and Christopher C. Joyner. New York: Cambridge University Press.

Hopewell, Kristen. 2013. "New Protagonists in Global Economic Governance: Brazilian Agribusiness at the WTO." *New Political Economy* 18(4):603–23.

Horsefield, J. Keith. 1969. *The International Monetary Fund, 1945–1965: Twenty Years of International Monetary Cooperation*. Washington, D.C.: International Monetary Fund.

Hülsse, Rainer. 2008. "Even Clubs Can't Do Without Legitimacy: Why the Anti-Money Laundering Blacklist Was Suspended." *Regulation & Governance* 2(4):459–79.

Hurd, Ian. 1999. "Legitimacy and Authority in International Politics." *International Organization* 53(02):379–408.

2008. *After Anarchy: Legitimacy and Power in the United Nations Security Council*. Princeton, NJ: Princeton University Press.

International Monetary Fund (IMF). 1999. *Orderly and Effective Insolvency Procedures: Key Issues*. Washington, D.C.: International Monetary Fund.

Johnson, Cathryn, Timothy J. Dowd, and Cecilia L. Ridgeway. 2006. "Legitimacy As a Social Process." *Annual Review of Sociology*:53–78.

Jönsson, Christer. 1995. "IGO-NGO Relations and HIV/AIDS: Innovation or Stalemate?" *Third World Quarterly* 16(3):459–76.

Kapur, Devesh, John P. Lewis, and Richard Webb. 1997. *The World Bank: Its First Half Century*, Vol. 1, History. Washington, D.C.: Brookings Institution Press.

Karpik, Lucien. 1990. "Technical and Political Knowledge: the Relationship of Lawyers and Other Legal Professions to the Market and the State." in *The Formation of Professions: Knowledge, State, and Strategy*, edited by Rolf Torstendahl and Michael Burrage. London: Sage.

1993. "French Lawyers and Political Liberalism." At Workshop on *Lawyers and Political Liberalism. International Institute in the Sociology of Law, Oñati*, Spain.

Keck, Margaret E., and Kathryn Sikkink. 1998. *Activists Beyond Borders: Advocacy Networks in International Politics*. Ithaca: Cornell University Press.

King, Brayden G., and Nicholas A. Pearce. 2010. "The Contentiousness of Markets: Politics, Social Movements, and Institutional Change in Markets." *Annual Review of Sociology* 36(1):249–67.

Krever, Tor. 2011. "The Legal Turn in Late Development Theory: The Rule of Law and the World Bank's Development Model." *Harvard Journal of International Law* 52:287–319.

Lamont, Michele, and Virag Molnar. 2002. "The Study of Boundaries in the Social Sciences." *Annual Review of Sociology* 28:167–95.

Larson, Magali S. 1977. *The Rise of Professionalism*. Berkeley: University of California Press.

Lemercier, Claire, and Jérôme Sgard. 2013. "Waiting for the Markets to Catch Up: The Construction of International Commercial Arbitration between Two Global Eras (1920–1960)." *Conference on Law and Globalization in a Comparative Perspective: The Interwar versus the Post-Cold War Periods*. European Center for International Relations, Sciences-Po, Paris.

Levmore, Saul. 2010. "Interest Groups and the Problem with Incrementalism." *University of Pennsylvania Law Review* 158(3):815–58.

Levy, Daniel. 2010. "Recursive Cosmopolitization: Argentina and the Global Human Rights Regime." *The British journal of sociology* 61(3):579–96.

Liang, Lily, and Sida Liu. Forthcoming. "Beyond the Manifesto: Mustafa Emirbayer and Relational Sociology." *Palgrave Handbook of Relational Sociology*.

Liu, Sida. 2008. "Globalization as Boundary-Blurring: International and Local Law firms in China's Corporate Law Market." *Law & Society Review* 42(4):771–804.

2010. "*Field and Ecology: Towards a General Theory of Social Space*." Department of Sociology, University of Wisconsin-Madison..

2011. *The Formation of a Social Space: Professions and the State in the Chinese Legal Services Market*, 1979–2009. University of Wisconsin-Madison.

Liu, Sida, and Hongqi Wu. 2016. "The Ecology of Organizational Growth: Chinese Law Firms in the Age of Globalization." *American Journal of Sociology* 122:798–837.

Liu, Sida, and Mustafa Emirbayer. 2016. "Field and Ecology." *Sociological Theory* 34:62–79.

Liu, Sida, and Terence C. Halliday. 2009. "Recursivity in Legal Change: Lawyers and Reforms of China's Criminal Procedural Law." *Law & Social Inquiry* 34(4):911–50.

Lloyd, Paulette, and Beth A. Simmons. 2015. "Framing for a New Transnational Legal Order: The Case of Human Trafficking." Pp. 400–38 in *Transnational Legal Orders*, edited by Terence C. Halliday and Gregory Shaffer. New York: Cambridge University Press.

Luhmann, Niklas. 1985. *A Sociological Theory of Law*. London: Routledge.

Macdonald, Roderick A. 2015. "When Lenders Have Too Much Cash and Borrowers Have Too Little Law: The Emergence of Secured Transactions Transnational Legal Orders." Pp. 114–54 in *Transnational Legal Orders*, edited by Terence C. Halliday and Gregory Shaffer. New York: Cambridge University Press.

Mahoney, James, and Kathleen Thelen (Eds.). 2010a. *Explaining Institutional Change: Ambiguity, Agency, and Power*. New York: Cambridge University Press.

2010b. "A Theory of Gradual Institutional Change." Pp. 1–37 in *Explaining Institutional Change: Ambiguity, Agency, and Power*, edited by James Mahoney and Kathleen Thelen. New York: Cambridge University Press.

Mallard, Grégoire. 2014. *Fallout: Nuclear Diplomacy in an Age of Global Fracture*. Chicago: University of Chicago Press.

March, James, and Herbert Simon. 1958. *Organizations*. New York: John Wiley & Sons.

Maton, John, and Carolyn Maton. 2007. "Independence Under Fire: Extra-legal Pressures and Coalition Building in WTO Dispute Settlement." *Journal of International Economic Law* 10(2):317–34.

Matteucci, Mario. 1956. "The Methods of the Unification of Law: General Report." Pp. 1–45. Rome: International Institute for the Unification of Private Law.

Mattli, Walter, and Tim Büthe. 2003. "Setting International Standards: Technological Rationality or Primacy of Power?" *World Politics* 56(1):1–42.

McCormack, Gerard. 2011. *Secured Credit and the Harmonisation of Law: The UNCITRAL Experience*. Cheltenham, UK; Northampton, MA: Edward Elgar.

McGoey, Linsey. 2012. "The Logic of Strategic Ignorance." *The British Journal of Sociology* 63(3):533–76.

Meernik, James. 2003. "Victor's Justice or the Law? Judging and Punishing at the International Criminal Tribunal for the Former Yugoslavia." *Journal of Conflict Resolution* 47(2):140–62.

Meernik, James, and Kimi King. 2003. "The Sentencing Determinants of the International Criminal Tribunal for the Former Yugoslavia: An Empirical and Doctrinal Analysis." *Leiden Journal of International Law* 16(4):717–50.

Meidinger, Errol E. 2001. "Lawmaking by Global Civil Society: the Forest Certification Program." in *International Conference on Social and Political Dimensions of Forest Certification*. University of Freiburg, Germany..

Mennicken, Andrea. 2010. "From Inspection to Auditing: Audit and Markets as Linked Ecologies." *Accounting, Organizations and Society* 35(3):334–59.

Merry, Sally Engle. 2003. "Constructing a Global Law – Violence against Women and the Human Rights System." *Law and Social Inquiry* 28(4):941–77.

2006a. *Human Rights and Gender Violence: Translating International Law into Local Justice*: University of Chicago Press.

2006b. "Transnational Human Rights and Local Activism: Mapping the Middle." *American Anthropologist* 108(1):38–51.

2013. "Ethnography of the Global." *Workshop on Empirical Research Methods, Center for the Study of Law and Society*, University of California Berkeley.

2015. "Firming Up Soft Law: The Impact of Indicators on Transnational Human Rights Legal Orders." Pp. 374–99 in *Transnational Legal Orders*, edited by Terence C. Halliday and Gregory Shaffer. New York: Cambridge University Press.

Mertz, Elizabeth. 2007. *The Language of Law School: Learning to "Think Like a Lawyer."* Oxford: Oxford University Press.

Mertz, Elizabeth, and Jothie Rajah. 2014. "Language-and-Law Scholarship: An Interdisciplinary Conversation and a Post-9/11 Example." *Annual Review of Law and Social Science* 10(1):169–83.

Meyer, John W. 2010. "World Society, Institutional Theories, and the Actor." *Annual Review of Sociology* 36:1–20.

Mingst, Karen A., and Margaret P. Karns. 2007. *The United Nations in the 21st Century*. Boulder, CO: Westview Press.

Morgan, Glenn. 2011. "On Terence C. Halliday and Bruce G. Carruthers *Bankrupt: Global Lawmaking and Systemic Financial Crisis:* International Rulemaking and National Implementations in the Formation of a Global Bankruptcy Regime." *Socio Economic Review* 9(2):381–85.

Morgan, Glenn, and Sigrid Quack. 2010. "Law as a Governing Institution." Pp. 275–308 in *The Oxford Handbook of Comparative Institutional Analysis*, edited by John L. Campbell, Glenn Morgan, Colin Crouch, Ove Kaj Pedersen, Richard Whitley. Oxford: Oxford University Press.

Moss, Gabriel, Ian Fletcher, and Stuart Isaacs (Eds.). 2002. *The EC Regulation on Insolvency Proceedings*. Oxford: Oxford University Press.

Munari, Francesco. 2012. "Competition in Liner Shipping." Pp. 3–27 in *The Hamburg Lectures on Maritime Affairs 2009 & 2010*, edited by Jürgen Basedow, Ulrich Magnus, and Rüdiger Wolfrum. Berlin, Heidelberg: Springer Berlin Heidelberg.

Murphy, Sean D. 2013. "Codification, Progressive Development, or Scholarly Analysis? The Art of Packaging the ILC's Work Product." Pp. 29–40 in *Responsibility of International Organizations*, edited by Maurizio Ragazzi. Hague: Brill Nihjoff.

Northedge, Frederick Samuel. 1986. *The League of Nations: Its Life and Times, 1920–1946*. Leicester: Leicester University Press.

Nourse, Victoria, and Gregory Shaffer. 2009. "Varieties of New Legal Realism: Can a New World Order Prompt a New Legal Theory." *Cornell Law Review* 95(1):61–138.

Ocasio, William. 2011. "Attention to Attention." *Organization Science* 22:1286–96.

Ofosu-Amaah, W. Paatii 2002. "Legal and Judicial Reform in Developing Countries: Reflections on World Bank Experience." *American Law and Business Review* 8:551–81.

Park, Robert E., Ernest W. Burgess, and R.D. Mackenzie. 1925. *The City* Chicago: University of Chicago Press.

Payne, Leigh. 2015. "The Justice Paradox? Transnational Legal Orders and Accountability for Past Human Rights Violations." Pp. 439–73 in *Transnational Legal Orders*, edited by Terence C. Halliday and Gregory Shaffer. New York: Cambridge University Press.

Payne, Rodger A., and Nayef H. Samhat. 2004. *Democratizing Global Politics: Discourse Norms, International Regimes, and Political Community*. Albany: State University of New York Press.

Peltzman, Sam. 1976. "Toward a More General Theory of Regulation." *Journal of Law and Economics* 19(2):211–40.

Perry-Kessaris, Amanda (Ed.). 2013. *Sociolegal Approaches to International Economic Law: Text, Context, Subtext*. London: Routledge.

2015. "Approaching the Econo-Socio-Legal." *Annual Review of Law and Social Science* 11(1):57–74.

Peters, Anne, Till Förster, and Lucy Koechlin. 2009. "Towards Non-State Actors as Effective, Legitimate, and Accountable Standard Setters." Pp. 492–562 in *Non-State Actors as Standard Setters*, edited by Anne Peters, Till Förster, and Lucy Koechlin. New York: Cambridge University Press.

Peters, Lena. 2011. *International Institute for the Unification of Private Law (UNIDROIT)*. The Netherlands: Kluwer Law International.

Pfeffer, Jeffrey, and G. Salancik. 1978. *The External Control of Organizations: A Resource Dependence Perspective*. New York: Harper & Row.

Pierson, Paul. 2004. *Politics in Time*. Princeton, NJ: Princeton University Press.

Pistor, Katharina, and Chenggang Xu. 2003. "Incomplete Law – A Conceptual and Analytical Framework and Its Application to the Evolution of Financial Market Regulation." *Journal of International Law and Politics* 35(4):931–1013.

Pollack, Mark A., and Gregory C. Shaffer. 2009. *When Cooperation Fails: The International Law and Politics of Genetically Modified Organisms*. Oxford: Oxford University.

Popielarz, Pamela A., and Zachary P. Neal. 2007. "The Niche as a Theoretical Tool." *Annual Review of Sociology* 33:65–84.

Potter, Pitman Benjamin. 1922. "League of Nations." Pp. 240–57 in *An Introduction to the Study of International Organization*, edited by Pitman Benjamin Potter. New York: Appleton-Centruy-Crofts, Inc.

Pottow, John. 2005. "Procedural Incrementalism: A Model for International Bankruptcy." *Virginia Journal of International Law* 45:935–1015.

Prebisch, Raul. 1964. *Towards a New Trade Policy for Development: Report by the Secretary-General of the United Nations Conference on Trade and Development*. United Nations: New York.

Price, Richard. 1998. "Reversing the Gun Sights: Transnational Civil Society Targets Land Mines." *International Organization* 52(3):613–44.

Price, Richard MacKay. 2003. "Review: Transnational Civil Society and Advocacy in World Politics." *World Politics* 55(4):579–606.

Quack, Sigrid. 2010. "Special Issue: Law, Expertise and Legitimacy in Transnational Economic Governance." *Socio Economic Review* 8(1):3–16.

Rajah, Jothie. 2008. "Policing Religion: Discursive Excursions into Singapore's Maintenance of Religious Harmony Act." Pp. 267–306 in *Examining Practice, Interrogating Theory: Comparative Legal Studies in Asia*: Brill.

2012. *Authoritarian Rule of Law: Legislation, Discourse and Legitimacy in Singapore*. New York: Cambridge University Press.

2015. "'Rule of Law' as Transnational Legal Order." Pp. 340–73 in *Transnational Legal Orders*, edited by Terence C. Halliday and Gregory Shaffer. New York: Cambridge University Press.

Rehder, Britta. 2006. "Lawyers as Institutional Entrepreneurs: How the Legal Profession Shaped the Regulation of Collective Bargaining in Germany." in *Max-Planck-Institute for the Study of Societies*.

Reubens, Edwin Pierce. 1981. *The Challenge of the New International Economic Order*. Boulder, CO: Westview Press.

Rosenne, Shabtai. 1960. "The International Law Commission, 1949–59." *British Yearbook of International Law* 36:104–73.

Santos, Boaventura De Sousa. 2006. *Another Production Is Possible: Beyond the Capitalist Canon*. London; New York: Verso.

Santos, Boaventura De Sousa, and César A. Rodríguez-Garavito (Eds.). 2005. *Law and Globalization from Below: Towards a Cosmopolitan Legality (Cambridge Studies in Law and Society)*. Cambridge: Cambridge University Press.

Santos, Boaventura de Sousa. 2000. "Law and Democracy: (Mis)trusting the Global Reform of Courts." Pp. 253–84 in *Globalizing institutions: case studies in regulation and innovation*, edited by Jenson Jane, Santos Boaventura de Sousa, W. Arthurs Harry, Buchanan Ruth, Merry Sally Engle, Paoli Maria Celia, W. Seidman Gay, White Lucie, Yngvesson Barbara, E. Fuat Keyman, Jenson Jane, Santos Boaventura de Sousa, Boaventura de Sousa Santos, and Jane Jenson. Aldershot; Burlington USA: Ashgate.

Sassen, Saskia. 2006. *Territory Authority Rights: From Medieval to Global Assemblages*. Princeton, NJ: Princeton University Press.

Schelin, Johan. 2009. "The UNCITRAL Convention on Carriage of Goods by Sea: Harmonization or De-Harmonization?" *Texas International Law Journal* 44:321–27.

Schmitthoff, Clive M. 1964. "The Law of International Trade, Its Growth, Forumlation and Operation." in *The Sources of the Law of International Trade, with Special Reference to East-West Trade*, edited by Clive M. Schmitthoff. Stevens & Sons: London.

Schwartz, Alan, and Robert E. Scott. 1995. "The Political Economy of Private Legislatures." *University of Pennsylvania Law Review* 143:595–654.

Scott, Robert E. 1994. "The Politics of Article 9." *Virginia Law Review* 80:1783–851.

Scott, W. Richard. 2004. "Reflections on a Half-Century of Organizational Sociology." *Annual Review of Sociology* 30:1–21.

Seabrooke, Leonard, and Eleni Tsingou. 2009. "Power Elites and Everyday Politics in International Financial Reform." *International Political Sociology* 3(4):457–61.

Sewell, William. 1996. "Three Temporalities: Toward an Eventful Sociology." Pp. 245–80 in *The Historic Turn in the Human Sciences*, edited by Terence McDonald. Ann Arbor, MI: University of Michigan Press.

Shaffer, Gregory. C. 2001. "The World Trade Organization Under Challenge: Democracy and the Law and Politics of the WTO's Treatment of Trade and Environment Matters." *Harvard Environmental Law Review* 25:1–93.

2003a. *Defending Interests: Public-Private Partnerships in W.T.O. Litigation*. Washington, D.C.: Brookings Institution.

2011. "Transnational Recursivity Theory: A Review Essay of Halliday & Carruthers' *Bankrupt*." *Socio-Economic Review* 9(2):371–94.

2012. "Transnational Legal Process and State Change." *Law and Social Inquiry* 37:229–64.

Shaffer, Gregory C., and Mark A. Pollack. 2010. "Hard vs. Soft Law: Alternatives, Complements and Antagonists in International Governance." *Minnesota Law Review* 94:706–99.

Shaffer, Gregory, and Tom Ginsburg. 2012. "The Empirical Turn in International Legal Scholarship." *American Journal of International Law* 106(1):1–46.

Sheng, Andrew. 2009. *From Asian to Global Financial Crisis: An Asian Regulator's View of Unfettered Finance in the 1990s and 2000s*. Cambridge: Cambridge University Press.

Sherer, Peter D., and Kyungmook Lee. 2002. "Institutional Change in Large Law Firms: A Resource Dependency and Institutional Perspective." *Academy of Management journal* 45(1):102–19.

Simma, Bruno, and Andreas L. Paulus. 1999. "The Responsibility of Individuals for Human Rights Abuses in Internal Conflicts: A Positivist View." *The American Journal of International Law* 93(2):302–16.

Simmons, Beth A. 2009. *Mobilizing for Human Rights: International Law in Domestic Politics*. New York: Cambridge University Press.

Sjostrom, William. 2004. "Ocean Shipping Cartels: A Survey." *Review of Network Economics* 3(2):107–34.

Skelcher, Chris, and Jacob Torfing. 2010. "Improving Democratic Governance through Institutional Design: Civic Participation and Democratic Ownership in Europe." *Regulation & Governance* 4(1):71–91.

Slaughter, Anna-Marie. 2004. *A New World Order*. Princeton: Princeton University Press.

Stigler, George J. 1971. "The Theory of Economic Regulation." *The Bell Journal of Economics and Management Science* 2(1):3–21.

Stinchcombe, Arthur S. 2001. *When Formality Works: Authority and Abstraction in Law and Organizations*. Chicago: University of Chicago Press.

Stone, Randall. 2011. *Controlling Institutions*. New York: Cambridge University Press.

Stone Sweet, Alec, and Thomas L. Brunell. 1998. "The European Court and the National Courts: A Statistical Analysis of Preliminary References, 1961–95." *Journal of European Public Policy* 5(1):66–97.

Sturley, Michael F. 1991. "The History of COGSA and the Hague Rules." *Journal of Maritime Law and Commerce* 22(1):1–58.

2009. "Modernizing and Reforming U.S. Maritime Law: The Impact of the Rotterdam Rules in the United States." *Texas International Law Journal* 44:427–55.

Sturley, Michael F., Tomotaka Fujita, and Gertjan van der Ziel. 2010. *The Rotterdam Rules*. London: Sweet and Maxwell.

Suchman, Mark C. 1995. "Managing Legitimacy: Strategic and Institutional Approaches." *Academy of Management Review* 20(3):571–610.

Swedberg, Richard. 2003. "The Case for an Economic Sociology of Law." *Theory and Society* 32:1–37.

2006. "Max Weber's Contribution to the Economic Sociology of Law." *Annual Review of Law and Social Science* 2(1):61–81.

Szasz, Paul. 1995a. "Remarks: Tinker, Catherine. The Role of Non-state Actors in International Law-Making During the UN Decade of International Law." *Proceedings of the Annual Meeting (American Society of International Law)* 89:177–80, 80–85.

1995b. "General Law-Making Processes." Pp. 35–108 in *United Nations Legal Order*, edited by Oscar Schachter and Christopher C. Joyner. New York: Cambridge University Press.

Thommen, T.K. 1968. *International Legislation on Shipping: A Report to the United Nations Conference on Trade and Development*. New York: United Nations.

Thornton, Patricia H., and William Ocasio. 2008. "Institutional Logics." Pp. 99–129 in *The SAGE Handbook of Organizational Institutionalism*, edited by R. Greenwood, C. Oliver, K. Sahlin-Andersson, and R. Suddaby. Thousand Oaks, CA: Sage.

Thornton, Patricia H., William Ocasio, and Michael Lounsbury. 2012. *The Institutional Logics Perspective: A New Approach to Culture, Structure, and Process*. New York: Oxford University Press.

Toye, John, and Richard Toye. 2004. *The UN and Global Political Economy: Trade, Finance, and Development*. Bloomington: Indiana University Press.

Trubek, David M., Patrick Cottrell, and Mark Nance. 2006. "'Soft Law', 'Hard Law', and EU Integration." Pp. 65–95 in *Law and New Governance in the EU and the US*, edited by Gráinne de Búrca and J. Scott. Oxford: Bloomsbury Publishing.

Tushman, Michael L., and Johann Peter Murmann. 1998. "Dominant Designs, Technology Cycles, and Organizational Outcomes." *Research in Organizational Behavior* 20:231–66.

UNCITRAL. 1992. "*Uniform Commercial Law in the Twenty-First Century: Proceedings of the Congress of the United Nations Commission on International Trade Law, 18–22 May 1992.*" New York: United Nations.

UNIDROIT. 1995. "Secretariat Report, Meeting of International Organisations Currently Involved in the Preparation of Legislation in the Field of Personal Property Security." Study Doc. LXXIIB, Doc. 1. Rome: International Institute for the Unification of Private Law.

United Nations. 1945. "Statute of the International Court of Justice." http://legal.un.org/avl/pdf/ha/sicj/icj_statute_e.pdf.

United Nations, Economic and Social Council. 1963. "United Nations Conference on Trade and Development: Interim Report on the Preparatory Committee on Its First Session." UN Doc. No. E/3720_E/CONF.46/PC/3.

US Federal, Maritime Commission, and Bureau of Trade Analysis. 2012. *Staff Report: Study of the 2008 Repreal of the Liner Conference Exemption from European Union Competition Law*. Washington, D.C,: Federal Maritime Commission.

van Dijk, Teun A. 2003. "Critical Discourse Analysis." Pp. 352–71 in *The Handbook of Discourse Analysis*. New York: Wiley-Blackwell.

Waldron, Jeremy. 2011. "Are Sovereigns Entitled to the Benefit of the International Rule of Law?" *European Journal of International Law* 22(2):315–43.

Wallerstein, Immanuel. 1984. *The Politics of the World-Economy: The States, The Movements, and the Civilizations*. New York: Cambridge University Press.

2005. "After Developmentalism and Globalization, What?" *Social Forces* 83:1263–78.

2002. "Opening Remarks: Legal Constraints in the Capitalist World-Economy." Transnational Legal Processes: Globalization and Power Disparities:61–64.

Waltz, Kenneth Neal. 1979. *Theory of International Politics*. Reading, MA: Addison-Wesley Pub. Co.

Weick, K.E. 1999. *Sensemaking in Organizations*. Thousands Oaks, CA: Sage.

Weiss, Charles. 2003. "Scientific Uncertainty and Science-Based Precaution." *International Environmental Agreements* 3(2):137–66.

Weiss, Friedl, and Armin J. Kammel. 2015. *The Changing Landscape of Global Financial Governance and the Role of Soft Law*. Leiden, The Netherlands: Brill Nijhoff.

Wesson, Robert G. 1971. "The United Nations in the World Outlook of the Soviet Union and the United States." in *Soviet and American Policies in the United Nations: A Twenty-Five Year Perspective*, edited by Alvin Z. Rubinstein and George Ginsburgs. New York: New York University Press.

Westbrook, Jay Lawrence. 1996. "Creating International Insolvency Law." *American Bankruptcy Law Journal* 70(4):563–63.

2000. "A Global Solution to Multinational Default." *Michigan Law Review* 98(7):2276–328.

Williamson, John. 1990. "What Washington Means by Policy Reform." in *Latin American Adjustment: How Much Has Happened.*, edited by John Williamson. Washington, D.C.: Peterson Institute for International Economics.

Wolfensohn, James D. 1997. "Forward." in *World Development Report 1997: The State in a Changing World*. Washington, D.C.: World Bank.

World Bank. 1999a. "Building Effective Insolvency Systems." in *Insolvency Systems in Asia An Efficiency Perspective: An Efficiency Perspective*. Sydney, Australia: OECD Publishing.

1999b. *Principles and Guidelines for Effective Insolvency and Creditor Rights Systems*. Washington, D.C.: World Bank.

2001. "*Key Principles and Features of Effective Insolvency Regimes*." Washington, D.C.: World Bank.

2003. "*Principles and Guidelines for Effective Insolvency and Creditor Rights Systems.*" Washington, D.C.: World Bank.

2005. *Principles for Effective Insolvency and Creditor Rights Systems*. Washington, D.C.: World Bank.

Wouters, Patricia. 2008. "Global Water Governance through Many Lenses." *Global Governance: A Review of Multilateralism and International Organizations* 14(4):523–34.

Yancey, Benjamin W. 1983. "Carriage of Goods: Hague, COGSA, Visby, and Hamburg Admiralty Law Institute Symposium on American and International Maritime Law: Comparative Aspects of Current Importance." *Tulane Law Review* 57(5):1238–59.

Zamora, Stephen. 1995. "Economic Relations and Development." Pp. 503–76 in *United Nations Legal Order*, edited by Oscar Schachter and Christopher C. Joyner. New York: Cambridge University Press.

Zerubavel, Eviatar. 2004. *Time Maps*. Chicago, IL: University of Chicago Press.

Zhao, Dingxin. 1998. "Ecologies of Social Movements: Student Mobilization during the 1989 Pro-democracy Movement in Beijing." *American Journal of Sociology* 103(6):1493–529.

Index

CAMBRIDGE STUDIES IN LAW AND SOCIETY

Books in the Series

Diseases of the Will Mariana Valverde

The Politics of Truth and Reconciliation in South Africa: Legitimizing the Post-Apartheid State Richard A. Wilson

Modernism and the Grounds of Law Peter Fitzpatrick

Unemployment and Government: Genealogies of the Social William Walters

Autonomy and Ethnicity: Negotiating Competing Claims in Multi-Ethnic States Yash Ghai

Constituting Democracy: Law, Globalism and South Africa's Political Reconstruction Heinz Klug

The Ritual of Rights in Japan: Law, Society, and Health Policy Eric A. Feldman

The Invention of the Passport: Surveillance, Citizenship and the State John Torpey

Governing Morals: A Social History of Moral Regulation Alan Hunt

The Colonies of Law: Colonialism, Zionism and Law in Early Mandate Palestine Ronen Shamir

Law and Nature David Delaney

Social Citizenship and Workfare in the United States and Western Europe: The Paradox of Inclusion Joel F. Handler

Law, Anthropology and the Constitution of the Social: Making Persons and Things Edited by Alain Pottage and Martha Mundy

Judicial Review and Bureaucratic Impact: International and Interdisciplinary Perspectives Edited by Marc Hertogh and Simon Halliday

Immigrants at the Margins: Law, Race, and Exclusion in Southern Europe Kitty Calavita

Lawyers and Regulation: The Politics of the Administrative Process Patrick Schmidt

Law and Globalization from Below: Toward a Cosmopolitan Legality Edited by Boaventura de Sousa Santos and Cesar A. Rodriguez-Garavito

Public Accountability: Designs, Dilemmas and Experiences Edited by Michael W. Dowdle

Law, Violence and Sovereignty among West Bank Palestinians Tobias Kelly

Legal Reform and Administrative Detention Powers in China Sarah Biddulph

The Practice of Human Rights: Tracking Law Between the Global and the Local Edited by Mark Goodale and Sally Engle Merry

Judges Beyond Politics in Democracy and Dictatorship: Lessons from Chile Lisa Hilbink

Paths to International Justice: Social and Legal Perspectives Edited by Marie-Bénédicte Dembour and Tobias Kelly

Law and Society in Vietnam: The Transition from Socialism in Comparative Perspective
Mark Sidel

Constitutionalizing Economic Globalization: Investment Rules and Democracy's Promise
David Schneiderman

The New World Trade Organization Knowledge Agreements: 2nd Edition
Christopher Arup

Justice and Reconciliation in Post-Apartheid South Africa Edited by François du Bois and Antje du Bois-Pedain

Militarization and Violence against Women in Conflict Zones in the Middle East: A Palestinian Case-Study Nadera Shalhoub-Kevorkian

Child Pornography and Sexual Grooming: Legal and Societal Responses Suzanne Ost

Darfur and the Crime of Genocide John Hagan and Wenona Rymond-Richmond

Fictions of Justice: The International Criminal Court and the Challenge of Legal Pluralism in Sub-Saharan Africa Kamari Maxine Clarke

Conducting Law and Society Research: Reflections on Methods and Practices
Simon Halliday and Patrick Schmidt

Planted Flags: Trees, Land, and Law in Israel/Palestine Irus Braverman

Culture under Cross-Examination: International Justice and the Special Court for Sierra Leone Tim Kelsall

Cultures of Legality: Judicialization and Political Activism in Latin America Javier Couso, Alexandra Huneeus, Rachel Sieder

Courting Democracy in Bosnia and Herzegovina: The Hague Tribunal's Impact in a Postwar State Lara J. Nettelfield

The Gacaca Courts and Post-Genocide Justice and Reconciliation in Rwanda: Justice without Lawyers Phil Clark

Law, Society, and History: Themes in the Legal Sociology and Legal History of Lawrence M. Friedman Robert W. Gordon and Morton J. Horwitz

After Abu Ghraib: Exploring Human Rights in America and the Middle East
Shadi Mokhtari

Adjudication in Religious Family Laws: Cultural Accommodation: Legal Pluralism, and Gender Equality in India Gopika Solanki

Water On Tap: Rights and Regulation in the Transnational Governance of Urban Water Services Bronwen Morgan

Elements of Moral Cognition: Rawls' Linguistic Analogy and the Cognitive Science of Moral and Legal Judgment John Mikhail

A Sociology of Transnational Constitutions: Social Foundations of the Post-National Legal Structure Chris Thornhill

Mitigation and Aggravation at Sentencing Edited by Julian Roberts

Institutional Inequality and the Mobilization of the Family and Medical Leave Act: Rights on Leave Catherine R. Albiston

Authoritarian Rule of Law: Legislation, Discourse and Legitimacy in Singapore Jothie Rajah

Law and Development and the Global Discourses of Legal Transfers Edited by John Gillespie and Pip Nicholson

Law against the State: Ethnographic Forays into Law's Transformations Edited by Julia Eckert, Brian Donahoe, Christian Strümpell and Zerrin Özlem Biner

Transnational Legal Process and State Change Edited by Gregory C. Shaffer

Legal Mobilization under Authoritarianism: The Case of Post-Colonial Hong Kong Edited by Waikeung Tam

Complementarity in the Line of Fire: The Catalysing Effect of the International Criminal Court in Uganda and Sudan Sarah M. H. Nouwen

Political and Legal Transformations of an Indonesian Polity: The Nagari from Colonisation to Decentralisation Franz von Benda-Beckmann and Keebet von Benda-Beckmann

Pakistan's Experience with Formal Law: An Alien Justice Osama Siddique

Human Rights under State-Enforced Religious Family Laws in Israel, Egypt, and India Yüksel Sezgin

Why Prison? Edited by David Scott

Law's Fragile State: Colonial, Authoritarian, and Humanitarian Legacies in Sudan Mark Fathi Massoud

Rights for Others: The Slow Home-Coming of Human Rights in the Netherlands Barbara Oomen

European States and their Muslim Citizens: The Impact of Institutions on Perceptions and Boundaries Edited by John R. Bowen, Christophe Bertossi, Jan Willem Duyvendak and Mona Lena Krook

Environmental Litigation in China Rachel E. Stern

Indigeneity and Legal Pluralism in India: Claims, Histories, Meanings Pooja Parmar

Paper Tiger: Law, Bureaucracy and the Developmental State in Himalayan India Nayanika Mathur

Religion, Law and Society Russell Sandberg

The Experiences of Face Veil Wearers in Europe and the Law Edited by Eva Brems

The Contentious History of the International Bill of Human Rights Christopher N. J. Roberts

Transnational Legal Orders Edited by Terence C. Halliday and Gregory Shaffer

Lost in China?, Law, Culture and Society in Post-1997 Hong Kong Carol A. G. Jones

Security Theology, Surveillance and the Politics of Fear Nadera Shalhoub-Kevorkian

Opposing the Rule of Law: How Myanmar's Courts Make Law and Order Nick Cheesman

The Ironies of Colonial Governance: Law, Custom and Justice in Colonial India James Jaffe

The Clinic and the Court: Law, Medicine and Anthropology Edited by Tobias Kelly, Ian Harper and Akshay Khanna

A World of Indicators: The Making of Government Knowledge Through Quantification Edited by Richard Rottenburg, Sally E. Merry, Sung-Joon Park and Johanna Mugler

Contesting Immigration Policy in Court: Legal Activism and its Radiating Effects in the United States and France Leila Kawar

The Quiet Power of Indicators: Measuring Governance, Corruption, and Rule of Law Edited by Sally Engle Merry, Kevin Davis, and Benedict Kingsbury

Investing in Authoritarian Rule: Punishment and Patronage in Rwanda's Gacaca Courts for Genocide Crimes Anuradha Chakravarty

Contractual Knowledge: One Hundred Years of Legal Experimentation in Global Markets Edited by Grégoire Mallard and Jérôme Sgard

Iraq and the Crimes of Aggressive War: The Legal Cynicism of Criminal Militarism John Hagan, Joshua Kaiser, and Anna Hanson

Culture in the Domains of Law Edited by René Provost

China and Islam: The Prophet, the Party, and Law Matthew S. Erie

Diversity in Practice: Race, Gender, and Class in Legal and Professional Careers Edited by Spencer Headworth and Robert Nelson

A Sociology of Transnational Constitutions: Social Foundations of the Post-National Legal Structure Chris Thornhill

Shifting Legal Visions: Judicial Change and Human Rights Trials in Latin America Ezequiel A. González Ocantos

The Demographic Transformations of Citizenship Heli Askola

Criminal Defense in China: The Politics of Lawyers at Work Sida Liu and Terence C. Halliday

Contesting Economic and Social Rights in Ireland: Constitution, State and Society, 1848–2016 Thomas Murray

Buried in the Heart: Women, Complex Victimhood and the War in Northern Uganda Erin Baines

Palaces of Hope: The Anthropology of Global Organizations Edited by Ronald Niezen and Maria Sapignoli

The Politics of Bureaucratic Corruption in Post-Transitional Eastern Europe Marina Zaloznaya

Revisiting the Law and Governance of Trafficking, Forced Labor and Modern Slavery Prabha Kotiswaran

Incitement on Trial: Prosecuting International Speech Crimes Richard Ashby Wilson

Criminalizing Children: A History of Welfare and the State in Australia David McCallum

Global Lawmakers: International Organizations in the Crafting of World Markets Susan Block-Lieb and Terence C. Halliday

For EU product safety concerns, contact us at Calle de José Abascal, 56–1°, 28003 Madrid, Spain or eugpsr@cambridge.org.

www.ingramcontent.com/pod-product-compliance
Lightning Source LLC
LaVergne TN
LVHW011532200926
848484LV00001B/239

* 9 7 8 1 1 0 7 1 8 7 5 8 0 *